The ONE YEAR® *Seasonal* BIBLE

Summer Devotions

Tyndale House Publishers, Inc.
Carol Stream, Illinois

CONTENTS

JULY

1

2 KINGS 18:13–19:37

In the fourteenth year of King Hezekiah's reign,* King Sennacherib of Assyria came to attack the fortified towns of Judah and conquered them. ¹⁴King Hezekiah sent this message to the king of Assyria at Lachish: "I have done wrong. I will pay whatever tribute money you demand if you will only withdraw." The king of Assyria then demanded a settlement of more than eleven tons of silver and one ton of gold.* ¹⁵To gather this amount, King Hezekiah used all the silver stored in the Temple of the LORD and in the palace treasury. ¹⁶Hezekiah even stripped the gold from the doors of the LORD's Temple and from the doorposts he had overlaid with gold, and he gave it all to the Assyrian king.

¹⁷Nevertheless, the king of Assyria sent his commander in chief, his field commander, and his chief of staff* from Lachish with a huge army to confront King Hezekiah in Jerusalem. The Assyrians took up a position beside the aqueduct that feeds water into the upper pool, near the road leading to the field where cloth is washed.* ¹⁸They summoned King Hezekiah, but the king sent these officials to meet with them: Eliakim son of Hilkiah, the palace administrator; Shebna the court secretary; and Joah son of Asaph, the royal historian.

¹⁹Then the Assyrian king's chief of staff told them to give this message to Hezekiah:

"This is what the great king of Assyria says: What are you trusting in that makes you so confident? ²⁰Do you think that mere words can substitute for military skill and strength? Who are you counting on, that you have rebelled against me? ²¹On Egypt? If you lean on Egypt, it will be like a reed that splinters beneath your weight and pierces your hand. Pharaoh, the king of Egypt, is completely unreliable!

²²"But perhaps you will say to me, 'We are trusting in the LORD our God!' But isn't he the one who was insulted by Hezekiah? Didn't Hezekiah tear down his shrines and altars and make everyone in Judah and Jerusalem worship only at the altar here in Jerusalem?

²³"I'll tell you what! Strike a bargain with my master, the king of Assyria. I will give you 2,000 horses if you can find that many men to ride on them! ²⁴With your tiny army, how can you think of challenging even the weakest contingent of my master's troops, even with the help of Egypt's chariots and charioteers? ²⁵What's more, do you think we have invaded your land without the LORD's direction? The LORD himself told us, 'Attack this land and destroy it!'"

²⁶Then Eliakim son of Hilkiah, Shebna, and Joah said to the Assyrian chief of staff, "Please speak to us in Aramaic, for we understand it well. Don't speak in Hebrew,* for the people on the wall will hear."

²⁷But Sennacherib's chief of staff replied, "Do you think my master sent this message only to you and your master? He wants all the people to hear it, for when we put this city under siege, they will suffer along with you. They will be so hungry and thirsty that they will eat their own dung and drink their own urine."

²⁸Then the chief of staff stood and shouted in Hebrew to the people on the wall, "Listen to this message from the great king of Assyria! ²⁹This is what the king

says: Don't let Hezekiah deceive you. He will never be able to rescue you from my power. [30]Don't let him fool you into trusting in the LORD by saying, 'The LORD will surely rescue us. This city will never fall into the hands of the Assyrian king!'

[31]"Don't listen to Hezekiah! These are the terms the king of Assyria is offering: Make peace with me—open the gates and come out. Then each of you can continue eating from your own grapevine and fig tree and drinking from your own well. [32]Then I will arrange to take you to another land like this one—a land of grain and new wine, bread and vineyards, olive groves and honey. Choose life instead of death!

"Don't listen to Hezekiah when he tries to mislead you by saying, 'The LORD will rescue us!' [33]Have the gods of any other nations ever saved their people from the king of Assyria? [34]What happened to the gods of Hamath and Arpad? And what about the gods of Sepharvaim, Hena, and Ivvah? Did any god rescue Samaria from my power? [35]What god of any nation has ever been able to save its people from my power? So what makes you think that the LORD can rescue Jerusalem from me?"

[36]But the people were silent and did not utter a word because Hezekiah had commanded them, "Do not answer him."

[37]Then Eliakim son of Hilkiah, the palace administrator; Shebna the court secretary; and Joah son of Asaph, the royal historian, went back to Hezekiah. They tore their clothes in despair, and they went in to see the king and told him what the Assyrian chief of staff had said.

19:1WHEN King Hezekiah heard their report, he tore his clothes and put on burlap and went into the Temple of the LORD. [2]And he sent Eliakim the palace administrator, Shebna the court secretary, and the leading priests, all dressed in burlap, to the prophet Isaiah son of Amoz. [3]They told him, "This is what King Hezekiah says: Today is a day of trouble, insults, and disgrace. It is like when a child is ready to be born, but the mother has no strength to deliver the baby. [4]But perhaps the LORD your God has heard the Assyrian chief of staff,* sent by the king to defy the living God, and will punish him for his words. Oh, pray for those of us who are left!"

[5]After King Hezekiah's officials delivered the king's message to Isaiah, [6]the prophet replied, "Say to your master, 'This is what the LORD says: Do not be disturbed by this blasphemous speech against me from the Assyrian king's messengers. [7]Listen! I myself will move against him,* and the king will receive a message that he is needed at home. So he will return to his land, where I will have him killed with a sword.'"

[8]Meanwhile, the Assyrian chief of staff left Jerusalem and went to consult the king of Assyria, who had left Lachish and was attacking Libnah.

[9]Soon afterward King Sennacherib received word that King Tirhakah of Ethiopia* was leading an army to fight against him. Before leaving to meet the attack, he sent messengers back to Hezekiah in Jerusalem with this message:

[10]"This message is for King Hezekiah of Judah. Don't let your God, in whom you trust, deceive you with promises that Jerusalem will not be captured by the king of Assyria. [11]You know perfectly well what the kings of Assyria have done wherever they have gone. They have completely destroyed everyone who stood in their way! Why should you be any different? [12]Have the gods of other nations rescued them—such nations as Gozan, Haran, Rezeph, and the people of Eden who were in Telassar? My predecessors destroyed them all! [13]What happened to the king of Hamath and the king of Arpad? What happened to the kings of Sepharvaim, Hena, and Ivvah?"

[14]After Hezekiah received the letter from the messengers and read it, he went up to the LORD's Temple and

spread it out before the LORD. ¹⁵And
Hezekiah prayed this prayer before the
LORD: "O LORD, God of Israel, you are enthroned between the mighty cherubim!
You alone are God of all the kingdoms of
the earth. You alone created the heavens
and the earth. ¹⁶Bend down, O LORD, and
listen! Open your eyes, O LORD, and see!
Listen to Sennacherib's words of defi-
ance against the living God.

¹⁷"It is true, LORD, that the kings of
Assyria have destroyed all these nations.
¹⁸And they have thrown the gods of
these nations into the fire and burned
them. But of course the Assyrians could
destroy them! They were not gods at all—
only idols of wood and stone shaped by
human hands. ¹⁹Now, O LORD our God,
rescue us from his power; then all the
kingdoms of the earth will know that you
alone, O LORD, are God."

²⁰Then Isaiah son of Amoz sent this
message to Hezekiah: "This is what
the LORD, the God of Israel, says: I have
heard your prayer about King Sennacherib of Assyria. ²¹And the LORD has
spoken this word against him:

"The virgin daughter of Zion
    despises you and laughs at you.
The daughter of Jerusalem
    shakes her head in derision
    as you flee.

²² "Whom have you been defying
    and ridiculing?
    Against whom did you raise
        your voice?
At whom did you look with such
        haughty eyes?
    It was the Holy One of Israel!
²³ By your messengers you have
        defied the Lord.
    You have said, 'With my many
        chariots
I have conquered the highest
        mountains—
    yes, the remotest peaks
        of Lebanon.
I have cut down its tallest cedars
    and its finest cypress trees.
I have reached its farthest corners
    and explored its deepest forests.

²⁴ I have dug wells in many foreign
        lands
    and refreshed myself with
        their water.
With the sole of my foot
    I stopped up all the rivers
        of Egypt!'

²⁵ "But have you not heard?
    I decided this long ago.
Long ago I planned it,
    and now I am making it happen.
I planned for you to crush
        fortified cities
    into heaps of rubble.
²⁶ That is why their people have so
        little power
    and are so frightened and
        confused.
They are as weak as grass,
    as easily trampled as tender
        green shoots.
They are like grass sprouting
        on a housetop,
    scorched before it can grow
        lush and tall.

²⁷ "But I know you well—
        where you stay
and when you come and go.
    I know the way you have raged
        against me.
²⁸ And because of your raging
        against me
    and your arrogance, which I have
        heard for myself,
I will put my hook in your nose
    and my bit in your mouth.
I will make you return
    by the same road on which
        you came."

²⁹Then Isaiah said to Hezekiah, "Here is
the proof that what I say is true:

"This year you will eat only what
        grows up by itself,
    and next year you will eat what
        springs up from that.
But in the third year you will plant
        crops and harvest them;
    you will tend vineyards and
        eat their fruit.
³⁰ And you who are left in Judah,

who have escaped the ravages
of the siege,
will put roots down in your own soil
and will grow up and flourish.
31 For a remnant of my people will
spread out from Jerusalem,
a group of survivors from
Mount Zion.
The passionate commitment of the
LORD of Heaven's Armies*
will make this happen!

32"And this is what the LORD says about
the king of Assyria:

"His armies will not enter Jerusalem.
They will not even shoot
an arrow at it.
They will not march outside its
gates with their shields
nor build banks of earth against
its walls.
33 The king will return to his own
country
by the same road on which
he came.
He will not enter this city,
says the LORD.
34 For my own honor and for the sake
of my servant David,
I will defend this city and
protect it."

35 That night the angel of the LORD
went out to the Assyrian camp and
killed 185,000 Assyrian soldiers.
When the surviving Assyrians* woke
up the next morning, they found
corpses everywhere. 36Then King Sennacherib of Assyria broke camp and
returned to his own land. He went
home to his capital of Nineveh and
stayed there.
37One day while he was worshiping in
the temple of his god Nisroch, his sons*
Adrammelech and Sharezer killed him
with their swords. They then escaped to
the land of Ararat, and another son, Esarhaddon, became the next king of Assyria.

18:13 The fourteenth year of Hezekiah's reign was 701 B.C.
18:14 Hebrew 300 talents [10 metric tons] of silver and
30 talents [1 metric ton] of gold. 18:17a Or the
rabshakeh; also in 18:19, 26, 27, 28, 37. 18:17b Or
bleached. 18:26 Hebrew in the dialect of Judah; also in
18:28. 19:4 Or the rabshakeh; also in 19:8.

19:7 Hebrew I will put a spirit in him. 19:9 Hebrew
of Cush. 19:31 As in Greek and Syriac versions, Latin
Vulgate, and an alternate reading of the Masoretic Text
(see also Isa 37:32); the other alternate reads the LORD.
19:35 Hebrew When they. 19:37 As in Greek version
and an alternate reading of the Masoretic Text (see also
Isa 37:38); the other alternate reading lacks his sons.

ACTS 21:1-17

After saying farewell to the Ephesian
elders, we [Luke, Paul, and their com-
panions] sailed straight to the island
of Cos. The next day we reached Rhodes
and then went to Patara. 2There we
boarded a ship sailing for Phoenicia.
3We sighted the island of Cyprus,
passed it on our left, and landed at the
harbor of Tyre, in Syria, where the ship
was to unload its cargo.
4We went ashore, found the local believers,* and stayed with them a week.
These believers prophesied through the
Holy Spirit that Paul should not go on to
Jerusalem. 5When we returned to the
ship at the end of the week, the entire
congregation, including wives and children, left the city and came down to the
shore with us. There we knelt, prayed,
6and said our farewells. Then we went
aboard, and they returned home.
7The next stop after leaving Tyre was
Ptolemais, where we greeted the brothers and sisters* and stayed for one day.
8The next day we went on to Caesarea
and stayed at the home of Philip the
Evangelist, one of the seven men who
had been chosen to distribute food. 9He
had four unmarried daughters who had
the gift of prophecy.
10Several days later a man named
Agabus, who also had the gift of prophecy, arrived from Judea. 11He came over,
took Paul's belt, and bound his own feet
and hands with it. Then he said, "The
Holy Spirit declares, 'So shall the owner
of this belt be bound by the Jewish leaders in Jerusalem and turned over to the
Gentiles.' " 12When we heard this, we
and the local believers all begged Paul
not to go on to Jerusalem.
13But he said, "Why all this weeping?
You are breaking my heart! I am ready
not only to be jailed at Jerusalem but
even to die for the sake of the Lord

Jesus." [14]When it was clear that we couldn't persuade him, we gave up and said, "The Lord's will be done."

[15]After this we packed our things and left for Jerusalem. [16]Some believers from Caesarea accompanied us, and they took us to the home of Mnason, a man originally from Cyprus and one of the early believers. [17]When we arrived, the brothers and sisters in Jerusalem welcomed us warmly.

21:4 Greek *disciples;* also in 21:16.　21:7 Greek *brothers;* also in 21:17.

PSALM 149:1-9

Praise the LORD!

Sing to the LORD a new song.
　　Sing his praises in the assembly
　　　of the faithful.

[2] O Israel, rejoice in your Maker.
　　O people of Jerusalem,* exult
　　　in your King.
[3] **Praise his name with dancing,**
　　accompanied by tambourine
　　and harp.
[4] **For the LORD delights in**
　　his people;
　　he crowns the humble
　　with victory.
[5] Let the faithful rejoice that he
　　honors them.
　　Let them sing for joy as they
　　　lie on their beds.

[6] Let the praises of God be in
　　their mouths,
　　and a sharp sword in their
　　　hands—
[7] to execute vengeance on
　　the nations
　　and punishment on
　　the peoples,
[8] to bind their kings with shackles
　　and their leaders with
　　　iron chains,
[9] to execute the judgment written
　　against them.
　　This is the glorious privilege
　　　of his faithful ones.

Praise the LORD!

149:2 Hebrew *Zion.*

PROVERBS 18:8

Rumors are dainty morsels that sink deep into one's heart.

JULY 2

2 KINGS 20:1–22:2

About that time Hezekiah became deathly ill, and the prophet Isaiah son of Amoz went to visit him. He gave the king this message: "This is what the LORD says: Set your affairs in order, for you are going to die. You will not recover from this illness."

[2]When Hezekiah heard this, he turned his face to the wall and prayed to the LORD, [3]"Remember, O LORD, how I have always been faithful to you and have served you single-mindedly, always doing what pleases you." Then he broke down and wept bitterly.

[4]But before Isaiah had left the middle courtyard, this message came to him from the LORD: [5]"Go back to Hezekiah, the leader of my people. Tell him, 'This is what the LORD, the God of your ancestor David, says: I have heard your prayer and seen your tears. I will heal you, and three days from now you will get out of bed and go to the Temple of the LORD. [6]I will add fifteen years to your life, and I will rescue you and this city from the king of Assyria. I will defend this city for my own honor and for the sake of my servant David.'"

[7]Then Isaiah said, "Make an ointment from figs." So Hezekiah's servants spread the ointment over the boil, and Hezekiah recovered!

[8]Meanwhile, Hezekiah had said to Isaiah, "What sign will the LORD give to prove that he will heal me and that I will go to the Temple of the LORD three days from now?"

[9]Isaiah replied, "This is the sign from the LORD to prove that he will do as he promised. Would you like the shadow on the sundial to go forward ten steps or backward ten steps?*"

[10]"The shadow always moves forward," Hezekiah replied, "so that would be easy. Make it go ten steps backward instead." [11]So Isaiah the prophet asked the LORD to do this, and he caused the shadow to move ten steps backward on the sundial* of Ahaz!

[12]Soon after this, Merodach-baladan son of Baladan, king of Babylon, sent Hezekiah his best wishes and a gift, for he had heard that Hezekiah had been very sick. [13]Hezekiah received the Babylonian envoys and showed them everything in his treasure-houses—the silver, the gold, the spices, and the aromatic oils. He also took them to see his armory and showed them everything in his royal treasuries! There was nothing in his palace or kingdom that Hezekiah did not show them.

[14]Then Isaiah the prophet went to King Hezekiah and asked him, "What did those men want? Where were they from?"

Hezekiah replied, "They came from the distant land of Babylon."

[15]"What did they see in your palace?" Isaiah asked.

"They saw everything," Hezekiah replied. "I showed them everything I own—all my royal treasuries."

[16]Then Isaiah said to Hezekiah, "Listen to this message from the LORD: [17]The time is coming when everything in your palace—all the treasures stored up by your ancestors until now—will be carried off to Babylon. Nothing will be left, says the LORD. [18]Some of your very own sons will be taken away into exile. They will become eunuchs who will serve in the palace of Babylon's king."

[19]Then Hezekiah said to Isaiah, "This message you have given me from the LORD is good." For the king was thinking, "At least there will be peace and security during my lifetime."

[20]The rest of the events in Hezekiah's reign, including the extent of his power and how he built a pool and dug a tunnel* to bring water into the city, are recorded in *The Book of the History of the Kings of Judah*. [21]Hezekiah died, and his son Manasseh became the next king.

[21:1]MANASSEH was twelve years old when he became king, and he reigned in Jerusalem fifty-five years. His mother was Hephzibah. [2]He did what was evil in the LORD's sight, following the detestable practices of the pagan nations that the LORD had driven from the land ahead of the Israelites. [3]He rebuilt the pagan shrines his father, Hezekiah, had destroyed. He constructed altars for Baal and set up an Asherah pole, just as King Ahab of Israel had done. He also bowed before all the powers of the heavens and worshiped them.

[4]He built pagan altars in the Temple of the LORD, the place where the LORD had said, "My name will remain in Jerusalem forever." [5]He built these altars for all the powers of the heavens in both courtyards of the LORD's Temple. [6]Manasseh also sacrificed his own son in the fire.* He practiced sorcery and divination, and he consulted with mediums and psychics. He did much that was evil in the LORD's sight, arousing his anger.

[7]Manasseh even made a carved image of Asherah and set it up in the Temple, the very place where the LORD had told David and his son Solomon: "My name will be honored forever in this Temple and in Jerusalem—the city I have chosen from among all the tribes of Israel. [8]If the Israelites will be careful to obey my commands—all the laws my servant Moses gave them—I will not send them into exile from this land that I gave their ancestors." [9]But the people refused to listen, and Manasseh led them to do even more evil than the pagan nations that the LORD had destroyed when the people of Israel entered the land.

[10]Then the LORD said through his servants the prophets: [11]"King Manasseh of Judah has done many detestable things. He is even more wicked than the Am-

orites, who lived in this land before Israel. He has caused the people of Judah to sin with his idols.* ¹²So this is what the LORD, the God of Israel, says: I will bring such disaster on Jerusalem and Judah that the ears of those who hear about it will tingle with horror. ¹³I will judge Jerusalem by the same standard I used for Samaria and the same measure* I used for the family of Ahab. I will wipe away the people of Jerusalem as one wipes a dish and turns it upside down. ¹⁴Then I will reject even the remnant of my own people who are left, and I will hand them over as plunder for their enemies. ¹⁵For they have done great evil in my sight and have angered me ever since their ancestors came out of Egypt."

¹⁶Manasseh also murdered many innocent people until Jerusalem was filled from one end to the other with innocent blood. This was in addition to the sin that he caused the people of Judah to commit, leading them to do evil in the LORD's sight.

¹⁷The rest of the events in Manasseh's reign and everything he did, including the sins he committed, are recorded in *The Book of the History of the Kings of Judah.* ¹⁸When Manasseh died, he was buried in the palace garden, the garden of Uzza. Then his son Amon became the next king.

¹⁹Amon was twenty-two years old when he became king, and he reigned in Jerusalem two years. His mother was Meshullemeth, the daughter of Haruz from Jotbah. ²⁰He did what was evil in the LORD's sight, just as his father, Manasseh, had done. ²¹He followed the example of his father, worshiping the same idols his father had worshiped. ²²He abandoned the LORD, the God of his ancestors, and he refused to follow the LORD's ways.

²³Then Amon's own officials conspired against him and assassinated him in his palace. ²⁴But the people of the land killed all those who had conspired against King Amon, and they made his son Josiah the next king.

²⁵The rest of the events in Amon's reign and what he did are recorded in

The Book of the History of the Kings of Judah. ²⁶He was buried in his tomb in the garden of Uzza. Then his son Josiah became the next king.

²²:¹JOSIAH was eight years old when he became king, and he reigned in Jerusalem thirty-one years. His mother was Jedidah, the daughter of Adaiah from Bozkath. ²He did what was pleasing in the LORD's sight and followed the example of his ancestor David. He did not turn away from doing what was right.

20:9 Or *The shadow on the sundial has gone forward ten steps; do you want it to go backward ten steps?*
20:11 Hebrew *the steps.*   20:20 Hebrew *watercourse.*
21:6 Or *also made his son pass through the fire.*
21:11 The Hebrew term (literally *round things*) probably alludes to dung; also in 21:21.   21:13 Hebrew *the same plumb line I used for Samaria and the same plumb bob.*

ACTS 21:18-36

The next day Paul went with us [Luke and Paul's other companions] to meet with James, and all the elders of the Jerusalem church were present. ¹⁹After greeting them, Paul gave a detailed account of the things God had accomplished among the Gentiles through his ministry.

²⁰After hearing this, they praised God. And then they said, "You know, dear brother, how many thousands of Jews have also believed, and they all follow the law of Moses very seriously. ²¹But the Jewish believers here in Jerusalem have been told that you are teaching all the Jews who live among the Gentiles to turn their backs on the laws of Moses. They've heard that you teach them not to circumcise their children or follow other Jewish customs. ²²What should we do? They will certainly hear that you have come.

²³"Here's what we want you to do. We have four men here who have completed their vow. ²⁴Go with them to the Temple and join them in the purification ceremony, paying for them to have their heads ritually shaved. Then everyone will know that the rumors are all false and that you yourself observe the Jewish laws. ²⁵"As for the Gentile believers, they

should do what we already told them in a letter: They should abstain from eating food offered to idols, from consuming blood or the meat of strangled animals, and from sexual immorality."

²⁶So Paul went to the Temple the next day with the other men. They had already started the purification ritual, so he publicly announced the date when their vows would end and sacrifices would be offered for each of them.

²⁷The seven days were almost ended when some Jews from the province of Asia saw Paul in the Temple and roused a mob against him. They grabbed him, ²⁸yelling, "Men of Israel, help us! This is the man who preaches against our people everywhere and tells everybody to disobey the Jewish laws. He speaks against the Temple—and even defiles this holy place by bringing in Gentiles.*" ²⁹(For earlier that day they had seen him in the city with Trophimus, a Gentile from Ephesus,* and they assumed Paul had taken him into the Temple.)

³⁰The whole city was rocked by these accusations, and a great riot followed. Paul was grabbed and dragged out of the Temple, and immediately the gates were closed behind him. ³¹As they were trying to kill him, word reached the commander of the Roman regiment that all Jerusalem was in an uproar. ³²He immediately called out his soldiers and officers* and ran down among the crowd. When the mob saw the commander and the troops coming, they stopped beating Paul.

³³Then the commander arrested him and ordered him bound with two chains. He asked the crowd who he was and what he had done. ³⁴Some shouted one thing and some another. Since he couldn't find out the truth in all the uproar and confusion, he ordered that Paul be taken to the fortress. ³⁵As Paul reached the stairs, the mob grew so violent the soldiers had to lift him to their shoulders to protect him. ³⁶And the crowd followed behind, shouting, "Kill him, kill him!"

21:28 Greek *Greeks.*   21:29 Greek *Trophimus, the Ephesian.*   21:32 Greek *centurions.*

PSALM 150:1-6

Praise the Lord!

Praise God in his sanctuary;
    praise him in his mighty heaven!
² Praise him for his mighty works;
    praise his unequaled greatness!
³ Praise him with a blast of the
        ram's horn;
    praise him with the lyre and harp!
⁴ Praise him with the tambourine
        and dancing;
    praise him with strings and flutes!
⁵ Praise him with a clash of cymbals;
    praise him with loud clanging
        cymbals.
⁶ Let everything that breathes sing
    praises to the Lord!

Praise the Lord!

PROVERBS 18:9-10

A lazy person is as bad as someone who destroys things. □ The name of the Lord is a strong fortress; the godly run to him and are safe.

JULY
3

2 KINGS 22:3–23:30

In the eighteenth year of his reign, King Josiah sent Shaphan son of Azaliah and grandson of Meshullam, the court secretary, to the Temple of the Lord. He told him, ⁴"Go to Hilkiah the high priest and have him count the money the gatekeepers have collected from the people at the Lord's Temple. ⁵Entrust this money to the men assigned to supervise the Temple's restoration. Then they can use it to pay workers to repair the Temple of the Lord. ⁶They will need to hire carpenters, builders, and masons. Also have them buy the timber and the finished stone needed to repair the Temple. ⁷But don't require the construction supervisors to keep account of the money they receive, for they are honest and trustworthy men."

[8]Hilkiah the high priest said to Shaphan the court secretary, "I have found the Book of the Law in the LORD's Temple!" Then Hilkiah gave the scroll to Shaphan, and he read it.

[9]Shaphan went to the king and reported, "Your officials have turned over the money collected at the Temple of the LORD to the workers and supervisors at the Temple." [10]Shaphan also told the king, "Hilkiah the priest has given me a scroll." So Shaphan read it to the king.

[11]When the king heard what was written in the Book of the Law, he tore his clothes in despair. [12]Then he gave these orders to Hilkiah the priest, Ahikam son of Shaphan, Acbor son of Micaiah, Shaphan the court secretary, and Asaiah the king's personal adviser: [13]"Go to the Temple and speak to the LORD for me and for the people and for all Judah. Inquire about the words written in this scroll that has been found. For the LORD's great anger is burning against us because our ancestors have not obeyed the words in this scroll. We have not been doing everything it says we must do."

[14]So Hilkiah the priest, Ahikam, Acbor, Shaphan, and Asaiah went to the New Quarter* of Jerusalem to consult with the prophet Huldah. She was the wife of Shallum son of Tikvah, son of Harhas, the keeper of the Temple wardrobe.

[15]She said to them, "The LORD, the God of Israel, has spoken! Go back and tell the man who sent you, [16]'This is what the LORD says: I am going to bring disaster on this city* and its people. All the words written in the scroll that the king of Judah has read will come true. [17]For my people have abandoned me and offered sacrifices to pagan gods, and I am very angry with them for everything they have done. My anger will burn against this place, and it will not be quenched.'

[18]"But go to the king of Judah who sent you to seek the LORD and tell him: 'This is what the LORD, the God of Israel,

says concerning the message you have just heard: [19]You were sorry and humbled yourself before the LORD when you heard what I said against this city and its people—that this land would be cursed and become desolate. You tore your clothing in despair and wept before me in repentance. And I have indeed heard you, says the LORD. [20]So I will not send the promised disaster until after you have died and been buried in peace. You will not see the disaster I am going to bring on this city.'"

So they took her message back to the king.

[23:1]THEN the king summoned all the elders of Judah and Jerusalem. [2]And the king went up to the Temple of the LORD with all the people of Judah and Jerusalem, along with the priests and the prophets—all the people from the least to the greatest. There the king read to them the entire Book of the Covenant that had been found in the LORD's Temple. [3]The king took his place of authority beside the pillar and renewed the covenant in the LORD's presence. He pledged to obey the LORD by keeping all his commands, laws, and decrees with all his heart and soul. In this way, he confirmed all the terms of the covenant that were written in the scroll, and all the people pledged themselves to the covenant.

[4]Then the king instructed Hilkiah the high priest and the priests of the second rank and the Temple gatekeepers to remove from the LORD's Temple all the articles that were used to worship Baal, Asherah, and all the powers of the heavens. The king had all these things burned outside Jerusalem on the terraces of the Kidron Valley, and he carried the ashes away to Bethel. [5]He did away with the idolatrous priests, who had been appointed by the previous kings of Judah, for they had offered sacrifices at the pagan shrines throughout Judah and even in the vicinity of Jerusalem. They had also offered sacrifices to Baal, and to the sun, the moon, the constellations, and to all

the powers of the heavens. [6]The king removed the Asherah pole from the LORD's Temple and took it outside Jerusalem to the Kidron Valley, where he burned it. Then he ground the ashes of the pole to dust and threw the dust over the graves of the people. [7]He also tore down the living quarters of the male and female shrine prostitutes that were inside the Temple of the LORD, where the women wove coverings for the Asherah pole.

[8]Josiah brought to Jerusalem all the priests who were living in other towns of Judah. He also defiled the pagan shrines, where they had offered sacrifices—all the way from Geba to Beersheba. He destroyed the shrines at the entrance to the gate of Joshua, the governor of Jerusalem. This gate was located to the left of the city gate as one enters the city. [9]The priests who had served at the pagan shrines were not allowed* to serve at the LORD's altar in Jerusalem, but they were allowed to eat unleavened bread with the other priests.

[10]Then the king defiled the altar of Topheth in the valley of Ben-Hinnom, so no one could ever again use it to sacrifice a son or daughter in the fire* as an offering to Molech. [11]He removed from the entrance of the LORD's Temple the horse statues that the former kings of Judah had dedicated to the sun. They were near the quarters of Nathan-melech the eunuch, an officer of the court.* The king also burned the chariots dedicated to the sun.

[12]Josiah tore down the altars that the kings of Judah had built on the palace roof above the upper room of Ahaz. The king destroyed the altars that Manasseh had built in the two courtyards of the LORD's Temple. He smashed them to bits* and scattered the pieces in the Kidron Valley. [13]The king also desecrated the pagan shrines east of Jerusalem, to the south of the Mount of Corruption, where King Solomon of Israel had built shrines for Ashtoreth, the detestable goddess of the Sidonians; and for Chemosh, the detestable god of the Moabites; and for Molech,* the vile god of the Ammonites. [14]He smashed the sacred pillars and cut down the Asherah poles. Then he desecrated these places by scattering human bones over them.

[15]The king also tore down the altar at Bethel—the pagan shrine that Jeroboam son of Nebat had made when he caused Israel to sin. He burned down the shrine and ground it to dust, and he burned the Asherah pole. [16]Then Josiah turned around and noticed several tombs in the side of the hill. He ordered that the bones be brought out, and he burned them on the altar at Bethel to desecrate it. (This happened just as the LORD had promised through the man of God when Jeroboam stood beside the altar at the festival.)

Then Josiah turned and looked up at the tomb of the man of God* who had predicted these things. [17]"What is that monument over there?" Josiah asked.

And the people of the town told him, "It is the tomb of the man of God who came from Judah and predicted the very things that you have just done to the altar at Bethel!"

[18]Josiah replied, "Leave it alone. Don't disturb his bones." So they did not burn his bones or those of the old prophet from Samaria.

[19]Then Josiah demolished all the buildings at the pagan shrines in the towns of Samaria, just as he had done at Bethel. They had been built by the various kings of Israel and had made the LORD* very angry. [20]He executed the priests of the pagan shrines on their own altars, and he burned human bones on the altars to desecrate them. Finally, he returned to Jerusalem.

[21]King Josiah then issued this order to all the people: "You must celebrate the Passover to the LORD your God, as required in this Book of the Covenant." [22]There had not been a Passover celebration like that since the time when the judges ruled in Israel, nor throughout all the years of the kings of Israel and Judah. [23]This Passover was celebrated to the LORD in Jerusalem in the eighteenth year of King Josiah's reign.

[24]Josiah also got rid of the mediums

and psychics, the household gods, the idols,* and every other kind of detestable practice, both in Jerusalem and throughout the land of Judah. He did this in obedience to the laws written in the scroll that Hilkiah the priest had found in the LORD's Temple. 25Never before had there been a king like Josiah, who turned to the LORD with all his heart and soul and strength, obeying all the laws of Moses. And there has never been a king like him since.

26Even so, the LORD was very angry with Judah because of all the wicked things Manasseh had done to provoke him. 27For the LORD said, "I will also banish Judah from my presence just as I have banished Israel. And I will reject my chosen city of Jerusalem and the Temple where my name was to be honored."

28The rest of the events in Josiah's reign and all his deeds are recorded in *The Book of the History of the Kings of Judah.*

29While Josiah was king, Pharaoh Neco, king of Egypt, went to the Euphrates River to help the king of Assyria. King Josiah and his army marched out to fight him,* but King Neco* killed him when they met at Megiddo. 30Josiah's officers took his body back in a chariot from Megiddo to Jerusalem and buried him in his own tomb. Then the people of the land anointed Josiah's son Jehoahaz and made him the next king.

22:14 Or *the Second Quarter,* a newer section of Jerusalem. Hebrew reads *the Mishneh.* 22:16 Hebrew *this place;* also in 22:19, 20. 23:9 Hebrew *did not come up.* 23:10 Or *to make a son or daughter pass through the fire.* 23:11 The meaning of the Hebrew is uncertain. 23:12 Or *He quickly removed them.* 23:13 Hebrew *Milcom,* a variant spelling of Molech. 23:16 As in Greek version; Hebrew lacks *when Jeroboam stood beside the altar at the festival. Then Josiah turned and looked up at the tomb of the man of God.* 23:19 As in Greek and Syriac versions and Latin Vulgate; Hebrew lacks *the LORD.* 23:24 The Hebrew term (literally *round things*) probably alludes to dung. 23:29a Or *Josiah went out to meet him.* 23:29b Hebrew *he.*

ACTS 21:37–22:16

As Paul was about to be taken inside, he said to the commander, "May I have a word with you?"

"Do you know Greek?" the commander asked, surprised. 38"Aren't you the Egyptian who led a rebellion some time ago and took 4,000 members of the Assassins out into the desert?"

39"No," Paul replied, "I am a Jew and a citizen of Tarsus in Cilicia, which is an important city. Please, let me talk to these people." 40The commander agreed, so Paul stood on the stairs and motioned to the people to be quiet. Soon a deep silence enveloped the crowd, and he addressed them in their own language, Aramaic.*

22:1"BROTHERS and esteemed fathers," Paul said, "listen to me as I offer my defense." 2When they heard him speaking in their own language,* the silence was even greater.

3Then Paul said, "I am a Jew, born in Tarsus, a city in Cilicia, and I was brought up and educated here in Jerusalem under Gamaliel. As his student, I was carefully trained in our Jewish laws and customs. I became very zealous to honor God in everything I did, just like all of you today. 4And I persecuted the followers of the Way, hounding some to death, arresting both men and women and throwing them in prison. 5The high priest and the whole council of elders can testify that this is so. For I received letters from them to our Jewish brothers in Damascus, authorizing me to bring the Christians from there to Jerusalem, in chains, to be punished.

6"As I was on the road, approaching Damascus about noon, a very bright light from heaven suddenly shone down around me. 7I fell to the ground and heard a voice saying to me, 'Saul, Saul, why are you persecuting me?'

8"'Who are you, lord?' I asked.

"And the voice replied, 'I am Jesus the Nazarene,* the one you are persecuting.' 9The people with me saw the light but didn't understand the voice speaking to me.

10"I asked, 'What should I do, Lord?'

"And the Lord told me, 'Get up and go into Damascus, and there you will be told everything you are to do.'

11"I was blinded by the intense light

and had to be led by the hand to Damascus by my companions. ¹²A man named Ananias lived there. He was a godly man, deeply devoted to the law, and well regarded by all the Jews of Damascus. ¹³He came and stood beside me and said, 'Brother Saul, regain your sight.' And that very moment I could see him!

¹⁴"Then he told me, 'The God of our ancestors has chosen you to know his will and to see the Righteous One and hear him speak. ¹⁵For you are to be his witness, telling everyone what you have seen and heard. ¹⁶What are you waiting for? Get up and be baptized. Have your sins washed away by calling on the name of the Lord."

21:40 Or *Hebrew.*   22:2 Greek *in Aramaic,* or *in Hebrew.* 22:8 Or *Jesus of Nazareth.*

PSALM 1:1-6

Oh, the joys of those who do not
follow the advice of the wicked,
or stand around with sinners,
or join in with mockers.
² **But they delight in the law**
of the LORD,
meditating on it day and night.
³ They are like trees planted along
the riverbank,
bearing fruit each season.
Their leaves never wither,
and they prosper in all they do.

⁴ But not the wicked!
They are like worthless chaff,
scattered by the wind.
⁵ They will be condemned at the
time of judgment.
Sinners will have no place among
the godly.
⁶ For the LORD watches over the path
of the godly,
but the path of the wicked leads
to destruction.

PROVERBS 18:11-12

The rich think of their wealth as a strong defense; they imagine it to be a high wall of safety. ☐Haughtiness goes before destruction; humility precedes honor.

JULY 4

2 KINGS 23:31–25:30

Jehoahaz was twenty-three years old when he became king, and he reigned in Jerusalem three months. His mother was Hamutal, the daughter of Jeremiah from Libnah. ³²He did what was evil in the LORD's sight, just as his ancestors had done.

³³Pharaoh Neco put Jehoahaz in prison at Riblah in the land of Hamath to prevent him from ruling* in Jerusalem. He also demanded that Judah pay 7,500 pounds of silver and 75 pounds of gold* as tribute.

³⁴Pharaoh Neco then installed Eliakim, another of Josiah's sons, to reign in place of his father, and he changed Eliakim's name to Jehoiakim. Jehoahaz was taken to Egypt as a prisoner, where he died.

³⁵In order to get the silver and gold demanded as tribute by Pharaoh Neco, Jehoiakim collected a tax from the people of Judah, requiring them to pay in proportion to their wealth.

³⁶Jehoiakim was twenty-five years old when he became king, and he reigned in Jerusalem eleven years. His mother was Zebidah, the daughter of Pedaiah from Rumah. ³⁷He did what was evil in the LORD's sight, just as his ancestors had done.

²⁴:¹DURING Jehoiakim's reign, King Nebuchadnezzar of Babylon invaded the land of Judah. Jehoiakim surrendered and paid him tribute for three years but then rebelled. ²Then the LORD sent bands of Babylonian,* Aramean, Moabite, and Ammonite raiders against Judah to destroy it, just as the LORD had promised through his prophets. ³These disasters happened to Judah because of the LORD's command. He had decided to banish Judah from his presence because of the many sins of Manasseh, ⁴who had

filled Jerusalem with innocent blood. The LORD would not forgive this.

⁵The rest of the events in Jehoiakim's reign and all his deeds are recorded in *The Book of the History of the Kings of Judah*. ⁶When Jehoiakim died, his son Jehoiachin became the next king.

⁷The king of Egypt did not venture out of his country after that, for the king of Babylon captured the entire area formerly claimed by Egypt—from the Brook of Egypt to the Euphrates River.

⁸Jehoiachin was eighteen years old when he became king, and he reigned in Jerusalem three months. His mother was Nehushta, the daughter of Elnathan from Jerusalem. ⁹Jehoiachin did what was evil in the LORD's sight, just as his father had done.

¹⁰During Jehoiachin's reign, the officers of King Nebuchadnezzar of Babylon came up against Jerusalem and besieged it. ¹¹Nebuchadnezzar himself arrived at the city during the siege. ¹²Then King Jehoiachin, along with the queen mother, his advisers, his commanders, and his officials, surrendered to the Babylonians.

In the eighth year of Nebuchadnezzar's reign, he took Jehoiachin prisoner. ¹³As the LORD had said beforehand, Nebuchadnezzar carried away all the treasures from the LORD's Temple and the royal palace. He stripped away* all the gold objects that King Solomon of Israel had placed in the Temple. ¹⁴King Nebuchadnezzar took all of Jerusalem captive, including all the commanders and the best of the soldiers, craftsmen, and artisans—10,000 in all. Only the poorest people were left in the land.

¹⁵Nebuchadnezzar led King Jehoiachin away as a captive to Babylon, along with the queen mother, his wives and officials, and all Jerusalem's elite. ¹⁶He also exiled 7,000 of the best troops and 1,000 craftsmen and artisans, all of whom were strong and fit for war. ¹⁷Then the king of Babylon installed Mattaniah, Jehoiachin's* uncle, as the next king, and he changed Mattaniah's name to Zedekiah.

¹⁸Zedekiah was twenty-one years old when he became king, and he reigned in Jerusalem eleven years. His mother was Hamutal, the daughter of Jeremiah from Libnah. ¹⁹But Zedekiah did what was evil in the LORD's sight, just as Jehoiakim had done. ²⁰These things happened because of the LORD's anger against the people of Jerusalem and Judah, until he finally banished them from his presence and sent them into exile.

Zedekiah rebelled against the king of Babylon.

²⁵:¹So on January 15,* during the ninth year of Zedekiah's reign, King Nebuchadnezzar of Babylon led his entire army against Jerusalem. They surrounded the city and built siege ramps against its walls. ²Jerusalem was kept under siege until the eleventh year of King Zedekiah's reign.

³By July 18 in the eleventh year of Zedekiah's reign,* the famine in the city had become very severe, and the last of the food was entirely gone. ⁴Then a section of the city wall was broken down, and all the soldiers fled. Since the city was surrounded by the Babylonians,* they waited for nightfall. Then they slipped through the gate between the two walls behind the king's garden and headed toward the Jordan Valley.*

⁵But the Babylonian* troops chased the king and caught him on the plains of Jericho, for his men had all deserted him and scattered. ⁶They took him to the king of Babylon at Riblah, where they pronounced judgment upon Zedekiah. ⁷They made Zedekiah watch as they slaughtered his sons. Then they gouged out Zedekiah's eyes, bound him in bronze chains, and led him away to Babylon.

⁸On August 14 of that year,* which was the nineteenth year of King Nebuchadnezzar's reign, Nebuzaradan, the captain of the guard and an official of the Babylonian king, arrived in Jerusalem. ⁹He burned down the Temple of the LORD, the royal palace, and all the houses of Jerusalem. He destroyed all the important buildings* in the city.

10Then he supervised the entire Babylonian army as they tore down the walls of Jerusalem on every side. 11Nebuzaradan, the captain of the guard, then took as exiles the rest of the people who remained in the city, the defectors who had declared their allegiance to the king of Babylon, and the rest of the population. 12But the captain of the guard allowed some of the poorest people to stay behind in Judah to care for the vineyards and fields.

13The Babylonians broke up the bronze pillars in front of the LORD's Temple, the bronze water carts, and the great bronze basin called the Sea, and they carried all the bronze away to Babylon. 14They also took all the ash buckets, shovels, lamp snuffers, dishes, and all the other bronze articles used for making sacrifices at the Temple. 15Nebuzaradan, the captain of the guard, also took the incense burners and basins, and all the other articles made of pure gold or silver.

16The weight of the bronze from the two pillars, the Sea, and the water carts was too great to be measured. These things had been made for the LORD's Temple in the days of King Solomon. 17Each of the pillars was 27 feet* tall. The bronze capital on top of each pillar was 7½ feet* high and was decorated with a network of bronze pomegranates all the way around.

18Nebuzaradan, the captain of the guard, took with him as prisoners Seraiah the high priest, Zephaniah the priest of the second rank, and the three chief gatekeepers. 19And from among the people still hiding in the city, he took an officer who had been in charge of the Judean army; five of the king's personal advisers; the army commander's chief secretary, who was in charge of recruitment; and sixty other citizens. 20Nebuzaradan, the captain of the guard, took them all to the king of Babylon at Riblah. 21And there at Riblah, in the land of Hamath, the king of Babylon had them all put to death. So the people of Judah were sent into exile from their land.

22Then King Nebuchadnezzar appointed Gedaliah son of Ahikam and grandson of Shaphan as governor over the people he had left in Judah. 23When all the army commanders and their men learned that the king of Babylon had appointed Gedaliah as governor, they went to see him at Mizpah. These included Ishmael son of Nethaniah, Johanan son of Kareah, Seraiah son of Tanhumeth the Netophathite, and Jezaniah* son of the Maacathite, and all their men.

24Gedaliah vowed to them that the Babylonian officials meant them no harm. "Don't be afraid of them. Live in the land and serve the king of Babylon, and all will go well for you," he promised.

25But in midautumn of that year,* Ishmael son of Nethaniah and grandson of Elishama, who was of the royal family, went to Mizpah with ten men and killed Gedaliah. He also killed all the Judeans and Babylonians who were with Gedaliah at Mizpah.

26Then all the people of Judah, from the least to the greatest, as well as the army commanders, fled in panic to Egypt, for they were afraid of what the Babylonians would do to them.

27In the thirty-seventh year of the exile of King Jehoiachin of Judah, Evil-merodach ascended to the Babylonian throne. He was kind to* Jehoiachin and released him from prison on April 2 of that year.* 28He spoke kindly to Jehoiachin and gave him a higher place than all the other exiled kings in Babylon. 29He supplied Jehoiachin with new clothes to replace his prison garb and allowed him to dine in the king's presence for the rest of his life. 30So the Babylonian king gave him a regular food allowance as long as he lived.

23:33a The meaning of the Hebrew is uncertain.
23:33b Hebrew *100 talents* [3,400 kilograms] *of silver and 1 talent* [34 kilograms] *of gold.*   24:2 Or *Chaldean.*
24:13 Or *He cut apart.*   24:17 Hebrew *his.*   25:1 Hebrew *on the tenth day of the tenth month,* of the ancient Hebrew lunar calendar. A number of events in 2 Kings can be cross-checked with dates in surviving Babylonian records and related accurately to our modern calendar. This day was January 15, 588 B.C.   25:3 Hebrew *By the ninth day of the [fourth] month* [in the eleventh year of Zedekiah's reign] (compare Jer 52:6 and the note there). This day was July 18, 586 B.C.; also see note on 25:1.   25:4a Or *the Chaldeans;* also in 25:13, 25, 26.   25:4b Hebrew *the Arabah.*
25:5 Or *Chaldean;* also in 25:10, 24.   25:8 Hebrew *On the seventh day of the fifth month,* of the ancient Hebrew lunar

calendar. This day was August 14, 586 B.C.; also see note on 25:1.   **25:9** Or *destroyed the houses of all the important people.*   **25:17a** Hebrew *18 cubits* [8.1 meters].
25:17b As in parallel texts at 1 Kgs 7:16, 2 Chr 3:15, and Jer 52:22, all of which read *5 cubits* [2.3 meters]; Hebrew reads *3 cubits,* which is 4.5 feet or 1.4 meters.   **25:23** As in parallel text at Jer 40:8; Hebrew reads *Jaazaniah,* a variant spelling of Jezaniah.   **25:25** Hebrew *in the seventh month,* of the ancient Hebrew lunar calendar. This month occurred within the months of October and November 586 B.C.; also see note on 25:1.   **25:27a** Hebrew *He raised the head of.* **25:27b** Hebrew *on the twenty-seventh day of the twelfth month,* of the ancient Hebrew lunar calendar. This day was April 2, 561 B.C.; also see note on 25:1.

ACTS 22:17–23:10

"**A**fter I [Paul] returned to Jerusalem, I was praying in the Temple and fell into a trance. ¹⁸I saw a vision of Jesus* saying to me, 'Hurry! Leave Jerusalem, for the people here won't accept your testimony about me.'

¹⁹"'But Lord,' I argued, 'they certainly know that in every synagogue I imprisoned and beat those who believed in you. ²⁰And I was in complete agreement when your witness Stephen was killed. I stood by and kept the coats they took off when they stoned him.'

²¹"But the Lord said to me, 'Go, for I will send you far away to the Gentiles!'"

²²The crowd listened until Paul said that word. Then they all began to shout, "Away with such a fellow! He isn't fit to live!" ²³They yelled, threw off their coats, and tossed handfuls of dust into the air.

²⁴The commander brought Paul inside and ordered him lashed with whips to make him confess his crime. He wanted to find out why the crowd had become so furious. ²⁵When they tied Paul down to lash him, Paul said to the officer* standing there, "Is it legal for you to whip a Roman citizen who hasn't even been tried?"

²⁶When the officer heard this, he went to the commander and asked, "What are you doing? This man is a Roman citizen!"

²⁷So the commander went over and asked Paul, "Tell me, are you a Roman citizen?"

"Yes, I certainly am," Paul replied.

²⁸"I am, too," the commander muttered, "and it cost me plenty!"

Paul answered, "But I am a citizen by birth!"

²⁹The soldiers who were about to interrogate Paul quickly withdrew when they heard he was a Roman citizen, and the commander was frightened because he had ordered him bound and whipped.

³⁰The next day the commander ordered the leading priests into session with the Jewish high council.* He wanted to find out what the trouble was all about, so he released Paul to have him stand before them.

^{23:1}GAZING intently at the high council,* Paul began: "Brothers, I have always lived before God with a clear conscience!"

²Instantly Ananias the high priest commanded those close to Paul to slap him on the mouth. ³But Paul said to him, "God will slap you, you corrupt hypocrite!* What kind of judge are you to break the law yourself by ordering me struck like that?"

⁴Those standing near Paul said to him, "Do you dare to insult God's high priest?"

⁵"I'm sorry, brothers. I didn't realize he was the high priest," Paul replied, "for the Scriptures say, 'You must not speak evil of any of your rulers.'*"

⁶Paul realized that some members of the high council were Sadducees and some were Pharisees, so he shouted, "Brothers, I am a Pharisee, as were my ancestors! And I am on trial because my hope is in the resurrection of the dead!"

⁷This divided the council—the Pharisees against the Sadducees—⁸for the Sadducees say there is no resurrection or angels or spirits, but the Pharisees believe in all of these. ⁹So there was a great uproar. Some of the teachers of religious law who were Pharisees jumped up and began to argue forcefully. "We see nothing wrong with him," they shouted. "Perhaps a spirit or an angel spoke to him." ¹⁰As the conflict grew more violent, the commander was afraid they would tear Paul apart. So he ordered his soldiers to go and rescue him by force and take him back to the fortress.

22:18 Greek *him.*   **22:25** Greek *the centurion;* also in 22:26.   **22:30** Greek *Sanhedrin.*   **23:1** Greek *Sanhedrin;* also in 23:6, 15, 20, 28.   **23:3** Greek *you whitewashed wall.*   **23:5** Exod 22:28.

PSALM 2:1-12

Why are the nations so angry?
Why do they waste their time
with futile plans?
2 The kings of the earth prepare
for battle;
the rulers plot together
against the LORD
and against his anointed one.
3 "Let us break their chains," they cry,
"and free ourselves from
slavery to God."

4 But the one who rules in heaven
laughs.
The Lord scoffs at them.
5 Then in anger he rebukes them,
terrifying them with his
fierce fury.
6 For the Lord declares, "I have placed
my chosen king on the throne
in Jerusalem,* on my holy
mountain."

7 The king proclaims the LORD's
decree:
"The LORD said to me, 'You
are my son.*
Today I have become
your Father.*
8 Only ask, and I will give you the
nations as your inheritance,
the whole earth as your
possession.
9 You will break* them with
an iron rod
and smash them like clay pots.'"

10 Now then, you kings, act wisely!
Be warned, you rulers of
the earth!
11 Serve the LORD with reverent fear,
and rejoice with trembling.
12 Submit to God's royal son,* or he
will become angry,
and you will be destroyed in the
midst of all your activities—
for his anger flares up in an instant.
But what joy for all who take
refuge in him!

2:6 Hebrew *on Zion.*   2:7a Or *Son;* also in 2:12.   2:7b Or
Today I reveal you as my son.   2:9 Greek version reads
rule. Compare Rev 2:27.   2:12 The meaning of the Hebrew
is uncertain.

PROVERBS 18:13

Spouting off before listening to the
facts is both shameful and foolish.

JULY
5

1 CHRONICLES 1:1–2:17

The descendants of Adam were* Seth,
Enosh, 2Kenan, Mahalalel, Jared,
3Enoch, Methuselah, Lamech,
4and Noah.
The sons of Noah were* Shem,
Ham, and Japheth.

5 The descendants of Japheth were
Gomer, Magog, Madai, Javan, Tubal,
Meshech, and Tiras.
6The descendants of Gomer were
Ashkenaz, Riphath,* and Togarmah.
7 The descendants of Javan were
Elishah, Tarshish, Kittim, and
Rodanim.

8The descendants of Ham were Cush,
Mizraim,* Put, and Canaan.
9The descendants of Cush were Seba,
Havilah, Sabtah, Raamah, and
Sabteca. The descendants of
Raamah were Sheba and Dedan.
10Cush was also the ancestor of
Nimrod, who was the first heroic
warrior on earth.
11Mizraim was the ancestor of the
Ludites, Anamites, Lehabites,
Naphtuhites, 12Pathrusites,
Casluhites, and the Caphtorites,
from whom the Philistines came.*
13Canaan's oldest son was Sidon, the
ancestor of the Sidonians. Canaan
was also the ancestor of the Hittites,
14Jebusites, Amorites, Girgashites,
15Hivites, Arkites, Sinites, 16Arvadites,
Zemarites, and Hamathites.

17 The descendants of Shem were
Elam, Asshur, Arphaxad, Lud, and
Aram.

The descendants of Aram were* Uz, Hul, Gether, and Mash.*

[18]Arphaxad was the father of Shelah. Shelah was the father of Eber.

[19]Eber had two sons. The first was named Peleg (which means "division"), for during his lifetime the people of the world were divided into different language groups. His brother's name was Joktan.

[20]Joktan was the ancestor of Almodad, Sheleph, Hazarmaveth, Jerah, [21]Hadoram, Uzal, Diklah, [22]Obal,* Abimael, Sheba, [23]Ophir, Havilah, and Jobab. All these were descendants of Joktan.

[24]So this is the family line descended from Shem: Arphaxad, Shelah,* [25]Eber, Peleg, Reu, [26]Serug, Nahor, Terah, [27]and Abram, later known as Abraham.

[28]The sons of Abraham were Isaac and Ishmael. [29]These are their genealogical records:

The sons of Ishmael were Nebaioth (the oldest), Kedar, Adbeel, Mibsam, [30]Mishma, Dumah, Massa, Hadad, Tema, [31]Jetur, Naphish, and Kedemah. These were the sons of Ishmael.

[32]The sons of Keturah, Abraham's concubine, were Zimran, Jokshan, Medan, Midian, Ishbak, and Shuah.

The sons of Jokshan were Sheba and Dedan.

[33]The sons of Midian were Ephah, Epher, Hanoch, Abida, and Eldaah. All these were descendants of Abraham through his concubine Keturah.

[34]Abraham was the father of Isaac. The sons of Isaac were Esau and Israel.*

[35]The sons of Esau were Eliphaz, Reuel, Jeush, Jalam, and Korah.

[36]The sons of Eliphaz were Teman, Omar, Zepho,* Gatam, Kenaz, and Amalek, who was born to Timna.*

[37]The sons of Reuel were Nahath, Zerah, Shammah, and Mizzah.

[38]The sons of Seir were Lotan, Shobal, Zibeon, Anah, Dishon, Ezer, and Dishan.

[39]The sons of Lotan were Hori and Heman.* Lotan's sister was named Timna.

[40]The sons of Shobal were Alvan,* Manahath, Ebal, Shepho,* and Onam.

The sons of Zibeon were Aiah and Anah.

[41]The son of Anah was Dishon.

The sons of Dishon were Hemdan,* Eshban, Ithran, and Keran.

[42]The sons of Ezer were Bilhan, Zaavan, and Akan.*

The sons of Dishan* were Uz and Aran.

[43]These are the kings who ruled in Edom before there were kings in Israel*:

Bela son of Beor, who ruled from his city of Dinhabah.

[44]When Bela died, Jobab son of Zerah from Bozrah became king.

[45]When Jobab died, Husham from the land of the Temanites became king.

[46]When Husham died, Hadad son of Bedad became king and ruled from the city of Avith. He was the one who destroyed the Midianite army in the land of Moab.

[47]When Hadad died, Samlah from the city of Masrekah became king.

[48]When Samlah died, Shaul from the city of Rehoboth on the river became king.

[49]When Shaul died, Baal-hanan son of Acbor became king.

[50]When Baal-hanan died, Hadad became king and ruled from the city of Pau.* His wife was Mehetabel, the daughter of Matred and granddaughter of Me-zahab. [51]Then Hadad died.

The clan leaders of Edom were Timna, Alvah,* Jetheth, [52]Oholibamah, Elah, Pinon, [53]Kenaz, Teman, Mibzar, [54]Magdiel, and Iram. These were the clan leaders of Edom.

2:1THE sons of Israel* were Reuben, Simeon, Levi, Judah, Issachar, Zebulun, 2Dan, Joseph, Benjamin, Naphtali, Gad, and Asher.

3Judah had three sons from Bathshua, a Canaanite woman. Their names were Er, Onan, and Shelah. But the LORD saw that the oldest son, Er, was a wicked man, so he killed him. 4Later Judah had twin sons from Tamar, his widowed daughter-in-law. Their names were Perez and Zerah. So Judah had five sons in all.

5The sons of Perez were Hezron and Hamul.

6The sons of Zerah were Zimri, Ethan, Heman, Calcol, and Darda*—five in all.

7The son of Carmi (a descendant of Zimri) was Achan,* who brought disaster on Israel by taking plunder that had been set apart for the LORD.*

8The son of Ethan was Azariah.

9The sons of Hezron were Jerahmeel, Ram, and Caleb.*

10 Ram was the father of Amminadab. Amminadab was the father of Nahshon, a leader of Judah.

11 Nahshon was the father of Salmon.* Salmon was the father of Boaz.

12 Boaz was the father of Obed. Obed was the father of Jesse.

13Jesse's first son was Eliab, his second was Abinadab, his third was Shimea, 14his fourth was Nethanel, his fifth was Raddai, 15his sixth was Ozem, and his seventh was David.

16Their sisters were named Zeruiah and Abigail. Zeruiah had three sons named Abishai, Joab, and Asahel. 17Abigail married a man named Jether, an Ishmaelite, and they had a son named Amasa.

1:1 Hebrew lacks *The descendants of Adam were.* 1:4 As in Greek version (see also Gen 5:3-32); Hebrew lacks *The sons of Noah were.* 1:6 As in some Hebrew manuscripts and Greek version (see also Gen 10:3); most Hebrew manuscripts read *Diphath.* 1:8 Or *Egypt;* also in 1:11. 1:12 Hebrew *Casluhites, from whom the Philistines came, Caphtorites.* See Jer 47:4; Amos 9:7. 1:17a As in one Hebrew manuscript and some Greek manuscripts (see also Gen 10:23); most Hebrew manuscripts lack *The descendants of Aram were.* 1:17b As in parallel text at Gen 10:23; Hebrew reads *and Meshech.* 1:22 As in some Hebrew manuscripts and Syriac version (see also Gen 10:28); most Hebrew manuscripts read *Ebal.* 1:24 Some Greek manuscripts read *Arphaxad, Cainan, Shelah.* See notes on Gen 10:24; 11:12-13. 1:34 *Israel* is the name that God gave to Jacob. 1:36a As in many Hebrew manuscripts and a few Greek manuscripts (see also Gen 36:11); most Hebrew manuscripts read *Zephi.* 1:36b As in some Greek manuscripts (see also Gen 36:12); Hebrew reads *Kenaz, Timna, and Amalek.* 1:39 As in parallel text at Gen 36:22; Hebrew reads *and Homam.* 1:40a As in many Hebrew manuscripts and a few Greek manuscripts (see also Gen 36:23); most Hebrew manuscripts read *Alian.* 1:40b As in some Hebrew manuscripts (see also Gen 36:23); most Hebrew manuscripts read *Shephi.* 1:41 As in many Hebrew manuscripts and some Greek manuscripts (see also Gen 36:26); most Hebrew manuscripts read *Hamran.* 1:42a As in many Hebrew and Greek manuscripts (see also Gen 36:27); most Hebrew manuscripts read *Jaakan.* 1:42b Hebrew *Dishon;* compare 1:38 and parallel text at Gen 36:28. 1:43 Or *before an Israelite king ruled over them.* 1:50 As in many Hebrew manuscripts, some Greek manuscripts, Syriac version, and Latin Vulgate (see also Gen 36:39); most Hebrew manuscripts read *Pai.* 1:51 As in parallel text at Gen 36:40; Hebrew reads *Aliah.* 2:1 *Israel* is the name that God gave to Jacob. 2:6 As in many Hebrew manuscripts, some Greek manuscripts, and Syriac version (see also 1 Kgs 4:31); Hebrew reads *Dara.* 2:7a Hebrew *Achar;* compare Josh 7:1. *Achar* means "disaster." 2:7b The Hebrew term used here refers to the complete consecration of things or people to the LORD, either by destroying them or by giving them as an offering. 2:9 Hebrew *Kelubai,* a variant spelling of Caleb; compare 2:18. 2:11 As in Greek version (see also Ruth 4:21); Hebrew reads *Salma.*

ACTS 23:11-35

That night the Lord appeared to Paul and said, "Be encouraged, Paul. Just as you have been a witness to me here in Jerusalem, you must preach the Good News in Rome as well."

12The next morning a group of Jews* got together and bound themselves with an oath not to eat or drink until they had killed Paul. 13There were more than forty of them in the conspiracy. 14They went to the leading priests and elders and told them, "We have bound ourselves with an oath to eat nothing until we have killed Paul. 15So you and the high council should ask the commander to bring Paul back to the council again. Pretend you want to examine his case more fully. We will kill him on the way."

16But Paul's nephew—his sister's son—heard of their plan and went to the fortress and told Paul. 17Paul called for one of the Roman officers* and said, "Take this young man to the commander. He has something important to tell him."

18So the officer did, explaining, "Paul, the prisoner, called me over and asked me to bring this young man to you because he has something to tell you."

¹⁹The commander took his hand, led him aside, and asked, "What is it you want to tell me?"

²⁰Paul's nephew told him, "Some Jews are going to ask you to bring Paul before the high council tomorrow, pretending they want to get some more information. ²¹But don't do it! There are more than forty men hiding along the way ready to ambush him. They have vowed not to eat or drink anything until they have killed him. They are ready now, just waiting for your consent."

²²"Don't let anyone know you told me this," the commander warned the young man.

²³Then the commander called two of his officers and ordered, "Get 200 soldiers ready to leave for Caesarea at nine o'clock tonight. Also take 200 spearmen and 70 mounted troops. ²⁴Provide horses for Paul to ride, and get him safely to Governor Felix." ²⁵Then he wrote this letter to the governor:

²⁶"From Claudius Lysias, to his Excellency, Governor Felix:
Greetings!

²⁷"This man was seized by some Jews, and they were about to kill him when I arrived with the troops. When I learned that he was a Roman citizen, I removed him to safety. ²⁸Then I took him to their high council to try to learn the basis of the accusations against him. ²⁹I soon discovered the charge was something regarding their religious law—certainly nothing worthy of imprisonment or death. ³⁰But when I was informed of a plot to kill him, I immediately sent him on to you. I have told his accusers to bring their charges before you."

³¹So that night, as ordered, the soldiers took Paul as far as Antipatris. ³²They returned to the fortress the next morning, while the mounted troops took him on to Caesarea. ³³When they arrived in Caesarea, they presented Paul and the letter to Governor Felix. ³⁴He read it and then asked Paul what province he was from. "Cilicia," Paul answered.

³⁵"I will hear your case myself when your accusers arrive," the governor told him. Then the governor ordered him kept in the prison at Herod's headquarters.*

23:12 Greek *the Jews*.   23:17 Greek *centurions;* also in 23:23.   23:35 Greek *Herod's Praetorium*.

PSALM 3:1-8
A psalm of David, regarding the time David fled from his son Absalom.

¹ O LORD, I have so many enemies;
   so many are against me.
² So many are saying,
   "God will never rescue him!"
                              *Interlude**

³ But you, O LORD, are a shield
      around me;
   you are my glory, the one who
      holds my head high.
⁴ I cried out to the LORD,
   and he answered me from his
      holy mountain.   *Interlude*

⁵ I lay down and slept,
   yet I woke up in safety,
   for the LORD was watching
      over me.
⁶ I am not afraid of ten thousand
      enemies
   who surround me on every side.

⁷ Arise, O LORD!
   Rescue me, my God!
   Slap all my enemies in the face!
   Shatter the teeth of the wicked!
⁸ Victory comes from you, O LORD.
   May you bless your people.
                              Interlude

3:2 Hebrew *Selah*. The meaning of this word is uncertain, though it is probably a musical or literary term. It is rendered *Interlude* throughout the Psalms.

PROVERBS 18:14-15
The human spirit can endure a sick body, but who can bear a crushed spirit? □ Intelligent people are always ready to learn. Their ears are open for knowledge.

JULY 6

1 CHRONICLES 2:18–4:4

Hezron's son Caleb had sons from his wife Azubah and from Jerioth.* Her sons were named Jesher, Shobab, and Ardon. ¹⁹After Azubah died, Caleb married Ephrathah,* and they had a son named Hur. ²⁰Hur was the father of Uri. Uri was the father of Bezalel.

²¹When Hezron was sixty years old, he married Gilead's sister, the daughter of Makir. They had a son named Segub. ²²Segub was the father of Jair, who ruled twenty-three towns in the land of Gilead. ²³(But Geshur and Aram captured the Towns of Jair* and also took Kenath and its sixty surrounding villages.) All these were descendants of Makir, the father of Gilead.

²⁴Soon after Hezron died in the town of Caleb-ephrathah, his wife Abijah gave birth to a son named Ashhur (the father of* Tekoa).

²⁵The sons of Jerahmeel, the oldest son of Hezron, were Ram (the firstborn), Bunah, Oren, Ozem, and Ahijah. ²⁶Jerahmeel had a second wife named Atarah. She was the mother of Onam.

²⁷The sons of Ram, the oldest son of Jerahmeel, were Maaz, Jamin, and Eker.

²⁸The sons of Onam were Shammai and Jada.

The sons of Shammai were Nadab and Abishur.

²⁹The sons of Abishur and his wife Abihail were Ahban and Molid.

³⁰The sons of Nadab were Seled and Appaim. Seled died without children, ³¹but Appaim had a son named Ishi. The son of Ishi was Sheshan. Sheshan had a descendant named Ahlai.

³²The sons of Jada, Shammai's brother, were Jether and Jonathan. Jether died without children, ³³but Jonathan had two sons named Peleth and Zaza.

These were all descendants of Jerahmeel.

³⁴Sheshan had no sons, though he did have daughters. He also had an Egyptian servant named Jarha. ³⁵Sheshan gave one of his daughters to be the wife of Jarha, and they had a son named Attai.

³⁶ Attai was the father of Nathan. Nathan was the father of Zabad.

³⁷ Zabad was the father of Ephlal. Ephlal was the father of Obed.

³⁸ Obed was the father of Jehu. Jehu was the father of Azariah.

³⁹ Azariah was the father of Helez. Helez was the father of Eleasah.

⁴⁰ Eleasah was the father of Sismai. Sismai was the father of Shallum.

⁴¹ Shallum was the father of Jekamiah. Jekamiah was the father of Elishama.

⁴²The descendants of Caleb, the brother of Jerahmeel, included Mesha (the firstborn), who became the father of Ziph. Caleb's descendants also included the sons of Mareshah, the father of Hebron.*

⁴³The sons of Hebron were Korah, Tappuah, Rekem, and Shema. ⁴⁴Shema was the father of Raham. Raham was the father of Jorkeam. Rekem was the father of Shammai. ⁴⁵The son of Shammai was Maon. Maon was the father of Beth-zur.

⁴⁶Caleb's concubine Ephah gave birth to Haran, Moza, and Gazez. Haran was the father of Gazez.

⁴⁷The sons of Jahdai were Regem, Jotham, Geshan, Pelet, Ephah, and Shaaph.

⁴⁸Another of Caleb's concubines, Maacah, gave birth to Sheber and Tirhanah. ⁴⁹She also gave birth to Shaaph (the father of Madmannah) and Sheva (the father of Macbenah and Gibea). Caleb also had a daughter named Acsah.

⁵⁰These were all descendants of Caleb.

The sons of Hur, the oldest son of Caleb's wife Ephrathah, were Shobal (the founder of Kiriath-jearim), ⁵¹Salma (the founder of Bethlehem), and Hareph (the founder of Beth-gader).

⁵²The descendants of Shobal (the founder of Kiriath-jearim) were Haroeh, half the Manahathites, ⁵³and the families of Kiriath-jearim—the Ithrites, Puthites, Shumathites, and Mishraites, from whom came the people of Zorah and Eshtaol.

⁵⁴The descendants of Salma were the people of Bethlehem, the Netophathites, Atroth-beth-joab, the other half of the Manahathites, the Zorites, ⁵⁵and the families of scribes living at Jabez—the Tirathites, Shimeathites, and Sucathites. All these were Kenites who descended from Hammath, the father of the family of Recab.*

3:1THESE are the sons of David who were born in Hebron:

The oldest was Amnon, whose mother was Ahinoam from Jezreel.

The second was Daniel, whose mother was Abigail from Carmel.

² The third was Absalom, whose mother was Maacah, the daughter of Talmai, king of Geshur.

The fourth was Adonijah, whose mother was Haggith.

³ The fifth was Shephatiah, whose mother was Abital.

The sixth was Ithream, whose mother was Eglah, David's wife.

⁴These six sons were born to David in Hebron, where he reigned seven and a half years.

Then David reigned another thirty-three years in Jerusalem. ⁵The sons born to David in Jerusalem included Shammua,* Shobab, Nathan, and Solomon. Their mother was Bathsheba,* the daughter of Ammiel. ⁶David also had nine other sons: Ibhar, Elishua,* Elpelet,* ⁷Nogah, Nepheg, Japhia, ⁸Elishama, Eliada, and Eliphelet.

⁹These were the sons of David, not including his sons born to his concubines. Their sister was named Tamar.

¹⁰The descendants of Solomon were Rehoboam, Abijah, Asa, Jehoshaphat, ¹¹Jehoram,* Ahaziah, Joash, ¹²Amaziah, Uzziah,* Jotham, ¹³Ahaz, Hezekiah, Manasseh, ¹⁴Amon, and Josiah.

¹⁵The sons of Josiah were Johanan (the oldest), Jehoiakim (the second), Zedekiah (the third), and Jehoahaz* (the fourth).

¹⁶The successors of Jehoiakim were his son Jehoiachin and his brother Zedekiah.*

¹⁷The sons of Jehoiachin,* who was taken prisoner by the Babylonians, were Shealtiel, ¹⁸Malkiram, Pedaiah, Shenazzar, Jekamiah, Hoshama, and Nedabiah.

¹⁹The sons of Pedaiah were Zerubbabel and Shimei.

The sons of Zerubbabel were Meshullam and Hananiah. (Their sister was Shelomith.) ²⁰His five other sons were Hashubah, Ohel, Berekiah, Hasadiah, and Jushab-hesed.

²¹The sons of Hananiah were Pelatiah and Jeshaiah. Jeshaiah's son was Rephaiah. Rephaiah's son was Arnan. Arnan's son was Obadiah. Obadiah's son was Shecaniah.

²²The descendants of Shecaniah were Shemaiah and his sons, Hattush, Igal, Bariah, Neariah, and Shaphat—six in all.

²³The sons of Neariah were Elioenai, Hizkiah, and Azrikam—three in all.

²⁴The sons of Elioenai were Hodaviah, Eliashib, Pelaiah, Akkub, Johanan, Delaiah, and Anani—seven in all.

4:1THE descendants of Judah were Perez, Hezron, Carmi, Hur, and Shobal. ²Shobal's son Reaiah was the father of Jahath. Jahath was the father of

Ahumai and Lahad. These were the families of the Zorathites.

³The descendants of* Etam were Jezreel, Ishma, Idbash, their sister Hazzelelponi, ⁴Penuel (the father of* Gedor), and Ezer (the father of Hushah). These were the descendants of Hur (the firstborn of Ephrathah), the ancestor of Bethlehem.

2:18 Or *Caleb had a daughter named Jerioth from his wife, Azubah.* The meaning of the Hebrew is uncertain. 2:19 Hebrew *Ephrath,* a variant spelling of Ephrathah; compare 2:50 and 4:4. 2:23 Or *captured Havvoth-jair.* 2:24 Or *the founder of;* also in 2:42, 45, 49. 2:42 Or *who founded Hebron.* The meaning of the Hebrew is uncertain. 2:55 Or *the founder of Beth-recab.* 3:5a As in Syriac version (see also 14:4; 2 Sam 5:14); Hebrew reads *Shimea.* 3:5b Hebrew *Bathshua,* a variant spelling of Bathsheba. 3:6a As in some Hebrew and Greek manuscripts (see also 14:5-7 and 2 Sam 5:15); most Hebrew manuscripts read *Elishama.* 3:6b Hebrew *Eliphelet;* compare parallel text at 14:5-7. 3:11 Hebrew *Joram,* a variant spelling of Jehoram. 3:12 Hebrew *Azariah,* a variant spelling of Uzziah. 3:15 Hebrew *Shallum,* another name for Jehoahaz. 3:16 Hebrew *The sons of Jehoiakim were his son Jeconiah* [a variant spelling of Jehoiachin] *and his son Zedekiah.* 3:17 Hebrew *Jeconiah,* a variant spelling of Jehoiachin. 4:3 As in Greek version; Hebrew reads *father of.* The meaning of the Hebrew is uncertain. 4:4 Or *the founder of;* also in 4:5, 12, 14, 17, 18, and perhaps other instances where the text reads *the father of.*

ACTS 24:1-27

Five days later Ananias, the high priest, arrived with some of the Jewish elders and the lawyer* Tertullus, to present their case against Paul to the governor. ²When Paul was called in, Tertullus presented the charges against Paul in the following address to the governor:

"Your Excellency, you have provided a long period of peace for us Jews and with foresight have enacted reforms for us. ³For all of this we are very grateful to you. ⁴But I don't want to bore you, so please give me your attention for only a moment. ⁵We have found this man to be a troublemaker who is constantly stirring up riots among the Jews all over the world. He is a ringleader of the cult known as the Nazarenes. ⁶Furthermore, he was trying to desecrate the Temple when we arrested him.* ⁸You can find out the truth of our accusations by examining him yourself." ⁹Then the other Jews chimed in, declaring that everything Tertullus said was true.

¹⁰The governor then motioned for Paul to speak. Paul said, "I know, sir, that you have been a judge of Jewish affairs for many years, so I gladly present my defense before you. ¹¹You can quickly discover that I arrived in Jerusalem no more than twelve days ago to worship at the Temple. ¹²My accusers never found me arguing with anyone in the Temple, nor stirring up a riot in any synagogue or on the streets of the city. ¹³These men cannot prove the things they accuse me of doing.

¹⁴"But I admit that I follow the Way, which they call a cult. I worship the God of our ancestors, and I firmly believe the Jewish law and everything written in the prophets. ¹⁵I have the same hope in God that these men have, that he will raise both the righteous and the unrighteous. ¹⁶Because of this, I always try to maintain a clear conscience before God and all people.

¹⁷"After several years away, I returned to Jerusalem with money to aid my people and to offer sacrifices to God. ¹⁸My accusers saw me in the Temple as I was completing a purification ceremony. There was no crowd around me and no rioting. ¹⁹But some Jews from the province of Asia were there—and they ought to be here to bring charges if they have anything against me! ²⁰Ask these men here what crime the Jewish high council* found me guilty of, ²¹except for the one time I shouted out, 'I am on trial before you today because I believe in the resurrection of the dead!'"

²²At that point Felix, who was quite familiar with the Way, adjourned the hearing and said, "Wait until Lysias, the garrison commander, arrives. Then I will decide the case." ²³He ordered an officer* to keep Paul in custody but to give him some freedom and allow his friends to visit him and take care of his needs.

²⁴A few days later Felix came back with his wife, Drusilla, who was Jewish. Sending for Paul, they listened as he told them about faith in Christ Jesus. ²⁵As he reasoned with them about righteousness and self-control and the

coming day of judgment, Felix became frightened. "Go away for now," he replied. "When it is more convenient, I'll call for you again." [26]He also hoped that Paul would bribe him, so he sent for him quite often and talked with him.

[27]After two years went by in this way, Felix was succeeded by Porcius Festus. And because Felix wanted to gain favor with the Jewish people, he left Paul in prison.

24:1 Greek *some elders and an orator.*   24:6 Some manuscripts add *We would have judged him by our law, [7]but Lysias, the commander of the garrison, came and violently took him away from us, [8]commanding his accusers to come before you.*   24:20 Greek *Sanhedrin.* 24:23 Greek *a centurion.*

PSALM 4:1-8

For the choir director: A psalm of David, to be accompanied by stringed instruments.

[1] **A**nswer me when I call to you,
    O God who declares me innocent.
  Free me from my troubles.
    Have mercy on me and hear
      my prayer.

[2] How long will you people ruin
      my reputation?
  How long will you make
      groundless accusations?
  How long will you continue
      your lies?   *Interlude*

[3] **You can be sure of this:**
  The LORD set apart the godly
    for himself.
  The LORD will answer when
    I call to him.

[4] Don't sin by letting anger
      control you.
  Think about it overnight and
      remain silent.   *Interlude*

[5] Offer sacrifices in the right spirit,
    and trust the LORD.

[6] Many people say, "Who will show
      us better times?"
  Let your face smile on us, LORD.

[7] You have given me greater joy
    than those who have abundant
      harvests of grain and new wine.

[8] In peace I will lie down and sleep,
    for you alone, O LORD, will
      keep me safe.

PROVERBS 18:16-18

Giving a gift can open doors; it gives access to important people! □ The first to speak in court sounds right— until the cross-examination begins. □ Casting lots can end arguments; it settles disputes between powerful opponents.

JULY 7

1 CHRONICLES 4:5–5:17

Ashhur (the father of Tekoa) had two wives, named Helah and Naarah. [6]Naarah gave birth to Ahuzzam, Hepher, Temeni, and Haahashtari. [7]Helah gave birth to Zereth, Izhar, Ethnan, [8]and Koz, who became the ancestor of Anub, Zobebah, and all the families of Aharhel son of Harum.

[9]There was a man named Jabez who was more honorable than any of his brothers. His mother named him Jabez* because his birth had been so painful. [10]He was the one who prayed to the God of Israel, "Oh, that you would bless me and expand my territory! Please be with me in all that I do, and keep me from all trouble and pain!" And God granted him his request.

[11]Kelub (the brother of Shuhah) was the father of Mehir. Mehir was the father of Eshton. [12]Eshton was the father of Beth-rapha, Paseah, and Tehinnah. Tehinnah was the father of Ir-nahash. These were the descendants of Recah.

[13]The sons of Kenaz were Othniel and Seraiah. Othniel's sons were Hathath and Meonothai.* [14]Meonothai was the father of Ophrah. Seraiah was the father of Joab, the founder of the Valley of Craftsmen,* so called because they were craftsmen.

15 The sons of Caleb son of Jephunneh were Iru, Elah, and Naam. The son of Elah was Kenaz.

16 The sons of Jehallelel were Ziph, Ziphah, Tiria, and Asarel.

17 The sons of Ezrah were Jether, Mered, Epher, and Jalon. One of Mered's wives became* the mother of Miriam, Shammai, and Ishbah (the father of Eshtemoa). 18 He married a woman from Judah, who became the mother of Jered (the father of Gedor), Heber (the father of Soco), and Jekuthiel (the father of Zanoah). Mered also married Bithia, a daughter of Pharaoh, and she bore him children.

19 Hodiah's wife was the sister of Naham. One of her sons was the father of Keilah the Garmite, and another was the father of Eshtemoa the Maacathite.

20 The sons of Shimon were Amnon, Rinnah, Ben-hanan, and Tilon.

The descendants of Ishi were Zoheth and Ben-zoheth.

21 Shelah was one of Judah's sons. The descendants of Shelah were Er (the father of Lecah); Laadah (the father of Mareshah); the families of linen workers at Beth-ashbea; 22 Jokim; the men of Cozeba; and Joash and Saraph, who ruled over Moab and Jashubi-lehem. These names all come from ancient records. 23 They were the pottery makers who lived in Netaim and Gederah. They lived there and worked for the king.

24 The sons of Simeon were Jemuel,* Jamin, Jarib, Zohar,* and Shaul.

25 The descendants of Shaul were Shallum, Mibsam, and Mishma.

26 The descendants of Mishma were Hammuel, Zaccur, and Shimei.

27 Shimei had sixteen sons and six daughters, but none of his brothers had large families. So Simeon's tribe never grew as large as the tribe of Judah.

28 They lived in Beersheba, Moladah, Hazar-shual, 29 Bilhah, Ezem, Tolad, 30 Bethuel, Hormah, Ziklag, 31 Beth-marcaboth, Hazar-susim, Beth-biri, and Shaaraim. These towns were under their control until the time of King David. 32 Their descendants also lived in Etam, Ain, Rimmon, Token, and Ashan—five towns 33 and their surrounding villages as far away as Baalath.* This was their territory, and these names are listed in their genealogical records.

34 Other descendants of Simeon included Meshobab, Jamlech, Joshah son of Amaziah, 35 Joel, Jehu son of Joshibiah, son of Seraiah, son of Asiel, 36 Elioenai, Jaakobah, Jesho-haiah, Asaiah, Adiel, Jesimiel, Benaiah, 37 and Ziza son of Shiphi, son of Allon, son of Jedaiah, son of Shimri, son of Shemaiah.

38 These were the names of some of the leaders of Simeon's wealthy clans. Their families grew, 39 and they traveled to the region of Gerar,* in the east part of the valley, seeking pastureland for their flocks. 40 They found lush pastures there, and the land was quiet and peaceful.

Some of Ham's descendants had been living in that region. 41 But during the reign of King Hezekiah of Judah, these leaders of Simeon invaded the region and completely destroyed* the homes of the descendants of Ham and of the Meunites. No trace of them remains today. They killed everyone who lived there and took the land for themselves, because they wanted its good pastureland for their flocks. 42 Five hundred of these invaders from the tribe of Simeon went to Mount Seir, led by Pelatiah, Neariah, Rephaiah, and Uzziel—all sons of Ishi. 43 They destroyed the few Amalekites who had survived, and they have lived there ever since.

5:1 THE oldest son of Israel* was Reuben. But since he dishonored his father by sleeping with one of his father's concubines, his birthright was given to the sons of his brother Joseph. For this reason, Reuben is not listed in the genealogical records as the firstborn son. ²The descendants of Judah became the most powerful tribe and provided a ruler for the nation,* but the birthright belonged to Joseph.

³The sons of Reuben, the oldest son of Israel, were Hanoch, Pallu, Hezron, and Carmi.

⁴The descendants of Joel were Shemaiah, Gog, Shimei, ⁵Micah, Reaiah, Baal, ⁶and Beerah. Beerah was the leader of the Reubenites when they were taken into captivity by King Tiglath-pileser* of Assyria.

⁷Beerah's* relatives are listed in their genealogical records by their clans: Jeiel (the leader), Zechariah, ⁸and Bela son of Azaz, son of Shema, son of Joel.

The Reubenites lived in the area that stretches from Aroer to Nebo and Baal-meon. ⁹And since they had so many livestock in the land of Gilead, they spread east toward the edge of the desert that stretches to the Euphrates River.

¹⁰During the reign of Saul, the Reubenites defeated the Hagrites in battle. Then they moved into the Hagrite settlements all along the eastern edge of Gilead.

¹¹Next to the Reubenites, the descendants of Gad lived in the land of Bashan as far east as Salecah. ¹²Joel was the leader in the land of Bashan, and Shapham was second-in-command, followed by Janai and Shaphat. ¹³Their relatives, the leaders of seven other clans, were Michael, Meshullam, Sheba, Jorai, Jacan, Zia, and Eber. ¹⁴These were all descendants of Abihail son of Huri, son of Jaroah, son of Gilead, son of Michael, son of Jeshishai, son of Jahdo, son of Buz. ¹⁵Ahi son of Abdiel, son of Guni, was the leader of their clans.

¹⁶The Gadite lived in the land of Gilead, in Bashan and its villages, and throughout all the pasturelands of Shar-

on. ¹⁷All of these were listed in the genealogical records during the days of King Jotham of Judah and King Jeroboam of Israel.

4:9 *Jabez* sounds like a Hebrew word meaning "distress" or "pain." **4:13** As in some Greek manuscripts and Latin Vulgate; Hebrew lacks *and Meonothai.* **4:14** Or *Joab, the father of Ge-harashim.* **4:17** Or *Jether's wife became;* Hebrew reads *She became.* **4:24a** As in Syriac version (see also Gen 46:10; Exod 6:15); Hebrew reads *Nemuel.* **4:24b** As in parallel texts at Gen 46:10 and Exod 6:15; Hebrew reads *Zerah.* **4:33** As in some Greek manuscripts (see also Josh 19:8); Hebrew reads *Baal.* **4:39** As in Greek version; Hebrew reads *Gedor.* **4:41** The Hebrew term used here refers to the complete consecration of things or people to the LORD, either by destroying them or by giving them as an offering. **5:1** *Israel* is the name that God gave to Jacob. **5:2** Or *and from Judah came a prince.* **5:6** Hebrew *Tilgath-pilneser,* a variant spelling of Tiglath-pileser; also in 5:26. **5:7** Hebrew *His.*

ACTS 25:1-27

Three days after Festus arrived in Caesarea to take over his new responsibilities, he left for Jerusalem, ²where the leading priests and other Jewish leaders met with him and made their accusations against Paul. ³They asked Festus as a favor to transfer Paul to Jerusalem (planning to ambush and kill him on the way). ⁴But Festus replied that Paul was at Caesarea and he himself would be returning there soon. ⁵So he said, "Those of you in authority can return with me. If Paul has done anything wrong, you can make your accusations."

⁶About eight or ten days later Festus returned to Caesarea, and on the following day he took his seat in court and ordered that Paul be brought in. ⁷When Paul arrived, the Jewish leaders from Jerusalem gathered around and made many serious accusations they couldn't prove.

⁸Paul denied the charges. "I am not guilty of any crime against the Jewish laws or the Temple or the Roman government," he said.

⁹Then Festus, wanting to please the Jews, asked him, "Are you willing to go to Jerusalem and stand trial before me there?"

¹⁰But Paul replied, "No! This is the official Roman court, so I ought to be tried right here. You know very well I am not guilty of harming the Jews. ¹¹If I have

done something worthy of death, I don't refuse to die. But if I am innocent, no one has a right to turn me over to these men to kill me. I appeal to Caesar!"

¹²Festus conferred with his advisers and then replied, "Very well! You have appealed to Caesar, and to Caesar you will go!"

¹³A few days later King Agrippa arrived with his sister, Bernice,* to pay their respects to Festus. ¹⁴During their stay of several days, Festus discussed Paul's case with the king. "There is a prisoner here," he told him, "whose case was left for me by Felix. ¹⁵When I was in Jerusalem, the leading priests and Jewish elders pressed charges against him and asked me to condemn him. ¹⁶I pointed out to them that Roman law does not convict people without a trial. They must be given an opportunity to confront their accusers and defend themselves.

¹⁷"When his accusers came here for the trial, I didn't delay. I called the case the very next day and ordered Paul brought in. ¹⁸But the accusations made against him weren't any of the crimes I expected. ¹⁹Instead, it was something about their religion and a dead man named Jesus, who Paul insists is alive. ²⁰I was at a loss to know how to investigate these things, so I asked him whether he would be willing to stand trial on these charges in Jerusalem. ²¹But Paul appealed to have his case decided by the emperor. So I ordered that he be held in custody until I could arrange to send him to Caesar."

²²"I'd like to hear the man myself," Agrippa said.

And Festus replied, "You will—tomorrow!"

²³So the next day Agrippa and Bernice arrived at the auditorium with great pomp, accompanied by military officers and prominent men of the city. Festus ordered that Paul be brought in. ²⁴Then Festus said, "King Agrippa and all who are here, this is the man whose death is demanded by all the Jews, both here and in Jerusalem. ²⁵But in my opinion he has

done nothing deserving death. However, since he appealed his case to the emperor, I have decided to send him to Rome.

²⁶"But what shall I write the emperor? For there is no clear charge against him. So I have brought him before all of you, and especially you, King Agrippa, so that after we examine him, I might have something to write. ²⁷For it makes no sense to send a prisoner to the emperor without specifying the charges against him!"

25:13 Greek *Agrippa the king and Bernice arrived.*

PSALM 5:1-12

For the choir director: A psalm of David, to be accompanied by the flute.

¹ **O Lᴏʀᴅ, hear me as I pray;**
   pay attention to my groaning.
² **Listen to my cry for help, my King**
      and my God,
   for I pray to no one but you.
³ Listen to my voice in the morning,
      Lᴏʀᴅ.
   Each morning I bring my requests
      to you and wait expectantly.

⁴ O God, you take no pleasure in
      wickedness;
   you cannot tolerate the sins
      of the wicked.
⁵ Therefore, the proud may not stand
      in your presence,
   for you hate all who do evil.
⁶ You will destroy those who tell lies.
   The Lᴏʀᴅ detests murderers
      and deceivers.

⁷ Because of your unfailing love,
      I can enter your house;
   I will worship at your Temple
      with deepest awe.
⁸ Lead me in the right path, O Lᴏʀᴅ,
      or my enemies will conquer me.
   Make your way plain for me
      to follow.

⁹ My enemies cannot speak a truthful
      word.
   Their deepest desire is to
      destroy others.

Their talk is foul, like the stench
  from an open grave.
Their tongues are filled with
  flattery.*
[10] O God, declare them guilty.
  Let them be caught in their
    own traps.
Drive them away because of their
  many sins,
  for they have rebelled against you.

[11] But let all who take refuge
  in you rejoice;
  let them sing joyful praises
    forever.
Spread your protection over them,
  that all who love your name may
    be filled with joy.
[12] For you bless the godly, O LORD;
  you surround them with your
    shield of love.

5:9 Greek version reads *with lies.* Compare Rom 3:12.

PROVERBS 18:19
An offended friend is harder to win
back than a fortified city. Arguments
separate friends like a gate locked with
bars.

JULY
8

1 CHRONICLES 5:18–6:81
There were 44,760 capable warriors in
the armies of Reuben, Gad, and the half-
tribe of Manasseh. They were all skilled
in combat and armed with shields,
swords, and bows. [19] They waged war
against the Hagrites, the Jeturites, the
Naphishites, and the Nodabites. [20] They
cried out to God during the battle, and
he answered their prayer because they
trusted in him. So the Hagrites and all
their allies were defeated. [21] The plunder taken from the Hagrites included
50,000 camels, 250,000 sheep and
goats, 2,000 donkeys, and 100,000 captives. [22] Many of the Hagrites were killed
in the battle because God was fighting
against them. The people of Reuben,
Gad, and Manasseh lived in their land
until they were taken into exile.

[23] The half-tribe of Manasseh was
very large and spread through the land
from Bashan to Baal-hermon, Senir, and
Mount Hermon. [24] These were the leaders of their clans: Epher,* Ishi, Eliel,
Azriel, Jeremiah, Hodaviah, and Jahdiel.
These men had a great reputation as
mighty warriors and leaders of their
clans.

[25] But these tribes were unfaithful to
the God of their ancestors. They worshiped the gods of the nations that God
had destroyed. [26] So the God of Israel
caused King Pul of Assyria (also known
as Tiglath-pileser) to invade the land
and take away the people of Reuben,
Gad, and the half-tribe of Manasseh as
captives. The Assyrians exiled them to
Halah, Habor, Hara, and the Gozan
River, where they remain to this day.

6:1 *THE sons of Levi were Gershon,
  Kohath, and Merari.
[2] The descendants of Kohath included
  Amram, Izhar, Hebron, and Uzziel.
[3] The children of Amram were Aaron,
  Moses, and Miriam.
The sons of Aaron were Nadab, Abihu,
  Eleazar, and Ithamar.
[4] Eleazar was the father of Phinehas.
  Phinehas was the father of Abishua.
[5] Abishua was the father of Bukki.
  Bukki was the father of Uzzi.
[6] Uzzi was the father of Zerahiah.
  Zerahiah was the father of Meraioth.
[7] Meraioth was the father of Amariah.
  Amariah was the father of Ahitub.
[8] Ahitub was the father of Zadok.
  Zadok was the father of Ahimaaz.
[9] Ahimaaz was the father of Azariah.
  Azariah was the father of Johanan.
[10] Johanan was the father of Azariah,
  the high priest at the Temple*
  built by Solomon in Jerusalem.
[11] Azariah was the father of Amariah.
  Amariah was the father of Ahitub.

¹² Ahitub was the father of Zadok. Zadok was the father of Shallum. ¹³ Shallum was the father of Hilkiah. Hilkiah was the father of Azariah. ¹⁴ Azariah was the father of Seraiah. Seraiah was the father of Jehozadak, ¹⁵who went into exile when the LORD sent the people of Judah and Jerusalem into captivity under Nebuchadnezzar.

¹⁶*The sons of Levi were Gershon,* Kohath, and Merari. ¹⁷ The descendants of Gershon included Libni and Shimei. ¹⁸The descendants of Kohath included Amram, Izhar, Hebron, and Uzziel. ¹⁹ The descendants of Merari included Mahli and Mushi.

The following were the Levite clans, listed according to their ancestral descent:

²⁰The descendants of Gershon included Libni, Jahath, Zimmah, ²¹Joah, Iddo, Zerah, and Jeatherai. ²² The descendants of Kohath included Amminadab, Korah, Assir, ²³Elkanah, Abiasaph,* Assir, ²⁴Tahath, Uriel, Uzziah, and Shaul. ²⁵ The descendants of Elkanah included Amasai, Ahimoth, ²⁶ Elkanah, Zophai, Nahath, ²⁷Eliab, Jeroham, Elkanah, and Samuel.* ²⁸The sons of Samuel were Joel* (the older) and Abijah (the second). ²⁹ The descendants of Merari included Mahli, Libni, Shimei, Uzzah, ³⁰Shimea, Haggiah, and Asaiah.

³¹David assigned the following men to lead the music at the house of the LORD after the Ark was placed there. ³² They ministered with music at the Tabernacle* until Solomon built the Temple of the LORD in Jerusalem. They carried out their work, following all the regulations handed down to them. ³³ These are the men who served, along with their sons:

Heman the musician was from the clan of Kohath. His genealogy was traced back through Joel, Samuel, ³⁴Elkanah, Jeroham, Eliel, Toah, ³⁵Zuph, Elkanah, Mahath, Amasai, ³⁶ Elkanah, Joel, Azariah, Zephaniah, ³⁷ Tahath, Assir, Abiasaph, Korah, ³⁸Izhar, Kohath, Levi, and Israel.* ³⁹Heman's first assistant was Asaph from the clan of Gershon.* Asaph's genealogy was traced back through Berekiah, Shimea, ⁴⁰Michael, Baaseiah, Malkijah, ⁴¹Ethni, Zerah, Adaiah, ⁴²Ethan, Zimmah, Shimei, ⁴³Jahath, Gershon, and Levi.

⁴⁴Heman's second assistant was Ethan from the clan of Merari. Ethan's genealogy was traced back through Kishi, Abdi, Malluch, ⁴⁵Hashabiah, Amaziah, Hilkiah, ⁴⁶Amzi, Bani, Shemer, ⁴⁷Mahli, Mushi, Merari, and Levi.

⁴⁸Their fellow Levites were appointed to various other tasks in the Tabernacle, the house of God.

⁴⁹Only Aaron and his descendants served as priests. They presented the offerings on the altar of burnt offering and the altar of incense, and they performed all the other duties related to the Most Holy Place. They made atonement for Israel by doing everything that Moses, the servant of God, had commanded them.

⁵⁰The descendants of Aaron were Eleazar, Phinehas, Abishua, ⁵¹Bukki, Uzzi, Zerahiah, ⁵²Meraioth, Amariah, Ahitub, ⁵³Zadok, and Ahimaaz.

⁵⁴This is a record of the towns and territory assigned by means of sacred lots to the descendants of Aaron, who were from the clan of Kohath. ⁵⁵ This territory included Hebron and its surrounding pasturelands in Judah, ⁵⁶but the fields and outlying areas belonging to the city were given to Caleb son of Jephunneh. ⁵⁷So the descendants of Aaron were given the following towns, each with its pasturelands: Hebron (a city of refuge),* Libnah, Jattir, Eshtemoa, ⁵⁸Holon,* Debir, ⁵⁹Ain,* Juttah,* and Beth-shemesh. ⁶⁰And from the territory of Benjamin they were given Gibeon,* Geba, Alemeth,

and Anathoth, each with its pasturelands. So thirteen towns were given to the descendants of Aaron. [61]The remaining descendants of Kohath received ten towns from the territory of the half-tribe of Manasseh by means of sacred lots.

[62]The descendants of Gershon received by sacred lots thirteen towns from the territories of Issachar, Asher, Naphtali, and from the Bashan area of Manasseh, east of the Jordan.

[63]The descendants of Merari received by sacred lots twelve towns from the territories of Reuben, Gad, and Zebulun.

[64]So the people of Israel assigned all these towns and pasturelands to the Levites. [65]The towns in the territories of Judah, Simeon, and Benjamin, mentioned above, were assigned to them by means of sacred lots.

[66]The descendants of Kohath were given the following towns from the territory of Ephraim, each with its pasturelands: [67]Shechem (a city of refuge in the hill country of Ephraim),* Gezer, [68]Jokmeam, Beth-horon, [69]Aijalon, and Gathrimmon. [70]The remaining descendants of Kohath were assigned the towns of Aner and Bileam from the territory of the half-tribe of Manasseh, each with its pasturelands.

[71]The descendants of Gershon received the towns of Golan (in Bashan) and Ashtaroth from the territory of the half-tribe of Manasseh, each with its pasturelands. [72]From the territory of Issachar, they were given Kedesh, Daberath, [73]Ramoth, and Anem, each with its pasturelands. [74]From the territory of Asher, they received Mashal, Abdon, [75]Hukok, and Rehob, each with its pasturelands. [76]From the territory of Naphtali, they were given Kedesh in Galilee, Hammon, and Kiriathaim, each with its pasturelands.

[77]The remaining descendants of Merari received the towns of Jokneam, Kartah,* Rimmon,* and Tabor from the territory of Zebulun, each with its pasturelands. [78]From the territory of

Reuben, east of the Jordan River opposite Jericho, they received Bezer (a desert town), Jahaz,* [79]Kedemoth, and Mephaath, each with its pasturelands. [80]And from the territory of Gad, they received Ramoth in Gilead, Mahanaim, [81]Heshbon, and Jazer, each with its pasturelands.

5:24 As in Greek version and Latin Vulgate; Hebrew reads *and Epher.*   6:1 Verses 6:1-15 are numbered 5:27-41 in Hebrew text.   6:10 Hebrew *the house.*   6:16a Verses 6:16-81 are numbered 6:1-66 in Hebrew text.   6:16b Hebrew *Gershom,* a variant spelling of Gershon (see 6:1); also in 6:17, 20, 43, 62, 71.   6:23 Hebrew *Ebiasaph,* a variant spelling of Abiasaph (also in 6:37); compare parallel text at Exod 6:24.   6:27 As in some Greek manuscripts   (see also 6:33-34); Hebrew lacks *and Samuel.*   6:28 As in some Greek manuscripts and the Syriac version (see also 6:33 and 1 Sam 8:2); Hebrew lacks *Joel.*   6:32 Hebrew *the Tabernacle, the Tent of Meeting.*   6:38 *Israel* is the name that God gave to Jacob.   6:39 Hebrew lacks *from the clan of Gershon;* see 6:43.   6:57 As in parallel text at Josh 21:13; Hebrew reads *were given the cities of refuge: Hebron, and the following towns, each with its pasturelands.*   6:58 As in parallel text at Josh 21:15; Hebrew reads *Hilen.*   6:59a As in parallel text at Josh 21:16; Hebrew reads *Ashan.*   6:59b As in Syriac version (see also Josh 21:16); Hebrew lacks *Juttah.*   6:60 As in parallel text at Josh 21:17; Hebrew lacks *Gibeon.*   6:66-67 As in parallel text at Josh 21:21. Hebrew text reads *were given the cities of refuge: Shechem in the hill country of Ephraim, and the following towns, each with its pasturelands.*   6:77a As in Greek version (see also Josh 21:34); Hebrew lacks *Jokneam, Kartah.*   6:77b As in Greek version (see also Josh 19:13); Hebrew reads *Rimmono.*   6:78 Hebrew *Jahzah,* a variant spelling of Jahaz.

ACTS 26:1-32

Then Agrippa said to Paul, "You may speak in your defense."

So Paul, gesturing with his hand, started his defense: [2]"I am fortunate, King Agrippa, that you are the one hearing my defense today against all these accusations made by the Jewish leaders, [3]for I know you are an expert on all Jewish customs and controversies. Now please listen to me patiently!

[4]"As the Jewish leaders are well aware, I was given a thorough Jewish training from my earliest childhood among my own people and in Jerusalem. [5]If they would admit it, they know that I have been a member of the Pharisees, the strictest sect of our religion. [6]Now I am on trial because of my hope in the fulfillment of God's promise made to our ancestors. [7]In fact, that is why the twelve tribes of Israel zealously worship God night and day, and they share the same hope I have. Yet, Your Majesty, they accuse me for having this hope! [8]Why does

it seem incredible to any of you that God can raise the dead?

9"I used to believe that I ought to do everything I could to oppose the very name of Jesus the Nazarene.* 10Indeed, I did just that in Jerusalem. Authorized by the leading priests, I caused many believers there to be sent to prison. And I cast my vote against them when they were condemned to death. 11Many times I had them punished in the synagogues to get them to curse Jesus.* I was so violently opposed to them that I even chased them down in foreign cities.

12"One day I was on such a mission to Damascus, armed with the authority and commission of the leading priests. 13About noon, Your Majesty, as I was on the road, a light from heaven brighter than the sun shone down on me and my companions. 14We all fell down, and I heard a voice saying to me in Aramaic,* 'Saul, Saul, why are you persecuting me? It is useless for you to fight against my will.*'

15"'Who are you, lord?' I asked.

"And the Lord replied, 'I am Jesus, the one you are persecuting. 16Now get to your feet! For I have appeared to you to appoint you as my servant and witness. You are to tell the world what you have seen and what I will show you in the future. 17And I will rescue you from both your own people and the Gentiles. Yes, I am sending you to the Gentiles 18to open their eyes, so they may turn from darkness to light and from the power of Satan to God. Then they will receive forgiveness for their sins and be given a place among God's people, who are set apart by faith in me.'

19"And so, King Agrippa, I obeyed that vision from heaven. 20I preached first to those in Damascus, then in Jerusalem and throughout all Judea, and also to the Gentiles, that all must repent of their sins and turn to God—and prove they have changed by the good things they do. 21Some Jews arrested me in the Temple for preaching this, and they tried to kill me. 22But God has protected me right up to this present time so I can testify to everyone, from the least to the greatest. **I teach nothing except what the prophets and Moses said would happen—**23that the Messiah would suffer and be the first to rise from the dead, and in this way announce God's light to Jews and Gentiles alike."

24Suddenly, Festus shouted, "Paul, you are insane. Too much study has made you crazy!"

25But Paul replied, "I am not insane, Most Excellent Festus. What I am saying is the sober truth. 26And King Agrippa knows about these things. I speak boldly, for I am sure these events are all familiar to him, for they were not done in a corner! 27King Agrippa, do you believe the prophets? I know you do—"

28Agrippa interrupted him. "Do you think you can persuade me to become a Christian so quickly?"*

29Paul replied, "Whether quickly or not, I pray to God that both you and everyone here in this audience might become the same as I am, except for these chains."

30Then the king, the governor, Bernice, and all the others stood and left. 31As they went out, they talked it over and agreed, "This man hasn't done anything to deserve death or imprisonment."

32And Agrippa said to Festus, "He could have been set free if he hadn't appealed to Caesar."

26:9 Or *Jesus of Nazareth.*   26:11 Greek *to blaspheme.*
26:14a Or *Hebrew.*   26:14b Greek *It is hard for you to kick against the oxgoads.*   26:28 Or "A little more, and your arguments would make me a Christian."

PSALM 6:1-10

*For the choir director: A psalm of David, to be accompanied by an eight-stringed instrument.**

1 O LORD, don't rebuke me
        in your anger
    or discipline me in your
        rage.
2 Have compassion on me, LORD,
        for I am weak.
    Heal me, LORD, for my bones
        are in agony.

3 I am sick at heart.
  How long, O Lord, until you
    restore me?

4 Return, O Lord, and rescue me.
  Save me because of your
    unfailing love.
5 For the dead do not remember you.
  Who can praise you from
    the grave?*

6 I am worn out from sobbing.
  All night I flood my bed
    with weeping,
  drenching it with my tears.
7 My vision is blurred by grief;
  my eyes are worn out because
    of all my enemies.

8 Go away, all you who do evil,
  for the Lord has heard my
    weeping.
9 The Lord has heard my plea;
  the Lord will answer my prayer.
10 May all my enemies be disgraced
    and terrified.
  May they suddenly turn back
    in shame.

6:title Hebrew *with stringed instruments; according to the
sheminith.*   6:5 Hebrew *from Sheol?*

PROVERBS 18:20-21
Wise words satisfy like a good meal;
the right words bring satisfaction.
□ The tongue can bring death or life;
those who love to talk will reap the consequences.

JULY
9

1 CHRONICLES 7:1–8:40
The four sons of Issachar were Tola,
Puah, Jashub, and Shimron.
2 The sons of Tola were Uzzi, Rephaiah,
Jeriel, Jahmai, Ibsam, and Shemuel.
Each of them was the leader of an

ancestral clan. At the time of King
David, the total number of mighty
warriors listed in the records of
these clans was 22,600.
3 The son of Uzzi was Izrahiah. The
sons of Izrahiah were Michael,
Obadiah, Joel, and Isshiah. These
five became the leaders of clans. 4 All
of them had many wives and many
sons, so the total number of men
available for military service among
their descendants was 36,000.
5 The total number of mighty warriors
from all the clans of the tribe of
Issachar was 87,000. All of them were
listed in their genealogical records.

6 Three of Benjamin's sons were Bela,
Beker, and Jediael.
7 The five sons of Bela were Ezbon,
Uzzi, Uzziel, Jerimoth, and Iri. Each
of them was the leader of an
ancestral clan. The total number of
mighty warriors from these clans
was 22,034, as listed in their
genealogical records.
8 The sons of Beker were Zemirah,
Joash, Eliezer, Elioenai, Omri,
Jeremoth, Abijah, Anathoth, and
Alemeth. 9 Each of them was the
leader of an ancestral clan. The total
number of mighty warriors and
leaders from these clans was 20,200,
as listed in their genealogical records.
10 The son of Jediael was Bilhan. The
sons of Bilhan were Jeush, Benjamin,
Ehud, Kenaanah, Zethan, Tarshish,
and Ahishahar. 11 Each of them was
the leader of an ancestral clan.
From these clans the total number
of mighty warriors ready for war
was 17,200.
12 The sons of Ir were Shuppim and
Huppim. Hushim was the son of Aher.

13 The sons of Naphtali were Jahzeel,*
Guni, Jezer, and Shillem.* They were
all descendants of Jacob's concubine
Bilhah.

14 The descendants of Manasseh
through his Aramean concubine
included Asriel. She also bore Makir,

the father of Gilead. [15]Makir found wives for* Huppim and Shuppim. Makir had a sister named Maacah. One of his descendants was Zelophehad, who had only daughters. [16]Makir's wife, Maacah, gave birth to a son whom she named Peresh. His brother's name was Sheresh. The sons of Peresh were Ulam and Rakem. [17]The son of Ulam was Bedan. All these were considered Gileadites, descendants of Makir son of Manasseh.

[18]Makir's sister Hammoleketh gave birth to Ishhod, Abiezer, and Mahlah. [19]The sons of Shemida were Ahian, Shechem, Likhi, and Aniam.

[20]The descendants of Ephraim were Shuthelah, Bered, Tahath, Eleadah, Tahath, [21]Zabad, Shuthelah, Ezer, and Elead. These two were killed trying to steal livestock from the local farmers near Gath. [22]Their father, Ephraim, mourned for them a long time, and his relatives came to comfort him. [23]Afterward Ephraim slept with his wife, and she became pregnant and gave birth to a son. Ephraim named him Beriah* because of the tragedy his family had suffered. [24]He had a daughter named Sheerah. She built the towns of Lower and Upper Beth-horon and Uzzen-sheerah.

[25]The descendants of Ephraim included Rephah, Resheph, Telah, Tahan, [26]Ladan, Ammihud, Elishama, [27]Nun, and Joshua.

[28]The descendants of Ephraim lived in the territory that included Bethel and its surrounding towns to the south, Naaran to the east, Gezer and its villages to the west, and Shechem and its surrounding villages to the north as far as Ayyah and its towns. [29]Along the border of Manasseh were the towns of Bethshan,* Taanach, Megiddo, Dor, and their surrounding villages. The descendants of Joseph son of Israel* lived in these towns.

[30]The sons of Asher were Imnah, Ishvah, Ishvi, and Beriah. They had a sister named Serah. [31]The sons of Beriah were Heber and Malkiel (the father of Birzaith). [32]The sons of Heber were Japhlet, Shomer, and Hotham. They had a sister named Shua. [33]The sons of Japhlet were Pasach, Bimhal, and Ashvath. [34]The sons of Shomer were Ahi,* Rohgah, Hubbah, and Aram. [35]The sons of his brother Helem* were Zophah, Imna, Shelesh, and Amal. [36]The sons of Zophah were Suah, Harnepher, Shual, Beri, Imrah, [37]Bezer, Hod, Shamma, Shilshah, Ithran,* and Beera. [38]The sons of Jether were Jephunneh, Pispah, and Ara. [39]The sons of Ulla were Arah, Hanniel, and Rizia.

[40]Each of these descendants of Asher was the head of an ancestral clan. They were all select men—mighty warriors and outstanding leaders. The total number of men available for military service was 26,000, as listed in their genealogical records.

[8:1]BENJAMIN's first son was Bela, the second was Ashbel, the third was Aharah, [2]the fourth was Nohah, and the fifth was Rapha. [3]The sons of Bela were Addar, Gera, Abihud,* [4]Abishua, Naaman, Ahoah, [5]Gera, Shephuphan, and Huram. [6]The sons of Ehud, leaders of the clans living at Geba, were exiled to Manahath. [7]Ehud's sons were Naaman, Ahijah, and Gera. Gera, who led them into exile, was the father of Uzza and Ahihud.*

[8]After Shaharaim divorced his wives Hushim and Baara, he had children in the land of Moab. [9]Hodesh, his new wife, gave birth to Jobab, Zibia, Mesha, Malcam, [10]Jeuz, Sakia, and Mirmah. These sons all became the leaders of clans. [11]Shaharaim's wife Hushim had

already given birth to Abitub and Elpaal. ¹²The sons of Elpaal were Eber, Misham, Shemed (who built the towns of Ono and Lod and their nearby villages), ¹³Beriah, and Shema. They were the leaders of the clans living in Aijalon, and they drove out the inhabitants of Gath. ¹⁴Ahio, Shashak, Jeremoth, ¹⁵Zebadiah, Arad, Eder, ¹⁶Michael, Ishpah, and Joha were the sons of Beriah.

¹⁷Zebadiah, Meshullam, Hizki, Heber, ¹⁸Ishmerai, Izliah, and Jobab were the sons of Elpaal.

¹⁹Jakim, Zicri, Zabdi, ²⁰Elienai, Zillethai, Eliel, ²¹Adaiah, Beraiah, and Shimrath were the sons of Shimei.

²²Ishpan, Eber, Eliel, ²³Abdon, Zicri, Hanan, ²⁴Hananiah, Elam, Anthothijah, ²⁵Iphdeiah, and Penuel were the sons of Shashak.

²⁶Shamsherai, Shehariah, Athaliah, ²⁷Jaareshiah, Elijah, and Zicri were the sons of Jeroham.

²⁸These were the leaders of the ancestral clans; they were listed in their genealogical records, and they all lived in Jerusalem.

²⁹Jeiel* (the father of* Gibeon) lived in the town of Gibeon. His wife's name was Maacah, ³⁰and his oldest son was named Abdon. Jeiel's other sons were Zur, Kish, Baal, Ner,* Nadab, ³¹Gedor, Ahio, Zechariah,* ³²and Mikloth, who was the father of Shimeam.* All these families lived near each other in Jerusalem.

³³ Ner was the father of Kish.
Kish was the father of Saul.
Saul was the father of Jonathan, Malkishua, Abinadab, and Esh-baal.

³⁴ Jonathan was the father of Merib-baal.
Merib-baal was the father of Micah.

³⁵ Micah was the father of Pithon, Melech, Tahrea,* and Ahaz.

³⁶ Ahaz was the father of Jadah.*
Jadah was the father of Alemeth, Azmaveth, and Zimri.
Zimri was the father of Moza.

³⁷ Moza was the father of Binea.

Binea was the father of Rephaiah.*
Rephaiah was the father of Eleasah.
Eleasah was the father of Azel.

³⁸Azel had six sons: Azrikam, Bokeru, Ishmael, Sheariah, Obadiah, and Hanan. These were the sons of Azel.

³⁹Azel's brother Eshek had three sons: the first was Ulam, the second was Jeush, and the third was Eliphelet. ⁴⁰Ulam's sons were all mighty warriors and expert archers. They had many sons and grandsons—150 in all.

All these were descendants of Benjamin.

7:13a As in parallel text at Gen 46:24; Hebrew reads *Jahziel*, a variant spelling of Jahzeel.   7:13b As in some Hebrew and Greek manuscripts (see also Gen 46:24); most Hebrew manuscripts read *Shallum*.   7:15 Or *Makir took a wife from*. The meaning of the Hebrew is uncertain. 7:23 *Beriah* sounds like a Hebrew term meaning "tragedy" or "misfortune."   7:29a Hebrew *Beth-shean*, a variant spelling of Beth-shan.   7:29b *Israel* is the name that God gave to Jacob.   7:34 Or *The sons of Shomer, his brother, were*.   7:35 Possibly another name for *Hotham*; compare 7:32.   7:37 Possibly another name for *Jether*; compare 7:38.   8:3 Possibly *Gera the father of Ehud*; compare 8:6. 8:7 Or *Gera, that is Heglam, was the father of Uzza and Ahihud*.   8:29a As in some Greek manuscripts (see also 9:35); Hebrew lacks *Jeiel*.   8:29b Or *the founder of*. 8:30 As in some Greek manuscripts (see also 9:36); Hebrew lacks *Ner*.   8:31 As in parallel text at 9:37; Hebrew reads *Zeker*, a variant spelling of Zechariah.   8:32 As in parallel text at 9:38; Hebrew reads *Shimeah*, a variant spelling of Shimeam.   8:35 As in parallel text at 9:41; Hebrew reads *Tarea*, a variant spelling of Tahrea.   8:36 As in parallel text at 9:42; Hebrew reads *Jehoaddah*, a variant spelling of Jadah.   8:37 As in parallel text at 9:43; Hebrew reads *Raphah*, a variant spelling of Rephaiah.

ACTS 27:1-20

When the time came, we [Luke, Paul, and his companions] set sail for Italy. Paul and several other prisoners were placed in the custody of a Roman officer* named Julius, a captain of the Imperial Regiment. ²Aristarchus, a Macedonian from Thessalonica, was also with us. We left on a ship whose home port was Adramyttium on the northwest coast of the province of Asia;* it was scheduled to make several stops at ports along the coast of the province.

³The next day when we docked at Sidon, Julius was very kind to Paul and let him go ashore to visit with friends so they could provide for his needs. ⁴Putting out to sea from there, we encountered strong headwinds that made it difficult to keep the ship on course, so

we sailed north of Cyprus between the island and the mainland. [5]Keeping to the open sea, we passed along the coast of Cilicia and Pamphylia, landing at Myra, in the province of Lycia. [6]There the commanding officer found an Egyptian ship from Alexandria that was bound for Italy, and he put us on board.

[7]We had several days of slow sailing, and after great difficulty we finally neared Cnidus. But the wind was against us, so we sailed across to Crete and along the sheltered coast of the island, past the cape of Salmone. [8]We struggled along the coast with great difficulty and finally arrived at Fair Havens, near the town of Lasea. [9]We had lost a lot of time. The weather was becoming dangerous for sea travel because it was so late in the fall,* and Paul spoke to the ship's officers about it.

[10]"Men," he said, "I believe there is trouble ahead if we go on—shipwreck, loss of cargo, and danger to our lives as well." [11]But the officer in charge of the prisoners listened more to the ship's captain and the owner than to Paul. [12]And since Fair Havens was an exposed harbor—a poor place to spend the winter—most of the crew wanted to go on to Phoenix, farther up the coast of Crete, and spend the winter there. Phoenix was a good harbor with only a southwest and northwest exposure.

[13]When a light wind began blowing from the south, the sailors thought they could make it. So they pulled up anchor and sailed close to the shore of Crete. [14]But the weather changed abruptly, and a wind of typhoon strength (called a "northeaster") caught the ship and blew it out to sea. [15]They couldn't turn the ship into the wind, so they gave up and let it run before the gale.

[16]We sailed along the sheltered side of a small island named Cauda,* where with great difficulty we hoisted aboard the lifeboat being towed behind us. [17]Then the sailors bound ropes around the hull of the ship to strengthen it. They were afraid of being driven across to the sandbars of Syrtis off the African coast, so they lowered the sea anchor to slow the ship and were driven before the wind.

[18]The next day, as gale-force winds continued to batter the ship, the crew began throwing the cargo overboard. [19]The following day they even took some of the ship's gear and threw it overboard. [20]The terrible storm raged for many days, blotting out the sun and the stars, until at last all hope was gone.

27:1 Greek *centurion;* similarly in 27:6, 11, 31, 43.
27:2 Asia was a Roman province in what is now western Turkey. 27:9 Greek *because the fast was now already gone by.* This fast was associated with the Day of Atonement *(Yom Kippur),* which occurred in late September or early October. 27:16 Some manuscripts read *Clauda.*

PSALM 7:1-17

A psalm of David, which he sang to the Lord concerning Cush of the tribe of Benjamin.

[1] I come to you for protection,
    O Lord my God.
    Save me from my persecutors—
        rescue me!
[2] If you don't, they will maul me
        like a lion,
    tearing me to pieces with no one
        to rescue me.
[3] O Lord my God, if I have done wrong
        or am guilty of injustice,
[4] if I have betrayed a friend
        or plundered my enemy
        without cause,
[5] then let my enemies capture me.
    Let them trample me into
        the ground
    and drag my honor in the dust.
                            Interlude

[6] Arise, O Lord, in anger!
    Stand up against the fury
        of my enemies!
    Wake up, my God, and
        bring justice!
[7] Gather the nations before you.
    Rule over them from on high.
[8]   The Lord judges the nations.
    Declare me righteous, O Lord,
        for I am innocent, O Most High!
[9] **End the evil of those who
        are wicked,
    and defend the righteous.**

For you look deep within the
　　mind and heart,
　O righteous God.

10 God is my shield,
　　saving those whose hearts
　　are true and right.
11 God is an honest judge.
　He is angry with the wicked
　　every day.

12 If a person does not repent,
　God* will sharpen his sword;
　he will bend and string his bow.
13 He will prepare his deadly weapons
　and shoot his flaming arrows.

14 The wicked conceive evil;
　they are pregnant with trouble
　and give birth to lies.
15 They dig a deep pit to trap others,
　then fall into it themselves.
16 The trouble they make for others
　backfires on them.
　The violence they plan falls
　on their own heads.

17 I will thank the LORD because
　he is just;
　I will sing praise to the name
　of the LORD Most High.

7:12 Hebrew *he.*

PROVERBS 18:22
The man who finds a wife finds a treasure, and he receives favor from the LORD.

JULY
10

1 CHRONICLES 9:1–10:14
So all Israel was listed in the genealogi-
cal records in *The Book of the Kings of
Israel.*
　The people of Judah were exiled to
Babylon because they were unfaithful
to the LORD. 2 The first of the exiles to re-
turn to their property in their former

towns were priests, Levites, Temple servants, and other Israelites. 3 Some of the
people from the tribes of Judah, Benjamin, Ephraim, and Manasseh came and
settled in Jerusalem.

4 One family that returned was that
　of Uthai son of Ammihud, son
　of Omri, son of Imri, son of Bani,
　a descendant of Perez son of Judah.
5 Others returned from the Shilonite
　clan, including Asaiah (the oldest)
　and his sons.
6 From the Zerahite clan, Jeuel returned
　with his relatives.
In all, 690 families from the tribe of Judah returned.

7 From the tribe of Benjamin came
　Sallu son of Meshullam, son of
　Hodaviah, son of Hassenuah;
　8 Ibneiah son of Jeroham; Elah son of
　Uzzi, son of Micri; and Meshullam
　son of Shephatiah, son of Reuel, son
　of Ibnijah.
9 These men were all leaders of clans,
and they were listed in their genealogical records. In all, 956 families from the
tribe of Benjamin returned.

10 Among the priests who returned were
　Jedaiah, Jehoiarib, Jakin, 11 Azariah
　son of Hilkiah, son of Meshullam, son
　of Zadok, son of Meraioth, son of
　Ahitub. Azariah was the chief officer
　of the house of God.
12 Other returning priests were Adaiah
　son of Jeroham, son of Pashhur, son
　of Malkijah, and Maasai son of Adiel,
　son of Jahzerah, son of Meshullam,
　son of Meshillemith, son of Immer.
13 In all, 1,760 priests returned. They
were heads of clans and very able men.
They were responsible for ministering
at the house of God.

14 The Levites who returned were
　Shemaiah son of Hasshub, son
　of Azrikam, son of Hashabiah, a
　descendant of Merari; 15 Bakbakkar;
　Heresh; Galal; Mattaniah son of
　Mica, son of Zicri, son of Asaph;
　16 Obadiah son of Shemaiah, son of

Galal, son of Jeduthun; and Berekiah son of Asa, son of Elkanah, who lived in the area of Netophah.

¹⁷ The gatekeepers who returned were Shallum, Akkub, Talmon, Ahiman, and their relatives. Shallum was the chief gatekeeper. ¹⁸Prior to this time, they were responsible for the King's Gate on the east side. These men served as gatekeepers for the camps of the Levites. ¹⁹Shallum was the son of Kore, a descendant of Abiasaph,* from the clan of Korah. He and his relatives, the Korahites, were responsible for guarding the entrance to the sanctuary, just as their ancestors had guarded the Tabernacle in the camp of the LORD.

²⁰Phinehas son of Eleazar had been in charge of the gatekeepers in earlier times, and the LORD had been with him. ²¹And later Zechariah son of Meshelemiah was responsible for guarding the entrance to the Tabernacle.*

²²In all, there were 212 gatekeepers in those days, and they were listed according to the genealogies in their villages. David and Samuel the seer had appointed their ancestors because they were reliable men. ²³These gatekeepers and their descendants, by their divisions, were responsible for guarding the entrance to the house of the LORD when that house was a tent. ²⁴The gatekeepers were stationed on all four sides—east, west, north, and south. ²⁵Their relatives in the villages came regularly to share their duties for seven-day periods.

²⁶The four chief gatekeepers, all Levites, were trusted officials, for they were responsible for the rooms and treasuries at the house of God. ²⁷They would spend the night around the house of God, since it was their duty to guard it and to open the gates every morning.

²⁸Some of the gatekeepers were assigned to care for the various articles used in worship. They checked them in and out to avoid any loss. ²⁹Others were responsible for the furnishings, the items in the sanctuary, and the supplies, such as choice flour, wine, olive oil, frankincense, and spices. ³⁰But it was the priests who blended the spices. ³¹Mattithiah, a Levite and the oldest son of Shallum the Korahite, was entrusted with baking the bread used in the offerings. ³²And some members of the clan of Kohath were in charge of preparing the bread to be set on the table each Sabbath day.

³³The musicians, all prominent Levites, lived at the Temple. They were exempt from other responsibilities since they were on duty at all hours. ³⁴All these men lived in Jerusalem. They were the heads of Levite families and were listed as prominent leaders in their genealogical records.

³⁵Jeiel (the father of* Gibeon) lived in the town of Gibeon. His wife's name was Maacah, ³⁶and his oldest son was named Abdon. Jeiel's other sons were Zur, Kish, Baal, Ner, Nadab, ³⁷Gedor, Ahio, Zechariah, and Mikloth. ³⁸Mikloth was the father of Shimeam. All these families lived near each other in Jerusalem.

³⁹ Ner was the father of Kish.
Kish was the father of Saul.
Saul was the father of Jonathan,
    Malkishua, Abinadab, and
    Esh-baal.
⁴⁰ Jonathan was the father of Merib-
    baal.
Merib-baal was the father of Micah.
⁴¹ The sons of Micah were Pithon,
    Melech, Tahrea, and Ahaz.*
⁴² Ahaz was the father of Jadah.*
Jadah was the father of Alemeth,
    Azmaveth, and Zimri.
Zimri was the father of Moza.
⁴³ Moza was the father of Binea.
Binea's son was Rephaiah.
Rephaiah's son was Eleasah.
Eleasah's son was Azel.
⁴⁴Azel had six sons, whose names were Azrikam, Bokeru, Ishmael, Sheariah, Obadiah, and Hanan. These were the sons of Azel.

10:1Now the Philistines attacked Israel, and the men of Israel fled before them. Many were slaughtered on the slopes of Mount Gilboa. 2The Philistines closed in on Saul and his sons, and they killed three of his sons—Jonathan, Abinadab, and Malkishua. 3The fighting grew very fierce around Saul, and the Philistine archers caught up with him and wounded him.

4Saul groaned to his armor bearer, "Take your sword and kill me before these pagan Philistines come to taunt and torture me."

But his armor bearer was afraid and would not do it. So Saul took his own sword and fell on it. 5When his armor bearer realized that Saul was dead, he fell on his own sword and died. 6So Saul and his three sons died there together, bringing his dynasty to an end.

7When all the Israelites in the Jezreel Valley saw that their army had fled and that Saul and his sons were dead, they abandoned their towns and fled. So the Philistines moved in and occupied their towns.

8The next day, when the Philistines went out to strip the dead, they found the bodies of Saul and his sons on Mount Gilboa. 9So they stripped off Saul's armor and cut off his head. Then they proclaimed the good news of Saul's death before their idols and to the people throughout the land of Philistia. 10They placed his armor in the temple of their gods, and they fastened his head to the temple of Dagon.

11But when everyone in Jabesh-gilead heard about everything the Philistines had done to Saul, 12all their mighty warriors brought the bodies of Saul and his sons back to Jabesh. Then they buried their bones beneath the great tree at Jabesh, and they fasted for seven days.

13So Saul died because he was unfaithful to the LORD. He failed to obey the LORD's command, and he even consulted a medium 14instead of asking the LORD for guidance. So the LORD killed him and turned the kingdom over to David son of Jesse.

9:19 Hebrew *Ebiasaph*, a variant spelling of Abiasaph; compare Exod 6:24.   9:21 Hebrew *Tent of Meeting*. 9:35 Or *the founder of*.   9:41 As in Syriac version and Latin Vulgate (see also 8:35); Hebrew lacks *and Ahaz*.   9:42 As in some Hebrew manuscripts and Greek version (see also 8:36); Hebrew reads *Jarah*.

ACTS 27:21-44

No one had eaten for a long time. Finally, Paul called the crew together and said, "Men, you should have listened to me in the first place and not left Crete. You would have avoided all this damage and loss. 22But take courage! None of you will lose your lives, even though the ship will go down. 23For last night an angel of the God to whom I belong and whom I serve stood beside me, 24and he said, 'Don't be afraid, Paul, for you will surely stand trial before Caesar! What's more, God in his goodness has granted safety to everyone sailing with you.' 25So take courage! For I believe God. It will be just as he said. 26But we will be shipwrecked on an island."

27About midnight on the fourteenth night of the storm, as we were being driven across the Sea of Adria,* the sailors sensed land was near. 28They dropped a weighted line and found that the water was 120 feet deep. But a little later they measured again and found it was only 90 feet deep.* 29At this rate they were afraid we would soon be driven against the rocks along the shore, so they threw out four anchors from the back of the ship and prayed for daylight.

30Then the sailors tried to abandon the ship; they lowered the lifeboat as though they were going to put out anchors from the front of the ship. 31But Paul said to the commanding officer and the soldiers, "You will all die unless the sailors stay aboard." 32So the soldiers cut the ropes to the lifeboat and let it drift away.

33Just as day was dawning, Paul urged everyone to eat. "You have been so worried that you haven't touched food for two weeks," he said. 34"Please eat something now for your own good. For not a hair of your heads will perish." 35Then he took some bread, gave thanks to God before them all, and broke off a piece and ate it. ³⁶Then everyone was encouraged and began to eat—³⁷all 276 of us who were on board. ³⁸After eating, the crew lightened the ship further by throwing the cargo of wheat overboard.

³⁹When morning dawned, they didn't recognize the coastline, but they saw a bay with a beach and wondered if they could get to shore by running the ship aground. ⁴⁰So they cut off the anchors and left them in the sea. Then they lowered the rudders, raised the foresail, and headed toward shore. ⁴¹But they hit a shoal and ran the ship aground too soon. The bow of the ship stuck fast, while the stern was repeatedly smashed by the force of the waves and began to break apart.

⁴²The soldiers wanted to kill the prisoners to make sure they didn't swim ashore and escape. ⁴³But the commanding officer wanted to spare Paul, so he didn't let them carry out their plan. Then he ordered all who could swim to jump overboard first and make for land. ⁴⁴The others held onto planks or debris from the broken ship.* So everyone escaped safely to shore.

27:27 The *Sea of Adria* includes the central portion of the Mediterranean.   27:28 Greek *20 fathoms . . . 15 fathoms* [37 meters . . . 27 meters].   27:44 Or *or were helped by members of the ship's crew.*

PSALM 8:1-9

For the choir director: A psalm of David, to be accompanied by a stringed instrument.

¹ **O** LORD, our Lord, your majestic
   name fills the earth!
   Your glory is higher than the
   heavens.
² You have taught children
   and infants
      to tell of your strength,*
   silencing your enemies
      and all who oppose you.

³ **When I look at the night sky
   and see the work of
   your fingers—
      the moon and the stars you set
      in place—**

⁴ **what are people that you should
   think about them,
   mere mortals that you should
   care for them?***
⁵ Yet you made them only a little
      lower than God*
   and crowned them* with glory
      and honor.
⁶ You gave them charge of everything
      you made,
   putting all things under their
      authority—
⁷ the flocks and the herds
      and all the wild animals,
⁸ the birds in the sky, the fish
      in the sea,
   and everything that swims the
      ocean currents.

⁹ O LORD, our Lord, your majestic
      name fills the earth!

8:TITLE Hebrew *according to the gittith.*   8:2 Greek version reads *to give you praise.* Compare Matt 21:16. 8:4 Hebrew *what is man that you should think of him, / the son of man that you should care for him?*   8:5a Or *Yet you made them only a little lower than the angels;* Hebrew reads *Yet you made him* [i.e., man] *a little lower than Elohim.*   8:5b Hebrew *him* [i.e., man]; similarly in 8:6.

PROVERBS 18:23-24

The poor plead for mercy; the rich answer with insults. □ There are "friends" who destroy each other, but a real friend sticks closer than a brother.

JULY
11

1 CHRONICLES 11:1–12:18

Then all Israel gathered before David at Hebron and told him, "We are your own flesh and blood. ²In the past,* even when Saul was king, you were the one who really led the forces of Israel. And the LORD your God told you, 'You will be the shepherd of my people Israel. You will be the leader of my people Israel.'"

³So there at Hebron, David made a covenant before the LORD with all the elders of Israel. And they anointed him

king of Israel, just as the Lord had promised through Samuel.

⁴Then David and all Israel went to Jerusalem (or Jebus, as it used to be called), where the Jebusites, the original inhabitants of the land, were living. ⁵The people of Jebus taunted David, saying, "You'll never get in here!" But David captured the fortress of Zion, which is now called the City of David.

⁶David had said to his troops, "Whoever is first to attack the Jebusites will become the commander of my armies!" And Joab, the son of David's sister Zeruiah, was first to attack, so he became the commander of David's armies.

⁷David made the fortress his home, and that is why it is called the City of David. ⁸He extended the city from the supporting terraces* to the surrounding area, while Joab rebuilt the rest of Jerusalem. ⁹And David became more and more powerful, because the Lord of Heaven's Armies was with him.

¹⁰These are the leaders of David's mighty warriors. Together with all Israel, they decided to make David their king, just as the Lord had promised concerning Israel.

¹¹Here is the record of David's mightiest warriors: The first was Jashobeam the Hacmonite, who was leader of the Three—the mightiest warriors among David's men.* He once used his spear to kill 300 enemy warriors in a single battle.

¹²Next in rank among the Three was Eleazar son of Dodai,* a descendant of Ahoah. ¹³He was with David in the battle against the Philistines at Pas-dammim. The battle took place in a field full of barley, and the Israelite army fled. ¹⁴But Eleazar and David* held their ground in the middle of the field and beat back the Philistines. So the Lord saved them by giving them a great victory.

¹⁵Once when David was at the rock near the cave of Adullam, the Philistine army was camped in the valley of Rephaim. The Three (who were among the Thirty—an elite group among David's fighting men) went down to meet him there. ¹⁶David was staying in the stronghold at the time, and a Philistine detachment had occupied the town of Bethlehem.

¹⁷David remarked longingly to his men, "Oh, how I would love some of that good water from the well by the gate in Bethlehem." ¹⁸So the Three broke through the Philistine lines, drew some water from the well by the gate in Bethlehem, and brought it back to David. But David refused to drink it. Instead, he poured it out as an offering to the Lord. ¹⁹"God forbid that I should drink this!" he exclaimed. "This water is as precious as the blood of these men* who risked their lives to bring it to me." So David did not drink it. These are examples of the exploits of the Three.

²⁰Abishai, the brother of Joab, was the leader of the Thirty.* He once used his spear to kill 300 enemy warriors in a single battle. It was by such feats that he became as famous as the Three. ²¹Abishai was the most famous of the Thirty and was their commander, though he was not one of the Three.

²²There was also Benaiah son of Jehoiada, a valiant warrior from Kabzeel. He did many heroic deeds, which included killing two champions* of Moab. Another time, on a snowy day, he chased a lion down into a pit and killed it. ²³Once, armed only with a club, he killed an Egyptian warrior who was 7½ feet* tall and whose spear was as thick as a weaver's beam. Benaiah wrenched the spear from the Egyptian's hand and killed him with it. ²⁴Deeds like these made Benaiah as famous as the three mightiest warriors. ²⁵He was more honored than the other members of the Thirty, though he was not one of the Three. And David made him captain of his bodyguard.

²⁶David's mighty warriors also included:

Asahel, Joab's brother;
Elhanan son of Dodo
    from Bethlehem;
²⁷ Shammah from Harod;*
Helez from Pelon;

²⁸ Ira son of Ikkesh from Tekoa;
Abiezer from Anathoth;
²⁹ Sibbecai from Hushah;
Zalmon* from Ahoah;
³⁰ Maharai from Netophah;
Heled son of Baanah from Netophah;
³¹ Ithai son of Ribai from Gibeah
(in the land of Benjamin);
Benaiah from Pirathon;
³² Hurai from near Nahale-gaash*;
Abi-albon* from Arabah;
³³ Azmaveth from Bahurim*;
Eliahba from Shaalbon;
³⁴ the sons of Jashen* from Gizon;
Jonathan son of Shagee from Harar;
³⁵ Ahiam son of Sharar* from Harar;
Eliphal son of Ur;
³⁶ Hepher from Mekerah;
Ahijah from Pelon;
³⁷ Hezro from Carmel;
Paarai* son of Ezbai;
³⁸ Joel, the brother of Nathan;
Mibhar son of Hagri;
³⁹ Zelek from Ammon;
Naharai from Beeroth, Joab's
armor bearer;
⁴⁰ Ira from Jattir;
Gareb from Jattir;
⁴¹ Uriah the Hittite;
Zabad son of Ahlai;
⁴² Adina son of Shiza, the Reubenite
leader who had thirty men with
him;
⁴³ Hanan son of Maacah;
Joshaphat from Mithna;
⁴⁴ Uzzia from Ashtaroth;
Shama and Jeiel, the sons of
Hotham, from Aroer;
⁴⁵ Jediael son of Shimri;
Joha, his brother, from Tiz;
⁴⁶ Eliel from Mahavah;
Jeribai and Joshaviah, the
sons of Elnaam;
Ithmah from Moab;
⁴⁷ Eliel and Obed;
Jaasiel from Zobah.*

¹²:¹THE following men joined David at
Ziklag while he was hiding from Saul son
of Kish. They were among the warriors
who fought beside David in battle. ²All
of them were expert archers, and they
could shoot arrows or sling stones with
their left hand as well as their right. They
were all relatives of Saul from the tribe
of Benjamin. ³Their leader was Ahiezer
son of Shemaah from Gibeah; his
brother Joash was second-in-command.
These were the other warriors:

Jeziel and Pelet, sons of Azmaveth;
Beracah;
Jehu from Anathoth;
⁴ Ishmaiah from Gibeon, a famous
warrior and leader among the
Thirty;
*Jeremiah, Jahaziel, Johanan, and
Jozabad from Gederah;
⁵ Eluzai, Jerimoth, Bealiah, Shemariah,
and Shephatiah from Haruph;
⁶ Elkanah, Isshiah, Azarel, Joezer, and
Jashobeam, who were Korahites;
⁷ Joelah and Zebadiah, sons of
Jeroham from Gedor.

⁸Some brave and experienced warriors from the tribe of Gad also defected
to David while he was at the stronghold
in the wilderness. They were expert with
both shield and spear, as fierce as lions
and as swift as deer on the mountains.

⁹ Ezer was their leader.
Obadiah was second.
Eliab was third.
¹⁰ Mishmannah was fourth.
Jeremiah was fifth.
¹¹ Attai was sixth.
Eliel was seventh.
¹² Johanan was eighth.
Elzabad was ninth.
¹³ Jeremiah was tenth.
Macbannai was eleventh.

¹⁴These warriors from Gad were army
commanders. The weakest among them
could take on a hundred regular troops,
and the strongest could take on a thousand! ¹⁵These were the men who crossed
the Jordan River during its seasonal
flooding at the beginning of the year and
drove out all the people living in the low-
lands on both the east and west banks.

¹⁶Others from Benjamin and Judah
came to David at the stronghold.

[17]David went out to meet them and said, "If you have come in peace to help me, we are friends. But if you have come to betray me to my enemies when I am innocent, then may the God of our ancestors see it and punish you."

[18]Then the Spirit came upon Amasai, the leader of the Thirty, and he said,

"We are yours, David!
    We are on your side, son of Jesse.
Peace and prosperity be with you,
    and success to all who help you,
for your God is the one who helps
    you."

So David let them join him, and he made them officers over his troops.

11:2 Or *For some time.*   11:8 Hebrew *the millo.* The meaning of the Hebrew is uncertain.   11:11 As in some Greek manuscripts (see also 2 Sam 23:8); Hebrew reads *leader of the Thirty,* or *leader of the captains.*   11:12 As in parallel text at 2 Sam 23:9 (see also 1 Chr 27:4); Hebrew reads *Dodo,* a variant spelling of Dodai.   11:14 Hebrew *they.*   11:19 Hebrew *Shall I drink the lifeblood of these men?*   11:20 As in Syriac version; Hebrew reads *the Three;* also in 11:21.   11:22 Or *two sons of Ariel.*   11:23 Hebrew *5 cubits* [2.3 meters].   11:27 As in parallel text at 2 Sam 23:25; Hebrew reads *Shammoth from Haror.*   11:29 As in parallel text at 2 Sam 23:28; Hebrew reads *Ilai.*   11:32a Or *from the ravines of Gaash.*   11:32b As in parallel text at 2 Sam 23:31; Hebrew reads *Abiel.*   11:33 As in parallel text at 2 Sam 23:31; Hebrew reads *Baharum.*   11:34 As in parallel text at 2 Sam 23:32; Hebrew reads *sons of Hashem.*   11:35 As in parallel text at 2 Sam 23:33; Hebrew reads *son of Sacar.*   11:37 As in parallel text at 2 Sam 23:35; Hebrew reads *Naarai.*   11:47 Or *the Mezobaite.*   12:4 Verses 12:4b-40 are numbered 12:5-41 in Hebrew text.

ACTS 28:1-31

Once we [Luke, Paul, and his companions] were safe on shore, we learned that we were on the island of Malta. [2]The people of the island were very kind to us. It was cold and rainy, so they built a fire on the shore to welcome us.

[3]As Paul gathered an armful of sticks and was laying them on the fire, a poisonous snake, driven out by the heat, bit him on the hand. [4]The people of the island saw it hanging from his hand and said to each other, "A murderer, no doubt! Though he escaped the sea, justice will not permit him to live." [5]But Paul shook off the snake into the fire and was unharmed. [6]The people waited for him to swell up or suddenly drop dead. But when they had waited a long time and saw that he wasn't harmed, they changed their minds and decided he was a god.

[7]Near the shore where we landed was an estate belonging to Publius, the chief official of the island. He welcomed us and treated us kindly for three days. [8]As it happened, Publius's father was ill with fever and dysentery. Paul went in and prayed for him, and laying his hands on him, he healed him. [9]Then all the other sick people on the island came and were healed. [10]As a result we were showered with honors, and when the time came to sail, people supplied us with everything we would need for the trip.

[11]It was three months after the shipwreck that we set sail on another ship that had wintered at the island—an Alexandrian ship with the twin gods* as its figurehead. [12]Our first stop was Syracuse,* where we stayed three days. [13]From there we sailed across to Rhegium.* A day later a south wind began blowing, so the following day we sailed up the coast to Puteoli. [14]There we found some believers,* who invited us to spend a week with them. And so we came to Rome.

[15]The brothers and sisters* in Rome had heard we were coming, and they came to meet us at the Forum* on the Appian Way. Others joined us at The Three Taverns.* When Paul saw them, he was encouraged and thanked God.

[16]When we arrived in Rome, Paul was permitted to have his own private lodging, though he was guarded by a soldier.

[17]Three days after Paul's arrival, he called together the local Jewish leaders. He said to them, "Brothers, I was arrested in Jerusalem and handed over to the Roman government, even though I had done nothing against our people or the customs of our ancestors. [18]The Romans tried me and wanted to release me, because they found no cause for the death sentence. [19]But when the Jewish leaders protested the decision, I felt it necessary to appeal to Caesar, even though I had no desire to press charges against my own people. [20]I asked you to

come here today so we could get acquainted and so I could explain to you that I am bound with this chain because I believe that the hope of Israel—the Messiah—has already come."

[21]They replied, "We have had no letters from Judea or reports against you from anyone who has come here. [22]But we want to hear what you believe, for the only thing we know about this movement is that it is denounced everywhere."

[23]So a time was set, and on that day a large number of people came to Paul's lodging. He explained and testified about the Kingdom of God and tried to persuade them about Jesus from the Scriptures. Using the law of Moses and the books of the prophets, he spoke to them from morning until evening. [24]Some were persuaded by the things he said, but others did not believe. [25]And after they had argued back and forth among themselves, they left with this final word from Paul: "The Holy Spirit was right when he said to your ancestors through Isaiah the prophet,

[26] 'Go and say to this people:
When you hear what I say,
    you will not understand.
When you see what I do,
    you will not comprehend.
[27] For the hearts of these people
    are hardened,
    and their ears cannot hear,
    and they have closed their eyes—
so their eyes cannot see,
    and their ears cannot hear,
    and their hearts cannot
        understand,
and they cannot turn to me
    and let me heal them.'*

[28]So I want you to know that this salvation from God has also been offered to the Gentiles, and they will accept it."*

[30]For the next two years, Paul lived in Rome at his own expense.* He welcomed all who visited him, [31]boldly proclaiming the Kingdom of God and teaching about the Lord Jesus Christ. And no one tried to stop him.

28:11 The *twin gods* were the Roman gods Castor and Pollux.   28:12 *Syracuse* was on the island of Sicily.
28:13 *Rhegium* was on the southern tip of Italy.
28:14 Greek *brothers.*   28:15a Greek *brothers.*
28:15b *The Forum* was about 43 miles (70 kilometers) from Rome.   28:15c *The Three Taverns* was about 35 miles (57 kilometers) from Rome.   28:26-27 Isa 6:9-10 (Greek version).   28:28 Some manuscripts add verse 29, *And when he had said these words, the Jews departed, greatly disagreeing with each other.*   28:30 Or *in his own rented quarters.*

PSALM 9:1-12

For the choir director: A psalm of David, to be sung to the tune "Death of the Son."

[1] I will praise you, Lᴏʀᴅ, with
        all my heart;
    I will tell of all the marvelous
        things you have done.
[2] I will be filled with joy because
        of you.
    I will sing praises to your name,
        O Most High.

[3] My enemies retreated;
    they staggered and died when
        you appeared.
[4] For you have judged in my favor;
    from your throne you have
        judged with fairness.
[5] You have rebuked the nations and
        destroyed the wicked;
    you have erased their names
        forever.
[6] The enemy is finished, in endless
        ruins;
    the cities you uprooted are
        now forgotten.

[7] But the Lᴏʀᴅ reigns forever,
    executing judgment from
        his throne.
[8] He will judge the world with justice
    and rule the nations with
        fairness.
[9] **The Lᴏʀᴅ is a shelter for the
        oppressed,
    a refuge in times of trouble.**
[10] **Those who know your name trust
        in you,
    for you, O Lᴏʀᴅ, do not
        abandon those who search
        for you.**

[11] Sing praises to the Lᴏʀᴅ who reigns
        in Jerusalem.*

Tell the world about his
unforgettable deeds.

12 For he who avenges murder cares
for the helpless.
He does not ignore the cries
of those who suffer.

9:11 Hebrew *Zion;* also in 9:14.

PROVERBS 19:1-3

Better to be poor and honest than to be dishonest and a fool. □ Enthusiasm without knowledge is no good; haste makes mistakes. □ People ruin their lives by their own foolishness and then are angry at the Lord.

JULY
12

1 CHRONICLES 12:19–14:17

Some men from Manasseh defected from the Israelite army and joined David when he set out with the Philistines to fight against Saul. But as it turned out, the Philistine rulers refused to let David and his men go with them. After much discussion, they sent them back, for they said, "It will cost us our heads if David switches loyalties to Saul and turns against us."

20Here is a list of the men from Manasseh who defected to David as he was returning to Ziklag: Adnah, Jozabad, Jediael, Michael, Jozabad, Elihu, and Zillethai. Each commanded 1,000 troops from the tribe of Manasseh. 21They helped David chase down bands of raiders, for they were all brave and able warriors who became commanders in his army. 22Day after day more men joined David until he had a great army, like the army of God.

23These are the numbers of armed warriors who joined David at Hebron. They were all eager to see David be-

come king instead of Saul, just as the Lord had promised.

24From the tribe of Judah, there were 6,800 warriors armed with shields and spears.

25From the tribe of Simeon, there were 7,100 brave warriors.

26From the tribe of Levi, there were 4,600 warriors. 27This included Jehoiada, leader of the family of Aaron, who had 3,700 under his command. 28This also included Zadok, a brave young warrior, with 22 members of his family who were all officers.

29From the tribe of Benjamin, Saul's relatives, there were 3,000 warriors. Most of the men from Benjamin had remained loyal to Saul until this time.

30From the tribe of Ephraim, there were 20,800 brave warriors, each highly respected in his own clan.

31From the half-tribe of Manasseh west of the Jordan, 18,000 men were designated by name to help David become king.

32From the tribe of Issachar, there were 200 leaders of the tribe with their relatives. All these men understood the signs of the times and knew the best course for Israel to take.

33From the tribe of Zebulun, there were 50,000 skilled warriors. They were fully armed and prepared for battle and completely loyal to David.

34From the tribe of Naphtali, there were 1,000 officers and 37,000 warriors armed with shields and spears.

35From the tribe of Dan, there were 28,600 warriors, all prepared for battle.

36From the tribe of Asher, there were 40,000 trained warriors, all prepared for battle.

37From the east side of the Jordan River—where the tribes of Reuben and Gad and the half-tribe of

Manasseh lived—there were 120,000 troops armed with every kind of weapon.

³⁸All these men came in battle array to Hebron with the single purpose of making David the king over all Israel. In fact, everyone in Israel agreed that David should be their king. ³⁹They feasted and drank with David for three days, for preparations had been made by their relatives for their arrival. ⁴⁰And people from as far away as Issachar, Zebulun, and Naphtali brought food on donkeys, camels, mules, and oxen. Vast supplies of flour, fig cakes, clusters of raisins, wine, olive oil, cattle, sheep, and goats were brought to the celebration. There was great joy throughout the land of Israel.

¹³:¹DAVID consulted with all his officials, including the generals and captains of his army.* ²Then he addressed the entire assembly of Israel as follows: "If you approve and if it is the will of the LORD our God, let us send messages to all the Israelites throughout the land, including the priests and Levites in their towns and pasturelands. Let us invite them to come and join us. ³It is time to bring back the Ark of our God, for we neglected it during the reign of Saul."

⁴The whole assembly agreed to this, for the people could see it was the right thing to do. ⁵So David summoned all Israel, from the Shihor Brook of Egypt in the south all the way to the town of Lebo-hamath in the north, to join in bringing the Ark of God from Kiriath-jearim. ⁶Then David and all Israel went to Baalah of Judah (also called Kiriath-jearim) to bring back the Ark of God, which bears the name* of the LORD who is enthroned between the cherubim. ⁷They placed the Ark of God on a new cart and brought it from Abinadab's house. Uzzah and Ahio were guiding the cart. ⁸David and all Israel were celebrating before God with all their might, singing songs and playing all kinds of musical instruments—lyres, harps, tambourines, cymbals, and trumpets.

⁹But when they arrived at the threshing floor of Nacon,* the oxen stumbled, and Uzzah reached out his hand to steady the Ark. ¹⁰Then the LORD's anger was aroused against Uzzah, and he struck him dead because he had laid his hand on the Ark. So Uzzah died there in the presence of God.

¹¹David was angry because the LORD's anger had burst out against Uzzah. He named that place Perez-uzzah (which means "to burst out against Uzzah"), as it is still called today.

¹²David was now afraid of God, and he asked, "How can I ever bring the Ark of God back into my care?" ¹³So David did not move the Ark into the City of David. Instead, he took it to the house of Obed-edom of Gath. ¹⁴The Ark of God remained there in Obed-edom's house for three months, and the LORD blessed the household of Obed-edom and everything he owned.

¹⁴:¹THEN King Hiram of Tyre sent messengers to David, along with cedar timber, and stonemasons and carpenters to build him a palace. ²And David realized that the LORD had confirmed him as king over Israel and had greatly blessed his kingdom for the sake of his people Israel.

³Then David married more wives in Jerusalem, and they had more sons and daughters. ⁴These are the names of David's sons who were born in Jerusalem: Shammua, Shobab, Nathan, Solomon, ⁵Ibhar, Elishua, Elpelet, ⁶Nogah, Nepheg, Japhia, ⁷Elishama, Eliada,* and Eliphelet.

⁸When the Philistines heard that David had been anointed king over all Israel, they mobilized all their forces to capture him. But David was told they were coming, so he marched out to meet them. ⁹The Philistines arrived and made a raid in the valley of Rephaim. ¹⁰So David asked God, "Should I go out to fight the Philistines? Will you hand them over to me?"

The LORD replied, "Yes, go ahead. I will hand them over to you."

¹¹So David and his troops went up to

Baal-perazim and defeated the Philistines there. "God did it!" David exclaimed. "He used me to burst through my enemies like a raging flood!" So they named that place Baal-perazim (which means "the Lord who bursts through"). [12]The Philistines had abandoned their gods there, so David gave orders to burn them.

[13]But after a while the Philistines returned and raided the valley again. [14]And once again David asked God what to do. "Do not attack them straight on," God replied. "Instead, circle around behind and attack them near the poplar* trees. [15]When you hear a sound like marching feet in the tops of the poplar trees, go out and attack! That will be the signal that God is moving ahead of you to strike down the Philistine army." [16]So David did what God commanded, and they struck down the Philistine army all the way from Gibeon to Gezer.

[17]So David's fame spread everywhere, and the Lord caused all the nations to fear David.

13:1 Hebrew *the commanders of thousands and of hundreds.*   13:6 Or *the Ark of God, where the Name is proclaimed—the name.*   13:9 As in parallel text at 2 Sam 6:6; Hebrew reads *Kidon.*   14:7 Hebrew *Beeliada,* a variant spelling of Eliada; compare 3:8 and parallel text at 2 Sam 5:16.   14:14 Or *aspen,* or *balsam;* also in 14:15. The exact identification of this tree is uncertain.

ROMANS 1:1-17

This letter is from Paul, a slave of Christ Jesus, chosen by God to be an apostle and sent out to preach his Good News. [2]God promised this Good News long ago through his prophets in the holy Scriptures. [3]The Good News is about his Son, Jesus. In his earthly life he was born into King David's family line, [4]and he was shown to be* the Son of God when he was raised from the dead by the power of the Holy Spirit.* He is Jesus Christ our Lord. [5]Through Christ, God has given us the privilege and authority* as apostles to tell Gentiles everywhere what God has done for them, so that they will believe and obey him, bringing glory to his name.

[6]And you are included among those Gentiles who have been called to belong to Jesus Christ. [7]I am writing to all of you in Rome who are loved by God and are called to be his own holy people.

May God our Father and the Lord Jesus Christ give you grace and peace.

[8]Let me say first that I thank my God through Jesus Christ for all of you, because your faith in him is being talked about all over the world. [9]God knows how often I pray for you. Day and night I bring you and your needs in prayer to God, whom I serve with all my heart* by spreading the Good News about his Son.

[10]One of the things I always pray for is the opportunity, God willing, to come at last to see you. [11]For I long to visit you so I can bring you some spiritual gift that will help you grow strong in the Lord. [12]When we get together, I want to encourage you in your faith, but I also want to be encouraged by yours.

[13]I want you to know, dear brothers and sisters,* that I planned many times to visit you, but I was prevented until now. I want to work among you and see spiritual fruit, just as I have seen among other Gentiles. [14]For I have a great sense of obligation to people in both the civilized world and the rest of the world,* to the educated and uneducated alike. [15]So I am eager to come to you in Rome, too, to preach the Good News.

[16]**For I am not ashamed of this Good News about Christ. It is the power of God at work, saving everyone who believes—the Jew first and also the Gentile.*** [17]This Good News tells us how God makes us right in his sight. This is accomplished from start to finish by faith. As the Scriptures say, "It is through faith that a righteous person has life."*

1:4a Or *and was designated.*   1:4b Or *by the Spirit of holiness;* or *in the new realm of the Spirit.*   1:5 Or *the grace.*   1:9 Or *in my spirit.*   1:13 Greek *brothers.*   1:14 Greek *to Greeks and barbarians.*   1:16 Greek *also the Greek.*   1:17 Or *"The righteous will live by faith."* Hab 2:4.

PSALM 9:13-20

Lord, have mercy on me.
See how my enemies torment me.

Snatch me back from the
jaws of death.
14 Save me so I can praise you publicly
at Jerusalem's gates,
so I can rejoice that you have
rescued me.

15 The nations have fallen into the pit
they dug for others.
Their own feet have been caught
in the trap they set.
16 The LORD is known for his justice.
The wicked are trapped by their
own deeds.   *Quiet Interlude**

17 The wicked will go down to the
grave.*
This is the fate of all the nations
who ignore God.
18 But the needy will not be ignored
forever;
the hopes of the poor will not
always be crushed.

19 Arise, O LORD!
Do not let mere mortals defy you!
Judge the nations!
20 Make them tremble in fear, O LORD.
Let the nations know they are
merely human.   *Interlude*

9:16 Hebrew *Higgaion Selah*. The meaning of this phrase is
uncertain.   9:17 Hebrew *to Sheol*.

PROVERBS 19:4-5
Wealth makes many "friends"; poverty
drives them all away. □A false witness
will not go unpunished, nor will a liar
escape.

JULY
13

1 CHRONICLES 15:1–16:36
David now built several buildings for
himself in the City of David. He also
prepared a place for the Ark of God and
set up a special tent for it. 2Then he
commanded, "No one except the Levites may carry the Ark of God. The
LORD has chosen them to carry the Ark
of the LORD and to serve him forever."

3Then David summoned all Israel to
Jerusalem to bring the Ark of the LORD
to the place he had prepared for it.
4This is the number of the descendants
of Aaron (the priests) and the Levites
who were called together:

5From the clan of Kohath, 120, with
Uriel as their leader.
6From the clan of Merari, 220, with
Asaiah as their leader.
7From the clan of Gershon,* 130, with
Joel as their leader.
8From the descendants of Elizaphan,
200, with Shemaiah as their leader.
9From the descendants of Hebron, 80,
with Eliel as their leader.
10From the descendants of Uzziel, 112,
with Amminadab as their leader.

11Then David summoned the priests,
Zadok and Abiathar, and these Levite
leaders: Uriel, Asaiah, Joel, Shemaiah,
Eliel, and Amminadab. 12He said to
them, "You are the leaders of the Levite
families. You must purify yourselves
and all your fellow Levites, so you can
bring the Ark of the LORD, the God of
Israel, to the place I have prepared for it.
13Because you Levites did not carry the
Ark the first time, the anger of the LORD
our God burst out against us. We failed
to ask God how to move it properly."
14So the priests and the Levites purified
themselves in order to bring the Ark of
the LORD, the God of Israel, to Jerusalem. 15Then the Levites carried the Ark
of God on their shoulders with its carrying poles, just as the LORD had instructed Moses.

16David also ordered the Levite leaders to appoint a choir of Levites who
were singers and musicians to sing
joyful songs to the accompaniment of
harps, lyres, and cymbals. 17So the Levites appointed Heman son of Joel
along with his fellow Levites: Asaph son
of Berekiah, and Ethan son of Kushaiah
from the clan of Merari. 18The follow-

ing men were chosen as their assistants: Zechariah, Jaaziel,* Shemiramoth, Jehiel, Unni, Eliab, Benaiah, Maaseiah, Mattithiah, Eliphelehu, Mikneiah, and the gatekeepers—Obed-edom and Jeiel.

¹⁹The musicians Heman, Asaph, and Ethan were chosen to sound the bronze cymbals. ²⁰Zechariah, Aziel, Shemiramoth, Jehiel, Unni, Eliab, Maaseiah, and Benaiah were chosen to play the harps.* ²¹Mattithiah, Eliphelehu, Mikneiah, Obed-edom, Jeiel, and Azaziah were chosen to play the lyres.* ²²Kenaniah, the head Levite, was chosen as the choir leader because of his skill.

²³Berekiah and Elkanah were chosen to guard* the Ark. ²⁴Shebaniah, Joshaphat, Nethanel, Amasai, Zechariah, Benaiah, and Eliezer—all of whom were priests—were chosen to blow the trumpets as they marched in front of the Ark of God. Obed-edom and Jehiah were chosen to guard the Ark.

²⁵Then David and the elders of Israel and the generals of the army* went to the house of Obed-edom to bring the Ark of the LORD's Covenant up to Jerusalem with a great celebration. ²⁶And because God was clearly helping the Levites as they carried the Ark of the LORD's Covenant, they sacrificed seven bulls and seven rams.

²⁷David was dressed in a robe of fine linen, as were all the Levites who carried the Ark, and also the singers, and Kenaniah the choir leader. David was also wearing a priestly garment.* ²⁸So all Israel brought up the Ark of the LORD's Covenant with shouts of joy, the blowing of rams' horns and trumpets, the crashing of cymbals, and loud playing on harps and lyres.

²⁹But as the Ark of the LORD's Covenant entered the City of David, Michal, the daughter of Saul, looked down from her window. When she saw King David skipping about and laughing with joy, she was filled with contempt for him.

^{16:1}THEY brought the Ark of God and placed it inside the special tent David had prepared for it. And they presented burnt offerings and peace offerings to God. ²When he had finished his sacrifices, David blessed the people in the name of the LORD. ³Then he gave to every man and woman in all Israel a loaf of bread, a cake of dates,* and a cake of raisins.

⁴David appointed the following Levites to lead the people in worship before the Ark of the LORD—to invoke his blessings, to give thanks, and to praise the LORD, the God of Israel. ⁵Asaph, the leader of this group, sounded the cymbals. Second to him was Zechariah, followed by Jeiel, Shemiramoth, Jehiel, Mattithiah, Eliab, Benaiah, Obed-edom, and Jeiel. They played the harps and lyres. ⁶The priests, Benaiah and Jahaziel, played the trumpets regularly before the Ark of God's Covenant.

⁷On that day David gave to Asaph and his fellow Levites this song of thanksgiving to the LORD:

⁸ Give thanks to the LORD and
proclaim his greatness.
Let the whole world know
what he has done.
⁹ Sing to him; yes, sing his praises.
Tell everyone about his
wonderful deeds.
¹⁰ Exult in his holy name;
rejoice, you who worship the LORD.
¹¹ Search for the LORD and for
his strength;
continually seek him.
¹² Remember the wonders he has
performed,
his miracles, and the rulings
he has given,
¹³ you children of his servant Israel,
you descendants of Jacob,
his chosen ones.

¹⁴ He is the LORD our God.
His justice is seen throughout
the land.
¹⁵ Remember his covenant forever—
the commitment he made to
a thousand generations.
¹⁶ This is the covenant he made with
Abraham

and the oath he swore to Isaac.
¹⁷ He confirmed it to Jacob as
    a decree,
    and to the people of Israel as
    a never-ending covenant:
¹⁸ "I will give you the land of Canaan
    as your special possession."

¹⁹ He said this when you were
    few in number,
    a tiny group of strangers
    in Canaan.
²⁰ They wandered from nation
    to nation,
    from one kingdom to another.
²¹ Yet he did not let anyone oppress
    them.
    He warned kings on their behalf:
²² "Do not touch my chosen people,
    and do not hurt my prophets."

²³ Let the whole earth sing to the LORD!
    Each day proclaim the good news
    that he saves.
²⁴ Publish his glorious deeds among
    the nations.
    Tell everyone about the amazing
    things he does.
²⁵ Great is the LORD! He is most
    worthy of praise!
    He is to be feared above all gods.
²⁶ The gods of other nations are
    mere idols,
    but the LORD made the heavens!
²⁷ Honor and majesty surround him;
    strength and joy fill his dwelling.

²⁸ O nations of the world, recognize
    the LORD,
    recognize that the LORD is
    glorious and strong.
²⁹ Give to the LORD the glory he deserves!
    Bring your offering and come
    into his presence.
    Worship the LORD in all his
    holy splendor.
³⁰   Let all the earth tremble
    before him.
    The world stands firm and
    cannot be shaken.

³¹ Let the heavens be glad, and the
    earth rejoice!

Tell all the nations, "The LORD
    reigns!"
³² Let the sea and everything in it
    shout his praise!
    Let the fields and their crops
    burst out with joy!
³³ Let the trees of the forest rustle
    with praise,
    for the LORD is coming to judge
    the earth.

³⁴ Give thanks to the LORD, for
    he is good!
    His faithful love endures
    forever.
³⁵ Cry out, "Save us, O God of our
    salvation!
    Gather and rescue us from
    among the nations,
    so we can thank your holy name
    and rejoice and praise you."

³⁶ Praise the LORD, the God of Israel,
    who lives from everlasting
    to everlasting!

And all the people shouted "Amen!" and
praised the LORD.

15:7 Hebrew *Gershom*, a variant spelling of Gershon.
15:18 Or *Zechariah son of Jaaziel;* or *Zechariah, Ben,
Jaaziel.* 15:20 Hebrew adds *according to Alamoth,*
which is probably a musical term. The meaning of the
Hebrew is uncertain. 15:21 Hebrew adds *according to the
Sheminith,* which is probably a musical term. The meaning
of the Hebrew is uncertain. 15:23 Hebrew *chosen as
gatekeepers for;* also in 15:24. 15:25 Hebrew *the
commanders of thousands.* 15:27 Hebrew *a linen ephod.*
16:3 Or *a portion of meat.* The meaning of the Hebrew is
uncertain.

ROMANS 1:18-32
But God shows his anger from heaven
against all sinful, wicked people who
suppress the truth by their wickedness.* ¹⁹ They know the truth about God
because he has made it obvious to them.
**²⁰For ever since the world was cre-
ated, people have seen the earth and
sky. Through everything God made,
they can clearly see his invisible
qualities—his eternal power and divine nature. So they have no excuse
for not knowing God.**
    ²¹Yes, they knew God, but they
wouldn't worship him as God or even
give him thanks. And they began to think

up foolish ideas of what God was like. As a result, their minds became dark and confused. ²²Claiming to be wise, they instead became utter fools. ²³And instead of worshiping the glorious, ever-living God, they worshiped idols made to look like mere people and birds and animals and reptiles.

²⁴So God abandoned them to do whatever shameful things their hearts desired. As a result, they did vile and degrading things with each other's bodies. ²⁵They traded the truth about God for a lie. So they worshiped and served the things God created instead of the Creator himself, who is worthy of eternal praise! Amen. ²⁶That is why God abandoned them to their shameful desires. Even the women turned against the natural way to have sex and instead indulged in sex with each other. ²⁷And the men, instead of having normal sexual relations with women, burned with lust for each other. Men did shameful things with other men, and as a result of this sin, they suffered within themselves the penalty they deserved.

²⁸Since they thought it foolish to acknowledge God, he abandoned them to their foolish thinking and let them do things that should never be done. ²⁹Their lives became full of every kind of wickedness, sin, greed, hate, envy, murder, quarreling, deception, malicious behavior, and gossip. ³⁰They are backstabbers, haters of God, insolent, proud, and boastful. They invent new ways of sinning, and they disobey their parents. ³¹They refuse to understand, break their promises, are heartless, and have no mercy. ³²They know God's justice requires that those who do these things deserve to die, yet they do them anyway. Worse yet, they encourage others to do them, too.

1:18 Or *who, by their wickedness, prevent the truth from being known.*

PSALM 10:1-15

⬤ Lord, why do you stand
    so far away?
  Why do you hide when I am
    in trouble?

² The wicked arrogantly hunt down
    the poor.
  Let them be caught in the evil
    they plan for others.
³ For they brag about their evil desires;
    they praise the greedy and curse
    the Lord.

⁴ The wicked are too proud
    to seek God.
  They seem to think that
    God is dead.
⁵ Yet they succeed in everything
    they do.
  They do not see your punishment
    awaiting them.
  They sneer at all their
    enemies.
⁶ They think, "Nothing bad will ever
    happen to us!
  We will be free of trouble
    forever!"

⁷ Their mouths are full of cursing,
    lies, and threats.*
  Trouble and evil are on the tips
    of their tongues.
⁸ They lurk in ambush in the
    villages,
    waiting to murder innocent
    people.
  They are always searching for
    helpless victims.
⁹ Like lions crouched in hiding,
    they wait to pounce on the
    helpless.
  Like hunters they capture the
    helpless
    and drag them away in nets.
¹⁰ Their helpless victims are crushed;
    they fall beneath the strength
    of the wicked.
¹¹ The wicked think, "God isn't
    watching us!
  He has closed his eyes and won't
    even see what we do!"

¹² Arise, O Lord!
  Punish the wicked, O God!
  Do not ignore the helpless!
¹³ Why do the wicked get away with
    despising God?

They think, "God will never
call us to account."
14 But you see the trouble and grief
they cause.
You take note of it and punish
them.
The helpless put their trust in you.
You defend the orphans.

15 Break the arms of these wicked,
evil people!
Go after them until the last one
is destroyed.

10:7 Greek version reads *cursing and bitterness.*
Compare Rom 3:14.

PROVERBS 19:6-7

Many seek favors from a ruler; everyone is the friend of a person who gives gifts! □ The relatives of the poor despise them; how much more will their friends avoid them! Though the poor plead with them, their friends are gone.

JULY
14

1 CHRONICLES 16:37–18:17

David arranged for Asaph and his fellow Levites to serve regularly before the Ark of the LORD's Covenant, doing whatever needed to be done each day. 38This group included Obed-edom (son of Jeduthun), Hosah, and sixty-eight other Levites as gatekeepers.

39Meanwhile, David stationed Zadok the priest and his fellow priests at the Tabernacle of the LORD at the place of worship in Gibeon, where they continued to minister before the LORD. 40They sacrificed the regular burnt offerings to the LORD each morning and evening on the altar set aside for that purpose, obeying everything written in the Law of the LORD, as he had commanded Israel. 41David also appointed Heman, Jeduthun, and the others chosen by name to

give thanks to the LORD, for "his faithful love endures forever." 42They used their trumpets, cymbals, and other instruments to accompany their songs of praise to God.* And the sons of Jeduthun were appointed as gatekeepers.

43Then all the people returned to their homes, and David turned and went home to bless his own family.

17:1WHEN David was settled in his palace, he summoned Nathan the prophet. "Look," David said, "I am living in a beautiful cedar palace,* but the Ark of the LORD's Covenant is out there under a tent!"

2Nathan replied to David, "Do whatever you have in mind, for God is with you."

3But that same night God said to Nathan,

4"Go and tell my servant David,
'This is what the LORD has declared:
You are not the one to build a house
for me to live in. 5I have never lived
in a house, from the day I brought
the Israelites out of Egypt until this
very day. My home has always been
a tent, moving from one place to
another in a Tabernacle. 6Yet no
matter where I have gone with the
Israelites, I have never once
complained to Israel's leaders,*
the shepherds of my people. I have
never asked them, "Why haven't
you built me a beautiful cedar
house?"'

7"Now go and say to my servant
David, 'This is what the LORD of
Heaven's Armies has declared:
I took you from tending sheep
in the pasture and selected you to be
the leader of my people Israel. 8I
have been with you wherever you
have gone, and I have destroyed all
your enemies before your eyes.
Now I will make your name as
famous as anyone who has ever lived
on the earth! 9And I will provide a
homeland for my people Israel,
planting them in a secure place
where they will never be disturbed.

Evil nations won't oppress them as they've done in the past, [10]starting from the time I appointed judges to rule my people Israel. And I will defeat all your enemies.

"'Furthermore, I declare that the LORD will build a house for you—a dynasty of kings! [11]For when you die and join your ancestors, I will raise up one of your descendants, one of your sons, and I will make his kingdom strong. [12]He is the one who will build a house—a temple—for me. And I will secure his throne forever. [13]I will be his father, and he will be my son. I will never take my favor from him as I took it from the one who ruled before you. [14]I will confirm him as king over my house and my kingdom for all time, and his throne will be secure forever.'"

[15]So Nathan went back to David and told him everything the LORD had said in this vision.

[16]Then King David went in and sat before the LORD and prayed,

"Who am I, O LORD God, and what is my family, that you have brought me this far? [17]And now, O God, in addition to everything else, you speak of giving your servant a lasting dynasty! You speak as though I were someone very great,* O LORD God!

[18]"What more can I say to you about the way you have honored me? You know what your servant is really like. [19]For the sake of your servant, O LORD, and according to your will, you have done all these great things and have made them known.

[20]"O LORD, there is no one like you. We have never even heard of another God like you! [21]What other nation on earth is like your people Israel? What other nation, O God, have you redeemed from slavery to be your own people? You made a great name for yourself when you redeemed your people from Egypt.

You performed awesome miracles and drove out the nations that stood in their way. [22]You chose Israel to be your very own people forever, and you, O LORD, became their God.

[23]"And now, O LORD, I am your servant; do as you have promised concerning me and my family. May it be a promise that will last forever. [24]And may your name be established and honored forever so that everyone will say, 'The LORD of Heaven's Armies, the God of Israel, is Israel's God!' And may the house of your servant David continue before you forever.

[25]"O my God, I have been bold enough to pray to you because you have revealed to your servant that you will build a house for him—a dynasty of kings! [26]For you are God, O LORD. And you have promised these good things to your servant. [27]And now, it has pleased you to bless the house of your servant, so that it will continue forever before you. For when you grant a blessing, O LORD, it is an eternal blessing!"

[18:1]AFTER this, David defeated and subdued the Philistines by conquering Gath and its surrounding towns. [2]David also conquered the land of Moab, and the Moabites who were spared became David's subjects and paid him tribute money.

[3]David also destroyed the forces of Hadadezer, king of Zobah, as far as Hamath,* when Hadadezer marched out to strengthen his control along the Euphrates River. [4]David captured 1,000 chariots, 7,000 charioteers, and 20,000 foot soldiers. He crippled all the chariot horses except enough for 100 chariots.

[5]When Arameans from Damascus arrived to help King Hadadezer, David killed 22,000 of them. [6]Then he placed several army garrisons* in Damascus, the Aramean capital, and the Arameans became David's subjects and paid him tribute money. So the LORD made David victorious wherever he went.

[7]David brought the gold shields of Hadadezer's officers to Jerusalem, [8]along with a large amount of bronze from Hadadezer's towns of Tebah* and Cun. Later Solomon melted the bronze and molded it into the great bronze basin called the Sea, the pillars, and the various bronze articles used at the Temple.

[9]When King Toi* of Hamath heard that David had destroyed the entire army of King Hadadezer of Zobah, [10]he sent his son Joram* to congratulate King David for his successful campaign. Hadadezer and Toi had been enemies and were often at war. Joram presented David with many gifts of gold, silver, and bronze.

[11]King David dedicated all these gifts to the LORD, along with the silver and gold he had taken from the other nations—from Edom, Moab, Ammon, Philistia, and Amalek.

[12]Abishai son of Zeruiah destroyed 18,000 Edomites in the Valley of Salt. [13]He placed army garrisons in Edom, and all the Edomites became David's subjects. In fact, the LORD made David victorious wherever he went.

[14]So David reigned over all Israel and did what was just and right for all his people. [15]Joab son of Zeruiah was commander of the army. Jehoshaphat son of Ahilud was the royal historian. [16]Zadok son of Ahitub and Ahimelech* son of Abiathar were the priests. Seraiah* was the court secretary. [17]Benaiah son of Jehoiada was captain of the king's bodyguard.* And David's sons served as the king's chief assistants.

16:42 Or to accompany the sacred music; or to accompany singing to God. 17:1 Hebrew a house of cedar. 17:6 As in Greek version (see also 2 Sam 7:7); Hebrew reads judges. 17:17 The meaning of the Hebrew is uncertain. 18:3 The meaning of the Hebrew is uncertain. 18:6 As in Greek version and Latin Vulgate (see also 2 Sam 8:6); Hebrew lacks several army garrisons. 18:8 Hebrew reads Tibhath, a variant spelling of Tebah; compare parallel text at 2 Sam 8:8. 18:9 As in parallel text at 2 Sam 8:9; Hebrew reads Tou; also in 18:10. 18:10 As in parallel text at 2 Sam 8:10; Hebrew reads Hadoram, a variant spelling of Joram. 18:16a As in some Hebrew manuscripts, Syriac version, and Latin Vulgate (see also 2 Sam 8:17); Hebrew manuscripts read Abimelech. 18:16b As in parallel text at 2 Sam 8:17; Hebrew reads Shavsha. 18:17 Hebrew of the Kerethites and Pelethites.

ROMANS 2:1-24

You may think you can condemn such people, but you are just as bad, and you have no excuse! When you say they are wicked and should be punished, you are condemning yourself, for you who judge others do these very same things. [2]And we know that God, in his justice, will punish anyone who does such things. [3]Since you judge others for doing these things, why do you think you can avoid God's judgment when you do the same things? [4]Don't you see how wonderfully kind, tolerant, and patient God is with you? Does this mean nothing to you? Can't you see that his kindness is intended to turn you from your sin?

[5]But because you are stubborn and refuse to turn from your sin, you are storing up terrible punishment for yourself. For a day of anger is coming, when God's righteous judgment will be revealed. [6]He will judge everyone according to what they have done. [7]He will give eternal life to those who keep on doing good, seeking after the glory and honor and immortality that God offers. [8]But he will pour out his anger and wrath on those who live for themselves, who refuse to obey the truth and instead live lives of wickedness. [9]There will be trouble and calamity for everyone who keeps on doing what is evil—for the Jew first and also for the Gentile.* [10]But there will be glory and honor and peace from God for all who do good—for the Jew first and also for the Gentile. [11]For God does not show favoritism.

[12]When the Gentiles sin, they will be destroyed, even though they never had God's written law. And the Jews, who do have God's law, will be judged by that law when they fail to obey it. [13]For merely listening to the law doesn't make us right with God. It is obeying the law that makes us right in his sight. [14]Even Gentiles, who do not have God's written law, show that they know his law when they instinctively obey it, even without having heard it. [15]They demonstrate that God's law is written in their hearts, for their own conscience and thoughts either accuse them

or tell them they are doing right. [16]And this is the message I proclaim—that the day is coming when God, through Christ Jesus, will judge everyone's secret life.

[17]You who call yourselves Jews are relying on God's law, and you boast about your special relationship with him. [18]You know what he wants; you know what is right because you have been taught his law. [19]You are convinced that you are a guide for the blind and a light for people who are lost in darkness. [20]You think you can instruct the ignorant and teach children the ways of God. For you are certain that God's law gives you complete knowledge and truth.

[21]Well then, if you teach others, why don't you teach yourself? You tell others not to steal, but do you steal? [22]You say it is wrong to commit adultery, but do you commit adultery? You condemn idolatry, but do you use items stolen from pagan temples?* [23]You are so proud of knowing the law, but you dishonor God by breaking it. [24]No wonder the Scriptures say, "The Gentiles blaspheme the name of God because of you."*

2:9 Greek *also for the Greek;* also in 2:10.   2:22 Greek *do you steal from temples?*   2:24 Isa 52:5 (Greek version).

PSALM 10:16-18

[The] LORD is king forever and ever! The godless nations will vanish from the land.
[17] LORD, you know the hopes of the helpless. Surely you will hear their cries and comfort them.
[18] You will bring justice to the orphans and the oppressed, so mere people can no longer terrify them.

PROVERBS 19:8-9

[To] acquire wisdom is to love oneself; people who cherish understanding will prosper. □ A false witness will not go unpunished, and a liar will be destroyed.

JULY 15

1 CHRONICLES 19:1–21:30

[S]ome time after this, King Nahash of the Ammonites died, and his son Hanun* became king. [2]David said, "I am going to show loyalty to Hanun because his father, Nahash, was always loyal to me." So David sent messengers to express sympathy to Hanun about his father's death.

But when David's ambassadors arrived in the land of Ammon, [3]the Ammonite commanders said to Hanun, "Do you really think these men are coming here to honor your father? No! David has sent them to spy out the land so they can come in and conquer it!" [4]So Hanun seized David's ambassadors and shaved them, cut off their robes at the buttocks, and sent them back to David in shame.

[5]When David heard what had happened to the men, he sent messengers to tell them, "Stay at Jericho until your beards grow out, and then come back." For they felt deep shame because of their appearance.

[6]When the people of Ammon realized how seriously they had angered David, Hanun and the Ammonites sent 75,000 pounds* of silver to hire chariots and charioteers from Aram-naharaim, Aram-maacah, and Zobah. [7]They also hired 32,000 chariots and secured the support of the king of Maacah and his army. These forces camped at Medeba, where they were joined by the Ammonite troops that Hanun had recruited from his own towns. [8]When David heard about this, he sent Joab and all his warriors to fight them. [9]The Ammonite troops came out and drew up their battle lines at the entrance of the city, while the other kings positioned themselves to fight in the open fields.

[10]When Joab saw that he would have to fight on both the front and the rear,

he chose some of Israel's elite troops and placed them under his personal command to fight the Arameans in the fields. [11]He left the rest of the army under the command of his brother Abishai, who was to attack the Ammonites. [12]"If the Arameans are too strong for me, then come over and help me," Joab told his brother. "And if the Ammonites are too strong for you, I will help you. [13]Be courageous! Let us fight bravely for our people and the cities of our God. May the LORD's will be done."

[14]When Joab and his troops attacked, the Arameans began to run away. [15]And when the Ammonites saw the Arameans running, they also ran from Abishai and retreated into the city. Then Joab returned to Jerusalem.

[16]The Arameans now realized that they were no match for Israel, so they sent messengers and summoned additional Aramean troops from the other side of the Euphrates River.* These troops were under the command of Shobach,* the commander of Hadadezer's forces.

[17]When David heard what was happening, he mobilized all Israel, crossed the Jordan River, and positioned his troops in battle formation. Then David engaged the Arameans in battle, and they fought against him. [18]But again the Arameans fled from the Israelites. This time David's forces killed 7,000 charioteers and 40,000 foot soldiers, including Shobach, the commander of their army. [19]When Hadadezer's allies saw that they had been defeated by Israel, they surrendered to David and became his subjects. After that, the Arameans were no longer willing to help the Ammonites.

[20:1]IN the spring of the year,* when kings normally go out to war, Joab led the Israelite army in successful attacks against the land of the Ammonites. In the process he laid siege to the city of Rabbah . However, David stayed behind in Jerusalem.

[2]When David arrived at Rabbah, he removed the crown from the king's head,* and it was placed on his own head. The crown was made of gold and set with gems, and he found that it weighed seventy-five pounds.* David took a vast amount of plunder from the city. [3]He also made slaves of the people of Rabbah and forced them to labor with* saws, iron picks, and iron axes.* That is how David dealt with the people of all the Ammonite towns. Then David and all the army returned to Jerusalem.

[4]After this, war broke out with the Philistines at Gezer. As they fought, Sibbecai from Hushah killed Saph,* a descendant of the giants,* and so the Philistines were subdued.

[5]During another battle with the Philistines, Elhanan son of Jair killed Lahmi, the brother of Goliath of Gath. The handle of Lahmi's spear was as thick as a weaver's beam!

[6]In another battle with the Philistines at Gath, they encountered a huge man with six fingers on each hand and six toes on each foot, twenty-four in all, who was also a descendant of the giants. [7]But when he defied and taunted Israel, he was killed by Jonathan, the son of David's brother Shimea.

[8]These Philistines were descendants of the giants of Gath, but David and his warriors killed them.

[21:1]SATAN rose up against Israel and caused David to take a census of the people of Israel. [2]So David said to Joab and the commanders of the army, "Take a census of all the people of Israel—from Beersheba in the south to Dan in the north—and bring me a report so I may know how many there are."

[3]But Joab replied, "May the LORD increase the number of his people a hundred times over! But why, my lord the king, do you want to do this? Are they not all your servants? Why must you cause Israel to sin?"

[4]But the king insisted that they take the census, so Joab traveled throughout all Israel to count the people. Then he returned to Jerusalem [5]and reported the number of people to David. There were

1,100,000 warriors in all Israel who could handle a sword, and 470,000 in Judah. [6]But Joab did not include the tribes of Levi and Benjamin in the census because he was so distressed at what the king had made him do.

[7]God was very displeased with the census, and he punished Israel for it. [8]Then David said to God, "I have sinned greatly by taking this census. Please forgive my guilt for doing this foolish thing."

[9]Then the LORD spoke to Gad, David's seer. This was the message: [10]"Go and say to David, 'This is what the LORD says: I will give you three choices. Choose one of these punishments, and I will inflict it on you.'"

[11]So Gad came to David and said, "These are the choices the LORD has given you. [12]You may choose three years of famine, three months of destruction by the sword of your enemies, or three days of severe plague as the angel of the LORD brings devastation throughout the land of Israel. Decide what answer I should give the LORD who sent me."

[13]"I'm in a desperate situation!" David replied to Gad. "But let me fall into the hands of the LORD, for his mercy is very great. Do not let me fall into human hands."

[14]So the LORD sent a plague upon Israel, and 70,000 people died as a result. [15]And God sent an angel to destroy Jerusalem. But just as the angel was preparing to destroy it, the LORD relented and said to the death angel, "Stop! That is enough!" At that moment the angel of the LORD was standing by the threshing floor of Araunah* the Jebusite.

[16]David looked up and saw the angel of the LORD standing between heaven and earth with his sword drawn, reaching out over Jerusalem. So David and the leaders of Israel put on burlap to show their deep distress and fell face down on the ground. [17]And David said to God, "I am the one who called for the census! I am the one who has sinned and done wrong! But these people are as innocent as sheep—what have they done? O LORD my God, let your anger fall against me

and my family, but do not destroy your people."

[18]Then the angel of the LORD told Gad to instruct David to go up and build an altar to the LORD on the threshing floor of Araunah the Jebusite. [19]So David went up to do what the LORD had commanded him through Gad. [20]Araunah, who was busy threshing wheat at the time, turned and saw the angel there. His four sons, who were with him, ran away and hid. [21]When Araunah saw David approaching, he left his threshing floor and bowed before David with his face to the ground.

[22]David said to Araunah, "Let me buy this threshing floor from you at its full price. Then I will build an altar to the LORD there, so that he will stop the plague."

[23]"Take it, my lord the king, and use it as you wish," Araunah said to David. "I will give the oxen for the burnt offerings, and the threshing boards for wood to build a fire on the altar, and the wheat for the grain offering. I will give it all to you."

[24]But King David replied to Araunah, "No, I insist on buying it for the full price. I will not take what is yours and give it to the LORD. I will not present burnt offerings that have cost me nothing!" [25]So David gave Araunah 600 pieces of gold* in payment for the threshing floor.

[26]David built an altar there to the LORD and sacrificed burnt offerings and peace offerings. And when David prayed, the LORD answered him by sending fire from heaven to burn up the offering on the altar. [27]Then the LORD spoke to the angel, who put the sword back into its sheath.

[28]When David saw that the LORD had answered his prayer, he offered sacrifices there at Araunah's threshing floor. [29]At that time the Tabernacle of the LORD and the altar of burnt offering that Moses had made in the wilderness were located at the place of worship in Gibeon. [30]But David was not able to go there to inquire of God, because he was terrified by the drawn sword of the angel of the LORD.

19:1 As in parallel text at 2 Sam 10:1; Hebrew lacks *Hanun.*   19:6 Hebrew *1,000 talents* [34,000 kilograms].   19:16a Hebrew *the river.*   19:16b As in parallel text

at 2 Sam 10:16; Hebrew reads *Shophach;* also in 19:18.
20:1 Hebrew *At the turn of the year.* The first day of the
year in the ancient Hebrew lunar calendar occurred in
March or April.   **20:2a** Or *from the head of Milcom* (as in
Greek version and Latin Vulgate). Milcom, also called
Molech, was the god of the Ammonites.   **20:2b** Hebrew
1 talent [34 kilograms].   **20:3a** Or *He also brought out the
people of Rabbah and cut them with.*   **20:3b** As in parallel
text at 2 Sam 12:31; Hebrew reads *and saws.*   **20:4a** As in
parallel text at 2 Sam 21:18; Hebrew reads *Sippai.*
20:4b Hebrew *descendant of the Rephaites;* also in 20:6, 8.
21:15 As in parallel text at 2 Sam 24:16; Hebrew reads
Ornan, another name for Araunah; also in 21:18-28.
21:25 Hebrew *600 shekels of gold,* about 15 pounds or
6.8 kilograms in weight.

ROMANS 2:25–3:8

The Jewish ceremony of circumcision
has value only if you obey God's law. But
if you don't obey God's law, you are no
better off than an uncircumcised Gentile. 26And if the Gentiles obey God's
law, won't God declare them to be his
own people? 27In fact, uncircumcised
Gentiles who keep God's law will condemn you Jews who are circumcised
and possess God's law but don't obey it.

28For you are not a true Jew just because you were born of Jewish parents
or because you have gone through the
ceremony of circumcision. 29**No, a true
Jew is one whose heart is right with
God. And true circumcision is not
merely obeying the letter of the law;
rather, it is a change of heart produced by God's Spirit. And a person
with a changed heart seeks praise***
from God, not from people.

3:1THEN what's the advantage of being a
Jew? Is there any value in the ceremony
of circumcision? 2Yes, there are great
benefits! First of all, the Jews were entrusted with the whole revelation of God.*

3True, some of them were unfaithful;
but just because they were unfaithful, does
that mean God will be unfaithful? 4Of
course not! Even if everyone else is a liar,
God is true. As the Scriptures say about
him,

"You will be proved right
in what you say,
and you will win your
case in court."*

5"But," some might say, "our sinful-
ness serves a good purpose, for it helps

people see how righteous God is. Isn't
it unfair, then, for him to punish us?"
(This is merely a human point of view.)
6Of course not! If God were not entirely
fair, how would he be qualified to judge
the world? 7"But," someone might still
argue, "how can God condemn me as a
sinner if my dishonesty highlights his
truthfulness and brings him more
glory?" 8And some people even slander
us by claiming that we say, "The more
we sin, the better it is!" Those who say
such things deserve to be condemned.

2:29 Or *receives praise.*   **3:2** Greek *the oracles of God.*
3:4 Ps 51:4 (Greek version).

PSALM 11:1-7
For the choir director: A psalm of David.

1 I trust in the LORD for protection.
So why do you say to me,
    "Fly like a bird to the mountains
        for safety!
2 The wicked are stringing their bows
    and fitting their arrows on the
        bowstrings.
They shoot from the shadows
    at those whose hearts are right.
3 The foundations of law and order
        have collapsed.
    What can the righteous do?"

4 But the LORD is in his holy Temple;
    the LORD still rules from heaven.
He watches everyone closely,
    examining every person on earth.
5 The LORD examines both the
        righteous and the wicked.
    He hates those who love
        violence.
6 He will rain down blazing coals
    and burning sulfur on the
        wicked,
punishing them with scorching
    winds.
7 For the righteous LORD
        loves justice.
    The virtuous will see his face.

PROVERBS 19:10-12

It isn't right for a fool to live in luxury or
for a slave to rule over princes! □ Sensi-
ble people control their temper; they

earn respect by overlooking wrongs. □The king's anger is like a lion's roar, but his favor is like dew on the grass.

JULY 16

1 CHRONICLES 22:1–23:32
Then David said, "This will be the location for the Temple of the LORD God and the place of the altar for Israel's burnt offerings!"

²So David gave orders to call together the foreigners living in Israel, and he assigned them the task of preparing finished stone for building the Temple of God. ³David provided large amounts of iron for the nails that would be needed for the doors in the gates and for the clamps, and he gave more bronze than could be weighed. ⁴He also provided innumerable cedar logs, for the men of Tyre and Sidon had brought vast amounts of cedar to David.

⁵David said, "My son Solomon is still young and inexperienced. And since the Temple to be built for the LORD must be a magnificent structure, famous and glorious throughout the world, I will begin making preparations for it now." So David collected vast amounts of building materials before his death.

⁶Then David sent for his son Solomon and instructed him to build a Temple for the LORD, the God of Israel. ⁷"My son, I wanted to build a Temple to honor the name of the LORD my God," David told him. ⁸"But the LORD said to me, 'You have killed many men in the battles you have fought. And since you have shed so much blood in my sight, you will not be the one to build a Temple to honor my name. ⁹But you will have a son who will be a man of peace. I will give him peace with his enemies in all the surrounding lands. His name will be Solomon,* and I

will give peace and quiet to Israel during his reign. ¹⁰He is the one who will build a Temple to honor my name. He will be my son, and I will be his father. And I will secure the throne of his kingdom over Israel forever.'

¹¹"Now, my son, may the LORD be with you and give you success as you follow his directions in building the Temple of the LORD your God. ¹²And may the LORD give you wisdom and understanding, that you may obey the Law of the LORD your God as you rule over Israel. ¹³For you will be successful if you carefully obey the decrees and regulations that the LORD gave to Israel through Moses. Be strong and courageous; do not be afraid or lose heart!

¹⁴"I have worked hard to provide materials for building the Temple of the LORD—nearly 4,000 tons of gold, 40,000 tons of silver,* and so much iron and bronze that it cannot be weighed. I have also gathered timber and stone for the walls, though you may need to add more. ¹⁵You have a large number of skilled stonemasons and carpenters and craftsmen of every kind. ¹⁶You have expert goldsmiths and silversmiths and workers of bronze and iron. Now begin the work, and may the LORD be with you!"

¹⁷Then David ordered all the leaders of Israel to assist Solomon in this project. ¹⁸"The LORD your God is with you," he declared. "He has given you peace with the surrounding nations. He has handed them over to me, and they are now subject to the LORD and his people. ¹⁹Now seek the LORD your God with all your heart and soul. Build the sanctuary of the LORD God so that you can bring the Ark of the LORD's Covenant and the holy vessels of God into the Temple built to honor the LORD's name."

²³:¹WHEN David was an old man, he appointed his son Solomon to be king over Israel. ²David summoned all the leaders of Israel, together with the priests and Levites. ³All the Levites who were thirty years old or older were counted, and the total came to 38,000. ⁴Then David said,

"From all the Levites, 24,000 will supervise the work at the Temple of the LORD. Another 6,000 will serve as officials and judges. [5]Another 4,000 will work as gatekeepers, and 4,000 will praise the LORD with the musical instruments I have made." [6]Then David divided the Levites into divisions named after the clans descended from the three sons of Levi—Gershon, Kohath, and Merari.

[7]The Gershonite family units were defined by their lines of descent from Libni* and Shimei, the sons of Gershon. [8]Three of the descendants of Libni were Jehiel (the family leader), Zetham, and Joel. [9]These were the leaders of the family of Libni.

Three of the descendants of Shimei were Shelomoth, Haziel, and Haran. [10]Four other descendants of Shimei were Jahath, Ziza,* Jeush, and Beriah. [11]Jahath was the family leader, and Ziza was next. Jeush and Beriah were counted as a single family because neither had many sons.

[12]Four of the descendants of Kohath were Amram, Izhar, Hebron, and Uzziel.

[13]The sons of Amram were Aaron and Moses. Aaron and his descendants were set apart to dedicate the most holy things, to offer sacrifices in the LORD's presence, to serve the LORD, and to pronounce blessings in his name forever.

[14]As for Moses, the man of God, his sons were included with the tribe of Levi. [15]The sons of Moses were Gershom and Eliezer. [16]The descendants of Gershom included Shebuel, the family leader. [17]Eliezer had only one son, Rehabiah, the family leader. Rehabiah had numerous descendants.

[18]The descendants of Izhar included Shelomith, the family leader.

[19]The descendants of Hebron included Jeriah (the family leader), Amariah (the second), Jahaziel (the third), and Jekameam (the fourth).

[20]The descendants of Uzziel included Micah (the family leader) and Isshiah (the second).

[21]The descendants of Merari included Mahli and Mushi.

The sons of Mahli were Eleazar and Kish. [22]Eleazar died with no sons, only daughters. His daughters married their cousins, the sons of Kish.

[23]Three of the descendants of Mushi were Mahli, Eder, and Jerimoth.

[24]These were the descendants of Levi by clans, the leaders of their family groups, registered carefully by name. Each had to be twenty years old or older to qualify for service in the house of the LORD. [25]For David said, "The LORD, the God of Israel, has given us peace, and he will always live in Jerusalem. [26]Now the Levites will no longer need to carry the Tabernacle and its furnishings from place to place." [27]In accordance with David's final instructions, all the Levites twenty years old or older were registered for service.

[28]The work of the Levites was to assist the priests, the descendants of Aaron, as they served at the house of the LORD. They also took care of the courtyards and side rooms, helped perform the ceremonies of purification, and served in many other ways in the house of God. [29]They were in charge of the sacred bread that was set out on the table, the choice flour for the grain offerings, the wafers made without yeast, the cakes cooked in olive oil, and the other mixed breads. They were also responsible to check all the weights and measures. [30]And each morning and evening they stood before the LORD to sing songs of thanks and praise to him. [31]They assisted with the burnt offerings that were presented to the LORD on Sabbath days, at new moon celebrations, and at all the appointed festivals. The required number of Levites served in the LORD's presence at all times, following all the procedures they had been given.

[32]And so, under the supervision of the priests, the Levites watched over the

Tabernacle and the Temple* and faithfully carried out their duties of service at the house of the LORD.

22:9 *Solomon* sounds like and is probably derived from the Hebrew word for "peace."   22:14 Hebrew *100,000 talents* [3,400 metric tons] *of gold, 1,000,000 talents* [34,000 metric tons] *of silver.*   23:7 Hebrew *Ladan* (also in 23:8, 9), a variant spelling of Libni; compare 6:17.   23:10 As in Greek version and Latin Vulgate (see also 23:11); Hebrew reads *Zina.*   23:32 Hebrew *the Tent of Meeting and the sanctuary.*

ROMANS 3:9-31

Well then, should we conclude that we Jews are better than others? No, not at all, for we have already shown that all people, whether Jews or Gentiles,* are under the power of sin. [10]As the Scriptures say,

"No one is righteous—
    not even one.
[11] No one is truly wise;
    no one is seeking God.
[12] All have turned away;
    all have become useless.
No one does good,
    not a single one."*
[13] "Their talk is foul, like the stench
        from an open grave.
    Their tongues are filled with lies."
    "Snake venom drips from their lips."*
[14]   "Their mouths are full of cursing
        and bitterness."*
[15] "They rush to commit murder.
[16]   Destruction and misery always
        follow them.
[17] They don't know where
        to find peace."*
[18]   "They have no fear of God at all."*

[19]Obviously, the law applies to those to whom it was given, for its purpose is to keep people from having excuses, and to show that the entire world is guilty before God. [20]For no one can ever be made right with God by doing what the law commands. The law simply shows us how sinful we are.

[21]**But now God has shown us a way to be made right with him without keeping the requirements of the law, as was promised in the writings of Moses* and the prophets long ago. [22]We are made right with God by placing our faith in Jesus Christ. And this is true for everyone who believes, no matter who we are.**

[23]For everyone has sinned; we all fall short of God's glorious standard. [24]Yet God, with undeserved kindness, declares that we are righteous. He did this through Christ Jesus when he freed us from the penalty for our sins. [25]For God presented Jesus as the sacrifice for sin. People are made right with God when they believe that Jesus sacrificed his life, shedding his blood. This sacrifice shows that God was being fair when he held back and did not punish those who sinned in times past, [26]for he was looking ahead and including them in what he would do in this present time. God did this to demonstrate his righteousness, for he himself is fair and just, and he declares sinners to be right in his sight when they believe in Jesus.

[27]Can we boast, then, that we have done anything to be accepted by God? No, because our acquittal is not based on obeying the law. It is based on faith. [28]So we are made right with God through faith and not by obeying the law.

[29]After all, is God the God of the Jews only? Isn't he also the God of the Gentiles? Of course he is. [30]There is only one God, and he makes people right with himself only by faith, whether they are Jews or Gentiles.* [31]Well then, if we emphasize faith, does this mean that we can forget about the law? Of course not! In fact, only when we have faith do we truly fulfill the law.

3:9 Greek *or Greeks.*   3:10-12 Pss 14:1-3; 53:1-3 (Greek version).   3:13 Pss 5:9 (Greek version); 140:3.   3:14 Ps 10:7 (Greek version).   3:15-17 Isa 59:7-8.   3:18 Ps 36:1.   3:21 Greek *in the law.*   3:30 Greek *whether they are circumcised or uncircumcised.*

PSALM 12:1-8

*For the choir director: A psalm of David, to be accompanied by an eight-stringed instrument.**

[1] **H**elp, O LORD, for the godly are
        fast disappearing!
    The faithful have vanished
        from the earth!
[2] Neighbors lie to each other,

speaking with flattering lips and deceitful hearts.

³ May the LORD cut off their
flattering lips
and silence their boastful tongues.

⁴ They say, "We will lie to our
hearts' content.
Our lips are our own—who can
stop us?"

⁵ The LORD replies, "I have seen
violence done to the helpless,
and I have heard the groans
of the poor.
Now I will rise up to rescue them,
as they have longed for me to do."

⁶ The LORD's promises are pure,
like silver refined in a furnace,
purified seven times over.

⁷ Therefore, LORD, we know you will
protect the oppressed,
preserving them forever from this
lying generation,

⁸ even though the wicked strut about,
and evil is praised throughout
the land.

12:TITLE Hebrew *according to the sheminith.*

PROVERBS 19:13-14

A foolish child* is a calamity to a father; a quarrelsome wife is as annoying as constant dripping. □ Fathers can give their sons an inheritance of houses and wealth, but only the LORD can give an understanding wife.

19:13 Hebrew *son;* also in 19:27.

JULY 17

1 CHRONICLES 24:1–26:11

This is how Aaron's descendants, the priests, were divided into groups for service. The sons of Aaron were Nadab, Abihu, Eleazar, and Ithamar. ²But Nadab and Abihu died before their father, and they had no sons. So only Eleazar

and Ithamar were left to carry on as priests.

³With the help of Zadok, who was a descendant of Eleazar, and of Ahimelech, who was a descendant of Ithamar, David divided Aaron's descendants into groups according to their various duties. ⁴Eleazar's descendants were divided into sixteen groups and Ithamar's into eight, for there were more family leaders among the descendants of Eleazar.

⁵All tasks were assigned to the various groups by means of sacred lots so that no preference would be shown, for there were many qualified officials serving God in the sanctuary from among the descendants of both Eleazar and Ithamar. ⁶Shemaiah son of Nethanel, a Levite, acted as secretary and wrote down the names and assignments in the presence of the king, the officials, Zadok the priest, Ahimelech son of Abiathar, and the family leaders of the priests and Levites. The descendants of Eleazar and Ithamar took turns casting lots.

⁷ The first lot fell to Jehoiarib.
The second lot fell to Jedaiah.

⁸ The third lot fell to Harim.
The fourth lot fell to Seorim.

⁹ The fifth lot fell to Malkijah.
The sixth lot fell to Mijamin.

¹⁰ The seventh lot fell to Hakkoz.
The eighth lot fell to Abijah.

¹¹ The ninth lot fell to Jeshua.
The tenth lot fell to Shecaniah.

¹² The eleventh lot fell to Eliashib.
The twelfth lot fell to Jakim.

¹³ The thirteenth lot fell to Huppah.
The fourteenth lot fell to Jeshebeab.

¹⁴ The fifteenth lot fell to Bilgah.
The sixteenth lot fell to Immer.

¹⁵ The seventeenth lot fell to Hezir.
The eighteenth lot fell to
Happizzez.

¹⁶ The nineteenth lot fell to Pethahiah.
The twentieth lot fell to Jehezkel.

¹⁷ The twenty-first lot fell to Jakin.
The twenty-second lot fell to Gamul.

¹⁸ The twenty-third lot fell to Delaiah.
The twenty-fourth lot fell to Maaziah.

¹⁹Each group carried out its appointed duties in the house of the LORD according to the procedures established by their ancestor Aaron in obedience to the commands of the LORD, the God of Israel.

²⁰These were the other family leaders descended from Levi:

From the descendants of Amram, the leader was Shebuel.*
From the descendants of Shebuel, the leader was Jehdeiah.
²¹From the descendants of Rehabiah, the leader was Isshiah.
²²From the descendants of Izhar, the leader was Shelomith.*
From the descendants of Shelomith, the leader was Jahath.
²³From the descendants of Hebron, Jeriah was the leader,* Amariah was second, Jahaziel was third, and Jekameam was fourth.
²⁴From the descendants of Uzziel, the leader was Micah.
From the descendants of Micah, the leader was Shamir, ²⁵along with Isshiah, the brother of Micah.
From the descendants of Isshiah, the leader was Zechariah.
²⁶From the descendants of Merari, the leaders were Mahli and Mushi.
From the descendants of Jaaziah, the leader was Beno.
²⁷From the descendants of Merari through Jaaziah, the leaders were Beno, Shoham, Zaccur, and Ibri.
²⁸From the descendants of Mahli, the leader was Eleazar, though he had no sons.
²⁹From the descendants of Kish, the leader was Jerahmeel.
³⁰From the descendants of Mushi, the leaders were Mahli, Eder, and Jerimoth.

These were the descendants of Levi in their various families. ³¹Like the descendants of Aaron, they were assigned to their duties by means of sacred lots, without regard to age or rank. Lots were drawn in the presence of King David, Zadok, Ahimelech, and the family leaders of the priests and the Levites.

²⁵:¹DAVID and the army commanders then appointed men from the families of Asaph, Heman, and Jeduthun to proclaim God's messages to the accompaniment of lyres, harps, and cymbals. Here is a list of their names and their work:

²From the sons of Asaph, there were Zaccur, Joseph, Nethaniah, and Asarelah. They worked under the direction of their father, Asaph, who proclaimed God's messages by the king's orders.
³From the sons of Jeduthun, there were Gedaliah, Zeri, Jeshaiah, Shimei,* Hashabiah, and Mattithiah, six in all. They worked under the direction of their father, Jeduthun, who proclaimed God's messages to the accompaniment of the lyre, offering thanks and praise to the LORD.
⁴From the sons of Heman, there were Bukkiah, Mattaniah, Uzziel, Shubael,* Jerimoth, Hananiah, Hanani, Eliathah, Giddalti, Romamti-ezer, Joshbekashah, Mallothi, Hothir, and Mahazioth. ⁵All these were the sons of Heman, the king's seer, for God had honored him with fourteen sons and three daughters.

⁶All these men were under the direction of their fathers as they made music at the house of the LORD. Their responsibilities included the playing of cymbals, harps, and lyres at the house of God. Asaph, Jeduthun, and Heman reported directly to the king. ⁷They and their families were all trained in making music before the LORD, and each of them—288 in all—was an accomplished musician. ⁸The musicians were appointed to their term of service by means of sacred lots, without regard to whether they were young or old, teacher or student.

⁹ The first lot fell to Joseph of the Asaph clan and twelve of his sons and relatives.*
The second lot fell to Gedaliah and twelve of his sons and relatives.

[10] The third lot fell to Zaccur and twelve of his sons and relatives.

[11] The fourth lot fell to Zeri* and twelve of his sons and relatives.

[12] The fifth lot fell to Nethaniah and twelve of his sons and relatives.

[13] The sixth lot fell to Bukkiah and twelve of his sons and relatives.

[14] The seventh lot fell to Asarelah* and twelve of his sons and relatives.

[15] The eighth lot fell to Jeshaiah and twelve of his sons and relatives.

[16] The ninth lot fell to Mattaniah and twelve of his sons and relatives.

[17] The tenth lot fell to Shimei and twelve of his sons and relatives.

[18] The eleventh lot fell to Uzziel* and twelve of his sons and relatives.

[19] The twelfth lot fell to Hashabiah and twelve of his sons and relatives.

[20] The thirteenth lot fell to Shubael and twelve of his sons and relatives.

[21] The fourteenth lot fell to Mattithiah and twelve of his sons and relatives.

[22] The fifteenth lot fell to Jerimoth* and twelve of his sons and relatives.

[23] The sixteenth lot fell to Hananiah and twelve of his sons and relatives.

[24] The seventeenth lot fell to Joshbekashah* and twelve of his sons and relatives.

[25] The eighteenth lot fell to Hanani and twelve of his sons and relatives.

[26] The nineteenth lot fell to Mallothi and twelve of his sons and relatives.

[27] The twentieth lot fell to Eliathah and twelve of his sons and relatives.

[28] The twenty-first lot fell to Hothir and twelve of his sons and relatives.

[29] The twenty-second lot fell to Giddalti and twelve of his sons and relatives.

[30] The twenty-third lot fell to Mahazioth and twelve of his sons and relatives.

[31] The twenty-fourth lot fell to Romamti-ezer and twelve of his sons and relatives.

26:1THESE are the divisions of the gatekeepers:

From the Korahites, there was Meshelemiah son of Kore, of the family of Abiasaph.* [2] The sons of Meshelemiah were Zechariah (the oldest), Jediael (the second), Zebadiah (the third), Jathniel (the fourth), [3]Elam (the fifth), Jehohanan (the sixth), and Eliehoenai (the seventh).

[4]The sons of Obed-edom, also gatekeepers, were Shemaiah (the oldest), Jehozabad (the second), Joah (the third), Sacar (the fourth), Nethanel (the fifth), [5]Ammiel (the sixth), Issachar (the seventh), and Peullethai (the eighth). God had richly blessed Obed-edom.

[6] Obed-edom's son Shemaiah had sons with great ability who earned positions of great authority in the clan. [7] Their names were Othni, Rephael, Obed, and Elzabad. Their relatives, Elihu and Semakiah, were also very capable men.

[8]All of these descendants of Obed-edom, including their sons and grandsons—sixty-two of them in all—were very capable men, well qualified for their work.

[9]Meshelemiah's eighteen sons and relatives were also very capable men.

[10]Hosah, of the Merari clan, appointed Shimri as the leader among his sons, though he was not the oldest. [11]His other sons included Hilkiah (the second), Tebaliah (the third), and Zechariah (the fourth). Hosah's sons and relatives, who served as gatekeepers, numbered thirteen in all.

24:20 Hebrew *Shubael* (also in 24:20b), a variant spelling of Shebuel; compare 23:16 and 26:24.   24:22 Hebrew *Shelomoth* (also in 24:22b), a variant spelling of Shelomith; compare 23:18.   24:23 Hebrew *From the descendants of Jeriah;* compare 23:19.   25:3 As in one Hebrew manuscript and some Greek manuscripts (see also 25:17); most Hebrew manuscripts lack *Shimei.*   25:4 Hebrew *Shebuel,* a variant spelling of Shubael; compare 25:20.   25:9 As in Greek version; Hebrew lacks *and twelve of his sons and relatives.*

25:11 Hebrew *Izri*, a variant spelling of Zeri; compare 25:3.
25:14 Hebrew *Jesarelah, a variant spelling of Asarelah;
compare 25:2.*   **25:18** Hebrew *Azarel*, a variant spelling
of Uzziel; compare 25:4.   **25:22** Hebrew *Jeremoth*, a
variant spelling of Jerimoth; compare 25:4.   **25:24** Hebrew
Joshbekasha, a variant spelling of Joshbekashah; compare
25:4.   **26:1** As in Greek version (see also Exod 6:24);
Hebrew reads *Asaph*.

ROMANS 4:1-12

Abraham was, humanly speaking, the
founder of our Jewish nation. What did
he discover about being made right with
God? ²**If his good deeds had made him
acceptable to God, he would have had
something to boast about. But that
was not God's way.** ³**For the Scriptures
tell us, "Abraham believed God, and
God counted him as righteous because of his faith."***

⁴When people work, their wages are
not a gift, but something they have
earned. ⁵But people are counted as righteous, not because of their work, but because of their faith in God who forgives
sinners. ⁶David also spoke of this when
he described the happiness of those who
are declared righteous without working
for it:

⁷ "Oh, what joy for those
      whose disobedience is forgiven,
      whose sins are put out of sight.
⁸ Yes, what joy for those
      whose record the LORD has
      cleared of sin."*

⁹Now, is this blessing only for the Jews,
or is it also for uncircumcised Gentiles?*
Well, we have been saying that Abraham
was counted as righteous by God because of his faith. ¹⁰But how did this
happen? Was he counted as righteous
only after he was circumcised, or was it
before he was circumcised? Clearly, God
accepted Abraham before he was circumcised! ¹¹Circumcision was a sign that Abraham already had faith and that God had
already accepted him and declared him
to be righteous—even before he was circumcised. So Abraham is the spiritual
father of those who have faith but have
not been circumcised. They are counted
as righteous because of their faith.
¹²And Abraham is also the spiritual
father of those who have been circumcised, but only if they have the same kind
of faith Abraham had before he was circumcised.

4:3 Gen 15:6.   **4:7-8** Ps 32:1-2 (Greek version).
4:9 Greek *is this blessing only for the circumcised,
or is it also for the uncircumcised?*

PSALM 13:1-6

For the choir director: A psalm of David.

¹ **O** LORD, how long will you forget
      me? Forever?
   How long will you look the
      other way?
² How long must I struggle with
      anguish in my soul,
   with sorrow in my heart every day?
   How long will my enemy have
      the upper hand?

³ Turn and answer me, O LORD my God!
   Restore the sparkle to my eyes,
      or I will die.
⁴ Don't let my enemies gloat, saying,
      "We have defeated him!"
   Don't let them rejoice at my
      downfall.

⁵ But I trust in your unfailing love.
   I will rejoice because you have
      rescued me.
⁶ I will sing to the LORD
   because he is good to me.

PROVERBS 19:15-16

Lazy people sleep soundly, but idleness
leaves them hungry. □ Keep the commandments and keep your life; despis-
ing them leads to death.

JULY 18

1 CHRONICLES 26:12-27:34

These divisions of the gatekeepers were
named for their family leaders, and like
the other Levites, they served at the

house of the LORD. [13] They were assigned by families for guard duty at the various gates, without regard to age or training, for it was all decided by means of sacred lots.

[14] The responsibility for the east gate went to Meshelemiah* and his group. The north gate was assigned to his son Zechariah, a man of unusual wisdom. [15] The south gate went to Obed-edom, and his sons were put in charge of the storehouse. [16] Shuppim and Hosah were assigned the west gate and the gateway leading up to the Temple.* Guard duties were divided evenly. [17] Six Levites were assigned each day to the east gate, four to the north gate, four to the south gate, and two pairs at the storehouse. [18] Six were assigned each day to the west gate, four to the gateway leading up to the Temple, and two to the courtyard.*

[19] These were the divisions of the gatekeepers from the clans of Korah and Merari.

[20] Other Levites, led by Ahijah, were in charge of the treasuries of the house of God and the treasuries of the gifts dedicated to the LORD. [21] From the family of Libni* in the clan of Gershon, Jehiel* was the leader. [22] The sons of Jehiel, Zetham and his brother Joel, were in charge of the treasuries of the house of the LORD.

[23] These are the leaders that descended from Amram, Izhar, Hebron, and Uzziel:

[24] From the clan of Amram, Shebuel was a descendant of Gershom son of Moses. He was the chief officer of the treasuries. [25] His relatives through Eliezer were Rehabiah, Jeshaiah, Joram, Zicri, and Shelomoth.

[26] Shelomoth and his relatives were in charge of the treasuries containing the gifts that King David, the family leaders, and the generals and captains* and other officers of the army had dedicated to the LORD. [27] These men dedicated some of the plunder they had gained in battle to maintain the house of the LORD. [28] Shelomoth* and his relatives also cared for the gifts dedicated to the LORD by Samuel the seer, Saul son of Kish, Abner son of Ner, and Joab son of Zeruiah. All the other dedicated gifts were in their care, too.

[29] From the clan of Izhar came Kenaniah. He and his sons were given administrative responsibilities* over Israel as officials and judges.

[30] From the clan of Hebron came Hashabiah. He and his relatives— 1,700 capable men—were put in charge of the Israelite lands west of the Jordan River. They were responsible for all matters related to the things of the LORD and the service of the king in that area.

[31] Also from the clan of Hebron came Jeriah,* who was the leader of the Hebronites according to the genealogical records. (In the fortieth year of David's reign, a search was made in the records, and capable men from the clan of Hebron were found at Jazer in the land of Gilead.) [32] There were 2,700 capable men among the relatives of Jeriah. King David sent them to the east side of the Jordan River and put them in charge of the tribes of Reuben and Gad and the half-tribe of Manasseh. They were responsible for all matters related to God and to the king.

[27:1] THIS is the list of Israelite generals and captains,* and their officers, who served the king by supervising the army divisions that were on duty each month of the year. Each division served for one month and had 24,000 troops.

[2] Jashobeam son of Zabdiel was commander of the first division of 24,000 troops, which was on duty during the first month. [3] He was a descendant of Perez and was in charge of all the army officers for the first month.

[4] Dodai, a descendant of Ahoah, was commander of the second division of 24,000 troops, which was on duty

during the second month. Mikloth was his chief officer.

5Benaiah son of Jehoiada the priest was commander of the third division of 24,000 troops, which was on duty during the third month. 6This was the Benaiah who commanded David's elite military group known as the Thirty. His son Ammizabad was his chief officer.

7Asahel, the brother of Joab, was commander of the fourth division of 24,000 troops, which was on duty during the fourth month. Asahel was succeeded by his son Zebadiah.

8Shammah* the Izrahite was commander of the fifth division of 24,000 troops, which was on duty during the fifth month.

9Ira son of Ikkesh from Tekoa was commander of the sixth division of 24,000 troops, which was on duty during the sixth month.

10Helez, a descendant of Ephraim from Pelon, was commander of the seventh division of 24,000 troops, which was on duty during the seventh month.

11Sibbecai, a descendant of Zerah from Hushah, was commander of the eighth division of 24,000 troops, which was on duty during the eighth month.

12Abiezer from Anathoth in the territory of Benjamin was commander of the ninth division of 24,000 troops, which was on duty during the ninth month.

13Maharai, a descendant of Zerah from Netophah, was commander of the tenth division of 24,000 troops, which was on duty during the tenth month.

14Benaiah from Pirathon in Ephraim was commander of the eleventh division of 24,000 troops, which was on duty during the eleventh month.

15Heled,* a descendant of Othniel from Netophah, was commander of the twelfth division of 24,000 troops, which was on duty during the twelfth month.

16The following were the tribes of Israel and their leaders:

Tribe	Leader
Reuben	Eliezer son of Zicri
Simeon	Shephatiah son of Maacah
17 Levi	Hashabiah son of Kemuel
Aaron (the priests)	Zadok
18 Judah	Elihu (a brother of David)
Issachar	Omri son of Michael
19 Zebulun	Ishmaiah son of Obadiah
Naphtali	Jeremoth son of Azriel
20 Ephraim	Hoshea son of Azaziah
Manasseh (west)	Joel son of Pedaiah
21 Manasseh in Gilead (east)	Iddo son of Zechariah
Benjamin	Jaasiel son of Abner
22 Dan	Azarel son of Jeroham

These were the leaders of the tribes of Israel.

23When David took his census, he did not count those who were younger than twenty years of age, because the Lord had promised to make the Israelites as numerous as the stars in heaven. 24Joab son of Zeruiah began the census but never finished it because* the anger of God fell on Israel. The total number was never recorded in King David's official records.

25Azmaveth son of Adiel was in charge of the palace treasuries.

Jonathan son of Uzziah was in charge of the regional treasuries throughout the towns, villages, and fortresses of Israel.

26Ezri son of Kelub was in charge of the field workers who farmed the king's lands.

27Shimei from Ramah was in charge of the king's vineyards.

Zabdi from Shepham was responsible for the grapes and the supplies of wine.

28Baal-hanan from Geder was in charge of the king's olive groves and sycamore-fig trees in the foothills of Judah.*

Joash was responsible for the supplies of olive oil.

²⁹Shitrai from Sharon was in charge of the cattle on the Sharon Plain.

Shaphat son of Adlai was responsible for the cattle in the valleys.

³⁰Obil the Ishmaelite was in charge of the camels.

Jehdeiah from Meronoth was in charge of the donkeys.

³¹Jaziz the Hagrite was in charge of the king's flocks of sheep and goats.

All these officials were overseers of King David's property.

³²Jonathan, David's uncle, was a wise counselor to the king, a man of great insight, and a scribe. Jehiel the Hacmonite was responsible for teaching the king's sons. ³³Ahithophel was the royal adviser. Hushai the Arkite was the king's friend. ³⁴Ahithophel was succeeded by Jehoiada son of Benaiah and by Abiathar. Joab was commander of the king's army.

26:14 Hebrew *Shelemiah*, a variant spelling of Meshelemiah; compare 26:2. **26:16** Or *the gate of Shalleketh on the upper road* (also in 26:18). The meaning of the Hebrew is uncertain. **26:18** Or *the colonnade*. The meaning of the Hebrew is uncertain. **26:21a** Hebrew *Ladan*, a variant spelling of Libni; compare 6:17. **26:21b** Hebrew *Jehieli* (also in 26:22), a variant spelling of Jehiel; compare 23:8. **26:26** Hebrew *the commanders of thousands and of hundreds.* **26:28** Hebrew *Shelomith*, a variant spelling of Shelomoth. **26:29** Or *were given outside work;* or *were given work away from the Temple area.* **26:31** Hebrew *Jerijah*, a variant spelling of Jeriah; compare 23:19. **27:1** Hebrew *commanders of thousands and of hundreds.* **27:8** Hebrew *Shamhuth*, a variant spelling of Shammah; compare 11:27 and 2 Sam 23:25. **27:15** Hebrew *Heldai*, a variant spelling of Heled; compare 11:30 and 2 Sam 23:29. **27:24** Or *never finished it, and yet.* **27:28** Hebrew *the Shephelah.*

ROMANS 4:13–5:5

Clearly, God's promise to give the whole earth to Abraham and his descendants was based not on his obedience to God's law, but on a right relationship with God that comes by faith. ¹⁴If God's promise is only for those who obey the law, then faith is not necessary and the promise is pointless. ¹⁵For the law always brings punishment on those who try to obey it. (The only way to avoid breaking the law is to have no law to break!)

¹⁶So the promise is received by faith. It is given as a free gift. And we are all certain to receive it, whether or not we live according to the law of Moses, if we have faith like Abraham's. For Abraham is the father of all who believe. ¹⁷That is what the Scriptures mean when God told him, "I have made you the father of many nations."* This happened because Abraham believed in the God who brings the dead back to life and who creates new things out of nothing.

¹⁸Even when there was no reason for hope, Abraham kept hoping—believing that he would become the father of many nations. For God had said to him, "That's how many descendants you will have!"* ¹⁹And Abraham's faith did not weaken, even though, at about 100 years of age, he figured his body was as good as dead—and so was Sarah's womb.

²⁰Abraham never wavered in believing God's promise. In fact, his faith grew stronger, and in this he brought glory to God. ²¹He was fully convinced that God is able to do whatever he promises. ²²And because of Abraham's faith, God counted him as righteous. ²³And when God counted him as righteous, it wasn't just for Abraham's benefit. It was recorded ²⁴for our benefit, too, assuring us that God will also count us as righteous if we believe in him, the one who raised Jesus our Lord from the dead. ²⁵He was handed over to die because of our sins, and he was raised to life to make us right with God.

⁵:¹THEREFORE, **since we have been made right in God's sight by faith, we have peace with God because of what Jesus Christ our Lord has done for us.** ²Because of our faith, Christ has brought us into this place of undeserved privilege where we now stand, and we confidently and joyfully look forward to sharing God's glory.

³We can rejoice, too, when we run into problems and trials, for we know that they help us develop endurance. ⁴And endurance develops strength of character, and character strengthens our confident hope of salvation. ⁵And this hope will not lead to disappointment. For we know how dearly God loves

us, because he has given us the Holy Spirit to fill our hearts with his love.

4:17 Gen 17:5. **4:18** Gen 15:5.

PSALM 14:1-7
For the choir director: A psalm of David.

¹ **O**nly fools say in their hearts,
"There is no God."
They are corrupt, and their actions
are evil;
not one of them does good!

² The Lord looks down from heaven
on the entire human race;
he looks to see if anyone is
truly wise,
if anyone seeks God.

³ But no, all have turned away;
all have become corrupt.*
No one does good,
not a single one!

⁴ Will those who do evil never
learn?
They eat up my people like bread
and wouldn't think of praying to
the Lord.

⁵ Terror will grip them,
for God is with those who
obey him.

⁶ The wicked frustrate the plans
of the oppressed,
but the Lord will protect his
people.

⁷ Who will come from Mount Zion
to rescue Israel?
When the Lord restores his
people,
Jacob will shout with joy, and
Israel will rejoice.

14:3 Greek version reads *have become useless.* Compare Rom 3:12.

PROVERBS 19:17
If you help the poor, you are lending to the Lord— and he will repay you!

JULY 19

1 CHRONICLES 28:1–29:30
David summoned all the officials of Israel to Jerusalem—the leaders of the tribes, the commanders of the army divisions, the other generals and captains,* the overseers of the royal property and livestock, the palace officials, the mighty men, and all the other brave warriors in the kingdom. ²David rose to his feet and said: "My brothers and my people! It was my desire to build a temple where the Ark of the Lord's Covenant, God's footstool, could rest permanently. I made the necessary preparations for building it, ³but God said to me, 'You must not build a temple to honor my name, for you are a warrior and have shed much blood.'

⁴"Yet the Lord, the God of Israel, has chosen me from among all my father's family to be king over Israel forever. For he has chosen the tribe of Judah to rule, and from among the families of Judah he chose my father's family. And from among my father's sons the Lord was pleased to make me king over all Israel. ⁵And from among my sons—for the Lord has given me many—he chose Solomon to succeed me on the throne of Israel and to rule over the Lord's kingdom. ⁶He said to me, 'Your son Solomon will build my Temple and its courtyards, for I have chosen him as my son, and I will be his father. ⁷And if he continues to obey my commands and regulations as he does now, I will make his kingdom last forever.'

⁸"So now, with God as our witness, and in the sight of all Israel—the Lord's assembly—I give you this charge. Be careful to obey all the commands of the Lord your God, so that you may continue to possess this good land and leave it to your children as a permanent inheritance.

⁹"And Solomon, my son, learn to know the God of your ancestors intimately. Worship and serve him with your whole

heart and a willing mind. For the LORD sees every heart and knows every plan and thought. If you seek him, you will find him. But if you forsake him, he will reject you forever. ¹⁰So take this seriously. The LORD has chosen you to build a Temple as his sanctuary. Be strong, and do the work."

¹¹Then David gave Solomon the plans for the Temple and its surroundings, including the entry room, the storerooms, the upstairs rooms, the inner rooms, and the inner sanctuary—which was the place of atonement. ¹²David also gave Solomon all the plans he had in mind* for the courtyards of the LORD's Temple, the outside rooms, the treasuries, and the rooms for the gifts dedicated to the LORD. ¹³The king also gave Solomon the instructions concerning the work of the various divisions of priests and Levites in the Temple of the LORD. And he gave specifications for the items in the Temple that were to be used for worship.

¹⁴David gave instructions regarding how much gold and silver should be used to make the items needed for service. ¹⁵He told Solomon the amount of gold needed for the gold lampstands and lamps, and the amount of silver for the silver lampstands and lamps, depending on how each would be used. ¹⁶He designated the amount of gold for the table on which the Bread of the Presence would be placed and the amount of silver for other tables.

¹⁷David also designated the amount of gold for the solid gold meat hooks used to handle the sacrificial meat and for the basins, pitchers, and dishes, as well as the amount of silver for every dish. ¹⁸He designated the amount of refined gold for the altar of incense. Finally, he gave him a plan for the LORD's "chariot"—the gold cherubim* whose wings were stretched out over the Ark of the LORD's Covenant. ¹⁹"Every part of this plan," David told Solomon, "was given to me in writing from the hand of the LORD.*"

²⁰Then David continued, "Be strong and courageous, and do the work. Don't be afraid or discouraged, for the LORD

God, my God, is with you. He will not fail you or forsake you. He will see to it that all the work related to the Temple of the LORD is finished correctly. ²¹The various divisions of priests and Levites will serve in the Temple of God. Others with skills of every kind will volunteer, and the officials and the entire nation are at your command."

²⁹:¹THEN King David turned to the entire assembly and said, "My son Solomon, whom God has clearly chosen as the next king of Israel, is still young and inexperienced. The work ahead of him is enormous, for the Temple he will build is not for mere mortals—it is for the LORD God himself! ²Using every resource at my command, I have gathered as much as I could for building the Temple of my God. Now there is enough gold, silver, bronze, iron, and wood, as well as great quantities of onyx, other precious stones, costly jewels, and all kinds of fine stone and marble.

³"And now, because of my devotion to the Temple of my God, I am giving all of my own private treasures of gold and silver to help in the construction. This is in addition to the building materials I have already collected for his holy Temple. ⁴I am donating more than 112 tons of gold* from Ophir and 262 tons of refined silver* to be used for overlaying the walls of the buildings ⁵and for the other gold and silver work to be done by the craftsmen. Now then, who will follow my example and give offerings to the LORD today?"

⁶Then the family leaders, the leaders of the tribes of Israel, the generals and captains of the army,* and the king's administrative officers all gave willingly. ⁷For the construction of the Temple of God, they gave about 188 tons of gold,* 10,000 gold coins,* 375 tons of silver,* 675 tons of bronze,* and 3,750 tons of iron.* ⁸They also contributed numerous precious stones, which were deposited in the treasury of the house of the LORD under the care of Jehiel, a descendant of Gershon. ⁹The people rejoiced over the

offerings, for they had given freely and wholeheartedly to the LORD, and King David was filled with joy.

¹⁰Then David praised the LORD in the presence of the whole assembly:

"O LORD, the God of our ancestor Israel,* may you be praised forever and ever! ¹¹Yours, O LORD, is the greatness, the power, the glory, the victory, and the majesty. Everything in the heavens and on earth is yours, O LORD, and this is your kingdom. We adore you as the one who is over all things. ¹²Wealth and honor come from you alone, for you rule over everything. Power and might are in your hand, and at your discretion people are made great and given strength.

¹³"O our God, we thank you and praise your glorious name! ¹⁴But who am I, and who are my people, that we could give anything to you? Everything we have has come from you, and we give you only what you first gave us! ¹⁵We are here for only a moment, visitors and strangers in the land as our ancestors were before us. Our days on earth are like a passing shadow, gone so soon without a trace.

¹⁶"O LORD our God, even this material we have gathered to build a Temple to honor your holy name comes from you! It all belongs to you! ¹⁷I know, my God, that you examine our hearts and rejoice when you find integrity there. You know I have done all this with good motives, and I have watched your people offer their gifts willingly and joyously.

¹⁸"O LORD, the God of our ancestors Abraham, Isaac, and Israel, make your people always want to obey you. See to it that their love for you never changes. ¹⁹Give my son Solomon the wholehearted desire to obey all your commands, laws, and decrees, and to do everything necessary to build this Temple, for which I have made these preparations."

²⁰Then David said to the whole assembly, "Give praise to the LORD your God!" And the entire assembly praised the LORD, the God of their ancestors, and they bowed low and knelt before the LORD and the king.

²¹The next day they brought 1,000 bulls, 1,000 rams, and 1,000 male lambs as burnt offerings to the LORD. They also brought liquid offerings and many other sacrifices on behalf of all Israel. ²²They feasted and drank in the LORD's presence with great joy that day.

And again they crowned David's son Solomon as their new king. They anointed him before the LORD as their leader, and they anointed Zadok as priest. ²³So Solomon took the throne of the LORD in place of his father, David, and he succeeded in everything, and all Israel obeyed him. ²⁴All the officials, the warriors, and the sons of King David pledged their loyalty to King Solomon. ²⁵And the LORD exalted Solomon in the sight of all Israel, and he gave Solomon greater royal splendor than any king in Israel before him.

²⁶So David son of Jesse reigned over all Israel. ²⁷He reigned over Israel for forty years, seven of them in Hebron and thirty-three in Jerusalem. ²⁸He died at a ripe old age, having enjoyed long life, wealth, and honor. Then his son Solomon ruled in his place.

²⁹All the events of King David's reign, from beginning to end, are written in *The Record of Samuel the Seer, The Record of Nathan the Prophet,* and *The Record of Gad the Seer.* ³⁰These accounts include the mighty deeds of his reign and everything that happened to him and to Israel and to all the surrounding kingdoms.

28:1 Hebrew *the commanders of thousands and commanders of hundreds.*   28:12 Or *the plans of the spirit that was with him.*   28:18 Hebrew *for the gold cherub chariot.*   28:19 Or *was written under the direction of the LORD.*   29:4a Hebrew *3,000 talents* [102 metric tons] *of gold.*   29:4b Hebrew *7,000 talents* [238 metric tons] *of silver.*   29:6 Hebrew *the commanders of thousands and commanders of hundreds.*   29:7a Hebrew *5,000 talents* [170 metric tons] *of gold.*   29:7b Hebrew *10,000 darics* [a Persian coin] *of gold,* about 185 pounds or 84 kilograms in weight.   29:7c Hebrew *10,000 talents* [340 metric tons] *of silver.*   29:7d Hebrew *18,000 talents* [612 metric tons] *of bronze.*   29:7e Hebrew *100,000 talents* [3,400 metric tons] *of iron.*   29:10 *Israel* is the name that God gave to Jacob.

ROMANS 5:6-21

When we were utterly helpless, Christ came at just the right time and died for us sinners. [7]Now, most people would not be willing to die for an upright person, though someone might perhaps be willing to die for a person who is especially good. [8]But God showed his great love for us by sending Christ to die for us while we were still sinners. [9]And since we have been made right in God's sight by the blood of Christ, he will certainly save us from God's condemnation. [10]For since our friendship with God was restored by the death of his Son while we were still his enemies, we will certainly be saved through the life of his Son. [11]So now we can rejoice in our wonderful new relationship with God because our Lord Jesus Christ has made us friends of God.

[12]When Adam sinned, sin entered the world. Adam's sin brought death, so death spread to everyone, for everyone sinned. [13]Yes, people sinned even before the law was given. But it was not counted as sin because there was not yet any law to break. [14]Still, everyone died—from the time of Adam to the time of Moses—even those who did not disobey an explicit commandment of God, as Adam did. Now Adam is a symbol, a representation of Christ, who was yet to come. [15]But there is a great difference between Adam's sin and God's gracious gift. For the sin of this one man, Adam, brought death to many. But even greater is God's wonderful grace and his gift of forgiveness to many through this other man, Jesus Christ. [16]And the result of God's gracious gift is very different from the result of that one man's sin. For Adam's sin led to condemnation, but God's free gift leads to our being made right with God, even though we are guilty of many sins. [17]For the sin of this one man, Adam, caused death to rule over many. But even greater is God's wonderful grace and his gift of righteousness, for all who receive it will live in triumph over sin and death through this one man, Jesus Christ.

[18]Yes, Adam's one sin brings condemnation for everyone, but Christ's one act of righteousness brings a right relationship with God and new life for everyone. [19]**Because one person disobeyed God, many became sinners. But because one other person obeyed God, many will be made righteous.**

[20]God's law was given so that all people could see how sinful they were. But as people sinned more and more, God's wonderful grace became more abundant. [21]So just as sin ruled over all people and brought them to death, now God's wonderful grace rules instead, giving us right standing with God and resulting in eternal life through Jesus Christ our Lord.

PSALM 15:1-5

A psalm of David.

[1] **W**ho may worship in your
      sanctuary, LORD?
   Who may enter your presence
      on your holy hill?
[2] Those who lead blameless lives and
      do what is right,
   speaking the truth from sincere
      hearts.
[3] Those who refuse to gossip
      or harm their neighbors
      or speak evil of their friends.
[4] Those who despise flagrant
      sinners,
   and honor the faithful followers
      of the LORD,
   and keep their promises even
      when it hurts.
[5] Those who lend money without
      charging interest,
   and who cannot be bribed to lie
      about the innocent.
   Such people will stand firm
      forever.

PROVERBS 19:18-19

Discipline your children while there is hope. Otherwise you will ruin their lives. □ Hot-tempered people must pay the penalty. If you rescue them once, you will have to do it again.

JULY
20

2 CHRONICLES 1:1–3:17

Solomon son of David took firm control of his kingdom, for the LORD his God was with him and made him very powerful.

²Solomon called together all the leaders of Israel—the generals and captains of the army,* the judges, and all the political and clan leaders. ³Then he led the entire assembly to the place of worship in Gibeon, for God's Tabernacle* was located there. (This was the Tabernacle that Moses, the LORD's servant, had made in the wilderness.)

⁴David had already moved the Ark of God from Kiriath-jearim to the tent he had prepared for it in Jerusalem. ⁵But the bronze altar made by Bezalel son of Uri and grandson of Hur was there* at Gibeon in front of the Tabernacle of the LORD. So Solomon and the people gathered in front of it to consult the LORD.* ⁶There in front of the Tabernacle, Solomon went up to the bronze altar in the LORD's presence and sacrificed 1,000 burnt offerings on it.

⁷That night God appeared to Solomon and said, "What do you want? Ask, and I will give it to you!"

⁸Solomon replied to God, "You showed faithful love to David, my father, and now you have made me king in his place. ⁹O LORD God, please continue to keep your promise to David my father, for you have made me king over a people as numerous as the dust of the earth! ¹⁰Give me the wisdom and knowledge to lead them properly,* for who could possibly govern this great people of yours?"

¹¹God said to Solomon, "Because your greatest desire is to help your people, and you did not ask for wealth, riches, fame, or even the death of your enemies or a long life, but rather you asked for wisdom and knowledge to properly govern my people—¹²I will certainly give you the wisdom and knowledge you requested. But I will also give you wealth, riches, and fame such as no other king has had before you or will ever have in the future!"

¹³Then Solomon returned to Jerusalem from the Tabernacle at the place of worship in Gibeon, and he reigned over Israel.

¹⁴Solomon built up a huge force of chariots and horses.* He had 1,400 chariots and 12,000 horses. He stationed some of them in the chariot cities and some near him in Jerusalem. ¹⁵The king made silver and gold as plentiful in Jerusalem as stone. And valuable cedar timber was as common as the sycamore-fig trees that grow in the foothills of Judah.* ¹⁶Solomon's horses were imported from Egypt* and from Cilicia*; the king's traders acquired them from Cilicia at the standard price. ¹⁷At that time chariots from Egypt could be purchased for 600 pieces of silver,* and horses for 150 pieces of silver.* They were then exported to the kings of the Hittites and the kings of Aram.

²:¹*SOLOMON decided to build a Temple to honor the name of the LORD, and also a royal palace for himself. ²*He enlisted a force of 70,000 laborers, 80,000 men to quarry stone in the hill country, and 3,600 foremen.

³Solomon also sent this message to King Hiram* at Tyre:

"Send me cedar logs as you did for my father, David, when he was building his palace. ⁴I am about to build a Temple to honor the name of the LORD my God. It will be a place set apart to burn fragrant incense before him, to display the special sacrificial bread, and to sacrifice burnt offerings each morning and evening, on the Sabbaths, at new moon celebrations, and at the other appointed festivals of the LORD our God. He has commanded Israel to do these things forever.

⁵"This must be a magnificent Temple because our God is greater than all other gods. ⁶But who can

really build him a worthy home? Not even the highest heavens can contain him! So who am I to consider building a Temple for him, except as a place to burn sacrifices to him?

7"So send me a master craftsman who can work with gold, silver, bronze, and iron, as well as with purple, scarlet, and blue cloth. He must be a skilled engraver who can work with the craftsmen of Judah and Jerusalem who were selected by my father, David.

8"Also send me cedar, cypress, and red sandalwood* logs from Lebanon, for I know that your men are without equal at cutting timber in Lebanon. I will send my men to help them. 9An immense amount of timber will be needed, for the Temple I am going to build will be very large and magnificent. 10In payment for your woodcutters, I will send 100,000 bushels of crushed wheat, 100,000 bushels of barley,* 110,000 gallons of wine, and 110,000 gallons of olive oil.*"

11King Hiram sent this letter of reply to Solomon:

"It is because the LORD loves his people that he has made you their king! 12Praise the LORD, the God of Israel, who made the heavens and the earth! He has given King David a wise son, gifted with skill and understanding, who will build a Temple for the LORD and a royal palace for himself.

13"I am sending you a master craftsman named Huram-abi, who is extremely talented. 14His mother is from the tribe of Dan in Israel, and his father is from Tyre. He is skillful at making things from gold, silver, bronze, and iron, and he also works with stone and wood. He can work with purple, blue, and scarlet cloth and fine linen. He is also an engraver and can follow any design given to him. He will work with your craftsmen and those appointed by my lord David, your father.

15"Send along the wheat, barley, olive oil, and wine that my lord has mentioned. 16We will cut whatever timber you need from the Lebanon mountains and will float the logs in rafts down the coast of the Mediterranean Sea* to Joppa. From there you can transport the logs up to Jerusalem."

17Solomon took a census of all foreigners in the land of Israel, like the census his father had taken, and he counted 153,600. 18He assigned 70,000 of them as common laborers, 80,000 as quarry workers in the hill country, and 3,600 as foremen.

3:1So Solomon began to build the Temple of the LORD in Jerusalem on Mount Moriah, where the LORD had appeared to David, his father. The Temple was built on the threshing floor of Araunah* the Jebusite, the site that David had selected. 2The construction began in midspring,* during the fourth year of Solomon's reign.

3These are the dimensions Solomon used for the foundation of the Temple of God (using the old standard of measurement).* It was 90 feet long and 30 feet wide.* 4The entry room at the front of the Temple was 30 feet* wide, running across the entire width of the Temple, and 30 feet* high. He overlaid the inside with pure gold.

5He paneled the main room of the Temple with cypress wood, overlaid it with fine gold, and decorated it with carvings of palm trees and chains. 6He decorated the walls of the Temple with beautiful jewels and with gold from the land of Parvaim. 7He overlaid the beams, thresholds, walls, and doors throughout the Temple with gold, and he carved figures of cherubim on the walls.

8He made the Most Holy Place 30 feet wide, corresponding to the width of the Temple, and 30 feet deep. He overlaid its interior with 23 tons* of fine gold. 9The gold nails that were used weighed 20 ounces* each. He also overlaid the walls of the upper rooms with gold.

[10]He made two figures shaped like cherubim, overlaid them with gold, and placed them in the Most Holy Place. [11]The total wingspan of the two cherubim standing side by side was 30 feet. One wing of the first figure was 7½ feet* long, and it touched the Temple wall. The other wing, also 7½ feet long, touched one of the wings of the second figure. [12]In the same way, the second figure had one wing 7½ feet long that touched the opposite wall. The other wing, also 7½ feet long, touched the wing of the first figure. [13]So the wingspan of the two cherubim side by side was 30 feet. They stood on their feet and faced out toward the main room of the Temple.

[14]Across the entrance of the Most Holy Place he hung a curtain made of fine linen, decorated with blue, purple, and scarlet thread and embroidered with figures of cherubim.

[15]For the front of the Temple, he made two pillars that were 27 feet* tall, each topped by a capital extending upward another 7½ feet. [16]He made a network of interwoven chains and used them to decorate the tops of the pillars. He also made 100 decorative pomegranates and attached them to the chains. [17]Then he set up the two pillars at the entrance of the Temple, one to the south of the entrance and the other to the north. He named the one on the south Jakin, and the one on the north Boaz.*

1:2 Hebrew *the commanders of thousands and of hundreds.* 1:3 Hebrew *Tent of Meeting;* also in 1:6, 13. 1:5a As in Greek version and Latin Vulgate, and some Hebrew manuscripts. Masoretic Text reads *he placed.* 1:5b Hebrew *to consult him.* 1:10 Hebrew *to go out and come in before this people.* 1:14 Or *charioteers;* also in 1:14b. 1:15 Hebrew *the Shephelah.* 1:16a Possibly *Muzur,* a district near Cilicia; also in 1:17. 1:16b Hebrew *Kue,* probably another name for Cilicia. 1:17a Hebrew *600 shekels of silver,* about 15 pounds or 6.8 kilograms in weight. 1:17b Hebrew *150 shekels,* about 3.8 pounds or 1.7 kilograms in weight. 2:1 Verse 2:1 is numbered 1:18 in Hebrew text. 2:2 Verses 2:2-18 are numbered 2:1-17 in Hebrew text. 2:3 Hebrew *Huram,* a variant spelling of Hiram; also in 2:11. 2:8 Or *juniper;* Hebrew reads *algum,* perhaps a variant spelling of *almug;* compare 9:10-11 and parallel text at 1 Kgs 10:11-12. 2:10a Hebrew *20,000 cors* [3,640 kiloliters] *of crushed wheat, 20,000 cors of barley.* 2:10b Hebrew

20,000 baths [420 kiloliters] *of wine, and 20,000 baths of olive oil.* 2:16 Hebrew *the sea.* 3:1 Hebrew reads Ornan, a variant spelling of Araunah; compare 2 Sam 24:16. 3:2 Hebrew *on the second day of the second month.* This day of the ancient Hebrew lunar calendar occurred in April or May. 3:3a The "old standard of measurement" was a cubit equal to 18 inches [46 centimeters]. The new standard was a cubit of approximately 21 inches [53 centimeters]. 3:3b Hebrew *60 cubits* [27.6 meters] *long and 20 cubits* [9.2 meters] *wide.* 3:4a Hebrew *20 cubits* [9.2 meters]; also in 3:8, 11, 13. 3:4b As in some Greek and Syriac manuscripts, which read *20 cubits* [9.2 meters]; Hebrew reads *120 cubits,* which is 180 feet or 55 meters. 3:8 Hebrew *600 talents* [20.4 metric tons]. 3:9 Hebrew *50 shekels* [570 grams]. 3:11 Hebrew *5 cubits* [2.3 meters]; also in 3:11b, 12, 15. 3:15 As in Syriac version (see also 1 Kgs 7:15; 2 Kgs 25:17; Jer 52:21), which reads *18 cubits* [8.3 meters]; Hebrew reads *35 cubits,* which is 52.5 feet or 16.5 meters. 3:17 *Jakin* probably means "he establishes"; *Boaz* probably means "in him is strength."

ROMANS 6:1-23

Well then, should we keep on sinning so that God can show us more and more of his wonderful grace? [2]Of course not! Since we have died to sin, how can we continue to live in it? [3]Or have you forgotten that when we were joined with Christ Jesus in baptism, we joined him in his death? [4]For we died and were buried with Christ by baptism. And just as Christ was raised from the dead by the glorious power of the Father, now we also may live new lives.

[5]Since we have been united with him in his death, we will also be raised to life as he was. [6]We know that our old sinful selves were crucified with Christ so that sin might lose its power in our lives. We are no longer slaves to sin. [7]For when we died with Christ we were set free from the power of sin. [8]And since we died with Christ, we know we will also live with him. [9]We are sure of this because Christ was raised from the dead, and he will never die again. Death no longer has any power over him. [10]When he died, he died once to break the power of sin. But now that he lives, he lives for the glory of God. [11]So you also should consider yourselves to be dead to the power of sin and alive to God through Christ Jesus.

[12]Do not let sin control the way you live;* do not give in to sinful desires. [13]Do not let any part of your body become an instrument of evil to serve sin. Instead, give yourselves completely to

God, for you were dead, but now you have new life. So use your whole body as an instrument to do what is right for the glory of God. [14]Sin is no longer your master, for you no longer live under the requirements of the law. Instead, you live under the freedom of God's grace.

[15]Well then, since God's grace has set us free from the law, does that mean we can go on sinning? Of course not! [16]Don't you realize that you become the slave of whatever you choose to obey? You can be a slave to sin, which leads to death, or you can choose to obey God, which leads to righteous living. [17]Thank God! Once you were slaves of sin, but now you wholeheartedly obey this teaching we have given you. [18]Now you are free from your slavery to sin, and you have become slaves to righteous living.

[19]Because of the weakness of your human nature, I am using the illustration of slavery to help you understand all this. Previously, you let yourselves be slaves to impurity and lawlessness, which led ever deeper into sin. Now you must give yourselves to be slaves to righteous living so that you will become holy.

[20]When you were slaves to sin, you were free from the obligation to do right. [21]And what was the result? You are now ashamed of the things you used to do, things that end in eternal doom. [22]**But now you are free from the power of sin and have become slaves of God. Now you do those things that lead to holiness and result in eternal life. [23]For the wages of sin is death, but the free gift of God is eternal life through Christ Jesus our Lord.**

6:12 Or *Do not let sin reign in your body, which is subject to death.*

PSALM 16:1-11
A psalm of David.

[1] **K**eep me safe, O God,
for I have come to you for refuge.

[2] I said to the LORD, "You are my Master!

Every good thing I have comes from you."
[3] The godly people in the land are my true heroes!
I take pleasure in them!
[4] Troubles multiply for those who chase after other gods.
I will not take part in their sacrifices of blood
or even speak the names of their gods.

[5] LORD, you alone are my inheritance, my cup of blessing.
You guard all that is mine.
[6] The land you have given me is a pleasant land.
What a wonderful inheritance!

[7] I will bless the LORD who guides me;
even at night my heart instructs me.
[8] I know the LORD is always with me.
I will not be shaken, for he is right beside me.

[9] No wonder my heart is glad, and I rejoice.*
My body rests in safety.
[10] For you will not leave my soul among the dead*
or allow your holy one* to rot in the grave.
[11] You will show me the way of life, granting me the joy of your presence
and the pleasures of living with you forever.*

16:9 Greek version reads *and my tongue shouts his praises.* Compare Acts 2:26.   16:10a Hebrew *in Sheol.*   16:10b Or *your Holy One.*   16:11 Greek version reads *You have shown me the way of life, / and you will fill me with the joy of your presence.* Compare Acts 2:28.

PROVERBS 19:20-21
Get all the advice and instruction you can, so you will be wise the rest of your life. □ You can make many plans, but the LORD's purpose will prevail.

JULY
21

2 CHRONICLES 4:1–6:11

Solomon* also made a bronze altar 30 feet long, 30 feet wide, and 15 feet high.* 2 Then he cast a great round basin, 15 feet across from rim to rim, called the Sea. It was 7½ feet deep and about 45 feet in circumference.* 3 It was encircled just below its rim by two rows of figures that resembled oxen. There were about six oxen per foot* all the way around, and they were cast as part of the basin.

4 The Sea was placed on a base of twelve bronze oxen, all facing outward. Three faced north, three faced west, three faced south, and three faced east, and the Sea rested on them. 5 The walls of the Sea were about three inches* thick, and its rim flared out like a cup and resembled a water lily blossom. It could hold about 16,500 gallons* of water.

6 He also made ten smaller basins for washing the utensils for the burnt offerings. He set five on the south side and five on the north. But the priests washed themselves in the Sea.

7 He then cast ten gold lampstands according to the specifications that had been given, and he put them in the Temple. Five were placed against the south wall, and five were placed against the north wall.

8 He also built ten tables and placed them in the Temple, five along the south wall and five along the north wall. Then he molded 100 gold basins.

9 He then built a courtyard for the priests, and also the large outer courtyard. He made doors for the courtyard entrances and overlaid them with bronze. 10 The great bronze basin called the Sea was placed near the southeast corner of the Temple.

11 Huram-abi also made the necessary washbasins, shovels, and bowls.

So at last Huram-abi completed everything King Solomon had assigned him to make for the Temple of God:

12 the two pillars;
   the two bowl-shaped capitals on top of the pillars;
   the two networks of interwoven chains that decorated the capitals;
13 the 400 pomegranates that hung from the chains on the capitals (two rows of pomegranates for each of the chain networks that decorated the capitals on top of the pillars);
14 the water carts holding the basins;
15 the Sea and the twelve oxen under it;
16 the ash buckets, the shovels, the meat hooks, and all the related articles.

Huram-abi made all these things of burnished bronze for the Temple of the LORD, just as King Solomon had directed. 17 The king had them cast in clay molds in the Jordan Valley between Succoth and Zarethan.* 18 Solomon used such great quantities of bronze that its weight could not be determined.

19 Solomon also made all the furnishings for the Temple of God:

   the gold altar;
   the tables for the Bread of the Presence;
20 the lampstands and their lamps of solid gold, to burn in front of the Most Holy Place as prescribed;
21 the flower decorations, lamps, and tongs—all of the purest gold;
22 the lamp snuffers, bowls, dishes, and incense burners—all of solid gold;
   the doors for the entrances to the Most Holy Place and the main room of the Temple, overlaid with gold.

5:1 So Solomon finished all his work on the Temple of the LORD. Then he brought all the gifts his father, David, had dedicated—the silver, the gold, and the various articles—and he stored them in the treasuries of the Temple of God.

2 Solomon then summoned to Jerusalem the elders of Israel and all the

heads of tribes—the leaders of the ancestral families of Israel. They were to
bring the Ark of the LORD's Covenant
to the Temple from its location in the
City of David, also known as Zion. ³So
all the men of Israel assembled before
the king at the annual Festival of Shelters, which is held in early autumn.*

⁴When all the elders of Israel arrived,
the Levites picked up the Ark. ⁵The
priests and Levites brought up the Ark
along with the special tent* and all the
sacred items that had been in it. ⁶There,
before the Ark, King Solomon and the
entire community of Israel sacrificed so
many sheep, goats, and cattle that no
one could keep count!

⁷Then the priests carried the Ark of
the LORD's Covenant into the inner
sanctuary of the Temple—the Most Holy
Place—and placed it beneath the wings
of the cherubim. ⁸The cherubim spread
their wings over the Ark, forming a
canopy over the Ark and its carrying
poles. ⁹These poles were so long that
their ends could be seen from the Temple's main room—the Holy Place*—but
not from the outside. They are still there
to this day. ¹⁰Nothing was in the Ark except the two stone tablets that Moses
had placed in it at Mount Sinai,* where
the LORD made a covenant with the people of Israel when they left Egypt.

¹¹Then the priests left the Holy Place.
All the priests who were present had purified themselves, whether or not they
were on duty that day. ¹²And the Levites
who were musicians—Asaph, Heman, Jeduthun, and all their sons and brothers—
were dressed in fine linen robes and
stood at the east side of the altar playing
cymbals, lyres, and harps. They were
joined by 120 priests who were playing
trumpets. ¹³The trumpeters and singers
performed together in unison to praise
and give thanks to the LORD. Accompanied by trumpets, cymbals, and other
instruments, they raised their voices and
praised the LORD with these words:

"He is good!
    His faithful love endures forever!"

At that moment a thick cloud filled
the Temple of the LORD. ¹⁴The priests
could not continue their service because
of the cloud, for the glorious presence
of the LORD filled the Temple of God.

⁶:¹THEN Solomon prayed, "O LORD, you
have said that you would live in a thick
cloud of darkness. ²Now I have built a
glorious Temple for you, a place where
you can live forever!"

³Then the king turned around to the
entire community of Israel standing before him and gave this blessing: ⁴"Praise
the LORD, the God of Israel, who has kept
the promise he made to my father, David. For he told my father, ⁵'From the day
I brought my people out of the land of
Egypt, I have never chosen a city among
any of the tribes of Israel as the place
where a Temple should be built to honor
my name. Nor have I chosen a king to
lead my people Israel. ⁶But now I have
chosen Jerusalem as the place for my
name to be honored, and I have chosen
David to be king over my people Israel.'"

⁷Then Solomon said, "My father, David, wanted to build this Temple to
honor the name of the LORD, the God of
Israel. ⁸But the LORD told him, 'You
wanted to build the Temple to honor
my name. Your intention is good, ⁹but
you are not the one to do it. One of your
own sons will build the Temple to
honor me.'

¹⁰"And now the LORD has fulfilled the
promise he made, for I have become
king in my father's place, and now I sit
on the throne of Israel, just as the LORD
promised. I have built this Temple to
honor the name of the LORD, the God of
Israel. ¹¹There I have placed the Ark,
which contains the covenant that the
LORD made with the people of Israel."

4:1a Or *Huram-abi;* Hebrew reads *He.*   4:1b Hebrew
20 cubits [9.2 meters] *long, 20 cubits wide, and 10 cubits*
[4.6 meters] *high.*   4:2 Hebrew *10 cubits* [4.6 meters]
across . . . 5 cubits [2.3 meters] *deep and 30 cubits*
[13.8 meters] *in circumference.*   4:3 Or *20 oxen per meter;*
Hebrew reads *10 per cubit.*   4:5a Hebrew *a handbreadth*
[8 centimeters].   4:5b Hebrew *3,000 baths* [63 kiloliters].
4:17 As in parallel text at 1 Kgs 7:46; Hebrew reads
Zeredah. 5:3 Hebrew *at the festival that is in the seventh
month.* The Festival of Shelters began on the fifteenth day
of the seventh month of the ancient Hebrew lunar calendar.

This day occurred in late September, October, or early
November.   **5:5** Hebrew *the Tent of Meeting;* i.e., the tent
mentioned in 2 Sam 6:17 and 1 Chr 16:1.   **5:9** As in
parallel text at 1 Kgs 8:8; Hebrew reads *from the Ark in
front of the Most Holy Place.*   **5:10** Hebrew *Horeb,* another
name for Sinai.

ROMANS 7:1-13

Now, dear brothers and sisters*—you
who are familiar with the law—don't
you know that the law applies only
while a person is living? ²For example,
when a woman marries, the law binds
her to her husband as long as he is alive.
But if he dies, the laws of marriage no
longer apply to her. ³So while her husband is alive, she would be committing
adultery if she married another man.
But if her husband dies, she is free from
that law and does not commit adultery
when she remarries.

⁴So, my dear brothers and sisters, this
is the point: You died to the power of
the law when you died with Christ. And
now you are united with the one who
was raised from the dead. As a result, we
can produce a harvest of good deeds for
God. ⁵When we were controlled by our
old nature,* sinful desires were at work
within us, and the law aroused these evil
desires that produced a harvest of sinful deeds, resulting in death. **⁶But now
we have been released from the law,
for we died to it and are no longer
captive to its power. Now we can
serve God, not in the old way of obeying the letter of the law, but in the
new way of living in the Spirit.**

⁷Well then, am I suggesting that the
law of God is sinful? Of course not! In
fact, it was the law that showed me my
sin. I would never have known that cov-
eting is wrong if the law had not said,
"You must not covet."* ⁸But sin used
this command to arouse all kinds of
covetous desires within me! If there
were no law, sin would not have that
power. ⁹At one time I lived without
understanding the law. But when I
learned the command not to covet, for
instance, the power of sin came to life,
¹⁰and I died. So I discovered that the
law's commands, which were supposed
to bring life, brought spiritual death in-

stead. ¹¹Sin took advantage of those
commands and deceived me; it used the
commands to kill me. ¹²But still, the law
itself is holy, and its commands are holy
and right and good.

¹³But how can that be? Did the law,
which is good, cause my death? Of
course not! Sin used what was good to
bring about my condemnation to death.
So we can see how terrible sin really is.
It uses God's good commands for its
own evil purposes.

7:1 Greek *brothers;* also in 7:4.   **7:5** Greek *When we were
in the flesh.*   **7:7** Exod 20:17; Deut 5:21.

PSALM 17:1-15
A prayer of David.

¹ **O** LORD, hear my plea for justice.
   Listen to my cry for help.
 Pay attention to my prayer,
   for it comes from honest lips.
² Declare me innocent,
   for you see those who do right.

³ You have tested my thoughts
     and examined my heart
     in the night.
   You have scrutinized me and
     found nothing wrong.
   I am determined not to sin
     in what I say.
⁴ I have followed your commands,
     which keep me from following
     cruel and evil people.
⁵ My steps have stayed on your path;
   I have not wavered from
     following you.

⁶ I am praying to you because I know
     you will answer, O God.
   Bend down and listen as I pray.
⁷ Show me your unfailing love in
     wonderful ways.
   By your mighty power you rescue
     those who seek refuge from
     their enemies.
⁸ Guard me as you would guard your
     own eyes.*
   Hide me in the shadow of your
     wings.
⁹ Protect me from wicked people who
     attack me,

from murderous enemies who
surround me.
10 They are without pity.
Listen to their boasting!
11 They track me down and
surround me,
watching for the chance to throw
me to the ground.
12 They are like hungry lions, eager
to tear me apart—
like young lions hiding in
ambush.

13 Arise, O LORD!
Stand against them, and bring
them to their knees!
Rescue me from the wicked with
your sword!
14 By the power of your hand,
O LORD,
destroy those who look to this
world for their reward.
But satisfy the hunger of your
treasured ones.
May their children have plenty,
leaving an inheritance for their
descendants.
15 Because I am righteous, I will
see you.
When I awake, I will see you face
to face and be satisfied.

17:8 Hebrew *as the pupil of your eye.*

PROVERBS 19:22-23
Loyalty makes a person attractive. It is
better to be poor than dishonest. □ Fear
of the LORD leads to life, bringing security and protection from harm.

JULY
22

2 CHRONICLES 6:12–8:10
Then Solomon stood before the altar of
the LORD in front of the entire community of Israel, and he lifted his hands
in prayer. 13Now Solomon had made a

bronze platform 7½ feet long, 7½ feet
wide, and 4½ feet high* and had placed
it at the center of the Temple's outer
courtyard. He stood on the platform,
and then he knelt in front of the entire
community of Israel and lifted his
hands toward heaven. 14He prayed,

"O LORD, God of Israel, there is no
God like you in all of heaven and
earth. You keep your covenant and
show unfailing love to all who walk
before you in wholehearted
devotion. 15You have kept your
promise to your servant David, my
father. You made that promise with
your own mouth, and with your own
hands you have fulfilled it today.

16"And now, O LORD, God of
Israel, carry out the additional
promise you made to your servant
David, my father. For you said to
him, 'If your descendants guard
their behavior and faithfully follow
my Law as you have done, one of
them will always sit on the throne of
Israel.' 17Now, O LORD, God of Israel,
fulfill this promise to your servant
David.

18"But will God really live on earth
among people? Why, even the
highest heavens cannot contain you.
How much less this Temple I have
built! 19Nevertheless, listen to my
prayer and my plea, O LORD my God.
Hear the cry and the prayer that
your servant is making to you. 20May
you watch over this Temple day and
night, this place where you have said
you would put your name. May you
always hear the prayers I make
toward this place. 21May you hear
the humble and earnest requests
from me and your people Israel
when we pray toward this place. Yes,
hear us from heaven where you live,
and when you hear, forgive.

22"If someone wrongs another
person and is required to take an
oath of innocence in front of your
altar at this Temple, 23then hear
from heaven and judge between

your servants—the accuser and the accused. Pay back the guilty as they deserve. Acquit the innocent because of their innocence.

24"If your people Israel are defeated by their enemies because they have sinned against you, and if they turn back and acknowledge your name and pray to you here in this Temple, 25 then hear from heaven and forgive the sin of your people Israel and return them to this land you gave to them and to their ancestors.

26"If the skies are shut up and there is no rain because your people have sinned against you, and if they pray toward this Temple and acknowledge your name and turn from their sins because you have punished them, 27 then hear from heaven and forgive the sins of your servants, your people Israel. Teach them to follow the right path, and send rain on your land that you have given to your people as their special possession.

28"If there is a famine in the land or a plague or crop disease or attacks of locusts or caterpillars, or if your people's enemies are in the land besieging their towns—whatever disaster or disease there is—29 and if your people Israel pray about their troubles or sorrow, raising their hands toward this Temple, 30 then hear from heaven where you live, and forgive. Give your people what their actions deserve, for you alone know each human heart. 31 Then they will fear you and walk in your ways as long as they live in the land you gave to our ancestors.

32"In the future, foreigners who do not belong to your people Israel will hear of you. They will come from distant lands when they hear of your great name and your strong hand and your powerful arm. And when they pray toward this Temple, 33 then hear from heaven where you live, and grant what they ask of you. In

this way, all the people of the earth will come to know and fear you, just as your own people Israel do. They, too, will know that this Temple I have built honors your name.

34"If your people go out where you send them to fight their enemies, and if they pray to you by turning toward this city you have chosen and toward this Temple I have built to honor your name, 35 then hear their prayers from heaven and uphold their cause.

36"If they sin against you—and who has never sinned?—you might become angry with them and let their enemies conquer them and take them captive to a foreign land far away or near. 37 But in that land of exile, they might turn to you in repentance and pray, 'We have sinned, done evil, and acted wickedly.' 38 If they turn to you with their whole heart and soul in the land of their captivity and pray toward the land you gave to their ancestors—toward this city you have chosen, and toward this Temple I have built to honor your name— 39 then hear their prayers and their petitions from heaven where you live, and uphold their cause. Forgive your people who have sinned against you.

40"O my God, may your eyes be open and your ears attentive to all the prayers made to you in this place.

41 "And now arise, O LORD God,
      and enter your resting
      place,
   along with the Ark, the symbol
      of your power.
   May your priests, O LORD God, be
      clothed with salvation;
      may your loyal servants rejoice
      in your goodness.
42 O LORD God, do not reject the
      king you have anointed.
   Remember your unfailing love
      for your servant David."

7:1WHEN Solomon finished praying, fire flashed down from heaven and burned up the burnt offerings and sacrifices, and the glorious presence of the LORD filled the Temple. 2The priests could not enter the Temple of the LORD because the glorious presence of the LORD filled it. 3When all the people of Israel saw the fire coming down and the glorious presence of the LORD filling the Temple, they fell face down on the ground and worshiped and praised the LORD, saying,

"He is good!
His faithful love endures forever!"

4Then the king and all the people offered sacrifices to the LORD. 5King Solomon offered a sacrifice of 22,000 cattle and 120,000 sheep and goats. And so the king and all the people dedicated the Temple of God. 6The priests took their assigned positions, and so did the Levites who were singing, "His faithful love endures forever!" They accompanied the singing with music from the instruments King David had made for praising the LORD. Across from the Levites, the priests blew the trumpets, while all Israel stood.

7Solomon then consecrated the central area of the courtyard in front of the LORD's Temple. He offered burnt offerings and the fat of peace offerings there, because the bronze altar he had built could not hold all the burnt offerings, grain offerings, and sacrificial fat.

8For the next seven days Solomon and all Israel celebrated the Festival of Shelters.* A large congregation had gathered from as far away as Lebo-hamath in the north and the Brook of Egypt in the south. 9On the eighth day they had a closing ceremony, for they had celebrated the dedication of the altar for seven days and the Festival of Shelters for seven days. 10Then at the end of the celebration,* Solomon sent the people home. They were all joyful and glad because the LORD had been so good to David and to Solomon and to his people Israel.

11So Solomon finished the Temple of the LORD, as well as the royal palace. He completed everything he had planned to do in the construction of the Temple and the palace. 12Then one night the LORD appeared to Solomon and said,

"I have heard your prayer and have chosen this Temple as the place for making sacrifices. 13At times I might shut up the heavens so that no rain falls, or command grasshoppers to devour your crops, or send plagues among you. 14Then if my people who are called by my name will humble themselves and pray and seek my face and turn from their wicked ways, I will hear from heaven and will forgive their sins and restore their land. 15My eyes will be open and my ears attentive to every prayer made in this place. 16For I have chosen this Temple and set it apart to be holy—a place where my name will be honored forever. I will always watch over it, for it is dear to my heart.

17"As for you, if you faithfully follow me as David your father did, obeying all my commands, decrees, and regulations, 18then I will establish the throne of your dynasty. For I made this covenant with your father, David, when I said, 'One of your descendants will always rule over Israel.'

19"But if you or your descendants abandon me and disobey the decrees and commands I have given you, and if you serve and worship other gods, 20then I will uproot the people from this land that I have given them. I will reject this Temple that I have made holy to honor my name. I will make it an object of mockery and ridicule among the nations. 21And though this Temple is impressive now, all who pass by will be appalled. They will ask, 'Why did the LORD do such terrible things to this land and to this Temple?'

22"And the answer will be,

'Because his people abandoned the LORD, the God of their ancestors, who brought them out of Egypt, and they worshiped other gods instead and bowed down to them. That is why he has brought all these disasters on them.'"

8:1IT took Solomon twenty years to build the LORD's Temple and his own royal palace. At the end of that time, **2**Solomon turned his attention to rebuilding the towns that King Hiram* had given him, and he settled Israelites in them.

3Solomon also fought against the town of Hamath-zobah and conquered it. **4**He rebuilt Tadmor in the wilderness and built towns in the region of Hamath as supply centers. **5**He fortified the towns of Upper Beth-horon and Lower Beth-horon, rebuilding their walls and installing barred gates. **6**He also rebuilt Baalath and other supply centers and constructed towns where his chariots and horses* could be stationed. He built everything he desired in Jerusalem and Lebanon and throughout his entire realm.

7There were still some people living in the land who were not Israelites, including the Hittites, Amorites, Perizzites, Hivites, and Jebusites. **8**These were descendants of the nations whom the people of Israel had not destroyed. So Solomon conscripted them for his labor force, and they serve in the labor force to this day. **9**But Solomon did not conscript any of the Israelites for his labor force. Instead, he assigned them to serve as fighting men, officers in his army, commanders of his chariots, and charioteers. **10**King Solomon appointed 250 of them to supervise the people.

6:13 Hebrew *5 cubits* [2.3 meters] *long, 5 cubits wide, and 3 cubits* [1.4 meters] *high.*   7:8 Hebrew *the festival* (also in 7:9); see note on 5:3.   7:10 Hebrew *Then on the twenty-third day of the seventh month.* This day of the ancient Hebrew lunar calendar occurred in October or early November.   8:2 Hebrew *Huram,* a variant spelling of Hiram; also in 8:18.   8:6 Or *and charioteers.*

ROMANS 7:14–8:8
So the trouble is not with the law, for it is spiritual and good. The trouble is with

me, [Paul] for I am all too human, a slave to sin. **15**I don't really understand myself, for I want to do what is right, but I don't do it. Instead, I do what I hate. **16**But if I know that what I am doing is wrong, this shows that I agree that the law is good. **17**So I am not the one doing wrong; it is sin living in me that does it.

18And I know that nothing good lives in me, that is, in my sinful nature.* I want to do what is right, but I can't. **19**I want to do what is good, but I don't. I don't want to do what is wrong, but I do it anyway. **20**But if I do what I don't want to do, I am not really the one doing wrong; it is sin living in me that does it.

21I have discovered this principle of life—that when I want to do what is right, I inevitably do what is wrong. **22**I love God's law with all my heart. **23**But there is another power* within me that is at war with my mind. This power makes me a slave to the sin that is still within me. **24**Oh, what a miserable person I am! Who will free me from this life that is dominated by sin and death? **25**Thank God! The answer is in Jesus Christ our Lord. So you see how it is: In my mind I really want to obey God's law, but because of my sinful nature I am a slave to sin.

8:1 So now there is no condemnation for those who belong to Christ Jesus. **2**And because you belong to him, the power* of the life-giving Spirit has freed you* from the power of sin that leads to death. **3**The law of Moses was unable to save us because of the weakness of our sinful nature.* So God did what the law could not do. He sent his own Son in a body like the bodies we sinners have. And in that body God declared an end to sin's control over us by giving his Son as a sacrifice for our sins. **4**He did this so that the just requirement of the law would be fully satisfied for us, who no longer follow our sinful nature but instead follow the Spirit.

5Those who are dominated by the sinful nature think about sinful things, but those who are controlled by the Holy Spirit think about things that please the

Spirit. [6]So letting your sinful nature control your mind leads to death. But letting the Spirit control your mind leads to life and peace. [7]For the sinful nature is always hostile to God. It never did obey God's laws, and it never will. [8]That's why those who are still under the control of their sinful nature can never please God.

7:18 Greek *my flesh;* also in 7:25.   7:23 Greek *law;* also in 7:23b.   8:2a Greek *the law;* also in 8:2b.   8:2b Some manuscripts read *me.*   8:3 Greek *our flesh;* similarly in 8:4, 5, 6, 7, 8, 9, 12.

PSALM 18:1-15

For the choir director: A psalm of David, the servant of the LORD. He sang this song to the LORD on the day the LORD rescued him from all his enemies and from Saul. He sang:

[1] I love you, LORD;
  you are my strength.
[2] The LORD is my rock, my fortress,
    and my savior;
  my God is my rock, in whom
    I find protection.
He is my shield, the power that
    saves me,
  and my place of safety.
[3] I called on the LORD, who is worthy
    of praise,
  and he saved me from my
    enemies.

[4] The ropes of death entangled me;
  floods of destruction swept
    over me.
[5] The grave* wrapped its ropes
    around me;
  death laid a trap in my path.
[6] But in my distress I cried out
    to the LORD;
  yes, I prayed to my God
    for help.
He heard me from his sanctuary;
  my cry to him reached his ears.

[7] Then the earth quaked and
    trembled.
The foundations of the
    mountains shook;
  they quaked because of his anger.
[8] Smoke poured from his nostrils;
  fierce flames leaped from
    his mouth.

Glowing coals blazed forth
    from him.
[9] He opened the heavens and came
    down;
  dark storm clouds were beneath
    his feet.
[10] Mounted on a mighty angelic
    being,* he flew,
  soaring on the wings of the wind.
[11] He shrouded himself in darkness,
  veiling his approach with dark
    rain clouds.
[12] Thick clouds shielded the
    brightness around him
  and rained down hail and
    burning coals.*
[13] The LORD thundered from heaven;
    the voice of the Most High
    resounded
  amid the hail and burning coals.
[14] He shot his arrows and scattered
    his enemies;
  his lightning flashed, and they
    were greatly confused.
[15] Then at your command, O LORD,
    at the blast of your breath,
  the bottom of the sea could be seen,
    and the foundations of the earth
    were laid bare.

18:5 Hebrew *Sheol.*   18:10 Hebrew *a cherub.*   18:12 Or *and lightning bolts;* also in 18:13.

PROVERBS 19:24-25

Lazy people take food in their hand but don't even lift it to their mouth. □ If you punish a mocker, the simpleminded will learn a lesson; if you correct the wise, they will be all the wiser.

JULY
23

2 CHRONICLES 8:11–10:19

Solomon moved his wife, Pharaoh's daughter, from the City of David to the new palace he had built for her. He said, "My wife must not live in King David's palace, for the Ark of the LORD has been there, and it is holy ground."

12Then Solomon presented burnt offerings to the LORD on the altar he had built for him in front of the entry room of the Temple. 13He offered the sacrifices for the Sabbaths, the new moon festivals, and the three annual festivals—the Passover celebration, the Festival of Harvest,* and the Festival of Shelters—as Moses had commanded.

14In assigning the priests to their duties, Solomon followed the regulations of his father, David. He also assigned the Levites to lead the people in praise and to assist the priests in their daily duties. And he assigned the gatekeepers to their gates by their divisions, following the commands of David, the man of God. 15Solomon did not deviate in any way from David's commands concerning the priests and Levites and the treasuries.

16So Solomon made sure that all the work related to building the Temple of the LORD was carried out, from the day its foundation was laid to the day of its completion.

17Later Solomon went to Ezion-geber and Elath,* ports along the shore of the Red Sea* in the land of Edom. 18Hiram sent him ships commanded by his own officers and manned by experienced crews of sailors. These ships sailed to Ophir with Solomon's men and brought back to Solomon almost seventeen tons* of gold.

9:1WHEN the queen of Sheba heard of Solomon's fame, she came to Jerusalem to test him with hard questions. She arrived with a large group of attendants and a great caravan of camels loaded with spices, large quantities of gold, and precious jewels. When she met with Solomon, she talked with him about everything she had on her mind. 2Solomon had answers for all her questions; nothing was too hard for him to explain to her. 3When the queen of Sheba realized how wise Solomon was, and when she saw the palace he had built, 4she was overwhelmed. She was also amazed

at the food on his tables, the organization of his officials and their splendid clothing, the cup-bearers and their robes, and the burnt offerings Solomon made at the Temple of the LORD.

5She exclaimed to the king, "Everything I heard in my country about your achievements* and wisdom is true! 6I didn't believe what was said until I arrived here and saw it with my own eyes. In fact, I had not heard the half of your great wisdom! It is far beyond what I was told. 7How happy your people must be! What a privilege for your officials to stand here day after day, listening to your wisdom! 8Praise the LORD your God, who delights in you and has placed you on the throne as king to rule for him. Because God loves Israel and desires this kingdom to last forever, he has made you king over them so you can rule with justice and righteousness."

9Then she gave the king a gift of 9,000 pounds* of gold, great quantities of spices, and precious jewels. Never before had there been spices as fine as those the queen of Sheba gave to King Solomon.

10(In addition, the crews of Hiram and Solomon brought gold from Ophir, and they also brought red sandalwood* and precious jewels. 11The king used the sandalwood to make steps* for the Temple of the LORD and the royal palace, and to construct lyres and harps for the musicians. Never before had such beautiful things been seen in Judah.)

12King Solomon gave the queen of Sheba whatever she asked for—gifts of greater value than the gifts she had given him. Then she and all her attendants returned to their own land.

13Each year Solomon received about 25 tons* of gold. 14This did not include the additional revenue he received from merchants and traders. All the kings of Arabia and the governors of the provinces also brought gold and silver to Solomon.

15King Solomon made 200 large shields of hammered gold, each weighing more than 15 pounds.* 16He also made 300 smaller shields of hammered gold, each weighing more than 7½ pounds.* The king placed these shields in the Palace of the Forest of Lebanon.

¹⁷Then the king made a huge throne, decorated with ivory and overlaid with pure gold. ¹⁸The throne had six steps, with a footstool of gold. There were armrests on both sides of the seat, and the figure of a lion stood on each side of the throne. ¹⁹There were also twelve other lions, one standing on each end of the six steps. No other throne in all the world could be compared with it!

²⁰All of King Solomon's drinking cups were solid gold, as were all the utensils in the Palace of the Forest of Lebanon. They were not made of silver, for silver was considered worthless in Solomon's day!

²¹The king had a fleet of trading ships* manned by the sailors sent by Hiram.* Once every three years the ships returned, loaded with gold, silver, ivory, apes, and peacocks.*

²²So King Solomon became richer and wiser than any other king on earth. ²³Kings from every nation came to consult him and to hear the wisdom God had given him. ²⁴Year after year everyone who visited brought him gifts of silver and gold, clothing, weapons, spices, horses, and mules.

²⁵Solomon had 4,000 stalls for his horses and chariots, and he had 12,000 horses.* He stationed some of them in the chariot cities, and some near him in Jerusalem. ²⁶He ruled over all the kings from the Euphrates River* in the north to the land of the Philistines and the border of Egypt in the south. ²⁷The king made silver as plentiful in Jerusalem as stone. And valuable cedar timber was as common as the sycamore-fig trees that grow in the foothills of Judah.* ²⁸Solomon's horses were imported from Egypt* and many other countries.

²⁹The rest of the events of Solomon's reign, from beginning to end, are recorded in *The Record of Nathan the Prophet,* and *The Prophecy of Ahijah*

from Shiloh, and also in *The Visions of Iddo the Seer,* concerning Jeroboam son of Nebat. ³⁰Solomon ruled in Jerusalem over all Israel for forty years. ³¹When he died, he was buried in the City of David, named for his father. Then his son Rehoboam became the next king.

¹⁰:¹REHOBOAM went to Shechem, where all Israel had gathered to make him king. ²When Jeroboam son of Nebat heard of this, he returned from Egypt, for he had fled to Egypt to escape from King Solomon. ³The leaders of Israel summoned him, and Jeroboam and all Israel went to speak with Rehoboam. ⁴"Your father was a hard master," they said. "Lighten the harsh labor demands and heavy taxes that your father imposed on us. Then we will be your loyal subjects."

⁵Rehoboam replied, "Come back in three days for my answer." So the people went away.

⁶Then King Rehoboam discussed the matter with the older men who had counseled his father, Solomon. "What is your advice?" he asked. "How should I answer these people?"

⁷The older counselors replied, "If you are good to these people and do your best to please them and give them a favorable answer, they will always be your loyal subjects."

⁸But Rehoboam rejected the advice of the older men and instead asked the opinion of the young men who had grown up with him and were now his advisers. ⁹"What is your advice?" he asked them. "How should I answer these people who want me to lighten the burdens imposed by my father?"

¹⁰The young men replied, "This is what you should tell those complainers who want a lighter burden: 'My little finger is thicker than my father's waist! ¹¹Yes, my father laid heavy burdens on you, but I'm going to make them even heavier! My father beat you with whips, but I will beat you with scorpions!'"

¹²Three days later Jeroboam and all the people returned to hear Rehoboam's

decision, just as the king had ordered. [13]But Rehoboam spoke harshly to them, for he rejected the advice of the older counselors [14]and followed the counsel of his younger advisers. He told the people, "My father laid* heavy burdens on you, but I'm going to make them even heavier! My father beat you with whips, but I will beat you with scorpions!"

[15]So the king paid no attention to the people. This turn of events was the will of God, for it fulfilled the LORD's message to Jeroboam son of Nebat through the prophet Ahijah from Shiloh.

[16]When all Israel realized* that the king had refused to listen to them, they responded,

"Down with the dynasty of David!
    We have no interest in the
        son of Jesse.
Back to your homes, O Israel!
    Look out for your own house,
        O David!"

So all the people of Israel returned home. [17]But Rehoboam continued to rule over the Israelites who lived in the towns of Judah.

[18]King Rehoboam sent Adoniram,* who was in charge of the labor force, to restore order, but the people of Israel stoned him to death. When this news reached King Rehoboam, he quickly jumped into his chariot and fled to Jerusalem. [19]And to this day the northern tribes of Israel have refused to be ruled by a descendant of David.

8:13 Or *Festival of Weeks.*   8:17a As in Greek version (see also 2 Kgs 14:22; 16:6); Hebrew reads *Eloth,* a variant spelling of Elath.   8:17b As in parallel text at 1 Kgs 9:26; Hebrew reads *the sea.*   8:18 Hebrew *450 talents* [15.3 metric tons].   9:5 Hebrew *your words.*   9:9 Hebrew *120 talents* [4,000 kilograms].   9:10 Hebrew *algum wood* (also in 9:11); perhaps a variant spelling of *almug.* Compare parallel text at 1 Kgs 10:11-12.   9:11 Or *gateways.* The meaning of the Hebrew is uncertain.   9:13 Hebrew *666 talents* [23 metric tons].   9:15 Hebrew *600 shekels* [6.8 kilograms].   9:16 Hebrew *300 shekels* [3.4 kilograms]. 9:21a Hebrew *fleet of ships that could sail to Tarshish.* 9:21b Hebrew *Huram,* a variant spelling of Hiram. 9:21c Or *and baboons.*   9:25 Or *12,000 charioteers.* 9:26 Hebrew *the river.*   9:27 Hebrew *the Shephelah.* 9:28 Possibly *Muzur,* a district near Cilicia.   10:14 As in Greek version and many Hebrew manuscripts (see also 1 Kgs 12:14); Masoretic Text reads *I will lay.*   10:16 As in Syriac version, Latin Vulgate, and many Hebrew manuscripts (see also 1 Kgs 12:16); Masoretic Text lacks *realized.* 10:18 Hebrew *Hadoram,* a variant spelling of Adoniram; compare 1 Kgs 4:6; 5:14; 12:18.

ROMANS 8:9-25

But you are not controlled by your sinful nature. You are controlled by the Spirit if you have the Spirit of God living in you. (And remember that those who do not have the Spirit of Christ living in them do not belong to him at all.) [10]And Christ lives within you, so even though your body will die because of sin, the Spirit gives you life* because you have been made right with God. [11]**The Spirit of God, who raised Jesus from the dead, lives in you. And just as God raised Christ Jesus from the dead, he will give life to your mortal bodies by this same Spirit living within you.**

[12]Therefore, dear brothers and sisters,* you have no obligation to do what your sinful nature urges you to do. [13]For if you live by its dictates, you will die. But if through the power of the Spirit you put to death the deeds of your sinful nature,* you will live. [14]For all who are led by the Spirit of God are children* of God.

[15]So you have not received a spirit that makes you fearful slaves. Instead, you received God's Spirit when he adopted you as his own children.* Now we call him, "Abba, Father."* [16]For his Spirit joins with our spirit to affirm that we are God's children. [17]And since we are his children, we are his heirs. In fact, together with Christ we are heirs of God's glory. But if we are to share his glory, we must also share his suffering.

[18]Yet what we suffer now is nothing compared to the glory he will reveal to us later. [19]For all creation is waiting eagerly for that future day when God will reveal who his children really are. [20]Against its will, all creation was subjected to God's curse. But with eager hope, [21]the creation looks forward to the day when it will join God's children in glorious freedom from death and decay. [22]For we know that all creation has been groaning as in the pains of childbirth right up to the present time. [23]And we believers also groan, even though we have the Holy Spirit within us as a foretaste of future glory, for we long for our

bodies to be released from sin and suffering. We, too, wait with eager hope for the day when God will give us our full rights as his adopted children,* including the new bodies he has promised us. 24We were given this hope when we were saved. (If we already have something, we don't need to hope* for it. 25But if we look forward to something we don't yet have, we must wait patiently and confidently.)

8:10 Or *your spirit is alive.*   8:12 Greek *brothers;* also in 8:29.   8:13 Greek *deeds of the body.*   8:14 Greek *sons;* also in 8:19.   8:15a Greek *you received a spirit of sonship.* 8:15b *Abba* is an Aramaic term for "father."   8:23 Greek *wait anxiously for sonship.*   8:24 Some manuscripts read *wait.*

PSALM 18:16-36

He [the LORD] reached down from
    heaven and rescued me;
    he drew me out of deep waters.
17 He rescued me from my powerful
    enemies,
    from those who hated me and
        were too strong for me.
18 They attacked me at a moment
        when I was in distress,
    but the LORD supported me.
19 He led me to a place of safety;
    he rescued me because he
        delights in me.
20 The LORD rewarded me for
        doing right;
    he restored me because
        of my innocence.
21 For I have kept the ways of
        the LORD;
    I have not turned from my God
        to follow evil.
22 I have followed all his regulations;
    I have never abandoned his
        decrees.
23 I am blameless before God;
    I have kept myself from sin.
24 The LORD rewarded me for
        doing right.
    He has seen my innocence.

25 To the faithful you show yourself
        faithful;
    to those with integrity you
        show integrity.
26 To the pure you show yourself pure,
    but to the wicked you show
        yourself hostile.
27 You rescue the humble,
    but you humiliate the proud.
28 You light a lamp for me.
    The LORD, my God, lights up my
        darkness.
29 In your strength I can crush an army;
    with my God I can scale any wall.
30 God's way is perfect.
    All the LORD's promises prove true.
    He is a shield for all who look
        to him for protection.
31 For who is God except the LORD?
    Who but our God is a solid rock?
32 God arms me with strength,
    and he makes my way perfect.
33 He makes me as surefooted
        as a deer,
    enabling me to stand on
        mountain heights.
34 He trains my hands for battle;
    he strengthens my arm to draw
        a bronze bow.
35 You have given me your shield
        of victory.
    Your right hand supports me;
    your help has made me great.
36 You have made a wide path
        for my feet
    to keep them from slipping.

PROVERBS 19:26

Children who mistreat their father or chase away their mother are an embarrassment and a public disgrace.

JULY
24

2 CHRONICLES 11:1–13:22

When Rehoboam arrived at Jerusalem, he mobilized the men of Judah and Benjamin—180,000 select troops—to fight against Israel and to restore the kingdom to himself.

²But the LORD said to Shemaiah, the man of God, ³"Say to Rehoboam son of Solomon, king of Judah, and to all the Israelites in Judah and Benjamin: ⁴'This is what the LORD says: Do not fight against your relatives. Go back home, for what has happened is my doing!' " So they obeyed the message of the LORD and did not fight against Jeroboam.

⁵Rehoboam remained in Jerusalem and fortified various towns for the defense of Judah. ⁶He built up Bethlehem, Etam, Tekoa, ⁷Beth-zur, Soco, Adullam, ⁸Gath, Mareshah, Ziph, ⁹Adoraim, Lachish, Azekah, ¹⁰Zorah, Aijalon, and Hebron. These became the fortified towns of Judah and Benjamin. ¹¹Rehoboam strengthened their defenses and stationed commanders in them, and he stored supplies of food, olive oil, and wine. ¹²He also put shields and spears in these towns as a further safety measure. So only Judah and Benjamin remained under his control.

¹³But all the priests and Levites living among the northern tribes of Israel sided with Rehoboam. ¹⁴The Levites even abandoned their pasturelands and property and moved to Judah and Jerusalem, because Jeroboam and his sons would not allow them to serve the LORD as priests. ¹⁵Jeroboam appointed his own priests to serve at the pagan shrines, where they worshiped the goat and calf idols he had made. ¹⁶From all the tribes of Israel, those who sincerely wanted to worship the LORD, the God of Israel, followed the Levites to Jerusalem, where they could offer sacrifices to the LORD, the God of their ancestors. ¹⁷This strengthened the kingdom of Judah, and for three years they supported Rehoboam son of Solomon, for during those years they faithfully followed in the footsteps of David and Solomon.

¹⁸Rehoboam married his cousin Mahalath, the daughter of David's son Jerimoth and of Abihail, the daughter of Eliab son of Jesse. ¹⁹Mahalath had three sons—Jeush, Shemariah, and Zaham.

²⁰Later Rehoboam married another cousin, Maacah, the daughter of Absa-lom. Maacah gave birth to Abijah, Attai, Ziza, and Shelomith. ²¹Rehoboam loved Maacah more than any of his other wives and concubines. In all, he had eighteen wives and sixty concubines, and they gave birth to twenty-eight sons and sixty daughters.

²²Rehoboam appointed Maacah's son Abijah as leader among the princes, making it clear that he would be the next king. ²³Rehoboam also wisely gave responsibilities to his other sons and stationed some of them in the fortified towns throughout the land of Judah and Benjamin. He provided them with generous provisions, and he found many wives for them.

¹²:¹BUT when Rehoboam was firmly established and strong, he abandoned the Law of the LORD, and all Israel followed him in this sin. ²Because they were unfaithful to the LORD, King Shishak of Egypt came up and attacked Jerusalem in the fifth year of King Rehoboam's reign. ³He came with 1,200 chariots, 60,000 horses,* and a countless army of foot soldiers, including Libyans, Sukkites, and Ethiopians.* ⁴Shishak conquered Judah's fortified towns and then advanced to attack Jerusalem.

⁵The prophet Shemaiah then met with Rehoboam and Judah's leaders, who had all fled to Jerusalem because of Shishak. Shemaiah told them, "This is what the LORD says: You have abandoned me, so I am abandoning you to Shishak."

⁶Then the leaders of Israel and the king humbled themselves and said, "The LORD is right in doing this to us!"

⁷When the LORD saw their change of heart, he gave this message to Shemaiah: "Since the people have humbled themselves, I will not completely destroy them and will soon give them some relief. I will not use Shishak to pour out my anger on Jerusalem. ⁸But they will become his subjects, so they will know the difference between serving me and serving earthly rulers."

⁹So King Shishak of Egypt came up and attacked Jerusalem. He ransacked

the treasuries of the Lord's Temple and the royal palace; he stole everything, including all the gold shields Solomon had made. [10]King Rehoboam later replaced them with bronze shields as substitutes, and he entrusted them to the care of the commanders of the guard who protected the entrance to the royal palace. [11]Whenever the king went to the Temple of the Lord, the guards would also take the shields and then return them to the guardroom. [12]Because Rehoboam humbled himself, the Lord's anger was turned away, and he did not destroy him completely. There were still some good things in the land of Judah.

[13]King Rehoboam firmly established himself in Jerusalem and continued to rule. He was forty-one years old when he became king, and he reigned seventeen years in Jerusalem, the city the Lord had chosen from among all the tribes of Israel as the place to honor his name. Rehoboam's mother was Naamah, a woman from Ammon. [14]But he was an evil king, for he did not seek the Lord with all his heart.

[15]The rest of the events of Rehoboam's reign, from beginning to end, are recorded in *The Record of Shemaiah the Prophet* and *The Record of Iddo the Seer*, which are part of the genealogical record. Rehoboam and Jeroboam were continually at war with each other. [16]When Rehoboam died, he was buried in the City of David. Then his son Abijah became the next king.

[13:1]Abijah began to rule over Judah in the eighteenth year of Jeroboam's reign in Israel. [2]He reigned in Jerusalem three years. His mother was Maacah,* the daughter of Uriel from Gibeah.

Then war broke out between Abijah and Jeroboam. [3]Judah, led by King Abijah, fielded 400,000 select warriors, while Jeroboam mustered 800,000 select troops from Israel.

[4]When the army of Judah arrived in the hill country of Ephraim, Abijah stood on Mount Zemaraim and shouted to Jeroboam and all Israel: "Listen to me!

[5]Don't you realize that the Lord, the God of Israel, made a lasting covenant* with David, giving him and his descendants the throne of Israel forever? [6]Yet Jeroboam son of Nebat, a mere servant of David's son Solomon, rebelled against his master. [7]Then a whole gang of scoundrels joined him, defying Solomon's son Rehoboam when he was young and inexperienced and could not stand up to them.

[8]"Do you really think you can stand against the kingdom of the Lord that is led by the descendants of David? You may have a vast army, and you have those gold calves that Jeroboam made as your gods. [9]But you have chased away the priests of the Lord (the descendants of Aaron) and the Levites, and you have appointed your own priests, just like the pagan nations. You let anyone become a priest these days! Whoever comes to be dedicated with a young bull and seven rams can become a priest of these so-called gods of yours!

[10]"But as for us, the Lord is our God, and we have not abandoned him. Only the descendants of Aaron serve the Lord as priests, and the Levites alone may help them in their work. [11]They present burnt offerings and fragrant incense to the Lord every morning and evening. They place the Bread of the Presence on the holy table, and they light the gold lampstand every evening. We are following the instructions of the Lord our God, but you have abandoned him. [12]So you see, God is with us. He is our leader. His priests blow their trumpets and lead us into battle against you. O people of Israel, do not fight against the Lord, the God of your ancestors, for you will not succeed!"

[13]Meanwhile, Jeroboam had secretly sent part of his army around behind the men of Judah to ambush them. [14]When Judah realized that they were being attacked from the front and the rear, they cried out to the Lord for help. Then the priests blew the trumpets, [15]and the men of Judah began to shout. At the sound of their battle cry, God defeated Jeroboam

and all Israel and routed them before Abijah and the army of Judah.

[16]The Israelite army fled from Judah, and God handed them over to Judah in defeat. [17]Abijah and his army inflicted heavy losses on them; 500,000 of Israel's select troops were killed that day. [18]So Judah defeated Israel on that occasion because they trusted in the LORD, the God of their ancestors. [19]Abijah and his army pursued Jeroboam's troops and captured some of his towns, including Bethel, Jeshanah, and Ephron, along with their surrounding villages.

[20]So Jeroboam of Israel never regained his power during Abijah's lifetime, and finally the LORD struck him down and he died. [21]Meanwhile, Abijah of Judah grew more and more powerful. He married fourteen wives and had twenty-two sons and sixteen daughters.

[22]The rest of the events of Abijah's reign, including his words and deeds, are recorded in *The Commentary of Iddo the Prophet.*

12:3a Or *charioteers,* or *horsemen.*   12:3b Hebrew *and Cushites.*   13:2 As in most Greek manuscripts and Syriac version (see also 2 Chr 11:20-21; 1 Kgs 15:2); Hebrew reads *Micaiah,* a variant spelling of Maacah.   13:5 Hebrew *a covenant of salt.*

ROMANS 8:26-39

And the Holy Spirit helps us in our weakness. For example, we don't know what God wants us to pray for. But the Holy Spirit prays for us with groanings that cannot be expressed in words. [27]And the Father who knows all hearts knows what the Spirit is saying, for the Spirit pleads for us believers in harmony with God's own will. [28]And we know that God causes everything to work together* for the good of those who love God and are called according to his purpose for them. [29]For God knew his people in advance, and he chose them to become like his Son, so that his Son would be the firstborn among many brothers and sisters. [30]And having chosen them, he called them to come to him. And having called them, he gave them right standing with himself. And having given them right standing, he gave them his glory.

[31]What shall we say about such wonderful things as these? If God is for us, who can ever be against us? [32]Since he did not spare even his own Son but gave him up for us all, won't he also give us everything else? [33]Who dares accuse us whom God has chosen for his own? No one—for God himself has given us right standing with himself. [34]Who then will condemn us? No one—for Christ Jesus died for us and was raised to life for us, and he is sitting in the place of honor at God's right hand, pleading for us.

[35]Can anything ever separate us from Christ's love? Does it mean he no longer loves us if we have trouble or calamity, or are persecuted, or hungry, or destitute, or in danger, or threatened with death? [36](As the Scriptures say, "For your sake we are killed every day; we are being slaughtered like sheep."*) [37]No, despite all these things, overwhelming victory is ours through Christ, who loved us.

[38]**And I am convinced that nothing can ever separate us from God's love. Neither death nor life, neither angels nor demons,* neither our fears for today nor our worries about tomorrow—not even the powers of hell can separate us from God's love. [39]No power in the sky above or in the earth below—indeed, nothing in all creation will ever be able to separate us from the love of God that is revealed in Christ Jesus our Lord.**

8:28 Some manuscripts read *And we know that everything works together.*   8:36 Ps 44:22.   8:38 Greek *nor rulers.*

PSALM 18:37-50

I chased my enemies and caught them;
   I did not stop until they
    were conquered.
[38] I struck them down so they could
   not get up;
   they fell beneath my feet.
[39] You have armed me with strength
   for the battle;
   you have subdued my enemies
    under my feet.
[40] You placed my foot on their necks.

I have destroyed all who
hated me.
41 They called for help, but no one
came to their rescue.
They even cried to the LORD, but
he refused to answer.
42 I ground them as fine as dust
in the wind.
I swept them into the gutter
like dirt.
43 You gave me victory over my
accusers.
You appointed me ruler
over nations;
people I don't even know now
serve me.
44 As soon as they hear of me, they
submit;
foreign nations cringe before me.
45 They all lose their courage
and come trembling from their
strongholds.

46 The LORD lives! Praise to my Rock!
May the God of my salvation
be exalted!
47 He is the God who pays back those
who harm me;
he subdues the nations under me
48   and rescues me from my enemies.
You hold me safe beyond the reach
of my enemies.
you save me from violent
opponents.
49 For this, O LORD, I will praise you
among the nations;
I will sing praises to your name.
50 You give great victories to your king;
you show unfailing love to your
anointed,
to David and all his descendants
forever.

PROVERBS 19:27-29
If you stop listening to instruction, my
child, you will turn your back on knowledge. □ A corrupt witness makes a
mockery of justice; the mouth of the
wicked gulps down evil. □ Punishment
is made for mockers, and the backs of
fools are made to be beaten.

JULY 25

2 CHRONICLES 14:1-16:14
1*When Abijah died, he was buried in
the City of David. Then his son Asa became the next king. There was peace in
the land for ten years. 2*Asa did what
was pleasing and good in the sight of
the LORD his God. 3He removed the foreign altars and the pagan shrines. He
smashed the sacred pillars and cut
down the Asherah poles. 4He commanded the people of Judah to seek the
LORD, the God of their ancestors, and to
obey his law and his commands. 5Asa
also removed the pagan shrines, as well
as the incense altars from every one
of Judah's towns. So Asa's kingdom enjoyed a period of peace. 6During those
peaceful years, he was able to build up
the fortified towns throughout Judah.
No one tried to make war against him at
this time, for the LORD was giving him
rest from his enemies.

7Asa told the people of Judah, "Let us
build towns and fortify them with walls,
towers, gates, and bars. The land is still
ours because we sought the LORD our
God, and he has given us peace on every
side." So they went ahead with these
projects and brought them to completion.

8King Asa had an army of 300,000
warriors from the tribe of Judah, armed
with large shields and spears. He also
had an army of 280,000 warriors from
the tribe of Benjamin, armed with small
shields and bows. Both armies were
composed of well-trained fighting men.

9Once an Ethiopian* named Zerah attacked Judah with an army of 1,000,000
men* and 300 chariots. They advanced
to the town of Mareshah, 10so Asa de-
ployed his armies for battle in the valley
north of Mareshah.* 11Then Asa cried
out to the LORD his God, "O LORD, no one
but you can help the powerless against
the mighty! Help us, O LORD our God, for

we trust in you alone. It is in your name that we have come against this vast horde. O Lord, you are our God; do not let mere men prevail against you!"

¹²So the Lord defeated the Ethiopians* in the presence of Asa and the army of Judah, and the enemy fled. ¹³Asa and his army pursued them as far as Gerar, and so many Ethiopians fell that they were unable to rally. They were destroyed by the Lord and his army, and the army of Judah carried off a vast amount of plunder.

¹⁴While they were at Gerar, they attacked all the towns in that area, and terror from the Lord came upon the people there. As a result, a vast amount of plunder was taken from these towns, too. ¹⁵They also attacked the camps of herdsmen and captured many sheep, goats, and camels before finally returning to Jerusalem.

¹⁵:¹THEN the Spirit of God came upon Azariah son of Oded, ²and he went out to meet King Asa as he was returning from the battle. "Listen to me, Asa!" he shouted. "Listen, all you people of Judah and Benjamin! The Lord will stay with you as long as you stay with him! Whenever you seek him, you will find him. But if you abandon him, he will abandon you. ³For a long time Israel was without the true God, without a priest to teach them, and without the Law to instruct them. ⁴But whenever they were in trouble and turned to the Lord, the God of Israel, and sought him out, they found him.

⁵"During those dark times, it was not safe to travel. Problems troubled the people of every land. ⁶Nation fought against nation, and city against city, for God was troubling them with every kind of problem. ⁷But as for you, be strong and courageous, for your work will be rewarded."

⁸When Asa heard this message from Azariah the prophet,* he took courage and removed all the detestable idols from the land of Judah and Benjamin and in the towns he had captured in the hill country of Ephraim. And he re-

paired the altar of the Lord, which stood in front of the entry room of the Lord's Temple.

⁹Then Asa called together all the people of Judah and Benjamin, along with the people of Ephraim, Manasseh, and Simeon who had settled among them. For many from Israel had moved to Judah during Asa's reign when they saw that the Lord his God was with him. ¹⁰The people gathered at Jerusalem in late spring,* during the fifteenth year of Asa's reign.

¹¹On that day they sacrificed to the Lord 700 cattle and 7,000 sheep and goats from the plunder they had taken in the battle. ¹²Then they entered into a covenant to seek the Lord, the God of their ancestors, with all their heart and soul. ¹³They agreed that anyone who refused to seek the Lord, the God of Israel, would be put to death—whether young or old, man or woman. ¹⁴They shouted out their oath of loyalty to the Lord with trumpets blaring and rams' horns sounding. ¹⁵All in Judah were happy about this covenant, for they had entered into it with all their heart. They earnestly sought after God, and they found him. And the Lord gave them rest from their enemies on every side.

¹⁶King Asa even deposed his grandmother* Maacah from her position as queen mother because she had made an obscene Asherah pole. He cut down her obscene pole, broke it up, and burned it in the Kidron Valley. ¹⁷Although the pagan shrines were not removed from Israel, Asa's heart remained completely faithful throughout his life. ¹⁸He brought into the Temple of God the silver and gold and the various items that he and his father had dedicated.

¹⁹So there was no more war until the thirty-fifth year of Asa's reign.

¹⁶:¹IN the thirty-sixth year of Asa's reign, King Baasha of Israel invaded Judah and fortified Ramah in order to prevent anyone from entering or leaving King Asa's territory in Judah.

²Asa responded by removing the

silver and gold from the treasuries of the Temple of the LORD and the royal palace. He sent it to King Ben-hadad of Aram, who was ruling in Damascus, along with this message:

> ³"Let there be a treaty between you and me like the one between your father and my father. See, I am sending you silver and gold. Break your treaty with King Baasha of Israel so that he will leave me alone."

⁴Ben-hadad agreed to King Asa's request and sent the commanders of his army to attack the towns of Israel. They conquered the towns of Ijon, Dan, Abel-beth-maacah,* and all the store cities in Naphtali. ⁵As soon as Baasha of Israel heard what was happening, he abandoned his project of fortifying Ramah and stopped all work on it. ⁶Then King Asa called out all the men of Judah to carry away the building stones and timbers that Baasha had been using to fortify Ramah. Asa used these materials to fortify the towns of Geba and Mizpah.

⁷At that time Hanani the seer came to King Asa and told him, "Because you have put your trust in the king of Aram instead of in the LORD your God, you missed your chance to destroy the army of the king of Aram. ⁸Don't you remember what happened to the Ethiopians* and Libyans and their vast army, with all of their chariots and charioteers?* At that time you relied on the LORD, and he handed them over to you. ⁹**The eyes of the LORD search the whole earth in order to strengthen those whose hearts are fully committed to him.** What a fool you have been! From now on you will be at war."

¹⁰Asa became so angry with Hanani for saying this that he threw him into prison and put him in stocks. At that time Asa also began to oppress some of his people.

¹¹The rest of the events of Asa's reign, from beginning to end, are recorded in *The Book of the Kings of Judah and Israel.* ¹²In the thirty-ninth year of his reign, Asa developed a serious foot disease. Yet even with the severity of his disease, he did not seek the LORD's help but turned only to his physicians. ¹³So he died in the forty-first year of his reign. ¹⁴He was buried in the tomb he had carved out for himself in the City of David. He was laid on a bed perfumed with sweet spices and fragrant ointments, and the people built a huge funeral fire in his honor.

14:1 Verse is numbered 13:23 in the Hebrew text.
14:2 Verses 14:2-15 are numbered 14:1-14 in Hebrew text.
14:9a Hebrew *a Cushite.*   14:9b Or *an army of thousands and thousands;* Hebrew reads *an army of a thousand thousands.*   14:10 Or *in the Zephathah Valley near Mareshah.*   14:12 Hebrew *Cushites;* also in 14:13.
15:8 As in Syriac version and Latin Vulgate (see also 15:1); Hebrew reads *from Oded the prophet.*   15:10 Hebrew *in the third month.* This month of the ancient Hebrew lunar calendar usually occurs within the months of May and June.   15:16 Hebrew *his mother.*   16:4 As in parallel text at 1 Kgs 15:20; Hebrew reads *Abel-maim,* a variant spelling of Abel-beth-maacah.   16:8a Hebrew *Cushites.*   16:8b Or *and horsemen?*

ROMANS 9:1-24

With Christ as my witness, I [Paul] speak with utter truthfulness. My conscience and the Holy Spirit confirm it. ²My heart is filled with bitter sorrow and unending grief ³for my people, my Jewish brothers and sisters.* I would be willing to be forever cursed—cut off from Christ!— if that would save them. ⁴They are the people of Israel, chosen to be God's adopted children.* God revealed his glory to them. He made covenants with them and gave them his law. He gave them the privilege of worshiping him and receiving his wonderful promises. ⁵Abraham, Isaac, and Jacob are their ancestors, and Christ himself was an Israelite as far as his human nature is concerned. And he is God, the one who rules over everything and is worthy of eternal praise! Amen.*

⁶Well then, has God failed to fulfill his promise to Israel? No, for not all who are born into the nation of Israel are truly members of God's people! ⁷Being descendants of Abraham doesn't make them truly Abraham's children. For the Scriptures say, "Isaac is the son through whom your descendants will be counted,"* though Abraham had other children, too. ⁸This means that Abraham's physical descendants are not

necessarily children of God. Only the children of the promise are considered to be Abraham's children. 9For God had promised, "I will return about this time next year, and Sarah will have a son."*

10This son was our ancestor Isaac. When he married Rebekah, she gave birth to twins.* 11But before they were born, before they had done anything good or bad, she received a message from God. (This message shows that God chooses people according to his own purposes; 12he calls people, but not according to their good or bad works.) She was told, "Your older son will serve your younger son."* 13In the words of the Scriptures, "I loved Jacob, but I rejected Esau."*

14Are we saying, then, that God was unfair? Of course not! 15For God said to Moses,

"I will show mercy to anyone
    I choose,
and I will show compassion
    to anyone I choose."*

16So it is God who decides to show mercy. We can neither choose it nor work for it.

17For the Scriptures say that God told Pharaoh, "I have appointed you for the very purpose of displaying my power in you and to spread my fame throughout the earth."* 18So you see, God chooses to show mercy to some, and he chooses to harden the hearts of others so they refuse to listen.

19Well then, you might say, "Why does God blame people for not responding? Haven't they simply done what he makes them do?"

20No, don't say that. Who are you, a mere human being, to argue with God? Should the thing that was created say to the one who created it, "Why have you made me like this?" 21When a potter makes jars out of clay, doesn't he have a right to use the same lump of clay to make one jar for decoration and another to throw garbage into? 22In the same way, even though God has the right to show his anger and his power, he is very

patient with those on whom his anger falls, who were made for destruction. 23He does this to make the riches of his glory shine even brighter on those to whom he shows mercy, who were prepared in advance for glory. 24And we are among those whom he selected, both from the Jews and from the Gentiles.

9:3 Greek *my brothers.* 9:4 Greek *chosen for sonship.* 9:5 Or *May God, the one who rules over everything, be praised forever. Amen.* 9:7 Gen 21:12. 9:9 Gen 18:10, 14. 9:10 Greek *she conceived children through this one man.* 9:12 Gen 25:23. 9:13 Mal 1:2-3. 9:15 Exod 33:19. 9:17 Exod 9:16 (Greek version).

PSALM 19:1-14
For the choir director: A psalm of David.

1 The heavens proclaim the glory
        of God.
    The skies display his craftsmanship.
2 Day after day they continue to speak;
        night after night they make
        him known.
3 They speak without a sound or word;
        their voice is never heard.*
4 Yet their message has gone
        throughout the earth,
    and their words to all the world.

    God has made a home in the
        heavens for the sun.
5 It bursts forth like a radiant
        bridegroom after his wedding.
    It rejoices like a great athlete
        eager to run the race.
6 The sun rises at one end of the
        heavens
    and follows its course to the
        other end.
    Nothing can hide from its heat.

7 The instructions of the LORD
        are perfect,
        reviving the soul.
    The decrees of the LORD are
        trustworthy,
        making wise the simple.
8 The commandments of the LORD
        are right,
        bringing joy to the heart.
    The commands of the LORD are clear,
        giving insight for living.
9 Reverence for the LORD is pure,
        lasting forever.

The laws of the LORD are true;
    each one is fair.
[10] They are more desirable than gold,
    even the finest gold.
They are sweeter than honey,
    even honey dripping from
    the comb.
[11] They are a warning to your servant,
    a great reward for those who
    obey them.

[12] How can I know all the sins lurking
    in my heart?
Cleanse me from these hidden
    faults.
[13] Keep your servant from deliberate
    sins!
Don't let them control me.
Then I will be free of guilt
    and innocent of great sin.

[14] May the words of my mouth
    and the meditation of my heart
be pleasing to you,
    O LORD, my rock and my redeemer.

19:3 Or *There is no speech or language where their voice is not heard.*

PROVERBS 20:1

Wine produces mockers; alcohol leads to brawls. Those led astray by drink cannot be wise.

JULY
26

2 CHRONICLES 17:1–18:34

Then Jehoshaphat, Asa's son, became the next king. He strengthened Judah to stand against any attack from Israel. [2]He stationed troops in all the fortified towns of Judah, and he assigned additional garrisons to the land of Judah and to the towns of Ephraim that his father, Asa, had captured.

[3]The LORD was with Jehoshaphat because he followed the example of his father's early years* and did not worship the images of Baal. [4]He sought his father's God and obeyed his commands instead of following the evil practices of the kingdom of Israel. [5]So the LORD established Jehoshaphat's control over the kingdom of Judah. All the people of Judah brought gifts to Jehoshaphat, so he became very wealthy and highly esteemed. [6]He was deeply committed to* the ways of the LORD. He removed the pagan shrines and Asherah poles from Judah.

[7]In the third year of his reign Jehoshaphat sent his officials to teach in all the towns of Judah. These officials included Ben-hail, Obadiah, Zechariah, Nethanel, and Micaiah. [8]He sent Levites along with them, including Shemaiah, Nethaniah, Zebadiah, Asahel, Shemiramoth, Jehonathan, Adonijah, Tobijah, and Tobadonijah. He also sent out the priests Elishama and Jehoram. [9]They took copies of the Book of the Law of the LORD and traveled around through all the towns of Judah, teaching the people.

[10]Then the fear of the LORD fell over all the surrounding kingdoms so that none of them wanted to declare war on Jehoshaphat. [11]Some of the Philistines brought him gifts and silver as tribute, and the Arabs brought 7,700 rams and 7,700 male goats.

[12]So Jehoshaphat became more and more powerful and built fortresses and storage cities throughout Judah. [13]He stored numerous supplies in Judah's towns and stationed an army of seasoned troops at Jerusalem. [14]His army was enrolled according to ancestral clans.

From Judah there were 300,000
    troops organized in units of 1,000,
    under the command of Adnah.
[15]Next in command was Jehohanan,
    who commanded 280,000 troops.
[16]Next was Amasiah son of Zicri,
    who volunteered for the LORD's
    service, with 200,000 troops under
    his command.
[17]From Benjamin there were 200,000
    troops equipped with bows and
    shields. They were under the

command of Eliada, a veteran soldier. [18]Next in command was Jehozabad, who commanded 180,000 armed men.

[19]These were the troops stationed in Jerusalem to serve the king, besides those Jehoshaphat stationed in the fortified towns throughout Judah.

[18:1]JEHOSHAPHAT enjoyed great riches and high esteem, and he made an alliance with Ahab of Israel by having his son marry Ahab's daughter. [2]A few years later he went to Samaria to visit Ahab, who prepared a great banquet for him and his officials. They butchered great numbers of sheep, goats, and cattle for the feast. Then Ahab enticed Jehoshaphat to join forces with him to recover Ramoth-gilead.

[3]"Will you go with me to Ramoth-gilead?" King Ahab of Israel asked King Jehoshaphat of Judah.

Jehoshaphat replied, "Why, of course! You and I are as one, and my troops are your troops. We will certainly join you in battle." [4]Then Jehoshaphat added, "But first let's find out what the LORD says."

[5]So the king of Israel summoned the prophets, 400 of them, and asked them, "Should we go to war against Ramoth-gilead, or should I hold back?"

They all replied, "Yes, go right ahead! God will give the king victory."

[6]But Jehoshaphat asked, "Is there not also a prophet of the LORD here? We should ask him the same question."

[7]The king of Israel replied to Jehoshaphat, "There is one more man who could consult the LORD for us, but I hate him. He never prophesies anything but trouble for me! His name is Micaiah son of Imlah."

Jehoshaphat replied, "That's not the way a king should talk! Let's hear what he has to say."

[8]So the king of Israel called one of his officials and said, "Quick! Bring Micaiah son of Imlah."

[9]King Ahab of Israel and King Jehoshaphat of Judah, dressed in their royal robes, were sitting on thrones at the threshing floor near the gate of Samaria. All of Ahab's prophets were prophesying there in front of them. [10]One of them, Zedekiah son of Kenaanah, made some iron horns and proclaimed, "This is what the LORD says: With these horns you will gore the Arameans to death!"

[11]All the other prophets agreed. "Yes," they said, "go up to Ramoth-gilead and be victorious, for the LORD will give the king victory!"

[12]Meanwhile, the messenger who went to get Micaiah said to him, "Look, all the prophets are promising victory for the king. Be sure that you agree with them and promise success."

[13]But Micaiah replied, "As surely as the LORD lives, I will say only what my God says."

[14]When Micaiah arrived before the king, Ahab asked him, "Micaiah, should we go to war against Ramoth-gilead, or should I hold back?"

Micaiah replied sarcastically, "Yes, go up and be victorious, for you will have victory over them!"

[15]But the king replied sharply, "How many times must I demand that you speak only the truth to me when you speak for the LORD?"

[16]Then Micaiah told him, "In a vision I saw all Israel scattered on the mountains, like sheep without a shepherd. And the LORD said, 'Their master has been killed.* Send them home in peace.'"

[17]"Didn't I tell you?" the king of Israel exclaimed to Jehoshaphat. "He never prophesies anything but trouble for me."

[18]Then Micaiah continued, "Listen to what the LORD says! I saw the LORD sitting on his throne with all the armies of heaven around him, on his right and on his left. [19]And the LORD said, 'Who can entice King Ahab of Israel to go into battle against Ramoth-gilead so he can be killed?'

"There were many suggestions, [20]and finally a spirit approached the LORD and said, 'I can do it!'

"'How will you do this?' the LORD asked.

²¹"And the spirit replied, 'I will go out and inspire all of Ahab's prophets to speak lies.'

"'You will succeed,' said the Lord. 'Go ahead and do it.'

²²"So you see, the Lord has put a lying spirit in the mouths of your prophets. For the Lord has pronounced your doom."

²³Then Zedekiah son of Kenaanah walked up to Micaiah and slapped him across the face. "Since when did the Spirit of the Lord leave me to speak to you?" he demanded.

²⁴And Micaiah replied, "You will find out soon enough when you are trying to hide in some secret room!"

²⁵"Arrest him!" the king of Israel ordered. "Take him back to Amon, the governor of the city, and to my son Joash. ²⁶Give them this order from the king: 'Put this man in prison, and feed him nothing but bread and water until I return safely from the battle!'"

²⁷But Micaiah replied, "If you return safely, it will mean that the Lord has not spoken through me!" Then he added to those standing around, "Everyone mark my words!"

²⁸So King Ahab of Israel and King Jehoshaphat of Judah led their armies against Ramoth-gilead. ²⁹The king of Israel said to Jehoshaphat, "As we go into battle, I will disguise myself so no one will recognize me, but you wear your royal robes." So the king of Israel disguised himself, and they went into battle.

³⁰Meanwhile, the king of Aram had issued these orders to his chariot commanders: "Attack only the king of Israel! Don't bother with anyone else." ³¹So when the Aramean chariot commanders saw Jehoshaphat in his royal robes, they went after him. "There is the king of Israel!" they shouted. But Jehoshaphat called out and the Lord saved him. God helped him by turning the attackers away from him. ³²As soon as the chariot commanders realized he was not the king of Israel, they stopped chasing him.

³³An Aramean soldier, however, randomly shot an arrow at the Israelite troops and hit the king of Israel between the joints of his armor. "Turn the horses* and get me out of here!" Ahab groaned to the driver of the chariot. "I'm badly wounded!"

³⁴The battle raged all that day, and the king of Israel propped himself up in his chariot facing the Arameans. In the evening, just as the sun was setting, he died.

17:3 Some Hebrew manuscripts read *the example of his father, David.*   17:6 Hebrew *His heart was courageous in.*   18:16 Hebrew *These people have no master.*   18:33 Hebrew *Turn your hand.*

ROMANS 9:25–10:13

Concerning the Gentiles, God says in the prophecy of Hosea,

"Those who were not my people,
    I will now call my people.
And I will love those
    whom I did not love before."*

²⁶And,

"Then, at the place where they
    were told,
    'You are not my people,'
there they will be called
    'children of the living God.'"*

²⁷And concerning Israel, Isaiah the prophet cried out,

"Though the people of Israel are as
    numerous as the sand of the
    seashore,
only a remnant will be saved.
²⁸ For the Lord will carry out his
    sentence upon the earth
    quickly and with finality."*

²⁹And Isaiah said the same thing in another place:

"If the Lord of Heaven's Armies
    had not spared a few of our
    children,
we would have been wiped out like
    Sodom,
    destroyed like Gomorrah."*

³⁰What does all this mean? Even though the Gentiles were not trying to follow God's standards, they were made right with God. And it was by faith that

this took place. [31]But the people of Israel, who tried so hard to get right with God by keeping the law, never succeeded. [32]Why not? Because they were trying to get right with God by keeping the law* instead of by trusting in him. They stumbled over the great rock in their path. [33]God warned them of this in the Scriptures when he said,

"I am placing a stone in Jerusalem*
    that makes people stumble,
a rock that makes them fall.
But anyone who trusts in him
    will never be disgraced."*

[10:1]DEAR brothers and sisters,* the longing of my heart and my prayer to God is for the people of Israel to be saved. [2]I know what enthusiasm they have for God, but it is misdirected zeal. [3]For they don't understand God's way of making people right with himself. Refusing to accept God's way, they cling to their own way of getting right with God by trying to keep the law. [4]For Christ has already accomplished the purpose for which the law was given.* As a result, all who believe in him are made right with God.

[5]For Moses writes that the law's way of making a person right with God requires obedience to all of its commands.* [6]But faith's way of getting right with God says, "Don't say in your heart, 'Who will go up to heaven' (to bring Christ down to earth). [7]And don't say, 'Who will go down to the place of the dead' (to bring Christ back to life again)." [8]In fact, it says,

"The message is very close at hand;
    it is on your lips and in your
    heart."*

And that message is the very message about faith that we preach: [9]**If you confess with your mouth that Jesus is Lord and believe in your heart that God raised him from the dead, you will be saved.** [10]For it is by believing in your heart that you are made right with God, and it is by confessing with your mouth that you are saved. [11]As the

Scriptures tell us, "Anyone who trusts in him will never be disgraced.*" [12]Jew and Gentile* are the same in this respect. They have the same Lord, who gives generously to all who call on him. [13]For "Everyone who calls on the name of the LORD will be saved."*

9:25 Hos 2:23.   9:26 Greek *sons of the living God.* Hos 1:10.   9:27-28 Isa 10:22-23 (Greek version). 9:29 Isa 1:9.   9:32 Greek *by works.*   9:33a Greek *in Zion.* 9:33b Isa 8:14; 28:16 (Greek version).   10:1 Greek *Brothers.*   10:4 Or *For Christ is the end of the law.* 10:5 See Lev 18:5.   10:6-8 Deut 30:12-14.   10:11 Isa 28:16 (Greek version).   10:12 Greek *and Greek.* 10:13 Joel 2:32.

PSALM 20:1-9
For the choir director: A psalm of David.

[1] In times of trouble, may the
        LORD answer your cry.
    May the name of the God
        of Jacob keep you safe
        from all harm.
[2] May he send you help from his
        sanctuary
    and strengthen you from
        Jerusalem.*
[3] May he remember all your gifts
    and look favorably on your burnt
        offerings.   *Interlude*

[4] May he grant your heart's
        desires
    and make all your plans
        succeed.
[5] May we shout for joy when we hear
        of your victory
    and raise a victory banner in the
        name of our God.
    May the LORD answer all your
        prayers.

[6] Now I know that the LORD rescues
        his anointed king.
    He will answer him from his
        holy heaven
    and rescue him by his great
        power.
[7] Some nations boast of their
        chariots and horses,
    but we boast in the name
        of the LORD our God.
[8] Those nations will fall down
        and collapse,

but we will rise up and stand
firm.

⁹ Give victory to our king, O LORD!
Answer our cry for help.

20:2 Hebrew *Zion*.

PROVERBS 20:2-3
The king's fury is like a lion's roar; to
rouse his anger is to risk your life.
□ Avoiding a fight is a mark of honor;
only fools insist on quarreling.

JULY 27

2 CHRONICLES 19:1–20:37
When King Jehoshaphat of Judah arrived safely home in Jerusalem, ²Jehu
son of Hanani the seer went out to meet
him. "Why should you help the wicked
and love those who hate the LORD?" he
asked the king. "Because of what you
have done, the LORD is very angry with
you. ³Even so, there is some good in you,
for you have removed the Asherah
poles throughout the land, and you have
committed yourself to seeking God."

⁴Jehoshaphat lived in Jerusalem, but
he went out among the people, traveling
from Beersheba to the hill country of
Ephraim, encouraging the people to return to the LORD, the God of their ancestors. ⁵He appointed judges throughout
the nation in all the fortified towns,
⁶and he said to them, "Always think
carefully before pronouncing judgment. Remember that you do not judge
to please people but to please the LORD.
He will be with you when you render the
verdict in each case. ⁷Fear the LORD and
judge with integrity, for the LORD our
God does not tolerate perverted justice,
partiality, or the taking of bribes."

⁸In Jerusalem, Jehoshaphat appointed
some of the Levites and priests and clan
leaders in Israel to serve as judges for
cases involving the LORD's regulations
and for civil disputes. ⁹These were his instructions to them: "You must always act
in the fear of the LORD, with faithfulness
and an undivided heart. ¹⁰Whenever a
case comes to you from fellow citizens in
an outlying town, whether a murder case
or some other violation of God's laws,
commands, decrees, or regulations, you
must warn them not to sin against the
LORD, so that he will not be angry with
you and them. Do this and you will not be
guilty.
¹¹"Amariah the high priest will have
final say in all cases involving the LORD.
Zebadiah son of Ishmael, a leader from
the tribe of Judah, will have final say in
all civil cases. The Levites will assist you
in making sure that justice is served.
Take courage as you fulfill your duties,
and may the LORD be with those who do
what is right."

²⁰:¹AFTER this, the armies of the Moabites, Ammonites, and some of the Meunites* declared war on Jehoshaphat.
²Messengers came and told Jehoshaphat, "A vast army from Edom* is
marching against you from beyond
the Dead Sea.* They are already at
Hazazon-tamar." (This was another name
for En-gedi.)

³Jehoshaphat was terrified by this
news and begged the LORD for guidance. He also ordered everyone in Judah
to begin fasting. ⁴So people from all the
towns of Judah came to Jerusalem to
seek the LORD's help.

⁵Jehoshaphat stood before the community of Judah and Jerusalem in front
of the new courtyard at the Temple of
the LORD. ⁶He prayed, "O LORD, God of
our ancestors, you alone are the God
who is in heaven. You are ruler of all the
kingdoms of the earth. You are powerful and mighty; no one can stand against
you! ⁷O our God, did you not drive out
those who lived in this land when your
people Israel arrived? And did you not
give this land forever to the descendants of your friend Abraham? ⁸Your
people settled here and built this Tem-

ple to honor your name. ⁹They said, 'Whenever we are faced with any calamity such as war,* plague, or famine, we can come to stand in your presence before this Temple where your name is honored. We can cry out to you to save us, and you will hear us and rescue us.'

¹⁰"And now see what the armies of Ammon, Moab, and Mount Seir are doing. You would not let our ancestors invade those nations when Israel left Egypt, so they went around them and did not destroy them. ¹¹Now see how they reward us! For they have come to throw us out of your land, which you gave us as an inheritance. ¹²O our God, won't you stop them? We are powerless against this mighty army that is about to attack us. We do not know what to do, but we are looking to you for help."

¹³As all the men of Judah stood before the LORD with their little ones, wives, and children, ¹⁴the Spirit of the LORD came upon one of the men standing there. His name was Jahaziel son of Zechariah, son of Benaiah, son of Jeiel, son of Mattaniah, a Levite who was a descendant of Asaph.

¹⁵He said, "Listen, all you people of Judah and Jerusalem! Listen, King Jehoshaphat! This is what the LORD says: Do not be afraid! Don't be discouraged by this mighty army, for the battle is not yours, but God's. ¹⁶Tomorrow, march out against them. You will find them coming up through the ascent of Ziz at the end of the valley that opens into the wilderness of Jeruel. ¹⁷But you will not even need to fight. Take your positions; then stand still and watch the LORD's victory. He is with you, O people of Judah and Jerusalem. Do not be afraid or discouraged. Go out against them tomorrow, for the LORD is with you!"

¹⁸Then King Jehoshaphat bowed low with his face to the ground. And all the people of Judah and Jerusalem did the same, worshiping the LORD. ¹⁹Then the Levites from the clans of Kohath and Korah stood to praise the LORD, the God of Israel, with a very loud shout.

²⁰Early the next morning the army of Judah went out into the wilderness of Tekoa. On the way Jehoshaphat stopped and said, "Listen to me, all you people of Judah and Jerusalem! Believe in the LORD your God, and you will be able to stand firm. Believe in his prophets, and you will succeed."

²¹After consulting the people, the king appointed singers to walk ahead of the army, singing to the LORD and praising him for his holy splendor. This is what they sang:

"Give thanks to the LORD;
    his faithful love endures forever!"

²²At the very moment they began to sing and give praise, the LORD caused the armies of Ammon, Moab, and Mount Seir to start fighting among themselves. ²³The armies of Moab and Ammon turned against their allies from Mount Seir and killed every one of them. After they had destroyed the army of Seir, they began attacking each other. ²⁴So when the army of Judah arrived at the lookout point in the wilderness, all they saw were dead bodies lying on the ground as far as they could see. Not a single one of the enemy had escaped.

²⁵King Jehoshaphat and his men went out to gather the plunder. They found vast amounts of equipment, clothing,* and other valuables—more than they could carry. There was so much plunder that it took three days just to collect it all! ²⁶On the fourth day they gathered in the Valley of Blessing,* which got its name that day because the people praised and thanked the LORD there. It is still called the Valley of Blessing today.

²⁷Then all the men returned to Jerusalem, with Jehoshaphat leading them, overjoyed that the LORD had given them victory over their enemies. ²⁸They marched into Jerusalem to the music of harps, lyres, and trumpets, and they proceeded to the Temple of the LORD.

²⁹When all the surrounding kingdoms heard that the LORD himself had fought against the enemies of Israel, the

fear of God came over them. [30]So Jehoshaphat's kingdom was at peace, for his God had given him rest on every side.

[31]So Jehoshaphat ruled over the land of Judah. He was thirty-five years old when he became king, and he reigned in Jerusalem twenty-five years. His mother was Azubah, the daughter of Shilhi.

[32]Jehoshaphat was a good king, following the ways of his father, Asa. He did what was pleasing in the LORD's sight. [33]During his reign, however, he failed to remove all the pagan shrines, and the people never fully committed themselves to follow the God of their ancestors.

[34]The rest of the events of Jehoshaphat's reign, from beginning to end, are recorded in *The Record of Jehu Son of Hanani,* which is included in *The Book of the Kings of Israel.*

[35]Some time later King Jehoshaphat of Judah made an alliance with King Ahaziah of Israel, who was very wicked.* [36]Together they built a fleet of trading ships* at the port of Ezion-geber. [37]Then Eliezer son of Dodavahu from Mareshah prophesied against Jehoshaphat. He said, "Because you have allied yourself with King Ahaziah, the LORD will destroy your work." So the ships met with disaster and never put out to sea.*

20:1 As in some Greek manuscripts (see also 26:7); Hebrew repeats *Ammonites.*   20:2a As in one Hebrew manuscript; most Hebrew manuscripts and ancient versions read *Aram.*   20:2b Hebrew *the sea.*   20:9 Or *sword of judgment;* or *sword, judgment.*   20:25 As in some Hebrew manuscripts and Latin Vulgate; most Hebrew manuscripts read *corpses.*   20:26 Hebrew *valley of Beracah.*   20:35 Or *who made him do what was wicked.*   20:36 Hebrew *fleet of ships that could go to Tarshish.*   20:37 Hebrew *never set sail for Tarshish.*

ROMANS 10:14–11:12

But how can they call on him to save them unless they believe in him? And how can they believe in him if they have never heard about him? And how can they hear about him unless someone tells them? [15]And how will anyone go and tell them without being sent? That is why the Scriptures say, "How beautiful are the feet of messengers who bring good news!"*

[16]But not everyone welcomes the Good News, for Isaiah the prophet said, "LORD, who has believed our message?"* [17]**So faith comes from hearing, that is, hearing the Good News about Christ.** [18]But I ask, have the people of Israel actually heard the message? Yes, they have:

"The message has gone throughout
    the earth,
  and the words to all the world."*

[19]But I ask, did the people of Israel really understand? Yes, they did, for even in the time of Moses, God said,

"I will rouse your jealousy through
    people who are not even
    a nation.
  I will provoke your anger through
    the foolish Gentiles."*

[20]And later Isaiah spoke boldly for God, saying,

"I was found by people who were
    not looking for me.
  I showed myself to those who
    were not asking for me."*

[21]But regarding Israel, God said,

"All day long I opened my arms
    to them,
  but they were disobedient and
    rebellious."*

11:1I ASK, then, has God rejected his own people, the nation of Israel? Of course not! I myself am an Israelite, a descendant of Abraham and a member of the tribe of Benjamin.

[2]No, God has not rejected his own people, whom he chose from the very beginning. Do you realize what the Scriptures say about this? Elijah the prophet complained to God about the people of Israel and said, [3]"LORD, they have killed your prophets and torn down your altars. I am the only one left, and now they are trying to kill me, too."*

[4]And do you remember God's reply? He said, "No, I have 7,000 others who have never bowed down to Baal!"*

[5]It is the same today, for a few of the

people of Israel* have remained faithful because of God's grace—his undeserved kindness in choosing them. ⁶And since it is through God's kindness, then it is not by their good works. For in that case, God's grace would not be what it really is—free and undeserved.

⁷So this is the situation: Most of the people of Israel have not found the favor of God they are looking for so earnestly. A few have—the ones God has chosen—but the hearts of the rest were hardened. ⁸As the Scriptures say,

"God has put them into a deep sleep. To this day he has shut their eyes so they do not see,
and closed their ears so they do not hear."*

⁹Likewise, David said,

"Let their bountiful table become a snare,
a trap that makes them think all is well.
Let their blessings cause them to stumble,
and let them get what they deserve.
¹⁰ Let their eyes go blind so they cannot see,
and let their backs be bent forever."*

¹¹Did God's people stumble and fall beyond recovery? Of course not! They were disobedient, so God made salvation available to the Gentiles. But he wanted his own people to become jealous and claim it for themselves. ¹²Now if the Gentiles were enriched because the people of Israel turned down God's offer of salvation, think how much greater a blessing the world will share when they finally accept it.

10:15 Isa 52:7.   10:16 Isa 53:1.   10:18 Ps 19:4.
10:19 Deut 32:21.   10:20 Isa 65:1 (Greek version).
10:21 Isa 65:2 (Greek version).   11:3 1 Kgs 19:10, 14.
11:4 1 Kgs 19:18.   11:5 Greek *for a remnant.*   11:8 Isa
29:10; Deut 29:4.   11:9-10 Ps 69:22-23 (Greek version).

PSALM 21:1-13
For the choir director: A psalm of David.

¹ **H**ow the king rejoices in your strength, O LORD!

He shouts with joy because you give him victory.
² For you have given him his heart's desire;
you have withheld nothing he requested.   *Interlude*

³ You welcomed him back with success and prosperity.
You placed a crown of finest gold on his head.
⁴ He asked you to preserve his life, and you granted his request.
The days of his life stretch on forever.
⁵ Your victory brings him great honor, and you have clothed him with splendor and majesty.
⁶ You have endowed him with eternal blessings
and given him the joy of your presence.
⁷ For the king trusts in the LORD.
The unfailing love of the Most High will keep him from stumbling.

⁸ You will capture all your enemies. Your strong right hand will seize all who hate you.
⁹ You will throw them in a flaming furnace
when you appear.
The LORD will consume them in his anger;
fire will devour them.
¹⁰ You will wipe their children from the face of the earth;
they will never have descendants.
¹¹ Although they plot against you, their evil schemes will never succeed.
¹² For they will turn and run
when they see your arrows aimed at them.
¹³ Rise up, O LORD, in all your power. With music and singing we celebrate your mighty acts.

PROVERBS 20:4-6
Those too lazy to plow in the right season will have no food at the harvest.
□ Though good advice lies deep within

the heart, a person with understanding will draw it out. □ Many will say they are loyal friends, but who can find one who is truly reliable?

JULY 28

2 CHRONICLES 21:1–23:21

When Jehoshaphat died, he was buried with his ancestors in the City of David. Then his son Jehoram became the next king.

2Jehoram's brothers—the other sons of Jehoshaphat—were Azariah, Jehiel, Zechariah, Azariahu, Michael, and Shephatiah; all these were the sons of Jehoshaphat king of Judah.* 3Their father had given each of them valuable gifts of silver, gold, and costly items, and also some of Judah's fortified towns. However, he designated Jehoram as the next king because he was the oldest. 4But when Jehoram had become solidly established as king, he killed all his brothers and some of the other leaders of Judah.

5Jehoram was thirty-two years old when he became king, and he reigned in Jerusalem eight years. 6But Jehoram followed the example of the kings of Israel and was as wicked as King Ahab, for he had married one of Ahab's daughters. So Jehoram did what was evil in the LORD's sight. 7But the LORD did not want to destroy David's dynasty, for he had made a covenant with David and promised that his descendants would continue to rule, shining like a lamp forever.

8During Jehoram's reign, the Edomites revolted against Judah and crowned their own king. 9So Jehoram went out with his full army and all his chariots. The Edomites surrounded him and his chariot commanders, but he went out at night

and attacked them* under cover of darkness. 10Even so, Edom has been independent from Judah to this day. The town of Libnah also revolted about that same time. All this happened because Jehoram had abandoned the LORD, the God of his ancestors. 11He had built pagan shrines in the hill country of Judah and had led the people of Jerusalem and Judah to give themselves to pagan gods and to go astray.

12Then Elijah the prophet wrote Jehoram this letter:

"This is what the LORD, the God of your ancestor David, says: You have not followed the good example of your father, Jehoshaphat, or your grandfather King Asa of Judah. 13Instead, you have been as evil as the kings of Israel. You have led the people of Jerusalem and Judah to worship idols, just as King Ahab did in Israel. And you have even killed your own brothers, men who were better than you. 14So now the LORD is about to strike you, your people, your children, your wives, and all that is yours with a heavy blow. 15You yourself will suffer with a severe intestinal disease that will get worse each day until your bowels come out."

16Then the LORD stirred up the Philistines and the Arabs, who lived near the Ethiopians,* to attack Jehoram. 17They marched against Judah, broke down its defenses, and carried away everything of value in the royal palace, including the king's sons and his wives. Only his youngest son, Ahaziah,* was spared.

18After all this, the LORD struck Jehoram with the severe intestinal disease. 19The disease grew worse and worse, and at the end of two years it caused his bowels to come out, and he died in agony. His people did not build a great funeral fire to honor him as they had done for his ancestors.

20Jehoram was thirty-two years old when he became king, and he reigned in

Jerusalem eight years. No one was sorry when he died. They buried him in the City of David, but not in the royal cemetery.

22:1THEN the people of Jerusalem made Ahaziah, Jehoram's youngest son, their next king, since the marauding bands who came with the Arabs* had killed all the older sons. So Ahaziah son of Jehoram reigned as king of Judah.

2Ahaziah was twenty-two* years old when he became king, and he reigned in Jerusalem one year. His mother was Athaliah, a granddaughter of King Omri. 3Ahaziah also followed the evil example of King Ahab's family, for his mother encouraged him in doing wrong. 4He did what was evil in the LORD's sight, just as Ahab's family had done. They even became his advisers after the death of his father, and they led him to ruin.

5Following their evil advice, Ahaziah joined King Joram,* the son of King Ahab of Israel, in his war against King Hazael of Aram at Ramoth-gilead. When the Arameans wounded Joram in the battle, 6he returned to Jezreel to recover from the wounds he had received at Ramoth.* Because Joram was wounded, King Ahaziah* of Judah went to Jezreel to visit him.

7But God had decided that this visit would be Ahaziah's downfall. While he was there, Ahaziah went out with Joram to meet Jehu son of Nimshi, whom the LORD had appointed to destroy the dynasty of Ahab.

8While Jehu was executing judgment against the family of Ahab, he happened to meet some of Judah's officials and Ahaziah's relatives* who were traveling with Ahaziah. So Jehu killed them all. 9Then Jehu's men searched for Ahaziah, and they found him hiding in the city of Samaria. They brought him to Jehu, who killed him. Ahaziah was given a decent burial because the people said, "He was the grandson of Jehoshaphat—a man who sought the LORD with all his heart." But none of the

surviving members of Ahaziah's family was capable of ruling the kingdom.

10When Athaliah, the mother of King Ahaziah of Judah, learned that her son was dead, she began to destroy the rest of Judah's royal family. 11But Ahaziah's sister Jehosheba,* the daughter of King Jehoram, took Ahaziah's infant son, Joash, and stole him away from among the rest of the king's children, who were about to be killed. She put Joash and his nurse in a bedroom. In this way, Jehosheba, wife of Jehoiada the priest and sister of Ahaziah, hid the child so that Athaliah could not murder him. 12Joash remained hidden in the Temple of God for six years while Athaliah ruled over the land.

23:1IN the seventh year of Athaliah's reign, Jehoiada the priest decided to act. He summoned his courage and made a pact with five army commanders: Azariah son of Jeroham, Ishmael son of Jehohanan, Azariah son of Obed, Maaseiah son of Adaiah, and Elishaphat son of Zicri. 2These men traveled secretly throughout Judah and summoned the Levites and clan leaders in all the towns to come to Jerusalem. 3They all gathered at the Temple of God, where they made a solemn pact with Joash, the young king.

Jehoiada said to them, "Here is the king's son! The time has come for him to reign! The LORD has promised that a descendant of David will be our king. 4This is what you must do. When you priests and Levites come on duty on the Sabbath, a third of you will serve as gatekeepers. 5Another third will go over to the royal palace, and the final third will be at the Foundation Gate. Everyone else should stay in the courtyards of the LORD's Temple. 6Remember, only the priests and Levites on duty may enter the Temple of the LORD, for they are set apart as holy. The rest of the people must obey the LORD's instructions and stay outside. 7You Levites, form a bodyguard around the king and keep your weapons in hand. Kill anyone who tries to enter the Temple. Stay with the king wherever he goes."

8So the Levites and all the people of Judah did everything as Jehoiada the priest ordered. The commanders took charge of the men reporting for duty that Sabbath, as well as those who were going off duty. Jehoiada the priest did not let anyone go home after their shift ended. 9Then Jehoiada supplied the commanders with the spears and the large and small shields that had once belonged to King David and were stored in the Temple of God. 10He stationed all the people around the king, with their weapons ready. They formed a line from the south side of the Temple around to the north side and all around the altar.

11Then Jehoiada and his sons brought out Joash, the king's son, placed the crown on his head, and presented him with a copy of God's laws.* They anointed him and proclaimed him king, and everyone shouted, "Long live the king!"

12When Athaliah heard the noise of the people running and the shouts of praise to the king, she hurried to the LORD's Temple to see what was happening. 13When she arrived, she saw the newly crowned king standing in his place of authority by the pillar at the Temple entrance. The commanders and trumpeters were surrounding him, and people from all over the land were rejoicing and blowing trumpets. Singers with musical instruments were leading the people in a great celebration. When Athaliah saw all this, she tore her clothes in despair and shouted, "Treason! Treason!"

14Then Jehoiada the priest ordered the commanders who were in charge of the troops, "Take her to the soldiers in front of the Temple,* and kill anyone who tries to rescue her." For the priest had said, "She must not be killed in the Temple of the LORD." 15So they seized her and led her out to the entrance of the Horse Gate on the palace grounds, and they killed her there.

16Then Jehoiada made a covenant between himself and the king and the people that they would be the LORD's people.

17And all the people went over to the temple of Baal and tore it down. They demolished the altars and smashed the idols, and they killed Mattan the priest of Baal in front of the altars.

18Jehoiada now put the priests and Levites in charge of the Temple of the LORD, following all the directions given by David. He also commanded them to present burnt offerings to the LORD, as prescribed by the Law of Moses, and to sing and rejoice as David had instructed. 19He also stationed gatekeepers at the gates of the LORD's Temple to keep out those who for any reason were ceremonially unclean.

20Then the commanders, nobles, rulers, and all the people of the land escorted the king from the Temple of the LORD. They went through the upper gate and into the palace, and they seated the king on the royal throne. 21So all the people of the land rejoiced, and the city was peaceful because Athaliah had been killed.

21:2 Hebrew *of Israel;* also in 21:4. The author of Chronicles sees Judah as representative of the true Israel. See also some Hebrew manuscripts, Greek and Syriac versions, and Latin Vulgate.   21:9 Or *he went out and escaped.* The meaning of the Hebrew is uncertain.   21:16 Hebrew *the Cushites.* 21:17 Hebrew *Jehoahaz,* a variant spelling of Ahaziah; compare 22:1.   22:1 Or *marauding bands of Arabs.* 22:2 As in some Greek manuscripts and Syriac version (see also 2 Kgs 8:26); Hebrew reads *forty-two.*   22:5 Hebrew *Jehoram,* a variant spelling of Joram; also in 22:6, 7. 22:6a Hebrew *Ramah,* a variant spelling of Ramoth. 22:6b As in some Hebrew manuscripts, Greek and Syriac versions, and Latin Vulgate (see also 2 Kgs 8:29); most Hebrew manuscripts read *Azariah.*   22:8 As in Greek version (see also 2 Kgs 10:13); Hebrew reads *and sons of the brothers of Ahaziah.*   22:11 As in parallel text at 2 Kgs 11:2; Hebrew omits *Ahaziah's sister* and reads *Jehoshabeath* [a variant spelling of Jehosheba].   23:11 Or *a copy of the covenant.*   23:14 Or *Bring her out from between the ranks;* or *Take her out of the Temple precincts.* The meaning of the Hebrew is uncertain.

ROMANS 11:13-36

I [Paul] am saying all this especially for you Gentiles. God has appointed me as the apostle to the Gentiles. I stress this, 14for I want somehow to make the people of Israel jealous of what you Gentiles have, so I might save some of them. 15For since their rejection meant that God offered salvation to the rest of the world, their acceptance will be even more wonderful. It will be life for those who were dead! [16]And since Abraham and the other patriarchs were holy, their descendants will also be holy—just as the entire batch of dough is holy because the portion given as an offering is holy. For if the roots of the tree are holy, the branches will be, too.

[17]But some of these branches from Abraham's tree—some of the people of Israel—have been broken off. And you Gentiles, who were branches from a wild olive tree, have been grafted in. So now you also receive the blessing God has promised Abraham and his children, sharing in the rich nourishment from the root of God's special olive tree. [18]But you must not brag about being grafted in to replace the branches that were broken off. You are just a branch, not the root.

[19]"Well," you may say, "those branches were broken off to make room for me." [20]Yes, but remember—those branches were broken off because they didn't believe in Christ, and you are there because you do believe. So don't think highly of yourself, but fear what could happen. [21]For if God did not spare the original branches, he won't* spare you either.

[22]Notice how God is both kind and severe. He is severe toward those who disobeyed, but kind to you if you continue to trust in his kindness. But if you stop trusting, you also will be cut off. [23]And if the people of Israel turn from their unbelief, they will be grafted in again, for God has the power to graft them back into the tree. [24]You, by nature, were a branch cut from a wild olive tree. So if God was willing to do something contrary to nature by grafting you into his cultivated tree, he will be far more eager to graft the original branches back into the tree where they belong.

[25]I want you to understand this mystery, dear brothers and sisters,* so that you will not feel proud about yourselves. Some of the people of Israel have hard hearts, but this will last only until the full number of Gentiles comes to Christ. [26]And so all Israel will be saved. As the Scriptures say,

"The one who rescues will come
    from Jerusalem,*
and he will turn Israel* away
    from ungodliness.
[27] And this is my covenant with them,
    that I will take away their sins."*

[28]Many of the people of Israel are now enemies of the Good News, and this benefits you Gentiles. Yet they are still the people he loves because he chose their ancestors Abraham, Isaac, and Jacob. [29]For God's gifts and his call can never be withdrawn. [30]Once, you Gentiles were rebels against God, but when the people of Israel rebelled against him, God was merciful to you instead. [31]Now they are the rebels, and God's mercy has come to you so that they, too, will share* in God's mercy. [32]For God has imprisoned everyone in disobedience so he could have mercy on everyone.

[33]**Oh, how great are God's riches and wisdom and knowledge! How impossible it is for us to understand his decisions and his ways!**

[34] For who can know the LORD's
        thoughts?
    Who knows enough to give
        him advice?*
[35] And who has given him so much
        that he needs to pay it back?*

[36]For everything comes from him and exists by his power and is intended for his glory. All glory to him forever! Amen.

11:21 Some manuscripts read *perhaps he won't.*
11:25 Greek *brothers.*   11:26a Greek *from Zion.*
11:26b Greek *Jacob.*   11:26-27 Isa 59:20-21; 27:9 (Greek version).   11:31 Other manuscripts read *will now share;* still others read *will someday share.*   11:34 Isa 40:13 (Greek version).   11:35 See Job 41:11.

PSALM 22:1-18
For the choir director: A psalm of David, to be sung to the tune "Doe of the Dawn."

[1] **M**y God, my God, why have you
        abandoned me?
    Why are you so far away when
        I groan for help?
[2] Every day I call to you, my God, but
        you do not answer.

Every night you hear my voice,
but I find no relief.

³ Yet you are holy,
enthroned on the praises of
Israel.
⁴ Our ancestors trusted in you,
and you rescued them.
⁵ They cried out to you and were
saved.
They trusted in you and were
never disgraced.

⁶ But I am a worm and not a man.
I am scorned and despised by all!
⁷ Everyone who sees me mocks me.
They sneer and shake their heads,
saying,
⁸ "Is this the one who relies on the
LORD?
Then let the LORD save him!
If the LORD loves him so much,
let the LORD rescue him!"

⁹ Yet you brought me safely from
my mother's womb
and led me to trust you at my
mother's breast.
¹⁰ I was thrust into your arms at
my birth.
You have been my God from the
moment I was born.

¹¹ Do not stay so far from me,
for trouble is near,
and no one else can help me.
¹² My enemies surround me like
a herd of bulls;
fierce bulls of Bashan have
hemmed me in!
¹³ Like lions they open their jaws
against me,
roaring and tearing into their
prey.
¹⁴ My life is poured out like water,
and all my bones are out of joint.
My heart is like wax,
melting within me.
¹⁵ My strength has dried up like
sunbaked clay.
My tongue sticks to the roof of my
mouth.
You have laid me in the dust and
left me for dead.

¹⁶ My enemies surround me like a pack
of dogs;
an evil gang closes in on me.
They have pierced my hands and
feet.
¹⁷ I can count all my bones.
My enemies stare at me and gloat.
¹⁸ They divide my garments among
themselves
and throw dice* for my clothing.

22:18 Hebrew *cast lots.*

PROVERBS 20:7
The godly walk with integrity; blessed
are their children who follow them.

JULY
29

2 CHRONICLES 24:1–25:28
Joash was seven years old when he became king, and he reigned in Jerusalem
forty years. His mother was Zibiah from
Beersheba. ²Joash did what was pleasing in the LORD's sight throughout the
lifetime of Jehoiada the priest. ³Jehoia-
da chose two wives for Joash, and he
had sons and daughters.

⁴At one point Joash decided to repair
and restore the Temple of the LORD.
⁵He summoned the priests and Levites
and gave them these instructions: "Go
to all the towns of Judah and collect the
required annual offerings, so that we
can repair the Temple of your God. Do
not delay!" But the Levites did not act
immediately.

⁶So the king called for Jehoiada the
high priest and asked him, "Why
haven't you demanded that the Levites
go out and collect the Temple taxes
from the towns of Judah and from Jerusalem? Moses, the servant of the LORD,
levied this tax on the community of Israel in order to maintain the Tabernacle
of the Covenant.*"

⁷Over the years the followers of

wicked Athaliah had broken into the Temple of God, and they had used all the dedicated things from the Temple of the LORD to worship the images of Baal.

8So now the king ordered a chest to be made and set outside the gate leading to the Temple of the LORD. 9Then a proclamation was sent throughout Judah and Jerusalem, telling the people to bring to the LORD the tax that Moses, the servant of God, had required of the Israelites in the wilderness. 10This pleased all the leaders and the people, and they gladly brought their money and filled the chest with it.

11Whenever the chest became full, the Levites would carry it to the king's officials. Then the court secretary and an officer of the high priest would come and empty the chest and take it back to the Temple again. This went on day after day, and a large amount of money was collected. 12The king and Jehoiada gave the money to the construction supervisors, who hired masons and carpenters to restore the Temple of the LORD. They also hired metalworkers, who made articles of iron and bronze for the LORD's Temple.

13The men in charge of the renovation worked hard and made steady progress. They restored the Temple of God according to its original design and strengthened it. 14When all the repairs were finished, they brought the remaining money to the king and Jehoiada. It was used to make various articles for the Temple of the LORD—articles for worship services and for burnt offerings, including ladles and other articles made of gold and silver. And the burnt offerings were sacrificed continually in the Temple of the LORD during the lifetime of Jehoiada the priest.

15Jehoiada lived to a very old age, finally dying at 130. 16He was buried among the kings in the City of David, because he had done so much good in Judah* for God and his Temple.

17But after Jehoiada's death, the leaders of Judah came and bowed before King Joash and persuaded him to listen to their advice. 18They decided to abandon the Temple of the LORD, the God of their ancestors, and they worshiped Asherah poles and idols instead! Because of this sin, divine anger fell on Judah and Jerusalem. 19Yet the LORD sent prophets to bring them back to him. The prophets warned them, but still the people would not listen.

20Then the Spirit of God came upon Zechariah son of Jehoiada the priest. He stood before the people and said, "This is what God says: Why do you disobey the LORD's commands and keep yourselves from prospering? You have abandoned the LORD, and now he has abandoned you!"

21Then the leaders plotted to kill Zechariah, and King Joash ordered that they stone him to death in the courtyard of the LORD's Temple. 22That was how King Joash repaid Jehoiada for his loyalty—by killing his son. Zechariah's last words as he died were, "May the LORD see what they are doing and avenge my death!"

23In the spring of the year* the Aramean army marched against Joash. They invaded Judah and Jerusalem and killed all the leaders of the nation. Then they sent all the plunder back to their king in Damascus. 24Although the Arameans attacked with only a small army, the LORD helped them conquer the much larger army of Judah. The people of Judah had abandoned the LORD, the God of their ancestors, so judgment was carried out against Joash.

25The Arameans withdrew, leaving Joash severely wounded. But his own officials plotted to kill him for murdering the son* of Jehoiada the priest. They assassinated him as he lay in bed. Then he was buried in the City of David, but not in the royal cemetery. 26The assassins were Jozacar,* the son of an Ammonite woman named Shimeath, and Jehozabad, the son of a Moabite woman named Shomer.*

27The account of the sons of Joash, the prophecies about him, and the record of his restoration of the Temple of God are written in *The Commentary on the Book of the Kings.* His son Amaziah became the next king.

25:1AMAZIAH was twenty-five years old when he became king, and he reigned in Jerusalem twenty-nine years. His mother was Jehoaddin* from Jerusalem. 2Amaziah did what was pleasing in the LORD's sight, but not wholeheartedly.

3When Amaziah was well established as king, he executed the officials who had assassinated his father. 4However, he did not kill the children of the assassins, for he obeyed the command of the LORD as written by Moses in the Book of the Law: "Parents must not be put to death for the sins of their children, nor children for the sins of their parents. Those deserving to die must be put to death for their own crimes."*

5Then Amaziah organized the army, assigning generals and captains* for all Judah and Benjamin. He took a census and found that he had an army of 300,000 select troops, twenty years old and older, all trained in the use of spear and shield. 6He also paid about 7,500 pounds* of silver to hire 100,000 experienced fighting men from Israel.

7But a man of God came to him and said, "Your Majesty, do not hire troops from Israel, for the LORD is not with Israel. He will not help those people of Ephraim! 8If you let them go with your troops into battle, you will be defeated by the enemy no matter how well you fight. God will overthrow you, for he has the power to help you or to trip you up."

9Amaziah asked the man of God, "But what about all that silver I paid to hire the army of Israel?"

The man of God replied, "The LORD is able to give you much more than this!" 10So Amaziah discharged the hired troops and sent them back to Ephraim. This made them very angry with Judah, and they returned home in a great rage.

11Then Amaziah summoned his courage and led his army to the Valley of Salt, where they killed 10,000 Edomite troops from Seir. 12They captured another 10,000 and took them to the top

of a cliff and threw them off, dashing them to pieces on the rocks below.

13Meanwhile, the hired troops that Amaziah had sent home raided several of the towns of Judah between Samaria and Beth-horon. They killed 3,000 people and carried off great quantities of plunder.

14When King Amaziah returned from slaughtering the Edomites, he brought with him idols taken from the people of Seir. He set them up as his own gods, bowed down in front of them, and offered sacrifices to them! 15This made the LORD very angry, and he sent a prophet to ask, "Why do you turn to gods who could not even save their own people from you?"

16But the king interrupted him and said, "Since when have I made you the king's counselor? Be quiet now before I have you killed!"

So the prophet stopped with this warning: "I know that God has determined to destroy you because you have done this and have refused to accept my counsel."

17After consulting with his advisers, King Amaziah of Judah sent this challenge to Israel's king Jehoash,* the son of Jehoahaz and grandson of Jehu: "Come and meet me in battle!"*

18But King Jehoash of Israel replied to King Amaziah of Judah with this story: "Out in the Lebanon mountains, a thistle sent a message to a mighty cedar tree: 'Give your daughter in marriage to my son.' But just then a wild animal of Lebanon came by and stepped on the thistle, crushing it!

19"You are saying, 'I have defeated Edom,' and you are very proud of it. But my advice is to stay at home. Why stir up trouble that will only bring disaster on you and the people of Judah?"

20But Amaziah refused to listen, for God was determined to destroy him for turning to the gods of Edom. 21So King Jehoash of Israel mobilized his army against King Amaziah of Judah. The two armies drew up their battle lines at Beth-shemesh in Judah. 22Judah was routed by the army of Israel, and its army scattered and fled for home. 23King Jehoash of Israel captured Judah's king, Amaziah son of Joash and grandson of Ahaziah, at Beth-shemesh. Then he brought him to Jerusalem, where he demolished 600 feet* of Jerusalem's wall, from the Ephraim Gate to the Corner Gate. 24He carried off all the gold and silver and all the articles from the Temple of God that had been in the care of Obed-edom. He also seized the treasures of the royal palace, along with hostages, and then returned to Samaria.

25King Amaziah of Judah lived on for fifteen years after the death of King Jehoash of Israel. 26The rest of the events in Amaziah's reign, from beginning to end, are recorded in *The Book of the Kings of Judah and Israel.*

27After Amaziah turned away from the LORD, there was a conspiracy against his life in Jerusalem, and he fled to Lachish. But his enemies sent assassins after him, and they killed him there. 28They brought his body back on a horse, and he was buried with his ancestors in the City of David.*

24:6 Hebrew *Tent of the Testimony.*   **24:16** Hebrew *in Israel.* The author of Chronicles sees Judah as representative of the true Israel.   **24:23** Hebrew *At the turn of the year.* The first day of the year in the ancient Hebrew lunar calendar occurred in March or April.   **24:25** As in Greek version and Latin Vulgate; Hebrew reads *sons.*   **24:26a** As in parallel text at 2 Kgs 12:21; Hebrew reads *Zabad.* **24:26b** As in parallel text at 2 Kgs 12:21; Hebrew reads *Shimrith,* a variant spelling of Shomer.   **25:1** As in parallel text at 2 Kgs 14:2; Hebrew reads *Jehoaddan,* a variant spelling of Jehoaddin.   **25:4** Deut 24:16.   **25:5** Hebrew *commanders of thousands and commanders of hundreds.* **25:6** Hebrew *100 talents* [3,400 kilograms]. **25:17a** Hebrew *Joash,* a variant spelling of Jehoash; also in 25:18, 21, 23, 25.   **25:17b** Hebrew *Come, let us look one another in the face.*   **25:23** Hebrew *400 cubits* [180 meters].   **25:28** As in some Hebrew manuscripts and other ancient versions (see also 2 Kgs 14:20); most Hebrew manuscripts read *the city of Judah.*

ROMANS 12:1-21

And so, dear brothers and sisters,* I plead with you to give your bodies to God because of all he has done for you. Let them be a living and holy sacrifice—the kind he will find acceptable. This is truly the way to worship him.* 2Don't copy the behavior and customs of this world, but let God transform you into a new person by changing the way you think. Then you will learn to know God's will for you, which is good and pleasing and perfect.

3Because of the privilege and authority* God has given me, I give each of you this warning: Don't think you are better than you really are. Be honest in your evaluation of yourselves, measuring yourselves by the faith God has given us.* 4Just as our bodies have many parts and each part has a special function, 5so it is with Christ's body. We are many parts of one body, and we all belong to each other.

6In his grace, God has given us different gifts for doing certain things well. So if God has given you the ability to prophesy, speak out with as much faith as God has given you. 7If your gift is serving others, serve them well. If you are a teacher, teach well. 8If your gift is to encourage others, be encouraging. If it is giving, give generously. If God has given you leadership ability, take the responsibility seriously. And if you have a gift for showing kindness to others, do it gladly.

9Don't just pretend to love others. Really love them. Hate what is wrong. Hold tightly to what is good. 10Love each other with genuine affection,* and take delight in honoring each other. 11Never be lazy, but work hard and serve the Lord enthusiastically.* 12Rejoice in our confident hope. Be patient in trouble, and keep on praying. 13When God's people are in need, be ready to help them. Always be eager to practice hospitality.

14Bless those who persecute you. Don't curse them; pray that God will bless them. 15Be happy with those who are happy, and weep with those who weep. 16Live in harmony with each other. Don't be too proud to enjoy the company of ordinary people. And don't think you know it all!

17Never pay back evil with more evil. Do things in such a way that everyone can see you are honorable. 18Do all that you can to live in peace with everyone.

19Dear friends, never take revenge. Leave that to the righteous anger of God. For the Scriptures say,

"I will take revenge;
    I will pay them back,"*
    says the LORD.

²⁰Instead,

"If your enemies are hungry, feed
    them.
If they are thirsty, give them
    something to drink.
In doing this, you will heap
    burning coals of shame
    on their heads."*

²¹Don't let evil conquer you, but con-
quer evil by doing good.

12:1a Greek *brothers.* 12:1b Or *This is your spiritual
worship;* or *This is your reasonable service.* 12:3a Or
Because of the grace; compare 1:5. 12:3b Or *by the faith
God has given you;* or *by the standard of our God-given
faith.* 12:10 Greek *with brotherly love.* 12:11 Or *but
serve the Lord with a zealous spirit;* or *but let the Spirit
excite you as you serve the Lord.* 12:19 Deut 32:35.
12:20 Prov 25:21-22.

PSALM 22:19-31

○ LORD, do not stay far away!
    You are my strength; come
    quickly to my aid!
²⁰ Save me from the sword;
    spare my precious life from
    these dogs.
²¹ Snatch me from the lion's jaws
    and from the horns of these
    wild oxen.

²² I will proclaim your name to my
    brothers and sisters.*
    I will praise you among your
    assembled people.
²³ Praise the LORD, all you who fear
    him!
    Honor him, all you descendants
    of Jacob!
    Show him reverence, all you
    descendants of Israel!
²⁴ For he has not ignored or
    belittled the suffering
    of the needy.
    He has not turned his back
    on them,
    but has listened to their cries
    for help.

²⁵ I will praise you in the great
    assembly.
    I will fulfill my vows in the

presence of those who
    worship you.
²⁶ The poor will eat and be satisfied.
    All who seek the LORD will praise
    him.
    Their hearts will rejoice with
    everlasting joy.
²⁷ The whole earth will acknowledge
    the LORD and return to him.
    All the families of the nations
    will bow down before him.
²⁸ For royal power belongs to the LORD.
    He rules all the nations.

²⁹ Let the rich of the earth feast and
    worship.
    Bow before him, all who
    are mortal,
    all whose lives will end
    as dust.
³⁰ Our children will also serve him.
    Future generations will hear
    about the wonders of
    the Lord.
³¹ His righteous acts will be told to
    those not yet born.
    They will hear about everything
    he has done.

22:22 Hebrew *my brothers.*

PROVERBS 20:8-10

When a king sits in judgment, he
weighs all the evidence, distinguishing
the bad from the good. □ Who can say,
"I have cleansed my heart; I am pure and
free from sin"? □ False weights and un-
equal measures*—the LORD detests
double standards of every kind.

20:10 Hebrew *A stone and a stone, an ephah and an ephah.*

JULY 30

2 CHRONICLES 26:1–28:27

All the people of Judah had crowned
Amaziah's sixteen-year-old son, Uzzi-
ah, as king in place of his father. ²After

his father's death, Uzziah rebuilt the town of Elath* and restored it to Judah.

³Uzziah was sixteen years old when he became king, and he reigned in Jerusalem fifty-two years. His mother was Jecoliah from Jerusalem. ⁴He did what was pleasing in the LORD's sight, just as his father, Amaziah, had done. ⁵Uzziah sought God during the days of Zechariah, who taught him to fear God.* And as long as the king sought guidance from the LORD, God gave him success.

⁶Uzziah declared war on the Philistines and broke down the walls of Gath, Jabneh, and Ashdod. Then he built new towns in the Ashdod area and in other parts of Philistia. ⁷God helped him in his wars against the Philistines, his battles with the Arabs of Gur,* and his wars with the Meunites. ⁸The Meunites* paid annual tribute to him, and his fame spread even to Egypt, for he had become very powerful.

⁹Uzziah built fortified towers in Jerusalem at the Corner Gate, at the Valley Gate, and at the angle in the wall. ¹⁰He also constructed forts in the wilderness and dug many water cisterns, because he kept great herds of livestock in the foothills of Judah* and on the plains. He was also a man who loved the soil. He had many workers who cared for his farms and vineyards, both on the hillsides and in the fertile valleys.

¹¹Uzziah had an army of well-trained warriors, ready to march into battle, unit by unit. This army had been mustered and organized by Jeiel, the secretary of the army, and his assistant, Maaseiah. They were under the direction of Hananiah, one of the king's officials. ¹²These regiments of mighty warriors were commanded by 2,600 clan leaders. ¹³The army consisted of 307,500 men, all elite troops. They were prepared to assist the king against any enemy.

¹⁴Uzziah provided the entire army with shields, spears, helmets, coats of mail, bows, and sling stones. ¹⁵And he produced machines mounted on the walls of Jerusalem, designed by experts to shoot arrows and hurl stones* from the towers and the corners of the wall. His fame spread far and wide, for the LORD gave him marvelous help, and he became very powerful.

¹⁶But when he had become powerful, he also became proud, which led to his downfall. He sinned against the LORD his God by entering the sanctuary of the LORD's Temple and personally burning incense on the incense altar. ¹⁷Azariah the high priest went in after him with eighty other priests of the LORD, all brave men. ¹⁸They confronted King Uzziah and said, "It is not for you, Uzziah, to burn incense to the LORD. That is the work of the priests alone, the descendants of Aaron who are set apart for this work. Get out of the sanctuary, for you have sinned. The LORD God will not honor you for this!"

¹⁹Uzziah, who was holding an incense burner, became furious. But as he was standing there raging at the priests before the incense altar in the LORD's Temple, leprosy* suddenly broke out on his forehead. ²⁰When Azariah the high priest and all the other priests saw the leprosy, they rushed him out. And the king himself was eager to get out because the LORD had struck him. ²¹So King Uzziah had leprosy until the day he died. He lived in isolation in a separate house, for he was excluded from the Temple of the LORD. His son Jotham was put in charge of the royal palace, and he governed the people of the land.

²²The rest of the events of Uzziah's reign, from beginning to end, are recorded by the prophet Isaiah son of Amoz. ²³When Uzziah died, he was buried with his ancestors; his grave was in a nearby burial field belonging to the kings, for the people said, "He had leprosy." And his son Jotham became the next king.

²⁷:¹JOTHAM was twenty-five years old when he became king, and he reigned in Jerusalem sixteen years. His mother was Jerusha, the daughter of Zadok. ²Jotham did what was pleasing in the

LORD's sight. He did everything his father, Uzziah, had done, except that Jotham did not sin by entering the Temple of the LORD. But the people continued in their corrupt ways.

3Jotham rebuilt the upper gate of the Temple of the LORD. He also did extensive rebuilding on the wall at the hill of Ophel. 4He built towns in the hill country of Judah and constructed fortresses and towers in the wooded areas. 5Jotham went to war against the Ammonites and conquered them. Over the next three years he received from them an annual tribute of 7,500 pounds* of silver, 50,000 bushels of wheat, and 50,000 bushels of barley.*

6King Jotham became powerful because he was careful to live in obedience to the LORD his God.

7The rest of the events of Jotham's reign, including all his wars and other activities, are recorded in *The Book of the Kings of Israel and Judah.* 8He was twenty-five years old when he became king, and he reigned in Jerusalem sixteen years. 9When Jotham died, he was buried in the City of David. And his son Ahaz became the next king.

28:1AHAZ was twenty years old when he became king, and he reigned in Jerusalem sixteen years. He did not do what was pleasing in the sight of the LORD, as his ancestor David had done. 2Instead, he followed the example of the kings of Israel. He cast metal images for the worship of Baal. 3He offered sacrifices in the valley of Ben-Hinnom, even sacrificing his own sons in the fire.* In this way, he followed the detestable practices of the pagan nations the LORD had driven from the land ahead of the Israelites. 4He offered sacrifices and burned incense at the pagan shrines and on the hills and under every green tree.

5Because of all this, the LORD his God allowed the king of Aram to defeat Ahaz and to exile large numbers of his people to Damascus. The armies of the king of Israel also defeated Ahaz and inflicted many casualties on his army. 6In a single day Pekah son of Remaliah, Israel's king, killed 120,000 of Judah's troops, all of them experienced warriors, because they had abandoned the LORD, the God of their ancestors. 7Then Zicri, a warrior from Ephraim, killed Maaseiah, the king's son; Azrikam, the king's palace commander; and Elkanah, the king's second-in-command. 8The armies of Israel captured 200,000 women and children from Judah and seized tremendous amounts of plunder, which they took back to Samaria.

9But a prophet of the LORD named Oded was there in Samaria when the army of Israel returned home. He went out to meet them and said, "The LORD, the God of your ancestors, was angry with Judah and let you defeat them. But you have gone too far, killing them without mercy, and all heaven is disturbed. 10And now you are planning to make slaves of these people from Judah and Jerusalem. What about your own sins against the LORD your God? 11Listen to me and return these prisoners you have taken, for they are your own relatives. Watch out, because now the LORD's fierce anger has been turned against you!"

12Then some of the leaders of Israel*—Azariah son of Jehohanan, Berekiah son of Meshillemoth, Jehizkiah son of Shallum, and Amasa son of Hadlai—agreed with this and confronted the men returning from battle. 13"You must not bring the prisoners here!" they declared. "We cannot afford to add to our sins and guilt. Our guilt is already great, and the LORD's fierce anger is already turned against Israel."

14So the warriors released the prisoners and handed over the plunder in the sight of the leaders and all the people. 15Then the four men just mentioned by name came forward and distributed clothes from the plunder to the prisoners who were naked. They provided clothing and sandals to wear, gave them enough food and drink, and dressed their wounds with olive oil. They put those who were weak on donkeys and took all the prisoners back to their own people in Jericho, the city of palms. Then they returned to Samaria.

¹⁶At that time King Ahaz of Judah asked the king of Assyria for help. ¹⁷The armies of Edom had again invaded Judah and taken captives. ¹⁸And the Philistines had raided towns located in the foothills of Judah* and in the Negev of Judah. They had already captured and occupied Beth-shemesh, Aijalon, Gederoth, Soco with its villages, Timnah with its villages, and Gimzo with its villages. ¹⁹The LORD was humbling Judah because of King Ahaz of Judah,* for he had encouraged his people to sin and had been utterly unfaithful to the LORD.

²⁰So when King Tiglath-pileser* of Assyria arrived, he attacked Ahaz instead of helping him. ²¹Ahaz took valuable items from the LORD's Temple, the royal palace, and from the homes of his officials and gave them to the king of Assyria as tribute. But this did not help him.

²²Even during this time of trouble, King Ahaz continued to reject the LORD. ²³He offered sacrifices to the gods of Damascus who had defeated him, for he said, "Since these gods helped the kings of Aram, they will help me, too, if I sacrifice to them." But instead, they led to his ruin and the ruin of all Judah.

²⁴The king took the various articles from the Temple of God and broke them into pieces. He shut the doors of the LORD's Temple so that no one could worship there, and he set up altars to pagan gods in every corner of Jerusalem. ²⁵He made pagan shrines in all the towns of Judah for offering sacrifices to other gods. In this way, he aroused the anger of the LORD, the God of his ancestors.

²⁶The rest of the events of Ahaz's reign and everything he did, from beginning to end, are recorded in *The Book of the Kings of Judah and Israel.* ²⁷When Ahaz died, he was buried in Jerusalem but not in the royal cemetery of

the kings of Judah. Then his son Hezekiah became the next king.

26:2 As in Greek version (see also 2 Kgs 14:22; 16:6); Hebrew reads *Eloth,* a variant spelling of Elath. 26:5 As in Syriac and Greek versions; Hebrew reads *who instructed him in divine visions.* 26:7 As in Greek version; Hebrew reads *Gur-baal.* 26:8 As in Greek version; Hebrew reads *Ammonites.* Compare 26:7. 26:10 Hebrew *the Shephelah.* 26:15 Or *to protect those who shot arrows and stones.* 26:19 Or *a contagious skin disease.* The Hebrew word used here and throughout this passage can describe various skin diseases. 27:5a Hebrew *100 talents* [3,400 kilograms]. 27:5b Hebrew *10,000 cors* [1,820 kiloliters] *of wheat, and 10,000 cors of barley.* 28:3 Or *even making his sons pass through the fire.* 28:12 Hebrew *Ephraim,* referring to the northern kingdom of Israel. 28:18 Hebrew *the Shephelah.* 28:19 Hebrew *of Israel;* also in 28:23, 27. The author of Chronicles sees Judah as representative of the true Israel. See also some Hebrew manuscripts, Greek and Syriac versions, and Latin Vulgate. 28:20 Hebrew *Tilgath-pilneser,* a variant spelling of Tiglath-pileser.

ROMANS 13:1-14

Everyone must submit to governing authorities. For all authority comes from God, and those in positions of authority have been placed there by God. ²So anyone who rebels against authority is rebelling against what God has instituted, and they will be punished. ³For the authorities do not strike fear in people who are doing right, but in those who are doing wrong. Would you like to live without fear of the authorities? Do what is right, and they will honor you. ⁴The authorities are God's servants, sent for your good. But if you are doing wrong, of course you should be afraid, for they have the power to punish you. They are God's servants, sent for the very purpose of punishing those who do what is wrong. ⁵So you must submit to them, not only to avoid punishment, but also to keep a clear conscience.

⁶Pay your taxes, too, for these same reasons. For government workers need to be paid. They are serving God in what they do. ⁷Give to everyone what you owe them: Pay your taxes and government fees to those who collect them, and give respect and honor to those who are in authority.

⁸Owe nothing to anyone—except for your obligation to love one another. If you love your neighbor, you will fulfill the requirements of God's law. ⁹For the commandments say, "You must not commit adultery. You must not

murder. You must not steal. You must not covet."* These—and other such commandments—are summed up in this one commandment: "Love your neighbor as yourself."* ¹⁰Love does no wrong to others, so love fulfills the requirements of God's law.

¹¹This is all the more urgent, for you know how late it is; time is running out. Wake up, for our salvation is nearer now than when we first believed. ¹²**The night is almost gone; the day of salvation will soon be here. So remove your dark deeds like dirty clothes, and put on the shining armor of right living.** ¹³Because we belong to the day, we must live decent lives for all to see. Don't participate in the darkness of wild parties and drunkenness, or in sexual promiscuity and immoral living, or in quarreling and jealousy. ¹⁴Instead, clothe yourself with the presence of the Lord Jesus Christ. And don't let yourself think about ways to indulge your evil desires.

13:9a Exod 20:13-15, 17.   13:9b Lev 19:18.

PSALM 23:1-6
A psalm of David.

¹ The Lord is my shepherd;
     I have all that I need.
² He lets me rest in green meadows;
     he leads me beside peaceful
          streams.
³   He renews my strength.
  He guides me along right paths,
     bringing honor to his name.
⁴ Even when I walk
     through the darkest valley,*
  I will not be afraid,
     for you are close beside me.
  Your rod and your staff
     protect and comfort me.
⁵ You prepare a feast for me
     in the presence of my enemies.
  You honor me by anointing my
          head with oil.
     My cup overflows with blessings.
⁶ Surely your goodness and unfailing
          love will pursue me
  all the days of my life,

and I will live in the house
     of the Lord
  forever.

23:4 Or *the dark valley of death.*

PROVERBS 20:11
Even children are known by the way they act, whether their conduct is pure, and whether it is right.

JULY 31

2 CHRONICLES 29:1-36
Hezekiah was twenty-five years old when he became the king of Judah, and he reigned in Jerusalem twenty-nine years. His mother was Abijah, the daughter of Zechariah. ²He did what was pleasing in the Lord's sight, just as his ancestor David had done.

³In the very first month of the first year of his reign, Hezekiah reopened the doors of the Temple of the Lord and repaired them. ⁴He summoned the priests and Levites to meet him at the courtyard east of the Temple. ⁵He said to them, "Listen to me, you Levites! Purify yourselves, and purify the Temple of the Lord, the God of your ancestors. Remove all the defiled things from the sanctuary. ⁶Our ancestors were unfaithful and did what was evil in the sight of the Lord our God. They abandoned the Lord and his dwelling place; they turned their backs on him. ⁷They also shut the doors to the Temple's entry room, and they snuffed out the lamps. They stopped burning incense and presenting burnt offerings at the sanctuary of the God of Israel.

⁸"That is why the Lord's anger has fallen upon Judah and Jerusalem. He has made them an object of dread, horror, and ridicule, as you can see with your own eyes. ⁹Because of this, our fa-

thers have been killed in battle, and our sons and daughters and wives have been captured. [10]But now I will make a covenant with the LORD, the God of Israel, so that his fierce anger will turn away from us. [11]My sons, do not neglect your duties any longer! The LORD has chosen you to stand in his presence, to minister to him, and to lead the people in worship and present offerings to him."

[12]Then these Levites got right to work:

From the clan of Kohath: Mahath son of Amasai and Joel son of Azariah.
From the clan of Merari: Kish son of Abdi and Azariah son of Jehallelel.
From the clan of Gershon: Joah son of Zimmah and Eden son of Joah.
[13] From the family of Elizaphan: Shimri and Jeiel.
From the family of Asaph: Zechariah and Mattaniah.
[14] From the family of Heman: Jehiel and Shimei.
From the family of Jeduthun: Shemaiah and Uzziel.

[15]These men called together their fellow Levites, and they all purified themselves. Then they began to cleanse the Temple of the LORD, just as the king had commanded. They were careful to follow all the LORD's instructions in their work. [16]The priests went into the sanctuary of the Temple of the LORD to cleanse it, and they took out to the Temple courtyard all the defiled things they found. From there the Levites carted it all out to the Kidron Valley.

[17]They began the work in early spring, on the first day of the new year,* and in eight days they had reached the entry room of the LORD's Temple. Then they purified the Temple of the LORD itself, which took another eight days. So the entire task was completed in sixteen days.

[18]Then the Levites went to King Hezekiah and gave him this report: "We have cleansed the entire Temple of the

LORD, the altar of burnt offering with all its utensils, and the table of the Bread of the Presence with all its utensils. [19]We have also recovered all the items discarded by King Ahaz when he was unfaithful and closed the Temple. They are now in front of the altar of the LORD, purified and ready for use."

[20]Early the next morning King Hezekiah gathered the city officials and went to the Temple of the LORD. [21]They brought seven bulls, seven rams, and seven male lambs as a burnt offering, together with seven male goats as a sin offering for the kingdom, for the Temple, and for Judah. The king commanded the priests, who were descendants of Aaron, to sacrifice the animals on the altar of the LORD.

[22]So they killed the bulls, and the priests took the blood and sprinkled it on the altar. Next they killed the rams and sprinkled their blood on the altar. And finally, they did the same with the male lambs. [23]The male goats for the sin offering were then brought before the king and the assembly of people, who laid their hands on them. [24]The priests then killed the goats as a sin offering and sprinkled their blood on the altar to make atonement for the sins of all Israel. The king had specifically commanded that this burnt offering and sin offering should be made for all Israel.

[25]King Hezekiah then stationed the Levites at the Temple of the LORD with cymbals, lyres, and harps. He obeyed all the commands that the LORD had given to King David through Gad, the king's seer, and the prophet Nathan. [26]The Levites then took their positions around the Temple with the instruments of David, and the priests took their positions with the trumpets.

[27]Then Hezekiah ordered that the burnt offering be placed on the altar. As the burnt offering was presented, songs of praise to the LORD were begun, accompanied by the trumpets and other instruments of David, the former king of Israel. [28]The entire assembly worshiped the LORD as the singers sang and the trumpets blew, until all the burnt offerings

were finished. [29]Then the king and everyone with him bowed down in worship. [30]King Hezekiah and the officials ordered the Levites to praise the LORD with the psalms written by David and by Asaph the seer. So they offered joyous praise and bowed down in worship.

[31]Then Hezekiah declared, "Now that you have consecrated yourselves to the LORD, bring your sacrifices and thanksgiving offerings to the Temple of the LORD." So the people brought their sacrifices and thanksgiving offerings, and all whose hearts were willing brought burnt offerings, too. [32]The people brought to the LORD 70 bulls, 100 rams, and 200 male lambs for burnt offerings. [33]They also brought 600 cattle and 3,000 sheep and goats as sacred offerings.

[34]But there were too few priests to prepare all the burnt offerings. So their relatives the Levites helped them until the work was finished and more priests had been purified, for the Levites had been more conscientious about purifying themselves than the priests had been. [35]There was an abundance of burnt offerings, along with the usual liquid offerings, and a great deal of fat from the many peace offerings.

So the Temple of the LORD was restored to service. [36]And Hezekiah and all the people rejoiced because of what God had done for the people, for everything had been accomplished so quickly.

29:17 Hebrew *on the first day of the first month.* This day in the ancient Hebrew lunar calendar occurred in March or early April, 715 B.C.

ROMANS 14:1-23

Accept other believers who are weak in faith, and don't argue with them about what they think is right or wrong. [2]For instance, one person believes it's all right to eat anything. But another believer with a sensitive conscience will eat only vegetables. [3]Those who feel free to eat anything must not look down on those who don't. And those who don't eat certain foods must not condemn those who do, for God has accepted them. [4]Who are you to condemn someone else's servants? They are responsible to the Lord, so let him judge whether they are right or wrong. And with the Lord's help, they will do what is right and will receive his approval.

[5]In the same way, some think one day is more holy than another day, while others think every day is alike. You should each be fully convinced that whichever day you choose is acceptable. [6]Those who worship the Lord on a special day do it to honor him. Those who eat any kind of food do so to honor the Lord, since they give thanks to God before eating. And those who refuse to eat certain foods also want to please the Lord and give thanks to God. [7]For we don't live for ourselves or die for ourselves. [8]If we live, it's to honor the Lord. And if we die, it's to honor the Lord. So whether we live or die, we belong to the Lord. [9]Christ died and rose again for this very purpose—to be Lord both of the living and of the dead.

[10]So why do you condemn another believer*? Why do you look down on another believer? Remember, we will all stand before the judgment seat of God. [11]For the Scriptures say,

> "'As surely as I live,' says the LORD,
> 'every knee will bend to me,
>> and every tongue will confess and give praise to God.*'"

[12]Yes, each of us will give a personal account to God. [13]So let's stop condemning each other. Decide instead to live in such a way that you will not cause another believer to stumble and fall.

[14]I know and am convinced on the authority of the Lord Jesus that no food, in and of itself, is wrong to eat. But if someone believes it is wrong, then for that person it is wrong. [15]And if another believer is distressed by what you eat, you are not acting in love if you eat it. Don't let your eating ruin someone for whom Christ died. [16]Then you will not be criticized for doing something you

believe is good. [17] For the Kingdom of God is not a matter of what we eat or drink, but of living a life of goodness and peace and joy in the Holy Spirit. [18] If you serve Christ with this attitude, you will please God, and others will approve of you, too. [19] **So then, let us aim for harmony in the church and try to build each other up.**

[20] **Don't tear apart the work of God over what you eat. Remember, all foods are acceptable, but it is wrong to eat something if it makes another person stumble.** [21] It is better not to eat meat or drink wine or do anything else if it might cause another believer to stumble. [22] You may believe there's nothing wrong with what you are doing, but keep it between yourself and God. Blessed are those who don't feel guilty for doing something they have decided is right. [23] But if you have doubts about whether or not you should eat something, you are sinning if you go ahead and do it. For you are not following your convictions. If you do anything you believe is not right, you are sinning.

14:10 Greek *your brother;* also in 14:10b, 13, 15, 21.
14:11 Or *confess allegiance to God.* Isa 49:18; 45:23 (Greek version).

PSALM 24:1-10
A psalm of David.

[1] **T**he earth is the LORD's, and
   everything in it.
The world and all its people
   belong to him.
[2] For he laid the earth's foundation
   on the seas
   and built it on the ocean depths.

[3] Who may climb the mountain
   of the LORD?
Who may stand in his holy place?
[4] Only those whose hands and
   hearts are pure,
   who do not worship idols
   and never tell lies.
[5] They will receive the LORD's blessing
   and have a right relationship with
   God their savior.
[6] Such people may seek you
   and worship in your presence,
   O God of Jacob.   *Interlude*

[7] Open up, ancient gates!
   Open up, ancient doors,
   and let the King of glory enter.
[8] Who is the King of glory?
   The LORD, strong and mighty;
   the LORD, invincible in battle.
[9] Open up, ancient gates!
   Open up, ancient doors,
   and let the King of glory enter.
[10] Who is the King of glory?
   The LORD of Heaven's Armies—
   he is the King of glory.   *Interlude*

PROVERBS 20:12
Ears to hear and eyes to see—both are gifts from the LORD.

AUGUST
1

2 CHRONICLES 30:1–31:21

King Hezekiah now sent word to all Israel and Judah, and he wrote letters of invitation to the people of Ephraim and Manasseh. He asked everyone to come to the Temple of the LORD at Jerusalem to celebrate the Passover of the LORD, the God of Israel. ²The king, his officials, and all the community of Jerusalem decided to celebrate Passover a month later than usual.* ³They were unable to celebrate it at the prescribed time because not enough priests could be purified by then, and the people had not yet assembled at Jerusalem.

⁴This plan for keeping the Passover seemed right to the king and all the people. ⁵So they sent a proclamation throughout all Israel, from Beersheba in the south to Dan in the north, inviting everyone to come to Jerusalem to celebrate the Passover of the LORD, the God of Israel. The people had not been celebrating it in great numbers as required in the Law.

⁶At the king's command, runners were sent throughout Israel and Judah. They carried letters that said:

"O people of Israel, return to the LORD, the God of Abraham, Isaac, and Israel,* so that he will return to the few of us who have survived the conquest of the Assyrian kings. ⁷Do not be like your ancestors and relatives who abandoned the LORD, the God of their ancestors, and became an object of derision, as you yourselves can see. ⁸Do not be stubborn, as they were, but submit yourselves to the LORD. Come to his Temple, which he has set apart as holy forever. Worship the LORD your God so that his fierce anger will turn away from you.

⁹"For if you return to the LORD, your relatives and your children will be treated mercifully by their captors, and they will be able to return to this land. For the LORD your God is gracious and merciful. If you return to him, he will not continue to turn his face from you."

¹⁰The runners went from town to town throughout Ephraim and Manasseh and as far as the territory of Zebulun. But most of the people just laughed at the runners and made fun of them. ¹¹However, some people from Asher, Manasseh, and Zebulun humbled themselves and went to Jerusalem.

¹²At the same time, God's hand was on the people in the land of Judah, giving them all one heart to obey the orders of the king and his officials, who were following the word of the LORD. ¹³So a huge crowd assembled at Jerusalem in midspring* to celebrate the Festival of Unleavened Bread. ¹⁴They set to work and removed the pagan altars from Jerusalem. They took away all the incense altars and threw them into the Kidron Valley.

¹⁵On the fourteenth day of the second month, one month later than usual,* the people slaughtered the Passover lamb. This shamed the priests and Levites, so they purified themselves and brought burnt offerings to the Temple of the LORD. ¹⁶Then they took their places at the Temple as prescribed in the Law of Moses, the man of God. The Levites brought the sacrificial blood to the priests, who then sprinkled it on the altar.

¹⁷Since many of the people had not purified themselves, the Levites had to slaughter their Passover lamb for them, to set them apart for the LORD. ¹⁸Most of those who came from Ephraim, Manasseh, Issachar, and Zebulun had not

purified themselves. But King Hezekiah prayed for them, and they were allowed to eat the Passover meal anyway, even though this was contrary to the requirements of the Law. For Hezekiah said, "May the LORD, who is good, pardon those [19]who decide to follow the LORD, the God of their ancestors, even though they are not properly cleansed for the ceremony." [20]And the LORD listened to Hezekiah's prayer and healed the people.

[21]So the people of Israel who were present in Jerusalem joyously celebrated the Festival of Unleavened Bread for seven days. Each day the Levites and priests sang to the LORD, accompanied by loud instruments.* [22]Hezekiah encouraged all the Levites regarding the skill they displayed as they served the LORD. The celebration continued for seven days. Peace offerings were sacrificed, and the people gave thanks to the LORD, the God of their ancestors.

[23]The entire assembly then decided to continue the festival another seven days, so they celebrated joyfully for another week. [24]King Hezekiah gave the people 1,000 bulls and 7,000 sheep and goats for offerings, and the officials donated 1,000 bulls and 10,000 sheep and goats. Meanwhile, many more priests purified themselves.

[25]The entire assembly of Judah rejoiced, including the priests, the Levites, all who came from the land of Israel, the foreigners who came to the festival, and all those who lived in Judah. [26]There was great joy in the city, for Jerusalem had not seen a celebration like this one since the days of Solomon, King David's son. [27]Then the priests and Levites stood and blessed the people, and God heard their prayer from his holy dwelling in heaven.

[31:1]WHEN the festival ended, the Israelites who attended went to all the towns of Judah, Benjamin, Ephraim, and Manasseh, and they smashed all the sacred pillars, cut down the Asherah poles, and removed the pagan shrines and altars. After this, the Israelites returned to their own towns and homes.

[2]Hezekiah then organized the priests and Levites into divisions to offer the burnt offerings and peace offerings, and to worship and give thanks and praise to the LORD at the gates of the Temple. [3]The king also made a personal contribution of animals for the daily morning and evening burnt offerings, the weekly Sabbath festivals, the monthly new moon festivals, and the annual festivals as prescribed in the Law of the LORD. [4]In addition, he required the people in Jerusalem to bring a portion of their goods to the priests and Levites, so they could devote themselves fully to the Law of the LORD.

[5]The people of Israel responded immediately and generously by bringing the first of their crops and grain, new wine, olive oil, honey, and all the produce of their fields. They brought a large quantity—a tithe of all they produced. [6]The people who had moved to Judah from Israel, and the people of Judah themselves, brought in the tithes of their cattle, sheep, and goats and a tithe of the things that had been dedicated to the LORD their God, and they piled them up in great heaps. [7]They began piling them up in late spring, and the heaps continued to grow until early autumn.* [8]When Hezekiah and his officials came and saw these huge piles, they thanked the LORD and his people Israel!

[9]"Where did all this come from?" Hezekiah asked the priests and Levites.

[10]And Azariah the high priest, from the family of Zadok, replied, "Since the people began bringing their gifts to the LORD's Temple, we have had enough to eat and plenty to spare. The LORD has blessed his people, and all this is left over."

[11]Hezekiah ordered that storerooms be prepared in the Temple of the LORD. When this was done, [12]the people faithfully brought all the tithes and gifts to the Temple. Conaniah the Levite was put in charge, assisted by his brother Shimei. [13]The supervisors under them were Jehiel, Azaziah, Nahath, Asahel, Jerimoth, Jozabad, Eliel, Ismakiah, Mahath, and Be-

naiah. These appointments were made by King Hezekiah and Azariah, the chief official in the Temple of God.

¹⁴Kore son of Imnah the Levite, who was the gatekeeper at the East Gate, was put in charge of distributing the voluntary offerings given to God, the gifts, and the things that had been dedicated to the LORD. ¹⁵His faithful assistants were Eden, Miniamin, Jeshua, Shemaiah, Amariah, and Shecaniah. They distributed the gifts among the families of priests in their towns by their divisions, dividing the gifts fairly among old and young alike. ¹⁶They distributed the gifts to all males three years old or older, regardless of their place in the genealogical records. The distribution went to all who would come to the LORD's Temple to perform their daily duties according to their divisions. ¹⁷They distributed gifts to the priests who were listed by their families in the genealogical records, and to the Levites twenty years old or older who were listed according to their jobs and their divisions. ¹⁸Food allotments were also given to the families of all those listed in the genealogical records, including their little babies, wives, sons, and daughters. For they had all been faithful in purifying themselves.

¹⁹As for the priests, the descendants of Aaron, who were living in the open villages around the towns, men were appointed by name to distribute portions to every male among the priests and to all the Levites listed in the genealogical records.

²⁰In this way, King Hezekiah handled the distribution throughout all Judah, doing what was pleasing and good in the sight of the LORD his God. ²¹In all that he did in the service of the Temple of God and in his efforts to follow God's laws and commands, Hezekiah sought his God wholeheartedly. As a result, he was very successful.

30:2 Hebrew *in the second month.* Passover was normally observed in the first month (of the ancient Hebrew lunar calendar). **30:6** *Israel* is the name that God gave to Jacob. **30:13** Hebrew *in the second month.* The second month of the ancient Hebrew lunar calendar usually occurs within the months of April and May. **30:15** Hebrew *On the fourteenth day of the second month.* Passover normally

began on the fourteenth day of the first month (see Lev 23:5). **30:21** Or *sang to the LORD with all their strength.* **31:7** Hebrew *in the third month . . . until the seventh month.* The third month of the ancient Hebrew lunar calendar usually occurs within the months of May and June; the seventh month usually occurs within September and October.

ROMANS 15:1-22

We [Paul and other Christians] who are strong must be considerate of those who are sensitive about things like this. We must not just please ourselves. ²We should help others do what is right and build them up in the Lord. ³For even Christ didn't live to please himself. As the Scriptures say, "The insults of those who insult you, O God, have fallen on me."* ⁴Such things were written in the Scriptures long ago to teach us. And the Scriptures give us hope and encouragement as we wait patiently for God's promises to be fulfilled.

⁵**May God, who gives this patience and encouragement, help you live in complete harmony with each other, as is fitting for followers of Christ Jesus. ⁶Then all of you can join together with one voice, giving praise and glory to God, the Father of our Lord Jesus Christ.**

⁷Therefore, accept each other just as Christ has accepted you so that God will be given glory. ⁸Remember that Christ came as a servant to the Jews* to show that God is true to the promises he made to their ancestors. ⁹He also came so that the Gentiles might give glory to God for his mercies to them. That is what the psalmist meant when he wrote:

"For this, I will praise you among
the Gentiles;
I will sing praises to your
name."*

¹⁰And in another place it is written,

"Rejoice with his people,
you Gentiles."*

¹¹And yet again,

"Praise the LORD, all you Gentiles.
Praise him, all you people
of the earth."*

12And in another place Isaiah said,

"The heir to David's throne*
    will come,
    and he will rule over the Gentiles.
    They will place their hope on him."*

13I pray that God, the source of hope, will fill you completely with joy and peace because you trust in him. Then you will overflow with confident hope through the power of the Holy Spirit.

14I am fully convinced, my dear brothers and sisters,* that you are full of goodness. You know these things so well you can teach each other all about them. 15Even so, I have been bold enough to write about some of these points, knowing that all you need is this reminder. For by God's grace, 16I am a special messenger from Christ Jesus to you Gentiles. I bring you the Good News so that I might present you as an acceptable offering to God, made holy by the Holy Spirit. 17So I have reason to be enthusiastic about all Christ Jesus has done through me in my service to God. 18Yet I dare not boast about anything except what Christ has done through me, bringing the Gentiles to God by my message and by the way I worked among them. 19They were convinced by the power of miraculous signs and wonders and by the power of God's Spirit.* In this way, I have fully presented the Good News of Christ from Jerusalem all the way to Illyricum.*

20My ambition has always been to preach the Good News where the name of Christ has never been heard, rather than where a church has already been started by someone else. 21I have been following the plan spoken of in the Scriptures, where it says,

"Those who have never been told
    about him will see,
    and those who have never heard
    of him will understand."*

22In fact, my visit to you has been delayed so long because I have been preaching in these places.

15:3 Greek *who insult you have fallen on me.* Ps 69:9.
15:8 Greek *servant of circumcision.*   15:9 Ps 18:49.

15:10 Deut 32:43.   15:11 Ps 117:1.   15:12a Greek *The root of Jesse.* David was the son of Jesse.   15:12b Isa 11:10 (Greek version).   15:14 Greek *brothers;* also in 15:30.   15:19a Other manuscripts read *the Spirit;* still others read *the Holy Spirit.*   15:19b *Illyricum* was a region northeast of Italy.   15:21 Isa 52:15 (Greek version).

*PSALM 25:1-15
A psalm of David.

1 ⬤ LORD, I give my life to you.
2   I trust in you, my God!
Do not let me be disgraced,
    or let my enemies rejoice
        in my defeat.
3 No one who trusts in you will ever
        be disgraced,
    but disgrace comes to those who
        try to deceive others.

4 Show me the right path, O LORD;
    point out the road for me
        to follow.
5 Lead me by your truth and teach me,
    for you are the God who saves me.
    All day long I put my hope in you.
6 Remember, O LORD, your
        compassion and unfailing love,
    which you have shown from
        long ages past.
7 Do not remember the rebellious
        sins of my youth.
    Remember me in the light of your
        unfailing love,
    for you are merciful, O LORD.

8 The LORD is good and does what
        is right;
    he shows the proper path to
        those who go astray.
9 He leads the humble in doing right,
    teaching them his way.
10 The LORD leads with unfailing love
        and faithfulness
    all who keep his covenant and
        obey his demands.

11 For the honor of your name, O LORD,
    forgive my many, many sins.
12 Who are those who fear
        the LORD?
    He will show them the path they
        should choose.
13 They will live in prosperity,
    and their children will inherit
        the land.

¹⁴ The Lᴏʀᴅ is a friend to those who
    fear him.
He teaches them his covenant.
¹⁵ My eyes are always on the Lᴏʀᴅ,
    for he rescues me from the traps
    of my enemies.

25 This psalm is a Hebrew acrostic poem; each verse begins
with a successive letter of the Hebrew alphabet.

PROVERBS 20:13-15

If you love sleep, you will end in poverty.
Keep your eyes open, and there will be
plenty to eat! □ The buyer haggles over
the price, saying, "It's worthless," then
brags about getting a bargain! □ Wise
words are more valuable than much gold
and many rubies.

AUGUST
2

2 CHRONICLES 32:1–33:13

After Hezekiah had faithfully carried
out this work, King Sennacherib of Assyria invaded Judah. He laid siege to the
fortified towns, giving orders for his
army to break through their walls.
²When Hezekiah realized that Sennacherib also intended to attack Jerusalem,
³he consulted with his officials and military advisers, and they decided to stop
the flow of the springs outside the city.
⁴They organized a huge work crew to
stop the flow of the springs, cutting
off the brook that ran through the fields.
For they said, "Why should the kings
of Assyria come here and find plenty of
water?"
⁵Then Hezekiah worked hard at repairing all the broken sections of the wall,
erecting towers, and constructing a second wall outside the first. He also re-
inforced the supporting terraces* in the
City of David and manufactured large
numbers of weapons and shields. ⁶He
appointed military officers over the people and assembled them before him in

the square at the city gate. Then Hezekiah
encouraged them by saying: ⁷"Be strong
and courageous! Don't be afraid or discouraged because of the king of Assyria
or his mighty army, for there is a power
far greater on our side! ⁸He may have a
great army, but they are merely men. We
have the Lᴏʀᴅ our God to help us and to
fight our battles for us!" Hezekiah's
words greatly encouraged the people.

⁹While King Sennacherib of Assyria
was still besieging the town of Lachish,
he sent his officers to Jerusalem with
this message for Hezekiah and all the
people in the city:

¹⁰"This is what King Sennacherib of
Assyria says: What are you trusting
in that makes you think you can
survive my siege of Jerusalem?
¹¹Hezekiah has said, 'The Lᴏʀᴅ our
God will rescue us from the king of
Assyria.' Surely Hezekiah is
misleading you, sentencing you to
death by famine and thirst! ¹²Don't
you realize that Hezekiah is the very
person who destroyed all the Lᴏʀᴅ's
shrines and altars? He commanded
Judah and Jerusalem to worship only
at the altar at the Temple and to
offer sacrifices on it alone.
¹³"Surely you must realize what
I and the other kings of Assyria
before me have done to all the
people of the earth! Were any of the
gods of those nations able to rescue
their people from my power?
¹⁴Which of their gods was able to
rescue its people from the destructive
power of my predecessors? What
makes you think your God can
rescue you from me? ¹⁵Don't let
Hezekiah deceive you! Don't let him
fool you like this! I say it again—no
god of any nation or kingdom has
ever yet been able to rescue his
people from me or my ancestors.
How much less will your God rescue
you from my power!"

¹⁶And Sennacherib's officers further
mocked the Lᴏʀᴅ God and his servant

Hezekiah, heaping insult upon insult. [17] The king also sent letters scorning the LORD, the God of Israel. He wrote, "Just as the gods of all the other nations failed to rescue their people from my power, so the God of Hezekiah will also fail." [18] The Assyrian officials who brought the letters shouted this in Hebrew* to the people gathered on the walls of the city, trying to terrify them so it would be easier to capture the city. [19] These officers talked about the God of Jerusalem as though he were one of the pagan gods, made by human hands.

[20] Then King Hezekiah and the prophet Isaiah son of Amoz cried out in prayer to God in heaven. [21] And the LORD sent an angel who destroyed the Assyrian army with all its commanders and officers. So Sennacherib was forced to return home in disgrace to his own land. And when he entered the temple of his god, some of his own sons killed him there with a sword.

[22] That is how the LORD rescued Hezekiah and the people of Jerusalem from King Sennacherib of Assyria and from all the others who threatened them. So there was peace throughout the land. [23] From then on King Hezekiah became highly respected among all the surrounding nations, and many gifts for the LORD arrived at Jerusalem, with valuable presents for King Hezekiah, too.

[24] About that time Hezekiah became deathly ill. He prayed to the LORD, who healed him and gave him a miraculous sign. [25] But Hezekiah did not respond appropriately to the kindness shown him, and he became proud. So the LORD's anger came against him and against Judah and Jerusalem. [26] Then Hezekiah humbled himself and repented of his pride, as did the people of Jerusalem. So the LORD's anger did not fall on them during Hezekiah's lifetime.

[27] Hezekiah was very wealthy and highly honored. He built special treasury buildings for his silver, gold, precious stones, and spices, and for his shields and other valuable items. [28] He also constructed many storehouses for his grain, new wine, and olive oil; and he made many stalls for his cattle and pens for his flocks of sheep and goats. [29] He built many towns and acquired vast flocks and herds, for God had given him great wealth. [30] He blocked up the upper spring of Gihon and brought the water down through a tunnel to the west side of the City of David. And so he succeeded in everything he did.

[31] However, when ambassadors arrived from Babylon to ask about the remarkable events that had taken place in the land, God withdrew from Hezekiah in order to test him and to see what was really in his heart.

[32] The rest of the events in Hezekiah's reign and his acts of devotion are recorded in *The Vision of the Prophet Isaiah Son of Amoz*, which is included in *The Book of the Kings of Judah and Israel*. [33] When Hezekiah died, he was buried in the upper area of the royal cemetery, and all Judah and Jerusalem honored him at his death. And his son Manasseh became the next king.

[33:1] MANASSEH was twelve years old when he became king, and he reigned in Jerusalem fifty-five years. [2] He did what was evil in the LORD's sight, following the detestable practices of the pagan nations that the LORD had driven from the land ahead of the Israelites. [3] He rebuilt the pagan shrines his father, Hezekiah, had broken down. He constructed altars for the images of Baal and set up Asherah poles. He also bowed before all the powers of the heavens and worshiped them.

[4] He built pagan altars in the Temple of the LORD, the place where the LORD had said, "My name will remain in Jerusalem forever." [5] He built these altars for all the powers of the heavens in both courtyards of the LORD's Temple. [6] Manasseh also sacrificed his own sons in the fire* in the valley of Ben-Hinnom. He practiced sorcery, divination, and witchcraft, and he consulted with mediums and psychics. He did much that

was evil in the LORD's sight, arousing his anger.

[7]Manasseh even took a carved idol he had made and set it up in God's Temple, the very place where God had told David and his son Solomon: "My name will be honored forever in this Temple and in Jerusalem—the city I have chosen from among all the tribes of Israel. [8]If the Israelites will be careful to obey my commands—all the laws, decrees, and regulations given through Moses—I will not send them into exile from this land that I set aside for your ancestors." [9]But Manasseh led the people of Judah and Jerusalem to do even more evil than the pagan nations that the LORD had destroyed when the people of Israel entered the land.

[10]The LORD spoke to Manasseh and his people, but they ignored all his warnings. [11]So the LORD sent the commanders of the Assyrian armies, and they took Manasseh prisoner. They put a ring through his nose, bound him in bronze chains, and led him away to Babylon. [12]But while in deep distress, Manasseh sought the LORD his God and sincerely humbled himself before the God of his ancestors. [13]And when he prayed, the LORD listened to him and was moved by his request. So the LORD brought Manasseh back to Jerusalem and to his kingdom. Then Manasseh finally realized that the LORD alone is God!

32:5 Hebrew *the millo.* The meaning of the Hebrew is uncertain.   32:18 Hebrew *in the dialect of Judah.*
33:6 Or *also made his sons pass through the fire.*

ROMANS 15:23–16:9

But now I [Paul] have finished my work in these regions, and after all these long years of waiting, I am eager to visit you. [24]I am planning to go to Spain, and when I do, I will stop off in Rome. And after I have enjoyed your fellowship for a little while, you can provide for my journey.

[25]But before I come, I must go to Jerusalem to take a gift to the believers there. [26]For you see, the believers in Macedonia and Achaia* have eagerly taken up an offering for the poor among the believers

in Jerusalem. [27]They were glad to do this because they feel they owe a real debt to them. Since the Gentiles received the spiritual blessings of the Good News from the believers in Jerusalem, they feel the least they can do in return is to help them financially. [28]As soon as I have delivered this money and completed this good deed of theirs, I will come to see you on my way to Spain. [29]And I am sure that when I come, Christ will richly bless our time together.

[30]Dear brothers and sisters, I urge you in the name of our Lord Jesus Christ to join in my struggle by praying to God for me. Do this because of your love for me, given to you by the Holy Spirit. [31]Pray that I will be rescued from those in Judea who refuse to obey God. Pray also that the believers there will be willing to accept the donation* I am taking to Jerusalem. [32]Then, by the will of God, I will be able to come to you with a joyful heart, and we will be an encouragement to each other.

[33]And now may God, who gives us his peace, be with you all. Amen.*

[16:1]I COMMEND to you our sister Phoebe, who is a deacon in the church in Cenchrea. [2]Welcome her in the Lord as one who is worthy of honor among God's people. Help her in whatever she needs, for she has been helpful to many, and especially to me.

[3]Give my greetings to Priscilla and Aquila, my co-workers in the ministry of Christ Jesus. [4]In fact, they once risked their lives for me. I am thankful to them, and so are all the Gentile churches. [5]Also give my greetings to the church that meets in their home.

Greet my dear friend Epenetus. He was the first person from the province of Asia to become a follower of Christ. [6]Give my greetings to Mary, who has worked so hard for your benefit. [7]Greet Andronicus and Junia,* my fellow Jews,* who were in prison with me. They are highly respected among the apostles and became followers of Christ before I did. [8]Greet Ampliatus, my dear friend in the

Lord. ⁹Greet Urbanus, our co-worker in Christ, and my dear friend Stachys.

15:26 *Macedonia* and *Achaia* were the northern and southern regions of Greece.   15:31 Greek *the ministry;* other manuscripts read *the gift.*   15:33 Some manuscripts omit *Amen.* One very early manuscript places 16:25-27 here.   16:7a *Junia* is a feminine name. Some late manuscripts accent the word so it reads *Junias,* a masculine name; still others read *Julia* (feminine).   16:7b Or *compatriots;* also in 16:21.

PSALM 25:16-22

Turn to me and have mercy,
for I am alone and in deep distress.
¹⁷ My problems go from bad to worse.
Oh, save me from them all!
¹⁸ Feel my pain and see my trouble.
Forgive all my sins.
¹⁹ See how many enemies I have
and how viciously they hate me!
²⁰ **Protect me! Rescue my life
from them!
Do not let me be disgraced, for
in you I take refuge.**
²¹ **May integrity and honesty
protect me,
for I put my hope in you.**

²² O God, ransom Israel
from all its troubles.

PROVERBS 20:16-18

Get security from someone who guarantees a stranger's debt. Get a deposit if he does it for foreigners.* □Stolen bread tastes sweet, but it turns to gravel in the mouth. □Plans succeed through good counsel; don't go to war without wise advice.

20:16 An alternate reading in the Hebrew text is *for a promiscuous woman.*

AUGUST 3

2 CHRONICLES 33:14–34:33

After this Manasseh rebuilt the outer wall of the City of David, from west of the Gihon Spring in the Kidron Valley to the Fish Gate, and continuing around the hill of Ophel. He built the wall very high. And he stationed his military officers in all of the fortified towns of Judah. ¹⁵Manasseh also removed the foreign gods and the idol from the Lord's Temple. He tore down all the altars he had built on the hill where the Temple stood and all the altars that were in Jerusalem, and he dumped them outside the city. ¹⁶Then he restored the altar of the Lord and sacrificed peace offerings and thanksgiving offerings on it. He also encouraged the people of Judah to worship the Lord, the God of Israel. ¹⁷However, the people still sacrificed at the pagan shrines, though only to the Lord their God.

¹⁸The rest of the events of Manasseh's reign, his prayer to God, and the words the seers spoke to him in the name of the Lord, the God of Israel, are recorded in *The Book of the Kings of Israel.* ¹⁹Manasseh's prayer, the account of the way God answered him, and an account of all his sins and unfaithfulness are recorded in *The Record of the Seers.** It includes a list of the locations where he built pagan shrines and set up Asherah poles and idols before he humbled himself and repented. ²⁰When Manasseh died, he was buried in his palace. Then his son Amon became the next king.

²¹Amon was twenty-two years old when he became king, and he reigned in Jerusalem two years. ²²He did what was evil in the Lord's sight, just as his father, Manasseh, had done. He worshiped and sacrificed to all the idols his father had made. ²³But unlike his father, he did not humble himself before the Lord. Instead, Amon sinned even more.

²⁴Then Amon's own officials conspired against him and assassinated him in his palace. ²⁵But the people of the land killed all those who had conspired against King Amon, and they made his son Josiah the next king.

³⁴:¹Josiah was eight years old when he became king, and he reigned in Jerusalem thirty-one years. ²He did what was pleasing in the Lord's sight and followed the example of his ancestor Da-

vid. He did not turn away from doing what was right.

³During the eighth year of his reign, while he was still young, Josiah began to seek the God of his ancestor David. Then in the twelfth year he began to purify Judah and Jerusalem, destroying all the pagan shrines, the Asherah poles, and the carved idols and cast images. ⁴He ordered that the altars of Baal be demolished and that the incense altars which stood above them be broken down. He also made sure that the Asherah poles, the carved idols, and the cast images were smashed and scattered over the graves of those who had sacrificed to them. ⁵He burned the bones of the pagan priests on their own altars, and so he purified Judah and Jerusalem.

⁶He did the same thing in the towns of Manasseh, Ephraim, and Simeon, even as far as Naphtali, and in the regions* all around them. ⁷He destroyed the pagan altars and the Asherah poles, and he crushed the idols into dust. He cut down all the incense altars throughout the land of Israel. Finally, he returned to Jerusalem.

⁸In the eighteenth year of his reign, after he had purified the land and the Temple, Josiah appointed Shaphan son of Azaliah, Maaseiah the governor of Jerusalem, and Joah son of Joahaz, the royal historian, to repair the Temple of the LORD his God. ⁹They gave Hilkiah the high priest the money that had been collected by the Levites who served as gatekeepers at the Temple of God. The gifts were brought by people from Manasseh, Ephraim, and from all the remnant of Israel, as well as from all Judah, Benjamin, and the people of Jerusalem.

¹⁰He entrusted the money to the men assigned to supervise the restoration of the LORD's Temple. Then they paid the workers who did the repairs and renovation of the Temple. ¹¹They hired carpenters and builders, who purchased finished stone for the walls and timber for the rafters and beams. They restored what earlier kings of Judah had allowed to fall into ruin.

¹²The workers served faithfully under the leadership of Jahath and Obadiah, Levites of the Merarite clan, and Zechariah and Meshullam, Levites of the Kohathite clan. Other Levites, all of whom were skilled musicians, ¹³were put in charge of the laborers of the various trades. Still others assisted as secretaries, officials, and gatekeepers.

¹⁴While they were bringing out the money collected at the LORD's Temple, Hilkiah the priest found the Book of the Law of the LORD that was written by Moses. ¹⁵Hilkiah said to Shaphan the court secretary, "I have found the Book of the Law in the LORD's Temple!" Then Hilkiah gave the scroll to Shaphan.

¹⁶Shaphan took the scroll to the king and reported, "Your officials are doing everything they were assigned to do. ¹⁷The money that was collected at the Temple of the LORD has been turned over to the supervisors and workmen." ¹⁸Shaphan also told the king, "Hilkiah the priest has given me a scroll." So Shaphan read it to the king.

¹⁹When the king heard what was written in the Law, he tore his clothes in despair. ²⁰Then he gave these orders to Hilkiah, Ahikam son of Shaphan, Acbor son of Micaiah,* Shaphan the court secretary, and Asaiah the king's personal adviser: ²¹"Go to the Temple and speak to the LORD for me and for all the remnant of Israel and Judah. Inquire about the words written in the scroll that has been found. For the LORD's great anger has been poured out on us because our ancestors have not obeyed the word of the LORD. We have not been doing everything this scroll says we must do."

²²So Hilkiah and the other men went to the New Quarter* of Jerusalem to consult with the prophet Huldah. She was the wife of Shallum son of Tikvah, son of Harhas,* the keeper of the Temple wardrobe.

²³She said to them, "The LORD, the God of Israel, has spoken! Go back and tell the man who sent you, ²⁴'This is what the LORD says: I am going to bring disaster on this city* and its people. All the curses

written in the scroll that was read to the king of Judah will come true. [25]For my people have abandoned me and offered sacrifices to pagan gods, and I am very angry with them for everything they have done. My anger will be poured out on this place, and it will not be quenched.'

[26]"But go to the king of Judah who sent you to seek the Lord and tell him: 'This is what the Lord, the God of Israel, says concerning the message you have just heard: [27]You were sorry and humbled yourself before God when you heard his words against this city and its people. You humbled yourself and tore your clothing in despair and wept before me in repentance. And I have indeed heard you, says the Lord. [28]So I will not send the promised disaster until after you have died and been buried in peace. You yourself will not see the disaster I am going to bring on this city and its people.'"

So they took her message back to the king.

[29]Then the king summoned all the elders of Judah and Jerusalem. [30]And the king went up to the Temple of the Lord with all the people of Judah and Jerusalem, along with the priests and the Levites—all the people from the greatest to the least. There the king read to them the entire Book of the Covenant that had been found in the Lord's Temple. [31]The king took his place of authority beside the pillar and renewed the covenant in the Lord's presence. He pledged to obey the Lord by keeping all his commands, laws, and decrees with all his heart and soul. He promised to obey all the terms of the covenant that were written in the scroll. [32]And he required everyone in Jerusalem and the people of Benjamin to make a similar pledge. The people of Jerusalem did so, renewing their covenant with God, the God of their ancestors.

[33]So Josiah removed all detestable idols from the entire land of Israel and required everyone to worship the Lord their God. And throughout the rest of his lifetime, they did not turn away from the Lord, the God of their ancestors.

33:19 Or *The Record of Hozai.* 34:6 As in Syriac version. Hebrew reads *in their temples,* or *in their ruins.* The meaning of the Hebrew is uncertain. 34:20 As in parallel text at 2 Kgs 22:12; Hebrew reads *Abdon son of Micah.* 34:22a Or *the Second Quarter,* a newer section of Jerusalem. Hebrew reads *the Mishneh.* 34:22b As in parallel text at 2 Kgs 22:14; Hebrew reads *son of Tokhath, son of Hasrah.* 34:24 Hebrew *this place;* also in 34:27, 28.

ROMANS 16:10-27

Greet Apelles, a good man whom Christ approves. And give my [Paul's] greetings to the believers from the household of Aristobulus. [11]Greet Herodion, my fellow Jew.* Greet the Lord's people from the household of Narcissus. [12]Give my greetings to Tryphena and Tryphosa, the Lord's workers, and to dear Persis, who has worked so hard for the Lord. [13]Greet Rufus, whom the Lord picked out to be his very own; and also his dear mother, who has been a mother to me.

[14]Give my greetings to Asyncritus, Phlegon, Hermes, Patrobas, Hermas, and the brothers and sisters* who meet with them. [15]Give my greetings to Philologus, Julia, Nereus and his sister, and to Olympas and all the believers who meet with them. [16]Greet each other in Christian love.* All the churches of Christ send you their greetings.

[17]And now I make one more appeal, my dear brothers and sisters. Watch out for people who cause divisions and upset people's faith by teaching things contrary to what you have been taught. Stay away from them. [18]Such people are not serving Christ our Lord; they are serving their own personal interests. By smooth talk and glowing words they deceive innocent people. [19]But everyone knows that you are obedient to the Lord. This makes me very happy. I want you to be wise in doing right and to stay innocent of any wrong. [20]The God of peace will soon crush Satan under your feet. May the grace of our Lord Jesus* be with you.

[21]Timothy, my fellow worker, sends you his greetings, as do Lucius, Jason, and Sosipater, my fellow Jews.

[22]I, Tertius, the one writing this letter for Paul, send my greetings, too, as one of the Lord's followers.

[23]Gaius says hello to you. He is my

host and also serves as host to the whole church. Erastus, the city treasurer, sends you his greetings, and so does our brother Quartus.*

25Now all glory to God, who is able to make you strong, just as my Good News says. This message about Jesus Christ has revealed his plan for you Gentiles, a plan kept secret from the beginning of time. 26But now as the prophets* foretold and as the eternal God has commanded, this message is made known to all Gentiles everywhere, so that they too might believe and obey him. 27All glory to the only wise God, through Jesus Christ, forever. Amen.

16:11 Or *compatriot.* 16:14 Greek *brothers;* also in 16:17. 16:16 Greek *with a sacred kiss.* 16:20 Some manuscripts read *Lord Jesus Christ.* 16:23 Some manuscripts add verse 24, *May the grace of our Lord Jesus Christ be with you all. Amen.* Still others add this sentence after verse 27. 16:26 Greek *the prophetic writings.*

PSALM 26:1-12
A psalm of David.

1 **D**eclare me innocent, O Lord,
    for I have acted with integrity;
    I have trusted in the Lord
        without wavering.
2 **Put me on trial, Lord, and cross-examine me.**
    Test my motives and my heart.
3 **For I am always aware of your unfailing love,**
    and I have lived according to your truth.
4 I do not spend time with liars
    or go along with hypocrites.
5 I hate the gatherings of those
        who do evil,
    and I refuse to join in with
        the wicked.
6 I wash my hands to declare
        my innocence.
    I come to your altar, O Lord,
7 singing a song of thanksgiving
    and telling of all your wonders.
8 I love your sanctuary, Lord,
    the place where your glorious
        presence dwells.

9 Don't let me suffer the fate
    of sinners.

Don't condemn me along
    with murderers.
10 Their hands are dirty with evil
        schemes,
    and they constantly take bribes.
11 But I am not like that; I live
        with integrity.
    So redeem me and show
        me mercy.
12 Now I stand on solid ground,
    and I will publicly praise
        the Lord.

PROVERBS 20:19
A gossip goes around telling secrets, so don't hang around with chatterers.

AUGUST 4

2 CHRONICLES 35:1–36:23
Then Josiah announced that the Passover of the Lord would be celebrated in Jerusalem, and so the Passover lamb was slaughtered on the fourteenth day of the first month.* 2Josiah also assigned the priests to their duties and encouraged them in their work at the Temple of the Lord. 3He issued this order to the Levites, who were to teach all Israel and who had been set apart to serve the Lord: "Put the holy Ark in the Temple that was built by Solomon son of David, the king of Israel. You no longer need to carry it back and forth on your shoulders. Now spend your time serving the Lord your God and his people Israel. 4Report for duty according to the family divisions of your ancestors, following the directions of King David of Israel and the directions of his son Solomon.

5"Then stand in the sanctuary at the place appointed for your family division and help the families assigned to you as they bring their offerings to the Temple. 6Slaughter the Passover lambs, purify yourselves, and prepare to help those who come. Follow all the directions that the LORD gave through Moses."

[7] Then Josiah provided 30,000 lambs and young goats for the people's Passover offerings, along with 3,000 cattle, all from the king's own flocks and herds. [8] The king's officials also made willing contributions to the people, priests, and Levites. Hilkiah, Zechariah, and Jehiel, the administrators of God's Temple, gave the priests 2,600 lambs and young goats and 300 cattle as Passover offerings. [9] The Levite leaders—Conaniah and his brothers Shemaiah and Nethanel, as well as Hashabiah, Jeiel, and Jozabad—gave 5,000 lambs and young goats and 500 cattle to the Levites for their Passover offerings.

[10] When everything was ready for the Passover celebration, the priests and the Levites took their places, organized by their divisions, as the king had commanded. [11] The Levites then slaughtered the Passover lambs and presented the blood to the priests, who sprinkled the blood on the altar while the Levites prepared the animals. [12] They divided the burnt offerings among the people by their family groups, so they could offer them to the LORD as prescribed in the Book of Moses. They did the same with the cattle. [13] Then they roasted the Passover lambs as prescribed; and they boiled the holy offerings in pots, kettles, and pans, and brought them out quickly so the people could eat them.

[14] Afterward the Levites prepared Passover offerings for themselves and for the priests—the descendants of Aaron—because the priests had been busy from morning till night offering the burnt offerings and the fat portions. The Levites took responsibility for all these preparations.

[15] The musicians, descendants of Asaph, were in their assigned places, following the commands that had been given by David, Asaph, Heman, and Jeduthun, the king's seer. The gatekeepers guarded the gates and did not need to leave their posts of duty, for their Passover offerings were prepared for them by their fellow Levites.

[16] The entire ceremony for the LORD's Passover was completed that day. All the burnt offerings were sacrificed on the altar of the LORD, as King Josiah had commanded. [17] All the Israelites present in Jerusalem celebrated Passover and the Festival of Unleavened Bread for seven days. [18] Never since the time of the prophet Samuel had there been such a Passover. None of the kings of Israel had ever kept a Passover as Josiah did, involving all the priests and Levites, all the people of Jerusalem, and people from all over Judah and Israel. [19] This Passover celebration took place in the eighteenth year of Josiah's reign.

[20] After Josiah had finished restoring the Temple, King Neco of Egypt led his army up from Egypt to do battle at Carchemish on the Euphrates River, and Josiah and his army marched out to fight him.* [21] But King Neco sent messengers to Josiah with this message:

> "What do you want with me, king of Judah? I have no quarrel with you today! I am on my way to fight another nation, and God has told me to hurry! Do not interfere with God, who is with me, or he will destroy you."

[22] But Josiah refused to listen to Neco, to whom God had indeed spoken, and he would not turn back. Instead, he disguised himself and led his army into battle on the plain of Megiddo. [23] But the enemy archers hit King Josiah with their arrows and wounded him. He cried out to his men, "Take me from the battle, for I am badly wounded!"

[24] So they lifted Josiah out of his chariot and placed him in another chariot. Then they brought him back to Jerusalem, where he died. He was buried there in the royal cemetery. And all Judah and Jerusalem mourned for him. [25] The prophet Jeremiah composed funeral songs for Josiah, and to this day choirs still sing these sad songs about his death.

These songs of sorrow have become a tradition and are recorded in *The Book of Laments*.

²⁶The rest of the events of Josiah's reign and his acts of devotion (carried out according to what was written in the Law of the LORD), ²⁷from beginning to end—all are recorded in *The Book of the Kings of Israel and Judah*.

³⁶:¹THEN the people of the land took Josiah's son Jehoahaz and made him the next king in Jerusalem.

²Jehoahaz* was twenty-three years old when he became king, and he reigned in Jerusalem three months.

³Then he was deposed by the king of Egypt, who demanded that Judah pay 7,500 pounds of silver and 75 pounds of gold* as tribute.

⁴The king of Egypt then installed Eliakim, the brother of Jehoahaz, as the next king of Judah and Jerusalem, and he changed Eliakim's name to Jehoiakim. Then Neco took Jehoahaz to Egypt as a prisoner.

⁵Jehoiakim was twenty-five years old when he became king, and he reigned in Jerusalem eleven years. He did what was evil in the sight of the LORD his God.

⁶Then King Nebuchadnezzar of Babylon came to Jerusalem and captured it, and he bound Jehoiakim in bronze chains and led him away to Babylon. ⁷Nebuchadnezzar also took some of the treasures from the Temple of the LORD, and he placed them in his palace* in Babylon.

⁸The rest of the events in Jehoiakim's reign, including all the evil things he did and everything found against him, are recorded in *The Book of the Kings of Israel and Judah*. Then his son Jehoiachin became the next king.

⁹Jehoiachin was eighteen* years old when he became king, and he reigned in Jerusalem three months and ten days. Jehoiachin did what was evil in the LORD's sight.

¹⁰In the spring of the year* King Nebuchadnezzar took Jehoiachin to Babylon. Many treasures from the Temple of the LORD were also taken to Babylon at that time. And Nebuchadnezzar installed Jehoiachin's uncle,* Zedekiah, as the next king in Judah and Jerusalem.

¹¹Zedekiah was twenty-one years old when he became king, and he reigned in Jerusalem eleven years. ¹²He did what was evil in the sight of the LORD his God, and he refused to humble himself when the prophet Jeremiah spoke to him directly from the LORD. ¹³He also rebelled against King Nebuchadnezzar, even though he had taken an oath of loyalty in God's name. Zedekiah was a hard and stubborn man, refusing to turn to the LORD, the God of Israel.

¹⁴Likewise, all the leaders of the priests and the people became more and more unfaithful. They followed all the pagan practices of the surrounding nations, desecrating the Temple of the LORD that had been consecrated in Jerusalem.

¹⁵The LORD, the God of their ancestors, repeatedly sent his prophets to warn them, for he had compassion on his people and his Temple. ¹⁶But the people mocked these messengers of God and despised their words. They scoffed at the prophets until the LORD's anger could no longer be restrained and nothing could be done.

¹⁷So the LORD brought the king of Babylon against them. The Babylonians* killed Judah's young men, even chasing after them into the Temple. They had no pity on the people, killing both young men and young women, the old and the infirm. God handed all of them over to Nebuchadnezzar. ¹⁸The king took home to Babylon all the articles, large and small, used in the Temple of God, and the treasures from both the LORD's Temple and from the palace of the king and his officials. ¹⁹Then his army burned the Temple of God, tore down the walls of Jerusalem, burned all the palaces, and completely destroyed everything of value.* ²⁰The few who survived were taken as exiles to Babylon, and they became servants to the king

and his sons until the kingdom of Persia came to power.

²¹So the message of the LORD spoken through Jeremiah was fulfilled. The land finally enjoyed its Sabbath rest, lying desolate until the seventy years were fulfilled, just as the prophet had said.

²²In the first year of King Cyrus of Persia,* the LORD fulfilled the prophecy he had given through Jeremiah.* He stirred the heart of Cyrus to put this proclamation in writing and to send it throughout his kingdom:

²³"This is what King Cyrus of Persia says:

"The LORD, the God of heaven, has given me all the kingdoms of the earth. He has appointed me to build him a Temple at Jerusalem, which is in Judah. Any of you who are the LORD's people may go there for this task. And may the LORD your God be with you!"

35:1 This day in the ancient Hebrew lunar calendar was April 5, 622 B.C.   35:20 Or *Josiah went out to meet him.* 36:2 Hebrew *Joahaz,* a variant spelling of Jehoahaz; also in 36:4.   36:3 Hebrew *100 talents* [3,400 kilograms] *of silver and 1 talent* [34 kilograms] *of gold.*   36:7 Or *temple.* 36:9 As in one Hebrew manuscript, some Greek manuscripts, and Syriac version (see also 2 Kgs 24:8); most Hebrew manuscripts read *eight.*   36:10a Hebrew *At the turn of the year.* The first day of this year in the ancient Hebrew lunar calendar was April 13, 597 B.C.   36:10b As in parallel text at 2 Kgs 24:17; Hebrew reads *brother,* or *relative.*   36:17 Or *Chaldeans.*   36:19 Or *destroyed all the valuable articles from the Temple.*   36:22a The first year of Cyrus's reign over Babylon was 538 B.C.   36:22b See Jer 25:11-12; 29:10.

1 CORINTHIANS 1:1-17

This letter is from Paul, chosen by the will of God to be an apostle of Christ Jesus, and from our brother Sosthenes.

²I am writing to God's church in Corinth,* to you who have been called by God to be his own holy people. He made you holy by means of Christ Jesus,* just as he did for all people everywhere who call on the name of our Lord Jesus Christ, their Lord and ours.

³May God our Father and the Lord Jesus Christ give you grace and peace.

⁴I always thank my God for you and for the gracious gifts he has given you, now that you belong to Christ Jesus. ⁵Through him, God has enriched your church in every way—with all of your eloquent words and all of your knowledge. ⁶This confirms that what I told you about Christ is true. ⁷**Now you have every spiritual gift you need as you eagerly wait for the return of our Lord Jesus Christ. ⁸He will keep you strong to the end so that you will be free from all blame on the day when our Lord Jesus Christ returns.** ⁹God will do this, for he is faithful to do what he says, and he has invited you into partnership with his Son, Jesus Christ our Lord.

¹⁰I appeal to you, dear brothers and sisters,* by the authority of our Lord Jesus Christ, to live in harmony with each other. Let there be no divisions in the church. Rather, be of one mind, united in thought and purpose. ¹¹For some members of Chloe's household have told me about your quarrels, my dear brothers and sisters. ¹²Some of you are saying, "I am a follower of Paul." Others are saying, "I follow Apollos," or "I follow Peter,*" or "I follow only Christ."

¹³Has Christ been divided into factions? Was I, Paul, crucified for you? Were any of you baptized in the name of Paul? Of course not! ¹⁴I thank God that I did not baptize any of you except Crispus and Gaius, ¹⁵for now no one can say they were baptized in my name. ¹⁶(Oh yes, I also baptized the household of Stephanas, but I don't remember baptizing anyone else.) ¹⁷For Christ didn't send me to baptize, but to preach the Good News—and not with clever speech, for fear that the cross of Christ would lose its power.

1:2a *Corinth* was the capital city of Achaia, the southern region of the Greek peninsula.   1:2b Or *because you belong to Christ Jesus.*   1:10 Greek *brothers;* also in 1:11, 26.   1:12 Greek *Cephas.*

PSALM 27:1-6
A psalm of David.

¹ The LORD is my light and
    my salvation—
  so why should I be afraid?
The LORD is my fortress, protecting
    me from danger,
  so why should I tremble?

² When evil people come to devour me,
  when my enemies and foes
     attack me,
  they will stumble and fall.
³ Though a mighty army surrounds
     me,
  my heart will not be afraid.
  Even if I am attacked,
     I will remain confident.

⁴ The one thing I ask of the LORD—
     the thing I seek most—
  is to live in the house of the LORD
     all the days of my life,
  delighting in the LORD's perfections
  and meditating in his Temple.
⁵ For he will conceal me there when
     troubles come;
  he will hide me in his sanctuary.
  He will place me out of reach
     on a high rock.
⁶ Then I will hold my head high
     above my enemies who
     surround me.
  At his sanctuary I will offer
     sacrifices with shouts of joy,
  singing and praising the LORD
     with music.

PROVERBS 20:20-21
If you insult your father or mother, your
light will be snuffed out in total darkness. □ An inheritance obtained too
early in life is not a blessing in the end.

AUGUST
5

EZRA 1:1-2:70
In the first year of King Cyrus of Persia,*
the LORD fulfilled the prophecy he had
given through Jeremiah.* He stirred the
heart of Cyrus to put this proclamation
in writing and to send it throughout his
kingdom:

²"This is what King Cyrus of Persia
says:

"The LORD, the God of heaven,
has given me all the kingdoms
of the earth. He has appointed me
to build him a Temple at Jerusalem,
which is in Judah. ³Any of you who
are his people may go to Jerusalem
in Judah to rebuild this Temple of
the LORD, the God of Israel, who
lives in Jerusalem. And may your
God be with you! ⁴Wherever this
Jewish remnant is found, let their
neighbors contribute toward their
expenses by giving them silver and
gold, supplies for the journey, and
livestock, as well as a voluntary
offering for the Temple of God in
Jerusalem."

⁵Then God stirred the hearts of the
priests and Levites and the leaders of
the tribes of Judah and Benjamin to go
to Jerusalem to rebuild the Temple of
the LORD. ⁶And all their neighbors assisted by giving them articles of silver
and gold, supplies for the journey, and
livestock. They gave them many valuable gifts in addition to all the voluntary
offerings.

⁷King Cyrus himself brought out the
articles that King Nebuchadnezzar had
taken from the LORD's Temple in Jerusalem and had placed in the temple of
his own gods. ⁸Cyrus directed Mithredath, the treasurer of Persia, to count
these items and present them to Sheshbazzar, the leader of the exiles returning to Judah.* ⁹This is a list of the items
that were returned:

gold basins	30
silver basins	1,000
silver incense burners*	29
¹⁰ gold bowls	30
silver bowls	410
other items	1,000

¹¹In all, there were 5,400 articles of
gold and silver. Sheshbazzar brought all
of these along when the exiles went
from Babylon to Jerusalem.

²:¹HERE is the list of the Jewish exiles of
the provinces who returned from their

captivity. King Nebuchadnezzar had deported them to Babylon, but now they returned to Jerusalem and the other towns in Judah where they originally lived. ²Their leaders were Zerubbabel, Jeshua, Nehemiah, Seraiah, Reelaiah, Mordecai, Bilshan, Mispar, Bigvai, Rehum, and Baanah.

This is the number of the men of Israel who returned from exile:

³ The family of Parosh........... 2,172
⁴ The family of Shephatiah 372
⁵ The family of Arah.............. 775
⁶ The family of Pahath-moab (descendants of Jeshua and Joab)..................... 2,812
⁷ The family of Elam............. 1,254
⁸ The family of Zattu 945
⁹ The family of Zaccai 760
¹⁰ The family of Bani.............. 642
¹¹ The family of Bebai.............. 623
¹² The family of Azgad 1,222
¹³ The family of Adonikam 666
¹⁴ The family of Bigvai........... 2,056
¹⁵ The family of Adin.............. 454
¹⁶ The family of Ater (descendants of Hezekiah)........ 98
¹⁷ The family of Bezai 323
¹⁸ The family of Jorah 112
¹⁹ The family of Hashum 223
²⁰ The family of Gibbar............. 95
²¹ The people of Bethlehem........ 123
²² The people of Netophah.......... 56
²³ The people of Anathoth......... 128
²⁴ The people of Beth-azmaveth*..... 42
²⁵ The people of Kiriath-jearim,* Kephirah, and Beeroth 743
²⁶ The people of Ramah and Geba... 621
²⁷ The people of Micmash.......... 122
²⁸ The people of Bethel and Ai 223
²⁹ The citizens of Nebo............. 52
³⁰ The citizens of Magbish.......... 156
³¹ The citizens of Elam 1,254
³² The citizens of Harim........... 320
³³ The citizens of Lod, Hadid, and Ono 725
³⁴ The citizens of Jericho 345
³⁵ The citizens of Senaah 3,630

³⁶These are the priests who returned from exile:

The family of Jedaiah (through the line of Jeshua) 973
³⁷ The family of Immer........... 1,052
³⁸ The family of Pashhur.......... 1,247
³⁹ The family of Harim 1,017

⁴⁰These are the Levites who returned from exile:

The families of Jeshua and Kadmiel (descendants of Hodaviah)......... 74
⁴¹ The singers of the family of Asaph 128
⁴² The gatekeepers of the families of Shallum, Ater, Talmon, Akkub, Hatita, and Shobai...................... 139

⁴³The descendants of the following Temple servants returned from exile:
Ziha, Hasupha, Tabbaoth,
⁴⁴ Keros, Siaha, Padon,
⁴⁵ Lebanah, Hagabah, Akkub,
⁴⁶ Hagab, Shalmai,* Hanan,
⁴⁷ Giddel, Gahar, Reaiah,
⁴⁸ Rezin, Nekoda, Gazzam,
⁴⁹ Uzza, Paseah, Besai,
⁵⁰ Asnah, Meunim, Nephusim,
⁵¹ Bakbuk, Hakupha, Harhur,
⁵² Bazluth, Mehida, Harsha,
⁵³ Barkos, Sisera, Temah,
⁵⁴ Neziah, and Hatipha.

⁵⁵The descendants of these servants of King Solomon returned from exile:
Sotai, Hassophereth, Peruda,
⁵⁶ Jaalah, Darkon, Giddel,
⁵⁷ Shephatiah, Hattil, Pokerethhazzebaim, and Ami.

⁵⁸In all, the Temple servants and the descendants of Solomon's servants numbered 392.

⁵⁹Another group returned at this time from the towns of Tel-melah, Telharsha, Kerub, Addan, and Immer. However, they could not prove that they or their families were descendants of Israel. ⁶⁰This group included the families of Delaiah, Tobiah, and Nekoda—a total of 652 people.

⁶¹Three families of priests—Hobaiah, Hakkoz, and Barzillai—also returned. (This Barzillai had married a woman who was a descendant of Barzillai of Gil-

ead, and he had taken her family name.) [62]They searched for their names in the genealogical records, but they were not found, so they were disqualified from serving as priests. [63]The governor told them not to eat the priests' share of food from the sacrifices until a priest could consult the LORD about the matter by using the Urim and Thummim—the sacred lots.

[64]So a total of 42,360 people returned to Judah, [65]in addition to 7,337 servants and 200 singers, both men and women. [66]They took with them 736 horses, 245 mules, [67]435 camels, and 6,720 donkeys.

[68]When they arrived at the Temple of the LORD in Jerusalem, some of the family leaders made voluntary offerings toward the rebuilding of God's Temple on its original site, [69]and each leader gave as much as he could. The total of their gifts came to 61,000 gold coins,* 6,250 pounds* of silver, and 100 robes for the priests.

[70]So the priests, the Levites, the singers, the gatekeepers, the Temple servants, and some of the common people settled in villages near Jerusalem. The rest of the people returned to their own towns throughout Israel.

1:1a The first year of Cyrus's reign over Babylon was 538 B.C. 1:1b See Jer 25:11-12; 29:10.   1:8 Hebrew *Sheshbazzar, the prince of Judah.*   1:9 The meaning of this Hebrew word is uncertain.   2:24 As in parallel text at Neh 7:28; Hebrew reads *Azmaveth.*   2:25 As in some Hebrew manuscripts and Greek version (see also Neh 7:29); Hebrew reads *Kiriath-arim.*   2:46 As in an alternate reading of the Masoretic Text (see also Neh 7:48); the other alternate reads *Shamlai.*   2:69a Hebrew *61,000 darics of gold,* about 1,100 pounds or 500 kilograms in weight.   2:69b Hebrew *5,000 minas* (3,000 kilograms).

1 CORINTHIANS 1:18–2:5

The message of the cross is foolish to those who are headed for destruction! But we who are being saved know it is the very power of God. [19]As the Scriptures say,

"I will destroy the wisdom of the wise
    and discard the intelligence
        of the intelligent."*

[20]So where does this leave the philosophers, the scholars, and the world's brilliant debaters? God has made the wisdom of this world look foolish. [21]Since God in his wisdom saw to it that the world would never know him through human wisdom, he has used our foolish preaching to save those who believe. [22]It is foolish to the Jews, who ask for signs from heaven. And it is foolish to the Greeks, who seek human wisdom. [23]So when we preach that Christ was crucified, the Jews are offended and the Gentiles say it's all nonsense.

[24]But to those called by God to salvation, both Jews and Gentiles,* Christ is the power of God and the wisdom of God. [25]This foolish plan of God is wiser than the wisest of human plans, and God's weakness is stronger than the greatest of human strength.

[26]Remember, dear brothers and sisters, that few of you were wise in the world's eyes or powerful or wealthy* when God called you. [27]Instead, God chose things the world considers foolish in order to shame those who think they are wise. And he chose things that are powerless to shame those who are powerful. [28]God chose things despised by the world,* things counted as nothing at all, and used them to bring to nothing what the world considers important. [29]As a result, no one can ever boast in the presence of God.

[30]God has united you with Christ Jesus. For our benefit God made him to be wisdom itself. Christ made us right with God; he made us pure and holy, and he freed us from sin. [31]Therefore, as the Scriptures say, "If you want to boast, boast only about the LORD."*

[2:1]WHEN I [Paul] first came to you, dear brothers and sisters,* I didn't use lofty words and impressive wisdom to tell you God's secret plan.* [2]For I decided that while I was with you I would forget everything except Jesus Christ, the one who was crucified. [3]I came to you in weakness—timid and trembling. [4]And my message and my preaching were very plain. Rather than using clever and persuasive speeches, I relied only on the power of the Holy Spirit. ⁵I did this so you would trust not in human wisdom but in the power of God.

1:19 Isa 29:14.   1:24 Greek *and Greeks*.   1:26 Or *high born*.   1:28 Or *God chose those who are low born*.   1:31 Jer 9:24.   2:1a Greek *brothers*.   2:1b Greek *God's mystery*; other manuscripts read *God's testimony*.

PSALM 27:7-14

Hear me as I pray, O LORD.
    Be merciful and answer me!
⁸ My heart has heard you say, "Come
        and talk with me."
    And my heart responds, "LORD,
        I am coming."
⁹ Do not turn your back on me.
    Do not reject your servant
        in anger.
    You have always been my helper.
    Don't leave me now; don't abandon
        me,
        O God of my salvation!
¹⁰ Even if my father and mother
        abandon me,
    the LORD will hold me close.

¹¹ Teach me how to live, O LORD.
    Lead me along the right path,
        for my enemies are waiting
        for me.
¹² Do not let me fall into their hands.
    For they accuse me of things
        I've never done;
    with every breath they threaten
        me with violence.
¹³ Yet I am confident I will see the
        LORD's goodness
    while I am here in the land
        of the living.

¹⁴ Wait patiently for the LORD.
    Be brave and courageous.
    Yes, wait patiently for the LORD.

PROVERBS 20:22-23

Don't say, "I will get even for this wrong." Wait for the LORD to handle the matter. □ The LORD detests double standards; he is not pleased by dishonest scales.

AUGUST 6

EZRA 3:1–4:23

In early autumn,* when the Israelites had settled in their towns, all the people assembled in Jerusalem with a unified purpose. ²Then Jeshua son of Jehozadak* joined his fellow priests and Zerubbabel son of Shealtiel with his family in rebuilding the altar of the God of Israel. They wanted to sacrifice burnt offerings on it, as instructed in the Law of Moses, the man of God. ³Even though the people were afraid of the local residents, they rebuilt the altar at its old site. Then they began to sacrifice burnt offerings on the altar to the LORD each morning and evening.

⁴They celebrated the Festival of Shelters as prescribed in the Law, sacrificing the number of burnt offerings specified for each day of the festival. ⁵They also offered the regular burnt offerings and the offerings required for the new moon celebrations and the annual festivals as prescribed by the LORD. The people also gave voluntary offerings to the LORD. ⁶Fifteen days before the Festival of Shelters began,* the priests had begun to sacrifice burnt offerings to the LORD. This was even before they had started to lay the foundation of the LORD's Temple.

⁷Then the people hired masons and carpenters and bought cedar logs from the people of Tyre and Sidon, paying them with food, wine, and olive oil. The logs were brought down from the Lebanon mountains and floated along the coast of the Mediterranean Sea* to Joppa, for King Cyrus had given permission for this.

⁸The construction of the Temple of God began in midspring,* during the second year after they arrived in Jerusalem. The work force was made up of everyone who had returned from exile, including Zerubbabel son of Shealtiel, Jeshua son of Jehozadak and his fellow

priests, and all the Levites. The Levites who were twenty years old or older were put in charge of rebuilding the LORD's Temple. ⁹The workers at the Temple of God were supervised by Jeshua with his sons and relatives, and Kadmiel and his sons, all descendants of Hodaviah.* They were helped in this task by the Levites of the family of Henadad.

¹⁰When the builders completed the foundation of the LORD's Temple, the priests put on their robes and took their places to blow their trumpets. And the Levites, descendants of Asaph, clashed their cymbals to praise the LORD, just as King David had prescribed. ¹¹With praise and thanks, they sang this song to the LORD:

"He is so good!
His faithful love for Israel
   endures forever!"

Then all the people gave a great shout, praising the LORD because the foundation of the LORD's Temple had been laid.

¹²But many of the older priests, Levites, and other leaders who had seen the first Temple wept aloud when they saw the new Temple's foundation. The others, however, were shouting for joy. ¹³The joyful shouting and weeping mingled together in a loud noise that could be heard far in the distance.

4:1THE enemies of Judah and Benjamin heard that the exiles were rebuilding a Temple to the LORD, the God of Israel. ²So they approached Zerubbabel and the other leaders and said, "Let us build with you, for we worship your God just as you do. We have sacrificed to him ever since King Esarhaddon of Assyria brought us here."

³But Zerubbabel, Jeshua, and the other leaders of Israel replied, "You may have no part in this work. We alone will build the Temple for the LORD, the God of Israel, just as King Cyrus of Persia commanded us."

⁴Then the local residents tried to discourage and frighten the people of Judah to keep them from their work.

⁵They bribed agents to work against them and to frustrate their plans. This went on during the entire reign of King Cyrus of Persia and lasted until King Darius of Persia took the throne.*

⁶Years later when Xerxes* began his reign, the enemies of Judah wrote a letter of accusation against the people of Judah and Jerusalem.

⁷Even later, during the reign of King Artaxerxes of Persia,* the enemies of Judah, led by Bishlam, Mithredath, and Tabeel, sent a letter to Artaxerxes in the Aramaic language, and it was translated for the king.

⁸*Rehum the governor and Shimshai the court secretary wrote the letter, telling King Artaxerxes about the situation in Jerusalem. ⁹They greeted the king for all their colleagues—the judges and local leaders, the people of Tarpel, the Persians, the Babylonians, and the people of Erech and Susa (that is, Elam). ¹⁰They also sent greetings from the rest of the people whom the great and noble Ashurbanipal* had deported and relocated in Samaria and throughout the neighboring lands of the province west of the Euphrates River.* ¹¹This is a copy of their letter:

"To King Artaxerxes, from your loyal subjects in the province west of the Euphrates River.

¹²"The king should know that the Jews who came here to Jerusalem from Babylon are rebuilding this rebellious and evil city. They have already laid the foundation and will soon finish its walls. ¹³And the king should know that if this city is rebuilt and its walls are completed, it will be much to your disadvantage, for the Jews will then refuse to pay their tribute, customs, and tolls to you.

¹⁴"Since we are your loyal subjects* and do not want to see the king dishonored in this way, we have sent the king this information. ¹⁵We suggest that a search be made in your ancestors' records, where you

will discover what a rebellious city this has been in the past. In fact, it was destroyed because of its long and troublesome history of revolt against the kings and countries who controlled it. [16]We declare to the king that if this city is rebuilt and its walls are completed, the province west of the Euphrates River will be lost to you."

[17]Then King Artaxerxes sent this reply:

"To Rehum the governor, Shimshai the court secretary, and their colleagues living in Samaria and throughout the province west of the Euphrates River. Greetings.

[18]"The letter you sent has been translated and read to me. [19]I ordered a search of the records and have found that Jerusalem has indeed been a hotbed of insurrection against many kings. In fact, rebellion and revolt are normal there! [20]Powerful kings have ruled over Jerusalem and the entire province west of the Euphrates River, receiving tribute, customs, and tolls. [21]Therefore, issue orders to have these men stop their work. That city must not be rebuilt except at my express command. [22]Be diligent, and don't neglect this matter, for we must not permit the situation to harm the king's interests."

[23]When this letter from King Artaxerxes was read to Rehum, Shimshai, and their colleagues, they hurried to Jerusalem. Then, with a show of strength, they forced the Jews to stop building.

3:1 Hebrew *in the seventh month*. The year is not specified, so it may have been during Cyrus's first year (538 B.C.) or second year (537 B.C.). The seventh month of the ancient Hebrew lunar calendar occurred within the months of September/October 538 B.C. and October/November 537 B.C.   3:2 Hebrew *Jozadak*, a variant spelling of Jehozadak; also in 3:8.   3:6 Hebrew *On the first day of the seventh month*. This day in the ancient Hebrew lunar calendar occurred in September or October. The Festival of Shelters began on the fifteenth day of the seventh month.   3:7 Hebrew *the sea*.   3:8 Hebrew *in the second month*. This month in the ancient Hebrew lunar calendar occurred within the months of April and May 536 B.C.   3:9 Hebrew *sons of Judah* (i.e., *bene Yehudah*). Bene might also be read here as the proper name Binnui; *Yehudah* is

probably another name for Hodaviah. Compare 2:40; Neh 7:43; 1 Esdras 5:58.   4:5 Darius reigned 521–486 B.C.   4:6 Hebrew *Ahasuerus*, another name for Xerxes. He reigned 486–465 B.C.   4:7 Artaxerxes reigned 465–424 B.C.   4:8 The original text of 4:8–6:18 is in Aramaic.   4:10a Aramaic *Osnappar*, another name for Ashurbanipal.   4:10b Aramaic *the province beyond the river;* also in 4:11, 16, 17, 20.   4:14 Aramaic *Since we eat the salt of the palace.*

1 CORINTHIANS 2:6–3:4

Yet when I [Paul] am among mature believers, I do speak with words of wisdom, but not the kind of wisdom that belongs to this world or to the rulers of this world, who are soon forgotten. [7]No, the wisdom we speak of is the mystery of God*—his plan that was previously hidden, even though he made it for our ultimate glory before the world began. [8]But the rulers of this world have not understood it; if they had, they would not have crucified our glorious Lord. [9]That is what the Scriptures mean when they say,

"No eye has seen, no ear has
          heard,
     and no mind has imagined
  what God has prepared
     for those who love him."*

[10]But* it was to us that God revealed these things by his Spirit. For his Spirit searches out everything and shows us God's deep secrets. [11]No one can know a person's thoughts except that person's own spirit, and no one can know God's thoughts except God's own Spirit. **[12]And we have received God's Spirit (not the world's spirit), so we can know the wonderful things God has freely given us.**

[13]When we tell you these things, we do not use words that come from human wisdom. Instead, we speak words given to us by the Spirit, using the Spirit's words to explain spiritual truths.* [14]But people who aren't spiritual* can't receive these truths from God's Spirit. It all sounds foolish to them and they can't understand it, for only those who are spiritual can understand what the Spirit means. [15]Those who are spiritual can evaluate all things, but they themselves cannot be evaluated by others. [16]For,

"Who can know the LORD's
thoughts?
Who knows enough to teach him?"*

But we understand these things, for we have the mind of Christ.

3:1DEAR brothers and sisters,* when I was with you I couldn't talk to you as I would to spiritual people.* I had to talk as though you belonged to this world or as though you were infants in the Christian life.* 2I had to feed you with milk, not with solid food, because you weren't ready for anything stronger. And you still aren't ready, 3for you are still controlled by your sinful nature. You are jealous of one another and quarrel with each other. Doesn't that prove you are controlled by your sinful nature? Aren't you living like people of the world? 4When one of you says, "I am a follower of Paul," and another says, "I follow Apollos," aren't you acting just like people of the world?

2:7 Greek *But we speak God's wisdom in a mystery.*
2:9 Isa 64:4.   2:10 Some manuscripts read *For.*   2:13 Or *explaining spiritual truths in spiritual language,* or *explaining spiritual truths to spiritual people.*   2:14 Or *who don't have the Spirit;* or *who have only physical life.*   2:16 Isa 40:13 (Greek version).   3:1a Greek *Brothers.*   3:1b Or *to people who have the Spirit.*   3:1c Greek *in Christ.*

PSALM 28:1-9
A psalm of David.

1 I pray to you, O LORD, my rock.
    Do not turn a deaf ear to me.
For if you are silent,
    I might as well give up and die.
2 Listen to my prayer for mercy
    as I cry out to you for help,
    as I lift my hands toward your
        holy sanctuary.

3 Do not drag me away with
        the wicked—
    with those who do evil—
those who speak friendly words
        to their neighbors
    while planning evil in their
        hearts.
4 Give them the punishment they so
        richly deserve!
    Measure it out in proportion to
        their wickedness.

Pay them back for all their evil
        deeds!
    Give them a taste of what they
        have done to others.
5 They care nothing for what the
        LORD has done
    or for what his hands have made.
So he will tear them down,
    and they will never be rebuilt!

6 Praise the LORD!
    For he has heard my cry for mercy.
7 The LORD is my strength and shield.
    I trust him with all my heart.
He helps me, and my heart is filled
        with joy.
    I burst out in songs of
        thanksgiving.

8 The LORD gives his people strength.
    He is a safe fortress for his
        anointed king.
9 Save your people!
    Bless Israel, your special
        possession.*
Lead them like a shepherd,
    and carry them in your
        arms forever.

28:9 Hebrew *Bless your inheritance.*

PROVERBS 20:24-25
The LORD directs our steps, so why try to understand everything along the way? □ Don't trap yourself by making a rash promise to God and only later counting the cost.

AUGUST 7

EZRA 4:24–6:22
So the work on the Temple of God in Jerusalem had stopped, and it remained at a standstill until the second year of the reign of King Darius of Persia.*

5:1AT that time the prophets Haggai and Zechariah son of Iddo prophesied to the Jews in Judah and Jerusalem. They prophesied in the name of the God of Israel who was over them. [2]Zerubbabel son of Shealtiel and Jeshua son of Jehozadak* responded by starting again to rebuild the Temple of God in Jerusalem. And the prophets of God were with them and helped them.

[3]But Tattenai, governor of the province west of the Euphrates River,* and Shethar-bozenai and their colleagues soon arrived in Jerusalem and asked, "Who gave you permission to rebuild this Temple and restore this structure?" [4]They also asked for the names of all the men working on the Temple. [5]But because their God was watching over them, the leaders of the Jews were not prevented from building until a report was sent to Darius and he returned his decision.

[6]This is a copy of the letter that Tattenai the governor, Shethar-bozenai, and the other officials of the province west of the Euphrates River sent to King Darius:

[7]"To King Darius. Greetings.

[8]"The king should know that we went to the construction site of the Temple of the great God in the province of Judah. It is being rebuilt with specially prepared stones, and timber is being laid in its walls. The work is going forward with great energy and success.

[9]"We asked the leaders, 'Who gave you permission to rebuild this Temple and restore this structure?' [10]And we demanded their names so that we could tell you who the leaders were.

[11]"This was their answer: 'We are the servants of the God of heaven and earth, and we are rebuilding the Temple that was built here many years ago by a great king of Israel. [12]But because our ancestors angered the God of heaven, he abandoned them to King Nebuchadnezzar of Babylon,* who destroyed this Temple and exiled the people to Babylonia. [13]However, King Cyrus of Babylon,* during the first year of his reign, issued a decree that the Temple of God should be rebuilt. [14]King Cyrus returned the gold and silver cups that Nebuchadnezzar had taken from the Temple of God in Jerusalem and had placed in the temple of Babylon. These cups were taken from that temple and presented to a man named Sheshbazzar, whom King Cyrus appointed as governor of Judah. [15]The king instructed him to return the cups to their place in Jerusalem and to rebuild the Temple of God there on its original site. [16]So this Sheshbazzar came and laid the foundations of the Temple of God in Jerusalem. The people have been working on it ever since, though it is not yet completed.'

[17]"Therefore, if it pleases the king, we request that a search be made in the royal archives of Babylon to discover whether King Cyrus ever issued a decree to rebuild God's Temple in Jerusalem. And then let the king send us his decision in this matter."

[6:1]So King Darius issued orders that a search be made in the Babylonian archives, which were stored in the treasury. [2]But it was at the fortress at Ecbatana in the province of Media that a scroll was found. This is what it said:

"Memorandum:

[3]"In the first year of King Cyrus's reign, a decree was sent out concerning the Temple of God at Jerusalem.

"Let the Temple be rebuilt on the site where Jews used to offer their sacrifices, using the original foundations. Its height will be ninety feet, and its width will be ninety feet.* [4]Every three layers of specially prepared stones will be topped by a layer of timber. All expenses will be paid by the royal treasury.

[5]Furthermore, the gold and silver cups, which were taken to Babylon by Nebuchadnezzar from the Temple of God in Jerusalem, must be returned to Jerusalem and put back where they belong. Let them be taken back to the Temple of God."

[6]So King Darius sent this message:

"Now therefore, Tattenai, governor of the province west of the Euphrates River,* and Shethar-bozenai, and your colleagues and other officials west of the Euphrates River—stay away from there! [7]Do not disturb the construction of the Temple of God. Let it be rebuilt on its original site, and do not hinder the governor of Judah and the elders of the Jews in their work.

[8]"Moreover, I hereby decree that you are to help these elders of the Jews as they rebuild this Temple of God. You must pay the full construction costs, without delay, from my taxes collected in the province west of the Euphrates River so that the work will not be interrupted.

[9]"Give the priests in Jerusalem whatever is needed in the way of young bulls, rams, and male lambs for the burnt offerings presented to the God of heaven. And without fail, provide them with as much wheat, salt, wine, and olive oil as they need each day. [10]Then they will be able to offer acceptable sacrifices to the God of heaven and pray for the welfare of the king and his sons.

[11]"Those who violate this decree in any way will have a beam pulled from their house. Then they will be tied to it and flogged, and their house will be reduced to a pile of rubble.* [12]May the God who has chosen the city of Jerusalem as the place to honor his name destroy any king or nation that violates this command and destroys this Temple.

"I, Darius, have issued this decree. Let it be obeyed with all diligence."

[13]Tattenai, governor of the province west of the Euphrates River, and Shethar-bozenai and their colleagues complied at once with the command of King Darius. [14]So the Jewish elders continued their work, and they were greatly encouraged by the preaching of the prophets Haggai and Zechariah son of Iddo. The Temple was finally finished, as had been commanded by the God of Israel and decreed by Cyrus, Darius, and Artaxerxes, the kings of Persia. [15]The Temple was completed on March 12,* during the sixth year of King Darius's reign.

[16]The Temple of God was then dedicated with great joy by the people of Israel, the priests, the Levites, and the rest of the people who had returned from exile. [17]During the dedication ceremony for the Temple of God, 100 young bulls, 200 rams, and 400 male lambs were sacrificed. And 12 male goats were presented as a sin offering for the twelve tribes of Israel. [18]Then the priests and Levites were divided into their various divisions to serve at the Temple of God in Jerusalem, as prescribed in the Book of Moses.

[19]On April 21* the returned exiles celebrated Passover. [20]The priests and Levites had purified themselves and were ceremonially clean. So they slaughtered the Passover lamb for all the returned exiles, for their fellow priests, and for themselves. [21]The Passover meal was eaten by the people of Israel who had returned from exile and by the others in the land who had turned from their immoral customs to worship the LORD, the God of Israel. [22]Then they celebrated the Festival of Unleavened Bread for seven days. There was great joy throughout the land because the LORD had caused the king of Assyria* to be favorable to them, so that he helped them to rebuild the Temple of God, the God of Israel.

4:24 The second year of Darius's reign was 520 B.C. The narrative started in 4:1-5 is resumed at verse 24.
5:2 Aramaic *Jozadak*, a variant spelling of Jehozadak.
5:3 Aramaic *the province beyond the river;* also in 5:6.
5:12 Aramaic *Nebuchadnezzar the Chaldean.* 5:13 King Cyrus of Persia is here identified as the king of Babylon because Persia had conquered the Babylonian Empire.

6:3 Aramaic *Its height will be 60 cubits* [27.6 meters], *and its width will be 60 cubits*. It is commonly held that this verse should be emended to read: "Its height will be 30 cubits [45 feet, or 13.8 meters], its length will be 60 cubits [90 feet, or 27.6 meters], and its width will be 20 meters [30 feet, or 9.2 meters]"; compare 1 Kgs 6:2. The emendation regarding the width is supported by the Syriac version. **6:6** Aramaic *the province beyond the river;* also in 6:6b, 8, 13. **6:11** Aramaic *a dunghill.* **6:15** Aramaic *on the third day of the month Adar,* of the ancient Hebrew lunar calendar. A number of events in Ezra can be cross-checked with dates in surviving Persian records and related accurately to our modern calendar. This day was March 12, 515 B.C. **6:19** Hebrew *On the fourteenth day of the first month,* of the ancient Hebrew lunar calendar. This day was April 21, 515 B.C.; also see note on 6:15. **6:22** King Darius of Persia is here identified as the king of Assyria because Persia had conquered the Babylonian Empire, which included the earlier Assyrian Empire.

1 CORINTHIANS 3:5-23

After all, who is Apollos? Who is Paul? We are only God's servants through whom you believed the Good News. Each of us did the work the Lord gave us. ⁶I planted the seed in your hearts, and Apollos watered it, but it was God who made it grow. **⁷It's not important who does the planting, or who does the watering. What's important is that God makes the seed grow. ⁸The one who plants and the one who waters work together with the same purpose. And both will be rewarded for their own hard work.** ⁹For we are both God's workers. And you are God's field. You are God's building.

¹⁰Because of God's grace to me, I have laid the foundation like an expert builder. Now others are building on it. But whoever is building on this foundation must be very careful. ¹¹For no one can lay any foundation other than the one we already have—Jesus Christ.

¹²Anyone who builds on that foundation may use a variety of materials—gold, silver, jewels, wood, hay, or straw. ¹³But on the judgment day, fire will reveal what kind of work each builder has done. The fire will show if a person's work has any value. ¹⁴If the work survives, that builder will receive a reward. ¹⁵But if the work is burned up, the builder will suffer great loss. The builder will be saved, but like someone barely escaping through a wall of flames.

¹⁶Don't you realize that all of you together are the temple of God and that the Spirit of God lives in* you? ¹⁷God will destroy anyone who destroys this temple. For God's temple is holy, and you are that temple.

¹⁸Stop deceiving yourselves. If you think you are wise by this world's standards, you need to become a fool to be truly wise. ¹⁹For the wisdom of this world is foolishness to God. As the Scriptures say,

"He traps the wise
in the snare of their
own cleverness."*

²⁰And again,

"The LORD knows the thoughts
of the wise;
he knows they are worthless."*

²¹So don't boast about following a particular human leader. For everything belongs to you—²²whether Paul or Apollos or Peter,* or the world, or life and death, or the present and the future. Everything belongs to you, ²³and you belong to Christ, and Christ belongs to God.

3:16 Or *among.*   **3:19** Job 5:13.   **3:20** Ps 94:11.
3:22 Greek *Cephas.*

PSALM 29:1-11
A psalm of David.

¹ **H**onor the LORD, you heavenly
    beings*;
    honor the LORD for his glory
    and strength.
² Honor the LORD for the glory
    of his name.
    Worship the LORD in the
    splendor of his holiness.

³ The voice of the LORD echoes
    above the sea.
    The God of glory thunders.
    The LORD thunders over the
    mighty sea.
⁴ The voice of the LORD is powerful;
    the voice of the LORD is majestic.
⁵ The voice of the LORD splits the
    mighty cedars;
    the LORD shatters the cedars
    of Lebanon.

⁶ He makes Lebanon's mountains
    skip like a calf;
  he makes Mount Hermon* leap
    like a young wild ox.
⁷ The voice of the LORD strikes
    with bolts of lightning.
⁸ The voice of the LORD makes the
    barren wilderness quake;
  the LORD shakes the wilderness
    of Kadesh.
⁹ The voice of the LORD twists
    mighty oaks*
  and strips the forests bare.
  In his Temple everyone shouts,
    "Glory!"

¹⁰ The LORD rules over the
    floodwaters.
  The LORD reigns as king forever.
¹¹ The LORD gives his people strength.
  The LORD blesses them with
    peace.

29:1 Hebrew *you sons of God.*   **29:6** Hebrew *Sirion,*
another name for Mount Hermon.   **29:9** Or *causes the
deer to writhe in labor.*

PROVERBS 20:26-27
A wise king scatters the wicked like
wheat, then runs his threshing wheel
over them. □ The LORD's light pene-
trates the human spirit,* exposing every
hidden motive.

20:27 Or *The human spirit is the LORD's light.*

AUGUST 8

EZRA 7:1–8:20
Many years later, during the reign of
King Artaxerxes of Persia,* there was a
man named Ezra. He was the son* of
Seraiah, son of Azariah, son of Hilkiah,
²son of Shallum, son of Zadok, son of
Ahitub, ³son of Amariah, son of Azariah,
son* of Meraioth, ⁴son of Zerahiah, son
of Uzzi, son of Bukki, ⁵son of Abishua,
son of Phinehas, son of Eleazar, son of
Aaron the high priest.* ⁶This Ezra was a

scribe who was well versed in the Law of
Moses, which the LORD, the God of Israel,
had given to the people of Israel. He
came up to Jerusalem from Babylon,
and the king gave him everything he
asked for, because the gracious hand
of the LORD his God was on him. ⁷Some
of the people of Israel, as well as some of
the priests, Levites, singers, gatekeepers,
and Temple servants, traveled up to Jerusalem with him in the seventh year of
King Artaxerxes' reign.
  ⁸Ezra arrived in Jerusalem in August*
of that year. ⁹He had arranged to leave
Babylon on April 8, the first day of the
new year,* and he arrived at Jerusalem
on August 4,* for the gracious hand of
his God was on him. ¹⁰This was because
Ezra had determined to study and obey
the Law of the LORD and to teach those
decrees and regulations to the people of
Israel.
  ¹¹King Artaxerxes had given a copy
of the following letter to Ezra, the priest
and scribe who studied and taught the
commands and decrees of the LORD to
Israel:

  ¹²*"From Artaxerxes, the king of
kings, to Ezra the priest, the teacher
of the law of the God of heaven.
  ¹³"I decree that any of the people
of Israel in my kingdom, including
the priests and Levites, may
volunteer to return to Jerusalem
with you. ¹⁴I and my council of
seven hereby instruct you to
conduct an inquiry into the situation
in Judah and Jerusalem, based on
your God's law, which is in your
hand. ¹⁵We also commission you to
take with you silver and gold, which
we are freely presenting as an
offering to the God of Israel who
lives in Jerusalem.
  ¹⁶"Furthermore, you are to take
any silver and gold that you may
obtain from the province of
Babylon, as well as the voluntary
offerings of the people and the
priests that are presented for the
Temple of their God in Jerusalem.

17 These donations are to be used specifically for the purchase of bulls, rams, male lambs, and the appropriate grain offerings and liquid offerings, all of which will be offered on the altar of the Temple of your God in Jerusalem. 18 Any silver and gold that is left over may be used in whatever way you and your colleagues feel is the will of your God.

19 "But as for the cups we are entrusting to you for the service of the Temple of your God, deliver them all to the God of Jerusalem. 20 If you need anything else for your God's Temple or for any similar needs, you may take it from the royal treasury.

21 "I, Artaxerxes the king, hereby send this decree to all the treasurers in the province west of the Euphrates River*: 'You are to give Ezra, the priest and teacher of the law of the God of heaven, whatever he requests of you. 22 You are to give him up to 7,500 pounds* of silver, 500 bushels* of wheat, 550 gallons of wine, 550 gallons of olive oil,* and an unlimited supply of salt. 23 Be careful to provide whatever the God of heaven demands for his Temple, for why should we risk bringing God's anger against the realm of the king and his sons? 24 I also decree that no priest, Levite, singer, gatekeeper, Temple servant, or other worker in this Temple of God will be required to pay tribute, customs, or tolls of any kind.'

25 "And you, Ezra, are to use the wisdom your God has given you to appoint magistrates and judges who know your God's laws to govern all the people in the province west of the Euphrates River. Teach the law to anyone who does not know it. 26 Anyone who refuses to obey the law of your God and the law of the king will be punished immediately, either by death, banishment, confiscation of goods, or imprisonment."

27 Praise the LORD, the God of our ancestors, who made the king want to beautify the Temple of the LORD in Jerusalem! 28 And praise him for demonstrating such unfailing love to me by honoring me before the king, his council, and all his mighty nobles! I felt encouraged because the gracious hand of the LORD my God was on me. And I gathered some of the leaders of Israel to return with me to Jerusalem.

8:1 HERE is a list of the family leaders and the genealogies of those who came with me from Babylon during the reign of King Artaxerxes:

2 From the family of Phinehas: Gershom.

From the family of Ithamar: Daniel.

From the family of David: Hattush, 3 a descendant of Shecaniah.

From the family of Parosh: Zechariah and 150 other men were registered.

4 From the family of Pahath-moab: Eliehoenai son of Zerahiah and 200 other men.

5 From the family of Zattu*: Shecaniah son of Jahaziel and 300 other men.

6 From the family of Adin: Ebed son of Jonathan and 50 other men.

7 From the family of Elam: Jeshaiah son of Athaliah and 70 other men.

8 From the family of Shephatiah: Zebadiah son of Michael and 80 other men.

9 From the family of Joab: Obadiah son of Jehiel and 218 other men.

10 From the family of Bani*: Shelomith son of Josiphiah and 160 other men.

11 From the family of Bebai: Zechariah son of Bebai and 28 other men.

12 From the family of Azgad: Johanan son of Hakkatan and 110 other men.

13 From the family of Adonikam, who came later*: Eliphelet, Jeuel, Shemaiah, and 60 other men.

¹⁴ From the family of Bigvai: Uthai, Zaccur, and 70 other men.

¹⁵I assembled the exiles at the Ahava Canal, and we camped there for three days while I went over the lists of the people and the priests who had arrived. I found that not one Levite had volunteered to come along. ¹⁶So I sent for Eliezer, Ariel, Shemaiah, Elnathan, Jarib, Elnathan, Nathan, Zechariah, and Meshullam, who were leaders of the people. I also sent for Joiarib and Elnathan, who were men of discernment. ¹⁷I sent them to Iddo, the leader of the Levites at Casiphia, to ask him and his relatives and the Temple servants to send us ministers for the Temple of God at Jerusalem.

¹⁸Since the gracious hand of our God was on us, they sent us a man named Sherebiah, along with eighteen of his sons and brothers. He was a very astute man and a descendant of Mahli, who was a descendant of Levi son of Israel.* ¹⁹They also sent Hashabiah, together with Jeshaiah from the descendants of Merari, and twenty of his sons and brothers, ²⁰and 220 Temple servants. The Temple servants were assistants to the Levites—a group of Temple workers first instituted by King David and his officials. They were all listed by name.

7:1a Artaxerxes reigned 465–424 B.C.   7:1b Or *descendant;* see 1 Chr 6:14.   7:3 Or *descendant;* see 1 Chr 6:6-10.   7:5 Or *the first priest.*   7:8 Hebrew *in the fifth month.* This month in the ancient Hebrew lunar calendar occurred within the months of August and September 458 B.C.   7:9a Hebrew *on the first day of the first month,* of the ancient Hebrew lunar calendar. This day was April 8, 458 B.C.; also see note on 6:15.   7:9b Hebrew *on the first day of the fifth month,* of the ancient Hebrew lunar calendar. This day was August 4, 458 B.C.; also see note on 6:15.   7:12 The original text of 7:12-26 is in Aramaic.   7:21 Aramaic *the province beyond the river;* also in 7:25.   7:22a Aramaic *100 talents* [3,400 kilograms].   7:22b Aramaic *100 cors* [18.2 kiloliters].   7:22c Aramaic *100 baths* [2.1 kiloliters] *of wine, 100 baths of olive oil.*   8:5 As in some Greek manuscripts (see also 1 Esdras 8:32); Hebrew lacks *Zattu.*   8:10 As in some Greek manuscripts (see also 1 Esdras 8:36); Hebrew lacks *Bani.*   8:13 Or *who were the last of his family.*   8:18 *Israel* is the name that God gave to Jacob.

1 CORINTHIANS 4:1-21

So look at Apollos and me [Paul] as mere servants of Christ who have been put in charge of explaining God's mysteries. ²Now, a person who is put in charge as a manager must be faithful. ³As for me, it matters very little how I might be evaluated by you or by any human authority. I don't even trust my own judgment on this point. ⁴My conscience is clear, but that doesn't prove I'm right. It is the Lord himself who will examine me and decide.

⁵So don't make judgments about anyone ahead of time—before the Lord returns. For he will bring our darkest secrets to light and will reveal our private motives. Then God will give to each one whatever praise is due.

⁶Dear brothers and sisters,* I have used Apollos and myself to illustrate what I've been saying. If you pay attention to what I have quoted from the Scriptures,* you won't be proud of one of your leaders at the expense of another. ⁷For what gives you the right to make such a judgment? What do you have that God hasn't given you? And if everything you have is from God, why boast as though it were not a gift?

⁸You think you already have everything you need. You think you are already rich. You have begun to reign in God's kingdom without us! I wish you really were reigning already, for then we would be reigning with you. ⁹Instead, I sometimes think God has put us apostles on display, like prisoners of war at the end of a victor's parade, condemned to die. We have become a spectacle to the entire world—to people and angels alike.

¹⁰Our dedication to Christ makes us look like fools, but you claim to be so wise in Christ! We are weak, but you are so powerful! You are honored, but we are ridiculed. ¹¹Even now we go hungry and thirsty, and we don't have enough clothes to keep warm. We are often beaten and have no home. ¹²We work wearily with our own hands to earn our living. We bless those who curse us. We are patient with those who abuse us. ¹³We appeal gently when evil things are said about us. Yet we are treated like the world's garbage, like everybody's trash—right up to the present moment.

¹⁴I am not writing these things to shame you, but to warn you as my beloved children. ¹⁵For even if you had ten thousand others to teach you about Christ, you have only one spiritual father. For I became your father in Christ Jesus when I preached the Good News to you. ¹⁶So I urge you to imitate me.

¹⁷That's why I have sent Timothy, my beloved and faithful child in the Lord. He will remind you of how I follow Christ Jesus, just as I teach in all the churches wherever I go.

¹⁸Some of you have become arrogant, thinking I will not visit you again. ¹⁹But I will come—and soon—if the Lord lets me, and then I'll find out whether these arrogant people just give pretentious speeches or whether they really have God's power. ²⁰For the Kingdom of God is not just a lot of talk; it is living by God's power. ²¹Which do you choose? Should I come with a rod to punish you, or should I come with love and a gentle spirit?

4:6a Greek *Brothers*.   4:6b Or *If you learn not to go beyond "what is written."*

PSALM 30:1-12

A psalm of David. A song for the dedication of the Temple.

¹ I will exalt you, Lord, for you
     rescued me.
  You refused to let my enemies
     triumph over me.
² O Lord my God, I cried to you
     for help,
  and you restored my health.
³ You brought me up from the
     grave,* O Lord.
  You kept me from falling into
     the pit of death.

⁴ Sing to the Lord, all you godly ones!
     Praise his holy name.
⁵ For his anger lasts only a moment,
     but his favor lasts a lifetime!
  Weeping may last through
     the night,
  but joy comes with the morning.

⁶ When I was prosperous, I said,
     "Nothing can stop me now!"

⁷ Your favor, O Lord, made me as
     secure as a mountain.
  Then you turned away from me,
     and I was shattered.

⁸ I cried out to you, O Lord.
  I begged the Lord for mercy,
     saying,
⁹ "What will you gain if I die,
     if I sink into the grave?
  Can my dust praise you?
     Can it tell of your faithfulness?
¹⁰ Hear me, Lord, and have mercy
     on me.
  Help me, O Lord."

¹¹ You have turned my mourning
     into joyful dancing.
  You have taken away my clothes
     of mourning and clothed me
     with joy,
¹² that I might sing praises to you and
     not be silent.
  O Lord my God, I will give you
     thanks forever!

30:3 Hebrew *from Sheol*.

PROVERBS 20:28-30

Unfailing love and faithfulness protect the king; his throne is made secure through love. □ The glory of the young is their strength; the gray hair of experience is the splendor of the old. □ Physical punishment cleanses away evil;* such discipline purifies the heart.

20:30 The meaning of the Hebrew is uncertain.

AUGUST 9

EZRA 8:21–9:15

And there by the Ahava Canal, I [Ezra] gave orders for all of us to fast and humble ourselves before our God. We prayed that he would give us a safe journey and protect us, our children, and our goods as we traveled. ²²For I was ashamed to ask the king for soldiers and horsemen* to accompany us and protect us from enemies along the way. After all, we had told the king, "Our God's hand of protection is on all who worship him, but his fierce anger rages against those who abandon him." ²³So we fasted and earnestly prayed that our God would take care of us, and he heard our prayer.

²⁴I appointed twelve leaders of the priests—Sherebiah, Hashabiah, and ten other priests—²⁵to be in charge of transporting the silver, the gold, the gold bowls, and the other items that the king, his council, his officials, and all the people of Israel had presented for the Temple of God. ²⁶I weighed the treasure as I gave it to them and found the totals to be as follows:

24 tons* of silver,
7,500 pounds* of silver articles,
7,500 pounds of gold,
²⁷ 20 gold bowls, equal in value
    to 1,000 gold coins,*
2 fine articles of polished bronze,
    as precious as gold.

²⁸And I said to these priests, "You and these treasures have been set apart as holy to the Lord. This silver and gold is a voluntary offering to the Lord, the God of our ancestors. ²⁹Guard these treasures well until you present them to the leading priests, the Levites, and the leaders of Israel, who will weigh them at the storerooms of the Lord's Temple in Jerusalem." ³⁰So the priests and the Levites accepted the task of transporting these treasures of silver and gold to the Temple of our God in Jerusalem.

³¹We broke camp at the Ahava Canal on April 19* and started off to Jerusalem. And the gracious hand of our God protected us and saved us from enemies and bandits along the way. ³²So we arrived safely in Jerusalem, where we rested for three days.

³³On the fourth day after our arrival, the silver, gold, and other valuables were weighed at the Temple of our God and entrusted to Meremoth son of Uriah the priest and to Eleazar son of Phinehas, along with Jozabad son of Jeshua and Noadiah son of Binnui—both of whom were Levites. ³⁴Everything was accounted for by number and weight, and the total weight was officially recorded.

³⁵Then the exiles who had come out of captivity sacrificed burnt offerings to the God of Israel. They presented twelve bulls for all the people of Israel, as well as ninety-six rams and seventy-seven male lambs. They also offered twelve male goats as a sin offering. All this was given as a burnt offering to the Lord. ³⁶The king's decrees were delivered to his highest officers and the governors of the province west of the Euphrates River,* who then cooperated by supporting the people and the Temple of God.

⁹:¹WHEN these things had been done, the Jewish leaders came to me and said, "Many of the people of Israel, and even some of the priests and Levites, have not kept themselves separate from the other peoples living in the land. They have taken up the detestable practices of the Canaanites, Hittites, Perizzites, Jebusites, Ammonites, Moabites, Egyptians, and Amorites. ²For the men of Israel have married women from these people and have taken them as wives for their sons. So the holy race has become polluted by these mixed marriages. Worse yet, the leaders and officials have led the way in this outrage."

³When I heard this, I tore my cloak and my shirt, pulled hair from my head and beard, and sat down utterly shocked. ⁴Then all who trembled at the words of the God of Israel came and sat with me because of this outrage committed by the returned exiles. And I sat there utterly appalled until the time of the evening sacrifice.

⁵At the time of the sacrifice, I stood up from where I had sat in mourning with my clothes torn. I fell to my knees and lifted my hands to the Lord my God. ⁶I prayed,

"O my God, I am utterly ashamed; I blush to lift up my face to you. For our sins are piled higher than our heads, and our guilt has reached to the heavens. [7] From the days of our ancestors until now, we have been steeped in sin. That is why we and our kings and our priests have been at the mercy of the pagan kings of the land. We have been killed, captured, robbed, and disgraced, just as we are today.

[8]"But now we have been given a brief moment of grace, for the LORD our God has allowed a few of us to survive as a remnant. He has given us security in this holy place. Our God has brightened our eyes and granted us some relief from our slavery. [9] For we were slaves, but in his unfailing love our God did not abandon us in our slavery. Instead, he caused the kings of Persia to treat us favorably. He revived us so we could rebuild the Temple of our God and repair its ruins. He has given us a protective wall in Judah and Jerusalem.

[10]"And now, O our God, what can we say after all of this? For once again we have abandoned your commands! [11] Your servants the prophets warned us when they said, 'The land you are entering to possess is totally defiled by the detestable practices of the people living there. From one end to the other, the land is filled with corruption. [12] Don't let your daughters marry their sons! Don't take their daughters as wives for your sons. Don't ever promote the peace and prosperity of those nations. If you follow these instructions, you will be strong and will enjoy the good things the land produces, and you will leave this prosperity to your children forever.'

[13]"Now we are being punished because of our wickedness and our great guilt. But we have actually been punished far less than we deserve, for you, our God, have

allowed some of us to survive as a remnant. [14] But even so, we are again breaking your commands and intermarrying with people who do these detestable things. Won't your anger be enough to destroy us, so that even this little remnant no longer survives? [15] O LORD, God of Israel, you are just. We come before you in our guilt as nothing but an escaped remnant, though in such a condition none of us can stand in your presence."

8:22 Or *charioteers.*   **8:26a** Hebrew *650 talents* [22 metric tons].   **8:26b** Hebrew *100 talents* [3,400 kilograms]; also in 8:26c.   **8:27** Hebrew *1,000 darics,* about 19 pounds or 8.6 kilograms in weight.   **8:31** Hebrew *on the twelfth day of the first month,* of the ancient Hebrew lunar calendar. This day was April 19, 458 B.C.; also see note on 6:15.   **8:36** Hebrew *the province beyond the river.*

1 CORINTHIANS 5:1-13

I [Paul] can hardly believe the report about the sexual immorality going on among you—something that even pagans don't do. I am told that a man in your church is living in sin with his stepmother.* [2] You are so proud of yourselves, but you should be mourning in sorrow and shame. And you should remove this man from your fellowship.

[3] Even though I am not with you in person, I am with you in the Spirit.* And as though I were there, I have already passed judgment on this man [4] in the name of the Lord Jesus. You must call a meeting of the church.* I will be present with you in spirit, and so will the power of our Lord Jesus. [5] Then you must throw this man out and hand him over to Satan so that his sinful nature will be destroyed* and he himself* will be saved on the day the Lord* returns.

[6] Your boasting about this is terrible. Don't you realize that this sin is like a little yeast that spreads through the whole batch of dough? [7] Get rid of the old "yeast" by removing this wicked person from among you. Then you will be like a fresh batch of dough made without yeast, which is what you really are. Christ, our Passover Lamb, has been sacrificed for us.* [8] So let us celebrate the festival, not with the old bread* of wickedness

and evil, but with the new bread* of sincerity and truth.

⁹When I wrote to you before, I told you not to associate with people who indulge in sexual sin. ¹⁰But I wasn't talking about unbelievers who indulge in sexual sin, or are greedy, or cheat people, or worship idols. You would have to leave this world to avoid people like that. ¹¹I meant that you are not to associate with anyone who claims to be a believer* yet indulges in sexual sin, or is greedy, or worships idols, or is abusive, or is a drunkard, or cheats people. Don't even eat with such people.

¹²It isn't my responsibility to judge outsiders, but it certainly is your responsibility to judge those inside the church who are sinning. **¹³God will judge those on the outside; but as the Scriptures say, "You must remove the evil person from among you."***

5:1 Greek *his father's wife*. 5:3 Or *in spirit*. 5:4 Or *In the name of the Lord Jesus, you must call a meeting of the church*. 5:5a Or *so that his body will be destroyed*; Greek reads *for the destruction of the flesh*. 5:5b Greek *and the spirit*. 5:5c Other manuscripts read *the Lord Jesus*; still others read *our Lord Jesus Christ*. 5:7 Greek *has been sacrificed*. 5:8a Greek *not with old leaven*. 5:8b Greek *but with unleavened [bread]*. 5:11 Greek *a brother*. 5:13 Deut 17:7.

PSALM 31:1-8

For the choir director: A psalm of David.

¹ **O** LORD, I have come to you for
    protection;
    don't let me be disgraced.
    Save me, for you do what is right.
² Turn your ear to listen to me;
    rescue me quickly.
  Be my rock of protection,
    a fortress where I will be safe.
³ You are my rock and my fortress.
    For the honor of your name, lead
    me out of this danger.
⁴ Pull me from the trap my enemies
    set for me,
    for I find protection in you alone.
⁵ I entrust my spirit into your hand.
    Rescue me, LORD, for you are
    a faithful God.

⁶ I hate those who worship worthless
    idols.

    I trust in the LORD.
⁷ I will be glad and rejoice in your
    unfailing love,
    for you have seen my troubles,
    and you care about the anguish
    of my soul.
⁸ You have not handed me over
    to my enemies
    but have set me in a safe place.

PROVERBS 21:1-2

The king's heart is like a stream of water directed by the LORD; he guides it wherever he pleases. □ People may be right in their own eyes, but the LORD examines their heart.

AUGUST 10

EZRA 10:1-44

While Ezra prayed and made this confession, weeping and lying face down on the ground in front of the Temple of God, a very large crowd of people from Israel—men, women, and children—gathered and wept bitterly with him. ²Then Shecaniah son of Jehiel, a descendant of Elam, said to Ezra, "We have been unfaithful to our God, for we have married these pagan women of the land. But in spite of this there is hope for Israel. ³Let us now make a covenant with our God to divorce our pagan wives and to send them away with their children. We will follow the advice given by you and by the others who respect the commands of our God. Let it be done according to the Law of God. ⁴Get up, for it is your duty to tell us how to proceed in setting things straight. We are behind you, so be strong and take action."

⁵So Ezra stood up and demanded that the leaders of the priests and the Levites and all the people of Israel swear that they would do as Shecaniah had said. And they all swore a solemn oath.

[6]Then Ezra left the front of the Temple of God and went to the room of Jehohanan son of Eliashib. He spent the night* there without eating or drinking anything. He was still in mourning because of the unfaithfulness of the returned exiles.

[7]Then a proclamation was made throughout Judah and Jerusalem that all the exiles should come to Jerusalem. [8]Those who failed to come within three days would, if the leaders and elders so decided, forfeit all their property and be expelled from the assembly of the exiles.

[9]Within three days, all the people of Judah and Benjamin had gathered in Jerusalem. This took place on December 19,* and all the people were sitting in the square before the Temple of God. They were trembling both because of the seriousness of the matter and because it was raining. [10]Then Ezra the priest stood and said to them: "You have committed a terrible sin. By marrying pagan women, you have increased Israel's guilt. [11]So now confess your sin to the LORD, the God of your ancestors, and do what he demands. Separate yourselves from the people of the land and from these pagan women."

[12]Then the whole assembly raised their voices and answered, "Yes, you are right; we must do as you say!" [13]Then they added, "This isn't something that can be done in a day or two, for many of us are involved in this extremely sinful affair. And this is the rainy season, so we cannot stay out here much longer. [14]Let our leaders act on behalf of us all. Let everyone who has a pagan wife come at a scheduled time, accompanied by the leaders and judges of his city, so that the fierce anger of our God concerning this affair may be turned away from us."

[15]Only Jonathan son of Asahel and Jahzeiah son of Tikvah opposed this course of action, and they were supported by Meshullam and Shabbethai the Levite.

[16]So this was the plan they followed.

Ezra selected leaders to represent their families, designating each of the representatives by name. On December 29,* the leaders sat down to investigate the matter. [17]By March 27, the first day of the new year,* they had finished dealing with all the men who had married pagan wives.

[18]These are the priests who had married pagan wives:

From the family of Jeshua son of Jehozadak* and his brothers: Maaseiah, Eliezer, Jarib, and Gedaliah. [19]They vowed to divorce their wives, and they each acknowledged their guilt by offering a ram as a guilt offering.

[20]From the family of Immer: Hanani and Zebadiah.

[21]From the family of Harim: Maaseiah, Elijah, Shemaiah, Jehiel, and Uzziah.

[22]From the family of Pashhur: Elioenai, Maaseiah, Ishmael, Nethanel, Jozabad, and Elasah.

[23]These are the Levites who were guilty: Jozabad, Shimei, Kelaiah (also called Kelita), Pethahiah, Judah, and Eliezer.

[24]This is the singer who was guilty: Eliashib.

These are the gatekeepers who were guilty: Shallum, Telem, and Uri.

[25]These are the other people of Israel who were guilty:

From the family of Parosh: Ramiah, Izziah, Malkijah, Mijamin, Eleazar, Hashabiah,* and Benaiah.

[26]From the family of Elam: Mattaniah, Zechariah, Jehiel, Abdi, Jeremoth, and Elijah.

[27]From the family of Zattu: Elioenai, Eliashib, Mattaniah, Jeremoth, Zabad, and Aziza.

[28]From the family of Bebai: Jehohanan, Hananiah, Zabbai, and Athlai.

[29]From the family of Bani: Meshullam, Malluch, Adaiah, Jashub, Sheal, and Jeremoth.

[30]From the family of Pahath-moab:

Adna, Kelal, Benaiah, Maaseiah, Mattaniah, Bezalel, Binnui, and Manasseh.

31From the family of Harim: Eliezer, Ishijah, Malkijah, Shemaiah, Shimeon, 32Benjamin, Malluch, and Shemariah.

33From the family of Hashum: Mattenai, Mattattah, Zabad, Eliphelet, Jeremai, Manasseh, and Shimei.

34From the family of Bani: Maadai, Amram, Uel, 35Benaiah, Bedeiah, Keluhi, 36Vaniah, Meremoth, Eliashib, 37Mattaniah, Mattenai, and Jaasu.

38From the family of Binnui*: Shimei, 39Shelemiah, Nathan, Adaiah, 40Macnadebai, Shashai, Sharai, 41Azarel, Shelemiah, Shemariah, 42Shallum, Amariah, and Joseph.

43From the family of Nebo: Jeiel, Mattithiah, Zabad, Zebina, Jaddai, Joel, and Benaiah.

44Each of these men had a pagan wife, and some even had children by these wives.*

10:6 As in parallel text at 1 Esdras 9:2; Hebrew reads He went.   10:9 Hebrew on the twentieth day of the ninth month, of the ancient Hebrew lunar calendar. This day was December 19, 458 B.C.; also see note on 6:15. 10:16 Hebrew On the first day of the tenth month, of the ancient Hebrew lunar calendar. This day was December 29, 458 B.C.; also see note on 6:15.   10:17 Hebrew By the first day of the first month, of the ancient Hebrew lunar calendar. This day was March 27, 457 B.C.; also see note on 6:15.   10:18 Hebrew Jozadak, a variant spelling of Jehozadak.   10:25 As in parallel text at 1 Esdras 9:26; Hebrew reads Malkijah.   10:37-38 As in Greek version; Hebrew reads Jaasu, 38Bani, Binnui.   10:44 Or and they sent them away with their children. The meaning of the Hebrew is uncertain.

1 CORINTHIANS 6:1-20

When one of you has a dispute with another believer, how dare you file a lawsuit and ask a secular court to decide the matter instead of taking it to other believers! 2Don't you realize that someday we believers will judge the world? And since you are going to judge the world, can't you decide even these little things among yourselves? 3Don't you realize that we will judge angels? So you should surely be able to resolve ordinary disputes in this life. 4If you have le-

gal disputes about such matters, why go to outside judges who are not respected by the church? 5I am saying this to shame you. Isn't there anyone in all the church who is wise enough to decide these issues? 6But instead, one believer* sues another—right in front of unbelievers!

7Even to have such lawsuits with one another is a defeat for you. Why not just accept the injustice and leave it at that? Why not let yourselves be cheated? 8Instead, you yourselves are the ones who do wrong and cheat even your fellow believers.*

9Don't you realize that those who do wrong will not inherit the Kingdom of God? Don't fool yourselves. Those who indulge in sexual sin, or who worship idols, or commit adultery, or are male prostitutes, or practice homosexuality, 10or are thieves, or greedy people, or drunkards, or are abusive, or cheat people—none of these will inherit the Kingdom of God. 11Some of you were once like that. But you were cleansed; you were made holy; you were made right with God by calling on the name of the Lord Jesus Christ and by the Spirit of our God.

12You say, "I am allowed to do anything"—but not everything is good for you. And even though "I am allowed to do anything," I must not become a slave to anything. 13You say, "Food was made for the stomach, and the stomach for food." (This is true, though someday God will do away with both of them.) But you can't say that our bodies were made for sexual immorality. They were made for the Lord, and the Lord cares about our bodies. 14And God will raise us from the dead by his power, just as he raised our Lord from the dead.

15Don't you realize that your bodies are actually parts of Christ? Should a man take his body, which is part of Christ, and join it to a prostitute? Never! 16And don't you realize that if a man joins himself to a prostitute, he becomes one body with her? For the Scriptures say, "The two are united into one."* ¹⁷But the person who is joined to the Lord is one spirit with him.

¹⁸Run from sexual sin! No other sin so clearly affects the body as this one does. For sexual immorality is a sin against your own body. ¹⁹**Don't you realize that your body is the temple of the Holy Spirit, who lives in you and was given to you by God? You do not belong to yourself, ²⁰for God bought you with a high price. So you must honor God with your body.**

6:6 Greek *one brother.*   6:8 Greek *even the brothers.* 6:16 Gen 2:24.

PSALM 31:9-18

Have mercy on me, Lᴏʀᴅ, for I am
    in distress.
Tears blur my eyes.
My body and soul are withering
    away.
¹⁰ I am dying from grief;
    my years are shortened by
      sadness.
Sin has drained my strength;
    I am wasting away from within.
¹¹ I am scorned by all my enemies
    and despised by my neighbors—
    even my friends are afraid to
      come near me.
When they see me on the street,
    they run the other way.
¹² I am ignored as if I were dead,
    as if I were a broken pot.
¹³ I have heard the many rumors
    about me,
    and I am surrounded by terror.
My enemies conspire against me,
    plotting to take my life.

¹⁴ But I am trusting you, O Lᴏʀᴅ,
    saying, "You are my God!"
¹⁵ My future is in your hands.
    Rescue me from those who hunt
      me down relentlessly.
¹⁶ Let your favor shine on your servant.
    In your unfailing love, rescue me.
¹⁷ Don't let me be disgraced, O Lᴏʀᴅ,
    for I call out to you for help.
Let the wicked be disgraced;
    let them lie silent in the grave.*
¹⁸ Silence their lying lips—

those proud and arrogant lips that
    accuse the godly.

31:17 Hebrew *in Sheol.*

PROVERBS 21:3

The Lᴏʀᴅ is more pleased when we do what is right and just than when we offer him sacrifices.

AUGUST 11

NEHEMIAH 1:1–3:14

These are the memoirs of Nehemiah son of Hacaliah.

In late autumn, in the month of Kislev, in the twentieth year of King Artaxerxes' reign,* I was at the fortress of Susa. ²Hanani, one of my brothers, came to visit me with some other men who had just arrived from Judah. I asked them about the Jews who had returned there from captivity and about how things were going in Jerusalem.

³They said to me, "Things are not going well for those who returned to the province of Judah. They are in great trouble and disgrace. The wall of Jerusalem has been torn down, and the gates have been destroyed by fire."

⁴When I heard this, I sat down and wept. In fact, for days I mourned, fasted, and prayed to the God of heaven. ⁵Then I said,

"O Lᴏʀᴅ, God of heaven, the great and awesome God who keeps his covenant of unfailing love with those who love him and obey his commands, ⁶listen to my prayer! Look down and see me praying night and day for your people Israel. I confess that we have sinned against you. Yes, even my own family and I have sinned! ⁷We have sinned terribly by not obeying the commands, decrees, and regulations that you gave us through your servant Moses.

8"Please remember what you told your servant Moses: 'If you are unfaithful to me, I will scatter you among the nations. 9But if you return to me and obey my commands and live by them, then even if you are exiled to the ends of the earth, I will bring you back to the place I have chosen for my name to be honored.'

10"The people you rescued by your great power and strong hand are your servants. 11O Lord, please hear my prayer! Listen to the prayers of those of us who delight in honoring you. Please grant me success today by making the king favorable to me.* Put it into his heart to be kind to me."

In those days I was the king's cup-bearer.

2:1EARLY the following spring, in the month of Nisan,* during the twentieth year of King Artaxerxes' reign, I was serving the king his wine. I had never before appeared sad in his presence. 2So the king asked me, "Why are you looking so sad? You don't look sick to me. You must be deeply troubled."

Then I was terrified, 3but I replied, "Long live the king! How can I not be sad? For the city where my ancestors are buried is in ruins, and the gates have been destroyed by fire."

4The king asked, "Well, how can I help you?"

With a prayer to the God of heaven, 5I replied, "If it please the king, and if you are pleased with me, your servant, send me to Judah to rebuild the city where my ancestors are buried."

6The king, with the queen sitting beside him, asked, "How long will you be gone? When will you return?" After I told him how long I would be gone, the king agreed to my request.

7I also said to the king, "If it please the king, let me have letters addressed to the governors of the province west of the Euphrates River,* instructing them to let me travel safely through their territories on my way to Judah. 8And please give me a letter addressed to Asaph, the manager of the king's forest, instructing him to give me timber. I will need it to make beams for the gates of the Temple fortress, for the city walls, and for a house for myself." And the king granted these requests, because the gracious hand of God was on me.

9When I came to the governors of the province west of the Euphrates River, I delivered the king's letters to them. The king, I should add, had sent along army officers and horsemen* to protect me. 10But when Sanballat the Horonite and Tobiah the Ammonite official heard of my arrival, they were very displeased that someone had come to help the people of Israel.

11So I arrived in Jerusalem. Three days later, 12I slipped out during the night, taking only a few others with me. I had not told anyone about the plans God had put in my heart for Jerusalem. We took no pack animals with us except the donkey I was riding. 13After dark I went out through the Valley Gate, past the Jackal's Well,* and over to the Dung Gate to inspect the broken walls and burned gates. 14Then I went to the Fountain Gate and to the King's Pool, but my donkey couldn't get through the rubble. 15So, though it was still dark, I went up the Kidron Valley* instead, inspecting the wall before I turned back and entered again at the Valley Gate.

16The city officials did not know I had been out there or what I was doing, for I had not yet said anything to anyone about my plans. I had not yet spoken to the Jewish leaders—the priests, the nobles, the officials, or anyone else in the administration. 17But now I said to them, "You know very well what trouble we are in. Jerusalem lies in ruins, and its gates have been destroyed by fire. Let us rebuild the wall of Jerusalem and end this disgrace!" 18Then I told them about how the gracious hand of God had been on me, and about my conversation with the king.

They replied at once, "Yes, let's rebuild the wall!" So they began the good work.

¹⁹But when Sanballat, Tobiah, and Geshem the Arab heard of our plan, they scoffed contemptuously. "What are you doing? Are you rebelling against the king?" they asked.

²⁰I replied, "The God of heaven will help us succeed. We, his servants, will start rebuilding this wall. But you have no share, legal right, or historic claim in Jerusalem."

³:¹THEN Eliashib the high priest and the other priests started to rebuild at the Sheep Gate. They dedicated it and set up its doors, building the wall as far as the Tower of the Hundred, which they dedicated, and the Tower of Hananel. ²People from the town of Jericho worked next to them, and beyond them was Zaccur son of Imri.

³The Fish Gate was built by the sons of Hassenaah. They laid the beams, set up its doors, and installed its bolts and bars. ⁴Meremoth son of Uriah and grandson of Hakkoz repaired the next section of wall. Beside him were Meshullam son of Berekiah and grandson of Meshezabel, and then Zadok son of Baana. ⁵Next were the people from Tekoa, though their leaders refused to work with the construction supervisors.

⁶The Old City Gate* was repaired by Joiada son of Paseah and Meshullam son of Besodeiah. They laid the beams, set up its doors, and installed its bolts and bars. ⁷Next to them were Melatiah from Gibeon, Jadon from Meronoth, people from Gibeon, and people from Mizpah, the headquarters of the governor of the province west of the Euphrates River.* ⁸Next was Uzziel son of Harhaiah, a goldsmith by trade, who also worked on the wall. Beyond him was Hananiah, a manufacturer of perfumes. They left out a section of Jerusalem as they built the Broad Wall.*

⁹Rephaiah son of Hur, the leader of

half the district of Jerusalem, was next to them on the wall. ¹⁰Next Jedaiah son of Harumaph repaired the wall across from his own house, and next to him was Hattush son of Hashabneiah. ¹¹Then came Malkijah son of Harim and Hasshub son of Pahath-moab, who repaired another section of the wall and the Tower of the Ovens. ¹²Shallum son of Hallohesh and his daughters repaired the next section. He was the leader of the other half of the district of Jerusalem.

¹³The Valley Gate was repaired by the people from Zanoah, led by Hanun. They set up its doors and installed its bolts and bars. They also repaired the 1,500 feet* of wall to the Dung Gate.

¹⁴The Dung Gate was repaired by Malkijah son of Recab, the leader of the Beth-hakkerem district. He rebuilt it, set up its doors, and installed its bolts and bars.

1:1 Hebrew *In the month of Kislev of the twentieth year.* A number of dates in the book of Nehemiah can be cross-checked with dates in surviving Persian records and related accurately to our modern calendar. This month of the ancient Hebrew lunar calendar occurred within the months of November and December 446 B.C. The *twentieth year* probably refers to the reign of King Artaxerxes I; compare 2:1; 5:14. 1:11 Hebrew *today in the sight of this man.* 2:1 Hebrew *In the month of Nisan.* This month of the ancient Hebrew lunar calendar occurred within the months of April and May 445 B.C. 2:7 Hebrew *the province beyond the river;* also in 2:9. 2:9 Or *charioteers.* 2:13 Or *Serpent's Well.* 2:15 Hebrew *the valley.* 3:6 Or *The Mishneh Gate,* or *The Jeshanah Gate.* 3:7 Hebrew *the province beyond the river.* 3:8 Or *They fortified Jerusalem up to the Broad Wall.* 3:13 Hebrew *1,000 cubits* [450 meters].

1 CORINTHIANS 7:1-24

Now regarding the questions you [Corinthians] asked in your letter. Yes, it is good to live a celibate life.* ²But because there is so much sexual immorality, each man should have his own wife, and each woman should have her own husband.

³The husband should fulfill his wife's sexual needs, and the wife should fulfill her husband's needs. ⁴The wife gives authority over her body to her husband, and the husband gives authority over his body to his wife.

⁵Do not deprive each other of sexual relations, unless you both agree to re-

frain from sexual intimacy for a limited time so you can give yourselves more completely to prayer. Afterward, you should come together again so that Satan won't be able to tempt you because of your lack of self-control. 6I say this as a concession, not as a command. 7But I wish everyone were single, just as I am. But God gives to some the gift of marriage, and to others the gift of singleness.

8So I say to those who aren't married and to widows—it's better to stay unmarried, just as I am. 9But if they can't control themselves, they should go ahead and marry. It's better to marry than to burn with lust.

10But for those who are married, I have a command that comes not from me, but from the Lord.* A wife must not leave her husband. 11But if she does leave him, let her remain single or else be reconciled to him. And the husband must not leave his wife.

12Now, I will speak to the rest of you, though I do not have a direct command from the Lord. If a Christian man* has a wife who is not a believer and she is willing to continue living with him, he must not leave her. 13And if a Christian woman has a husband who is not a believer and he is willing to continue living with her, she must not leave him. 14For the Christian wife brings holiness to her marriage, and the Christian husband* brings holiness to his marriage. Otherwise, your children would not be holy, but now they are holy. 15(But if the husband or wife who isn't a believer insists on leaving, let them go. In such cases the Christian husband or wife* is no longer bound to the other, for God has called you* to live in peace.) 16Don't you wives realize that your husbands might be saved because of you? And don't you husbands realize that your wives might be saved because of you?

17Each of you should continue to live in whatever situation the Lord has placed you, and remain as you were when God first called you. This is my rule for all the churches. 18For instance, a man who was circumcised before he became a believer should not try to reverse it. And the man who was uncircumcised when he became a believer should not be circumcised now. 19For it makes no difference whether or not a man has been circumcised. The important thing is to keep God's commandments.

20Yes, each of you should remain as you were when God called you. 21Are you a slave? Don't let that worry you—but if you get a chance to be free, take it. 22And remember, if you were a slave when the Lord called you, you are now free in the Lord. And if you were free when the Lord called you, you are now a slave of Christ. 23God paid a high price for you, so don't be enslaved by the world.* 24Each of you, dear brothers and sisters,* should remain as you were when God first called you.

7:1 Greek *It is good for a man not to touch a woman.*
7:10 See Matt 5:32; 19:9; Mark 10:11-12; Luke 16:18.
7:12 Greek *a brother.* 7:14 Greek *the brother.*
7:15a Greek *the brother or sister.* 7:15b Some manuscripts read *us.* 7:23 Greek *don't become slaves of people.* 7:24 Greek *brothers;* also in 7:29.

PSALM 31:19-24

How great is the goodness
    you have stored up for those
        who fear you.
You lavish it on those who come
        to you for protection,
    blessing them before the
        watching world.
20 You hide them in the shelter
        of your presence,
    safe from those who
        conspire against them.
You shelter them in your
        presence,
    far from accusing tongues.

21 Praise the LORD,
    for he has shown me the
        wonders of his unfailing
        love.
He kept me safe when my city
        was under attack.
22 In panic I cried out,
    "I am cut off from the LORD!"
But you heard my cry for mercy
    and answered my call for help.

²³ **Love the Lord, all you godly ones!**
    For the Lord protects those who
        are loyal to him,
    but he harshly punishes the
        arrogant.
²⁴ **So be strong and courageous,**
    all you who put your hope
        in the Lord!

PROVERBS 21:4
Haughty eyes, a proud heart, and evil
actions are all sin.

AUGUST 12

NEHEMIAH 3:15–5:13
The Fountain Gate was repaired by
Shallum* son of Col-hozeh, the leader
of the Mizpah district. He rebuilt it,
roofed it, set up its doors, and installed
its bolts and bars. Then he repaired the
wall of the pool of Siloam* near the
king's garden, and he rebuilt the wall as
far as the stairs that descend from the
City of David. ¹⁶Next to him was Nehemiah son of Azbuk, the leader of half
the district of Beth-zur. He rebuilt the
wall from a place across from the tombs
of David's family as far as the water reservoir and the House of the Warriors.

¹⁷Next to him, repairs were made by a
group of Levites working under the supervision of Rehum son of Bani. Then
came Hashabiah, the leader of half the
district of Keilah, who supervised the
building of the wall on behalf of his own
district. ¹⁸Next down the line were his
countrymen led by Binnui* son of Henadad, the leader of the other half of the
district of Keilah.

¹⁹Next to them, Ezer son of Jeshua,
the leader of Mizpah, repaired another
section of wall across from the ascent to
the armory near the angle in the wall.
²⁰Next to him was Baruch son of Zabbai,
who zealously repaired an additional

section from the angle to the door of
the house of Eliashib the high priest.
²¹Meremoth son of Uriah and grandson
of Hakkoz rebuilt another section of
the wall extending from the door of Eliashib's house to the end of the house.

²²The next repairs were made by the
priests from the surrounding region.
²³After them, Benjamin and Hasshub
repaired the section across from their
house, and Azariah son of Maaseiah and
grandson of Ananiah repaired the section across from his house. ²⁴Next was
Binnui son of Henadad, who rebuilt another section of the wall from Azariah's
house to the angle and the corner. ²⁵Pa-
lal son of Uzai carried on the work from
a point opposite the angle and the tower
that projects up from the king's upper
house beside the court of the guard.
Next to him were Pedaiah son of Pa-
rosh, ²⁶with the Temple servants living
on the hill of Ophel, who repaired the
wall as far as a point across from the
Water Gate to the east and the projecting tower. ²⁷Then came the people of
Tekoa, who repaired another section
across from the great projecting tower
and over to the wall of Ophel.

²⁸Above the Horse Gate, the priests
repaired the wall. Each one repaired the
section immediately across from his
own house. ²⁹Next Zadok son of Immer
also rebuilt the wall across from his
own house, and beyond him was Shemaiah son of Shecaniah, the gatekeeper
of the East Gate. ³⁰Next Hananiah
son of Shelemiah and Hanun, the sixth
son of Zalaph, repaired another section,
while Meshullam son of Berekiah rebuilt the wall across from where he
lived. ³¹Malkijah, one of the goldsmiths,
repaired the wall as far as the housing
for the Temple servants and merchants,
across from the Inspection Gate. Then
he continued as far as the upper room
at the corner. ³²The other goldsmiths
and merchants repaired the wall from
that corner to the Sheep Gate.

^{4:1}*Sanballat was very angry when he
learned that we were rebuilding the

wall. He flew into a rage and mocked the Jews, [2] saying in front of his friends and the Samarian army officers, "What does this bunch of poor, feeble Jews think they're doing? Do they think they can build the wall in a single day by just offering a few sacrifices?* Do they actually think they can make something of stones from a rubbish heap—and charred ones at that?"

[3] Tobiah the Ammonite, who was standing beside him, remarked, "That stone wall would collapse if even a fox walked along the top of it!"

[4] Then I prayed, "Hear us, our God, for we are being mocked. May their scoffing fall back on their own heads, and may they themselves become captives in a foreign land! [5] Do not ignore their guilt. Do not blot out their sins, for they have provoked you to anger here in front of* the builders."

[6] At last the wall was completed to half its height around the entire city, for the people had worked with enthusiasm.

[7] *But when Sanballat and Tobiah and the Arabs, Ammonites, and Ashdodites heard that the work was going ahead and that the gaps in the wall of Jerusalem were being repaired, they were furious. [8] They all made plans to come and fight against Jerusalem and throw us into confusion. [9] But we prayed to our God and guarded the city day and night to protect ourselves.

[10] Then the people of Judah began to complain, "The workers are getting tired, and there is so much rubble to be moved. We will never be able to build the wall by ourselves."

[11] Meanwhile, our enemies were saying, "Before they know what's happening, we will swoop down on them and kill them and end their work."

[12] The Jews who lived near the enemy came and told us again and again, "They will come from all directions and attack us!"* [13] So I placed armed guards behind the lowest parts of the wall in the exposed areas. I stationed the people to stand guard by families, armed with swords, spears, and bows.

[14] Then as I looked over the situation, I called together the nobles and the rest of the people and said to them, "Don't be afraid of the enemy! Remember the Lord, who is great and glorious, and fight for your brothers, your sons, your daughters, your wives, and your homes!"

[15] When our enemies heard that we knew of their plans and that God had frustrated them, we all returned to our work on the wall. [16] But from then on, only half my men worked while the other half stood guard with spears, shields, bows, and coats of mail. The leaders stationed themselves behind the people of Judah [17] who were building the wall. The laborers carried on their work with one hand supporting their load and one hand holding a weapon. [18] All the builders had a sword belted to their side. The trumpeter stayed with me to sound the alarm.

[19] Then I explained to the nobles and officials and all the people, "The work is very spread out, and we are widely separated from each other along the wall. [20] When you hear the blast of the trumpet, rush to wherever it is sounding. Then our God will fight for us!"

[21] We worked early and late, from sunrise to sunset. And half the men were always on guard. [22] I also told everyone living outside the walls to stay in Jerusalem. That way they and their servants could help with guard duty at night and work during the day. [23] During this time, none of us—not I, nor my relatives, nor my servants, nor the guards who were with me—ever took off our clothes. We carried our weapons with us at all times, even when we went for water.*

[5:1] ABOUT this time some of the men and their wives raised a cry of protest against their fellow Jews. [2] They were saying, "We have such large families. We need more food to survive."

[3] Others said, "We have mortgaged our fields, vineyards, and homes to get food during the famine."

[4] And others said, "We have had to borrow money on our fields and vineyards to pay our taxes. [5] We belong to the

same family as those who are wealthy, and our children are just like theirs. Yet we must sell our children into slavery just to get enough money to live. We have already sold some of our daughters, and we are helpless to do anything about it, for our fields and vineyards are already mortgaged to others."

⁶When I heard their complaints, I was very angry. ⁷After thinking it over, I spoke out against these nobles and officials. I told them, "You are hurting your own relatives by charging interest when they borrow money!" Then I called a public meeting to deal with the problem.

⁸At the meeting I said to them, "We are doing all we can to redeem our Jewish relatives who have had to sell themselves to pagan foreigners, but you are selling them back into slavery again. How often must we redeem them?" And they had nothing to say in their defense.

⁹Then I pressed further, "What you are doing is not right! Should you not walk in the fear of our God in order to avoid being mocked by enemy nations? ¹⁰I myself, as well as my brothers and my workers, have been lending the people money and grain, but now let us stop this business of charging interest. ¹¹You must restore their fields, vineyards, olive groves, and homes to them this very day. And repay the interest you charged when you lent them money, grain, new wine, and olive oil."

¹²They replied, "We will give back everything and demand nothing more from the people. We will do as you say." Then I called the priests and made the nobles and officials swear to do what they had promised.

¹³I shook out the folds of my robe and said, "If you fail to keep your promise, may God shake you like this from your homes and from your property!" The whole assembly responded, "Amen," and they praised the LORD. And the people did as they had promised.

3:15a As in Syriac version; Hebrew reads *Shallun*.
3:15b Hebrew *pool of Shelah,* another name for the pool of Siloam.   3:18 As in a few Hebrew manuscripts, some Greek manuscripts, and Syriac version (see also 3:24; 10:9); most Hebrew manuscripts read *Bavvai*.

4:1 Verses 4:1-6 are numbered 3:33-38 in Hebrew text.
4:2 The meaning of the Hebrew is uncertain.   4:5 Or *for they have thrown insults in the face of.*   4:7 Verses 4:7-23 are numbered 4:1-17 in Hebrew text.   4:12 The meaning of the Hebrew is uncertain.   4:23 Or *Each carried his weapon in his right hand.* Hebrew reads *Each his weapon the water.* The meaning of the Hebrew is uncertain.

1 CORINTHIANS 7:25-40

Now regarding your question about the young women who are not yet married. I [Paul] do not have a command from the Lord for them. But the Lord in his mercy has given me wisdom that can be trusted, and I will share it with you. ²⁶Because of the present crisis,* I think it is best to remain as you are. ²⁷If you have a wife, do not seek to end the marriage. If you do not have a wife, do not seek to get married. ²⁸But if you do get married, it is not a sin. And if a young woman gets married, it is not a sin. However, those who get married at this time will have troubles, and I am trying to spare you those problems.

²⁹But let me say this, dear brothers and sisters: The time that remains is very short. So from now on, those with wives should not focus only on their marriage. ³⁰Those who weep or who rejoice or who buy things should not be absorbed by their weeping or their joy or their possessions. ³¹Those who use the things of the world should not become attached to them. For this world as we know it will soon pass away.

³²I want you to be free from the concerns of this life. An unmarried man can spend his time doing the Lord's work and thinking how to please him. ³³But a married man has to think about his earthly responsibilities and how to please his wife. ³⁴His interests are divided. In the same way, a woman who is no longer married or has never been married can be devoted to the Lord and holy in body and in spirit. But a married woman has to think about her earthly responsibilities and how to please her husband. ³⁵I am saying this for your benefit, not to place restrictions on you. I want you to do whatever will help you serve the Lord best, with as few distractions as possible.

³⁶But if a man thinks that he's treating his fiancée improperly and will inevitably give in to his passion, let him marry her as he wishes. It is not a sin. ³⁷But if he has decided firmly not to marry and there is no urgency and he can control his passion, he does well not to marry. ³⁸So the person who marries his fiancée does well, and the person who doesn't marry does even better.

³⁹A wife is bound to her husband as long as he lives. If her husband dies, she is free to marry anyone she wishes, but only if he loves the Lord.* ⁴⁰But in my opinion it would be better for her to stay single, and I think I am giving you counsel from God's Spirit when I say this.

7:26 Or *the pressures of life.*   **7:39** Greek *but only in the Lord.*

PSALM 32:1-11
A psalm* of David.

¹ **O**h, what joy for those
   whose disobedience is forgiven,
   whose sin is put out of sight!
² Yes, what joy for those
   whose record the Lord has
      cleared of guilt,*
   whose lives are lived in complete
      honesty!
³ When I refused to confess my sin,
   my body wasted away,
   and I groaned all day long.
⁴ Day and night your hand of
      discipline was heavy on me.
   My strength evaporated like
      water in the summer heat.
                                    Interlude

⁵ Finally, I confessed all my sins to you
   and stopped trying to hide my
      guilt.
   I said to myself, "I will confess my
      rebellion to the Lord."
   And you forgave me! All my
      guilt is gone.   *Interlude*

⁶ Therefore, let all the godly pray to
   you while there is still time,
   that they may not drown in the
   floodwaters of judgment.
⁷ For you are my hiding place;

you protect me from trouble.
You surround me with songs of
   victory.   *Interlude*

⁸ The Lord says, "I will guide you
   along the best pathway
      for your life.
   I will advise you and watch
      over you.
⁹ Do not be like a senseless horse or
      mule
   that needs a bit and bridle to keep
      it under control."

¹⁰ Many sorrows come to the wicked,
   but unfailing love surrounds
      those who trust the Lord.
¹¹ So rejoice in the Lord and be glad,
   all you who obey him!
   Shout for joy, all you whose hearts
      are pure!

32:TITLE Hebrew *maskil.* This may be a literary or musical term.   **32:2** Greek version reads *of sin.* Compare Rom 4:7.

PROVERBS 21:5-7
Good planning and hard work lead to prosperity, but hasty shortcuts lead to poverty. □Wealth created by a lying tongue is a vanishing mist and a deadly trap.* □The violence of the wicked sweeps them away, because they refuse to do what is just.

21:6 As in Greek version; Hebrew reads *mist for those who seek death.*

AUGUST
13

NEHEMIAH 5:14–7:73a
For the entire twelve years that I was governor of Judah—from the twentieth year to the thirty-second year of the reign of King Artaxerxes*—neither I nor my officials drew on our official food allowance. ¹⁵The former governors, in contrast, had laid heavy burdens on the people, demanding a daily ration of food and wine, besides forty

pieces* of silver. Even their assistants took advantage of the people. But because I feared God, I did not act that way.

16I also devoted myself to working on the wall and refused to acquire any land. And I required all my servants to spend time working on the wall. 17I asked for nothing, even though I regularly fed 150 Jewish officials at my table, besides all the visitors from other lands! 18The provisions I paid for each day included one ox, six choice sheep or goats, and a large number of poultry. And every ten days we needed a large supply of all kinds of wine. Yet I refused to claim the governor's food allowance because the people already carried a heavy burden.

19Remember, O my God, all that I have done for these people, and bless me for it.

6:1SANBALLAT, Tobiah, Geshem the Arab, and the rest of our enemies found out that I had finished rebuilding the wall and that no gaps remained—though we had not yet set up the doors in the gates. 2So Sanballat and Geshem sent a message asking me to meet them at one of the villages* in the plain of Ono.

But I realized they were plotting to harm me, 3so I replied by sending this message to them: "I am engaged in a great work, so I can't come. Why should I stop working to come and meet with you?"

4Four times they sent the same message, and each time I gave the same reply. 5The fifth time, Sanballat's servant came with an open letter in his hand, 6and this is what it said:

"There is a rumor among the surrounding nations, and Geshem* tells me it is true, that you and the Jews are planning to rebel and that is why you are building the wall. According to his reports, you plan to be their king. 7He also reports that you have appointed prophets in Jerusalem to proclaim about you, 'Look! There is a king in Judah!'

"You can be very sure that this report will get back to the king, so I suggest that you come and talk it over with me."

8I replied, "There is no truth in any part of your story. You are making up the whole thing."

9They were just trying to intimidate us, imagining that they could discourage us and stop the work. So I continued the work with even greater determination.*

10Later I went to visit Shemaiah son of Delaiah and grandson of Mehetabel, who was confined to his home. He said, "Let us meet together inside the Temple of God and bolt the doors shut. Your enemies are coming to kill you tonight."

11But I replied, "Should someone in my position run from danger? Should someone in my position enter the Temple to save his life? No, I won't do it!" 12I realized that God had not spoken to him, but that he had uttered this prophecy against me because Tobiah and Sanballat had hired him. 13They were hoping to intimidate me and make me sin. Then they would be able to accuse and discredit me.

14Remember, O my God, all the evil things that Tobiah and Sanballat have done. And remember Noadiah the prophet and all the prophets like her who have tried to intimidate me.

15So on October 2* the wall was finished—just fifty-two days after we had begun. 16When our enemies and the surrounding nations heard about it, they were frightened and humiliated. They realized this work had been done with the help of our God.

17During those fifty-two days, many letters went back and forth between Tobiah and the nobles of Judah. 18For many in Judah had sworn allegiance to him because his father-in-law was Shecaniah son of Arah, and his son Jehohanan was married to the daughter of Meshullam son of Berekiah. 19They kept telling me about Tobiah's good deeds, and then they told him everything I said. And Tobiah kept sending threatening letters to intimidate me.

7:1AFTER the wall was finished and I had set up the doors in the gates, the gatekeepers, singers, and Levites were appointed. **2**I gave the responsibility of governing Jerusalem to my brother Hanani, along with Hananiah, the commander of the fortress, for he was a faithful man who feared God more than most. **3**I said to them, "Do not leave the gates open during the hottest part of the day.* And even while the gatekeepers are on duty, have them shut and bar the doors. Appoint the residents of Jerusalem to act as guards, everyone on a regular watch. Some will serve at sentry posts and some in front of their own homes."

4At that time the city was large and spacious, but the population was small, and none of the houses had been rebuilt. **5**So my God gave me the idea to call together all the nobles and leaders of the city, along with the ordinary citizens, for registration. I had found the genealogical record of those who had first returned to Judah. This is what was written there:

6Here is the list of the Jewish exiles of the provinces who returned from their captivity. King Nebuchadnezzar had deported them to Babylon, but now they returned to Jerusalem and the other towns in Judah where they originally lived. **7**Their leaders were Zerubbabel, Jeshua, Nehemiah, Seraiah,* Reelaiah,* Nahamani, Mordecai, Bilshan, Mispar,* Bigvai, Rehum,* and Baanah.

This is the number of the men of Israel who returned from exile:
8 The family of Parosh 2,172
9 The family of Shephatiah 372
10 The family of Arah 652
11 The family of Pahath-moab (descendants of Jeshua and Joab) 2,818

12 The family of Elam 1,254
13 The family of Zattu......... 845
14 The family of Zaccai........ 760
15 The family of Bani* 648
16 The family of Bebai 628
17 The family of Azgad 2,322
18 The family of Adonikam..... 667
19 The family of Bigvai 2,067
20 The family of Adin 655
21 The family of Ater (descendants of Hezekiah)............... 98
22 The family of Hashum....... 328
23 The family of Bezai......... 324
24 The family of Jorah*........ 112
25 The family of Gibbar* 95
26 The people of Bethlehem and Netophah 188
27 The people of Anathoth 128
28 The people of Beth-azmaveth............. 42
29 The people of Kiriath-jearim, Kephirah, and Beeroth 743
30 The people of Ramah and Geba..................... 621
31 The people of Micmash...... 122
32 The people of Bethel and Ai.. 123
33 The people of Nebo.......... 52
34 The citizens of Elam....... 1,254
35 The citizens of Harim 320
36 The citizens of Jericho....... 345
37 The citizens of Lod, Hadid, and Ono 721
38 The citizens of Senaah..... 3,930

39These are the priests who returned from exile:
The family of Jedaiah (through the line of Jeshua)......... 973
40 The family of Immer 1,052
41 The family of Pashhur 1,247
42 The family of Harim....... 1,017

43These are the Levites who returned from exile:
The families of Jeshua and Kadmiel (descendants of Hodaviah*).............. 74
44 The singers of the family of Asaph 148
45 The gatekeepers of the families of Shallum, Ater, Talmon, Akkub, Hatita, and Shobai 138

46The descendants of the following Temple servants returned from exile:

Ziha, Hasupha, Tabbaoth,
47 Keros, Siaha,* Padon,
48 Lebanah, Hagabah, Shalmai,
49 Hanan, Giddel, Gahar,
50 Reaiah, Rezin, Nekoda,
51 Gazzam, Uzza, Paseah,
52 Besai, Meunim, Nephusim,*
53 Bakbuk, Hakupha, Harhur,
54 Bazluth,* Mehida, Harsha,
55 Barkos, Sisera, Temah,
56 Neziah, and Hatipha.

57 The descendants of these servants of King Solomon returned from exile:

Sotai, Hassophereth, Peruda,*
58 Jaalah,* Darkon, Giddel,
59 Shephatiah, Hattil, Pokereth-hazzebaim, and Ami.*

60In all, the Temple servants and the descendants of Solomon's servants numbered 392.

61Another group returned at this time from the towns of Tel-melah, Tel-harsha, Kerub, Addan,* and Immer. However, they could not prove that they or their families were descendants of Israel. 62This group included the families of Delaiah, Tobiah, and Nekoda—a total of 642 people.

63Three families of priests—Hobaiah, Hakkoz, and Barzillai—also returned. (This Barzillai had married a woman who was a descendant of Barzillai of Gilead, and he had taken her family name.) 64They searched for their names in the genealogical records, but they were not found, so they were disqualified from serving as priests. 65The governor told them not to eat the priests' share of food from the sacrifices until a priest could consult the LORD about the matter by using the Urim and Thummim—the sacred lots.

66So a total of 42,360 people returned to Judah, 67in addition to 7,337 servants and 245 singers,

both men and women. 68They took with them 736 horses, 245 mules,* 69435 camels, and 6,720 donkeys.

70Some of the family leaders gave gifts for the work. The governor gave to the treasury 1,000 gold coins,* 50 gold basins, and 530 robes for the priests. 71The other leaders gave to the treasury a total of 20,000 gold coins* and some 2,750 pounds* of silver for the work. 72The rest of the people gave 20,000 gold coins, about 2,500 pounds* of silver, and 67 robes for the priests.

73So the priests, the Levites, the gatekeepers, the singers, the Temple servants, and some of the common people settled near Jerusalem. The rest of the people returned to their own towns throughout Israel.

5:14 That is, 445–433 B.C.   5:15 Hebrew *40 shekels* [1 pound, or 456 grams].   6:2 As in Greek version; Hebrew reads *at Kephirim*.   6:6 Hebrew *Gashmu*, a variant spelling of Geshem.   6:9 As in Greek version; Hebrew reads *But now to strengthen my hands*.
6:15 Hebrew *on the twenty-fifth day of the month Elul*, of the ancient Hebrew lunar calendar. This day was October 2, 445 B.C.; also see note on 1:1.   7:3 Or *Keep the gates of Jerusalem closed until the sun is hot*.   7:7a As in parallel text at Ezra 2:2; Hebrew reads *Azariah*.   7:7b As in parallel text at Ezra 2:2; Hebrew reads *Raamiah*.
7:7c As in parallel text at Ezra 2:2; Hebrew reads *Mispereth*.
7:7d As in parallel text at Ezra 2:2; Hebrew reads *Nehum*.
7:15 As in parallel text at Ezra 2:10; Hebrew reads *Binnui*.
7:24 As in parallel text at Ezra 2:18; Hebrew reads *Hariph*.
7:25 As in parallel text at Ezra 2:20; Hebrew reads *Gibeon*.
7:43 As in parallel text at Ezra 2:40; Hebrew reads *Hodevah*.
7:47 As in parallel text at Ezra 2:44; Hebrew reads *Sia*.
7:52 As in parallel text at Ezra 2:50; Hebrew reads *Nephushesim*.   7:54 As in parallel text at Ezra 2:52; Hebrew reads *Bazlith*.   7:57 As in parallel text at Ezra 2:55; Hebrew reads *Sotai, Sophereth, Perida*.   7:58 As in parallel text at Ezra 2:56; Hebrew reads *Jaala*.
7:59 As in parallel text at Ezra 2:57; Hebrew reads *Amon*.
7:61 As in parallel text at Ezra 2:59; Hebrew reads *Addon*.
7:68 As in some Hebrew manuscripts (see also Ezra 2:66); most Hebrew manuscripts lack this verse. Verses 7:69-73 are numbered 7:68-72 in Hebrew text.   7:70 Hebrew *1,000 darics of gold*, about 19 pounds or 8.6 kilograms in weight.   7:71a Hebrew *20,000 darics of gold*, about 375 pounds or 170 kilograms in weight; also in 7:72.   7:71b Hebrew *2,200 minas* [1,300 kilograms].
7:72 Hebrew *2,000 minas* [1,200 kilograms].

1 CORINTHIANS 8:1-13

Now regarding your [Corinthians] question about food that has been offered to idols. Yes, we know that "we all have knowledge" about this issue. But while knowledge makes us feel important, it is love that strengthens the church. 2Anyone who claims to know all the answers doesn't really know very much. ³But the person who loves God is the one whom God recognizes.*

⁴So, what about eating meat that has been offered to idols? Well, we all know that an idol is not really a god and that there is only one God. ⁵There may be so-called gods both in heaven and on earth, and some people actually worship many gods and many lords. ⁶But we know that there is only one God, the Father, who created everything, and we live for him. And there is only one Lord, Jesus Christ, through whom God made everything and through whom we have been given life.

⁷However, not all believers know this. Some are accustomed to thinking of idols as being real, so when they eat food that has been offered to idols, they think of it as the worship of real gods, and their weak consciences are violated. ⁸It's true that we can't win God's approval by what we eat. We don't lose anything if we don't eat it, and we don't gain anything if we do.

⁹But you must be careful so that your freedom does not cause others with a weaker conscience to stumble. ¹⁰For if others see you—with your "superior knowledge"—eating in the temple of an idol, won't they be encouraged to violate their conscience by eating food that has been offered to an idol? ¹¹So because of your superior knowledge, a weak believer* for whom Christ died will be destroyed. ¹²And when you sin against other believers* by encouraging them to do something they believe is wrong, you are sinning against Christ. ¹³So if what I eat causes another believer to sin, I will never eat meat again as long as I live—for I don't want to cause another believer to stumble.

8:3 Some manuscripts read *the person who loves has full knowledge.*   8:11 Greek *brother;* also in 8:13.
8:12 Greek *brothers.*

PSALM 33:1-11

Let the godly sing for joy to the
        LORD;
    it is fitting for the pure to
        praise him.
² **Praise the LORD with melodies
        on the lyre;
    make music for him on the
        ten-stringed harp.**
³ **Sing a new song of praise to him;
    play skillfully on the harp, and
        sing with joy.**
⁴ For the word of the LORD holds true,
    and we can trust everything
        he does.
⁵ He loves whatever is just and good;
    the unfailing love of the LORD fills
        the earth.

⁶ The LORD merely spoke,
    and the heavens were created.
He breathed the word,
    and all the stars were born.
⁷ He assigned the sea its boundaries
    and locked the oceans in vast
        reservoirs.
⁸ Let the whole world fear the LORD,
    and let everyone stand in awe
        of him.
⁹ For when he spoke, the world began!
    It appeared at his command.

¹⁰ The LORD frustrates the plans
        of the nations
    and thwarts all their schemes.
¹¹ But the LORD's plans stand firm
        forever;
    his intentions can never
        be shaken.

PROVERBS 21:8-10

The guilty walk a crooked path; the innocent travel a straight road. □It's better to live alone in the corner of an attic than with a quarrelsome wife in a lovely home. □Evil people desire evil; their neighbors get no mercy from them.

AUGUST
14

NEHEMIAH 7:73b–9:21

In October,* when the Israelites had settled in their towns, 8:1all the people assembled with a unified purpose at the square just inside the Water Gate. They asked Ezra the scribe to bring out the Book of the Law of Moses, which the LORD had given for Israel to obey.

2So on October 8* Ezra the priest brought the Book of the Law before the assembly, which included the men and women and all the children old enough to understand. 3He faced the square just inside the Water Gate from early morning until noon and read aloud to everyone who could understand. All the people listened closely to the Book of the Law.

4Ezra the scribe stood on a high wooden platform that had been made for the occasion. To his right stood Mattithiah, Shema, Anaiah, Uriah, Hilkiah, and Maaseiah. To his left stood Pedaiah, Mishael, Malkijah, Hashum, Hashbaddanah, Zechariah, and Meshullam. 5Ezra stood on the platform in full view of all the people. When they saw him open the book, they all rose to their feet.

6Then Ezra praised the LORD, the great God, and all the people chanted, "Amen! Amen!" as they lifted their hands. Then they bowed down and worshiped the LORD with their faces to the ground.

7The Levites—Jeshua, Bani, Sherebiah, Jamin, Akkub, Shabbethai, Hodiah, Maaseiah, Kelita, Azariah, Jozabad, Hanan, and Pelaiah—then instructed the people in the Law while everyone remained in their places. 8They read from the Book of the Law of God and clearly explained the meaning of what was being read, helping the people understand each passage.

9Then Nehemiah the governor, Ezra the priest and scribe, and the Levites who were interpreting for the people said to them, "Don't mourn or weep on such a day as this! For today is a sacred day before the LORD your God." For the people had all been weeping as they listened to the words of the Law.

10And Nehemiah* continued, "Go and celebrate with a feast of rich foods and sweet drinks, and share gifts of food with people who have nothing prepared. This is a sacred day before our Lord. Don't be dejected and sad, for the joy of the LORD is your strength!"

11And the Levites, too, quieted the people, telling them, "Hush! Don't weep! For this is a sacred day." 12So the people went away to eat and drink at a festive meal, to share gifts of food, and to celebrate with great joy because they had heard God's words and understood them.

13On October 9* the family leaders of all the people, together with the priests and Levites, met with Ezra the scribe to go over the Law in greater detail. 14As they studied the Law, they discovered that the LORD had commanded through Moses that the Israelites should live in shelters during the festival to be held that month.* 15He had said that a proclamation should be made throughout their towns and in Jerusalem, telling the people to go to the hills to get branches from olive, wild olive,* myrtle, palm, and other leafy trees. They were to use these branches to make shelters in which they would live during the festival, as prescribed in the Law.

16So the people went out and cut branches and used them to build shelters on the roofs of their houses, in their courtyards, in the courtyards of God's Temple, or in the squares just inside the Water Gate and the Ephraim Gate. 17So everyone who had returned from captivity lived in these shelters during the festival, and they were all filled with great joy! The Israelites had not celebrated like this since the days of Joshua* son of Nun.

18Ezra read from the Book of the Law of God on each of the seven days of the festival. Then on the eighth day they held a solemn assembly, as was required by law.

⁹:¹On October 31* the people assembled again, and this time they fasted and dressed in burlap and sprinkled dust on their heads. ²Those of Israelite descent separated themselves from all foreigners as they confessed their own sins and the sins of their ancestors. ³They remained standing in place for three hours* while the Book of the Law of the LORD their God was read aloud to them. Then for three more hours they confessed their sins and worshiped the LORD their God. ⁴The Levites—Jeshua, Bani, Kadmiel, Shebaniah, Bunni, Sherebiah, Bani, and Kenani—stood on the stairway of the Levites and cried out to the LORD their God with loud voices.

⁵Then the leaders of the Levites—Jeshua, Kadmiel, Bani, Hashabneiah, Sherebiah, Hodiah, Shebaniah, and Pethahiah—called out to the people: "Stand up and praise the LORD your God, for he lives from everlasting to everlasting!" Then they prayed:

"May your glorious name be praised! May it be exalted above all blessing and praise!

⁶"You alone are the LORD. You made the skies and the heavens and all the stars. You made the earth and the seas and everything in them. You preserve them all, and the angels of heaven worship you.

⁷"You are the LORD God, who chose Abram and brought him from Ur of the Chaldeans and renamed him Abraham. ⁸When he had proved himself faithful, you made a covenant with him to give him and his descendants the land of the Canaanites, Hittites, Amorites, Perizzites, Jebusites, and Girgashites. And you have done what you promised, for you are always true to your word.

⁹"You saw the misery of our ancestors in Egypt, and you heard their cries from beside the Red Sea.*

¹⁰You displayed miraculous signs and wonders against Pharaoh, his officials, and all his people, for you knew how arrogantly they were treating our ancestors. You have a glorious reputation that has never been forgotten. ¹¹You divided the sea for your people so they could walk through on dry land! And then you hurled their enemies into the depths of the sea. They sank like stones beneath the mighty waters. ¹²You led our ancestors by a pillar of cloud during the day and a pillar of fire at night so that they could find their way.

¹³"You came down at Mount Sinai and spoke to them from heaven. You gave them regulations and instructions that were just, and decrees and commands that were good. ¹⁴You instructed them concerning your holy Sabbath. And you commanded them, through Moses your servant, to obey all your commands, decrees, and instructions.

¹⁵"You gave them bread from heaven when they were hungry and water from the rock when they were thirsty. You commanded them to go and take possession of the land you had sworn to give them.

¹⁶"But our ancestors were proud and stubborn, and they paid no attention to your commands. ¹⁷They refused to obey and did not remember the miracles you had done for them. Instead, they became stubborn and appointed a leader to take them back to their slavery in Egypt! But you are a God of forgiveness, gracious and merciful, slow to become angry, and rich in unfailing love. You did not abandon them, ¹⁸even when they made an idol shaped like a calf and said, 'This is your god who brought you out of Egypt!' They committed terrible blasphemies.

¹⁹"But in your great mercy you did not abandon them to die in the

wilderness. The pillar of cloud still led them forward by day, and the pillar of fire showed them the way through the night. [20]You sent your good Spirit to instruct them, and you did not stop giving them manna from heaven or water for their thirst. [21]For forty years you sustained them in the wilderness, and they lacked nothing. Their clothes did not wear out, and their feet did not swell!"

7:73 Hebrew *in the seventh month.* This month of the ancient Hebrew lunar calendar occurred within the months of October and November 445 B.C.   8:2 Hebrew *on the first day of the seventh month,* of the ancient Hebrew lunar calendar. This day was October 8, 445 B.C.; also see note on 1:1.   8:10 Hebrew *he.*   8:13 Hebrew *On the second day,* of the seventh month of the ancient Hebrew lunar calendar. This day was October 9, 445 B.C.; also see notes on 1:1 and 8:2.   8:14 Hebrew *in the seventh month.* This month of the ancient Hebrew lunar calendar usually occurs within the months of September and October. See Lev 23:39-43.   8:15 Or *pine;* Hebrew reads *oil tree.*   8:17 Hebrew *Jeshua,* a variant spelling of Joshua.   9:1 Hebrew *On the twenty-fourth day of that same month,* the seventh month of the ancient Hebrew lunar calendar. This day was October 31, 445 B.C.; also see notes on 1:1 and 8:2.   9:3 Hebrew *for a quarter of a day.*   9:9 Hebrew *sea of reeds.*

1 CORINTHIANS 9:1-18

Am I [Paul] not as free as anyone else? Am I not an apostle? Haven't I seen Jesus our Lord with my own eyes? Isn't it because of my work that you belong to the Lord? [2]Even if others think I am not an apostle, I certainly am to you. You yourselves are proof that I am the Lord's apostle.

[3]This is my answer to those who question my authority.* [4]Don't we have the right to live in your homes and share your meals? [5]Don't we have the right to bring a Christian wife with us as the other disciples and the Lord's brothers do, and as Peter* does? [6]Or is it only Barnabas and I who have to work to support ourselves?

[7]What soldier has to pay his own expenses? What farmer plants a vineyard and doesn't have the right to eat some of its fruit? What shepherd cares for a flock of sheep and isn't allowed to drink some of the milk? [8]Am I expressing merely a human opinion, or does the law say the same thing? [9]For the law of Moses says, "You must not muzzle an ox to keep it from eating as it treads out the

grain."* Was God thinking only about oxen when he said this? [10]Wasn't he actually speaking to us? Yes, it was written for us, so that the one who plows and the one who threshes the grain might both expect a share of the harvest.

[11]Since we have planted spiritual seed among you, aren't we entitled to a harvest of physical food and drink? [12]If you support others who preach to you, shouldn't we have an even greater right to be supported? But we have never used this right. We would rather put up with anything than be an obstacle to the Good News about Christ.

[13]Don't you realize that those who work in the temple get their meals from the offerings brought to the temple? And those who serve at the altar get a share of the sacrificial offerings. [14]In the same way, the Lord ordered that those who preach the Good News should be supported by those who benefit from it. [15]Yet I have never used any of these rights. And I am not writing this to suggest that I want to start now. In fact, I would rather die than lose my right to boast about preaching without charge. [16]Yet preaching the Good News is not something I can boast about. I am compelled by God to do it. How terrible for me if I didn't preach the Good News!

[17]If I were doing this on my own initiative, I would deserve payment. But I have no choice, for God has given me this sacred trust. [18]What then is my pay? It is the opportunity to preach the Good News without charging anyone. That's why I never demand my rights when I preach the Good News.

9:3 Greek *those who examine me.*   9:5 Greek *Cephas.*   9:9 Deut 25:4.

PSALM 33:12-22

What joy for the nation whose God is the LORD,
    whose people he has chosen
        as his inheritance.

[13] The LORD looks down from heaven
    and sees the whole human race.
[14] From his throne he observes
    all who live on the earth.

¹⁵ He made their hearts,
    so he understands everything
        they do.
¹⁶ The best-equipped army cannot
        save a king,
    nor is great strength enough
        to save a warrior.
¹⁷ Don't count on your warhorse
        to give you victory—
    for all its strength, it cannot
        save you.

¹⁸ But the LORD watches over those
        who fear him,
    those who rely on his unfailing
        love.
¹⁹ He rescues them from death
    and keeps them alive in times
        of famine.

²⁰ **We put our hope in the LORD.**
    He is our help and our shield.
²¹ **In him our hearts rejoice,**
    for we trust in his holy name.
²² **Let your unfailing love surround**
        us, LORD,
    for our hope is in you alone.

PROVERBS 21:11-12
If you punish a mocker, the simpleminded become wise; if you instruct
the wise, they will be all the wiser. □ The
Righteous One* knows what is going
on in the homes of the wicked; he will
bring disaster on them.

21:12 Or *The righteous man.*

AUGUST
15

NEHEMIAH 9:22–10:39
    "Then you [the LORD] helped our
ancestors conquer kingdoms and
nations, and you placed your people
in every corner of the land.* They
took over the land of King Sihon
of Heshbon and the land of King Og
of Bashan. ²³ You made their

descendants as numerous as the
stars in the sky and brought them
into the land you had promised to
their ancestors.
    ²⁴"They went in and took
possession of the land. You subdued
whole nations before them. Even the
Canaanites, who inhabited the land,
were powerless! Your people could
deal with these nations and their
kings as they pleased. ²⁵Our
ancestors captured fortified cities
and fertile land. They took over
houses full of good things, with
cisterns already dug and vineyards
and olive groves and fruit trees in
abundance. So they ate until they
were full and grew fat and enjoyed
themselves in all your blessings.
    ²⁶"But despite all this, they were
disobedient and rebelled against
you. They turned their backs on
your Law, they killed your prophets
who warned them to return to you,
and they committed terrible
blasphemies. ²⁷So you handed them
over to their enemies, who made
them suffer. But in their time of
trouble they cried to you, and you
heard them from heaven. In your
great mercy, you sent them
liberators who rescued them from
their enemies.
    ²⁸"But as soon as they were at
peace, your people again committed
evil in your sight, and once more you
let their enemies conquer them. Yet
whenever your people turned and
cried to you again for help, you
listened once more from heaven. In
your wonderful mercy, you rescued
them many times!
    ²⁹"You warned them to return to
your Law, but they became proud
and obstinate and disobeyed your
commands. They did not follow
your regulations, by which people
will find life if only they obey. They
stubbornly turned their backs on
you and refused to listen. ³⁰In your
love, you were patient with them for
many years. You sent your Spirit,

who warned them through the prophets. But still they wouldn't listen! So once again you allowed the peoples of the land to conquer them. ³¹But in your great mercy, you did not destroy them completely or abandon them forever. What a gracious and merciful God you are!

³²"And now, our God, the great and mighty and awesome God, who keeps his covenant of unfailing love, do not let all the hardships we have suffered seem insignificant to you. Great trouble has come upon us and upon our kings and leaders and priests and prophets and ancestors—all of your people—from the days when the kings of Assyria first triumphed over us until now. ³³Every time you punished us you were being just. We have sinned greatly, and you gave us only what we deserved. ³⁴Our kings, leaders, priests, and ancestors did not obey your Law or listen to the warnings in your commands and laws. ³⁵Even while they had their own kingdom, they did not serve you, though you showered your goodness on them. You gave them a large, fertile land, but they refused to turn from their wickedness.

³⁶"So now today we are slaves in the land of plenty that you gave our ancestors for their enjoyment! We are slaves here in this good land. ³⁷The lush produce of this land piles up in the hands of the kings whom you have set over us because of our sins. They have power over us and our livestock. We serve them at their pleasure, and we are in great misery."

³⁸*The people responded, "In view of all this,* we are making a solemn promise and putting it in writing. On this sealed document are the names of our leaders and Levites and priests."

¹⁰:¹*THE document was ratified and sealed with the following names:

The governor:
Nehemiah son of Hacaliah, and also Zedekiah.
²The following priests:
Seraiah, Azariah, Jeremiah,
³Pashhur, Amariah, Malkijah,
⁴Hattush, Shebaniah, Malluch,
⁵Harim, Meremoth, Obadiah,
⁶Daniel, Ginnethon, Baruch,
⁷Meshullam, Abijah, Mijamin,
⁸Maaziah, Bilgai, and Shemaiah.
These were the priests.
⁹The following Levites:
Jeshua son of Azaniah, Binnui from the family of Henadad, Kadmiel,
¹⁰and their fellow Levites:
Shebaniah, Hodiah, Kelita, Pelaiah, Hanan, ¹¹Mica, Rehob, Hashabiah,
¹²Zaccur, Sherebiah, Shebaniah,
¹³Hodiah, Bani, and Beninu.
¹⁴The following leaders:
Parosh, Pahath-moab, Elam, Zattu, Bani, ¹⁵Bunni, Azgad, Bebai,
¹⁶Adonijah, Bigvai, Adin, ¹⁷Ater, Hezekiah, Azzur, ¹⁸Hodiah, Hashum, Bezai, ¹⁹Hariph, Anathoth, Nebai,
²⁰Magpiash, Meshullam, Hezir,
²¹Meshezabel, Zadok, Jaddua,
²²Pelatiah, Hanan, Anaiah, ²³Hoshea, Hananiah, Hasshub, ²⁴Hallohesh, Pilha, Shobek, ²⁵Rehum, Hashabnah, Maaseiah, ²⁶Ahiah, Hanan, Anan,
²⁷Malluch, Harim, and Baanah.

²⁸Then the rest of the people—the priests, Levites, gatekeepers, singers, Temple servants, and all who had separated themselves from the pagan people of the land in order to obey the Law of God, together with their wives, sons, daughters, and all who were old enough to understand—²⁹joined their leaders and bound themselves with an oath. They swore a curse on themselves if they failed to obey the Law of God as issued by his servant Moses. They solemnly promised to carefully follow all the commands, regulations, and decrees of the LORD our Lord:

³⁰"We promise not to let our daughters marry the pagan people

of the land, and not to let our sons marry their daughters.

31"We also promise that if the people of the land should bring any merchandise or grain to be sold on the Sabbath or on any other holy day, we will refuse to buy it. Every seventh year we will let our land rest, and we will cancel all debts owed to us.

32"In addition, we promise to obey the command to pay the annual Temple tax of one-eighth of an ounce of silver* for the care of the Temple of our God. 33This will provide for the Bread of the Presence; for the regular grain offerings and burnt offerings; for the offerings on the Sabbaths, the new moon celebrations, and the annual festivals; for the holy offerings; and for the sin offerings to make atonement for Israel. It will provide for everything necessary for the work of the Temple of our God.

34"We have cast sacred lots to determine when—at regular times each year—the families of the priests, Levites, and the common people should bring wood to God's Temple to be burned on the altar of the LORD our God, as is written in the Law.

35"We promise to bring the first part of every harvest to the LORD's Temple year after year—whether it be a crop from the soil or from our fruit trees. 36We agree to give God our oldest sons and the firstborn of all our herds and flocks, as prescribed in the Law. We will present them to the priests who minister in the Temple of our God. 37We will store the produce in the storerooms of the Temple of our God. We will bring the best of our flour and other grain offerings, the best of our fruit, and the best of our new wine and olive oil. And we promise to bring to the Levites a tenth of everything our land produces, for it is the Levites who

collect the tithes in all our rural towns.

38"A priest—a descendant of Aaron—will be with the Levites as they receive these tithes. And a tenth of all that is collected as tithes will be delivered by the Levites to the Temple of our God and placed in the storerooms. 39The people and the Levites must bring these offerings of grain, new wine, and olive oil to the storerooms and place them in the sacred containers near the ministering priests, the gatekeepers, and the singers.

"We promise together not to neglect the Temple of our God."

9:22 The meaning of the Hebrew is uncertain.
9:38a Verse 9:38 is numbered 10:1 in Hebrew text.
9:38b Or *In spite of all this.*   10:1 Verses 10:1-39 are numbered 10:2-40 in Hebrew text.   10:32 Hebrew *tax of ⅓ of a shekel* [4 grams].

1 CORINTHIANS 9:19–10:13

Even though I [Paul] am a free man with no master, I have become a slave to all people to bring many to Christ. 20When I was with the Jews, I lived like a Jew to bring the Jews to Christ. When I was with those who follow the Jewish law, I too lived under that law. Even though I am not subject to the law, I did this so I could bring to Christ those who are under the law. 21When I am with the Gentiles who do not follow the Jewish law,* I too live apart from that law so I can bring them to Christ. But I do not ignore the law of God; I obey the law of Christ.

22When I am with those who are weak, I share their weakness, for I want to bring the weak to Christ. Yes, I try to find common ground with everyone, doing everything I can to save some. 23I do everything to spread the Good News and share in its blessings.

24Don't you realize that in a race everyone runs, but only one person gets the prize? So run to win! 25All athletes are disciplined in their training. They do it to win a prize that will fade away, but we do it for an eternal prize. 26So I run with purpose in every step. I am not just shadowboxing. 27I discipline my body like an athlete, training it to do what it should. Otherwise, I fear that after preaching to others I myself might be disqualified.

10:1I DON'T want you to forget, dear brothers and sisters,* about our ancestors in the wilderness long ago. All of them were guided by a cloud that moved ahead of them, and all of them walked through the sea on dry ground. 2In the cloud and in the sea, all of them were baptized as followers of Moses. 3All of them ate the same spiritual food, 4and all of them drank the same spiritual water. For they drank from the spiritual rock that traveled with them, and that rock was Christ. 5Yet God was not pleased with most of them, and their bodies were scattered in the wilderness.

6These things happened as a warning to us, so that we would not crave evil things as they did, 7or worship idols as some of them did. As the Scriptures say, "The people celebrated with feasting and drinking, and they indulged in pagan revelry."* 8And we must not engage in sexual immorality as some of them did, causing 23,000 of them to die in one day.

9Nor should we put Christ* to the test, as some of them did and then died from snakebites. 10And don't grumble as some of them did, and then were destroyed by the angel of death. 11These things happened to them as examples for us. They were written down to warn us who live at the end of the age.

12If you think you are standing strong, be careful not to fall. 13**The temptations in your life are no different from what others experience. And God is faithful. He will not allow the temptation to be more than you can stand. When you are tempted, he will show you a way out so that you can endure.**

9:21 Greek *those without the law.*   10:1 Greek *brothers.*
10:7 Exod 32:6.   10:9 Some manuscripts read *the Lord.*

*PSALM 34:1-10

A psalm of David, regarding the time he pretended to be insane in front of Abimelech, who sent him away.

1 I will praise the LORD at all times.
   I will constantly speak
      his praises.
2 I will boast only in the LORD;
   let all who are helpless
      take heart.
3 Come, let us tell of the LORD's
      greatness;
   let us exalt his name together.

4 I prayed to the LORD, and he
      answered me.
   He freed me from all my fears.
5 Those who look to him for help will
      be radiant with joy;
   no shadow of shame will darken
      their faces.
6 In my desperation I prayed, and the
      LORD listened;
   he saved me from all my
      troubles.
7 For the angel of the LORD is
      a guard;
   he surrounds and defends all who
      fear him.

8 Taste and see that the LORD
      is good.
   Oh, the joys of those who take
      refuge in him!
9 Fear the LORD, you his godly
      people,
   for those who fear him will have
      all they need.
10 Even strong young lions sometimes
      go hungry,
   but those who trust in the LORD
      will lack no good thing.

34 This psalm is a Hebrew acrostic poem; each verse begins with a successive letter of the Hebrew alphabet.

PROVERBS 21:13
Those who shut their ears to the cries of the poor will be ignored in their own time of need.

AUGUST
16

NEHEMIAH 11:1–12:26

The leaders of the people were living in Jerusalem, the holy city. A tenth of the people from the other towns of Judah and Benjamin were chosen by sacred lots to live there, too, while the rest stayed where they were. [2] And the people commended everyone who volunteered to resettle in Jerusalem.

[3] Here is a list of the names of the provincial officials who came to live in Jerusalem. (Most of the people, priests, Levites, Temple servants, and descendants of Solomon's servants continued to live in their own homes in the various towns of Judah, [4] but some of the people from Judah and Benjamin resettled in Jerusalem.)

From the tribe of Judah:
Athaiah son of Uzziah, son of Zechariah, son of Amariah, son of Shephatiah, son of Mahalalel, of the family of Perez. [5] Also Maaseiah son of Baruch, son of Col-hozeh, son of Hazaiah, son of Adaiah, son of Joiarib, son of Zechariah, of the family of Shelah.* [6] There were 468 descendants of Perez who lived in Jerusalem—all outstanding men.
[7] From the tribe of Benjamin:
Sallu son of Meshullam, son of Joed, son of Pedaiah, son of Kolaiah, son of Maaseiah, son of Ithiel, son of Jeshaiah. [8] After him were Gabbai and Sallai and a total of 928 relatives. [9] Their chief officer was Joel son of Zicri, who was assisted by Judah son of Hassenuah, second-in-command over the city.
[10] From the priests:
Jedaiah son of Joiarib; Jakin; [11] and Seraiah son of Hilkiah, son of Meshullam, son of Zadok, son of Meraioth, son of Ahitub, the supervisor of the Temple of God.

[12] Also 822 of their associates, who worked at the Temple. Also Adaiah son of Jeroham, son of Pelaliah, son of Amzi, son of Zechariah, son of Pashhur, son of Malkijah, [13] along with 242 of his associates, who were heads of their families. Also Amashsai son of Azarel, son of Ahzai, son of Meshillemoth, son of Immer, [14] and 128 of his* outstanding associates. Their chief officer was Zabdiel son of Haggedolim.
[15] From the Levites:
Shemaiah son of Hasshub, son of Azrikam, son of Hashabiah, son of Bunni. [16] Also Shabbethai and Jozabad, who were in charge of the work outside the Temple of God. [17] Also Mattaniah son of Mica, son of Zabdi, a descendant of Asaph, who led in thanksgiving and prayer. Also Bakbukiah, who was Mattaniah's assistant, and Abda son of Shammua, son of Galal, son of Jeduthun. [18] In all, there were 284 Levites in the holy city.
[19] From the gatekeepers:
Akkub, Talmon, and 172 of their associates, who guarded the gates.

[20] The other priests, Levites, and the rest of the Israelites lived wherever their family inheritance was located in any of the towns of Judah. [21] The Temple servants, however, whose leaders were Ziha and Gishpa, all lived on the hill of Ophel.

[22] The chief officer of the Levites in Jerusalem was Uzzi son of Bani, son of Hashabiah, son of Mattaniah, son of Mica, a descendant of Asaph, whose family served as singers at God's Temple. [23] Their daily responsibilities were carried out according to the terms of a royal command.

[24] Pethahiah son of Meshezabel, a descendant of Zerah son of Judah, was the royal adviser in all matters of public administration.

[25] As for the surrounding villages with their open fields, some of the people of

Judah lived in Kiriath-arba with its settlements, Dibon with its settlements, and Jekabzeel with its villages. 26They also lived in Jeshua, Moladah, Beth-pelet, 27Hazar-shual, Beersheba with its settlements, 28Ziklag, and Meconah with its settlements. 29They also lived in En-rimmon, Zorah, Jarmuth, 30Zanoah, and Adullam with their surrounding villages. They also lived in Lachish with its nearby fields and Azekah with its surrounding villages. So the people of Judah were living all the way from Beersheba in the south to the valley of Hinnom.

31Some of the people of Benjamin lived at Geba, Micmash, Aija, and Bethel with its settlements. 32They also lived in Anathoth, Nob, Ananiah, 33Hazor, Ramah, Gittaim, 34Hadid, Zeboim, Neballat, 35Lod, Ono, and the Valley of Craftsmen.* 36Some of the Levites who lived in Judah were sent to live with the tribe of Benjamin.

12:1HERE is the list of the priests and Levites who returned with Zerubbabel son of Shealtiel and Jeshua the high priest:

Seraiah, Jeremiah, Ezra,
2 Amariah, Malluch, Hattush,
3 Shecaniah, Harim,* Meremoth,
4 Iddo, Ginnethon,* Abijah,
5 Miniamin, Moadiah,* Bilgah,
6 Shemaiah, Joiarib, Jedaiah,
7 Sallu, Amok, Hilkiah, and Jedaiah.

These were the leaders of the priests and their associates in the days of Jeshua.

8The Levites who returned with them were Jeshua, Binnui, Kadmiel, Sherebi-ah, Judah, and Mattaniah, who with his associates was in charge of the songs of thanksgiving. 9Their associates, Bakbukiah and Unni, stood opposite them during the service.

10 Jeshua the high priest was the father of Joiakim.
Joiakim was the father of Eliashib.
Eliashib was the father of Joiada.
11 Joiada was the father of Johanan.*
Johanan was the father of Jaddua.

12Now when Joiakim was high priest, the family leaders of the priests were as follows:

Meraiah was leader of the family of Seraiah.
Hananiah was leader of the family of Jeremiah.
13 Meshullam was leader of the family of Ezra.
Jehohanan was leader of the family of Amariah.
14 Jonathan was leader of the family of Malluch.*
Joseph was leader of the family of Shecaniah.*
15 Adna was leader of the family of Harim.
Helkai was leader of the family of Meremoth.*
16 Zechariah was leader of the family of Iddo.
Meshullam was leader of the family of Ginnethon.
17 Zicri was leader of the family of Abijah.
There was also a* leader of the family of Miniamin.
Piltai was leader of the family of Moadiah.
18 Shammua was leader of the family of Bilgah.
Jehonathan was leader of the family of Shemaiah.
19 Mattenai was leader of the family of Joiarib.
Uzzi was leader of the family of Jedaiah.
20 Kallai was leader of the family of Sallu.*
Eber was leader of the family of Amok.
21 Hashabiah was leader of the family of Hilkiah.
Nethanel was leader of the family of Jedaiah.

22A record of the Levite families was kept during the years when Eliashib, Joiada, Johanan, and Jaddua served as high priest. Another record of the priests was kept during the reign of Darius the Persian.* 23A record of the heads of the

Levite families was kept in *The Book of History* down to the days of Johanan, the grandson* of Eliashib.

²⁴These were the family leaders of the Levites: Hashabiah, Sherebiah, Jeshua, Binnui,* Kadmiel, and other associates, who stood opposite them during the ceremonies of praise and thanksgiving, one section responding to the other, as commanded by David, the man of God. ²⁵This included Mattaniah, Bakbukiah, and Obadiah.

Meshullam, Talmon, and Akkub were the gatekeepers in charge of the storerooms at the gates. ²⁶These all served in the days of Joiakim son of Jeshua, son of Jehozadak,* and in the days of Nehemiah the governor and of Ezra the priest and scribe.

11:5 Hebrew *son of the Shilonite.*   **11:14** As in Greek version; Hebrew reads *their.*   **11:35** Or *and Ge-harashim.*   **12:3** Hebrew *Rehum;* compare 7:42; 12:15; Ezra 2:39.   **12:4** As in some Hebrew manuscripts and Latin Vulgate (see also 12:16); most Hebrew manuscripts read *Gennethoi.*   **12:5** Hebrew *Mijamin, Maadiah;* compare 12:17.   **12:11** Hebrew *Jonathan;* compare 12:22.   **12:14a** As in Greek version (see also 10:4; 12:2); Hebrew reads *Malluchi.*   **12:14b** As in many Hebrew manuscripts, some Greek manuscripts, and Syriac version (see also 12:3); most Hebrew manuscripts read *Shebaniah.*   **12:15** As in some Greek manuscripts (see also 12:3); Hebrew reads *Meraioth.*   **12:17** Hebrew lacks the name of this family leader.   **12:20** Hebrew *Sallai;* compare 12:7.   **12:22** *Darius the Persian* is probably Darius II, who reigned 423–404 B.C., or possibly Darius III, who reigned 336–331 B.C.   **12:23** Hebrew *son;* compare 12:10-11.   **12:24** Hebrew *son of* (i.e., *ben*), which should probably be read here as the proper name Binnui; compare Ezra 3:9 and the note there.   **12:26** Hebrew *Jozadak,* a variant spelling of Jehozadak.

1 CORINTHIANS 10:14-33

So, my dear friends, flee from the worship of idols. ¹⁵You are reasonable people. Decide for yourselves if what I am saying is true. ¹⁶When we bless the cup at the Lord's Table, aren't we sharing in the blood of Christ? And when we break the bread, aren't we sharing in the body of Christ? ¹⁷And though we are many, we all eat from one loaf of bread, showing that we are one body. ¹⁸Think about the people of Israel. Weren't they united by eating the sacrifices at the altar?

¹⁹What am I trying to say? Am I saying that food offered to idols has some significance, or that the idols are real gods? ²⁰No, not at all. I am saying that these sacrifices are offered to demons, not to God. And I don't want you to participate with demons. ²¹You cannot drink from the cup of the Lord and from the cup of demons, too. You cannot eat at the Lord's Table and at the table of demons, too. ²²What? Do we dare to rouse the Lord's jealousy? Do you think we are stronger than he is?

²³You say, "I am allowed to do anything"*—but not everything is good for you. You say, "I am allowed to do anything"—but not everything is beneficial. ²⁴Don't be concerned for your own good but for the good of others.

²⁵So you may eat any meat that is sold in the marketplace without raising questions of conscience. ²⁶For "the earth is the LORD's, and everything in it."*

²⁷If someone who isn't a believer asks you home for dinner, accept the invitation if you want to. Eat whatever is offered to you without raising questions of conscience. ²⁸(But suppose someone tells you, "This meat was offered to an idol." Don't eat it, out of consideration for the conscience of the one who told you. ²⁹It might not be a matter of conscience for you, but it is for the other person.) For why should my freedom be limited by what someone else thinks? ³⁰If I can thank God for the food and enjoy it, why should I be condemned for eating it?

³¹**So whether you eat or drink, or whatever you do, do it all for the glory of God. ³²Don't give offense to Jews or Gentiles* or the church of God. ³³I, too, try to please everyone in everything I do. I don't just do what is best for me; I do what is best for others so that many may be saved.**

10:23 Greek *All things are lawful;* also in 10:23b.   **10:26** Ps 24:1.   **10:32** Greek *or Greeks.*

PSALM 34:11-22

Come, my children, and listen to me,
    and I will teach you to fear
    the LORD.
¹² Does anyone want to live a life
    that is long and prosperous?

¹³ Then keep your tongue from
     speaking evil
     and your lips from telling lies!
¹⁴ Turn away from evil and do good.
     Search for peace, and work to
     maintain it.

¹⁵ The eyes of the LORD watch over
     those who do right;
     his ears are open to their cries
     for help.
¹⁶ But the LORD turns his face against
     those who do evil;
     he will erase their memory from
     the earth.
¹⁷ The LORD hears his people when
     they call to him for help.
     He rescues them from all their
     troubles.
¹⁸ The LORD is close to the
     brokenhearted;
     he rescues those whose spirits
     are crushed.

¹⁹ The righteous person faces many
     troubles,
     but the LORD comes to the rescue
     each time.
²⁰ For the LORD protects the bones
     of the righteous;
     not one of them is broken!

²¹ Calamity will surely overtake the
     wicked,
     and those who hate the righteous
     will be punished.
²² But the LORD will redeem those who
     serve him.
     No one who takes refuge in him
     will be condemned.

PROVERBS 21:14-16

A secret gift calms anger; a bribe under the table pacifies fury. □ Justice is a joy to the godly, but it terrifies evildoers. □ The person who strays from common sense will end up in the company of the dead.

AUGUST 17

NEHEMIAH 12:27–13:31

For the dedication of the new wall of Jerusalem, the Levites throughout the land were asked to come to Jerusalem to assist in the ceremonies. They were to take part in the joyous occasion with their songs of thanksgiving and with the music of cymbals, harps, and lyres. ²⁸The singers were brought together from the region around Jerusalem and from the villages of the Netophathites. ²⁹They also came from Beth-gilgal and the rural areas near Geba and Azmaveth, for the singers had built their own settlements around Jerusalem. ³⁰The priests and Levites first purified themselves; then they purified the people, the gates, and the wall.

³¹I led the leaders of Judah to the top of the wall and organized two large choirs to give thanks. One of the choirs proceeded southward* along the top of the wall to the Dung Gate. ³²Hoshaiah and half the leaders of Judah followed them, ³³along with Azariah, Ezra, Meshullam, ³⁴Judah, Benjamin, Shemaiah, and Jeremiah. ³⁵Then came some priests who played trumpets, including Zechariah son of Jonathan, son of Shemaiah, son of Mattaniah, son of Micaiah, son of Zaccur, a descendant of Asaph. ³⁶And Zechariah's colleagues were Shemaiah, Azarel, Milalai, Gilalai, Maai, Nethanel, Judah, and Hanani. They used the musical instruments prescribed by David, the man of God. Ezra the scribe led this procession. ³⁷At the Fountain Gate they went straight up the steps on the ascent of the city wall toward the City of David. They passed the house of David and then proceeded to the Water Gate on the east.

³⁸The second choir giving thanks went northward* around the other way to meet them. I followed them, together with the other half of the people, along the top of the wall past the Tower of the Ovens to the Broad Wall, ³⁹then past the

Ephraim Gate to the Old City Gate,* past the Fish Gate and the Tower of Hananel, and on to the Tower of the Hundred. Then we continued on to the Sheep Gate and stopped at the Guard Gate.

⁴⁰The two choirs that were giving thanks then proceeded to the Temple of God, where they took their places. So did I, together with the group of leaders who were with me. ⁴¹We went together with the trumpet-playing priests—Eliakim, Maaseiah, Miniamin, Micaiah, Elioenai, Zechariah, and Hananiah—⁴²and the singers—Maaseiah, Shemaiah, Eleazar, Uzzi, Jehohanan, Malkijah, Elam, and Ezer. They played and sang loudly under the direction of Jezrahiah the choir director.

⁴³Many sacrifices were offered on that joyous day, for God had given the people cause for great joy. The women and children also participated in the celebration, and the joy of the people of Jerusalem could be heard far away.

⁴⁴On that day men were appointed to be in charge of the storerooms for the offerings, the first part of the harvest, and the tithes. They were responsible to collect from the fields outside the towns the portions required by the Law for the priests and Levites. For all the people of Judah took joy in the priests and Levites and their work. ⁴⁵They performed the service of their God and the service of purification, as commanded by David and his son Solomon, and so did the singers and the gatekeepers. ⁴⁶The custom of having choir directors to lead the choirs in hymns of praise and thanksgiving to God began long ago in the days of David and Asaph. ⁴⁷So now, in the days of Zerubbabel and of Nehemiah, all Israel brought a daily supply of food for the singers, the gatekeepers, and the Levites. The Levites, in turn, gave a portion of what they received to the priests, the descendants of Aaron.

¹³:¹On that same day, as the Book of Moses was being read to the people, the passage was found that said no Ammonite or Moabite should ever be permitted to enter the assembly of God.* ²For they had not provided the Israelites with food and water in the wilderness. Instead, they hired Balaam to curse them, though our God turned the curse into a blessing. ³When this passage of the Law was read, all those of foreign descent were immediately excluded from the assembly.

⁴Before this had happened, Eliashib the priest, who had been appointed as supervisor of the storerooms of the Temple of our God and who was also a relative of Tobiah, ⁵had converted a large storage room and placed it at Tobiah's disposal. The room had previously been used for storing the grain offerings, the frankincense, various articles for the Temple, and the tithes of grain, new wine, and olive oil (which were prescribed for the Levites, the singers, and the gatekeepers), as well as the offerings for the priests.

⁶I was not in Jerusalem at that time, for I had returned to King Artaxerxes of Babylon in the thirty-second year of his reign,* though I later asked his permission to return. ⁷When I arrived back in Jerusalem, I learned about Eliashib's evil deed in providing Tobiah with a room in the courtyards of the Temple of God. ⁸I became very upset and threw all of Tobiah's belongings out of the room. ⁹Then I demanded that the rooms be purified, and I brought back the articles for God's Temple, the grain offerings, and the frankincense.

¹⁰I also discovered that the Levites had not been given their prescribed portions of food, so they and the singers who were to conduct the worship services had all returned to work their fields. ¹¹I immediately confronted the leaders and demanded, "Why has the Temple of God been neglected?" Then I called all the Levites back again and restored them to their proper duties. ¹²And once more all the people of Judah began bringing their tithes of grain, new wine, and olive oil to the Temple storerooms.

¹³I assigned supervisors for the storerooms: Shelemiah the priest, Zadok the

scribe, and Pedaiah, one of the Levites. And I appointed Hanan son of Zaccur and grandson of Mattaniah as their assistant. These men had an excellent reputation, and it was their job to make honest distributions to their fellow Levites.

14Remember this good deed, O my God, and do not forget all that I have faithfully done for the Temple of my God and its services.

15In those days I saw men of Judah treading out their winepresses on the Sabbath. They were also bringing in grain, loading it on donkeys, and bringing their wine, grapes, figs, and all sorts of produce to Jerusalem to sell on the Sabbath. So I rebuked them for selling their produce on that day. 16Some men from Tyre, who lived in Jerusalem, were bringing in fish and all kinds of merchandise. They were selling it on the Sabbath to the people of Judah—and in Jerusalem at that!

17So I confronted the nobles of Judah. "Why are you profaning the Sabbath in this evil way?" I asked. 18"Wasn't it just this sort of thing that your ancestors did that caused our God to bring all this trouble upon us and our city? Now you are bringing even more wrath upon Israel by permitting the Sabbath to be desecrated in this way!"

19Then I commanded that the gates of Jerusalem should be shut as darkness fell every Friday evening,* not to be opened until the Sabbath ended. I sent some of my own servants to guard the gates so that no merchandise could be brought in on the Sabbath day. 20The merchants and tradesmen with a variety of wares camped outside Jerusalem once or twice. 21But I spoke sharply to them and said, "What are you doing out here, camping around the wall? If you do this again, I will arrest you!" And that was the last time they came on the Sabbath. 22Then I commanded the Levites to purify themselves and to guard the gates in order to preserve the holiness of the Sabbath.

Remember this good deed also, O my God! Have compassion on me according to your great and unfailing love.

23About the same time I realized that some of the men of Judah had married women from Ashdod, Ammon, and Moab. 24Furthermore, half their children spoke the language of Ashdod or of some other people and could not speak the language of Judah at all. 25So I confronted them and called down curses on them. I beat some of them and pulled out their hair. I made them swear in the name of God that they would not let their children intermarry with the pagan people of the land.

26"Wasn't this exactly what led King Solomon of Israel into sin?" I demanded. "There was no king from any nation who could compare to him, and God loved him and made him king over all Israel. But even he was led into sin by his foreign wives. 27How could you even think of committing this sinful deed and acting unfaithfully toward God by marrying foreign women?"

28One of the sons of Joiada son of Eliashib the high priest had married a daughter of Sanballat the Horonite, so I banished him from my presence.

29Remember them, O my God, for they have defiled the priesthood and the solemn vows of the priests and Levites.

30So I purged out everything foreign and assigned tasks to the priests and Levites, making certain that each knew his work. 31I also made sure that the supply of wood for the altar and the first portions of the harvest were brought at the proper times.

Remember this in my favor, O my God.

12:31 Hebrew *to the right.*   12:38 Hebrew *to the left.*
12:39 Or *the Mishneh Gate,* or *the Jeshanah Gate.*
13:1 See Deut 23:3-6.   13:6 King Artaxerxes of Persia is here identified as the king of Babylon because Persia had conquered the Babylonian Empire. The thirty-second year of Artaxerxes was 433 B.C.   13:19 Hebrew *on the day before the Sabbath.*

1 CORINTHIANS 11:1-16

And you [Corinthians] should imitate me [Paul], just as I imitate Christ.

²I am so glad that you always keep me in your thoughts, and that you are following the teachings I passed on to you. ³But there is one thing I want you to know: The head of every man is Christ, the head of woman is man, and the head of Christ is God.* ⁴A man dishonors his head* if he covers his head while praying or prophesying. ⁵But a woman dishonors her head* if she prays or prophesies without a covering on her head, for this is the same as shaving her head. ⁶Yes, if she refuses to wear a head covering, she should cut off all her hair! But since it is shameful for a woman to have her hair cut or her head shaved, she should wear a covering.*

⁷A man should not wear anything on his head when worshiping, for man is made in God's image and reflects God's glory. And woman reflects man's glory. ⁸For the first man didn't come from woman, but the first woman came from man. ⁹And man was not made for woman, but woman was made for man. ¹⁰For this reason, and because the angels are watching, a woman should wear a covering on her head to show she is under authority.*

¹¹**But among the Lord's people, women are not independent of men, and men are not independent of women.** ¹²**For although the first woman came from man, every other man was born from a woman, and everything comes from God.**

¹³Judge for yourselves. Is it right for a woman to pray to God in public without covering her head? ¹⁴Isn't it obvious that it's disgraceful for a man to have long hair? ¹⁵And isn't long hair a woman's pride and joy? For it has been given to her as a covering. ¹⁶But if anyone wants to argue about this, I simply say that we have no other custom than this, and neither do God's other churches.

11:3 Or *to know: The source of every man is Christ, the source of woman is man, and the source of Christ is God.* Or *to know: Every man is responsible to Christ, a woman is responsible to her husband, and Christ is responsible to God.*

11:4 Or *dishonors Christ.*   11:5 Or *dishonors her husband.*   11:6 Or *should have long hair.*   11:10 Greek *should have an authority on her head.*

PSALM 35:1-16

A psalm of David.

¹ **O** Lord, oppose those who
     oppose me.
  Fight those who fight against me.
² Put on your armor, and take up
     your shield.
  Prepare for battle, and come
     to my aid.
³ Lift up your spear and javelin
     against those who pursue me.
  Let me hear you say,
     "I will give you victory!"
⁴ Bring shame and disgrace on those
     trying to kill me;
  turn them back and humiliate
     those who want to harm me.
⁵ Blow them away like chaff in the
     wind—
  a wind sent by the angel of the
     Lord.
⁶ Make their path dark and slippery,
  with the angel of the Lord
     pursuing them.
⁷ I did them no wrong, but they laid
     a trap for me.
  I did them no wrong, but they dug
     a pit to catch me.
⁸ So let sudden ruin come upon them!
  Let them be caught in the trap
     they set for me!
  Let them be destroyed in the pit
     they dug for me.

⁹ Then I will rejoice in the Lord.
  I will be glad because he
     rescues me.
¹⁰ With every bone in my body I will
     praise him:
  "Lord, who can compare with
     you?
  Who else rescues the helpless
     from the strong?
  Who else protects the helpless
     and poor from those who rob
     them?"

¹¹ Malicious witnesses testify
     against me.

They accuse me of crimes I know
nothing about.
12 They repay me evil for good.
I am sick with despair.
13 Yet when they were ill, I grieved
for them.
I denied myself by fasting
for them,
but my prayers returned
unanswered.
14 I was sad, as though they were my
friends or family,
as if I were grieving for my
own mother.
15 But they are glad now that I am
in trouble;
they gleefully join together
against me.
I am attacked by people I don't
even know;
they slander me constantly.
16 They mock me and call me names;
they snarl at me.

PROVERBS 21:17-18
Those who love pleasure become poor;
those who love wine and luxury will
never be rich. □ The wicked are punished in place of the godly, and traitors
in place of the honest.

AUGUST
18

ESTHER 1:1–3:15
These events happened in the days
of King Xerxes,* who reigned over
127 provinces stretching from India to
Ethiopia.* 2At that time Xerxes ruled his
empire from his royal throne at the fortress of Susa. 3In the third year of his
reign, he gave a banquet for all his
nobles and officials. He invited all the
military officers of Persia and Media as
well as the princes and nobles of the
provinces. 4The celebration lasted
180 days—a tremendous display of the
opulent wealth of his empire and the
pomp and splendor of his majesty.
5When it was all over, the king gave a
banquet for all the people, from the
greatest to the least, who were in the
fortress of Susa. It lasted for seven days
and was held in the courtyard of the
palace garden. 6The courtyard was
beautifully decorated with white cotton
curtains and blue hangings, which were
fastened with white linen cords and
purple ribbons to silver rings embed-
ded in marble pillars. Gold and silver
couches stood on a mosaic pavement of
porphyry, marble, mother-of-pearl, and
other costly stones.
7Drinks were served in gold goblets
of many designs, and there was an
abundance of royal wine, reflecting the
king's generosity. 8By edict of the king,
no limits were placed on the drinking,
for the king had instructed all his palace
officials to serve each man as much as
he wanted.
9At the same time, Queen Vashti gave
a banquet for the women in the royal
palace of King Xerxes.
10On the seventh day of the feast,
when King Xerxes was in high spirits
because of the wine, he told the seven
eunuchs who attended him—Mehu-
man, Biztha, Harbona, Bigtha, Abagtha,
Zethar, and Carcas—11to bring Queen
Vashti to him with the royal crown on
her head. He wanted the nobles and all
the other men to gaze on her beauty, for
she was a very beautiful woman. 12But
when they conveyed the king's order
to Queen Vashti, she refused to come.
This made the king furious, and he
burned with anger.
13He immediately consulted with his
wise advisers, who knew all the Persian
laws and customs, for he always asked
their advice. 14The names of these men
were Carshena, Shethar, Admatha, Tarshish, Meres, Marsena, and Memucan—
seven nobles of Persia and Media. They
met with the king regularly and held the
highest positions in the empire.
15"What must be done to Queen Vashti?" the king demanded. "What penalty

does the law provide for a queen who refuses to obey the king's orders, properly sent through his eunuchs?"

[16]Memucan answered the king and his nobles, "Queen Vashti has wronged not only the king but also every noble and citizen throughout your empire. [17]Women everywhere will begin to despise their husbands when they learn that Queen Vashti has refused to appear before the king. [18]Before this day is out, the wives of all the king's nobles throughout Persia and Media will hear what the queen did and will start treating their husbands the same way. There will be no end to their contempt and anger.

[19]"So if it please the king, we suggest that you issue a written decree, a law of the Persians and Medes that cannot be revoked. It should order that Queen Vashti be forever banished from the presence of King Xerxes, and that the king should choose another queen more worthy than she. [20]When this decree is published throughout the king's vast empire, husbands everywhere, whatever their rank, will receive proper respect from their wives!"

[21]The king and his nobles thought this made good sense, so he followed Memucan's counsel. [22]He sent letters to all parts of the empire, to each province in its own script and language, proclaiming that every man should be the ruler of his own home and should say whatever he pleases.*

2:1But after Xerxes' anger had subsided, he began thinking about Vashti and what she had done and the decree he had made. [2]So his personal attendants suggested, "Let us search the empire to find beautiful young virgins for the king. [3]Let the king appoint agents in each province to bring these beautiful young women into the royal harem at the fortress of Susa. Hegai, the king's eunuch in charge of the harem, will see that they are all given beauty treatments. [4]After that, the young woman who most pleases the king will be made queen instead of Vashti." This advice

was very appealing to the king, so he put the plan into effect.

[5]At that time there was a Jewish man in the fortress of Susa whose name was Mordecai son of Jair. He was from the tribe of Benjamin and was a descendant of Kish and Shimei. [6]His family* had been among those who, with King Jehoiachin* of Judah, had been exiled from Jerusalem to Babylon by King Nebuchadnezzar. [7]This man had a very beautiful and lovely young cousin, Hadassah, who was also called Esther. When her father and mother died, Mordecai adopted her into his family and raised her as his own daughter.

[8]As a result of the king's decree, Esther, along with many other young women, was brought to the king's harem at the fortress of Susa and placed in Hegai's care. [9]Hegai was very impressed with Esther and treated her kindly. He quickly ordered a special menu for her and provided her with beauty treatments. He also assigned her seven maids specially chosen from the king's palace, and he moved her and her maids into the best place in the harem.

[10]Esther had not told anyone of her nationality and family background, because Mordecai had directed her not to do so. [11]Every day Mordecai would take a walk near the courtyard of the harem to find out about Esther and what was happening to her.

[12]Before each young woman was taken to the king's bed, she was given the prescribed twelve months of beauty treatments—six months with oil of myrrh, followed by six months with special perfumes and ointments. [13]When it was time for her to go to the king's palace, she was given her choice of whatever clothing or jewelry she wanted to take from the harem. [14]That evening she was taken to the king's private rooms, and the next morning she was brought to the second harem,* where the king's wives lived. There she would be under the care of Shaashgaz, the king's eunuch in charge of the concubines. She would never go to the king again unless he had

especially enjoyed her and requested her by name.

¹⁵Esther was the daughter of Abihail, who was Mordecai's uncle. (Mordecai had adopted his younger cousin Esther.) When it was Esther's turn to go to the king, she accepted the advice of Hegai, the eunuch in charge of the harem. She asked for nothing except what he suggested, and she was admired by everyone who saw her.

¹⁶Esther was taken to King Xerxes at the royal palace in early winter* of the seventh year of his reign. ¹⁷And the king loved Esther more than any of the other young women. He was so delighted with her that he set the royal crown on her head and declared her queen instead of Vashti. ¹⁸To celebrate the occasion, he gave a great banquet in Esther's honor for all his nobles and officials, declaring a public holiday for the provinces and giving generous gifts to everyone.

¹⁹Even after all the young women had been transferred to the second harem* and Mordecai had become a palace official,* ²⁰Esther continued to keep her family background and nationality a secret. She was still following Mordecai's directions, just as she did when she lived in his home.

²¹One day as Mordecai was on duty at the king's gate, two of the king's eunuchs, Bigthana* and Teresh—who were guards at the door of the king's private quarters—became angry at King Xerxes and plotted to assassinate him. ²²But Mordecai heard about the plot and gave the information to Queen Esther. She then told the king about it and gave Mordecai credit for the report. ²³When an investigation was made and Mordecai's story was found to be true, the two men were impaled on a sharpened pole. This was all recorded in *The Book of the History of King Xerxes' Reign.*

³:¹SOME time later King Xerxes promoted Haman son of Hammedatha the Agagite over all the other nobles, making him the most powerful official in the empire. ²All the king's officials would bow down before Haman to show him respect whenever he passed by, for so the king had commanded. But Mordecai refused to bow down or show him respect.

³Then the palace officials at the king's gate asked Mordecai, "Why are you disobeying the king's command?" ⁴They spoke to him day after day, but still he refused to comply with the order. So they spoke to Haman about this to see if he would tolerate Mordecai's conduct, since Mordecai had told them he was a Jew.

⁵When Haman saw that Mordecai would not bow down or show him respect, he was filled with rage. ⁶He had learned of Mordecai's nationality, so he decided it was not enough to lay hands on Mordecai alone. Instead, he looked for a way to destroy all the Jews throughout the entire empire of Xerxes.

⁷So in the month of April,* during the twelfth year of King Xerxes' reign, lots were cast in Haman's presence (the lots were called *purim*) to determine the best day and month to take action. And the day selected was March 7, nearly a year later.*

⁸Then Haman approached King Xerxes and said, "There is a certain race of people scattered through all the provinces of your empire who keep themselves separate from everyone else. Their laws are different from those of any other people, and they refuse to obey the laws of the king. So it is not in the king's interest to let them live. ⁹If it please the king, issue a decree that they be destroyed, and I will give 10,000 large sacks* of silver to the government administrators to be deposited in the royal treasury."

¹⁰The king agreed, confirming his decision by removing his signet ring from his finger and giving it to Haman son of Hammedatha the Agagite, the enemy of the Jews. ¹¹The king said, "The money and the people are both yours to do with as you see fit."

¹²So on April 17* the king's secretaries were summoned, and a decree was

written exactly as Haman dictated. It was sent to the king's highest officers, the governors of the respective provinces, and the nobles of each province in their own scripts and languages. The decree was written in the name of King Xerxes and sealed with the king's signet ring. [13]Dispatches were sent by swift messengers into all the provinces of the empire, giving the order that all Jews—young and old, including women and children—must be killed, slaughtered, and annihilated on a single day. This was scheduled to happen on March 7 of the next year.* The property of the Jews would be given to those who killed them.

[14]A copy of this decree was to be issued as law in every province and proclaimed to all peoples, so that they would be ready to do their duty on the appointed day. [15]At the king's command, the decree went out by swift messengers, and it was also proclaimed in the fortress of Susa. Then the king and Haman sat down to drink, but the city of Susa fell into confusion.

1:1a Hebrew *Ahasuerus*, another name for Xerxes; also throughout the book of Esther. Xerxes reigned 486–465 B.C. 1:1b Hebrew *to Cush.* 1:22 Or *and should speak in the language of his own people.* 2:6a Hebrew *He.* 2:6b Hebrew *Jeconiah*, a variant spelling of Jehoiachin. 2:14 Or *to another part of the harem.* 2:16 Hebrew *in the tenth month, the month of Tebeth.* A number of dates in the book of Esther can be cross-checked with dates in surviving Persian records and related accurately to our modern calendar. This month of the ancient Hebrew lunar calendar occurred within the months of December 479 B.C. and January 478 B.C. 2:19a The meaning of the Hebrew is uncertain. 2:19b Hebrew *and Mordecai was sitting in the gate of the king.* 2:21 Hebrew *Bigthan;* compare 6:2. 3:7a Hebrew *in the first month, the month of Nisan.* This month of the ancient Hebrew lunar calendar occurred within the months of April and May 474 B.C.; also see note on 2:16. 3:7b As in Greek version, which reads *the thirteenth day of the twelfth month, the month of Adar* (see also 3:13). Hebrew reads *in the twelfth month,* of the ancient Hebrew lunar calendar. The date selected was March 7, 473 B.C.; also see note on 2:16. 3:9 Hebrew *10,000 talents,* about 375 tons or 340 metric tons in weight. 3:12 Hebrew *On the thirteenth day of the first month,* of the ancient Hebrew lunar calendar. This day was April 17, 474 B.C.; also see note on 2:16. 3:13 Hebrew *on the thirteenth day of the twelfth month, the month of Adar,* of the ancient Hebrew lunar calendar. The date selected was March 7, 473 B.C.; also see note on 2:16.

1 CORINTHIANS 11:17-34

But in the following instructions, I [Paul] cannot praise you [Corinthians]. For it sounds as if more harm than good is done when you meet together. [18]First,

I hear that there are divisions among you when you meet as a church, and to some extent I believe it. [19]But, of course, there must be divisions among you so that you who have God's approval will be recognized!

[20]When you meet together, you are not really interested in the Lord's Supper. [21]For some of you hurry to eat your own meal without sharing with others. As a result, some go hungry while others get drunk. [22]What? Don't you have your own homes for eating and drinking? Or do you really want to disgrace God's church and shame the poor? What am I supposed to say? Do you want me to praise you? Well, I certainly will not praise you for this!

[23]For I pass on to you what I received from the Lord himself. On the night when he was betrayed, the Lord Jesus took some bread [24]and gave thanks to God for it. Then he broke it in pieces and said, "This is my body, which is given for you.* Do this to remember me." [25]In the same way, he took the cup of wine after supper, saying, "This cup is the new covenant between God and his people—an agreement confirmed with my blood. Do this to remember me as often as you drink it." [26]For every time you eat this bread and drink this cup, you are announcing the Lord's death until he comes again.

[27]So anyone who eats this bread or drinks this cup of the Lord unworthily is guilty of sinning against* the body and blood of the Lord. [28]That is why you should examine yourself before eating the bread and drinking the cup. [29]For if you eat the bread or drink the cup without honoring the body of Christ,* you are eating and drinking God's judgment upon yourself. [30]That is why many of you are weak and sick and some have even died.

[31]But if we would examine ourselves, we would not be judged by God in this way. [32]Yet when we are judged by the Lord, we are being disciplined so that we will not be condemned along with the world.

33 So, my dear brothers and sisters,* when you gather for the Lord's Supper, wait for each other. 34 If you are really hungry, eat at home so you won't bring judgment upon yourselves when you meet together. I'll give you instructions about the other matters after I arrive.

11:24 Greek *which is for you;* other manuscripts read *which is broken for you.* 11:27 Or *is responsible for.* 11:29 Greek *the body;* other manuscripts read *the Lord's body.* 11:33 Greek *brothers.*

PSALM 35:17-28

How long, O Lord, will you look
on and do nothing?
Rescue me from their fierce
attacks.
Protect my life from these lions!
18 Then I will thank you in front of the
great assembly.
I will praise you before all the
people.
19 Don't let my treacherous enemies
rejoice over my defeat.
Don't let those who hate me
without cause gloat over
my sorrow.
20 They don't talk of peace;
they plot against innocent people
who mind their own business.
21 They shout, "Aha! Aha!
With our own eyes we saw
him do it!"

22 O Lord, you know all about this.
Do not stay silent.
Do not abandon me now, O Lord.
23 Wake up! Rise to my defense!
Take up my case, my God and my
Lord.
24 Declare me not guilty, O Lord my
God, for you give justice.
Don't let my enemies laugh about
me in my troubles.
25 Don't let them say, "Look, we got
what we wanted!
Now we will eat him alive!"

26 May those who rejoice at my
troubles
be humiliated and disgraced.
May those who triumph over me
be covered with shame and
dishonor.

27 But give great joy to those who
came to my defense.
Let them continually say,
"Great is the Lord,
who delights in blessing his
servant with peace!"
28 Then I will proclaim your justice,
and I will praise you all day long.

PROVERBS 21:19-20

It's better to live alone in the desert than with a quarrelsome, complaining wife. □ The wise have wealth and luxury, but fools spend whatever they get.

AUGUST 19

ESTHER 4:1–7:10

When Mordecai learned about all that had been done, he tore his clothes, put on burlap and ashes, and went out into the city, crying with a loud and bitter wail. 2 He went as far as the gate of the palace, for no one was allowed to enter the palace gate while wearing clothes of mourning. 3 And as news of the king's decree reached all the provinces, there was great mourning among the Jews. They fasted, wept, and wailed, and many people lay in burlap and ashes.

4 When Queen Esther's maids and eunuchs came and told her about Mordecai, she was deeply distressed. She sent clothing to him to replace the burlap, but he refused it. 5 Then Esther sent for Hathach, one of the king's eunuchs who had been appointed as her attendant. She ordered him to go to Mordecai and find out what was troubling him and why he was in mourning. 6 So Hathach went out to Mordecai in the square in front of the palace gate.

7 Mordecai told him the whole story, including the exact amount of money Haman had promised to pay into the royal treasury for the destruction of the

Jews. [8]Mordecai gave Hathach a copy of the decree issued in Susa that called for the death of all Jews. He asked Hathach to show it to Esther and explain the situation to her. He also asked Hathach to direct her to go to the king to beg for mercy and plead for her people. [9]So Hathach returned to Esther with Mordecai's message.

[10]Then Esther told Hathach to go back and relay this message to Mordecai: [11]"All the king's officials and even the people in the provinces know that anyone who appears before the king in his inner court without being invited is doomed to die unless the king holds out his gold scepter. And the king has not called for me to come to him for thirty days." [12]So Hathach* gave Esther's message to Mordecai.

[13]Mordecai sent this reply to Esther: "Don't think for a moment that because you're in the palace you will escape when all other Jews are killed. [14]If you keep quiet at a time like this, deliverance and relief for the Jews will arise from some other place, but you and your relatives will die. Who knows if perhaps you were made queen for just such a time as this?"

[15]Then Esther sent this reply to Mordecai: [16]"Go and gather together all the Jews of Susa and fast for me. Do not eat or drink for three days, night or day. My maids and I will do the same. And then, though it is against the law, I will go in to see the king. If I must die, I must die." [17]So Mordecai went away and did everything as Esther had ordered him.

[5:1]ON the third day of the fast, Esther put on her royal robes and entered the inner court of the palace, just across from the king's hall. The king was sitting on his royal throne, facing the entrance. [2]When he saw Queen Esther standing there in the inner court, he welcomed her and held out the gold scepter to her. So Esther approached and touched the end of the scepter.

[3]Then the king asked her, "What do you want, Queen Esther? What is your request? I will give it to you, even if it is half the kingdom!"

[4]And Esther replied, "If it please the king, let the king and Haman come today to a banquet I have prepared for the king."

[5]The king turned to his attendants and said, "Tell Haman to come quickly to a banquet, as Esther has requested." So the king and Haman went to Esther's banquet.

[6]And while they were drinking wine, the king said to Esther, "Now tell me what you really want. What is your request? I will give it to you, even if it is half the kingdom!"

[7]Esther replied, "This is my request and deepest wish. [8]If I have found favor with the king, and if it pleases the king to grant my request and do what I ask, please come with Haman tomorrow to the banquet I will prepare for you. Then I will explain what this is all about."

[9]Haman was a happy man as he left the banquet! But when he saw Mordecai sitting at the palace gate, not standing up or trembling nervously before him, Haman became furious. [10]However, he restrained himself and went on home.

Then Haman gathered together his friends and Zeresh, his wife, [11]and boasted to them about his great wealth and his many children. He bragged about the honors the king had given him and how he had been promoted over all the other nobles and officials.

[12]Then Haman added, "And that's not all! Queen Esther invited only me and the king himself to the banquet she prepared for us. And she has invited me to dine with her and the king again tomorrow!" [13]Then he added, "But this is all worth nothing as long as I see Mordecai the Jew just sitting there at the palace gate."

[14]So Haman's wife, Zeresh, and all his friends suggested, "Set up a sharpened pole that stands seventy-five feet* tall, and in the morning ask the king to impale Mordecai on it. When this is done, you can go on your merry way to the banquet with the king." This pleased Haman, and he ordered the pole set up.

6:1THAT night the king had trouble sleeping, so he ordered an attendant to bring the book of the history of his reign so it could be read to him. 2In those records he discovered an account of how Mordecai had exposed the plot of Bigthana and Teresh, two of the eunuchs who guarded the door to the king's private quarters. They had plotted to assassinate King Xerxes.

3"What reward or recognition did we ever give Mordecai for this?" the king asked.

His attendants replied, "Nothing has been done for him."

4"Who is that in the outer court?" the king inquired. As it happened, Haman had just arrived in the outer court of the palace to ask the king to impale Mordecai on the pole he had prepared.

5So the attendants replied to the king, "Haman is out in the court."

"Bring him in," the king ordered. 6So Haman came in, and the king said, "What should I do to honor a man who truly pleases me?"

Haman thought to himself, "Whom would the king wish to honor more than me?" 7So he replied, "If the king wishes to honor someone, 8he should bring out one of the king's own royal robes, as well as a horse that the king himself has ridden—one with a royal emblem on its head. 9Let the robes and the horse be handed over to one of the king's most noble officials. And let him see that the man whom the king wishes to honor is dressed in the king's robes and led through the city square on the king's horse. Have the official shout as they go, 'This is what the king does for someone he wishes to honor!'"

10"Excellent!" the king said to Haman. "Quick! Take the robes and my horse, and do just as you have said for Mordecai the Jew, who sits at the gate of the palace. Leave out nothing you have suggested!"

11So Haman took the robes and put them on Mordecai, placed him on the king's own horse, and led him through the city square, shouting, "This is what the king does for someone he wishes to honor!" 12Afterward Mordecai returned to the palace gate, but Haman hurried home dejected and completely humiliated.

13When Haman told his wife, Zeresh, and all his friends what had happened, his wise advisers and his wife said, "Since Mordecai—this man who has humiliated you—is of Jewish birth, you will never succeed in your plans against him. It will be fatal to continue opposing him."

14While they were still talking, the king's eunuchs arrived and quickly took Haman to the banquet Esther had prepared.

7:1So the king and Haman went to Queen Esther's banquet. 2On this second occasion, while they were drinking wine, the king again said to Esther, "Tell me what you want, Queen Esther. What is your request? I will give it to you, even if it is half the kingdom!"

3Queen Esther replied, "If I have found favor with the king, and if it pleases the king to grant my request, I ask that my life and the lives of my people will be spared. 4For my people and I have been sold to those who would kill, slaughter, and annihilate us. If we had merely been sold as slaves, I could remain quiet, for that would be too trivial a matter to warrant disturbing the king."

5"Who would do such a thing?" King Xerxes demanded. "Who would be so presumptuous as to touch you?"

6Esther replied, "This wicked Haman is our adversary and our enemy." Haman grew pale with fright before the king and queen. 7Then the king jumped to his feet in a rage and went out into the palace garden.

Haman, however, stayed behind to plead for his life with Queen Esther, for he knew that the king intended to kill him. 8In despair he fell on the couch where Queen Esther was reclining, just as the king was returning from the palace garden.

The king exclaimed, "Will he even assault the queen right here in the palace, before my very eyes?" And as soon as the king spoke, his attendants covered Haman's face, signaling his doom.

⁹Then Harbona, one of the king's eunuchs, said, "Haman has set up a sharpened pole that stands seventy-five feet* tall in his own courtyard. He intended to use it to impale Mordecai, the man who saved the king from assassination."

"Then impale Haman on it!" the king ordered. ¹⁰So they impaled Haman on the pole he had set up for Mordecai, and the king's anger subsided.

4:12 As in Greek version; Hebrew reads *they*.
5:14 Hebrew *50 cubits* [22.5 meters].   7:9 Hebrew *50 cubits* [22.5 meters].

1 CORINTHIANS 12:1-26

Now, dear brothers and sisters,* regarding your [Corinthians] question about the special abilities the Spirit gives us. I [Paul] don't want you to misunderstand this. ²You know that when you were still pagans, you were led astray and swept along in worshiping speechless idols. ³So I want you to know that no one speaking by the Spirit of God will curse Jesus, and no one can say Jesus is Lord, except by the Holy Spirit.

⁴There are different kinds of spiritual gifts, but the same Spirit is the source of them all. ⁵There are different kinds of service, but we serve the same Lord. ⁶God works in different ways, but it is the same God who does the work in all of us.

⁷A spiritual gift is given to each of us so we can help each other. ⁸To one person the Spirit gives the ability to give wise advice*; to another the same Spirit gives a message of special knowledge.* ⁹The same Spirit gives great faith to another, and to someone else the one Spirit gives the gift of healing. ¹⁰He gives one person the power to perform miracles, and another the ability to prophesy. He gives someone else the ability to discern whether a message is from the Spirit of God or from another spirit. Still another person is given the ability to speak in unknown languages,* while another is given the ability to interpret what is being said. ¹¹It is the one and only Spirit who distributes all these gifts. He alone decides which gift each person should have.

¹²**The human body has many parts, but the many parts make up one whole body. So it is with the body of Christ. ¹³Some of us are Jews, some are Gentiles,* some are slaves, and some are free. But we have all been baptized into one body by one Spirit, and we all share the same Spirit.***

¹⁴Yes, the body has many different parts, not just one part. ¹⁵If the foot says, "I am not a part of the body because I am not a hand," that does not make it any less a part of the body. ¹⁶And if the ear says, "I am not part of the body because I am not an eye," would that make it any less a part of the body? ¹⁷If the whole body were an eye, how would you hear? Or if your whole body were an ear, how would you smell anything?

¹⁸But our bodies have many parts, and God has put each part just where he wants it. ¹⁹How strange a body would be if it had only one part! ²⁰Yes, there are many parts, but only one body. ²¹The eye can never say to the hand, "I don't need you." The head can't say to the feet, "I don't need you."

²²In fact, some parts of the body that seem weakest and least important are actually the most necessary. ²³And the parts we regard as less honorable are those we clothe with the greatest care. So we carefully protect those parts that should not be seen, ²⁴while the more honorable parts do not require this special care. So God has put the body together such that extra honor and care are given to those parts that have less dignity. ²⁵This makes for harmony among the members, so that all the members care for each other. ²⁶If one part suffers, all the parts suffer with it, and if one part is honored, all the parts are glad.

12:1 Greek *brothers.*   12:8a Or *gives a word of wisdom.*
12:8b Or *gives a word of knowledge.*   12:10 Or *in various tongues;* also in 12:28, 30.   12:13a Greek *some are Greeks.*
12:13b Greek *we were all given one Spirit to drink.*

PSALM 36:1-12
For the choir director: A psalm of David,
the servant of the LORD.

¹ **S**in whispers to the wicked, deep
within their hearts.
They have no fear of God at all.
² In their blind conceit,
they cannot see how wicked they
really are.
³ Everything they say is crooked and
deceitful.
They refuse to act wisely or do
good.
⁴ They lie awake at night, hatching
sinful plots.
Their actions are never good.
They make no attempt to turn
from evil.

⁵ Your unfailing love, O LORD, is as
vast as the heavens;
your faithfulness reaches beyond
the clouds.
⁶ Your righteousness is like the
mighty mountains,
your justice like the ocean
depths.
You care for people and animals
alike, O LORD.
⁷ How precious is your unfailing
love, O God!
All humanity finds shelter
in the shadow of your wings.
⁸ You feed them from the abundance
of your own house,
letting them drink from your river
of delights.
⁹ For you are the fountain of life,
the light by which we see.

¹⁰ Pour out your unfailing love on
those who love you;
give justice to those with honest
hearts.
¹¹ Don't let the proud trample me
or the wicked push me around.
¹² Look! Those who do evil have
fallen!
They are thrown down, never to
rise again.

PROVERBS 21:21-22
Whoever pursues righteousness and
unfailing love will find life, righteousness, and honor. ☐ The wise conquer
the city of the strong and level the fortress in which they trust.

AUGUST
20

ESTHER 8:1-10:3
On that same day King Xerxes gave the
property of Haman, the enemy of the
Jews, to Queen Esther. Then Mordecai
was brought before the king, for Esther
had told the king how they were related.
² The king took off his signet ring—
which he had taken back from Haman—
and gave it to Mordecai. And Esther appointed Mordecai to be in charge of
Haman's property.

³ Then Esther went again before the
king, falling down at his feet and begging him with tears to stop the evil plot
devised by Haman the Agagite against
the Jews. ⁴Again the king held out the
gold scepter to Esther. So she rose and
stood before him.

⁵Esther said, "If it please the king, and
if I have found favor with him, and if he
thinks it is right, and if I am pleasing to
him, let there be a decree that reverses
the orders of Haman son of Hammedatha the Agagite, who ordered that Jews
throughout all the king's provinces
should be destroyed. ⁶For how can I endure to see my people and my family
slaughtered and destroyed?"

⁷Then King Xerxes said to Queen Esther and Mordecai the Jew, "I have given
Esther the property of Haman, and he
has been impaled on a pole because he
tried to destroy the Jews. ⁸Now go ahead
and send a message to the Jews in the
king's name, telling them whatever you
want, and seal it with the king's signet

ring. But remember that whatever has already been written in the king's name and sealed with his signet ring can never be revoked."

⁹So on June 25* the king's secretaries were summoned, and a decree was written exactly as Mordecai dictated. It was sent to the Jews and to the highest officers, the governors, and the nobles of all the 127 provinces stretching from India to Ethiopia.* The decree was written in the scripts and languages of all the peoples of the empire, including that of the Jews. ¹⁰The decree was written in the name of King Xerxes and sealed with the king's signet ring. Mordecai sent the dispatches by swift messengers, who rode fast horses especially bred for the king's service.

¹¹The king's decree gave the Jews in every city authority to unite to defend their lives. They were allowed to kill, slaughter, and annihilate anyone of any nationality or province who might attack them or their children and wives, and to take the property of their enemies. ¹²The day chosen for this event throughout all the provinces of King Xerxes was March 7 of the next year.*

¹³A copy of this decree was to be issued as law in every province and proclaimed to all peoples, so that the Jews would be ready to take revenge on their enemies on the appointed day. ¹⁴So urged on by the king's command, the messengers rode out swiftly on fast horses bred for the king's service. The same decree was also proclaimed in the fortress of Susa.

¹⁵Then Mordecai left the king's presence, wearing the royal robe of blue and white, the great crown of gold, and an outer cloak of fine linen and purple. And the people of Susa celebrated the new decree. ¹⁶The Jews were filled with joy and gladness and were honored everywhere. ¹⁷In every province and city, wherever the king's decree arrived, the Jews rejoiced and had a great celebration and declared a public festival and holiday. And many of the people of the land

became Jews themselves, for they feared what the Jews might do to them.

⁹:¹So on March 7* the two decrees of the king were put into effect. On that day, the enemies of the Jews had hoped to overpower them, but quite the opposite happened. It was the Jews who overpowered their enemies. ²The Jews gathered in their cities throughout all the king's provinces to attack anyone who tried to harm them. But no one could make a stand against them, for everyone was afraid of them. ³And all the nobles of the provinces, the highest officers, the governors, and the royal officials helped the Jews for fear of Mordecai. ⁴For Mordecai had been promoted in the king's palace, and his fame spread throughout all the provinces as he became more and more powerful.

⁵So the Jews went ahead on the appointed day and struck down their enemies with the sword. They killed and annihilated their enemies and did as they pleased with those who hated them. ⁶In the fortress of Susa itself, the Jews killed 500 men. ⁷They also killed Parshandatha, Dalphon, Aspatha, ⁸Poratha, Adalia, Aridatha, ⁹Parmashta, Arisai, Aridai, and Vaizatha—¹⁰the ten sons of Haman son of Hammedatha, the enemy of the Jews. But they did not take any plunder.

¹¹That very day, when the king was informed of the number of people killed in the fortress of Susa, ¹²he called for Queen Esther. He said, "The Jews have killed 500 men in the fortress of Susa alone, as well as Haman's ten sons. If they have done that here, what has happened in the rest of the provinces? But now, what more do you want? It will be granted to you; tell me and I will do it."

¹³Esther responded, "If it please the king, give the Jews in Susa permission to do again tomorrow as they have done today, and let the bodies of Haman's ten sons be impaled on a pole."

¹⁴So the king agreed, and the decree was announced in Susa. And they impaled the bodies of Haman's ten sons.

¹⁵Then the Jews at Susa gathered together on March 8* and killed 300 more men, and again they took no plunder.

¹⁶Meanwhile, the other Jews throughout the king's provinces had gathered together to defend their lives. They gained relief from all their enemies, killing 75,000 of those who hated them. But they did not take any plunder. ¹⁷This was done throughout the provinces on March 7, and on March 8 they rested,* celebrating their victory with a day of feasting and gladness. ¹⁸(The Jews at Susa killed their enemies on March 7 and again on March 8, then rested on March 9,* making that their day of feasting and gladness.) ¹⁹So to this day, rural Jews living in remote villages celebrate an annual festival and holiday on the appointed day in late winter,* when they rejoice and send gifts of food to each other.

²⁰Mordecai recorded these events and sent letters to the Jews near and far, throughout all the provinces of King Xerxes, ²¹calling on them to celebrate an annual festival on these two days.* ²²He told them to celebrate these days with feasting and gladness and by giving gifts of food to each other and presents to the poor. This would commemorate a time when the Jews gained relief from their enemies, when their sorrow was turned into gladness and their mourning into joy.

²³So the Jews accepted Mordecai's proposal and adopted this annual custom. ²⁴Haman son of Hammedatha the Agagite, the enemy of the Jews, had plotted to crush and destroy them on the date determined by casting lots (the lots were called *purim*). ²⁵But when Esther came before the king, he issued a decree causing Haman's evil plot to backfire, and Haman and his sons were impaled on a sharpened pole. ²⁶That is why this celebration is called Purim, because it is the ancient word for casting lots.

So because of Mordecai's letter and because of what they had experienced, ²⁷the Jews throughout the realm agreed to inaugurate this tradition and to pass it on to their descendants and to all who became Jews. They declared they would never fail to celebrate these two prescribed days at the appointed time each year. ²⁸These days would be remembered and kept from generation to generation and celebrated by every family throughout the provinces and cities of the empire. This Festival of Purim would never cease to be celebrated among the Jews, nor would the memory of what happened ever die out among their descendants.

²⁹Then Queen Esther, the daughter of Abihail, along with Mordecai the Jew, wrote another letter putting the queen's full authority behind Mordecai's letter to establish the Festival of Purim. ³⁰Letters wishing peace and security were sent to the Jews throughout the 127 provinces of the empire of Xerxes. ³¹These letters established the Festival of Purim—an annual celebration of these days at the appointed time, decreed by both Mordecai the Jew and Queen Esther. (The people decided to observe this festival, just as they had decided for themselves and their descendants to establish the times of fasting and mourning.) ³²So the command of Esther confirmed the practices of Purim, and it was all written down in the records.

¹⁰:¹KING Xerxes imposed a tribute throughout his empire, even to the distant coastlands. ²His great achievements and the full account of the greatness of Mordecai, whom the king had promoted, are recorded in *The Book of the History of the Kings of Media and Persia.* ³Mordecai the Jew became the prime minister, with authority next to that of King Xerxes himself. He was very great among the Jews, who held him in high esteem, because he continued to work for the good of his people and to speak up for the welfare of all their descendants.

8:9a Hebrew *on the twenty-third day of the third month, the month of Sivan,* of the ancient Hebrew lunar calendar. This day was June 25, 474 B.C.; also see note on 2:16. 8:9b Hebrew *to Cush.*   8:12 Hebrew *the thirteenth day of the twelfth month, the month of Adar,* of the ancient

Hebrew lunar calendar. The date selected was March 7, 473 B.C.; also see note on 2:16.   **9:1** Hebrew *the thirteenth day of the twelfth month, the month of Adar,* of the ancient Hebrew lunar calendar. This day was March 7, 473 B.C.; also see note on 2:16.   **9:15** Hebrew *the fourteenth day of the month of Adar,* of the Hebrew lunar calendar. This day was March 8, 473 B.C.; also see note on 2:16.   **9:17** Hebrew *on the thirteenth day of the month of Adar, and on the fourteenth day they rested.* These days were March 7 and 8, 473 B.C.; also see note on 2:16.   **9:18** Hebrew *killed their enemies on the thirteenth day and the fourteenth day, and then rested on the fifteenth day,* of the Hebrew month of Adar.   **9:19** Hebrew *on the fourteenth day of the month of Adar.* This day of the Hebrew lunar calendar occurs in February or March.   **9:21** Hebrew *on the fourteenth and fifteenth days of Adar,* of the Hebrew lunar calendar.

1 CORINTHIANS 12:27–13:13

All of you [believers] together are Christ's body, and each of you is a part of it. 28Here are some of the parts God has appointed for the church:

> first are apostles,
> second are prophets,
> third are teachers,
> then those who do miracles,
> those who have the gift of healing,
> those who can help others,
> those who have the gift of
>   leadership,
> those who speak in unknown
>   languages.

29Are we all apostles? Are we all prophets? Are we all teachers? Do we all have the power to do miracles? 30Do we all have the gift of healing? Do we all have the ability to speak in unknown languages? Do we all have the ability to interpret unknown languages? Of course not! 31So you should earnestly desire the most helpful gifts.

But now let me show you a way of life that is best of all.

13:1If I could speak all the languages of earth and of angels, but didn't love others, I would only be a noisy gong or a clanging cymbal. 2If I had the gift of prophecy, and if I understood all of God's secret plans and possessed all knowledge, and if I had such faith that I could move mountains, but didn't love others, I would be nothing. 3If I gave everything I have to the poor and even sacrificed my body, I could boast about

it;* but if I didn't love others, I would have gained nothing.

4Love is patient and kind. Love is not jealous or boastful or proud 5or rude. It does not demand its own way. It is not irritable, and it keeps no record of being wronged. 6It does not rejoice about injustice but rejoices whenever the truth wins out. 7Love never gives up, never loses faith, is always hopeful, and endures through every circumstance.

8Prophecy and speaking in unknown languages* and special knowledge will become useless. But love will last forever! 9Now our knowledge is partial and incomplete, and even the gift of prophecy reveals only part of the whole picture! 10But when full understanding comes, these partial things will become useless.

11When I was a child, I spoke and thought and reasoned as a child. But when I grew up, I put away childish things. 12Now we see things imperfectly as in a cloudy mirror, but then we will see everything with perfect clarity.* All that I know now is partial and incomplete, but then I will know everything completely, just as God now knows me completely.

13**Three things will last forever— faith, hope, and love—and the greatest of these is love.**

13:3 Some manuscripts read *sacrificed my body to be burned.*   **13:8** Or *in tongues.*   **13:12** Greek *see face to face.*

*PSALM 37:1-11
A psalm of David.

> 1 **D**on't worry about the wicked
>   or envy those who do wrong.
> 2 For like grass, they soon fade away.
>   Like spring flowers, they
>   soon wither.
>
> 3 Trust in the LORD and do good.
>   Then you will live safely in the
>   land and prosper.
> 4 Take delight in the LORD,
>   and he will give you your heart's
>   desires.
>
> 5 Commit everything you do
>   to the LORD.

Trust him, and he will help you.
6 He will make your innocence radiate
like the dawn,
and the justice of your cause will
shine like the noonday sun.

7 Be still in the presence of the LORD,
and wait patiently for him to act.
Don't worry about evil people
who prosper
or fret about their wicked
schemes.

8 Stop being angry!
Turn from your rage!
Do not lose your temper—
it only leads to harm.
9 For the wicked will be destroyed,
but those who trust in the LORD
will possess the land.

10 Soon the wicked will disappear.
Though you look for them, they
will be gone.
11 The lowly will possess the land
and will live in peace and
prosperity.

37 This psalm is a Hebrew acrostic poem; each stanza
begins with a successive letter of the Hebrew alphabet.

PROVERBS 21:23-24

Watch your tongue and keep your
mouth shut, and you will stay out of trouble. □ Mockers are proud and haughty;
they act with boundless arrogance.

AUGUST
21

JOB 1:1–3:26

There once was a man named Job who
lived in the land of Uz. He was blameless—a man of complete integrity. He
feared God and stayed away from evil.
2 He had seven sons and three daughters. 3 He owned 7,000 sheep, 3,000
camels, 500 teams of oxen, and 500 female donkeys, and he employed many

servants. He was, in fact, the richest person in that entire area.

4 Job's sons would take turns preparing feasts in their homes, and they
would also invite their three sisters to
celebrate with them. 5 When these
celebrations ended—sometimes after
several days—Job would purify his children. He would get up early in the
morning and offer a burnt offering for
each of them. For Job said to himself,
"Perhaps my children have sinned and
have cursed God in their hearts." This
was Job's regular practice.

6 One day the members of the heavenly court* came to present themselves
before the LORD, and the Accuser, Satan,* came with them. 7 "Where have
you come from?" the LORD asked Satan.

Satan answered the LORD, "I have
been patrolling the earth, watching
everything that's going on."

8 Then the LORD asked Satan, "Have
you noticed my servant Job? He is the
finest man in all the earth. He is blameless—a man of complete integrity. He
fears God and stays away from evil."

9 Satan replied to the LORD, "Yes, but
Job has good reason to fear God. 10 You
have always put a wall of protection
around him and his home and his property. You have made him prosper in
everything he does. Look how rich he is!
11 But reach out and take away everything he has, and he will surely curse
you to your face!"

12 "All right, you may test him," the
LORD said to Satan. "Do whatever you
want with everything he possesses, but
don't harm him physically." So Satan
left the LORD's presence.

13 One day when Job's sons and
daughters were feasting at the oldest
brother's house, 14 a messenger arrived
at Job's home with this news: "Your
oxen were plowing, with the donkeys
feeding beside them, 15 when the Sabeans raided us. They stole all the animals
and killed all the farmhands. I am the
only one who escaped to tell you."

16 While he was still speaking, another messenger arrived with this news:

"The fire of God has fallen from heaven and burned up your sheep and all the shepherds. I am the only one who escaped to tell you."

¹⁷While he was still speaking, a third messenger arrived with this news: "Three bands of Chaldean raiders have stolen your camels and killed your servants. I am the only one who escaped to tell you."

¹⁸While he was still speaking, another messenger arrived with this news: "Your sons and daughters were feasting in their oldest brother's home. ¹⁹Suddenly, a powerful wind swept in from the wilderness and hit the house on all sides. The house collapsed, and all your children are dead. I am the only one who escaped to tell you."

²⁰Job stood up and tore his robe in grief. Then he shaved his head and fell to the ground to worship. ²¹He said,

"I came naked from my mother's
     womb,
   and I will be naked when I leave.
The LORD gave me what I had,
   and the LORD has taken it away.
Praise the name of the LORD!"

²²In all of this, Job did not sin by blaming God.

²:¹ONE day the members of the heavenly court* came again to present themselves before the LORD, and the Accuser, Satan,* came with them. ²"Where have you come from?" the LORD asked Satan.

Satan answered the LORD, "I have been patrolling the earth, watching everything that's going on."

³Then the LORD asked Satan, "Have you noticed my servant Job? He is the finest man in all the earth. He is blameless—a man of complete integrity. He fears God and stays away from evil. And he has maintained his integrity, even though you urged me to harm him without cause."

⁴Satan replied to the LORD, "Skin for skin! A man will give up everything he has to save his life. ⁵But reach out and

take away his health, and he will surely curse you to your face!"

⁶"All right, do with him as you please," the LORD said to Satan. "But spare his life." ⁷So Satan left the LORD's presence, and he struck Job with terrible boils from head to foot.

⁸Job scraped his skin with a piece of broken pottery as he sat among the ashes. ⁹His wife said to him, "Are you still trying to maintain your integrity? Curse God and die."

¹⁰But Job replied, "You talk like a foolish woman. Should we accept only good things from the hand of God and never anything bad?" So in all this, Job said nothing wrong.

¹¹When three of Job's friends heard of the tragedy he had suffered, they got together and traveled from their homes to comfort and console him. Their names were Eliphaz the Temanite, Bildad the Shuhite, and Zophar the Naamathite. ¹²When they saw Job from a distance, they scarcely recognized him. Wailing loudly, they tore their robes and threw dust into the air over their heads to show their grief. ¹³Then they sat on the ground with him for seven days and nights. No one said a word to Job, for they saw that his suffering was too great for words.

³:¹AT last Job spoke, and he cursed the day of his birth. ²He said:

³ "Let the day of my birth be erased,
     and the night I was conceived.
⁴ Let that day be turned to darkness.
     Let it be lost even to God on high,
     and let no light shine on it.
⁵ Let the darkness and utter gloom
     claim that day for its own.
   Let a black cloud overshadow it,
     and let the darkness terrify it.
⁶ Let that night be blotted off the
     calendar,
   never again to be counted among
     the days of the year,
   never again to appear among
     the months.
⁷ Let that night be childless.
     Let it have no joy.

8 Let those who are experts at
   cursing—
      whose cursing could rouse
         Leviathan*—
      curse that day.
9 Let its morning stars remain dark.
   Let it hope for light, but in vain;
      may it never see the morning
         light.
10 Curse that day for failing to shut my
      mother's womb,
   for letting me be born to see
      all this trouble.

11 "Why wasn't I born dead?
   Why didn't I die as I came from
      the womb?
12 Why was I laid on my mother's lap?
   Why did she nurse me at her
      breasts?
13 Had I died at birth, I would now be
      at peace.
   I would be asleep and at rest.
14 I would rest with the world's kings
      and prime ministers,
   whose great buildings now lie
      in ruins.
15 I would rest with princes, rich
      in gold,
   whose palaces were filled with
      silver.
16 Why wasn't I buried like a stillborn
      child,
   like a baby who never lives
      to see the light?
17 For in death the wicked cause
      no trouble,
   and the weary are at rest.
18 Even captives are at ease in death,
   with no guards to curse them.
19 Rich and poor are both there,
   and the slave is free from his
      master.

20 "Oh, why give light to those in
      misery,
   and life to those who are bitter?
21 They long for death, and it won't
      come.
   They search for death more
      eagerly than for hidden
         treasure.
22 They're filled with joy when they
      finally die,
   and rejoice when they find the
      grave.
23 Why is life given to those with no
      future,
   those God has surrounded with
      difficulties?
24 I cannot eat for sighing;
   my groans pour out like water.
25 What I always feared has happened
      to me.
   What I dreaded has come true.
26 I have no peace, no quietness.
   I have no rest; only trouble
      comes."

1:6a Hebrew *the sons of God.*   1:6b Hebrew *and the satan;*
similarly throughout this chapter.   2:1a Hebrew *the sons of
God.*   2:1b Hebrew *and the satan;* similarly throughout
this chapter.   3:8 The identification of Leviathan is
disputed, ranging from an earthly creature to a mythical sea
monster in ancient literature.

1 CORINTHIANS 14:1-17

Let love be your highest goal! But you should also desire the special abilities the Spirit gives—especially the ability to prophesy. ²For if you have the ability to speak in tongues,* you will be talking only to God, since people won't be able to understand you. You will be speaking by the power of the Spirit, but it will all be mysterious. ³But one who prophesies strengthens others, encourages them, and comforts them. ⁴A person who speaks in tongues is strengthened personally, but one who speaks a word of prophecy strengthens the entire church.

⁵I wish you could all speak in tongues, but even more I wish you could all prophesy. For prophecy is greater than speaking in tongues, unless someone interprets what you are saying so that the whole church will be strengthened.

⁶Dear brothers and sisters,* if I should come to you speaking in an unknown language,* how would that help you? But if I bring you a revelation or some special knowledge or prophecy or teaching, that will be helpful. ⁷Even lifeless instruments like the flute or the harp must play the notes clearly, or no one will recognize the melody. ⁸And if the bugler doesn't

sound a clear call, how will the soldiers know they are being called to battle?

⁹It's the same for you. If you speak to people in words they don't understand, how will they know what you are saying? You might as well be talking into empty space.

¹⁰There are many different languages in the world, and every language has meaning. ¹¹But if I don't understand a language, I will be a foreigner to someone who speaks it, and the one who speaks it will be a foreigner to me. ¹²And the same is true for you. Since you are so eager to have the special abilities the Spirit gives, seek those that will strengthen the whole church.

¹³So anyone who speaks in tongues should pray also for the ability to interpret what has been said. ¹⁴For if I pray in tongues, my spirit is praying, but I don't understand what I am saying.

¹⁵Well then, what shall I do? I will pray in the spirit,* and I will also pray in words I understand. I will sing in the spirit, and I will also sing in words I understand. ¹⁶For if you praise God only in the spirit, how can those who don't understand you praise God along with you? How can they join you in giving thanks when they don't understand what you are saying? ¹⁷You will be giving thanks very well, but it won't strengthen the people who hear you.

14:2 Or *in unknown languages;* also in 14:4, 5, 13, 14, 18, 22, 26, 27, 28, 39.   14:6a Greek *brothers;* also in 14:20, 26, 39.   14:6b Or *in tongues;* also in 14:19, 23. 14:15 Or *in the Spirit;* also in 14:15b, 16.

PSALM 37:12-29

The wicked plot against the godly;
    they snarl at them in defiance.
¹³ But the Lord just laughs,
    for he sees their day of judgment
        coming.

¹⁴ The wicked draw their swords
    and string their bows
to kill the poor and the oppressed,
    to slaughter those who do right.
¹⁵ But their swords will stab their own
        hearts,
    and their bows will be broken.

¹⁶ It is better to be godly and have
        little
    than to be evil and rich.
¹⁷ For the strength of the wicked will
        be shattered,
    but the Lord takes care of the
        godly.

¹⁸ Day by day the Lord takes care
        of the innocent,
    and they will receive an
        inheritance that lasts forever.
¹⁹ They will not be disgraced in hard
        times;
    even in famine they will have
        more than enough.

²⁰ But the wicked will die.
    The Lord's enemies are like
        flowers in a field—
    they will disappear like smoke.

²¹ The wicked borrow and never repay,
    but the godly are generous givers.
²² Those the Lord blesses will possess
        the land,
    but those he curses will die.

²³ The Lord directs the steps
        of the godly.
    He delights in every detail
        of their lives.
²⁴ Though they stumble, they will
        never fall,
    for the Lord holds them
        by the hand.

²⁵ **Once I was young, and now
        I am old.
    Yet I have never seen the godly
        abandoned
    or their children begging for
        bread.**
²⁶ **The godly always give generous
        loans to others,
    and their children are a
        blessing.**

²⁷ Turn from evil and do good,
    and you will live in the land
        forever.
²⁸ For the Lord loves justice,
    and he will never abandon
        the godly.

He will keep them safe forever,
   but the children of the wicked
      will die.
²⁹ The godly will possess the land
   and will live there forever.

PROVERBS 21:25-26

Despite their desires, the lazy will come to ruin, for their hands refuse to work. □Some people are always greedy for more, but the godly love to give!

AUGUST 22

JOB 4:1–7:21

Then Eliphaz the Temanite replied to Job:

² "Will you be patient and let me
      say a word?
   For who could keep from
      speaking out?

³ "In the past you have encouraged
      many people;
   you have strengthened those who
      were weak.
⁴ Your words have supported those
      who were falling;
   you encouraged those with shaky
      knees.
⁵ But now when trouble strikes, you
      lose heart.
   You are terrified when it touches
      you.
⁶ Doesn't your reverence for God give
      you confidence?
   Doesn't your life of integrity give
      you hope?

⁷ "Stop and think! Do the innocent
      die?
   When have the upright been
      destroyed?
⁸ My experience shows that those
      who plant trouble

and cultivate evil will harvest
   the same.
⁹ A breath from God destroys them.
   They vanish in a blast of his anger.
¹⁰ The lion roars and the wildcat snarls,
   but the teeth of strong lions will
      be broken.
¹¹ The fierce lion will starve for lack
      of prey,
   and the cubs of the lioness will
      be scattered.

¹² "This truth was given to me
      in secret,
   as though whispered in my ear.
¹³ It came to me in a disturbing vision
      at night,
   when people are in a deep sleep.
¹⁴ Fear gripped me,
   and my bones trembled.
¹⁵ A spirit* swept past my face,
   and my hair stood on end.*
¹⁶ The spirit stopped, but I couldn't see
      its shape.
   There was a form before my eyes.
   In the silence I heard a voice say,
¹⁷ 'Can a mortal be innocent before
      God?
   Can anyone be pure before the
      Creator?'

¹⁸ "If God does not trust his own angels
   and has charged his messengers
      with foolishness,
¹⁹ how much less will he trust people
      made of clay!
   They are made of dust, crushed
      as easily as a moth.
²⁰ They are alive in the morning but
      dead by evening,
   gone forever without a trace.
²¹ Their tent-cords are pulled and the
      tent collapses,
   and they die in ignorance.

⁵:¹ "CRY for help, but will anyone
      answer you?
   Which of the angels* will help
      you?
² Surely resentment destroys the fool,
   and jealousy kills the simple.
³ I have seen that fools may be
      successful for the moment,

but then comes sudden disaster.
⁴ Their children are abandoned far
  from help;
    they are crushed in court with
      no one to defend them.
⁵ The hungry devour their harvest,
    even when it is guarded by
      brambles.*
    The thirsty pant after their
      wealth.
⁶ But evil does not spring from the
    soil,
    and trouble does not sprout from
      the earth.
⁷ People are born for trouble
    as readily as sparks fly up from
      a fire.

⁸ "If I were you, I would go to God
    and present my case to him.
⁹ He does great things too marvelous
    to understand.
    He performs countless miracles.
¹⁰ He gives rain for the earth
    and water for the fields.
¹¹ He gives prosperity to the poor
    and protects those who suffer.
¹² He frustrates the plans of schemers
    so the work of their hands will not
      succeed.
¹³ He traps the wise in their own
    cleverness
    so their cunning schemes are
      thwarted.
¹⁴ They find it is dark in the daytime,
    and they grope at noon as if it
      were night.
¹⁵ He rescues the poor from the
    cutting words of the strong,
    and rescues them from the
      clutches of the powerful.
¹⁶ And so at last the poor have hope,
    and the snapping jaws of the
      wicked are shut.

¹⁷ "But consider the joy of those
    corrected by God!
    Do not despise the discipline of
      the Almighty when you sin.
¹⁸ For though he wounds, he also
    bandages.
    He strikes, but his hands also heal.

¹⁹ From six disasters he will rescue
    you;
    even in the seventh, he will keep
      you from evil.
²⁰ He will save you from death in time
    of famine,
    from the power of the sword in
      time of war.
²¹ You will be safe from slander
    and have no fear when
      destruction comes.
²² You will laugh at destruction and
    famine;
    wild animals will not terrify you.
²³ You will be at peace with the stones
    of the field,
    and its wild animals will be at
      peace with you.
²⁴ You will know that your home
    is safe.
    When you survey your
      possessions, nothing will be
        missing.
²⁵ You will have many children;
    your descendants will be as
      plentiful as grass!
²⁶ You will go to the grave at a ripe
    old age,
    like a sheaf of grain harvested
      at the proper time!

²⁷ "We have studied life and found all
    this to be true.
    Listen to my counsel, and apply
      it to yourself."

⁶:¹THEN Job spoke again:

² "If my misery could be weighed
    and my troubles be put on the
      scales,
³ they would outweigh all the sands
    of the sea.
    That is why I spoke impulsively.
⁴ For the Almighty has struck me
    down with his arrows.
    Their poison infects my spirit.
    God's terrors are lined up
      against me.
⁵ Don't I have a right to complain?
    Don't wild donkeys bray when
      they find no grass,
    and oxen bellow when they have
      no food?

⁶ Don't people complain about
    unsalted food?
    Does anyone want the tasteless
      white of an egg?*
⁷ My appetite disappears when I look
    at it;
    I gag at the thought of eating it!

⁸ "Oh, that I might have my request,
    that God would grant my desire.
⁹ I wish he would crush me.
    I wish he would reach out his
      hand and kill me.
¹⁰ At least I can take comfort in this:
    Despite the pain,
    I have not denied the words of the
      Holy One.
¹¹ But I don't have the strength to
    endure.
    I have nothing to live for.
¹² Do I have the strength of a stone?
    Is my body made of bronze?
¹³ No, I am utterly helpless,
    without any chance of success.

¹⁴ "One should be kind to a fainting
    friend,
    but you accuse me without any
      fear of the Almighty.*
¹⁵ My brothers, you have proved as
    unreliable as a seasonal brook
    that overflows its banks in the
      spring
¹⁶   when it is swollen with ice and
    melting snow.
¹⁷ But when the hot weather arrives,
    the water disappears.
    The brook vanishes in the heat.
¹⁸ The caravans turn aside to be
    refreshed,
    but there is nothing to drink, so
      they die.
¹⁹ The caravans from Tema search for
    this water;
    the travelers from Sheba hope
      to find it.
²⁰ They count on it but are
    disappointed.
    When they arrive, their hopes are
      dashed.
²¹ You, too, have given no help.
    You have seen my calamity, and
      you are afraid.

²² But why? Have I ever asked you
    for a gift?
    Have I begged for anything of
      yours for myself?
²³ Have I asked you to rescue me from
    my enemies,
    or to save me from ruthless
      people?
²⁴ Teach me, and I will keep quiet.
    Show me what I have done wrong.
²⁵ Honest words can be painful,
    but what do your criticisms
      amount to?
²⁶ Do you think your words are
    convincing
    when you disregard my cry
      of desperation?
²⁷ You would even send an orphan
    into slavery*
    or sell a friend.
²⁸ Look at me!
    Would I lie to your face?
²⁹ Stop assuming my guilt,
    for I have done no wrong.
³⁰ Do you think I am lying?
    Don't I know the difference
      between right and wrong?

⁷:¹ "Is not all human life a struggle?
    Our lives are like that of a hired
      hand,
² like a worker who longs for the
    shade,
    like a servant waiting to be paid.
³ I, too, have been assigned months
    of futility,
    long and weary nights of misery.
⁴ Lying in bed, I think, 'When will it
    be morning?'
    But the night drags on, and I toss
      till dawn.
⁵ My body is covered with maggots
    and scabs.
    My skin breaks open, oozing
      with pus.

⁶ "My days fly faster than a weaver's
    shuttle.
    They end without hope.
⁷ O God, remember that my life is
    but a breath,
    and I will never again feel
      happiness.

⁸ You see me now, but not for long.
    You will look for me, but I will
        be gone.
⁹ Just as a cloud dissipates and
        vanishes,
    those who die* will not come back.
¹⁰ They are gone forever from their
        home—
    never to be seen again.

¹¹ "I cannot keep from speaking.
    I must express my anguish.
    My bitter soul must complain.
¹² Am I a sea monster or a dragon
        that you must place me under
        guard?
¹³ I think, 'My bed will comfort me,
    and sleep will ease my misery,'
¹⁴ but then you shatter me with
        dreams
    and terrify me with visions.
¹⁵ I would rather be strangled—
    rather die than suffer like this.
¹⁶ I hate my life and don't want to go
        on living.
    Oh, leave me alone for my few
        remaining days.

¹⁷ "What are people, that you should
        make so much of us,
    that you should think of us so
        often?
¹⁸ For you examine us every morning
    and test us every moment.
¹⁹ Why won't you leave me alone,
    at least long enough for me to
        swallow!
²⁰ If I have sinned, what have I done
        to you,
    O watcher of all humanity?
    Why make me your target?
    Am I a burden to you?
²¹ Why not just forgive my sin
    and take away my guilt?
    For soon I will lie down in the dust
        and die.
    When you look for me, I will
        be gone."

4:15a Or *wind;* also in 4:16.   4:15b Or *its wind sent
shivers up my spine.*   5:1 Hebrew *the holy ones.*   5:5 The
meaning of the Hebrew for this phrase is uncertain.
6:6 Or *the tasteless juice of the mallow plant?*   6:14 Or
friend, / or he might lose his fear of the Almighty.
6:27 Hebrew *even gamble over an orphan.*   7:9 Hebrew
who go down to Sheol.

1 CORINTHIANS 14:18-40

❙ [Paul] thank God that I speak in tongues more than any of you. ¹⁹But in a church meeting I would rather speak five understandable words to help others than ten thousand words in an unknown language.

²⁰Dear brothers and sisters, don't be childish in your understanding of these things. Be innocent as babies when it comes to evil, but be mature in understanding matters of this kind. ²¹It is written in the Scriptures*:

"I will speak to my own people
    through strange languages
    and through the lips of foreigners.
But even then, they will not listen
    to me,"*
    says the LORD.

²²So you see that speaking in tongues is a sign, not for believers, but for unbelievers. Prophecy, however, is for the benefit of believers, not unbelievers. ²³Even so, if unbelievers or people who don't understand these things come into your church meeting and hear everyone speaking in an unknown language, they will think you are crazy. ²⁴But if all of you are prophesying, and unbelievers or people who don't understand these things come into your meeting, they will be convicted of sin and judged by what you say. ²⁵As they listen, their secret thoughts will be exposed, and they will fall to their knees and worship God, declaring, "God is truly here among you."

²⁶Well, my brothers and sisters, let's summarize. When you meet together, one will sing, another will teach, another will tell some special revelation God has given, one will speak in tongues, and another will interpret what is said. But everything that is done must strengthen all of you.

²⁷No more than two or three should speak in tongues. They must speak one at a time, and someone must interpret what they say. ²⁸But if no one is present who can interpret, they must be silent in

your church meeting and speak in tongues to God privately.

²⁹Let two or three people prophesy, and let the others evaluate what is said. ³⁰But if someone is prophesying and another person receives a revelation from the Lord, the one who is speaking must stop. ³¹In this way, all who prophesy will have a turn to speak, one after the other, so that everyone will learn and be encouraged. ³²Remember that people who prophesy are in control of their spirit and can take turns. ³³For God is not a God of disorder but of peace, as in all the meetings of God's holy people.*

³⁴Women should be silent during the church meetings. It is not proper for them to speak. They should be submissive, just as the law says. ³⁵If they have any questions, they should ask their husbands at home, for it is improper for women to speak in church meetings.*

³⁶Or do you think God's word originated with you Corinthians? Are you the only ones to whom it was given? ³⁷If you claim to be a prophet or think you are spiritual, you should recognize that what I am saying is a command from the Lord himself. ³⁸But if you do not recognize this, you yourself will not be recognized.*

³⁹So, my dear brothers and sisters, be eager to prophesy, and don't forbid speaking in tongues. ⁴⁰But be sure that everything is done properly and in order.

14:21a Greek *in the law.*   14:21b Isa 28:11-12.
14:33 The phrase *as in all the meetings of God's holy people* could instead be joined to the beginning of 14:34.
14:35 Some manuscripts place verses 34-35 after 14:40.
14:38 Some manuscripts read *If you are ignorant of this, stay in your ignorance.*

PSALM 37:30-40

**The godly offer good counsel;
      they teach right from wrong.**
³¹ **They have made God's law
         their own,
      so they will never slip from
         his path.**

³² The wicked wait in ambush for
         the godly,
      looking for an excuse to kill them.
³³ But the LORD will not let the wicked
         succeed

or let the godly be condemned
         when they are put on trial.

³⁴ Put your hope in the LORD.
      Travel steadily along his path.
   He will honor you by giving you
         the land.
      You will see the wicked destroyed.

³⁵ I have seen wicked and ruthless
         people
      flourishing like a tree in its
         native soil.
³⁶ But when I looked again, they
         were gone!
      Though I searched for them,
         I could not find them!

³⁷ Look at those who are honest
         and good,
      for a wonderful future awaits
         those who love peace.
³⁸ But the rebellious will be destroyed;
      they have no future.

³⁹ The LORD rescues the godly;
      he is their fortress in times
         of trouble.
⁴⁰ The LORD helps them,
      rescuing them from the wicked.
   He saves them,
      and they find shelter in him.

PROVERBS 21:27
The sacrifice of an evil person is detestable, especially when it is offered with wrong motives.

AUGUST 23

JOB 8:1–11:20
Then Bildad the Shuhite replied to Job:

² "How long will you go on like this?
      You sound like a blustering wind.
³ Does God twist justice?
      Does the Almighty twist what
         is right?

4 Your children must have sinned
    against him,
      so their punishment was well
        deserved.
5 But if you pray to God
    and seek the favor of the Almighty,
6 and if you are pure and live with
    integrity,
      he will surely rise up and restore
        your happy home.
7 And though you started with little,
    you will end with much.

8 "Just ask the previous generation.
    Pay attention to the experience
      of our ancestors.
9 For we were born but yesterday and
    know nothing.
      Our days on earth are as fleeting
        as a shadow.
10 But those who came before us will
    teach you.
      They will teach you the wisdom
        of old.

11 "Can papyrus reeds grow tall
    without a marsh?
      Can marsh grass flourish without
        water?
12 While they are still flowering, not
    ready to be cut,
      they begin to wither more quickly
        than grass.
13 The same happens to all who forget
    God.
      The hopes of the godless
        evaporate.
14 Their confidence hangs by a thread.
    They are leaning on a spider's
      web.
15 They cling to their home for
    security, but it won't last.
      They try to hold it tight, but it will
        not endure.
16 The godless seem like a lush plant
    growing in the sunshine,
      its branches spreading across
        the garden.
17 Its roots grow down through a
    pile of stones;
      it takes hold on a bed of rocks.
18 But when it is uprooted,
    it's as though it never existed!

19 That's the end of its life,
    and others spring up from the
      earth to replace it.

20 "But look, God will not reject a
    person of integrity,
      nor will he lend a hand to the
        wicked.
21 He will once again fill your mouth
    with laughter
      and your lips with shouts of joy.
22 Those who hate you will be clothed
    with shame,
      and the home of the wicked
        will be destroyed."

9:1 THEN Job spoke again:

2 "Yes, I know all this is true in
    principle.
      But how can a person be declared
        innocent in God's sight?
3 If someone wanted to take God to
    court,*
      would it be possible to answer
        him even once in a thousand
          times?
4 For God is so wise and so mighty.
    Who has ever challenged him
      successfully?

5 "Without warning, he moves the
    mountains,
      overturning them in his anger.
6 He shakes the earth from its place,
    and its foundations tremble.
7 If he commands it, the sun
    won't rise
      and the stars won't shine.
8 He alone has spread out the heavens
    and marches on the waves
      of the sea.
9 He made all the stars—the Bear
    and Orion,
      the Pleiades and the
        constellations of the southern
          sky.
10 He does great things too marvelous
    to understand.
      He performs countless miracles.

11 "Yet when he comes near, I cannot
    see him.

When he moves by, I do not see
    him go.
12 If he snatches someone in death,
    who can stop him?
    Who dares to ask, 'What are
    you doing?'
13 And God does not restrain his anger.
    Even the monsters of the sea* are
    crushed beneath his feet.

14 "So who am I, that I should try to
    answer God
    or even reason with him?
15 Even if I were right, I would have
    no defense.
    I could only plead for mercy.
16 And even if I summoned him and
    he responded,
    I'm not sure he would listen
    to me.
17 For he attacks me with a storm
    and repeatedly wounds me
    without cause.
18 He will not let me catch my breath,
    but fills me instead with bitter
    sorrows.
19 If it's a question of strength, he's the
    strong one.
    If it's a matter of justice, who
    dares to summon him to court?
20 Though I am innocent, my own
    mouth would pronounce me
    guilty.
    Though I am blameless, it* would
    prove me wicked.

21 "I am innocent,
    but it makes no difference
    to me—
    I despise my life.
22 Innocent or wicked, it is all the same
    to God.
    That's why I say, 'He destroys both
    the blameless and the wicked.'
23 When a plague* sweeps through,
    he laughs at the death of the
    innocent.
24 The whole earth is in the hands
    of the wicked,
    and God blinds the eyes of the
    judges.
    If he's not the one who does it,
    who is?

25 "My life passes more swiftly than
    a runner.
    It flees away without a glimpse
    of happiness.
26 It disappears like a swift papyrus
    boat,
    like an eagle swooping down on
    its prey.
27 If I decided to forget my complaints,
    to put away my sad face and be
    cheerful,
28 I would still dread all the pain,
    for I know you will not find me
    innocent, O God.
29 Whatever happens, I will be found
    guilty.
    So what's the use of trying?
30 Even if I were to wash myself
    with soap
    and clean my hands with lye,
31 you would plunge me into a muddy
    ditch,
    and my own filthy clothing would
    hate me.

32 "God is not a mortal like me,
    so I cannot argue with him or
    take him to trial.
33 If only there were a mediator
    between us,
    someone who could bring us
    together.
34 The mediator could make God stop
    beating me,
    and I would no longer live in
    terror of his punishment.
35 Then I could speak to him without
    fear,
    but I cannot do that in my
    own strength.

10:1"I AM disgusted with my life.
    Let me complain freely.
    My bitter soul must complain.
2 I will say to God, 'Don't simply
    condemn me—
    tell me the charge you are
    bringing against me.
3 What do you gain by oppressing
    me?
    Why do you reject me, the work
    of your own hands,

while smiling on the schemes of
the wicked?

⁴ Are your eyes like those of a human?
Do you see things only as people
see them?

⁵ Is your lifetime only as long as ours?
Is your life so short

⁶ that you must quickly probe
for my guilt
and search for my sin?

⁷ Although you know I am not guilty,
no one can rescue me from
your hands.

⁸ "'You formed me with your hands;
you made me,
yet now you completely destroy
me.

⁹ Remember that you made me from
dust—
will you turn me back to dust so
soon?

¹⁰ You guided my conception
and formed me in the womb.*

¹¹ You clothed me with skin
and flesh,
and you knit my bones and sinews
together.

¹² You gave me life and showed me
your unfailing love.
My life was preserved by your
care.

¹³ "'Yet your real motive—
your true intent—

¹⁴ was to watch me, and if I sinned,
you would not forgive my guilt.

¹⁵ If I am guilty, too bad for me;
and even if I'm innocent, I can't
hold my head high,
because I am filled with shame
and misery.

¹⁶ And if I hold my head high, you hunt
me like a lion
and display your awesome power
against me.

¹⁷ Again and again you witness
against me.
You pour out your growing
anger on me
and bring fresh armies
against me.

¹⁸ "'Why, then, did you deliver me
from my mother's womb?
Why didn't you let me die
at birth?

¹⁹ It would be as though I had never
existed,
going directly from the womb to
the grave.

²⁰ I have only a few days left, so leave
me alone,
that I may have a moment of
comfort

²¹ before I leave—never to return—
for the land of darkness and utter
gloom.

²² It is a land as dark as midnight,
a land of gloom and confusion,
where even the light is dark as
midnight.'"

¹¹:¹THEN Zophar the Naamathite replied to Job:

² "Shouldn't someone answer this
torrent of words?
Is a person proved innocent just
by a lot of talking?

³ Should I remain silent while you
babble on?
When you mock God, shouldn't
someone make you ashamed?

⁴ You claim, 'My beliefs are pure,'
and 'I am clean in the sight
of God.'

⁵ If only God would speak;
if only he would tell you what he
thinks!

⁶ If only he would tell you the secrets
of wisdom,
for true wisdom is not a simple
matter.
Listen! God is doubtless punishing
you
far less than you deserve!

⁷ "Can you solve the mysteries of God?
Can you discover everything
about the Almighty?

⁸ Such knowledge is higher than the
heavens—
and who are you?
It is deeper than the underworld*—
what do you know?

⁹ It is broader than the earth
   and wider than the sea.
¹⁰ If God comes and puts a person
      in prison
   or calls the court to order, who
      can stop him?
¹¹ For he knows those who are false,
   and he takes note of all their sins.
¹² An empty-headed person won't
      become wise
   any more than a wild donkey can
      bear a human child.*

¹³ "If only you would prepare your
      heart
   and lift up your hands to him
      in prayer!
¹⁴ Get rid of your sins,
   and leave all iniquity behind you.
¹⁵ Then your face will brighten with
      innocence.
   You will be strong and free of
      fear.
¹⁶ You will forget your misery;
   it will be like water flowing away.
¹⁷ Your life will be brighter than the
      noonday.
   Even darkness will be as bright
      as morning.
¹⁸ Having hope will give you courage.
   You will be protected and will
      rest in safety.
¹⁹ You will lie down unafraid,
   and many will look to you
      for help.
²⁰ But the wicked will be blinded.
   They will have no escape.
   Their only hope is death."

9:3 Or *If God wanted to take someone to court.*
9:13 Hebrew *the helpers of Rahab,* the name of a mythical
sea monster that represents chaos in ancient literature.
9:20 Or *he.*   9:23 Or *disaster.*   10:10 Hebrew *You
poured me out like milk / and curdled me like cheese.*
11:8 Hebrew *than Sheol.*   11:12 Or *than a wild male
donkey can bear a tame colt.*

1 CORINTHIANS 15:1-28

Let me [Paul] now remind you, dear
brothers and sisters,* of the Good News
I preached to you before. You welcomed it then, and you still stand firm
in it. ²It is this Good News that saves you
if you continue to believe the message I
told you—unless, of course, you be-

lieved something that was never true in
the first place.*

³I passed on to you what was most important and what had also been passed
on to me. Christ died for our sins, just as
the Scriptures said. ⁴He was buried, and
he was raised from the dead on the third
day, just as the Scriptures said. ⁵He was
seen by Peter* and then by the Twelve .
⁶After that, he was seen by more than
500 of his followers* at one time, most
of whom are still alive, though some have
died. ⁷Then he was seen by James and
later by all the apostles. ⁸Last of all, as
though I had been born at the wrong
time, I also saw him. ⁹For I am the least of
all the apostles. In fact, I'm not even worthy to be called an apostle after the way I
persecuted God's church.

¹⁰But whatever I am now, it is all because God poured out his special favor
on me—and not without results. For I
have worked harder than any of the other
apostles; yet it was not I but God who was
working through me by his grace. ¹¹So it
makes no difference whether I preach or
they preach, for we all preach the same
message you have already believed.

¹²But tell me this—since we preach
that Christ rose from the dead, why are
some of you saying there will be no resurrection of the dead? ¹³For if there is
no resurrection of the dead, then Christ
has not been raised either. ¹⁴And if
Christ has not been raised, then all our
preaching is useless, and your faith is
useless. ¹⁵And we apostles would all be
lying about God—for we have said that
God raised Christ from the grave. But
that can't be true if there is no resurrection of the dead. ¹⁶And if there is no resurrection of the dead, then Christ has
not been raised. ¹⁷And if Christ has not
been raised, then your faith is useless
and you are still guilty of your sins. ¹⁸In
that case, all who have died believing in
Christ are lost! ¹⁹And if our hope in Christ
is only for this life, we are more to be
pitied than anyone in the world.

²⁰But in fact, Christ has been raised
from the dead. He is the first of a great
harvest of all who have died.

²¹**So you see, just as death came into the world through a man, now the resurrection from the dead has begun through another man.** ²²Just as everyone dies because we all belong to Adam, everyone who belongs to Christ will be given new life. ²³But there is an order to this resurrection: Christ was raised as the first of the harvest; then all who belong to Christ will be raised when he comes back.

²⁴After that the end will come, when he will turn the Kingdom over to God the Father, having destroyed every ruler and authority and power. ²⁵For Christ must reign until he humbles all his enemies beneath his feet. ²⁶And the last enemy to be destroyed is death. ²⁷For the Scriptures say, "God has put all things under his authority."* (Of course, when it says "all things are under his authority," that does not include God himself, who gave Christ his authority.) ²⁸Then, when all things are under his authority, the Son will put himself under God's authority, so that God, who gave his Son authority over all things, will be utterly supreme over everything everywhere.

15:1 Greek *brothers;* also in 15:31, 50, 58.   15:2 Or *unless you never believed it in the first place.*   15:5 Greek *Cephas.* 15:6 Greek *the brothers.*   15:27 Ps 8:6.

PSALM 38:1-22
A psalm of David, asking God to remember him.

¹ **O** LORD, don't rebuke me in
    your anger
    or discipline me in your rage!
² Your arrows have struck deep,
    and your blows are crushing me.
³ Because of your anger, my whole
        body is sick;
    my health is broken because
        of my sins.
⁴ My guilt overwhelms me—
    it is a burden too heavy to bear.
⁵ My wounds fester and stink
    because of my foolish sins.
⁶ I am bent over and racked
        with pain.
    All day long I walk around filled
        with grief.

⁷ A raging fever burns within me,
    and my health is broken.
⁸ I am exhausted and completely
        crushed.
    My groans come from an
        anguished heart.

⁹ You know what I long for,
        Lord;
    you hear my every sigh.
¹⁰ My heart beats wildly, my strength
        fails,
    and I am going blind.
¹¹ My loved ones and friends
        stay away, fearing my
        disease.
    Even my own family stands
        at a distance.
¹² Meanwhile, my enemies lay traps
        to kill me.
    Those who wish me harm make
        plans to ruin me.
    All day long they plan their
        treachery.

¹³ But I am deaf to all their threats.
    I am silent before them as one
        who cannot speak.
¹⁴ I choose to hear nothing,
    and I make no reply.
¹⁵ For I am waiting for you,
        O LORD.
    You must answer for me, O Lord
        my God.
¹⁶ I prayed, "Don't let my enemies gloat
        over me
    or rejoice at my downfall."

¹⁷ I am on the verge of collapse,
    facing constant pain.
¹⁸ But I confess my sins;
    I am deeply sorry for what
        I have done.
¹⁹ I have many aggressive enemies;
    they hate me without reason.
²⁰ They repay me evil for good
    and oppose me for pursuing
        good.
²¹ Do not abandon me, O LORD.
    Do not stand at a distance,
        my God.
²² Come quickly to help me,
    O Lord my savior.

PROVERBS 21:28-29

A false witness will be cut off, but a credible witness will be allowed to speak. □ The wicked bluff their way through, but the virtuous think before they act.

AUGUST 24

JOB 12:1–15:35

Then Job spoke again:

2 "You people really know everything, don't you?
And when you die, wisdom will die with you!

3 Well, I know a few things myself—
and you're no better than I am.
Who doesn't know these things you've been saying?

4 Yet my friends laugh at me,
for I call on God and expect an answer.
I am a just and blameless man,
yet they laugh at me.

5 People who are at ease mock those in trouble.
They give a push to people who are stumbling.

6 But robbers are left in peace,
and those who provoke God live in safety—
though God keeps them in his power.

7 "Just ask the animals, and they will teach you.
Ask the birds of the sky, and they will tell you.

8 Speak to the earth, and it will instruct you.
Let the fish in the sea speak to you.

9 For they all know
that my disaster* has come from the hand of the Lord.

10 For the life of every living thing is in his hand,
and the breath of every human being.

11 The ear tests the words it hears
just as the mouth distinguishes between foods.

12 Wisdom belongs to the aged,
and understanding to the old.

13 "But true wisdom and power are found in God;
counsel and understanding are his.

14 What he destroys cannot be rebuilt.
When he puts someone in prison, there is no escape.

15 If he holds back the rain, the earth becomes a desert.
If he releases the waters, they flood the earth.

16 Yes, strength and wisdom are his;
deceivers and deceived are both in his power.

17 He leads counselors away, stripped of good judgment;
wise judges become fools.

18 He removes the royal robe of kings.
They are led away with ropes around their waist.

19 He leads priests away, stripped of status;
he overthrows those with long years in power.

20 He silences the trusted adviser
and removes the insight of the elders.

21 He pours disgrace upon princes
and disarms the strong.

22 "He uncovers mysteries hidden in darkness;
he brings light to the deepest gloom.

23 He builds up nations, and he destroys them.
He expands nations, and he abandons them.

24 He strips kings of understanding
and leaves them wandering in a pathless wasteland.

25 They grope in the darkness without a light.

He makes them stagger like
drunkards.

13:1"LOOK, I have seen all this with my
own eyes
and heard it with my own ears,
and now I understand.
2 I know as much as you do.
You are no better than I am.
3 As for me, I would speak directly
to the Almighty.
I want to argue my case with God
himself.
4 As for you, you smear me with lies.
As physicians, you are worthless
quacks.
5 If only you could be silent!
That's the wisest thing you
could do.
6 Listen to my charge;
pay attention to my arguments.

7 "Are you defending God with lies?
Do you make your dishonest
arguments for his sake?
8 Will you slant your testimony in his
favor?
Will you argue God's case for
him?
9 What will happen when he finds
out what you are doing?
Can you fool him as easily as you
fool people?
10 No, you will be in trouble with him
if you secretly slant your
testimony in his favor.
11 Doesn't his majesty terrify you?
Doesn't your fear of him
overwhelm you?
12 Your platitudes are as valuable as
ashes.
Your defense is as fragile as
a clay pot.

13 "Be silent now and leave me alone.
Let me speak, and I will face the
consequences.
14 Yes, I will take my life in my hands
and say what I really think.
15 God might kill me, but I have no
other hope.
I am going to argue my case with
him.

16 But this is what will save me—I am
not godless.
If I were, I could not stand before
him.

17 "Listen closely to what I am about
to say.
Hear me out.
18 I have prepared my case;
I will be proved innocent.
19 Who can argue with me over this?
And if you prove me wrong, I will
remain silent and die.

20 "O God, grant me these two things,
and then I will be able to face you.
21 Remove your heavy hand from me,
and don't terrify me with your
awesome presence.
22 Now summon me, and I will answer!
Or let me speak to you, and you
reply.
23 Tell me, what have I done wrong?
Show me my rebellion and my sin.
24 Why do you turn away from me?
Why do you treat me as your
enemy?
25 Would you terrify a leaf blown
by the wind?
Would you chase dry straw?

26 "You write bitter accusations
against me
and bring up all the sins
of my youth.
27 You put my feet in stocks.
You examine all my paths.
You trace all my footprints.
28 I waste away like rotting wood,
like a moth-eaten coat.

14:1"How frail is humanity!
How short is life, how full of
trouble!
2 We blossom like a flower and then
wither.
Like a passing shadow, we quickly
disappear.
3 Must you keep an eye on such a frail
creature
and demand an accounting
from me?
4 Who can bring purity out of an
impure person?

No one!
⁵ You have decided the length
of our lives.
You know how many months we
will live,
and we are not given a minute
longer.
⁶ So leave us alone and let us rest!
We are like hired hands, so let us
finish our work in peace.

⁷ "Even a tree has more hope!
If it is cut down, it will sprout
again
and grow new branches.
⁸ Though its roots have grown old in
the earth
and its stump decays,
⁹ at the scent of water it will bud
and sprout again like a new
seedling.

¹⁰ "But when people die, their strength
is gone.
They breathe their last, and then
where are they?
¹¹ As water evaporates from a lake
and a river disappears in drought,
¹² people are laid to rest and do not
rise again.
Until the heavens are no more,
they will not wake up
nor be roused from their sleep.

¹³ "I wish you would hide me in the
grave*
and forget me there until your
anger has passed.
But mark your calendar to think
of me again!
¹⁴ Can the dead live again?
If so, this would give me hope
through all my years of
struggle,
and I would eagerly await the
release of death.
¹⁵ You would call and I would answer,
and you would yearn for me, your
handiwork.
¹⁶ For then you would guard my steps,
instead of watching for my sins.
¹⁷ My sins would be sealed in a pouch,
and you would cover my guilt.

¹⁸ "But instead, as mountains fall
and crumble
and as rocks fall from a cliff,
¹⁹ as water wears away the stones
and floods wash away the soil,
so you destroy people's hope.
²⁰ You always overpower them, and
they pass from the scene.
You disfigure them in death and
send them away.
²¹ They never know if their children
grow up in honor
or sink to insignificance.
²² They suffer painfully;
their life is full of trouble."

¹⁵:¹THEN Eliphaz the Temanite replied:

² "A wise man wouldn't answer with
such empty talk!
You are nothing but a windbag.
³ The wise don't engage in empty
chatter.
What good are such words?
⁴ Have you no fear of God,
no reverence for him?
⁵ Your sins are telling your mouth
what to say.
Your words are based on clever
deception.
⁶ Your own mouth condemns you,
not I.
Your own lips testify against you.

⁷ "Were you the first person ever
born?
Were you born before the hills
were made?
⁸ Were you listening at God's secret
council?
Do you have a monopoly on
wisdom?
⁹ What do you know that we don't?
What do you understand that we
do not?
¹⁰ On our side are aged, gray-haired
men
much older than your father!

¹¹ "Is God's comfort too little
for you?
Is his gentle word not enough?
¹² What has taken away your reason?
What has weakened your vision,*

¹³ that you turn against God
   and say all these evil things?
¹⁴ Can any mortal be pure?
   Can anyone born of a woman
      be just?
¹⁵ Look, God does not even trust the
      angels.*
   Even the heavens are not
      absolutely pure in his sight.
¹⁶ How much less pure is a corrupt and
      sinful person
   with a thirst for wickedness!

¹⁷ "If you will listen, I will show you.
   I will answer you from my own
      experience.
¹⁸ And it is confirmed by the reports
      of wise men
   who have heard the same thing
      from their fathers—
¹⁹ from those to whom the land was
      given
   long before any foreigners arrived.

²⁰ "The wicked writhe in pain
      throughout their lives.
   Years of trouble are stored up for
      the ruthless.
²¹ The sound of terror rings in
      their ears,
   and even on good days they fear
      the attack of the destroyer.
²² They dare not go out into the
      darkness
   for fear they will be murdered.
²³ They wander around, saying, 'Where
      can I find bread?'*
   They know their day of
      destruction is near.
²⁴ That dark day terrifies them.
   They live in distress and anguish,
      like a king preparing for battle.
²⁵ For they shake their fists at God,
      defying the Almighty.
²⁶ Holding their strong shields,
      they defiantly charge against him.

²⁷ "These wicked people are heavy and
      prosperous;
   their waists bulge with fat.
²⁸ But their cities will be ruined.
   They will live in abandoned
      houses

that are ready to tumble down.
²⁹ Their riches will not last,
   and their wealth will not endure.
   Their possessions will no longer
      spread across the horizon.

³⁰ "They will not escape the darkness.
   The burning sun will wither
      their shoots,
   and the breath of God will destroy
      them.
³¹ Let them no longer fool themselves
      by trusting in empty riches,
   for emptiness will be their only
      reward.
³² Like trees, they will be cut down in
      the prime of life;
   their branches will never again
      be green.
³³ They will be like a vine whose grapes
      are harvested too early,
   like an olive tree that loses its
      blossoms before the fruit
      can form.
³⁴ For the godless are barren.
   Their homes, enriched through
      bribery, will burn.
³⁵ They conceive trouble and give
      birth to evil.
   Their womb produces deceit."

12:9 Hebrew *that this.*   **14:13** Hebrew *in Sheol.*
15:12 Or *Why do your eyes flash with anger;* Hebrew reads
Why do your eyes blink.   **15:15** Hebrew *the holy ones.*
15:23 Greek version reads *He is appointed to be food for
a vulture.*

1 CORINTHIANS 15:29-58

If the dead will not be raised, what
point is there in people being baptized
for those who are dead? Why do it unless the dead will someday rise again?

³⁰And why should we ourselves risk
our lives hour by hour? ³¹For I swear,
dear brothers and sisters, that I face
death daily. This is as certain as my pride
in what Christ Jesus our Lord has done in
you. ³²And what value was there in fighting wild beasts—those people of Ephesus*—if there will be no resurrection
from the dead? And if there is no resurrection, "Let's feast and drink, for tomorrow we die!"* ³³Don't be fooled by those
who say such things, for "bad company

corrupts good character." ³⁴Think carefully about what is right, and stop sinning. For to your shame I say that some of you don't know God at all.

³⁵But someone may ask, "How will the dead be raised? What kind of bodies will they have?" ³⁶What a foolish question! When you put a seed into the ground, it doesn't grow into a plant unless it dies first. ³⁷And what you put in the ground is not the plant that will grow, but only a bare seed of wheat or whatever you are planting. ³⁸Then God gives it the new body he wants it to have. A different plant grows from each kind of seed. ³⁹Similarly there are different kinds of flesh—one kind for humans, another for animals, another for birds, and another for fish.

⁴⁰There are also bodies in the heavens and bodies on the earth. The glory of the heavenly bodies is different from the glory of the earthly bodies. ⁴¹The sun has one kind of glory, while the moon and stars each have another kind. And even the stars differ from each other in their glory.

⁴²It is the same way with the resurrection of the dead. Our earthly bodies are planted in the ground when we die, but they will be raised to live forever. ⁴³Our bodies are buried in brokenness, but they will be raised in glory. They are buried in weakness, but they will be raised in strength. ⁴⁴They are buried as natural human bodies, but they will be raised as spiritual bodies. For just as there are natural bodies, there are also spiritual bodies.

⁴⁵The Scriptures tell us, "The first man, Adam, became a living person."* But the last Adam—that is, Christ—is a life-giving Spirit. ⁴⁶What comes first is the natural body, then the spiritual body comes later. ⁴⁷Adam, the first man, was made from the dust of the earth, while Christ, the second man, came from heaven. ⁴⁸Earthly people are like the earthly man, and heavenly people are like the heavenly man. ⁴⁹Just as we are now like the earthly man, we will someday be like* the heavenly man.

⁵⁰What I am saying, dear brothers and sisters, is that our physical bodies cannot inherit the Kingdom of God. These dying bodies cannot inherit what will last forever.

⁵¹But let me reveal to you a wonderful secret. We will not all die, but we will all be transformed! ⁵²It will happen in a moment, in the blink of an eye, when the last trumpet is blown. For when the trumpet sounds, those who have died will be raised to live forever. And we who are living will also be transformed. ⁵³For our dying bodies must be transformed into bodies that will never die; our mortal bodies must be transformed into immortal bodies.

⁵⁴Then, when our dying bodies have been transformed into bodies that will never die,* this Scripture will be fulfilled:

**"Death is swallowed up in
     victory.***
⁵⁵ **O death, where is your victory?
     O death, where is your sting?*"**

⁵⁶**For sin is the sting that results in death, and the law gives sin its power.** ⁵⁷**But thank God! He gives us victory over sin and death through our Lord Jesus Christ.**

⁵⁸So, my dear brothers and sisters, be strong and immovable. Always work enthusiastically for the Lord, for you know that nothing you do for the Lord is ever useless.

15:32a Greek *fighting wild beasts in Ephesus.*   15:32b Isa 22:13.   15:45 Gen 2:7.   15:49 Some manuscripts read *let us be like.*   15:54a Some manuscripts add *and our mortal bodies have been transformed into immortal bodies.*   15:54b Isa 25:8.   15:55 Hos 13:14 (Greek version).

PSALM 39:1-13

For Jeduthun, the choir director: A psalm of David.

¹ **I** said to myself, "I will watch what I do
     and not sin in what I say.
I will hold my tongue
     when the ungodly are around me."
² But as I stood there in silence—
     not even speaking of good
          things—

the turmoil within me grew worse.
3 The more I thought about it,
    the hotter I got,
        igniting a fire of words:
4 "LORD, remind me how brief my
        time on earth will be.
    Remind me that my days are
        numbered—
    how fleeting my life is.
5 You have made my life no longer
        than the width of my hand.
    My entire lifetime is just a
        moment to you;
    at best, each of us is but a breath."
                                    Interlude

6 We are merely moving shadows,
    and all our busy rushing ends in
        nothing.
    We heap up wealth,
        not knowing who will spend it.
7 And so, Lord, where do I put my
        hope?
    My only hope is in you.
8 Rescue me from my rebellion.
    Do not let fools mock me.
9 I am silent before you; I won't say
        a word,
    for my punishment is from you.
10 But please stop striking me!
    I am exhausted by the blows from
        your hand.
11 When you discipline us for our sins,
    you consume like a moth what is
        precious to us.
    Each of us is but a breath.
                                    Interlude

12 Hear my prayer, O LORD!
    Listen to my cries for help!
    Don't ignore my tears.
    For I am your guest—
        a traveler passing through,
    as my ancestors were before me.
13 Leave me alone so I can smile again
    before I am gone and exist no
        more.

PROVERBS 21:30-31
No human wisdom or understanding
or plan can stand against the LORD.
□ The horse is prepared for the day of
battle, but the victory belongs to the
LORD.

AUGUST 25

JOB 16:1–19:29
Then Job spoke again:

2 "I have heard all this before.
    What miserable comforters
        you are!
3 Won't you ever stop blowing hot air?
    What makes you keep on talking?
4 I could say the same things if you
        were in my place.
    I could spout off criticism and
        shake my head at you.
5 But if it were me, I would encourage
        you.
    I would try to take away your
        grief.
6 Instead, I suffer if I defend myself,
    and I suffer no less if I refuse
        to speak.

7 "O God, you have ground me down
    and devastated my family.
8 As if to prove I have sinned, you've
        reduced me to skin and bones.
    My gaunt flesh testifies
        against me.
9 God hates me and angrily tears
        me apart.
    He snaps his teeth at me
    and pierces me with his eyes.
10 People jeer and laugh at me.
    They slap my cheek in contempt.
    A mob gathers against me.
11 God has handed me over to sinners.
    He has tossed me into the hands
        of the wicked.

12 "I was living quietly until he
        shattered me.
    He took me by the neck and broke
        me in pieces.
    Then he set me up as his target,
13   and now his archers surround me.
    His arrows pierce me without
        mercy.
    The ground is wet with my
        blood.*

14 Again and again he smashes
   against me,
      charging at me like a warrior.
15 I wear burlap to show my grief.
   My pride lies in the dust.
16 My eyes are red with weeping;
   dark shadows circle my eyes.
17 Yet I have done no wrong,
   and my prayer is pure.

18 "O earth, do not conceal my blood.
   Let it cry out on my behalf.
19 Even now my witness is in heaven.
   My advocate is there on high.
20 My friends scorn me,
   but I pour out my tears to God.
21 I need someone to mediate between
   God and me,
      as a person mediates between
      friends.
22 For soon I must go down that road
   from which I will never return.

17:1"My spirit is crushed,
   and my life is nearly snuffed out.
   The grave is ready to receive me.
2 I am surrounded by mockers.
   I watch how bitterly they
   taunt me.

3 "You must defend my innocence,
   O God,
      since no one else will stand up
      for me.
4 You have closed their minds to
   understanding,
      but do not let them triumph.
5 They betray their friends for their
   own advantage,
      so let their children faint with
      hunger.

6 "God has made a mockery of me
   among the people;
      they spit in my face.
7 My eyes are swollen with weeping,
   and I am but a shadow of my
   former self.
8 The virtuous are horrified when
   they see me.
      The innocent rise up against the
      ungodly.
9 The righteous keep moving forward,
   and those with clean hands
   become stronger and stronger.

10 "As for all of you, come back with a
   better argument,
      though I still won't find a wise
      man among you.
11 My days are over.
   My hopes have disappeared.
   My heart's desires are broken.
12 These men say that night is day;
   they claim that the darkness is
   light.
13 What if I go to the grave*
   and make my bed in darkness?
14 What if I call the grave my father,
   and the maggot my mother or my
   sister?
15 Where then is my hope?
   Can anyone find it?
16 No, my hope will go down with me
   to the grave.
      We will rest together in the dust!"

18:1Then Bildad the Shuhite replied:

2 "How long before you stop talking?
   Speak sense if you want us to
   answer!
3 Do you think we are mere animals?
   Do you think we are stupid?
4 You may tear out your hair in anger,
   but will that destroy the earth?
   Will it make the rocks tremble?

5 "Surely the light of the wicked will
   be snuffed out.
      The sparks of their fire will
      not glow.
6 The light in their tent will grow
   dark.
      The lamp hanging above them
      will be quenched.
7 The confident stride of the wicked
   will be shortened.
      Their own schemes will be their
      downfall.
8 The wicked walk into a net.
   They fall into a pit.
9 A trap grabs them by the heel.
   A snare holds them tight.
10 A noose lies hidden on the ground.
   A rope is stretched across their
   path.

11 "Terrors surround the wicked
    and trouble them at every step.
12 Hunger depletes their strength,
    and calamity waits for them to
        stumble.
13 Disease eats their skin;
    death devours their limbs.
14 They are torn from the security of
        their homes
    and are brought down to the king
        of terrors.
15 The homes of the wicked will
        burn down;
    burning sulfur rains on their
        houses.
16 Their roots will dry up,
    and their branches will wither.
17 All memory of their existence will
        fade from the earth,
    No one will remember their
        names.
18 They will be thrust from light into
        darkness,
    driven from the world.
19 They will have neither children nor
        grandchildren,
    nor any survivor in the place
        where they lived.
20 People in the west are appalled at
        their fate;
    people in the east are horrified.
21 They will say, 'This was the home
        of a wicked person,
    the place of one who rejected
        God.'"

19:1 THEN Job spoke again:

2 "How long will you torture me?
    How long will you try to crush me
        with your words?
3 You have already insulted me ten
        times.
    You should be ashamed of
        treating me so badly.
4 Even if I have sinned,
    that is my concern, not yours.
5 You think you're better than I am,
    using my humiliation as evidence
        of my sin.
6 But it is God who has wronged me,
    capturing me in his net.*

7 "I cry out, 'Help!' but no one
        answers me.
    I protest, but there is no justice.
8 God has blocked my way so I cannot
        move.
    He has plunged my path into
        darkness.
9 He has stripped me of my honor
    and removed the crown from my
        head.
10 He has demolished me on every side,
        and I am finished.
    He has uprooted my hope like
        a fallen tree.
11 His fury burns against me;
    he counts me as an enemy.
12 His troops advance.
    They build up roads to attack me.
    They camp all around my tent.

13 "My relatives stay far away,
    and my friends have turned
        against me.
14 My family is gone,
    and my close friends have
        forgotten me.
15 My servants and maids consider
        me a stranger.
    I am like a foreigner to them.
16 When I call my servant, he doesn't
        come;
    I have to plead with him!
17 My breath is repulsive to my wife.
    I am rejected by my own family.
18 Even young children despise me.
    When I stand to speak, they turn
        their backs on me.
19 My close friends detest me.
    Those I loved have turned
        against me.
20 I have been reduced to skin
        and bones
    and have escaped death by the
        skin of my teeth.

21 "Have mercy on me, my friends,
        have mercy,
    for the hand of God has
        struck me.
22 Must you also persecute me, like
        God does?
    Haven't you chewed me up
        enough?

23 "Oh, that my words could be
     recorded.
   Oh, that they could be inscribed
     on a monument,
24 carved with an iron chisel and filled
     with lead,
   engraved forever in the rock.

25 "But as for me, I know that my
     Redeemer lives,
   and he will stand upon the earth
     at last.
26 And after my body has decayed,
     yet in my body I will see God!*
27 I will see him for myself.
   Yes, I will see him with my
     own eyes.
   I am overwhelmed at the thought!

28 "How dare you go on persecuting
     me,
   saying, 'It's his own fault'?
29 You should fear punishment
     yourselves,
   for your attitude deserves
     punishment.
   Then you will know that there is
     indeed a judgment."

16:13 Hebrew *my gall.*   17:13 Hebrew *to Sheol;* also in
17:16.   19:6 Or *for I am like a city under siege.*   19:26 Or
without my body I will see God! The meaning of the Hebrew
is uncertain.

1 CORINTHIANS 16:1-24

Now regarding your [Corinthians]
question about the money being collected for God's people in Jerusalem.
You should follow the same procedure I
gave to the churches in Galatia. ²On the
first day of each week, you should each
put aside a portion of the money you
have earned. Don't wait until I get there
and then try to collect it all at once.
³When I come, I will write letters of recommendation for the messengers you
choose to deliver your gift to Jerusalem.
⁴And if it seems appropriate for me to
go along, they can travel with me.

⁵I am coming to visit you after I have
been to Macedonia,* for I am planning
to travel through Macedonia. ⁶Perhaps I
will stay awhile with you, possibly all
winter, and then you can send me on my
way to my next destination. ⁷This time I

don't want to make just a short visit and
then go right on. I want to come and
stay awhile, if the Lord will let me. ⁸In
the meantime, I will be staying here at
Ephesus until the Festival of Pentecost.
⁹There is a wide-open door for a great
work here, although many oppose me.

¹⁰When Timothy comes, don't intimidate him. He is doing the Lord's work,
just as I am. ¹¹Don't let anyone treat him
with contempt. Send him on his way
with your blessing when he returns to
me. I expect him to come with the other
believers.*

¹²Now about our brother Apollos—I
urged him to visit you with the other believers, but he was not willing to go right
now. He will see you later when he has
the opportunity.

¹³Be on guard. Stand firm in the faith.
Be courageous.* Be strong. ¹⁴And do
everything with love.

¹⁵You know that Stephanas and his
household were the first of the harvest of
believers in Greece,* and they are spend-
ing their lives in service to God's people. I
urge you, dear brothers and sisters,* ¹⁶to
submit to them and others like them
who serve with such devotion. ¹⁷I am
very glad that Stephanas, Fortunatus, and
Achaicus have come here. They have
been providing the help you weren't here
to give me. ¹⁸They have been a wonderful
encouragement to me, as they have been
to you. You must show your appreciation
to all who serve so well.

¹⁹The churches here in the province
of Asia* send greetings in the Lord, as
do Aquila and Priscilla* and all the others who gather in their home for church
meetings. ²⁰All the brothers and sisters
here send greetings to you. Greet each
other with Christian love.*

²¹HERE IS MY GREETING IN MY OWN
HANDWRITING—PAUL.

²²If anyone does not love the Lord,
that person is cursed. Our Lord, come!*

²³May the grace of the Lord Jesus be
with you.

²⁴My love to all of you in Christ Jesus.*

16:5 *Macedonia* was in the northern region of Greece.
16:11 Greek *with the brothers;* also in 16:12.
16:13 Greek *Be men.*   16:15a Greek *in Achaia,* the

southern region of the Greek peninsula.   **16:15b** Greek *brothers;* also in 16:20.   **16:19a** *Asia* was a Roman province in what is now western Turkey.   **16:19b** Greek *Prisca.*   **16:20** Greek *with a sacred kiss.*   **16:22** From Aramaic, *Marana tha.* Some manuscripts read *Maran atha, "Our Lord has come."*   **16:24** Some manuscripts add *Amen.*

PSALM 40:1-10

For the choir director: A psalm of David.

¹ I waited patiently for the Lord
to help me,
and he turned to me and heard
my cry.
² He lifted me out of the pit of
despair,
out of the mud and the mire.
He set my feet on solid ground
and steadied me as I walked
along.
³ He has given me a new song to sing,
a hymn of praise to our God.
Many will see what he has done and
be amazed.
They will put their trust in
the Lord.

⁴ Oh, the joys of those who trust
the Lord,
who have no confidence in the
proud
or in those who worship idols.
⁵ **O Lord my God, you have
performed many wonders
for us.
Your plans for us are too
numerous to list.
You have no equal.
If I tried to recite all your
wonderful deeds,
I would never come to the end
of them.**

⁶ You take no delight in sacrifices
or offerings.
Now that you have made me
listen, I finally understand*—
you don't require burnt offerings
or sin offerings.
⁷ Then I said, "Look, I have come.
As is written about me in the
Scriptures:
⁸ I take joy in doing your will, my God,
for your instructions are written
on my heart."

⁹ I have told all your people about
your justice.
I have not been afraid to speak
out,
as you, O Lord, well know.
¹⁰ I have not kept the good news of
your justice hidden in my heart;
I have talked about your
faithfulness and saving power.
I have told everyone in the great
assembly
of your unfailing love and
faithfulness.

40:6 Greek text reads *You have given me a body.* Compare Heb 10:5.

PROVERBS 22:1

Choose a good reputation over great riches; being held in high esteem is better than silver or gold.

AUGUST 26

JOB 20:1–22:30

Then Zophar the Naamathite replied:

² "I must reply
because I am greatly disturbed.
³ I've had to endure your insults,
but now my spirit prompts me
to reply.

⁴ "Don't you realize that from the
beginning of time,
ever since people were first
placed on the earth,
⁵ the triumph of the wicked has been
short-lived
and the joy of the godless has
been only temporary?
⁶ Though the pride of the godless
reaches to the heavens
and their heads touch the clouds,
⁷ yet they will vanish forever,
thrown away like their own dung.
Those who knew them will ask,
'Where are they?'

8 They will fade like a dream and not
   be found.
    They will vanish like a vision in
       the night.
9 Those who once saw them will see
   them no more.
    Their families will never see
       them again.
10 Their children will beg from
    the poor,
     for they must give back their
        stolen riches.
11 Though they are young,
    their bones will lie in the dust.

12 "They enjoyed the sweet taste
    of wickedness,
     letting it melt under their tongue.
13 They savored it,
    holding it long in their mouths.
14 But suddenly the food in their
    bellies turns sour,
     a poisonous venom in their
        stomach.
15 They will vomit the wealth they
    swallowed.
     God won't let them keep it down.
16 They will suck the poison of cobras.
    The viper will kill them.
17 They will never again enjoy streams
    of olive oil
     or rivers of milk and honey.
18 They will give back everything they
    worked for.
     Their wealth will bring them
        no joy.
19 For they oppressed the poor and left
    them destitute.
     They foreclosed on their homes.
20 They were always greedy and never
    satisfied.
     Nothing remains of all the things
        they dreamed about.
21 Nothing is left after they finish
    gorging themselves.
     Therefore, their prosperity will
        not endure.

22 "In the midst of plenty, they will run
    into trouble
     and be overcome by misery.
23 May God give them a bellyful of
    trouble.

May God rain down his anger
   upon them.
24 When they try to escape an iron
   weapon,
    a bronze-tipped arrow will pierce
       them.
25 The arrow is pulled from their back,
    and the arrowhead glistens with
       blood.*
   The terrors of death are upon them.
26   Their treasures will be thrown
          into deepest darkness.
   A wildfire will devour their goods,
      consuming all they have left.
27 The heavens will reveal their guilt,
    and the earth will testify against
       them.
28 A flood will sweep away their house.
    God's anger will descend on them
       in torrents.
29 This is the reward that God gives the
    wicked.
     It is the inheritance decreed
        by God."

21:1 THEN Job spoke again:

2 "Listen closely to what I am saying.
   That's one consolation you can
      give me.
3 Bear with me, and let me speak.
   After I have spoken, you may
      resume mocking me.

4 "My complaint is with God, not
   with people.
    I have good reason to be so
       impatient.
5 Look at me and be stunned.
   Put your hand over your mouth
      in shock.
6 When I think about what I am
   saying, I shudder.
    My body trembles.

7 "Why do the wicked prosper,
   growing old and powerful?
8 They live to see their children grow
   up and settle down,
    and they enjoy their
       grandchildren.
9 Their homes are safe from every
   fear,
    and God does not punish them.

¹⁰ Their bulls never fail to breed.
   Their cows bear calves and never
      miscarry.
¹¹ They let their children frisk about
      like lambs.
   Their little ones skip and dance.
¹² They sing with tambourine and
      harp.
   They celebrate to the sound
      of the flute.
¹³ They spend their days in prosperity,
      then go down to the grave* in
         peace.
¹⁴ And yet they say to God, 'Go away.
   We want no part of you and your
      ways.
¹⁵ Who is the Almighty, and why
      should we obey him?
   What good will it do us to pray?'
¹⁶ (They think their prosperity is of
      their own doing,
   but I will have nothing to do with
      that kind of thinking.)

¹⁷ "Yet the light of the wicked never
      seems to be extinguished.
   Do they ever have trouble?
   Does God distribute sorrows to
      them in anger?
¹⁸ Are they driven before the wind
      like straw?
   Are they carried away by the
      storm like chaff?
   Not at all!

¹⁹ "'Well,' you say, 'at least God will
      punish their children!'
   But I say he should punish the
      ones who sin,
   so that they understand his
      judgment.
²⁰ Let them see their destruction with
      their own eyes.
   Let them drink deeply of the
      anger of the Almighty.
²¹ For they will not care what happens
      to their family
   after they are dead.

²² "But who can teach a lesson to God,
      since he judges even the most
         powerful?
²³ One person dies in prosperity,

   completely comfortable and
      secure,
²⁴ the picture of good health,
   vigorous and fit.
²⁵ Another person dies in bitter
      poverty,
   never having tasted the good life.
²⁶ But both are buried in the same
      dust,
   both eaten by the same maggots.

²⁷ "Look, I know what you're thinking.
   I know the schemes you plot
      against me.
²⁸ You will tell me of rich and wicked
      people
   whose houses have vanished
      because of their sins.
²⁹ But ask those who have been
      around,
   and they will tell you the truth.
³⁰ Evil people are spared in times
      of calamity
   and are allowed to escape
      disaster.
³¹ No one criticizes them openly
   or pays them back for what they
      have done.
³² When they are carried to the grave,
   an honor guard keeps watch at
      their tomb.
³³ A great funeral procession goes to
      the cemetery.
   Many pay their respects as the
      body is laid to rest,
   and the earth gives sweet repose.

³⁴ "How can your empty clichés
      comfort me?
   All your explanations are lies!"

²²:¹THEN Eliphaz the Temanite replied:

² "Can a person do anything to help
      God?
   Can even a wise person be helpful
      to him?
³ Is it any advantage to the Almighty
      if you are righteous?
   Would it be any gain to him if you
      were perfect?
⁴ Is it because you're so pious that he
      accuses you
   and brings judgment against you?

5 No, it's because of your wickedness!
There's no limit to your sins.

6 "For example, you must have lent
money to your friend
and demanded clothing as
security.
Yes, you stripped him to the bone.
7 You must have refused water for
the thirsty
and food for the hungry.
8 You probably think the land belongs
to the powerful
and only the privileged have a
right to it!
9 You must have sent widows away
empty-handed
and crushed the hopes of
orphans.
10 That is why you are surrounded
by traps
and tremble from sudden fears.
11 That is why you cannot see in the
darkness,
and waves of water cover you.

12 "God is so great—higher than the
heavens,
higher than the farthest stars.
13 But you reply, 'That's why God can't
see what I am doing!
How can he judge through the
thick darkness?
14 For thick clouds swirl about him,
and he cannot see us.
He is way up there, walking on the
vault of heaven.'

15 "Will you continue on the old paths
where evil people have walked?
16 They were snatched away in the
prime of life,
the foundations of their lives
washed away.
17 For they said to God, 'Leave us alone!
What can the Almighty do to us?'
18 Yet he was the one who filled their
homes with good things,
so I will have nothing to do with
that kind of thinking.

19 "The righteous will be happy to see
the wicked destroyed,

and the innocent will laugh in
contempt.
20 They will say, 'See how our enemies
have been destroyed.
The last of them have been
consumed in the fire.'

21 "Submit to God, and you will have
peace;
then things will go well for you.
22 Listen to his instructions,
and store them in your heart.
23 If you return to the Almighty, you
will be restored—
so clean up your life.
24 If you give up your lust for money
and throw your precious gold
into the river,
25 the Almighty himself will be your
treasure.
He will be your precious silver!

26 "Then you will take delight in the
Almighty
and look up to God.
27 You will pray to him, and he will
hear you,
and you will fulfill your vows
to him.
28 You will succeed in whatever you
choose to do,
and light will shine on the road
ahead of you.
29 If people are in trouble and you say,
'Help them,'
God will save them.
30 Even sinners will be rescued;
they will be rescued because your
hands are pure."

20:25 Hebrew *with gall.*   21:13 Hebrew *to Sheol.*

2 CORINTHIANS 1:1-11
This letter is from Paul, chosen by the
will of God to be an apostle of Christ
Jesus, and from our brother Timothy.

I am writing to God's church in
Corinth and to all of his holy people
throughout Greece.*

2May God our Father and the Lord
Jesus Christ give you grace and peace.

3**All praise to God, the Father of our
Lord Jesus Christ. God is our merciful
Father and the source of all comfort.**

4He comforts us in all our troubles so that we can comfort others. When they are troubled, we will be able to give them the same comfort God has given us. 5For the more we suffer for Christ, the more God will shower us with his comfort through Christ. 6Even when we are weighed down with troubles, it is for your comfort and salvation! For when we ourselves are comforted, we will certainly comfort you. Then you can patiently endure the same things we suffer. 7We are confident that as you share in our sufferings, you will also share in the comfort God gives us.

8We think you ought to know, dear brothers and sisters,* about the trouble we went through in the province of Asia. We were crushed and overwhelmed beyond our ability to endure, and we thought we would never live through it. 9In fact, we expected to die. But as a result, we stopped relying on ourselves and learned to rely only on God, who raises the dead. 10And he did rescue us from mortal danger, and he will rescue us again. We have placed our confidence in him, and he will continue to rescue us. 11And you are helping us by praying for us. Then many people will give thanks because God has graciously answered so many prayers for our safety.

1:1 Greek *Achaia,* the southern region of the Greek peninsula.   1:8 Greek *brothers.*

PSALM 40:11-17
    Lord, don't hold back your tender
        mercies from me.
        Let your unfailing love and
            faithfulness always protect me.
12 For troubles surround me—
        too many to count!
    My sins pile up so high
        I can't see my way out.
    They outnumber the hairs on
            my head.
        I have lost all courage.

13 Please, Lord, rescue me!
        Come quickly, Lord, and help me.
14 May those who try to destroy me

be humiliated and put to shame.
    May those who take delight in my
            trouble
        be turned back in disgrace.
15 Let them be horrified by their
            shame,
        for they said, "Aha! We've got
            him now!"

16 But may all who search for you
        be filled with joy and gladness
            in you.
    May those who love your salvation
        repeatedly shout, "The Lord
            is great!"

17 As for me, since I am poor and
            needy,
        let the Lord keep me in his
            thoughts.
    You are my helper and my savior.
        O my God, do not delay.

PROVERBS 22:2-4
The rich and poor have this in common: The Lord made them both. □ A prudent person foresees danger and takes precautions. The simpleton goes blindly on and suffers the consequences. □ True humility and fear of the Lord lead to riches, honor, and long life.

AUGUST
27

JOB 23:1–27:23
Then Job spoke again:

2 "My complaint today is still a bitter
            one,
        and I try hard not to groan aloud.
3 If only I knew where to find God,
        I would go to his court.
4 I would lay out my case
        and present my arguments.
5 Then I would listen to his reply
        and understand what he says
            to me.

6 Would he use his great power to
   argue with me?
   No, he would give me a fair
      hearing.
7 Honest people can reason with him,
   so I would be forever acquitted by
      my judge.
8 I go east, but he is not there.
   I go west, but I cannot find him.
9 I do not see him in the north, for he
      is hidden.
   I look to the south, but he is
      concealed.

10 "But he knows where I am going.
   And when he tests me, I will come
      out as pure as gold.
11 For I have stayed on God's paths;
   I have followed his ways and not
      turned aside.
12 I have not departed from his
      commands,
   but have treasured his words
      more than daily food.
13 But once he has made his decision,
      who can change his mind?
   Whatever he wants to do, he does.
14 So he will do to me whatever he has
      planned.
   He controls my destiny.
15 No wonder I am so terrified in his
      presence.
   When I think of it, terror
      grips me.
16 God has made me sick at heart;
   the Almighty has terrified me.
17 Darkness is all around me;
   thick, impenetrable darkness is
      everywhere.

24:1 "WHY doesn't the Almighty bring
      the wicked to judgment?
   Why must the godly wait for
      him in vain?
2 Evil people steal land by moving the
      boundary markers.
   They steal livestock and put them
      in their own pastures.
3 They take the orphan's donkey
   and demand the widow's ox as
      security for a loan.
4 The poor are pushed off the path;

the needy must hide together for
      safety.
5 Like wild donkeys in the wilderness,
   the poor must spend all their time
      looking for food,
   searching even in the desert for
      food for their children.
6 They harvest a field they do not own,
   and they glean in the vineyards
      of the wicked.
7 All night they lie naked in the cold,
   without clothing or covering.
8 They are soaked by mountain
      showers,
   and they huddle against the rocks
      for want of a home.

9 "The wicked snatch a widow's child
      from her breast,
   taking the baby as security
      for a loan.
10 The poor must go about naked,
      without any clothing.
   They harvest food for others
      while they themselves are
      starving.
11 They press out olive oil without
      being allowed to taste it,
   and they tread in the winepress as
      they suffer from thirst.
12 The groans of the dying rise from
      the city,
   and the wounded cry for help,
      yet God ignores their moaning.

13 "Wicked people rebel against
      the light.
   They refuse to acknowledge its
      ways
   or stay in its paths.
14 The murderer rises in the early
      dawn
   to kill the poor and needy;
      at night he is a thief.
15 The adulterer waits for the twilight,
   saying, 'No one will see me then.'
   He hides his face so no one will
      know him.
16 Thieves break into houses at night
   and sleep in the daytime.
   They are not acquainted with
      the light.
17 The black night is their morning.

They ally themselves with the
  terrors of the darkness.
18 "But they disappear like foam down
    a river.
  Everything they own is cursed,
    and they are afraid to enter their
    own vineyards.
19 The grave* consumes sinners
    just as drought and heat consume
    snow.
20 Their own mothers will forget them.
    Maggots will find them sweet
      to eat.
  No one will remember them.
    Wicked people are broken like a
    tree in the storm.
21 They cheat the woman who has no
    son to help her.
  They refuse to help the needy
    widow.

22 "God, in his power, drags away
    the rich.
  They may rise high, but they have
    no assurance of life.
23 They may be allowed to live in
    security,
  but God is always watching them.
24 And though they are great now,
    in a moment they will be gone like
    all others,
  cut off like heads of grain.
25 Can anyone claim otherwise?
  Who can prove me wrong?"

25:1THEN Bildad the Shuhite replied:

2 "God is powerful and dreadful.
  He enforces peace in the heavens.
3 Who is able to count his heavenly
    army?
  Doesn't his light shine on all the
    earth?
4 How can a mortal be innocent
    before God?
  Can anyone born of a woman
    be pure?
5 God is more glorious than the
    moon;
  he shines brighter than the stars.
6 In comparison, people are maggots;
  we mortals are mere worms."

26:1THEN Job spoke again:

2 "How you have helped the
    powerless!
  How you have saved the weak!
3 How you have enlightened my
    stupidity!
  What wise advice you have
    offered!
4 Where have you gotten all these
    wise sayings?
  Whose spirit speaks through you?

5 "The dead tremble—
    those who live beneath the
    waters.
6 The underworld* is naked in God's
    presence.
  The place of destruction* is
    uncovered.
7 God stretches the northern sky over
    empty space
  and hangs the earth on nothing.
8 He wraps the rain in his thick
    clouds,
  and the clouds don't burst with
    the weight.
9 He covers the face of the moon,*
  shrouding it with his clouds.
10 He created the horizon when he
    separated the waters;
  he set the boundary between day
    and night.
11 The foundations of heaven tremble;
  they shudder at his rebuke.
12 By his power the sea grew calm.
  By his skill he crushed the great
    sea monster.*
13 His Spirit made the heavens
    beautiful,
  and his power pierced the gliding
    serpent.
14 These are just the beginning of all
    that he does,
  merely a whisper of his power.
  Who, then, can comprehend the
    thunder of his power?"

27:1JOB continued speaking:

2 "I vow by the living God, who has
    taken away my rights,
  by the Almighty who has
    embittered my soul—

3 As long as I live,
while I have breath from God,
4 my lips will speak no evil,
and my tongue will speak
no lies.
5 I will never concede that you are
right;
I will defend my integrity until
I die.
6 I will maintain my innocence
without wavering.
My conscience is clear for as long
as I live.

7 "May my enemy be punished like
the wicked,
my adversary like those who
do evil.
8 For what hope do the godless have
when God cuts them off
and takes away their life?
9 Will God listen to their cry
when trouble comes upon
them?
10 Can they take delight in the
Almighty?
Can they call to God at
any time?
11 I will teach you about God's
power.
I will not conceal anything
concerning the Almighty.
12 But you have seen all this,
yet you say all these useless
things to me.

13 "This is what the wicked will
receive from God;
this is their inheritance from
the Almighty.
14 They may have many children,
but the children will die in war
or starve to death.
15 Those who survive will die
of a plague,
and not even their widows will
mourn them.

16 "Evil people may have piles
of money
and may store away mounds
of clothing.

17 But the righteous will wear that
clothing,
and the innocent will divide
that money.
18 The wicked build houses as fragile
as a spider's web,*
as flimsy as a shelter made
of branches.
19 The wicked go to bed rich
but wake to find that all their
wealth is gone.
20 Terror overwhelms them like
a flood,
and they are blown away in the
storms of the night.
21 The east wind carries them away,
and they are gone.
It sweeps them away.
22 It whirls down on them without
mercy.
They struggle to flee from
its power.
23 But everyone jeers at them
and mocks them."

24:19 Hebrew *Sheol.*   26:6a Hebrew *Sheol.*
26:6b Hebrew *Abaddon.*   26:9 Or *covers his*
throne.   26:12 Hebrew *Rahab,* the name of a mythical
sea monster that represents chaos in ancient literature.
27:18 As in Greek and Syriac versions (see also 8:14);
Hebrew reads *a moth.*

2 CORINTHIANS 1:12–2:11

We [Paul and his co-workers] can say
with confidence and a clear conscience
that we have lived with a God-given holiness* and sincerity in all our dealings.
We have depended on God's grace, not
on our own human wisdom. That is how
we have conducted ourselves before the
world, and especially toward you. 13Our
letters have been straightforward, and
there is nothing written between the
lines and nothing you can't understand.
I hope someday you will fully understand us, 14even if you don't understand
us now. Then on the day when the Lord
Jesus* returns, you will be proud of us in
the same way we are proud of you.

15Since I was so sure of your understanding and trust, I wanted to give you
a double blessing by visiting you twice—
16first on my way to Macedonia and
again when I returned from Macedo-

nia.* Then you could send me on my way to Judea.

¹⁷You may be asking why I changed my plan. Do you think I make my plans carelessly? Do you think I am like people of the world who say "Yes" when they really mean "No"? ¹⁸As surely as God is faithful, my word to you does not waver between "Yes" and "No." ¹⁹For Jesus Christ, the Son of God, does not waver between "Yes" and "No." He is the one whom Silas,* Timothy, and I preached to you, and as God's ultimate "Yes," he always does what he says. ²⁰For all of God's promises have been fulfilled in Christ with a resounding "Yes!" And through Christ, our "Amen" (which means "Yes") ascends to God for his glory.

²¹**It is God who enables us, along with you, to stand firm for Christ. He has commissioned us, ²²and he has identified us as his own by placing the Holy Spirit in our hearts as the first installment that guarantees everything he has promised us.**

²³Now I call upon God as my witness that I am telling the truth. The reason I didn't return to Corinth was to spare you from a severe rebuke. ²⁴But that does not mean we want to dominate you by telling you how to put your faith into practice. We want to work together with you so you will be full of joy, for it is by your own faith that you stand firm.

²:¹So I decided that I would not bring you grief with another painful visit. ²For if I cause you grief, who will make me glad? Certainly not someone I have grieved. ³That is why I wrote to you as I did, so that when I do come, I won't be grieved by the very ones who ought to give me the greatest joy. Surely you all know that my joy comes from your being joyful. ⁴I wrote that letter in great anguish, with a troubled heart and many tears. I didn't want to grieve you, but I wanted to let you know how much love I have for you.

⁵I am not overstating it when I say that the man who caused all the trouble hurt all of you more than he hurt me.

⁶Most of you opposed him, and that was punishment enough. ⁷Now, however, it is time to forgive and comfort him. Otherwise he may be overcome by discouragement. ⁸So I urge you now to reaffirm your love for him.

⁹I wrote to you as I did to test you and see if you would fully comply with my instructions. ¹⁰When you forgive this man, I forgive him, too. And when I forgive whatever needs to be forgiven, I do so with Christ's authority for your benefit, ¹¹so that Satan will not outsmart us. For we are familiar with his evil schemes.

1:12 Some manuscripts read *honesty.*   1:14 Some manuscripts read *our Lord Jesus.*   1:16 *Macedonia* was in the northern region of Greece.   1:19 Greek *Silvanus.*

PSALM 41:1-13
For the choir director: A psalm of David.

¹ **O**h, the joys of those who are kind
    to the poor!
  The LORD rescues them when
    they are in trouble.
² The LORD protects them
    and keeps them alive.
  He gives them prosperity in
    the land
    and rescues them from their
    enemies.
³ The LORD nurses them when they
    are sick
    and restores them to health.

⁴ "O LORD," I prayed, "have mercy
    on me.
  Heal me, for I have sinned
    against you."
⁵ But my enemies say nothing but evil
    about me.
  "How soon will he die and be
    forgotten?" they ask.
⁶ They visit me as if they were my
    friends,
    but all the while they gather
    gossip,
    and when they leave, they spread
    it everywhere.
⁷ All who hate me whisper about me,
    imagining the worst.
⁸ "He has some fatal disease,"
    they say.

"He will never get out of that
bed!"

⁹ Even my best friend, the one I
trusted completely,
the one who shared my food, has
turned against me.

¹⁰ Lᴏʀᴅ, have mercy on me.
Make me well again, so I can pay
them back!

¹¹ I know you are pleased with me,
for you have not let my enemies
triumph over me.

¹² You have preserved my life because
I am innocent;
you have brought me into your
presence forever.

¹³ Praise the Lᴏʀᴅ, the God of Israel,
who lives from everlasting to
everlasting.
Amen and amen!

PROVERBS 22:5-6

Corrupt people walk a thorny, treacherous road; whoever values life will avoid
it. □ Direct your children onto the right
path, and when they are older, they will
not leave it.

AUGUST
28

JOB 28:1–30:31

"**P**eople know where to mine silver
and how to refine gold.

² They know where to dig iron from
the earth
and how to smelt copper from
rock.

³ They know how to shine light
in the darkness
and explore the farthest regions
of the earth
as they search in the dark for ore.

⁴ They sink a mine shaft into the earth
far from where anyone lives.

They descend on ropes, swinging
back and forth.

⁵ Food is grown on the earth above,
but down below, the earth is
melted as by fire.

⁶ Here the rocks contain precious
lapis lazuli,
and the dust contains gold.

⁷ These are treasures no bird of prey
can see,
no falcon's eye observe.

⁸ No wild animal has walked upon
these treasures;
no lion has ever set his paw there.

⁹ People know how to tear apart
flinty rocks
and overturn the roots of
mountains.

¹⁰ They cut tunnels in the rocks
and uncover precious stones.

¹¹ They dam up the trickling streams
and bring to light the hidden
treasures.

¹² "But do people know where to find
wisdom?
Where can they find
understanding?

¹³ No one knows where to find it,
for it is not found among the
living.

¹⁴ 'It is not here,' says the ocean.
'Nor is it here,' says the sea.

¹⁵ It cannot be bought with gold.
It cannot be purchased with
silver.

¹⁶ It's worth more than all the gold
of Ophir,
greater than precious onyx or
lapis lazuli.

¹⁷ Wisdom is more valuable than gold
and crystal.
It cannot be purchased with
jewels mounted in fine gold.

¹⁸ Coral and jasper are worthless in
trying to get it.
The price of wisdom is far
above rubies.

¹⁹ Precious peridot from Ethiopia*
cannot be exchanged for it.
It's worth more than the purest
gold.

20 "But do people know where to find
wisdom?
Where can they find
understanding?
21 It is hidden from the eyes of all
humanity.
Even the sharp-eyed birds in the
sky cannot discover it.
22 Destruction* and Death say,
'We've heard only rumors of
where wisdom can be found.'

23 "God alone understands the way to
wisdom;
he knows where it can be found,
24 for he looks throughout the whole
earth
and sees everything under the
heavens.
25 He decided how hard the winds
should blow
and how much rain should fall.
26 He made the laws for the rain
and laid out a path for the
lightning.
27 Then he saw wisdom and
evaluated it.
He set it in place and examined
it thoroughly.
28 And this is what he says to all
humanity:
'The fear of the Lord is true wisdom;
to forsake evil is real
understanding.'"

29:1 JOB continued speaking:

2 "I long for the years gone by
when God took care of me,
3 when he lit up the way before me
and I walked safely through the
darkness.
4 When I was in my prime,
God's friendship was felt in
my home.
5 The Almighty was still with me,
and my children were around me.
6 My cows produced milk in
abundance,
and my groves poured out
streams of olive oil.

7 "Those were the days when I went
to the city gate

and took my place among the
honored leaders.
8 The young stepped aside when they
saw me,
and even the aged rose in respect
at my coming.
9 The princes stood in silence
and put their hands over their
mouths.
10 The highest officials of the city
stood quietly,
holding their tongues in respect.

11 "All who heard me praised me.
All who saw me spoke well of me.
12 For I assisted the poor in their need
and the orphans who required
help.
13 I helped those without hope, and
they blessed me.
And I caused the widows' hearts
to sing for joy.
14 Everything I did was honest.
Righteousness covered me like
a robe,
and I wore justice like a turban.
15 I served as eyes for the blind
and feet for the lame.
16 I was a father to the poor
and assisted strangers who
needed help.
17 I broke the jaws of godless
oppressors
and plucked their victims from
their teeth.

18 "I thought, 'Surely I will die
surrounded by my family
after a long, good life.*
19 For I am like a tree whose roots
reach the water,
whose branches are refreshed
with the dew.
20 New honors are constantly
bestowed on me,
and my strength is continually
renewed.'

21 "Everyone listened to my advice.
They were silent as they waited
for me to speak.
22 And after I spoke, they had nothing
to add,

for my counsel satisfied them.
23 They longed for me to speak as
people long for rain.
They drank my words like a
refreshing spring rain.
24 When they were discouraged,
I smiled at them.
My look of approval was precious
to them.
25 Like a chief, I told them what to do.
I lived like a king among
his troops
and comforted those who
mourned.

30:1 "BUT now I am mocked by people
younger than I,
by young men whose fathers are
not worthy to run with my
sheepdogs.
2 A lot of good they are to me—
those worn-out wretches!
3 They are gaunt with hunger
and flee to the deserts,
to desolate and gloomy
wastelands.
4 They pluck wild greens from
among the bushes
and eat from the roots of broom
trees.
5 They are driven from human
society,
and people shout at them as if
they were thieves.
6 So now they live in frightening
ravines,
in caves and among the rocks.
7 They sound like animals howling
among the bushes,
huddled together beneath the
nettles.
8 They are nameless fools,
outcasts from society.

9 "And now they mock me with
vulgar songs!
They taunt me!
10 They despise me and won't come
near me,
except to spit in my face.
11 For God has cut my bowstring.
He has humbled me,

so they have thrown off all
restraint.
12 These outcasts oppose me to my
face.
They send me sprawling
and lay traps in my path.
13 They block my road
and do everything they can to
destroy me.
They know I have no one to help me.
14 They come at me from all
directions.
They jump on me when I am
down.
15 I live in terror now.
My honor has blown away in
the wind,
and my prosperity has vanished
like a cloud.

16 "And now my life seeps away.
Depression haunts my days.
17 At night my bones are filled
with pain,
which gnaws at me relentlessly.
18 With a strong hand, God grabs
my shirt.
He grips me by the collar of
my coat.
19 He has thrown me into the mud.
I'm nothing more than dust
and ashes.

20 "I cry to you, O God, but you
don't answer.
I stand before you, but you don't
even look.
21 You have become cruel toward me.
You use your power to persecute
me.
22 You throw me into the
whirlwind
and destroy me in the storm.
23 And I know you are sending me
to my death—
the destination of all who live.

24 "Surely no one would turn against
the needy
when they cry for help in their
trouble.
25 Did I not weep for those in trouble?

Was I not deeply grieved for the
needy?
26 So I looked for good, but evil
came instead.
I waited for the light, but
darkness fell.
27 My heart is troubled and restless.
Days of suffering torment me.
28 I walk in gloom, without sunlight.
I stand in the public square and
cry for help.
29 Instead, I am considered a brother
to jackals
and a companion to owls.
30 My skin has turned dark,
and my bones burn with fever.
31 My harp plays sad music,
and my flute accompanies those
who weep."

28:19 Hebrew *from Cush.*   28:22 Hebrew *Abaddon.*
29:18 Hebrew *after I have counted my days like sand.*

2 CORINTHIANS 2:12-17

When I [Paul] came to the city of Troas
to preach the Good News of Christ, the
Lord opened a door of opportunity for
me. 13But I had no peace of mind because my dear brother Titus hadn't yet
arrived with a report from you. So I said
good-bye and went on to Macedonia to
find him.

14**But thank God! He has made us
his captives and continues to lead us
along in Christ's triumphal procession. Now he uses us to spread the
knowledge of Christ everywhere, like
a sweet perfume.** 15Our lives are a
Christ-like fragrance rising up to God.
But this fragrance is perceived differently by those who are being saved and
by those who are perishing. 16To those
who are perishing, we are a dreadful
smell of death and doom. But to those
who are being saved, we are a life-giving
perfume. And who is adequate for such
a task as this?

17You see, we are not like the many
hucksters* who preach for personal
profit. We preach the word of God with
sincerity and with Christ's authority,
knowing that God is watching us.

2:17 Some manuscripts read *the rest of the hucksters.*

PSALM 42:1-11
For the choir director: A psalm of the
descendants of Korah.*

1 **A**s the deer longs for streams
of water,
so I long for you, O God.
2 I thirst for God, the living God.
When can I go and stand
before him?
3 Day and night I have only tears
for food,
while my enemies continually
taunt me, saying,
"Where is this God of yours?"

4 My heart is breaking
as I remember how it used to be:
I walked among the crowds
of worshipers,
leading a great procession to the
house of God,
singing for joy and giving thanks
amid the sound of a great
celebration!

5 Why am I discouraged?
Why is my heart so sad?
I will put my hope in God!
I will praise him again—
my Savior and 6my God!

Now I am deeply discouraged,
but I will remember you—
even from distant Mount Hermon,
the source of the Jordan,
from the land of Mount Mizar.
7 I hear the tumult of the raging seas
as your waves and surging tides
sweep over me.
8 But each day the LORD pours his
unfailing love upon me,
and through each night I sing
his songs,
praying to God who gives me life.

9 "O God my rock," I cry,
"Why have you forgotten me?
Why must I wander around
in grief,
oppressed by my enemies?"
10 Their taunts break my bones.
They scoff, "Where is this God
of yours?"

11 Why am I discouraged?
Why is my heart so sad?
I will put my hope in God!
I will praise him again—
my Savior and my God!

42:TITLE Hebrew *maskil*. This may be a literary or
musical term.

PROVERBS 22:7
Just as the rich rule the poor, so the bor-
rower is servant to the lender.

AUGUST
29

JOB 31:1–33:33
"I [Job] made a covenant with my
eyes
not to look with lust at a young
woman.
2 For what has God above chosen
for us?
What is our inheritance from the
Almighty on high?
3 Isn't it calamity for the wicked
and misfortune for those who
do evil?
4 Doesn't he see everything I do
and every step I take?

5 "Have I lied to anyone
or deceived anyone?
6 Let God weigh me on the scales
of justice,
for he knows my integrity.
7 If I have strayed from his pathway,
or if my heart has lusted for what
my eyes have seen,
or if I am guilty of any other sin,
8 then let someone else eat the crops
I have planted.
Let all that I have planted be
uprooted.

9 "If my heart has been seduced by a
woman,
or if I have lusted for my
neighbor's wife,

10 then let my wife belong to* another
man;
let other men sleep with her.
11 For lust is a shameful sin,
a crime that should be punished.
12 It is a fire that burns all the way
to hell.*
It would wipe out everything
I own.

13 "If I have been unfair to my male
or female servants
when they brought their
complaints to me,
14 how could I face God?
What could I say when he
questioned me?
15 For God created both me and my
servants.
He created us both in the womb.

16 "Have I refused to help the poor,
or crushed the hopes of widows?
17 Have I been stingy with my food
and refused to share it with
orphans?
18 No, from childhood I have cared for
orphans like a father,
and all my life I have cared for
widows.
19 Whenever I saw the homeless
without clothes
and the needy with nothing
to wear,
20 did they not praise me
for providing wool clothing
to keep them warm?

21 "If I raised my hand against an
orphan,
knowing the judges would take
my side,
22 then let my shoulder be wrenched
out of place!
Let my arm be torn from its
socket!
23 That would be better than facing
God's judgment.
For if the majesty of God opposes
me, what hope is there?

24 "Have I put my trust in money
or felt secure because of my
gold?

²⁵ Have I gloated about my wealth
   and all that I own?

²⁶ "Have I looked at the sun shining
       in the skies,
   or the moon walking down its
       silver pathway,
²⁷ and been secretly enticed in
       my heart
   to throw kisses at them
       in worship?
²⁸ If so, I should be punished
       by the judges,
   for it would mean I had denied
       the God of heaven.

²⁹ "Have I ever rejoiced when disaster
       struck my enemies,
   or become excited when harm
       came their way?
³⁰ No, I have never sinned by cursing
       anyone
   or by asking for revenge.

³¹ "My servants have never said,
   'He let others go hungry.'
³² I have never turned away a stranger
   but have opened my doors to
       everyone.

³³ "Have I tried to hide my sins like
       other people do,
   concealing my guilt in my heart?
³⁴ Have I feared the crowd
   or the contempt of the masses,
   so that I kept quiet and stayed
       indoors?

³⁵ "If only someone would listen to me!
   Look, I will sign my name to my
       defense.
   Let the Almighty answer me.
   Let my accuser write out the
       charges against me.
³⁶ I would face the accusation proudly.
   I would wear it like a crown.
³⁷ For I would tell him exactly what
       I have done.
   I would come before him like
       a prince.

³⁸ "If my land accuses me
   and all its furrows cry out
       together,
³⁹ or if I have stolen its crops

or murdered its owners,
⁴⁰ then let thistles grow on that land
       instead of wheat,
   and weeds instead of barley."

Job's words are ended.

^{32:1} Job's three friends refused to reply further to him because he kept insisting on his innocence. ² Then Elihu son of Barakel the Buzite, of the clan of Ram, became angry. He was angry because Job refused to admit that he had sinned and that God was right in punishing him. ³ He was also angry with Job's three friends, for they made God* appear to be wrong by their inability to answer Job's arguments. ⁴ Elihu had waited for the others to speak to Job because they were older than he. ⁵ But when he saw that they had no further reply, he spoke out angrily. ⁶ Elihu son of Barakel the Buzite said,

"I am young and you are old,
   so I held back from telling you
       what I think.
⁷ I thought, 'Those who are older
       should speak,
   for wisdom comes with age.'
⁸ **But there is a spirit* within
       people,
   the breath of the Almighty
       within them,
   that makes them intelligent.**
⁹ **Sometimes the elders are
       not wise.
   Sometimes the aged do not
       understand justice.**
¹⁰ So listen to me,
   and let me tell you what I think.

¹¹ "I have waited all this time,
   listening very carefully to your
       arguments,
   listening to you grope for words.
¹² I have listened,
   but not one of you has refuted Job
   or answered his arguments.
¹³ And don't tell me, 'He is too wise
       for us.
   Only God can convince him.'
¹⁴ If Job had been arguing with me,

I would not answer with your
kind of logic!
¹⁵ You sit there baffled,
with nothing more to say.
¹⁶ Should I continue to wait, now that
you are silent?
Must I also remain silent?
¹⁷ No, I will say my piece.
I will speak my mind.
¹⁸ For I am full of pent-up words,
and the spirit within me urges
me on.
¹⁹ I am like a cask of wine without
a vent,
like a new wineskin ready
to burst!
²⁰ I must speak to find relief,
so let me give my answers.
²¹ I won't play favorites
or try to flatter anyone.
²² For if I tried flattery,
my Creator would soon
destroy me.

^{33:1}"LISTEN to my words, Job;
pay attention to what I have
to say.
² Now that I have begun to speak,
let me continue.
³ I speak with all sincerity;
I speak the truth.
⁴ For the Spirit of God has made me,
and the breath of the Almighty
gives me life.
⁵ Answer me, if you can;
make your case and take your
stand.
⁶ Look, you and I both belong to God.
I, too, was formed from clay.
⁷ So you don't need to be afraid
of me.
I won't come down hard on you.

⁸ "You have spoken in my hearing,
and I have heard your very words.
⁹ You said, 'I am pure; I am without
sin;
I am innocent; I have no guilt.
¹⁰ God is picking a quarrel with me,
and he considers me his enemy.
¹¹ He puts my feet in the stocks
and watches my every move.'

¹² "But you are wrong, and I will show
you why.
For God is greater than any
human being.
¹³ So why are you bringing a charge
against him?
Why say he does not respond to
people's complaints?
¹⁴ For God speaks again and again,
though people do not
recognize it.
¹⁵ He speaks in dreams, in visions
of the night,
when deep sleep falls on people
as they lie in their beds.
¹⁶ He whispers in their ears
and terrifies them with warnings.
¹⁷ He makes them turn from doing
wrong;
he keeps them from pride.
¹⁸ He protects them from the grave,
from crossing over the river
of death.

¹⁹ "Or God disciplines people with pain
on their sickbeds,
with ceaseless aching in their
bones.
²⁰ They lose their appetite
for even the most delicious food.
²¹ Their flesh wastes away,
and their bones stick out.
²² They are at death's door;
the angels of death wait for them.

²³ "But if an angel from heaven
appears—
a special messenger to intercede
for a person
and declare that he is upright—
²⁴ he will be gracious and say,
'Rescue him from the grave,
for I have found a ransom for
his life.'
²⁵ Then his body will become as
healthy as a child's,
firm and youthful again.
²⁶ When he prays to God,
he will be accepted.
And God will receive him with joy
and restore him to good standing.
²⁷ He will declare to his friends,
'I sinned and twisted the truth,

but it was not worth it.*
28 God rescued me from the grave,
and now my life is filled
with light.'

29 "Yes, God does these things
again and again for people.
30 He rescues them from the grave
so they may enjoy the light of life.
31 Mark this well, Job. Listen to me,
for I have more to say.
32 But if you have anything to say,
go ahead.
Speak, for I am anxious to see
you justified.
33 But if not, then listen to me.
Keep silent and I will teach
you wisdom!"

31:10 Hebrew *grind for.*   31:12 Hebrew *to Abaddon.*
32:3 As in ancient Hebrew scribal tradition; the Masoretic
Text reads *Job.*   32:8 Or *Spirit;* also in 32:18.
33:27 Greek version reads *but he* [God] *did not punish
me as my sin deserved.*

2 CORINTHIANS 3:1-18

Are we [Paul and his co-workers] beginning to praise ourselves again? Are we like others, who need to bring you letters of recommendation, or who ask you to write such letters on their behalf? Surely not! 2 The only letter of recommendation we need is you yourselves. Your lives are a letter written in our* hearts; everyone can read it and recognize our good work among you. 3 Clearly, you are a letter from Christ showing the result of our ministry among you. This "letter" is written not with pen and ink, but with the Spirit of the living God. It is carved not on tablets of stone, but on human hearts.

4 We are confident of all this because of our great trust in God through Christ. 5 It is not that we think we are qualified to do anything on our own. Our qualification comes from God. 6 He has enabled us to be ministers of his new covenant. This is a covenant not of written laws, but of the Spirit. The old written covenant ends in death; but under the new covenant, the Spirit gives life.

7 The old way,* with laws etched in stone, led to death, though it began with such glory that the people of Israel could not bear to look at Moses' face. For his face shone with the glory of God, even though the brightness was already fading away. 8 Shouldn't we expect far greater glory under the new way, now that the Holy Spirit is giving life? 9 If the old way, which brings condemnation, was glorious, how much more glorious is the new way, which makes us right with God! 10 In fact, that first glory was not glorious at all compared with the overwhelming glory of the new way. 11 So if the old way, which has been replaced, was glorious, how much more glorious is the new, which remains forever!

12 Since this new way gives us such confidence, we can be very bold. 13 We are not like Moses, who put a veil over his face so the people of Israel would not see the glory, even though it was destined to fade away. 14 But the people's minds were hardened, and to this day whenever the old covenant is being read, the same veil covers their minds so they cannot understand the truth. And this veil can be removed only by believing in Christ. 15 Yes, even today when they read Moses' writings, their hearts are covered with that veil, and they do not understand.

16 But whenever someone turns to the Lord, the veil is taken away. 17 For the Lord is the Spirit, and wherever the Spirit of the Lord is, there is freedom. 18 So all of us who have had that veil removed can see and reflect the glory of the Lord. And the Lord—who is the Spirit—makes us more and more like him as we are changed into his glorious image.

3:2 Some manuscripts read *your.*   3:7 Or *ministry;* also in 3:8, 9, 10, 11, 12.

PSALM 43:1-5

Declare me innocent, O God!
Defend me against these
ungodly people.
Rescue me from these unjust
liars.

2 For you are God, my only safe haven.
Why have you tossed me aside?
Why must I wander around in grief,

oppressed by my enemies?
3 Send out your light and your truth;
   let them guide me.
Let them lead me to your holy
      mountain,
   to the place where you live.
4 There I will go to the altar of God,
   to God—the source of all my joy.
I will praise you with my harp,
   O God, my God!

5 Why am I discouraged?
   Why is my heart so sad?
I will put my hope in God!
   I will praise him again—
   my Savior and my God!

PROVERBS 22:8-9

Those who plant injustice will harvest disaster, and their reign of terror will come to an end.* □Blessed are those who are generous, because they feed the poor.

22:8 The Greek version includes an additional proverb: *God blesses a man who gives cheerfully, / but his worthless deeds will come to an end.* Compare 2 Cor 9:7.

AUGUST
30

JOB 34:1–36:33
Then Elihu said:

2 "Listen to me, you wise men.
   Pay attention, you who have
      knowledge.
3 Job said, 'The ear tests the words
      it hears
   just as the mouth distinguishes
      between foods.'
4 So let us discern for ourselves what
      is right;
   let us learn together what is good.
5 For Job also said, 'I am innocent,
   but God has taken away my rights.
6 I am innocent, but they call me a liar.
   My suffering is incurable, though
      I have not sinned.'

7 "Tell me, has there ever been a man
      like Job,
   with his thirst for irreverent talk?
8 He chooses evil people as
      companions.
   He spends his time with wicked
      men.
9 He has even said, 'Why waste time
      trying to please God?'

10 "Listen to me, you who have
      understanding.
   Everyone knows that God
      doesn't sin!
   The Almighty can do no wrong.
11 He repays people according to their
      deeds.
   He treats people as they deserve.
12 Truly, God will not do wrong.
   The Almighty will not twist
      justice.
13 Did someone else put the world in
      his care?
   Who set the whole world in
      place?
14 If God were to take back his spirit
      and withdraw his breath,
15 all life would cease,
   and humanity would turn again
      to dust.

16 "Now listen to me if you are wise.
   Pay attention to what I say.
17 Could God govern if he hated
      justice?
   Are you going to condemn the
      almighty judge?
18 For he says to kings, 'You are
      wicked,'
   and to nobles, 'You are unjust.'
19 He doesn't care how great a person
      may be,
   and he pays no more attention to
      the rich than to the poor.
   He made them all.
20 In a moment they die.
   In the middle of the night they
      pass away;
   the mighty are removed without
      human hand.

21 "For God watches how people live;
   he sees everything they do.

22 No darkness is thick enough
　　to hide the wicked from his eyes.
23 We don't set the time
　　when we will come before God
　　　in judgment.
24 He brings the mighty to ruin without
　　asking anyone,
　　and he sets up others in their
　　　place.
25 He knows what they do,
　　and in the night he overturns and
　　　destroys them.
26 He strikes them down because they
　　are wicked,
　　doing it openly for all to see.
27 For they turned away from
　　following him.
　　They have no respect for any
　　　of his ways.
28 They cause the poor to cry out,
　　catching God's attention.
　　He hears the cries of the needy.
29 But if he chooses to remain quiet,
　　who can criticize him?
　　When he hides his face, no one can
　　　find him,
　　whether an individual or a nation.
30 He prevents the godless from ruling
　　so they cannot be a snare to
　　　the people.

31 "Why don't people say to God,
　　'I have sinned,
　　but I will sin no more'?
32 Or 'I don't know what evil I have
　　done—tell me.
　　If I have done wrong, I will stop
　　　at once'?

33 "Must God tailor his justice to your
　　demands?
　　But you have rejected him!
　　The choice is yours, not mine.
　　Go ahead, share your wisdom
　　　with us.
34 After all, bright people will tell me,
　　and wise people will hear me say,
35 'Job speaks out of ignorance;
　　his words lack insight.'
36 Job, you deserve the maximum
　　penalty
　　for the wicked way you have
　　　talked.

37 For you have added rebellion
　　to your sin;
　　you show no respect,
　　and you speak many angry words
　　　against God."

35:1 THEN Elihu said:

2 "Do you think it is right for you
　　to claim,
　　'I am righteous before God'?
3 For you also ask, 'What's in
　　it for me?
　　What's the use of living a
　　righteous life?'

4 "I will answer you
　　and all your friends, too.
5 Look up into the sky,
　　and see the clouds high
　　above you.
6 If you sin, how does that affect God?
　　Even if you sin again and again,
　　what effect will it have on him?
7 If you are good, is this some great
　　gift to him?
　　What could you possibly give
　　him?
8 No, your sins affect only people
　　like yourself,
　　and your good deeds also affect
　　only humans.

9 "People cry out when they are
　　oppressed.
　　They groan beneath the power
　　of the mighty.
10 Yet they don't ask, 'Where is God my
　　Creator,
　　the one who gives songs in the
　　night?
11 Where is the one who makes us
　　smarter than the animals
　　and wiser than the birds of the
　　sky?'
12 And when they cry out, God does
　　not answer
　　because of their pride.
13 But it is wrong to say God doesn't
　　listen,
　　to say the Almighty isn't
　　concerned.
14 You say you can't see him,

but he will bring justice if you will
    only wait.*
15 You say he does not respond to
    sinners with anger
    and is not greatly concerned
        about wickedness.*
16 But you are talking nonsense, Job.
    You have spoken like a fool."

36:1 ELIHU continued speaking:

2 "Let me go on, and I will show you
    the truth.
    For I have not finished defending
        God!
3 I will present profound arguments
    for the righteousness of my
        Creator.
4 I am telling you nothing but the
    truth,
    for I am a man of great
        knowledge.

5 "God is mighty, but he does not
    despise anyone!
    He is mighty in both power and
        understanding.
6 He does not let the wicked live
    but gives justice to the afflicted.
7 He never takes his eyes off the
    innocent,
    but he sets them on thrones
        with kings
    and exalts them forever.
8 If they are bound in chains
    and caught up in a web of trouble,
9 he shows them the reason.
    He shows them their sins of pride.
10 He gets their attention
    and commands that they turn
        from evil.

11 "If they listen and obey God,
    they will be blessed with
        prosperity throughout their
        lives.
    All their years will be pleasant.
12 But if they refuse to listen to him,
    they will be killed by the sword*
    and die from lack of
        understanding.
13 For the godless are full of
    resentment.
    Even when he punishes them,

they refuse to cry out to him for
    help.
14 They die when they are young,
    after wasting their lives in
        immoral living.
15 But by means of their suffering, he
    rescues those who suffer.
    For he gets their attention
        through adversity.

16 "God is leading you away from
    danger, Job,
    to a place free from distress.
    He is setting your table with the
        best food.
17 But you are obsessed with whether
    the godless will be judged.
    Don't worry, judgment and justice
        will be upheld.
18 But watch out, or you may be
    seduced by wealth.*
    Don't let yourself be bribed
        into sin.
19 Could all your wealth*
    or all your mighty efforts
    keep you from distress?
20 Do not long for the cover of night,
    for that is when people will be
        destroyed.*
21 Be on guard! Turn back from evil,
    for God sent this suffering
    to keep you from a life of evil.

22 "Look, God is all-powerful.
    Who is a teacher like him?
23 No one can tell him what to do,
    or say to him, 'You have done
        wrong.'
24 Instead, glorify his mighty works,
    singing songs of praise.
25 Everyone has seen these things,
    though only from a distance.

26 "Look, God is greater than we can
    understand.
    His years cannot be counted.
27 He draws up the water vapor
    and then distills it into rain.
28 The rain pours down from the
    clouds,
    and everyone benefits.
29 Who can understand the spreading
    of the clouds

and the thunder that rolls forth
from heaven?
30 See how he spreads the lightning
around him
and how it lights up the depths
of the sea.
31 By these mighty acts he nourishes*
the people,
giving them food in abundance.
32 He fills his hands with lightning
bolts
and hurls each at its target.
33 The thunder announces his
presence;
the storm announces his
indignant anger.*"

35:13-14 These verses can also be translated as follows: [13]*Indeed, God doesn't listen to their empty plea; / the Almighty is not concerned. / [14]How much less will he listen when you say you don't see him, / and that your case is before him and you're waiting for justice.*   **35:15** As in Greek and Latin versions; the meaning of this Hebrew word is uncertain.   **36:12** Or *they will cross the river* [of death].   **36:18** Or *But don't let your anger lead you to mockery.*   **36:19** Or *Could all your cries for help.*   **36:16-20** The meaning of the Hebrew in this passage is uncertain.   **36:31** Or *he governs.*   **36:33** Or *even the cattle know when a storm is coming.* The meaning of the Hebrew is uncertain.

2 CORINTHIANS 4:1-12

Therefore, since God in his mercy has given us [Paul and his co-workers] this new way,* we never give up. 2We reject all shameful deeds and underhanded methods. We don't try to trick anyone or distort the word of God. We tell the truth before God, and all who are honest know this.

3If the Good News we preach is hidden behind a veil, it is hidden only from people who are perishing. 4Satan, who is the god of this world, has blinded the minds of those who don't believe. They are unable to see the glorious light of the Good News. They don't understand this message about the glory of Christ, who is the exact likeness of God.

5You see, we don't go around preaching about ourselves. We preach that Jesus Christ is Lord, and we ourselves are your servants for Jesus' sake. 6For God, who said, "Let there be light in the darkness," has made this light shine in our hearts so we could know the glory of God that is seen in the face of Jesus Christ.

7**We now have this light shining in our hearts, but we ourselves are like fragile clay jars containing this great treasure.* This makes it clear that our great power is from God, not from ourselves.**

8We are pressed on every side by troubles, but we are not crushed. We are perplexed, but not driven to despair. 9We are hunted down, but never abandoned by God. We get knocked down, but we are not destroyed. 10Through suffering, our bodies continue to share in the death of Jesus so that the life of Jesus may also be seen in our bodies.

11Yes, we live under constant danger of death because we serve Jesus, so that the life of Jesus will be evident in our dying bodies. 12So we live in the face of death, but this has resulted in eternal life for you.

4:1 Or *ministry.*   **4:7** Greek *We now have this treasure in clay jars.*

PSALM 44:1-8

For the choir director: A psalm* of the descendants of Korah.

1 O God, we have heard it with our
own ears—
our ancestors have told us
of all you did in their day,
in days long ago:
2 You drove out the pagan nations
by your power
and gave all the land to our
ancestors.
You crushed their enemies
and set our ancestors free.
3 They did not conquer the land
with their swords;
it was not their own strong arm
that gave them victory.
It was your right hand and strong
arm
and the blinding light from your
face that helped them,
for you loved them.

4 You are my King and my God.
You command victories for Israel.*

5 Only by your power can we push
  back our enemies;
    only in your name can we trample
    our foes.
6 I do not trust in my bow;
    I do not count on my sword to
    save me.
7 You are the one who gives us victory
  over our enemies;
    you disgrace those who hate us.
8 O God, we give glory to you all day
  long
    and constantly praise your name.

Interlude

44:TITLE Hebrew *maskil*. This may be a literary or musical
term.   44:4 Hebrew *for Jacob*. The names "Jacob" and
"Israel" are often interchanged throughout the Old
Testament, referring sometimes to the individual patriarch
and sometimes to the nation.

PROVERBS 22:10-12

Throw out the mocker, and fighting
goes, too. Quarrels and insults will disappear. □ Whoever loves a pure heart
and gracious speech will have the king
as a friend. □ The LORD preserves those
with knowledge, but he ruins the plans
of the treacherous.

AUGUST
31

JOB 37:1–39:30
"My [Elihu's] heart pounds as
    I think of this.
  It trembles within me.
2 Listen carefully to the thunder of
  God's voice
    as it rolls from his mouth.
3 It rolls across the heavens,
    and his lightning flashes in every
    direction.
4 Then comes the roaring of the
  thunder—
    the tremendous voice of his
    majesty.
  He does not restrain it when
    he speaks.

5 God's voice is glorious in the
  thunder.
  We can't even imagine the
    greatness of his power.
6 "He directs the snow to fall on
  the earth
    and tells the rain to pour
    down.
7 Then everyone stops working
    so they can watch his power.
8 The wild animals take cover
    and stay inside their dens.
9 The stormy wind comes from its
  chamber,
    and the driving winds bring
    the cold.
10 God's breath sends the ice,
    freezing wide expanses
    of water.
11 He loads the clouds with moisture,
    and they flash with his lightning.
12 The clouds churn about at his
  direction.
  They do whatever he commands
    throughout the earth.
13 He makes these things happen
    either to punish people
    or to show his unfailing love.

14 "Pay attention to this, Job.
  Stop and consider the wonderful
    miracles of God!
15 Do you know how God controls the
  storm
    and causes the lightning to flash
    from his clouds?
16 Do you understand how he moves
  the clouds
    with wonderful perfection and
    skill?
17 When you are sweltering in your
  clothes
    and the south wind dies down and
    everything is still,
18 he makes the skies reflect the heat
    like a bronze mirror.
  Can you do that?

19 "So teach the rest of us what to say
  to God.
  We are too ignorant to make our
    own arguments.

20 Should God be notified that I want
   to speak?
   Can people even speak when they
   are confused?*
21 We cannot look at the sun,
   for it shines brightly in the sky
   when the wind clears away the
   clouds.
22 So also, golden splendor comes from
   the mountain of God.*
   He is clothed in dazzling
   splendor.
23 We cannot imagine the power
   of the Almighty;
   but even though he is just and
   righteous,
   he does not destroy us.
24 No wonder people everywhere
   fear him.
   All who are wise show him
   reverence."

38:1Then the Lord answered Job from
the whirlwind:

2 "Who is this that questions my
   wisdom
   with such ignorant words?
3 Brace yourself like a man,
   because I have some questions
   for you,
   and you must answer them.

4 "Where were you when I laid the
   foundations of the earth?
   Tell me, if you know so much.
5 Who determined its dimensions
   and stretched out the surveying
   line?
6 What supports its foundations,
   and who laid its cornerstone
7 as the morning stars sang together
   and all the angels* shouted
   for joy?

8 "Who kept the sea inside its
   boundaries
   as it burst from the womb,
9 and as I clothed it with clouds
   and wrapped it in thick darkness?
10 For I locked it behind barred gates,
   limiting its shores.
11 I said, 'This far and no farther will
   you come.

Here your proud waves must
   stop!'
12 "Have you ever commanded the
   morning to appear
   and caused the dawn to rise in
   the east?
13 Have you made daylight spread to
   the ends of the earth,
   to bring an end to the night's
   wickedness?
14 As the light approaches,
   the earth takes shape like clay
   pressed beneath a seal;
   it is robed in brilliant colors.*
15 The light disturbs the wicked
   and stops the arm that is raised
   in violence.

16 "Have you explored the springs
   from which the seas come?
   Have you explored their depths?
17 Do you know where the gates of
   death are located?
   Have you seen the gates of utter
   gloom?
18 Do you realize the extent of the
   earth?
   Tell me about it if you know!

19 "Where does light come from,
   and where does darkness go?
20 Can you take each to its home?
   Do you know how to get there?
21 But of course you know all this!
   For you were born before it was all
   created,
   and you are so very experienced!

22 "Have you visited the storehouses
   of the snow
   or seen the storehouses of hail?
23 (I have reserved them as weapons
   for the time of trouble,
   for the day of battle and war.)
24 Where is the path to the source
   of light?
   Where is the home of the east
   wind?

25 "Who created a channel for the
   torrents of rain?
   Who laid out the path for the
   lightning?

26 Who makes the rain fall on barren
        land,
    in a desert where no one lives?
27 Who sends rain to satisfy the
        parched ground
    and make the tender grass
        spring up?

28 "Does the rain have a father?
    Who gives birth to the dew?
29 Who is the mother of the ice?
    Who gives birth to the frost from
        the heavens?
30 For the water turns to ice as hard
        as rock,
    and the surface of the water
        freezes.

31 "Can you direct the movement of
        the stars—
    binding the cluster of the Pleiades
        or loosening the cords of Orion?
32 Can you direct the sequence of the
        seasons
    or guide the Bear with her cubs
        across the heavens?
33 Do you know the laws of the
        universe?
    Can you use them to regulate
        the earth?

34 "Can you shout to the clouds
    and make it rain?
35 Can you make lightning appear
    and cause it to strike as you
        direct?
36 Who gives intuition to the heart
    and instinct to the mind?
37 Who is wise enough to count all
        the clouds?
    Who can tilt the water jars of
        heaven
38 when the parched ground is dry
    and the soil has hardened into
        clods?

39 "Can you stalk prey for a lioness
    and satisfy the young lions'
        appetites
40 as they lie in their dens
    or crouch in the thicket?
41 Who provides food for the ravens
    when their young cry out to God
    and wander about in hunger?

39:1"Do you know when the wild goats
        give birth?
    Have you watched as deer are
        born in the wild?
2 Do you know how many months
    they carry their young?
    Are you aware of the time of their
        delivery?
3 They crouch down to give birth to
        their young
    and deliver their offspring.
4 Their young grow up in the open
        fields,
    then leave home and never return.

5 "Who gives the wild donkey its
        freedom?
    Who untied its ropes?
6 I have placed it in the wilderness;
    its home is the wasteland.
7 It hates the noise of the city
    and has no driver to shout at it.
8 The mountains are its pastureland,
    where it searches for every blade
        of grass.

9 "Will the wild ox consent to being
        tamed?
    Will it spend the night in your
        stall?
10 Can you hitch a wild ox to a plow?
    Will it plow a field for you?
11 Given its strength, can you trust it?
    Can you leave and trust the ox
        to do your work?
12 Can you rely on it to bring home
        your grain
    and deliver it to your threshing
        floor?

13 "The ostrich flaps her wings grandly,
    but they are no match for the
        feathers of the stork.
14 She lays her eggs on top of the earth,
    letting them be warmed in the
        dust.
15 She doesn't worry that a foot might
        crush them
    or a wild animal might destroy
        them.
16 She is harsh toward her young,
    as if they were not her own.
    She doesn't care if they die.

¹⁷ For God has deprived her of wisdom.
   He has given her no understanding.
¹⁸ But whenever she jumps up to run,
   she passes the swiftest horse with
      its rider.

¹⁹ "Have you given the horse its
      strength
   or clothed its neck with a flowing
      mane?
²⁰ Did you give it the ability to leap like
      a locust?
   Its majestic snorting is terrifying!
²¹ It paws the earth and rejoices in its
      strength
   when it charges out to battle.
²² It laughs at fear and is unafraid.
   It does not run from the sword.
²³ The arrows rattle against it,
   and the spear and javelin flash.
²⁴ It paws the ground fiercely
   and rushes forward into battle
      when the ram's horn blows.
²⁵ It snorts at the sound of the horn.
   It senses the battle in the
      distance.
   It quivers at the captain's
      commands and the noise
         of battle.

²⁶ "Is it your wisdom that makes the
      hawk soar
   and spread its wings toward
      the south?
²⁷ Is it at your command that the
      eagle rises
   to the heights to make its nest?
²⁸ It lives on the cliffs,
   making its home on a distant,
      rocky crag.
²⁹ From there it hunts its prey,
   keeping watch with piercing eyes.
³⁰ Its young gulp down blood.
   Where there's a carcass, there
      you'll find it."

37:20 Or *speak without being swallowed up?* 37:22 Or
from the north; or from the abode. 38:7 Hebrew *the sons
of God.* 38:14 Or *its features stand out like folds in a robe.*

2 CORINTHIANS 4:13–5:10

But we [Paul and his co-workers] continue to preach because we have the
same kind of faith the psalmist had

when he said, "I believed in God, so I
spoke."* ¹⁴We know that God, who
raised the Lord Jesus,* will also raise us
with Jesus and present us to himself together with you. ¹⁵All of this is for your
benefit. And as God's grace reaches
more and more people, there will be
great thanksgiving, and God will receive
more and more glory.

¹⁶That is why we never give up.
Though our bodies are dying, our spirits
are* being renewed every day. **¹⁷For
our present troubles are small and
won't last very long. Yet they produce
for us a glory that vastly outweighs
them and will last forever! ¹⁸So we
don't look at the troubles we can see
now; rather, we fix our gaze on things
that cannot be seen. For the things
we see now will soon be gone, but the
things we cannot see will last forever.**

⁵:¹FOR we know that when this earthly
tent we live in is taken down (that is,
when we die and leave this earthly
body), we will have a house in heaven, an
eternal body made for us by God himself and not by human hands. ²We grow
weary in our present bodies, and we
long to put on our heavenly bodies like
new clothing. ³For we will put on heavenly bodies; we will not be spirits without bodies.* ⁴While we live in these
earthly bodies, we groan and sigh, but
it's not that we want to die and get rid of
these bodies that clothe us. Rather, we
want to put on our new bodies so that
these dying bodies will be swallowed up
by life. ⁵God himself has prepared us
for this, and as a guarantee he has given
us his Holy Spirit.

⁶So we are always confident, even
though we know that as long as we live
in these bodies we are not at home with
the Lord. ⁷For we live by believing and
not by seeing. ⁸Yes, we are fully confident, and we would rather be away from
these earthly bodies, for then we will be
at home with the Lord. ⁹So whether we
are here in this body or away from this
body, our goal is to please him. ¹⁰For we

must all stand before Christ to be judged. We will each receive whatever we deserve for the good or evil we have done in this earthly body.

4:13 Ps 116:10.   4:14 Some manuscripts read *who raised Jesus.*   4:16 Greek *our inner being is.*   5:3 Greek *we will not be naked.*

PSALM 44:9-26

But now you [God] have tossed us aside in dishonor.
 You no longer lead our armies to battle.
10 You make us retreat from our enemies
 and allow those who hate us to plunder our land.
11 You have butchered us like sheep
 and scattered us among the nations.
12 You sold your precious people for a pittance,
 making nothing on the sale.
13 You let our neighbors mock us.
 We are an object of scorn and derision to those around us.
14 You have made us the butt of their jokes;
 they shake their heads at us in scorn.
15 We can't escape the constant humiliation;
 shame is written across our faces.
16 All we hear are the taunts of our mockers.
 All we see are our vengeful enemies.

17 All this has happened though we have not forgotten you.
 We have not violated your covenant.
18 Our hearts have not deserted you.
 We have not strayed from your path.
19 Yet you have crushed us in the jackal's desert home.
 You have covered us with darkness and death.
20 If we had forgotten the name of our God
 or spread our hands in prayer to foreign gods,
21 God would surely have known it,
 for he knows the secrets of every heart.
22 But for your sake we are killed every day;
 we are being slaughtered like sheep.

23 Wake up, O Lord! Why do you sleep?
 Get up! Do not reject us forever.
24 Why do you look the other way?
 Why do you ignore our suffering and oppression?
25 We collapse in the dust,
 lying face down in the dirt.
26 Rise up! Help us!
 Ransom us because of your unfailing love.

PROVERBS 22:13

The lazy person claims, "There's a lion out there! If I go outside, I might be killed!"

SEPTEMBER

1

JOB 40:1–42:17

Then the LORD said to Job,

2 "Do you still want to argue with
the Almighty?
You are God's critic, but do you
have the answers?"

3 Then Job replied to the LORD,

4 "I am nothing—how could I ever
find the answers?
I will cover my mouth with
my hand.
5 I have said too much already.
I have nothing more to say."

6 Then the LORD answered Job from
the whirlwind:

7 "Brace yourself like a man,
because I have some questions
for you,
and you must answer them.

8 "Will you discredit my justice
and condemn me just to prove
you are right?
9 Are you as strong as God?
Can you thunder with a voice
like his?
10 All right, put on your glory and
splendor,
your honor and majesty.
11 Give vent to your anger.
Let it overflow against the proud.
12 Humiliate the proud with a glance;
walk on the wicked where they
stand.
13 Bury them in the dust.
Imprison them in the world
of the dead.
14 Then even I would praise you,

for your own strength would
save you.

15 "Take a look at Behemoth,*
which I made, just as I made you.
It eats grass like an ox.
16 See its powerful loins
and the muscles of its belly.
17 Its tail is as strong as a cedar.
The sinews of its thighs are knit
tightly together.
18 Its bones are tubes of bronze.
Its limbs are bars of iron.
19 It is a prime example of God's
handiwork,
and only its Creator can
threaten it.
20 The mountains offer it their best
food,
where all the wild animals play.
21 It lies under the lotus plants,*
hidden by the reeds in the marsh.
22 The lotus plants give it shade
among the willows beside
the stream.
23 It is not disturbed by the raging
river,
not concerned when the swelling
Jordan rushes around it.
24 No one can catch it off guard
or put a ring in its nose and
lead it away.

41:1* "CAN you catch Leviathan* with
a hook
or put a noose around its jaw?
2 Can you tie it with a rope through
the nose
or pierce its jaw with a spike?
3 Will it beg you for mercy
or implore you for pity?
4 Will it agree to work for you,
to be your slave for life?
5 Can you make it a pet like a bird,
or give it to your little girls to
play with?
6 Will merchants try to buy it
to sell it in their shops?
7 Will its hide be hurt by spears

or its head by a harpoon?

8 If you lay a hand on it,
   you will certainly remember the
      battle that follows.
   You won't try that again!

9*No, it is useless to try to capture it.
   The hunter who attempts it will
      be knocked down.

10 And since no one dares to disturb it,
   who then can stand up to me?

11 Who has given me anything that I
      need to pay back?
   Everything under heaven is mine.

12 "I want to emphasize Leviathan's
      limbs
   and its enormous strength and
      graceful form.

13 Who can strip off its hide,
   and who can penetrate its double
      layer of armor?*

14 Who could pry open its jaws?
   For its teeth are terrible!

15 Its scales are like rows of shields
   tightly sealed together.

16 They are so close together
   that no air can get between them.

17 Each scale sticks tight to the next.
   They interlock and cannot be
      penetrated.

18 "When it sneezes, it flashes light!
   Its eyes are like the red of dawn.

19 Lightning leaps from its mouth;
   flames of fire flash out.

20 Smoke streams from its nostrils
   like steam from a pot heated over
      burning rushes.

21 Its breath would kindle coals,
   for flames shoot from its mouth.

22 "The tremendous strength in
      Leviathan's neck
   strikes terror wherever it goes.

23 Its flesh is hard and firm
   and cannot be penetrated.

24 Its heart is hard as rock,
   hard as a millstone.

25 When it rises, the mighty are afraid,
   gripped by terror.

26 No sword can stop it,
   no spear, dart, or javelin.

27 Iron is nothing but straw to that
      creature,
   and bronze is like rotten wood.

28 Arrows cannot make it flee.
   Stones shot from a sling are like
      bits of grass.

29 Clubs are like a blade of grass,
   and it laughs at the swish of
      javelins.

30 Its belly is covered with scales as
      sharp as glass.
   It plows up the ground as it drags
      through the mud.

31 "Leviathan makes the water boil
      with its commotion.
   It stirs the depths like a pot
      of ointment.

32 The water glistens in its wake,
   making the sea look white.

33 Nothing on earth is its equal,
   no other creature so fearless.

34 Of all the creatures, it is the proudest.
   It is the king of beasts."

42:1THEN Job replied to the LORD:

2 "I know that you can do anything,
   and no one can stop you.

3 You asked, 'Who is this that
      questions my wisdom with
      such ignorance?'
   It is I—and I was talking about
      things I knew nothing about,
      things far too wonderful for me.

4 You said, 'Listen and I will speak!
   I have some questions for you,
   and you must answer them.'

5 I had only heard about you before,
   but now I have seen you with my
      own eyes.

6 I take back everything I said,
   and I sit in dust and ashes to show
      my repentance."

7After the LORD had finished speaking to Job, he said to Eliphaz the Temanite: "I am angry with you and your two friends, for you have not spoken accurately about me, as my servant Job has. 8So take seven bulls and seven rams and go to my servant Job and offer a burnt offering for yourselves. My servant Job will pray for you, and I will accept his prayer on your behalf. I will not treat you as you deserve, for you have not spoken accurately about me, as my servant Job has." [9]So Eliphaz the Temanite, Bildad the Shuhite, and Zophar the Naamathite did as the LORD commanded them, and the LORD accepted Job's prayer.

[10]When Job prayed for his friends, the LORD restored his fortunes. In fact, the LORD gave him twice as much as before! [11]Then all his brothers, sisters, and former friends came and feasted with him in his home. And they consoled him and comforted him because of all the trials the LORD had brought against him. And each of them brought him a gift of money* and a gold ring.

[12]So the LORD blessed Job in the second half of his life even more than in the beginning. For now he had 14,000 sheep, 6,000 camels, 1,000 teams of oxen, and 1,000 female donkeys. [13]He also gave Job seven more sons and three more daughters. [14]He named his first daughter Jemimah, the second Keziah, and the third Keren-happuch. [15]In all the land no women were as lovely as the daughters of Job. And their father put them into his will along with their brothers.

[16]Job lived 140 years after that, living to see four generations of his children and grandchildren. [17]Then he died, an old man who had lived a long, full life.

40:15 The identification of Behemoth is disputed, ranging from an earthly creature to a mythical sea monster in ancient literature.   **40:21** Or *bramble bushes;* also in 40:22.   **41:1a** Verses 41:1-8 are numbered 40:25-32 in Hebrew text.   **41:1b** The identification of Leviathan is disputed, ranging from an earthly creature to a mythical sea monster in ancient literature.   **41:9** Verses 41:9-34 are numbered 41:1-26 in Hebrew text.   **41:13** As in Greek version; Hebrew reads *its bridle?*   **42:11** Hebrew *a kesitah;* the value or weight of the kesitah is no longer known.

2 CORINTHIANS 5:11-21

Because we [Paul and his co-workers] understand our fearful responsibility to the Lord, we work hard to persuade others. God knows we are sincere, and I hope you [Corinthians] know this, too. [12]Are we commending ourselves to you again? No, we are giving you a reason to be proud of us,* so you can answer those who brag about having a spectac-

ular ministry rather than having a sincere heart. [13]If it seems we are crazy, it is to bring glory to God. And if we are in our right minds, it is for your benefit. [14]**Either way, Christ's love controls us.* Since we believe that Christ died for all, we also believe that we have all died to our old life.*** [15]He died for everyone so that those who receive his new life will no longer live for themselves. Instead, they will live for Christ, who died and was raised for them.

[16]So we have stopped evaluating others from a human point of view. At one time we thought of Christ merely from a human point of view. How differently we know him now! [17]This means that anyone who belongs to Christ has become a new person. The old life is gone; a new life has begun!

[18]And all of this is a gift from God, who brought us back to himself through Christ. And God has given us this task of reconciling people to him. [19]For God was in Christ, reconciling the world to himself, no longer counting people's sins against them. And he gave us this wonderful message of reconciliation. [20]So we are Christ's ambassadors; God is making his appeal through us. We speak for Christ when we plead, "Come back to God!" [21]For God made Christ, who never sinned, to be the offering for our sin,* so that we could be made right with God through Christ.

5:12 Some manuscripts read *proud of yourselves.*   **5:14a** Or *urges us on.*   **5:14b** Greek *Since one died for all, then all died.*   **5:21** Or *to become sin itself.*

PSALM 45:1-17

For the choir director: A love song to be sung to the tune "Lilies." A psalm of the descendants of Korah.*

[1] **B**eautiful words stir my heart.
    I will recite a lovely poem about the king,
    for my tongue is like the pen of a skillful poet.

[2] You are the most handsome of all.
    Gracious words stream from your lips.

God himself has blessed you
forever.

³ Put on your sword, O mighty warrior!
You are so glorious, so majestic!

⁴ In your majesty, ride out to victory,
defending truth, humility, and
justice.
Go forth to perform awe-
inspiring deeds!

⁵ Your arrows are sharp, piercing
your enemies' hearts.
The nations fall beneath
your feet.

⁶ Your throne, O God,* endures
forever and ever.
You rule with a scepter of justice.

⁷ You love justice and hate evil.
Therefore God, your God, has
anointed you,
pouring out the oil of joy on you
more than on anyone else.

⁸ Myrrh, aloes, and cassia perfume
your robes.
In ivory palaces the music of
strings entertains you.

⁹ Kings' daughters are among your
noble women.
At your right side stands the queen,
wearing jewelry of finest gold
from Ophir!

¹⁰ Listen to me, O royal daughter; take
to heart what I say.
Forget your people and your
family far away.

¹¹ For your royal husband delights in
your beauty;
honor him, for he is your lord.

¹² The princess of Tyre* will shower
you with gifts.
The wealthy will beg your favor.

¹³ The bride, a princess, looks glorious
in her golden gown.

¹⁴ In her beautiful robes, she is led
to the king,
accompanied by her bridesmaids.

¹⁵ What a joyful and enthusiastic
procession
as they enter the king's palace!

¹⁶ Your sons will become kings like
their father.

You will make them rulers over
many lands.

¹⁷ I will bring honor to your name in
every generation.
Therefore, the nations will praise
you forever and ever.

45:TITLE Hebrew *maskil*. This may be a literary or musical term.   **45:6** Or *Your divine throne.*   **45:12** Hebrew *The daughter of Tyre.*

PROVERBS 22:14
The mouth of an immoral woman is a dangerous trap; those who make the LORD angry will fall into it.

SEPTEMBER 2

ECCLESIASTES 1:1–3:22
These are the words of the Teacher,* King David's son, who ruled in Jerusalem.

²"Everything is meaningless," says the Teacher, "completely meaningless!"

³What do people get for all their hard work under the sun? ⁴Generations come and generations go, but the earth never changes. ⁵The sun rises and the sun sets, then hurries around to rise again. ⁶The wind blows south, and then turns north. Around and around it goes, blowing in circles. ⁷Rivers run into the sea, but the sea is never full. Then the water returns again to the rivers and flows out again to the sea. ⁸Everything is wearisome beyond description. No matter how much we see, we are never satisfied. No matter how much we hear, we are not content.

⁹History merely repeats itself. It has all been done before. Nothing under the sun is truly new. ¹⁰Sometimes people say, "Here is something new!" But actually it is old; nothing is ever truly new. ¹¹We don't remember what happened in the past, and in future generations, no one will re-member what we are doing now.

¹²I, the Teacher, was king of Israel,

and I lived in Jerusalem. [13]I devoted myself to search for understanding and to explore by wisdom everything being done under heaven. I soon discovered that God has dealt a tragic existence to the human race. [14]I observed everything going on under the sun, and really, it is all meaningless—like chasing the wind.

[15] What is wrong cannot be made right.
   What is missing cannot be
      recovered.

[16]I said to myself, "Look, I am wiser than any of the kings who ruled in Jerusalem before me. I have greater wisdom and knowledge than any of them." [17]So I set out to learn everything from wisdom to madness and folly. But I learned firsthand that pursuing all this is like chasing the wind.

[18] The greater my wisdom, the greater
      my grief.
   To increase knowledge only
      increases sorrow.

[2:1]I SAID to myself, "Come on, let's try pleasure. Let's look for the 'good things' in life." But I found that this, too, was meaningless. [2]So I said, "Laughter is silly. What good does it do to seek pleasure?" [3]After much thought, I decided to cheer myself with wine. And while still seeking wisdom, I clutched at foolishness. In this way, I tried to experience the only happiness most people find during their brief life in this world.

[4]I also tried to find meaning by building huge homes for myself and by planting beautiful vineyards. [5]I made gardens and parks, filling them with all kinds of fruit trees. [6]I built reservoirs to collect the water to irrigate my many flourishing groves. [7]I bought slaves, both men and women, and others were born into my household. I also owned large herds and flocks, more than any of the kings who had lived in Jerusalem before me. [8]I collected great sums of silver and gold, the treasure of many kings and provinces. I hired wonderful singers, both men and women, and had many beautiful concubines. I had everything a man could desire!

[9]So I became greater than all who had lived in Jerusalem before me, and my wisdom never failed me. [10]Anything I wanted, I would take. I denied myself no pleasure. I even found great pleasure in hard work, a reward for all my labors. [11]But as I looked at everything I had worked so hard to accomplish, it was all so meaningless—like chasing the wind. There was nothing really worthwhile anywhere.

[12]So I decided to compare wisdom with foolishness and madness (for who can do this better than I, the king?*). [13]I thought, "Wisdom is better than foolishness, just as light is better than darkness. [14]For the wise can see where they are going, but fools walk in the dark." Yet I saw that the wise and the foolish share the same fate. [15]Both will die. So I said to myself, "Since I will end up the same as the fool, what's the value of all my wisdom? This is all so meaningless!" [16]For the wise and the foolish both die. The wise will not be remembered any longer than the fool. In the days to come, both will be forgotten.

[17]So I came to hate life because everything done here under the sun is so troubling. Everything is meaningless—like chasing the wind.

[18]I came to hate all my hard work here on earth, for I must leave to others everything I have earned. [19]And who can tell whether my successors will be wise or foolish? Yet they will control everything I have gained by my skill and hard work under the sun. How meaningless! [20]So I gave up in despair, questioning the value of all my hard work in this world.

[21]Some people work wisely with knowledge and skill, then must leave the fruit of their efforts to someone who hasn't worked for it. This, too, is meaningless, a great tragedy. [22]So what do people get in this life for all their hard work and anxiety? [23]Their days of labor are filled with pain and grief; even at night their minds cannot rest. It is all meaningless.

²⁴So I decided there is nothing better than to enjoy food and drink and to find satisfaction in work. Then I realized that these pleasures are from the hand of God. ²⁵For who can eat or enjoy anything apart from him?* ²⁶God gives wisdom, knowledge, and joy to those who please him. But if a sinner becomes wealthy, God takes the wealth away and gives it to those who please him. This, too, is meaningless—like chasing the wind.

3:1 FOR everything there is a season,
    a time for every activity under
    heaven.
² A time to be born and a time to die.
    A time to plant and a time
    to harvest.
³ A time to kill and a time to heal.
    A time to tear down and a time
    to build up.
⁴ A time to cry and a time to laugh.
    A time to grieve and a time
    to dance.
⁵ A time to scatter stones and a time
    to gather stones.
    A time to embrace and a time
    to turn away.
⁶ A time to search and a time to quit
    searching.
    A time to keep and a time to
    throw away.
⁷ A time to tear and a time to mend.
    A time to be quiet and a time
    to speak.
⁸ A time to love and a time to hate.
    A time for war and a time for
    peace.

⁹What do people really get for all their hard work? ¹⁰I have seen the burden God has placed on us all. ¹¹Yet God has made everything beautiful for its own time. He has planted eternity in the human heart, but even so, people cannot see the whole scope of God's work from beginning to end. ¹²So I concluded there is nothing better than to be happy and enjoy ourselves as long as we can. ¹³And people should eat and drink and enjoy the fruits of their labor, for these are gifts from God. ¹⁴And I know that whatever God does

is final. Nothing can be added to it or taken from it. God's purpose is that people should fear him. ¹⁵What is happening now has happened before, and what will happen in the future has happened before, because God makes the same things happen over and over again.

¹⁶I also noticed that under the sun there is evil in the courtroom. Yes, even the courts of law are corrupt! ¹⁷I said to myself, "In due season God will judge everyone, both good and bad, for all their deeds."

¹⁸I also thought about the human condition—how God proves to people that they are like animals. ¹⁹For people and animals share the same fate—both breathe* and both must die. So people have no real advantage over the animals. How meaningless! ²⁰Both go to the same place—they came from dust and they return to dust. ²¹For who can prove that the human spirit goes up and the spirit of animals goes down into the earth? ²²So I saw that there is nothing better for people than to be happy in their work. That is why we are here! No one will bring us back from death to enjoy life after we die.

1:1 Hebrew *Qoheleth;* this term is rendered "the Teacher" throughout this book.   2:12 The meaning of the Hebrew is uncertain.   2:25 As in Greek and Syriac versions; Hebrew reads *apart from me?*   3:19 Or *both have the same spirit.*

2 CORINTHIANS 6:1-13

As God's partners,* we [Paul and his co-workers] beg you [Corinthians] not to accept this marvelous gift of God's kindness and then ignore it. ²For God says,

"At just the right time, I heard you.
    On the day of salvation, I helped
    you."*

Indeed, the "right time" is now. Today is the day of salvation.

³We live in such a way that no one will stumble because of us, and no one will find fault with our ministry. ⁴In everything we do, we show that we are true ministers of God. We patiently endure troubles and hardships and calamities of every kind. ⁵We have been beaten, been

put in prison, faced angry mobs, worked to exhaustion, endured sleepless nights, and gone without food. 6We prove ourselves by our purity, our understanding, our patience, our kindness, by the Holy Spirit within us,* and by our sincere love. 7We faithfully preach the truth. God's power is working in us. We use the weapons of righteousness in the right hand for attack and the left hand for defense. 8We serve God whether people honor us or despise us, whether they slander us or praise us. We are honest, but they call us impostors. 9We are ignored, even though we are well known. We live close to death, but we are still alive. We have been beaten, but we have not been killed. 10Our hearts ache, but we always keep joy. We are poor, but we give spiritual riches to others. We own nothing, and yet we have everything.

11Oh, dear Corinthian friends! We have spoken honestly with you, and our hearts are open to you. 12There is no lack of love on our part, but you have withheld your love from us. 13I am asking you to respond as if you were my own children. Open your hearts to us!

6:1 Or As we work together.   **6:2** Isa 49:8 (Greek version).
6:6 Or by our holiness of spirit.

PSALM 46:1-11
*For the choir director: A song of the descendants of Korah, to be sung by soprano voices.**

1 **God is our refuge and strength,
    always ready to help in times
    of trouble.**
2 **So we will not fear when
    earthquakes come
    and the mountains crumble
    into the sea.**
3 Let the oceans roar and foam.
    Let the mountains tremble
        as the waters surge!   *Interlude*

4 A river brings joy to the city
        of our God,
    the sacred home of the Most High.
5 God dwells in that city; it cannot
        be destroyed.

From the very break of day, God
    will protect it.
6 The nations are in chaos,
    and their kingdoms crumble!
God's voice thunders,
    and the earth melts!
7 The LORD of Heaven's Armies is
        here among us;
    the God of Israel* is our fortress.
                                Interlude

8 Come, see the glorious works
        of the LORD:
    See how he brings destruction
        upon the world.
9 He causes wars to end throughout
        the earth.
    He breaks the bow and snaps
        the spear;
    he burns the shields with fire.

10 "Be still, and know that I am God!
    I will be honored by every nation.
    I will be honored throughout the
        world."

11 The LORD of Heaven's Armies
        is here among us;
    the God of Israel is our fortress.
                                Interlude

46:TITLE Hebrew according to alamoth.   **46:7** Hebrew of Jacob; also in 46:11. See note on 44:4.

PROVERBS 22:15
A youngster's heart is filled with foolishness, but physical discipline will drive it far away.

SEPTEMBER
3

ECCLESIASTES 4:1–6:12
Again, I [the Teacher] observed all the oppression that takes place under the sun. I saw the tears of the oppressed, with no one to comfort them. The oppressors have great power, and their victims are helpless. 2So I concluded that

the dead are better off than the living. [3]But most fortunate of all are those who are not yet born. For they have not seen all the evil that is done under the sun.

[4]Then I observed that most people are motivated to success because they envy their neighbors. But this, too, is meaningless—like chasing the wind.

[5] "Fools fold their idle hands,
     leading them to ruin."

[6]And yet,

"Better to have one handful with
     quietness
     than two handfuls with hard work
     and chasing the wind."

[7]I observed yet another example of something meaningless under the sun. [8]This is the case of a man who is all alone, without a child or a brother, yet who works hard to gain as much wealth as he can. But then he asks himself, "Who am I working for? Why am I giving up so much pleasure now?" It is all so meaningless and depressing.

[9]Two people are better off than one, for they can help each other succeed. [10]If one person falls, the other can reach out and help. But someone who falls alone is in real trouble. [11]Likewise, two people lying close together can keep each other warm. But how can one be warm alone? [12]A person standing alone can be attacked and defeated, but two can stand back-to-back and conquer. Three are even better, for a triple-braided cord is not easily broken.

[13]It is better to be a poor but wise youth than an old and foolish king who refuses all advice. [14]Such a youth could rise from poverty and succeed. He might even become king, though he has been in prison. [15]But then everyone rushes to the side of yet another youth* who replaces him. [16]Endless crowds stand around him,* but then another generation grows up and rejects him, too. So it is all meaningless—like chasing the wind.

[5:1]As you enter the house of God, keep your ears open and your mouth shut. It is

evil to make mindless offerings to God. [2]Don't make rash promises, and don't be hasty in bringing matters before God. After all, God is in heaven, and you are here on earth. So let your words be few.

[3] Too much activity gives you restless dreams; too many words make you a fool.

[4]When you make a promise to God, don't delay in following through, for God takes no pleasure in fools. Keep all the promises you make to him. [5]It is better to say nothing than to make a promise and not keep it. [6]Don't let your mouth make you sin. And don't defend yourself by telling the Temple messenger that the promise you made was a mistake. That would make God angry, and he might wipe out everything you have achieved.

[7]Talk is cheap, like daydreams and other useless activities. Fear God instead.

[8]Don't be surprised if you see a poor person being oppressed by the powerful and if justice is being miscarried throughout the land. For every official is under orders from higher up, and matters of justice get lost in red tape and bureaucracy. [9]Even the king milks the land for his own profit!*

[10]Those who love money will never have enough. How meaningless to think that wealth brings true happiness! [11]The more you have, the more people come to help you spend it. So what good is wealth—except perhaps to watch it slip through your fingers!

[12]People who work hard sleep well, whether they eat little or much. But the rich seldom get a good night's sleep.

[13]There is another serious problem I have seen under the sun. Hoarding riches harms the saver. [14]Money is put into risky investments that turn sour, and everything is lost. In the end, there is nothing left to pass on to one's children. [15]We all come to the end of our lives as naked and empty-handed as on the day we were born. We can't take our riches with us.

[16]And this, too, is a very serious problem. People leave this world no better

off than when they came. All their hard work is for nothing—like working for the wind. [17] Throughout their lives, they live under a cloud—frustrated, discouraged, and angry.

[18] Even so, I have noticed one thing, at least, that is good. It is good for people to eat, drink, and enjoy their work under the sun during the short life God has given them, and to accept their lot in life. [19] And it is a good thing to receive wealth from God and the good health to enjoy it. To enjoy your work and accept your lot in life—this is indeed a gift from God. [20] God keeps such people so busy enjoying life that they take no time to brood over the past.

[6:1] THERE is another serious tragedy I have seen under the sun, and it weighs heavily on humanity. [2] God gives some people great wealth and honor and everything they could ever want, but then he doesn't give them the chance to enjoy these things. They die, and someone else, even a stranger, ends up enjoying their wealth! This is meaningless—a sickening tragedy.

[3] A man might have a hundred children and live to be very old. But if he finds no satisfaction in life and doesn't even get a decent burial, it would have been better for him to be born dead. [4] His birth would have been meaningless, and he would have ended in darkness. He wouldn't even have had a name, [5] and he would never have seen the sun or known of its existence. Yet he would have had more peace than in growing up to be an unhappy man. [6] He might live a thousand years twice over but still not find contentment. And since he must die like everyone else—well, what's the use?

[7] All people spend their lives scratching for food, but they never seem to have enough. [8] So are wise people really better off than fools? Do poor people gain anything by being wise and knowing how to act in front of others?

[9] Enjoy what you have rather than desiring what you don't have. Just dreaming about nice things is meaningless—like chasing the wind.

[10] Everything has already been decided. It was known long ago what each person would be. So there's no use arguing with God about your destiny.

[11] The more words you speak, the less they mean. So what good are they?

[12] In the few days of our meaningless lives, who knows how our days can best be spent? Our lives are like a shadow. Who can tell what will happen on this earth after we are gone?

4:15 Hebrew *the second youth.*   **4:16** Hebrew *There is no end to all the people, to all those who are before them.* **5:9** The meaning of the Hebrew in verses 8 and 9 is uncertain.

2 CORINTHIANS 6:14–7:7

Don't team up with those who are unbelievers. How can righteousness be a partner with wickedness? How can light live with darkness? [15] What harmony can there be between Christ and the devil*? How can a believer be a partner with an unbeliever? [16] And what union can there be between God's temple and idols? For we are the temple of the living God. As God said:

> "I will live in them
>   and walk among them.
> I will be their God,
>   and they will be my people.*
> [17] Therefore, come out from among
>   unbelievers,
>   and separate yourselves from
>   them, says the LORD.
> Don't touch their filthy things,
>   and I will welcome you.*
> [18] And I will be your Father,
>   and you will be my sons and
>   daughters,
>   says the LORD Almighty.*"

[7:1] BECAUSE we have these promises, dear friends, let us cleanse ourselves from everything that can defile our body or spirit. And let us work toward complete holiness because we fear God.

[2] Please open your hearts to us. We have not done wrong to anyone, nor led anyone astray, nor taken advantage of anyone. [3] I'm not saying this to condemn

you. I said before that you are in our hearts, and we live or die together with you. ⁴I have the highest confidence in you, and I take great pride in you. You have greatly encouraged me and made me happy despite all our troubles.

⁵When we arrived in Macedonia, there was no rest for us. We faced conflict from every direction, with battles on the outside and fear on the inside. ⁶But God, who encourages those who are discouraged, encouraged us by the arrival of Titus. ⁷His presence was a joy, but so was the news he brought of the encouragement he received from you. When he told us how much you long to see me, and how sorry you are for what happened, and how loyal you are to me, I was filled with joy!

6:15 Greek *Beliar;* various other manuscripts render this proper name of the devil as *Belian, Beliab,* or *Belial.*
6:16 Lev 26:12; Ezek 37:27.   **6:17** Isa 52:11; Ezek 20:34 (Greek version).   **6:18** 2 Sam 7:14.

PSALM 47:1-9

For the choir director: A psalm of the descendants of Korah.

¹ **C**ome, everyone! Clap your hands!
     Shout to God with joyful praise!
² For the LORD Most High is awesome.
     He is the great King of all the
          earth.
³ He subdues the nations before us,
     putting our enemies beneath
          our feet.
⁴ He chose the Promised Land as our
          inheritance,
     the proud possession of Jacob's
          descendants, whom he loves.
                                Interlude

⁵ God has ascended with a mighty
          shout.
     The LORD has ascended with
          trumpets blaring.
⁶ Sing praises to God, sing praises;
     sing praises to our King, sing
          praises!
⁷ For God is the King over all the earth.
     Praise him with a psalm!
⁸ God reigns above the nations,
     sitting on his holy throne.

⁹ The rulers of the world have
          gathered together
     with the people of the God
          of Abraham.
   For all the kings of the earth belong
          to God.
     He is highly honored everywhere.

PROVERBS 22:16

A person who gets ahead by oppressing the poor or by showering gifts on the rich will end in poverty.

SEPTEMBER 4

ECCLESIASTES 7:1-9:18

A good reputation is more valuable
          than costly perfume.
     And the day you die is better than
          the day you are born.
² Better to spend your time at funerals
          than at parties.
     After all, everyone dies—
     .so the living should take this
          to heart.
³ Sorrow is better than laughter,
     for sadness has a refining
          influence on us.
⁴ A wise person thinks a lot
          about death,
     while a fool thinks only about
          having a good time.

⁵ Better to be criticized by a wise
          person
     than to be praised by a fool.
⁶ A fool's laughter is quickly gone,
     like thorns crackling in a fire.
     This also is meaningless.

⁷ Extortion turns wise people into fools,
     and bribes corrupt the heart.

⁸ Finishing is better than starting.
     Patience is better than pride.

⁹ Control your temper,
     for anger labels you a fool.

[10] Don't long for "the good old days." This is not wise.

[11] Wisdom is even better when you
have money.
Both are a benefit as you go
through life.
[12] Wisdom and money can get you
almost anything,
but only wisdom can save
your life.

[13] Accept the way God does things,
for who can straighten what he
has made crooked?
[14] Enjoy prosperity while you can,
but when hard times strike,
realize that both come
from God.
Remember that nothing is certain
in this life.

[15] I have seen everything in this meaningless life, including the death of good young people and the long life of wicked people. [16] So don't be too good or too wise! Why destroy yourself? [17] On the other hand, don't be too wicked either. Don't be a fool! Why die before your time? [18] Pay attention to these instructions, for anyone who fears God will avoid both extremes.*

[19] One wise person is stronger than ten leading citizens of a town!

[20] Not a single person on earth is always good and never sins.

[21] Don't eavesdrop on others—you may hear your servant curse you. [22] For you know how often you yourself have cursed others.

[23] I have always tried my best to let wisdom guide my thoughts and actions. I said to myself, "I am determined to be wise." But it didn't work. [24] Wisdom is always distant and difficult to find. [25] I searched everywhere, determined to find wisdom and to understand the reason for things. I was determined to prove to myself that wickedness is stupid and that foolishness is madness.

[26] I discovered that a seductive woman* is a trap more bitter than death. Her passion is a snare, and her soft hands are chains. Those who are pleasing to God will escape her, but sinners will be caught in her snare.

[27] "This is my conclusion," says the Teacher. "I discovered this after looking at the matter from every possible angle. [28] Though I have searched repeatedly, I have not found what I was looking for. Only one out of a thousand men is virtuous, but not one woman! [29] But I did find this: God created people to be virtuous, but they have each turned to follow their own downward path."

[8:1] How wonderful to be wise,
to analyze and interpret things.
Wisdom lights up a person's face,
softening its harshness.

[2] Obey the king since you vowed to God that you would. [3] Don't try to avoid doing your duty, and don't stand with those who plot evil, for the king can do whatever he wants. [4] His command is backed by great power. No one can resist or question it. [5] Those who obey him will not be punished. Those who are wise will find a time and a way to do what is right, [6] for there is a time and a way for everything, even when a person is in trouble.

[7] Indeed, how can people avoid what they don't know is going to happen? [8] None of us can hold back our spirit from departing. None of us has the power to prevent the day of our death. There is no escaping that obligation, that dark battle. And in the face of death, wickedness will certainly not rescue the wicked.

[9] I have thought deeply about all that goes on here under the sun, where people have the power to hurt each other. [10] I have seen wicked people buried with honor. Yet they were the very ones who frequented the Temple and are now praised* in the same city where they committed their crimes! This, too, is meaningless. [11] When a crime is not punished quickly, people feel it is safe to do wrong. [12] But even though a person sins a hundred times and still lives a long time, I know that those who fear God will be better off. [13] The wicked will

not prosper, for they do not fear God. Their days will never grow long like the evening shadows.

[14]And this is not all that is meaningless in our world. In this life, good people are often treated as though they were wicked, and wicked people are often treated as though they were good. This is so meaningless!

[15]So I recommend having fun, because there is nothing better for people in this world than to eat, drink, and enjoy life. That way they will experience some happiness along with all the hard work God gives them under the sun.

[16]In my search for wisdom and in my observation of people's burdens here on earth, I discovered that there is ceaseless activity, day and night. [17]I realized that no one can discover everything God is doing under the sun. Not even the wisest people discover everything, no matter what they claim.

[9:1]THIS, too, I carefully explored: Even though the actions of godly and wise people are in God's hands, no one knows whether God will show them favor. [2]The same destiny ultimately awaits everyone, whether righteous or wicked, good or bad,* ceremonially clean or unclean, religious or irreligious. Good people receive the same treatment as sinners, and people who make promises to God are treated like people who don't.

[3]It seems so tragic that everyone under the sun suffers the same fate. That is why people are not more careful to be good. Instead, they choose their own mad course, for they have no hope. There is nothing ahead but death anyway. [4]There is hope only for the living. As they say, "It's better to be a live dog than a dead lion!"

[5]The living at least know they will die, but the dead know nothing. They have no further reward, nor are they remembered. [6]Whatever they did in their lifetime—loving, hating, envying—is all long gone. They no longer play a part in anything here on earth. [7]So go ahead.

Eat your food with joy, and drink your wine with a happy heart, for God approves of this! [8]Wear fine clothes, with a splash of cologne!

[9]Live happily with the woman you love through all the meaningless days of life that God has given you under the sun. The wife God gives you is your reward for all your earthly toil. [10]Whatever you do, do well. For when you go to the grave,* there will be no work or planning or knowledge or wisdom.

[11]I have observed something else under the sun. The fastest runner doesn't always win the race, and the strongest warrior doesn't always win the battle. The wise sometimes go hungry, and the skillful are not necessarily wealthy. And those who are educated don't always lead successful lives. It is all decided by chance, by being in the right place at the right time.

[12]People can never predict when hard times might come. Like fish in a net or birds in a trap, people are caught by sudden tragedy.

[13]Here is another bit of wisdom that has impressed me as I have watched the way our world works. [14]There was a small town with only a few people, and a great king came with his army and besieged it. [15]A poor, wise man knew how to save the town, and so it was rescued. But afterward no one thought to thank him. [16]So even though wisdom is better than strength, those who are wise will be despised if they are poor. What they say will not be appreciated for long.

[17] Better to hear the quiet words
        of a wise person
    than the shouts of a foolish
        king.
[18] Better to have wisdom than
        weapons of war,
    but one sinner can destroy much
        that is good.

7:18 Or *will follow them both.*   7:26 Hebrew *a woman.*
8:10 As in some Hebrew manuscripts and Greek version; many Hebrew manuscripts read *and are forgotten.*   9:2 As in Greek and Syriac versions and Latin Vulgate; Hebrew lacks *or bad.*   9:10 Hebrew *to Sheol.*

2 CORINTHIANS 7:8-16

I [Paul] am not sorry that I sent that severe letter to you [Corinthians], though I was sorry at first, for I know it was painful to you for a little while. ⁹Now I am glad I sent it, not because it hurt you, but because the pain caused you to repent and change your ways. It was the kind of sorrow God wants his people to have, so you were not harmed by us in any way. **¹⁰For the kind of sorrow God wants us to experience leads us away from sin and results in salvation. There's no regret for that kind of sorrow. But worldly sorrow, which lacks repentance, results in spiritual death.**

¹¹Just see what this godly sorrow produced in you! Such earnestness, such concern to clear yourselves, such indignation, such alarm, such longing to see me, such zeal, and such a readiness to punish wrong. You showed that you have done everything necessary to make things right. ¹²My purpose, then, was not to write about who did the wrong or who was wronged. I wrote to you so that in the sight of God you could see for yourselves how loyal you are to us. ¹³We have been greatly encouraged by this.

In addition to our own encouragement, we were especially delighted to see how happy Titus was about the way all of you welcomed him and set his mind* at ease. ¹⁴I had told him how proud I was of you—and you didn't disappoint me. I have always told you the truth, and now my boasting to Titus has also proved true! ¹⁵Now he cares for you more than ever when he remembers the way all of you obeyed him and welcomed him with such fear and deep respect. ¹⁶I am very happy now because I have complete confidence in you.

7:13 Greek *his spirit.*

PSALM 48:1-14

A song. A psalm of the descendants of Korah.

¹ **H**ow great is the LORD,
how deserving of praise,
in the city of our God,
which sits on his holy mountain!

² It is high and magnificent;
the whole earth rejoices to see it!
Mount Zion, the holy mountain,*
is the city of the great King!
³ God himself is in Jerusalem's towers,
revealing himself as its defender.

⁴ The kings of the earth joined forces
and advanced against the city.
⁵ But when they saw it, they were
stunned;
they were terrified and ran away.
⁶ They were gripped with terror
and writhed in pain like a woman
in labor.
⁷ You destroyed them like the mighty
ships of Tarshish
shattered by a powerful east wind.

⁸ We had heard of the city's glory,
but now we have seen it
ourselves—
the city of the LORD of Heaven's
Armies.
It is the city of our God;
he will make it safe forever.
                                    Interlude

⁹ O God, we meditate on your
unfailing love
as we worship in your Temple.
¹⁰ As your name deserves, O God,
you will be praised to the ends
of the earth.
Your strong right hand is filled
with victory.
¹¹ Let the people on Mount Zion
rejoice.
Let all the towns of Judah be glad
because of your justice.

¹² Go, inspect the city of Jerusalem.*
Walk around and count the
many towers.
¹³ Take note of the fortified walls,
and tour all the citadels,
that you may describe them
to future generations.
¹⁴ For that is what God is like.
He is our God forever and ever,
and he will guide us until we die.

48:2 Or *Mount Zion, in the far north;* Hebrew reads *Mount Zion, the heights of Zaphon.* 48:12 Hebrew *Zion.*

PROVERBS 22:17-19

Listen to the words of the wise; apply your heart to my instruction. For it is good to keep these sayings in your heart and always ready on your lips. I am teaching you today—yes, you—so you will trust in the LORD.

SEPTEMBER 5

ECCLESIASTES 10:1–12:14

As dead flies cause even a bottle
of perfume to stink,
so a little foolishness spoils great
wisdom and honor.

2 A wise person chooses the right road;
a fool takes the wrong one.

3 You can identify fools
just by the way they walk down
the street!

4 If your boss is angry at you, don't quit!
A quiet spirit can overcome even
great mistakes.

5 There is another evil I have seen under the sun. Kings and rulers make a grave mistake 6 when they give great authority to foolish people and low positions to people of proven worth. 7 I have even seen servants riding horseback like princes—and princes walking like servants!

8 When you dig a well,
you might fall in.
When you demolish an old wall,
you could be bitten by a snake.

9 When you work in a quarry,
stones might fall and crush you.
When you chop wood,
there is danger with each stroke
of your ax.

10 Using a dull ax requires great
strength,
so sharpen the blade.
That's the value of wisdom;
it helps you succeed.

11 If a snake bites before you charm it,
what's the use of being a snake
charmer?

12 Wise words bring approval,
but fools are destroyed by their
own words.

13 Fools base their thoughts on foolish
assumptions,
so their conclusions will be
wicked madness;
14   they chatter on and on.

No one really knows what is going
to happen;
no one can predict the future.

15 Fools are so exhausted by a little work
that they can't even find their
way home.

16 What sorrow for the land ruled
by a servant,*
the land whose leaders feast
in the morning.

17 Happy is the land whose king
is a noble leader
and whose leaders feast at the
proper time
to gain strength for their work,
not to get drunk.

18 Laziness leads to a sagging roof;
idleness leads to a leaky house.

19 A party gives laughter,
wine gives happiness,
and money gives everything!

20 Never make light of the king, even
in your thoughts.
And don't make fun of the
powerful, even in your own
bedroom.
For a little bird might deliver your
message
and tell them what you said.

11:1 SEND your grain across the seas,
and in time, profits will flow
back to you.*

² But divide your investments among
  many places,*
    for you do not know what risks
      might lie ahead.

³ When clouds are heavy, the rains
  come down.
    Whether a tree falls north or
      south, it stays where it falls.

⁴ Farmers who wait for perfect
  weather never plant.
    If they watch every cloud, they
      never harvest.

⁵Just as you cannot understand the
path of the wind or the mystery of a tiny
baby growing in its mother's womb,* so
you cannot understand the activity of
God, who does all things.

⁶Plant your seed in the morning and
keep busy all afternoon, for you don't
know if profit will come from one activity or another—or maybe both.

⁷Light is sweet; how pleasant to see a
new day dawning.

⁸When people live to be very old, let
them rejoice in every day of life. But let
them also remember there will be many
dark days. Everything still to come is
meaningless.

⁹Young people,* it's wonderful to be
young! Enjoy every minute of it. Do
everything you want to do; take it all in.
But remember that you must give an account to God for everything you do. ¹⁰So
refuse to worry, and keep your body
healthy. But remember that youth, with
a whole life before you, is meaningless.

¹²:¹Don't let the excitement of youth
cause you to forget your Creator.
Honor him in your youth before you
grow old and say, "Life is not pleasant
anymore."** ²Remember him before the
light of the sun, moon, and stars is dim to
your old eyes, and rain clouds continually darken your sky. ³Remember him
before your legs—the guards of your
house—start to tremble; and before your
shoulders—the strong men—stoop. Remember him before your teeth—your
few remaining servants—stop grinding;

and before your eyes—the women looking through the windows—see dimly.

⁴Remember him before the door to
life's opportunities is closed and the
sound of work fades. Now you rise at
the first chirping of the birds, but then
all their sounds will grow faint.

⁵Remember him before you become
fearful of falling and worry about danger in the streets; before your hair turns
white like an almond tree in bloom, and
you drag along without energy like a dying grasshopper, and the caperberry no
longer inspires sexual desire. Remember him before you near the grave, your
everlasting home, when the mourners
will weep at your funeral.

⁶Yes, remember your Creator now
while you are young, before the silver
cord of life snaps and the golden bowl
is broken. Don't wait until the water
jar is smashed at the spring and the pul-
ley is broken at the well. ⁷For then the
dust will return to the earth, and the
spirit will return to God who gave it.

⁸"Everything is meaningless," says
the Teacher, "completely meaningless."

⁹Keep this in mind: The Teacher was
considered wise, and he taught the people everything he knew. He listened
carefully to many proverbs, studying and
classifying them. ¹⁰The Teacher sought
to find just the right words to express
truths clearly.*

¹¹The words of the wise are like cattle
prods—painful but helpful. Their collected sayings are like a nail-studded
stick with which a shepherd* drives the
sheep.

¹²But, my child,* let me give you some
further advice: Be careful, for writing
books is endless, and much study wears
you out.

¹³That's the whole story. Here now is
my final conclusion: Fear God and obey
his commands, for this is everyone's
duty. ¹⁴God will judge us for everything
we do, including every secret thing,
whether good or bad.

10:16 Or *a child.*   11:1 Or *Give generously, / for your gifts
will return to you later.* Hebrew reads *Throw your bread on
the waters, / for after many days you will find it again.*

11:2 Hebrew *among seven or even eight.*   11:5 Some manuscripts read *Just as you cannot understand how breath comes to a tiny baby in its mother's womb.*
11:9 Hebrew *Young man.*   12:10 Or *sought to write what was upright and true.*   12:11 Or *one shepherd.*
12:12 Hebrew *my son.*

2 CORINTHIANS 8:1-15

Now I [Paul] want you to know, dear brothers and sisters,* what God in his kindness has done through the churches in Macedonia. ²They are being tested by many troubles, and they are very poor. But they are also filled with abundant joy, which has overflowed in rich generosity.

³For I can testify that they gave not only what they could afford, but far more. And they did it of their own free will. ⁴They begged us again and again for the privilege of sharing in the gift for the believers in Jerusalem. ⁵They even did more than we had hoped, for their first action was to give themselves to the Lord and to us, just as God wanted them to do.

⁶So we have urged Titus, who encouraged your giving in the first place, to return to you and encourage you to finish this ministry of giving. ⁷Since you excel in so many ways—in your faith, your gifted speakers, your knowledge, your enthusiasm, and your love from us*—I want you to excel also in this gracious act of giving.

⁸I am not commanding you to do this. But I am testing how genuine your love is by comparing it with the eagerness of the other churches.

⁹You know the generous grace of our Lord Jesus Christ. Though he was rich, yet for your sakes he became poor, so that by his poverty he could make you rich.

¹⁰Here is my advice: It would be good for you to finish what you started a year ago. Last year you were the first who wanted to give, and you were the first to begin doing it. ¹¹Now you should finish what you started. Let the eagerness you showed in the beginning be matched now by your giving. Give in proportion to what you have. ¹²Whatever you give is acceptable if you give it eagerly. And give according to what you have, not what you don't have. ¹³Of course, I don't mean your giving should make life easy for others and hard for yourselves. I only mean that there should be some equality. ¹⁴Right now you have plenty and can help those who are in need. Later, they will have plenty and can share with you when you need it. In this way, things will be equal. ¹⁵As the Scriptures say,

"Those who gathered a lot had
    nothing left over,
and those who gathered only a
    little had enough."*

8:1 Greek *brothers.*   8:7 Some manuscripts read *your love for us.*   8:15 Exod 16:18.

PSALM 49:1-20

For the choir director: A psalm of the descendants of Korah.

¹ Listen to this, all you people!
    Pay attention, everyone in the
        world!
² High and low,
    rich and poor—listen!
³ For my words are wise,
    and my thoughts are filled
        with insight.
⁴ I listen carefully to many proverbs
    and solve riddles with inspiration
        from a harp.

⁵ Why should I fear when trouble
        comes,
    when enemies surround me?
⁶ They trust in their wealth
    and boast of great riches.
⁷ Yet they cannot redeem themselves
        from death*
    by paying a ransom to God.
⁸ Redemption does not come
        so easily,
    for no one can ever pay enough
⁹ to live forever
    and never see the grave.

¹⁰ Those who are wise must finally die,
    just like the foolish and senseless,
        leaving all their wealth behind.
¹¹ The grave is their eternal home,
    where they will stay forever.

They may name their estates after
  themselves,
¹² but their fame will not last.
  They will die, just like animals.
¹³ This is the fate of fools,
  though they are remembered as
    being wise.*   *Interlude*

¹⁴ Like sheep, they are led to
    the grave,*
  where death will be their
    shepherd.
  In the morning the godly will rule
    over them.
  Their bodies will rot in the grave,
    far from their grand estates.
¹⁵ But as for me, God will redeem my
    life.
  He will snatch me from the power
    of the grave.   *Interlude*

¹⁶ So don't be dismayed when the
    wicked grow rich
  and their homes become ever
    more splendid.
¹⁷ For when they die, they take nothing
    with them.
  Their wealth will not follow them
    into the grave.
¹⁸ In this life they consider themselves
    fortunate
  and are applauded for their
    success.
¹⁹ But they will die like all before them
  and never again see the light
    of day.
²⁰ People who boast of their wealth
    don't understand;
  they will die, just like animals.

49:7 Or *no one can redeem the life of another.*   49:13 The
meaning of the Hebrew is uncertain.   49:14 Hebrew *Sheol;*
also in 49:14b, 15.

PROVERBS 22:20-21

I have written thirty sayings* for you,
filled with advice and knowledge. In
this way, you may know the truth and
take an accurate report to those who
sent you.

22:20 Or *excellent sayings;* the meaning of the Hebrew is
uncertain.

SEPTEMBER 6

SONG OF SONGS 1:1–4:16
This is Solomon's song of songs, more
wonderful than any other.

*Young Woman**
² Kiss me and kiss me again,
  for your love is sweeter
    than wine.
³ How fragrant your cologne;
  your name is like its spreading
    fragrance.
  No wonder all the young women
    love you!
⁴ Take me with you; come, let's run!
  The king has brought me
    into his bedroom.

Young Women of Jerusalem
  How happy we are for you,
    O king.
  We praise your love even more
    than wine.

Young Woman
  How right they are to adore you.

⁵ I am dark but beautiful,
  O women of Jerusalem—
dark as the tents of Kedar,
  dark as the curtains of Solomon's
    tents.
⁶ Don't stare at me because I am
    dark—
  the sun has darkened my skin.
  My brothers were angry with me;
    they forced me to care for their
      vineyards,
    so I couldn't care for myself—
      my own vineyard.

⁷ Tell me, my love, where are you
    leading your flock today?
  Where will you rest your sheep
    at noon?
  For why should I wander like
    a prostitute*
  among your friends and their
    flocks?

Young Man

8 If you don't know, O most beautiful
 woman,
   follow the trail of my flock,
   and graze your young goats by the
     shepherds' tents.
9 You are as exciting, my darling,
   as a mare among Pharaoh's
     stallions.
10 How lovely are your cheeks;
   your earrings set them afire!
   How lovely is your neck,
   enhanced by a string of jewels.
11 We will make for you earrings
   of gold
   and beads of silver.

Young Woman

12 The king is lying on his couch,
   enchanted by the fragrance
   of my perfume.
13 My lover is like a sachet of myrrh
   lying between my breasts.
14 He is like a bouquet of sweet henna
   blossoms
   from the vineyards of En-gedi.

Young Man

15 How beautiful you are, my darling,
   how beautiful!
   Your eyes are like doves.

Young Woman

16 You are so handsome, my love,
   pleasing beyond words!
   The soft grass is our bed;
17   fragrant cedar branches are the
     beams of our house,
   and pleasant smelling firs are
     the rafters.

Young Woman

2:1 I am the spring crocus blooming on
   the Sharon Plain,*
   the lily of the valley.

Young Man

2 Like a lily among thistles
   is my darling among young
   women.

Young Woman

3 Like the finest apple tree in
   the orchard

is my lover among other young
   men.
I sit in his delightful shade
   and taste his delicious fruit.
4 He escorts me to the banquet hall;
   it's obvious how much he
     loves me.
5 Strengthen me with raisin cakes,
   refresh me with apples,
   for I am weak with love.
6 His left arm is under my head,
   and his right arm embraces me.

7 Promise me, O women of Jerusalem,
   by the gazelles and wild deer,
   not to awaken love until the time
   is right.*

8 Ah, I hear my lover coming!
   He is leaping over the mountains,
   bounding over the hills.
9 My lover is like a swift gazelle
   or a young stag.
   Look, there he is behind the wall,
   looking through the window,
   peering into the room.

10 My lover said to me,
   "Rise up, my darling!
   Come away with me, my fair one!
11 Look, the winter is past,
   and the rains are over and gone.
12 The flowers are springing up,
   the season of singing birds*
     has come,
   and the cooing of turtledoves
     fills the air.
13 The fig trees are forming young fruit,
   and the fragrant grapevines
   are blossoming.
   Rise up, my darling!
   Come away with me, my fair one!"

Young Man

14 My dove is hiding behind the rocks,
   behind an outcrop on the cliff.
   Let me see your face;
   let me hear your voice.
   For your voice is pleasant,
   and your face is lovely.

Young Women of Jerusalem

15 Catch all the foxes,
   those little foxes,

before they ruin the vineyard of love,
for the grapevines are blossoming!

Young Woman
16 My lover is mine, and I am his.
He browses among the lilies.
17 Before the dawn breezes blow
and the night shadows flee,
return to me, my love, like a gazelle
or a young stag on the rugged
mountains.*

Young Woman
3:1 ONE night as I lay in bed, I yearned
for my lover.
I yearned for him, but he did not
come.
2 So I said to myself, "I will get up and
roam the city,
searching in all its streets and
squares.
I will search for the one I love."
So I searched everywhere but did
not find him.
3 The watchmen stopped me as they
made their rounds,
and I asked, "Have you seen the
one I love?"
4 Then scarcely had I left them
when I found my love!
I caught and held him tightly,
then I brought him to my
mother's house,
into my mother's bed, where
I had been conceived.

5 Promise me, O women of Jerusalem,
by the gazelles and wild deer,
not to awaken love until the time
is right.*

Young Women of Jerusalem
6 Who is this sweeping in from
the wilderness
like a cloud of smoke?
Who is it, fragrant with myrrh and
frankincense
and every kind of spice?
7 Look, it is Solomon's carriage,
surrounded by sixty heroic men,
the best of Israel's soldiers.
8 They are all skilled swordsmen,
experienced warriors.
Each wears a sword on his thigh,
ready to defend the king against
an attack in the night.
9 King Solomon's carriage is built
of wood imported from Lebanon.
10 Its posts are silver,
its canopy gold;
its cushions are purple.
It was decorated with love
by the young women of Jerusalem.

Young Woman
11 Come out to see King Solomon,
young women of Jerusalem.*
He wears the crown his mother gave
him on his wedding day,
his most joyous day.

Young Man
4:1 You are beautiful, my darling,
beautiful beyond words.
Your eyes are like doves
behind your veil.
Your hair falls in waves,
like a flock of goats winding
down the slopes of Gilead.
2 Your teeth are as white as sheep,
recently shorn and freshly
washed.
Your smile is flawless,
each tooth matched with its twin.*
3 Your lips are like scarlet ribbon;
your mouth is inviting.
Your cheeks are like rosy
pomegranates
behind your veil.
4 Your neck is as beautiful as the
tower of David,
jeweled with the shields
of a thousand heroes.
5 Your breasts are like two fawns,
twin fawns of a gazelle grazing
among the lilies.
6 Before the dawn breezes blow
and the night shadows flee,
I will hurry to the mountain
of myrrh
and to the hill of frankincense.
7 You are altogether beautiful,
my darling,
beautiful in every way.

8 Come with me from Lebanon,
my bride,
come with me from Lebanon.

Come down* from Mount Amana,
from the peaks of Senir and
Hermon,
where the lions have their dens
and leopards live among the hills.

⁹ You have captured my heart,
my treasure,* my bride.
You hold it hostage with one glance
of your eyes,
with a single jewel of your
necklace.
¹⁰ Your love delights me,
my treasure, my bride.
Your love is better than wine,
your perfume more fragrant
than spices.
¹¹ Your lips are as sweet as nectar,
my bride.
Honey and milk are under
your tongue.
Your clothes are scented
like the cedars of Lebanon.

¹² You are my private garden, my
treasure, my bride,
a secluded spring, a hidden
fountain.
¹³ Your thighs shelter a paradise
of pomegranates
with rare spices—
henna with nard,
¹⁴   nard and saffron,
fragrant calamus and cinnamon,
with all the trees of frankincense,
myrrh, and aloes,
and every other lovely spice.
¹⁵ You are a garden fountain,
a well of fresh water
streaming down from Lebanon's
mountains.

Young Woman
¹⁶ Awake, north wind!
Rise up, south wind!
Blow on my garden
and spread its fragrance all
around.
Come into your garden, my love;
taste its finest fruits.

1:1 The headings identifying the speakers are not in the
original text, though the Hebrew usually gives clues by
means of the gender of the person speaking.   1:7 Hebrew
like a veiled woman.   2:1 Traditionally rendered *I am the*

rose of Sharon. Sharon Plain is a region in the coastal plain
of Palestine.   2:7 Or *not to awaken love until it is ready.*
2:12 Or *the season of pruning vines.*   2:17 Or *on the hills
of Bether.*   3:5 Or *not to awaken love until it is ready.*
3:11 Hebrew *of Zion.*   4:2 Hebrew *Not one is missing; each
has a twin.*   4:8 Or *Look down.*   4:9 Hebrew *my sister;*
also in 4:10, 12.

2 CORINTHIANS 8:16-24

But thank God! He has given Titus
the same enthusiasm for you [Corinthi-
ans] that I [Paul] have. ¹⁷Titus welcomed our request that he visit you
again. In fact, he himself was very eager
to go and see you. ¹⁸We are also sending
another brother with Titus. All the
churches praise him as a preacher of
the Good News. ¹⁹He was appointed by
the churches to accompany us as we
take the offering to Jerusalem*—a service that glorifies the Lord and shows
our eagerness to help.

²⁰We are traveling together to guard
against any criticism for the way we are
handling this generous gift. ²¹We are
careful to be honorable before the Lord,
but we also want everyone else to see
that we are honorable.

²²We are also sending with them another of our brothers who has proven
himself many times and has shown on
many occasions how eager he is. He is
now even more enthusiastic because of
his great confidence in you. ²³If anyone
asks about Titus, say that he is my partner who works with me to help you. And
the brothers with him have been sent by
the churches,* and they bring honor to
Christ. ²⁴So show them your love, and
prove to all the churches that our boasting about you is justified.

8:19 See 1 Cor 16:3-4.   8:23 Greek *are apostles of the
churches.*

PSALM 50:1-23
A psalm of Asaph.

¹ **The Lᴏʀᴅ, the Mighty One, is God,
and he has spoken;
he has summoned all humanity
from where the sun rises to
where it sets.**
² **From Mount Zion, the perfection
of beauty,**

God shines in glorious radiance.

³ Our God approaches,
  and he is not silent.
Fire devours everything in his way,
  and a great storm rages around
    him.
⁴ He calls on the heavens above
    and earth below
  to witness the judgment
    of his people.
⁵ "Bring my faithful people to me—
  those who made a covenant with
    me by giving sacrifices."
⁶ Then let the heavens proclaim
    his justice,
  for God himself will be the judge.
                                    Interlude

⁷ "O my people, listen as I speak.
  Here are my charges against you,
    O Israel:
  I am God, your God!
⁸ I have no complaint about your
    sacrifices
  or the burnt offerings you
    constantly offer.
⁹ But I do not need the bulls from
    your barns
  or the goats from your pens.
¹⁰ For all the animals of the forest
    are mine,
  and I own the cattle on a
    thousand hills.
¹¹ I know every bird on the mountains,
  and all the animals of the field
    are mine.
¹² If I were hungry, I would not tell you,
  for all the world is mine and
    everything in it.
¹³ Do I eat the meat of bulls?
  Do I drink the blood of goats?
¹⁴ Make thankfulness your sacrifice
    to God,
  and keep the vows you made
    to the Most High.
¹⁵ Then call on me when you are
    in trouble,
  and I will rescue you,
  and you will give me glory."

¹⁶ But God says to the wicked:
  "Why bother reciting my decrees

and pretending to obey my
    covenant?
¹⁷ For you refuse my discipline
  and treat my words like
    trash.
¹⁸ When you see thieves, you approve
    of them,
  and you spend your time with
    adulterers.
¹⁹ Your mouth is filled with
    wickedness,
  and your tongue is full of lies.
²⁰ You sit around and slander your
    brother—
  your own mother's son.
²¹ While you did all this, I remained
    silent,
  and you thought I didn't care.
  But now I will rebuke you,
    listing all my charges against
      you.
²² Repent, all of you who forget me,
  or I will tear you apart,
  and no one will help you.
²³ But giving thanks is a sacrifice that
    truly honors me.
  If you keep to my path,
  I will reveal to you the salvation
    of God."

PROVERBS 22:22-23
Don't rob the poor just because you
can, or exploit the needy in court. For
the LORD is their defender. He will ruin
anyone who ruins them.

SEPTEMBER 7

SONG OF SONGS 5:1–8:14

Young Man
I have entered my garden, my
    treasure,* my bride!
  I gather myrrh with my spices
and eat honeycomb with my honey.
  I drink wine with my milk.

Young Women of Jerusalem
 Oh, lover and beloved, eat and drink!
  Yes, drink deeply of your love!

Young Woman
 2 I slept, but my heart was awake,
  when I heard my lover knocking
   and calling:
 "Open to me, my treasure, my
  darling,
  my dove, my perfect one.
 My head is drenched with dew,
  my hair with the dampness
   of the night."

 3 But I responded,
 "I have taken off my robe.
  Should I get dressed again?
 I have washed my feet.
  Should I get them soiled?"

 4 My lover tried to unlatch the door,
  and my heart thrilled within me.
 5 I jumped up to open the door for
  my love,
  and my hands dripped with
   perfume.
 My fingers dripped with lovely
  myrrh
  as I pulled back the bolt.
 6 I opened to my lover,
  but he was gone!
  My heart sank.
 I searched for him
  but could not find him anywhere.
 I called to him,
  but there was no reply.
 7 The night watchmen found me
  as they made their rounds.
 They beat and bruised me
  and stripped off my veil,
  those watchmen on the walls.

 8 Make this promise, O women of
  Jerusalem—
 If you find my lover,
  tell him I am weak with love.

Young Women of Jerusalem
 9 Why is your lover better than
  all others,
  O woman of rare beauty?
 What makes your lover so special
  that we must promise this?

Young Woman
 10 My lover is dark and dazzling,
  better than ten thousand others!
 11 His head is finest gold,
  his wavy hair is black as a raven.
 12 His eyes sparkle like doves
  beside springs of water;
 they are set like jewels
  washed in milk.
 13 His cheeks are like gardens of spices
  giving off fragrance.
 His lips are like lilies,
  perfumed with myrrh.
 14 His arms are like rounded bars
  of gold,
  set with beryl.
 His body is like bright ivory,
  glowing with lapis lazuli.
 15 His legs are like marble pillars
  set in sockets of finest gold.
 His posture is stately,
  like the noble cedars of Lebanon.
 16 His mouth is sweetness itself;
  he is desirable in every way.
 Such, O women of Jerusalem,
  is my lover, my friend.

Young Women of Jerusalem
 6:1 WHERE has your lover gone,
  O woman of rare beauty?
 Which way did he turn
  so we can help you find him?

Young Woman
 2 My lover has gone down to his
  garden,
  to his spice beds,
 to browse in the gardens
  and gather the lilies.
 3 I am my lover's, and my lover
  is mine.
 He browses among the lilies.

Young Man
 4 You are beautiful, my darling,
  like the lovely city of Tirzah.
 Yes, as beautiful as Jerusalem,
  as majestic as an army with
   billowing banners.
 5 Turn your eyes away,
  for they overpower me.
 Your hair falls in waves,

like a flock of goats winding down
the slopes of Gilead.
6 Your teeth are as white as sheep
that are freshly washed.
Your smile is flawless,
each tooth matched with its twin.*
7 Your cheeks are like rosy
pomegranates
behind your veil.

8 Even among sixty queens
and eighty concubines
and countless young women,
9 I would still choose my dove, my
perfect one—
the favorite of her mother,
dearly loved by the one who
bore her.
The young women see her and
praise her;
even queens and royal concubines
sing her praises:
10 "Who is this, arising like the dawn,
as fair as the moon,
as bright as the sun,
as majestic as an army with
billowing banners?"

11 I went down to the grove of walnut
trees
and out to the valley to see the
new spring growth,
to see whether the grapevines had
budded
or the pomegranates were
in bloom.
12 Before I realized it,
I found myself in the royal chariot
with my beloved.*

Young Women of Jerusalem
13*Return, return to us, O maid of
Shulam.
Come back, come back, that we
may see you again.

Young Man
Why do you stare at this young
woman of Shulam,
as she moves so gracefully
between two lines of dancers?*

7:1*How beautiful are your sandaled
feet,

O queenly maiden.
Your rounded thighs are like jewels,
the work of a skilled craftsman.
2 Your navel is perfectly formed
like a goblet filled with mixed
wine.
Between your thighs lies a mound
of wheat
bordered with lilies.
3 Your breasts are like two fawns,
twin fawns of a gazelle.
4 Your neck is as beautiful as an ivory
tower.
Your eyes are like the sparkling
pools in Heshbon
by the gate of Bath-rabbim.
Your nose is as fine as the tower
of Lebanon
overlooking Damascus.
5 Your head is as majestic as Mount
Carmel,
and the sheen of your hair
radiates royalty.
The king is held captive by
its tresses.
6 Oh, how beautiful you are!
How pleasing, my love, how
full of delights!
7 You are slender like a palm tree,
and your breasts are like its
clusters of fruit.
8 I said, "I will climb the palm tree
and take hold of its fruit."
May your breasts be like grape
clusters,
and the fragrance of your breath
like apples.
9 May your kisses be as exciting as the
best wine,
flowing gently over lips and teeth.*

Young Woman
10 I am my lover's,
and he claims me as his own.
11 Come, my love, let us go out to the
fields
and spend the night among the
wildflowers.*
12 Let us get up early and go to the
vineyards
to see if the grapevines have
budded,

if the blossoms have opened,
and if the pomegranates have
bloomed.
There I will give you my love.
¹³ There the mandrakes give off their
fragrance,
and the finest fruits are at
our door,
new delights as well as old,
which I have saved for you,
my lover.

Young Woman
^{8:1} OH, I wish you were my brother,
who nursed at my mother's
breasts.
Then I could kiss you no matter
who was watching,
and no one would criticize me.
² I would bring you to my childhood
home,
and there you would teach me.*
I would give you spiced wine
to drink,
my sweet pomegranate wine.
³ Your left arm would be under
my head,
and your right arm would
embrace me.

⁴ Promise me, O women of Jerusalem,
not to awaken love until the time
is right.*

Young Women of Jerusalem
⁵ Who is this sweeping in from
the desert,
leaning on her lover?

Young Woman
I aroused you under the apple tree,
where your mother gave you
birth,
where in great pain she
delivered you.
⁶ Place me like a seal over your heart,
like a seal on your arm.
For love is as strong as death,
its jealousy* as enduring as
the grave.*
Love flashes like fire,
the brightest kind of flame.
⁷ Many waters cannot quench love,
nor can rivers drown it.

If a man tried to buy love
with all his wealth,
his offer would be utterly
scorned.

The Young Woman's Brothers
⁸ We have a little sister
too young to have breasts.
What will we do for our sister
if someone asks to marry her?
⁹ If she is a virgin, like a wall,
we will protect her with a silver
tower.
But if she is promiscuous, like
a swinging door,
we will block her door with
a cedar bar.

Young Woman
¹⁰ I was a virgin, like a wall;
now my breasts are like towers.
When my lover looks at me,
he is delighted with what he sees.

¹¹ Solomon has a vineyard at Baal-
hamon,
which he leases out to tenant
farmers.
Each of them pays a thousand
pieces of silver*
for harvesting its fruit.
¹² But my vineyard is mine to give,
and Solomon need not pay a
thousand pieces of silver.
But I will give two hundred pieces
to those who care for its vines.

Young Man
¹³ O my darling, lingering in the
gardens,
your companions are fortunate
to hear your voice.
Let me hear it, too!

Young Woman
¹⁴ Come away, my love! Be like a gazelle
or a young stag on the mountains
of spices.

5:1 Hebrew *my sister;* also in 5:2.   **6:6** Hebrew *Not one is
missing; each has a twin.*   **6:12** Or *among the royal
chariots of my people,* or *among the chariots of
Amminadab.* The meaning of the Hebrew is uncertain.
6:13a Verse 6:13 is numbered 7:1 in Hebrew text.
6:13b Or *as you would at the movements of two armies?* or
as you would at the dance of Mahanaim? The meaning of
the Hebrew is uncertain.   **7:1** Verses 7:1-13 are numbered
7:2-14 in Hebrew text.   **7:9** As in Greek and Syriac

versions and Latin Vulgate; Hebrew reads *over lips of sleepers.*   **7:11** Or *in the villages.*   **8:2** Or *there she will teach me; or there she bore me.*   **8:4** Or *not to awaken love until it is ready.*   **8:6a** Or *its passion.*   **8:6b** Hebrew as *Sheol.*   **8:11** Hebrew *1,000 shekels of silver.*

2 CORINTHIANS 9:1-15

❚ [Paul] really don't need to write to you about this ministry of giving for the believers in Jerusalem.* ²For I know how eager you are to help, and I have been boasting to the churches in Macedonia that you in Greece* were ready to send an offering a year ago. In fact, it was your enthusiasm that stirred up many of the Macedonian believers to begin giving.

³But I am sending these brothers to be sure you really are ready, as I have been telling them, and that your money is all collected. I don't want to be wrong in my boasting about you. ⁴We would be embarrassed—not to mention your own embarrassment—if some Macedonian believers came with me and found that you weren't ready after all I had told them! ⁵So I thought I should send these brothers ahead of me to make sure the gift you promised is ready. But I want it to be a willing gift, not one given grudgingly.

⁶Remember this—a farmer who plants only a few seeds will get a small crop. But the one who plants generously will get a generous crop. ⁷You must each decide in your heart how much to give. And don't give reluctantly or in response to pressure. "For God loves a person who gives cheerfully."* ⁸And God will generously provide all you need. Then you will always have everything you need and plenty left over to share with others. ⁹As the Scriptures say,

"They share freely and give
　　generously to the poor.
Their good deeds will be
　　remembered forever."*

¹⁰For God is the one who provides seed for the farmer and then bread to eat. In the same way, he will provide and increase your resources and then produce a great harvest of generosity* in you. ¹¹Yes, you will be enriched in every way so that you can always be generous. And when we take your gifts to those who need them, they will thank God. ¹²So two good things will result from this ministry of giving—the needs of the believers in Jerusalem will be met, and they will joyfully express their thanks to God.

¹³As a result of your ministry, they will give glory to God. For your generosity to them and to all believers will prove that you are obedient to the Good News of Christ. ¹⁴And they will pray for you with deep affection because of the overflowing grace God has given to you. ¹⁵Thank God for this gift* too wonderful for words!

9:1 Greek *about the offering for the saints.*   **9:2** Greek *in Achaia,* the southern region of the Greek peninsula. *Macedonia* was in the northern region of Greece.   **9:7** See footnote on Prov 22:8.   **9:9** Ps 112:9.   **9:10** Greek *righteousness.*   **9:15** Greek *his gift.*

PSALM 51:1-19

For the choir director: A psalm of David, regarding the time Nathan the prophet came to him after David had committed adultery with Bathsheba.

¹ **Have mercy on me, O God,
　　because of your unfailing love.
Because of your great
　　compassion,
　　blot out the stain of my sins.**
² **Wash me clean from my guilt.
　　Purify me from my sin.**
³ For I recognize my rebellion;
　　it haunts me day and night.
⁴ Against you, and you alone, have
　　I sinned;
　　I have done what is evil in your
　　　　sight.
　　You will be proved right in what
　　　　you say,
　　and your judgment against me
　　　　is just.*
⁵ For I was born a sinner—
　　yes, from the moment my mother
　　　　conceived me.
⁶ But you desire honesty from the
　　womb,*
　　teaching me wisdom even there.

⁷ Purify me from my sins,* and I will
　　be clean;

wash me, and I will be whiter
than snow.
8 Oh, give me back my joy again;
you have broken me—
now let me rejoice.
9 Don't keep looking at my sins.
Remove the stain of my guilt.
10 Create in me a clean heart,
O God.
Renew a loyal spirit within me.
11 Do not banish me from your
presence,
and don't take your Holy Spirit*
from me.

12 Restore to me the joy of your
salvation,
and make me willing to obey you.
13 Then I will teach your ways to rebels,
and they will return to you.
14 Forgive me for shedding blood,
O God who saves;
then I will joyfully sing of your
forgiveness.
15 Unseal my lips, O Lord,
that my mouth may praise you.

16 You do not desire a sacrifice, or I
would offer one.
You do not want a burnt offering.
17 The sacrifice you desire is a broken
spirit.
You will not reject a broken and
repentant heart, O God.
18 Look with favor on Zion and help
her;
rebuild the walls of Jerusalem.
19 Then you will be pleased with
sacrifices offered in the right
spirit—
with burnt offerings and whole
burnt offerings.
Then bulls will again be sacrificed
on your altar.

51:4 Greek version reads *and you will win your case in
court.* Compare Rom 3:4.　　**51:6** Or *from the heart;* Hebrew
reads *in the inward parts.*　　**51:7** Hebrew *Purify me with
the hyssop branch.*　　**51:11** Or *your spirit of holiness.*

PROVERBS 22:24-25
Don't befriend angry people or associate with hot-tempered people, or you
will learn to be like them and endanger
your soul.

SEPTEMBER
8

ISAIAH 1:1–2:22
These are the visions that Isaiah son of
Amoz saw concerning Judah and Jeru-
salem. He saw these visions during the
years when Uzziah, Jotham, Ahaz, and
Hezekiah were kings of Judah.*

2 Listen, O heavens! Pay attention,
earth!
This is what the LORD says:
"The children I raised and cared for
have rebelled against me.
3 Even an ox knows its owner,
and a donkey recognizes its
master's care—
but Israel doesn't know its master.
My people don't recognize my
care for them."
4 Oh, what a sinful nation they are—
loaded down with a burden
of guilt.
They are evil people,
corrupt children who have
rejected the LORD.
They have despised the Holy One
of Israel
and turned their backs on him.

5 Why do you continue to invite
punishment?
Must you rebel forever?
Your head is injured,
and your heart is sick.
6 You are battered from head
to foot—
covered with bruises, welts, and
infected wounds—
without any soothing ointments
or bandages.
7 Your country lies in ruins,
and your towns are burned.
Foreigners plunder your fields
before your eyes
and destroy everything they see.
8 Beautiful Jerusalem* stands
abandoned

like a watchman's shelter
in a vineyard,
like a lean-to in a cucumber field
after the harvest,
like a helpless city under siege.
⁹ If the LORD of Heaven's Armies
had not spared a few of us,*
we would have been wiped out
like Sodom,
destroyed like Gomorrah.

¹⁰ Listen to the LORD, you leaders
of "Sodom."
Listen to the law of our God,
people of "Gomorrah."
¹¹ "What makes you think I want all
your sacrifices?"
says the LORD.
"I am sick of your burnt offerings
of rams
and the fat of fattened cattle.
I get no pleasure from the blood
of bulls and lambs and goats.
¹² When you come to worship me,
who asked you to parade through
my courts with all your
ceremony?
¹³ Stop bringing me your meaningless
gifts;
the incense of your offerings
disgusts me!
As for your celebrations of the new
moon and the Sabbath
and your special days for fasting—
they are all sinful and false.
I want no more of your pious
meetings.
¹⁴ I hate your new moon celebrations
and your annual festivals.
They are a burden to me. I cannot
stand them!
¹⁵ When you lift up your hands in
prayer, I will not look.
Though you offer many prayers,
I will not listen,
for your hands are covered with
the blood of innocent victims.
¹⁶ Wash yourselves and be clean!
Get your sins out of my sight.
Give up your evil ways.
¹⁷ Learn to do good.
Seek justice.
Help the oppressed.

Defend the cause of orphans.
Fight for the rights of widows.

¹⁸ "Come now, let's settle this,"
says the LORD.
"Though your sins are like scarlet,
I will make them as white
as snow.
Though they are red like crimson,
I will make them as white
as wool.
¹⁹ If you will only obey me,
you will have plenty to eat.
²⁰ But if you turn away and refuse
to listen,
you will be devoured by the sword
of your enemies.
I, the LORD, have spoken!"

²¹ See how Jerusalem, once so
faithful,
has become a prostitute.
Once the home of justice and
righteousness,
she is now filled with murderers.
²² Once like pure silver,
you have become like worthless
slag.
Once so pure,
you are now like watered-down
wine.
²³ Your leaders are rebels,
the companions of thieves.
All of them love bribes
and demand payoffs,
but they refuse to defend the cause
of orphans
or fight for the rights of widows.

²⁴ Therefore, the Lord, the LORD of
Heaven's Armies,
the Mighty One of Israel, says,
"I will take revenge on my enemies
and pay back my foes!
²⁵ I will raise my fist against you.
I will melt you down and skim
off your slag.
I will remove all your impurities.
²⁶ Then I will give you good judges
again
and wise counselors like you
used to have.

Then Jerusalem will again be called
the Home of Justice
and the Faithful City."

27 Zion will be restored by justice;
those who repent will be revived
by righteousness.
28 But rebels and sinners will be
completely destroyed,
and those who desert the LORD
will be consumed.

29 You will be ashamed of your
idol worship
in groves of sacred oaks.
You will blush because you
worshiped
in gardens dedicated to idols.
30 You will be like a great tree with
withered leaves,
like a garden without water.
31 The strongest among you will
disappear like straw;
their evil deeds will be the spark
that sets it on fire.
They and their evil works will burn
up together,
and no one will be able to put
out the fire.

2:1 THIS is a vision that Isaiah son of Amoz
saw concerning Judah and Jerusalem:

2 In the last days, the mountain
of the LORD's house
will be the highest of all—
the most important place on
earth.
It will be raised above the other hills,
and people from all over the
world will stream there to
worship.
3 People from many nations will
come and say,
"Come, let us go up to the mountain
of the LORD,
to the house of Jacob's God.
There he will teach us his ways,
and we will walk in his paths."
For the LORD's teaching will go out
from Zion;
his word will go out from
Jerusalem.

4 The LORD will mediate between
nations
and will settle international
disputes.
They will hammer their swords into
plowshares
and their spears into pruning
hooks.
Nation will no longer fight against
nation,
nor train for war anymore.

5 Come, descendants of Jacob,
let us walk in the light of the
LORD!
6 For the LORD has rejected his people,
the descendants of Jacob,
because they have filled their land
with practices from the East
and with sorcerers, as the
Philistines do.
They have made alliances with
pagans.
7 Israel is full of silver and gold;
there is no end to its treasures.
Their land is full of warhorses;
there is no end to its chariots.
8 Their land is full of idols;
the people worship things they
have made
with their own hands.
9 So now they will be humbled,
and all will be brought low—
do not forgive them.
10 Crawl into caves in the rocks.
Hide in the dust
from the terror of the LORD
and the glory of his majesty.
11 Human pride will be brought down,
and human arrogance will be
humbled.
Only the LORD will be exalted
on that day of judgment.

12 For the LORD of Heaven's Armies
has a day of reckoning.
He will punish the proud and mighty
and bring down everything
that is exalted.
13 He will cut down the tall cedars
of Lebanon
and all the mighty oaks of Bashan.
14 He will level all the high mountains

and all the lofty hills.
¹⁵ He will break down every high tower
and every fortified wall.
¹⁶ He will destroy all the great trading
ships*
and every magnificent vessel.
¹⁷ Human pride will be humbled,
and human arrogance will be
brought down.
Only the LORD will be exalted
on that day of judgment.

¹⁸ Idols will completely disappear.
¹⁹ When the LORD rises to shake
the earth,
his enemies will crawl into holes
in the ground.
They will hide in caves in the rocks
from the terror of the LORD
and the glory of his majesty.
²⁰ On that day of judgment they will
abandon the gold and silver
idols
they made for themselves
to worship.
They will leave their gods to the
rodents and bats,
²¹   while they crawl away into caverns
and hide among the jagged rocks
in the cliffs.
They will try to escape the terror
of the LORD
and the glory of his majesty
as he rises to shake the earth.
²² Don't put your trust in mere humans.
They are as frail as breath.
What good are they?

1:1 These kings reigned from 792 to 686 B.C.   1:8 Hebrew
The daughter of Zion.   1:9 Greek version reads *a few of our
children.* Compare Rom 9:29.   2:16 Hebrew *every ship of
Tarshish.*

2 CORINTHIANS 10:1-18

Now I, Paul, appeal to you [Corinthians]
with the gentleness and kindness of
Christ—though I realize you think I am
timid in person and bold only when I
write from far away. ² Well, I am begging you now so that when I come I
won't have to be bold with those who
think we act from human motives.

³ We are human, but we don't wage
war as humans do. ⁴*We use God's

mighty weapons, not worldly weapons,
to knock down the strongholds of human reasoning and to destroy false arguments. ⁵ We destroy every proud
obstacle that keeps people from knowing God. We capture their rebellious
thoughts and teach them to obey Christ.
⁶And after you have become fully obe-
dient, we will punish everyone who remains disobedient.

⁷Look at the obvious facts.* Those
who say they belong to Christ must recognize that we belong to Christ as much
as they do. ⁸I may seem to be boasting
too much about the authority given to us
by the Lord. But our authority builds you
up; it doesn't tear you down. So I will not
be ashamed of using my authority.

⁹I'm not trying to frighten you by my
letters. ¹⁰For some say, "Paul's letters
are demanding and forceful, but in person he is weak, and his speeches are
worthless!" ¹¹Those people should realize that our actions when we arrive in
person will be as forceful as what we say
in our letters from far away.

¹²Oh, don't worry; we wouldn't dare
say that we are as wonderful as these
other men who tell you how important
they are! But they are only comparing
themselves with each other, using
themselves as the standard of measurement. How ignorant!

¹³We will not boast about things done
outside our area of authority. We will
boast only about what has happened
within the boundaries of the work God
has given us, which includes our working
with you. ¹⁴We are not reaching beyond
these boundaries when we claim authority over you, as if we had never visited
you. For we were the first to travel all the
way to Corinth with the Good News of
Christ.

¹⁵Nor do we boast and claim credit for
the work someone else has done. In-
stead, we hope that your faith will grow
so that the boundaries of our work
among you will be extended. ¹⁶Then we
will be able to go and preach the Good
News in other places far beyond you,
where no one else is working. Then there

will be no question of our boasting about work done in someone else's territory. [17]As the Scriptures say, "If you want to boast, boast only about the LORD."*

[18]When people commend themselves, it doesn't count for much. The important thing is for the Lord to commend them.

10:4 English translations divide verses 4 and 5 in various ways. 10:7 Or *You look at things only on the basis of appearance.* 10:17 Jer 9:24.

PSALM 52:1-9

For the choir director: A psalm of David, regarding the time Doeg the Edomite said to Saul, "David has gone to see Ahimelech."*

[1] **W**hy do you boast about your
        crimes, great warrior?
    Don't you realize God's justice
        continues forever?
[2] All day long you plot destruction.
    Your tongue cuts like a sharp
        razor;
    you're an expert at telling lies.
[3] You love evil more than good
    and lies more than truth.
                                Interlude

[4] You love to destroy others with
        your words,
    you liar!
[5] But God will strike you down once
        and for all.
    He will pull you from your home
    and uproot you from the land
        of the living.   *Interlude*

[6] The righteous will see it and be
        amazed.
    They will laugh and say,
[7] "Look what happens to mighty
        warriors
    who do not trust in God.
    They trust their wealth instead
        and grow more and more bold
        in their wickedness."

[8] But I am like an olive tree, thriving
        in the house of God.
    I will always trust in God's
        unfailing love.
[9] I will praise you forever, O God,
    for what you have done.

I will trust in your good name
    in the presence of your faithful
        people.

52:TITLE Hebrew *maskil.* This may be a literary or musical term.

PROVERBS 22:26-27
Don't agree to guarantee another person's debt or put up security for someone else. If you can't pay it, even your bed will be snatched from under you.

SEPTEMBER
9

ISAIAH 3:1–5:30
The Lord, the LORD of Heaven's
        Armies,
    will take away from Jerusalem
        and Judah
everything they depend on:
    every bit of bread
    and every drop of water,
[2] all their heroes and soldiers,
    judges and prophets,
    fortune-tellers and elders,
[3] army officers and high officials,
    advisers, skilled craftsmen, and
        astrologers.

[4] I will make boys their leaders,
    and toddlers their rulers.
[5] People will oppress each other—
    man against man,
    neighbor against neighbor.
Young people will insult their elders,
    and vulgar people will sneer
        at the honorable.

[6] In those days a man will say to his
        brother,
    "Since you have a coat, you be our
        leader!
    Take charge of this heap of ruins!"
[7] But he will reply,
    "No! I can't help.
    I don't have any extra food or clothes.
    Don't put me in charge!"

⁸ For Jerusalem will stumble,
and Judah will fall,
because they speak out against the
LORD and refuse to obey him.
They provoke him to his face.
⁹ The very look on their faces gives
them away.
They display their sin like the
people of Sodom
and don't even try to hide it.
They are doomed!
They have brought destruction
upon themselves.

¹⁰ Tell the godly that all will be well
for them.
They will enjoy the rich reward
they have earned!
¹¹ But the wicked are doomed,
for they will get exactly what
they deserve.

¹² Childish leaders oppress my people,
and women rule over them.
O my people, your leaders mislead
you;
they send you down the wrong
road.

¹³ The LORD takes his place in court
and presents his case against his
people!
¹⁴ The LORD comes forward to
pronounce judgment
on the elders and rulers
of his people:
"You have ruined Israel, my vineyard.
Your houses are filled with
things stolen from the poor.
¹⁵ How dare you crush my people,
grinding the faces of the poor
into the dust?"
demands the Lord, the LORD
of Heaven's Armies.

¹⁶ The LORD says, "Beautiful Zion*
is haughty:
craning her elegant neck,
flirting with her eyes,
walking with dainty steps,
tinkling her ankle bracelets.
¹⁷ So the Lord will send scabs on
her head;

the LORD will make beautiful
Zion bald."

¹⁸ On that day of judgment
the Lord will strip away
everything that makes her
beautiful:
ornaments, headbands, crescent
necklaces,
¹⁹ earrings, bracelets, and veils;
²⁰ scarves, ankle bracelets, sashes,
perfumes, and charms;
²¹ rings, jewels,
²² party clothes, gowns, capes, and
purses;
²³ mirrors, fine linen garments,
head ornaments, and shawls.

²⁴ Instead of smelling of sweet
perfume, she will stink.
She will wear a rope for a sash,
and her elegant hair will fall out.
She will wear rough burlap instead
of rich robes.
Shame will replace her beauty.*
²⁵ The men of the city will be killed
with the sword,
and her warriors will die in battle.
²⁶ The gates of Zion will weep and
mourn.
The city will be like a ravaged
woman,
huddled on the ground.

⁴:¹IN that day so few men will be left that
seven women will fight for each man,
saying, "Let us all marry you! We will
provide our own food and clothing.
Only let us take your name so we won't
be mocked as old maids."

² But in that day, the branch* of the
LORD
will be beautiful and glorious;
the fruit of the land will be the pride
and glory
of all who survive in Israel.
³ All who remain in Zion
will be a holy people—
those who survive the destruction
of Jerusalem
and are recorded among the living.
⁴ The Lord will wash the filth from
beautiful Zion*

and cleanse Jerusalem of its
  bloodstains
with the hot breath of fiery
  judgment.
5 Then the LORD will provide shade
  for Mount Zion
and all who assemble there.
He will provide a canopy of cloud
  during the day
and smoke and flaming fire at night,
  covering the glorious land.
6 It will be a shelter from daytime
  heat
and a hiding place from storms
  and rain.

5:1 Now I will sing for the one I love
  a song about his vineyard:
My beloved had a vineyard
  on a rich and fertile hill.
2 He plowed the land, cleared its
  stones,
and planted it with the best vines.
In the middle he built a watchtower
  and carved a winepress in the
  nearby rocks.
Then he waited for a harvest
  of sweet grapes,
but the grapes that grew were
  bitter.

3 Now, you people of Jerusalem
  and Judah,
  you judge between me and my
  vineyard.
4 What more could I have done for
  my vineyard
  that I have not already done?
When I expected sweet grapes,
  why did my vineyard give me
  bitter grapes?

5 Now let me tell you
  what I will do to my vineyard:
I will tear down its hedges
  and let it be destroyed.
I will break down its walls
  and let animals trample it.
6 I will make it a wild place
  where the vines are not pruned
  and the ground is not hoed,
  a place overgrown with briers and
  thorns.

I will command the clouds
  to drop no rain on it.

7 The nation of Israel is the vineyard
  of the LORD of Heaven's
  Armies.
The people of Judah are his
  pleasant garden.
He expected a crop of justice,
  but instead he found oppression.
He expected to find righteousness,
  but instead he heard cries of
  violence.

8 What sorrow for you who buy up
  house after house and field
  after field,
  until everyone is evicted and you
  live alone in the land.
9 But I have heard the LORD of
  Heaven's Armies
  swear a solemn oath:
"Many houses will stand deserted;
  even beautiful mansions will be
  empty.
10 Ten acres* of vineyard will not
  produce even six gallons*
  of wine.
  Ten baskets of seed will yield only
  one basket* of grain."

11 What sorrow for those who get up
  early in the morning
  looking for a drink of alcohol
and spend long evenings drinking
  wine
  to make themselves flaming
  drunk.
12 They furnish wine and lovely music
  at their grand parties—
  lyre and harp, tambourine and
  flute—
but they never think about the LORD
  or notice what he is doing.

13 So my people will go into exile far
  away
  because they do not know me.
Those who are great and honored
  will starve,
  and the common people will die
  of thirst.
14 The grave* is licking its lips in
  anticipation,

opening its mouth wide.
The great and the lowly
    and all the drunken mob will be
    swallowed up.
¹⁵ Humanity will be destroyed, and
    people brought down;
    even the arrogant will lower their
    eyes in humiliation.
¹⁶ But the Lord of Heaven's Armies
    will be exalted by his justice.
The holiness of God will be
    displayed by his righteousness.
¹⁷ In that day lambs will find good
    pastures,
    and fattened sheep and young
    goats* will feed among
    the ruins.

¹⁸ What sorrow for those who drag
    their sins behind them
    with ropes made of lies,
    who drag wickedness behind
    them like a cart!
¹⁹ They even mock God and say,
    "Hurry up and do something!
    We want to see what you can do.
    Let the Holy One of Israel carry out
    his plan,
    for we want to know what it is."

²⁰ What sorrow for those who say
    that evil is good and good is evil,
    that dark is light and light is dark,
    that bitter is sweet and sweet is
    bitter.
²¹ What sorrow for those who are wise
    in their own eyes
    and think themselves so clever.
²² What sorrow for those who are
    heroes at drinking wine
    and boast about all the alcohol
    they can hold.
²³ They take bribes to let the wicked
    go free,
    and they punish the innocent.

²⁴ Therefore, just as fire licks up
    stubble
    and dry grass shrivels in the flame,
so their roots will rot
    and their flowers wither.
For they have rejected the law of the
    Lord of Heaven's Armies;

they have despised the word of
    the Holy One of Israel.
²⁵ That is why the Lord's anger burns
    against his people,
    and why he has raised his fist to
    crush them.
The mountains tremble,
    and the corpses of his people
    litter the streets like garbage.
But even then the Lord's anger is
    not satisfied.
    His fist is still poised to strike!

²⁶ He will send a signal to distant
    nations far away
    and whistle to those at the ends
    of the earth.
They will come racing toward
    Jerusalem.
²⁷ They will not get tired or stumble.
    They will not stop for rest
    or sleep.
Not a belt will be loose,
    not a sandal strap broken.
²⁸ Their arrows will be sharp
    and their bows ready for battle.
Sparks will fly from their horses'
    hooves,
    and the wheels of their chariots
    will spin like a whirlwind.
²⁹ They will roar like lions,
    like the strongest of lions.
Growling, they will pounce on their
    victims and carry them off,
    and no one will be there to rescue
    them.
³⁰ They will roar over their victims on
    that day of destruction
    like the roaring of the sea.
If someone looks across the land,
    only darkness and distress will be
    seen;
    even the light will be darkened by
    clouds.

3:16 Or *The women of Zion* (with corresponding changes
to plural forms through verse 24); Hebrew reads *The
daughters of Zion;* also in 3:17.   3:24 As in Dead Sea
Scrolls; Masoretic Text reads *robes / because instead of
beauty.*   4:2 Or *the Branch.*   4:4 Or *from the women
of Zion;* Hebrew reads *from the daughters of Zion.*
5:10a Hebrew *A ten yoke,* that is, the area of land plowed
by ten teams of oxen in one day.   5:10b Hebrew *a bath*
[21 liters].   5:10c Hebrew *A homer* [5 bushels or
182 liters] *of seed will yield only an ephah* [20 quarts or
22 liters].   5:14 Hebrew *Sheol.*   5:17 As in Greek version;
Hebrew reads *and strangers.*

2 CORINTHIANS 11:1-15

I [Paul] hope you [Corinthians] will put up with a little more of my foolishness. Please bear with me. ²For I am jealous for you with the jealousy of God himself. I promised you as a pure bride* to one husband—Christ. ³But I fear that somehow your pure and undivided devotion to Christ will be corrupted, just as Eve was deceived by the cunning ways of the serpent. ⁴You happily put up with whatever anyone tells you, even if they preach a different Jesus than the one we preach, or a different kind of Spirit than the one you received, or a different kind of gospel than the one you believed.

⁵But I don't consider myself inferior in any way to these "super apostles" who teach such things. ⁶I may be unskilled as a speaker, but I'm not lacking in knowledge. We have made this clear to you in every possible way.

⁷Was I wrong when I humbled myself and honored you by preaching God's Good News to you without expecting anything in return? ⁸I "robbed" other churches by accepting their contributions so I could serve you at no cost. ⁹And when I was with you and didn't have enough to live on, I did not become a financial burden to anyone. For the brothers who came from Macedonia brought me all that I needed. I have never been a burden to you, and I never will be. ¹⁰As surely as the truth of Christ is in me, no one in all of Greece* will ever stop me from boasting about this. ¹¹Why? Because I don't love you? God knows that I do.

¹²But I will continue doing what I have always done. This will undercut those who are looking for an opportunity to boast that their work is just like ours. ¹³These people are false apostles. They are deceitful workers who disguise themselves as apostles of Christ. **¹⁴But I am not surprised! Even Satan disguises himself as an angel of light. ¹⁵So it is no wonder that his servants also disguise themselves as servants of righteousness. In the end they will get the punishment their wicked deeds deserve.**

11:2 Greek *a virgin.* 11:10 Greek *Achaia,* the southern region of the Greek peninsula.

PSALM 53:1-6

For the choir director: A meditation; a psalm of David.*

¹ **O**nly fools say in their hearts,
  "There is no God."
 They are corrupt, and their actions
   are evil;
  not one of them does good!

² God looks down from heaven
  on the entire human race;
 he looks to see if anyone is truly
   wise,
  if anyone seeks God.

³ But no, all have turned away;
  all have become corrupt.*
 No one does good,
  not a single one!

⁴ Will those who do evil never
   learn?
 They eat up my people like bread
  and wouldn't think of praying to
   God.

⁵ Terror will grip them,
  terror like they have never known
   before.
 God will scatter the bones of your
   enemies.
 You will put them to shame, for
  God has rejected them.

⁶ Who will come from Mount Zion to
   rescue Israel?
 When God restores his people,
 Jacob will shout with joy, and
  Israel will rejoice.

53:TITLE Hebrew *maskil.* This may be a literary or musical term. 53:3 Greek version reads *have become useless.* Compare Rom 3:12.

PROVERBS 22:28-29

Don't cheat your neighbor by moving the ancient boundary markers set up by previous generations. □ Do you see any truly competent workers? They will serve kings rather than working for ordinary people.

SEPTEMBER 10

ISAIAH 6:1–7:25

It was in the year King Uzziah died* that I [Isaiah] saw the Lord. He was sitting on a lofty throne, and the train of his robe filled the Temple. ²Attending him were mighty seraphim, each having six wings. With two wings they covered their faces, with two they covered their feet, and with two they flew. ³They were calling out to each other,

"Holy, holy, holy is the LORD of Heaven's Armies!
The whole earth is filled with his glory!"

⁴Their voices shook the Temple to its foundations, and the entire building was filled with smoke.

⁵Then I said, "It's all over! I am doomed, for I am a sinful man. I have filthy lips, and I live among a people with filthy lips. Yet I have seen the King, the LORD of Heaven's Armies."

⁶Then one of the seraphim flew to me with a burning coal he had taken from the altar with a pair of tongs. ⁷He touched my lips with it and said, "See, this coal has touched your lips. Now your guilt is removed, and your sins are forgiven."

⁸Then I heard the Lord asking, "Whom should I send as a messenger to this people? Who will go for us?"

I said, "Here I am. Send me."

⁹And he said, "Yes, go, and say to this people,

'Listen carefully, but do not understand.
Watch closely, but learn nothing.'
¹⁰ Harden the hearts of these people.
Plug their ears and shut their eyes.
That way, they will not see with their eyes,
nor hear with their ears,
nor understand with their hearts
and turn to me for healing."*

¹¹Then I said, "Lord, how long will this go on?"

And he replied,

"Until their towns are empty, their houses are deserted,
and the whole country is a wasteland;
¹² until the LORD has sent everyone away,
and the entire land of Israel lies deserted.
¹³ If even a tenth—a remnant—survive, it will be invaded again and burned.
But as a terebinth or oak tree leaves a stump when it is cut down,
so Israel's stump will be a holy seed."

⁷:¹WHEN Ahaz, son of Jotham and grandson of Uzziah, was king of Judah, King Rezin of Syria* and Pekah son of Remaliah, the king of Israel, set out to attack Jerusalem. However, they were unable to carry out their plan.

²The news had come to the royal court of Judah: "Syria is allied with Israel* against us!" So the hearts of the king and his people trembled with fear, like trees shaking in a storm.

³Then the LORD said to Isaiah, "Take your son Shear-jashub* and go out to meet King Ahaz. You will find him at the end of the aqueduct that feeds water into the upper pool, near the road leading to the field where cloth is washed.* ⁴Tell him to stop worrying. Tell him he doesn't need to fear the fierce anger of those two burned-out embers, King Rezin of Syria and Pekah son of Remaliah. ⁵Yes, the kings of Syria and Israel are plotting against him, saying, ⁶'We will attack Judah and capture it for ourselves. Then we will install the son of Tabeel as Judah's king.' ⁷But this is what the Sovereign LORD says:

"This invasion will never happen; it will never take place;
⁸ for Syria is no stronger than its capital, Damascus,

and Damascus is no stronger than
its king, Rezin.
As for Israel, within sixty-five years
it will be crushed and completely
destroyed.
⁹ Israel is no stronger than its capital,
Samaria,
and Samaria is no stronger than
its king, Pekah son of Remaliah.
Unless your faith is firm,
I cannot make you stand firm."

¹⁰Later, the Lᴏʀᴅ sent this message to
King Ahaz: ¹¹"Ask the Lᴏʀᴅ your God for
a sign of confirmation, Ahaz. Make it as
difficult as you want—as high as heaven
or as deep as the place of the dead.*"

¹²But the king refused. "No," he said,
"I will not test the Lᴏʀᴅ like that."

¹³Then Isaiah said, "Listen well, you
royal family of David! Isn't it enough to
exhaust human patience? Must you exhaust the patience of my God as well?
¹⁴All right then, the Lord himself will
give you the sign. Look! The virgin* will
conceive a child! She will give birth to a
son and will call him Immanuel (which
means 'God is with us'). ¹⁵By the time
this child is old enough to choose what
is right [and] reject what is wrong, he will
be eating yogurt* and honey. ¹⁶For before the child is that old, the lands of both
the two kings you fear so much will both be
deserted.

¹⁷"Then the Lᴏʀᴅ will bring things on
you, your nation, and your family unlike
anything since Israel broke away from
Judah. He will bring the king of Assyria
upon you!"

¹⁸In that day the Lᴏʀᴅ will whistle for
the army of southern Egypt and for the
army of Assyria. They will swarm around
you like flies and bees. ¹⁹They will come
in vast hordes and settle in the fertile
areas and also in the desolate valleys,
caves, and thorny places. ²⁰In that day
the Lord will hire a "razor" from beyond
the Euphrates River*—the king of Assyria—and use it to shave off everything:
your land, your crops, and your people.*

²¹In that day a farmer will be fortunate to have a cow and two sheep or

goats left. ²²Nevertheless, there will be
enough milk for everyone because so
few people will be left in the land. They
will eat their fill of yogurt and honey.
²³In that day the lush vineyards, now
worth 1,000 pieces of silver,* will become patches of briers and thorns.
²⁴The entire land will become a vast ex-
panse of briers and thorns, a hunting
ground overrun by wildlife. ²⁵No one
will go to the fertile hillsides where the
gardens once grew, for briers and
thorns will cover them. Cattle, sheep,
and goats will graze there.

6:1 King Uzziah died in 740 ʙ.ᴄ.   6:9-10 Greek version
reads *And he said, "Go and say to this people, / 'When you
hear what I say, you will not understand. / When you see
what I do, you will not comprehend.' / For the hearts of
these people are hardened, / and their ears cannot hear,
and they have closed their eyes— / so their eyes cannot see,
/ and their ears cannot hear, / and their hearts cannot
understand, / and they cannot turn to me and let me heal
them."* Compare Matt 13:14-15; Mark 4:12; Luke 8:10;
Acts 28:26-27.   7:1 Hebrew *Aram;* also in 7:2, 4, 5, 8.
7:2 Hebrew *Ephraim,* referring to the northern kingdom of
Israel; also in 7:5, 8, 9, 17.   7:3a *Shear-jashub* means "A
remnant will return."   7:3b Or *bleached.*   7:11 Hebrew *as
deep as Sheol.*   7:14 Or *young woman.*   7:15 Or *curds;*
also in 7:22.   7:20a Hebrew *the river.*   7:20b Hebrew
shave off the head, the hair of the legs, and the beard.
7:23 Hebrew *1,000 shekels of silver,* about 25 pounds or
11.4 kilograms in weight.

2 CORINTHIANS 11:16-33

Again I [Paul] say, don't think that I am a
fool to talk like this. But even if you do,
listen to me, as you would to a foolish
person, while I also boast a little. ¹⁷Such
boasting is not from the Lord, but I am
acting like a fool. ¹⁸And since others
boast about their human achievements,
I will, too. ¹⁹After all, you think you are
so wise, but you enjoy putting up with
fools! ²⁰You put up with it when someone enslaves you, takes everything you
have, takes advantage of you, takes control of everything, and slaps you in the
face. ²¹I'm ashamed to say that we've
been too "weak" to do that!

But whatever they dare to boast
about—I'm talking like a fool again—I
dare to boast about it, too. ²²Are they He-
brews? So am I. Are they Israelites? So am
I. Are they descendants of Abraham? So
am I. ²³Are they servants of Christ? I
know I sound like a madman, but I have
served him far more! I have worked

harder, been put in prison more often, been whipped times without number, and faced death again and again. 24Five different times the Jewish leaders gave me thirty-nine lashes. 25Three times I was beaten with rods. Once I was stoned. Three times I was shipwrecked. Once I spent a whole night and a day adrift at sea. 26I have traveled on many long journeys. I have faced danger from rivers and from robbers. I have faced danger from my own people, the Jews, as well as from the Gentiles. I have faced danger in the cities, in the deserts, and on the seas. And I have faced danger from men who claim to be believers but are not.* 27I have worked hard and long, enduring many sleepless nights. I have been hungry and thirsty and have often gone without food. I have shivered in the cold, without enough clothing to keep me warm.

28Then, besides all this, I have the daily burden of my concern for all the churches. 29Who is weak without my feeling that weakness? Who is led astray, and I do not burn with anger?

30If I must boast, I would rather boast about the things that show how weak I am. 31God, the Father of our Lord Jesus, who is worthy of eternal praise, knows I am not lying. 32When I was in Damascus, the governor under King Aretas kept guards at the city gates to catch me. 33I had to be lowered in a basket through a window in the city wall to escape from him.

11:26 Greek *from false brothers.*

PSALM 54:1-7
For the choir director: A psalm* of David, regarding the time the Ziphites came and said to Saul, "We know where David is hiding." To be accompanied by stringed instruments.

1 **C**ome with great power, O God,
    and rescue me!
  Defend me with your might.
2 Listen to my prayer, O God.
    Pay attention to my plea.
3 For strangers are attacking me;

    violent people are trying
      to kill me.
  They care nothing for God.
                          Interlude

4 But God is my helper.
    The Lord keeps me alive!
5 May the evil plans of my enemies be
      turned against them.
    Do as you promised and put an
      end to them.

6 I will sacrifice a voluntary offering
      to you;
    I will praise your name, O LORD,
      for it is good.
7 For you have rescued me from my
      troubles
    and helped me to triumph over
      my enemies.

54:TITLE Hebrew *maskil.* This may be a literary or musical term.

PROVERBS 23:1-3
While dining with a ruler, pay attention to what is put before you. If you are a big eater, put a knife to your throat; don't desire all the delicacies, for he might be trying to trick you.

SEPTEMBER
11

ISAIAH 8:1-9:21
Then the LORD said to me [Isaiah], "Make a large signboard and clearly write this name on it: Maher-shalal-hash-baz.*" 2I asked Uriah the priest and Zechariah son of Jeberekiah, both known as honest men, to witness my doing this.

3Then I slept with my wife, and she became pregnant and gave birth to a son. And the LORD said, "Call him Maher-shalal-hash-baz. 4For before this child is old enough to say 'Papa' or 'Mama,' the king of Assyria will carry away both the abundance of Damascus and the riches of Samaria."

⁵Then the LORD spoke to me again and said, ⁶"My care for the people of Judah is like the gently flowing waters of Shiloah, but they have rejected it. They are rejoicing over what will happen to* King Rezin and King Pekah.* ⁷Therefore, the Lord will overwhelm them with a mighty flood from the Euphrates River*—the king of Assyria and all his glory. This flood will overflow all its channels ⁸and sweep into Judah until it is chin deep. It will spread its wings, submerging your land from one end to the other, O Immanuel.

⁹ "Huddle together, you nations, and
    be terrified.
Listen, all you distant lands.
Prepare for battle, but you will be
    crushed!
Yes, prepare for battle, but you
    will be crushed!
¹⁰ Call your councils of war, but they
    will be worthless.
Develop your strategies, but they
    will not succeed.
For God is with us!*"

¹¹The LORD has given me a strong warning not to think like everyone else does. He said,

¹² "Don't call everything a conspiracy,
    like they do,
and don't live in dread of what
    frightens them.
¹³ Make the LORD of Heaven's Armies
    holy in your life.
He is the one you should fear.
He is the one who should make
    you tremble.
¹⁴   He will keep you safe.
But to Israel and Judah
    he will be a stone that makes
        people stumble,
    a rock that makes them fall.
And for the people of Jerusalem
    he will be a trap and a snare.
¹⁵ Many will stumble and fall,
    never to rise again.
    They will be snared and captured."

¹⁶ Preserve the teaching of God;
    entrust his instructions to those
        who follow me.
¹⁷ I will wait for the LORD,
    who has turned away from the
        descendants of Jacob.
    I will put my hope in him.

¹⁸I and the children the LORD has given me serve as signs and warnings to Israel from the LORD of Heaven's Armies who dwells in his Temple on Mount Zion.

¹⁹Someone may say to you, "Let's ask the mediums and those who consult the spirits of the dead. With their whisperings and mutterings, they will tell us what to do." But shouldn't people ask God for guidance? Should the living seek guidance from the dead?

²⁰Look to God's instructions and teachings! People who contradict his word are completely in the dark. ²¹They will go from one place to another, weary and hungry. And because they are hungry, they will rage and curse their king and their God. They will look up to heaven ²²and down at the earth, but wherever they look, there will be trouble and anguish and dark despair. They will be thrown out into the darkness.

⁹:¹*NEVERTHELESS, that time of darkness and despair will not go on forever. The land of Zebulun and Naphtali will be humbled, but there will be a time in the future when Galilee of the Gentiles, which lies along the road that runs between the Jordan and the sea, will be filled with glory.

²*The people who walk in darkness
    will see a great light.
For those who live in a land of deep
    darkness,*
    a light will shine.
³ You will enlarge the nation of Israel,
    and its people will rejoice.
They will rejoice before you
    as people rejoice at the harvest
    and like warriors dividing the
        plunder.
⁴ For you will break the yoke
    of their slavery

and lift the heavy burden from
their shoulders.
You will break the oppressor's rod,
just as you did when you
destroyed the army of Midian.
⁵ The boots of the warrior
and the uniforms bloodstained
by war
will all be burned.
They will be fuel for the fire.

⁶ **For a child is born to us,**
a son is given to us.
The government will rest on his
shoulders.
And he will be called:
Wonderful Counselor,*
Mighty God,
Everlasting Father, Prince
of Peace.
⁷ His government and its peace
will never end.
He will rule with fairness and
justice from the throne of his
ancestor David
for all eternity.
The passionate commitment of the
LORD of Heaven's Armies
will make this happen!

⁸ The Lord has spoken out against
Jacob;
his judgment has fallen upon Israel.
⁹ And the people of Israel* and
Samaria,
who spoke with such pride and
arrogance,
will soon know it.
¹⁰ They said, "We will replace the
broken bricks of our ruins with
finished stone,
and replant the felled sycamore-
fig trees with cedars."

¹¹ But the LORD will bring Rezin's
enemies against Israel
and stir up all their foes.
¹² The Syrians* from the east and the
Philistines from the west
will bare their fangs and devour
Israel.
But even then the LORD's anger will
not be satisfied.

His fist is still poised to strike.

¹³ For after all this punishment, the
people will still not repent.
They will not seek the LORD of
Heaven's Armies.
¹⁴ Therefore, in a single day the LORD
will destroy both the head and
the tail,
the noble palm branch and the
lowly reed.
¹⁵ The leaders of Israel are the head,
and the lying prophets are
the tail.
¹⁶ For the leaders of the people have
misled them.
They have led them down the
path of destruction.
¹⁷ That is why the Lord takes no
pleasure in the young men
and shows no mercy even to the
widows and orphans.
For they are all wicked hypocrites,
and they all speak foolishness.
But even then the LORD's anger will
not be satisfied.
His fist is still poised to strike.

¹⁸ This wickedness is like a
brushfire.
It burns not only briers and
thorns
but also sets the forests ablaze.
Its burning sends up clouds
of smoke.
¹⁹ The land will be blackened
by the fury of the LORD of
Heaven's Armies.
The people will be fuel for the fire,
and no one will spare even his
own brother.
²⁰ They will attack their neighbor on
the right
but will still be hungry.
They will devour their neighbor
on the left
but will not be satisfied.
In the end they will even eat their
own children.*
²¹ Manasseh will feed on Ephraim,
Ephraim will feed on Manasseh,
and both will devour Judah.

But even then the LORD's anger will
not be satisfied.
His fist is still poised to strike.

8:1 *Maher-shalal-hash-baz* means "Swift to plunder and
quick to carry away." 8:6a Or *They are rejoicing because
of.* 8:6b Hebrew *and the son of Remaliah.* 8:7 Hebrew
the river. 8:10 Hebrew *Immanuel!* 9:1 Verse 9:1 is
numbered 8:23 in Hebrew text. 9:2a Verses 9:2-21 are
numbered 9:1-20 in Hebrew text. 9:2b Greek version
reads *a land where death casts its shadow.* Compare Matt
4:16. 9:6 Or *Wonderful, Counselor.* 9:9 Hebrew *of
Ephraim,* referring to the northern kingdom of Israel.
9:12 Hebrew *Arameans.* 9:20 Or *eat their own arms.*

2 CORINTHIANS 12:1-10

This boasting will do no good, but I [Paul]
must go on. I will reluctantly tell about
visions and revelations from the Lord.
²I* was caught up to the third heaven
fourteen years ago. Whether I was in my
body or out of my body, I don't know—
only God knows. ³Yes, only God knows
whether I was in my body or outside my
body. But I do know ⁴that I was caught
up* to paradise and heard things so as-
tounding that they cannot be expressed
in words, things no human is allowed to
tell.

⁵That experience is worth boasting
about, but I'm not going to do it. I will
boast only about my weaknesses. ⁶If I
wanted to boast, I would be no fool in
doing so, because I would be telling the
truth. But I won't do it, because I don't
want anyone to give me credit beyond
what they can see in my life or hear in
my message, ⁷even though I have received such wonderful revelations from
God. So to keep me from becoming
proud, I was given a thorn in my flesh, a
messenger from Satan to torment me
and keep me from becoming proud.

⁸Three different times I begged the
Lord to take it away. ⁹Each time he said,
"My grace is all you need. My power
works best in weakness." So now I am
glad to boast about my weaknesses, so
that the power of Christ can work
through me. ¹⁰That's why I take pleasure
in my weaknesses, and in the insults,
hardships, persecutions, and troubles
that I suffer for Christ. For when I am
weak, then I am strong.

12:2 Greek *I know a man in Christ who.* 12:3-4 Greek
But I know such a man, 'that he was caught up.

PSALM 55:1-23

For the choir director: A psalm of David, to
be accompanied by stringed instruments.*

¹ Listen to my prayer, O God.
    Do not ignore my cry for help!
² Please listen and answer me,
    for I am overwhelmed by my
        troubles.
³ My enemies shout at me,
    making loud and wicked threats.
They bring trouble on me
    and angrily hunt me down.

⁴ My heart pounds in my chest.
    The terror of death assaults me.
⁵ Fear and trembling overwhelm me,
    and I can't stop shaking.
⁶ Oh, that I had wings like a dove;
    then I would fly away and rest!
⁷ I would fly far away
    to the quiet of the wilderness.
                                    Interlude
⁸ How quickly I would escape—
    far from this wild storm of hatred.

⁹ Confuse them, Lord, and frustrate
        their plans,
    for I see violence and conflict in
        the city.
¹⁰ Its walls are patrolled day and night
        against invaders,
    but the real danger is wickedness
        within the city.
¹¹ Everything is falling apart;
    threats and cheating are rampant
        in the streets.

¹² It is not an enemy who taunts me—
    I could bear that.
It is not my foes who so arrogantly
        insult me—
    I could have hidden from them.
¹³ Instead, it is you—my equal,
    my companion and close friend.
¹⁴ What good fellowship we once
        enjoyed
    as we walked together to the
        house of God.

¹⁵ Let death stalk my enemies;
    let the grave* swallow them alive,
    for evil makes its home within
        them.

¹⁶ But I will call on God,
and the LORD will rescue me.
¹⁷ Morning, noon, and night
I cry out in my distress,
and the LORD hears my voice.
¹⁸ He ransoms me and keeps me safe
from the battle waged
against me,
though many still oppose me.
¹⁹ God, who has ruled forever,
will hear me and humble them.
Interlude
For my enemies refuse to change
their ways;
they do not fear God.

²⁰ As for my companion, he betrayed
his friends;
he broke his promises.
²¹ His words are as smooth as butter,
but in his heart is war.
His words are as soothing as lotion,
but underneath are daggers!

²² Give your burdens to the LORD,
and he will take care of you.
He will not permit the godly
to slip and fall.

²³ But you, O God, will send the
wicked
down to the pit of destruction.
Murderers and liars will die
young,
but I am trusting you to save me.

55:TITLE Hebrew *maskil*. This may be a literary or musical
term.   55:15 Hebrew *let Sheol*.

PROVERBS 23:4-5
Don't wear yourself out trying to get
rich. Be wise enough to know when to
quit. In the blink of an eye wealth disappears, for it will sprout wings and fly
away like an eagle.

SEPTEMBER 12

ISAIAH 10:1–11:16
What sorrow awaits the unjust judges
and those who issue unfair laws.
² They deprive the poor of justice
and deny the rights of the needy
among my people.
They prey on widows
and take advantage of orphans.
³ What will you do when I punish you,
when I send disaster upon you
from a distant land?
To whom will you turn for help?
Where will your treasures
be safe?
⁴ You will stumble along as prisoners
or lie among the dead.
But even then the LORD's anger will
not be satisfied.
His fist is still poised to strike.

⁵ "What sorrow awaits Assyria, the
rod of my anger.
I use it as a club to express
my anger.
⁶ I am sending Assyria against
a godless nation,
against a people with whom
I am angry.
Assyria will plunder them,
trampling them like dirt beneath
its feet.
⁷ But the king of Assyria will not
understand that he is my tool;
his mind does not work that way.
His plan is simply to destroy,
to cut down nation after nation.
⁸ He will say,
'Each of my princes will soon
be a king.
⁹ We destroyed Calno just as we did
Carchemish.
Hamath fell before us as
Arpad did.
And we destroyed Samaria just
as we did Damascus.

10 Yes, we have finished off many
       a kingdom
    whose gods were greater than
       those in Jerusalem and
       Samaria.
11 So we will defeat Jerusalem and
       her gods,
    just as we destroyed Samaria
       with hers.'"

12After the Lord has used the king of
Assyria to accomplish his purposes on
Mount Zion and in Jerusalem, he will
turn against the king of Assyria and
punish him—for he is proud and arrogant. 13He boasts,

   "By my own powerful arm I have
      done this.
    With my own shrewd wisdom
       I planned it.
    I have broken down the defenses
       of nations
    and carried off their treasures.
    I have knocked down their kings
       like a bull.
14 I have robbed their nests of riches
    and gathered up kingdoms as a
       farmer gathers eggs.
    No one can even flap a wing
       against me
    or utter a peep of protest."

15 But can the ax boast greater power
       than the person who uses it?
    Is the saw greater than the person
       who saws?
    Can a rod strike unless a hand
       moves it?
    Can a wooden cane walk by itself?
16 Therefore, the Lord, the LORD of
       Heaven's Armies,
    will send a plague among
       Assyria's proud troops,
    and a flaming fire will consume
       its glory.
17 The LORD, the Light of Israel, will
       be a fire;
    the Holy One will be a flame.
    He will devour the thorns and briers
       with fire,
    burning up the enemy in a single
       night.

18 The LORD will consume Assyria's glory
       like a fire consumes a forest
       in a fruitful land;
    it will waste away like sick people
       in a plague.
19 Of all that glorious forest, only a few
       trees will survive—
    so few that a child could count
       them!

20 In that day the remnant left in Israel,
       the survivors in the house
       of Jacob,
    will no longer depend on allies
       who seek to destroy them.
    But they will faithfully trust the LORD,
       the Holy One of Israel.
21 A remnant will return;*
    yes, the remnant of Jacob will
       return to the Mighty God.
22 But though the people of Israel are
       as numerous
       as the sand of the seashore,
    only a remnant of them will return.
    The LORD has rightly decided to
       destroy his people.
23 Yes, the Lord, the LORD of Heaven's
       Armies,
    has already decided to destroy the
       entire land.*

24So this is what the Lord, the LORD of
Heaven's Armies, says: "O my people in
Zion, do not be afraid of the Assyrians
when they oppress you with rod and
club as the Egyptians did long ago. 25In
a little while my anger against you will
end, and then my anger will rise up to
destroy them." 26The LORD of Heaven's
Armies will lash them with his whip, as
he did when Gideon triumphed over the
Midianites at the rock of Oreb, or when
the LORD's staff was raised to drown the
Egyptian army in the sea.

27 In that day the LORD will end the
       bondage of his people.
    He will break the yoke of slavery
       and lift it from their shoulders.*

28 Look, the Assyrians are now at Aiath.
       They are passing through Migron
       and are storing their equipment
       at Micmash.

²⁹ They are crossing the pass
  and are camping at Geba.
Fear strikes the town of Ramah.
  All the people of Gibeah, the
    hometown of Saul,
  are running for their lives.
³⁰ Scream in terror,
  you people of Gallim!
Shout out a warning to Laishah.
  Oh, poor Anathoth!
³¹ There go the people of Madmenah,
    all fleeing.
  The citizens of Gebim are trying
    to hide.
³² The enemy stops at Nob for the rest
    of that day.
  He shakes his fist at beautiful
    Mount Zion, the mountain
    of Jerusalem.

³³ But look! The Lord, the LORD of
    Heaven's Armies,
  will chop down the mighty tree
    of Assyria with great power!
  He will cut down the proud.
  That lofty tree will be brought
    down.
³⁴ He will cut down the forest trees
    with an ax.
  Lebanon will fall to the Mighty
    One.*

¹¹:¹Out of the stump of David's family*
    will grow a shoot—
  yes, a new Branch bearing fruit
    from the old root.
² And the Spirit of the LORD will rest
    on him—
  the Spirit of wisdom and
    understanding,
  the Spirit of counsel and might,
    the Spirit of knowledge and the
    fear of the LORD.
³ He will delight in obeying the LORD.
  He will not judge by appearance
  nor make a decision based on
    hearsay.
⁴ He will give justice to the poor
  and make fair decisions for the
    exploited.
The earth will shake at the force
    of his word,

and one breath from his mouth
  will destroy the wicked.
⁵ He will wear righteousness like a belt
  and truth like an undergarment.

⁶ **In that day the wolf and the lamb
    will live together;
  the leopard will lie down with
    the baby goat.
The calf and the yearling will be
    safe with the lion,
  and a little child will lead
    them all.**
⁷ The cow will graze near the bear.
  The cub and the calf will lie down
    together.
  The lion will eat hay like a cow.
⁸ The baby will play safely near the
    hole of a cobra.
  Yes, a little child will put its hand
    in a nest of deadly snakes
    without harm.
⁹ Nothing will hurt or destroy in all
    my holy mountain,
  for as the waters fill the sea,
  so the earth will be filled with
    people who know the LORD.

¹⁰ In that day the heir to David's throne*
    will be a banner of salvation
    to all the world.
  The nations will rally to him,
    and the land where he lives
    will be a glorious place.*
¹¹ In that day the Lord will reach out
    his hand a second time
  to bring back the remnant of his
    people—
  those who remain in Assyria and
    northern Egypt;
    in southern Egypt, Ethiopia,*
    and Elam;
    in Babylonia,* Hamath, and
    all the distant coastlands.
¹² He will raise a flag among the
    nations
  and assemble the exiles of Israel.
  He will gather the scattered people
    of Judah
  from the ends of the earth.
¹³ Then at last the jealousy between
    Israel* and Judah will end.

They will not be rivals anymore.
14 They will join forces to swoop down
on Philistia to the west.
Together they will attack and
plunder the nations to the east.
They will occupy the lands of Edom
and Moab,
and Ammon will obey them.
15 The LORD will make a dry path
through the gulf of the Red Sea.*
He will wave his hand over the
Euphrates River,*
sending a mighty wind to divide it
into seven streams
so it can easily be crossed on foot.
16 He will make a highway for the
remnant of his people,
the remnant coming from Assyria,
just as he did for Israel long ago
when they returned from Egypt.

10:21 Hebrew *Shear-jashub;* see 7:3; 8:18.
10:22-23 Greek version reads *only a remnant of them will
be saved. / For he will carry out his sentence quickly and
with finality and righteousness; / for God will carry out his
sentence upon all the world with finality.* Compare Rom
9:27-28.   10:27 As in Greek version; Hebrew reads
The yoke will be broken, / for you have grown so fat.
10:34 Or *with an ax / as even the mighty trees of Lebanon
fall.*   11:1 Hebrew *the stump of the line of Jesse.* Jesse was
King David's father.   11:10a Hebrew *the root of Jesse.*
11:10b Greek version reads *In that day the heir to David's
throne* [literally *the root of Jesse*] *will come, / and he will
rule over the Gentiles. / They will place their hopes on him.*
Compare Rom 15:12.   11:11a Hebrew *in Pathros, Cush.*
11:11b Hebrew *in Shinar.*   11:13 Hebrew *Ephraim,*
referring to the northern kingdom of Israel.
11:15a Hebrew *will destroy the tongue of the sea
of Egypt.*   11:15b Hebrew *the river.*

2 CORINTHIANS 12:11-21

You [Corinthians] have made me [Paul]
act like a fool—boasting like this.* You
ought to be writing commendations for
me, for I am not at all inferior to these
"super apostles," even though I am
nothing at all. 12When I was with you, I
certainly gave you proof that I am an
apostle. For I patiently did many signs
and wonders and miracles among you.
13The only thing I failed to do, which I
do in the other churches, was to become a financial burden to you. Please
forgive me for this wrong!

14Now I am coming to you for the
third time, and I will not be a burden to
you. I don't want what you have—I want
you. After all, children don't provide for
their parents. Rather, parents provide

for their children. 15I will gladly spend
myself and all I have for you, even
though it seems that the more I love
you, the less you love me.

16Some of you admit I was not a burden to you. But others still think I was
sneaky and took advantage of you by
trickery. 17But how? Did any of the men
I sent to you take advantage of you?
18When I urged Titus to visit you and
sent our other brother with him, did Titus take advantage of you? No! For we
have the same spirit and walk in each
other's steps, doing things the same
way.

19Perhaps you think we're saying
these things just to defend ourselves.
No, we tell you this as Christ's servants,
and with God as our witness. Everything
we do, dear friends, is to strengthen
you. 20For I am afraid that when I come I
won't like what I find, and you won't like
my response. I am afraid that I will find
quarreling, jealousy, anger, selfishness,
slander, gossip, arrogance, and dis-
orderly behavior. 21Yes, I am afraid that
when I come again, God will humble me
in your presence. And I will be grieved
because many of you have not given up
your old sins. You have not repented of
your impurity, sexual immorality, and
eagerness for lustful pleasure.

12:11 Some manuscripts omit *boasting like this.*

PSALM 56:1-13

*For the choir director: A psalm of David,
regarding the time the Philistines seized
him in Gath. To be sung to the tune "Dove
on Distant Oaks."*

1 O God, have mercy on me,
for people are hounding me.
My foes attack me all day long.
2 I am constantly hounded by those
who slander me,
and many are boldly attacking me.
3 But when I am afraid,
I will put my trust in you.
4 I praise God for what he has
promised.
I trust in God, so why should
I be afraid?

What can mere mortals
   do to me?

5 They are always twisting what I say;
      they spend their days plotting to
      harm me.
6 They come together to spy
      on me—
      watching my every step, eager
      to kill me.
7 Don't let them get away with their
      wickedness;
      in your anger, O God, bring
      them down.

8 You keep track of all my sorrows.*
      You have collected all my tears in
      your bottle.
      You have recorded each one in
      your book.

9 My enemies will retreat when I call
      to you for help.
      This I know: God is on my side!
10 I praise God for what he has
      promised;
      Yes, I praise the LORD for what
      he has promised.
11 I trust in God, so why should I be
      afraid?
      What can mere mortals do to me?

12 I will fulfill my vows to you,
      O God,
      and will offer a sacrifice of thanks
      for your help.
13 For you have rescued me from
      death;
      you have kept my feet from
      slipping.
   So now I can walk in your presence,
      O God,
      in your life-giving light.

56:8 Or *my wanderings*.

PROVERBS 23:6-8

Don't eat with people who are stingy;
don't desire their delicacies. They are
always thinking about how much it
costs.* "Eat and drink," they say, but
they don't mean it. You will throw up
what little you've eaten, and your com-
pliments will be wasted.

23:7 The meaning of the Hebrew is uncertain.

SEPTEMBER 13

ISAIAH 12:1–14:32

In that day you [Israel] will sing:
   "I will praise you, O LORD!
You were angry with me, but
   not any more.
Now you comfort me.
2 See, God has come to save me.
   I will trust in him and not be
   afraid.
The LORD GOD is my strength
   and my song;
   he has given me victory."

3 With joy you will drink deeply
      from the fountain of salvation!
4 In that wonderful day you will sing:
      "Thank the LORD! Praise his name!
Tell the nations what he has done.
   Let them know how mighty he is!
5 Sing to the LORD, for he has done
      wonderful things.
   Make known his praise around
      the world.
6 Let all the people of Jerusalem*
      shout his praise with joy!
   For great is the Holy One of Israel
      who lives among you."

13:1Isaiah son of Amoz received this
message concerning the destruction of
Babylon:

2 "Raise a signal flag on a bare hilltop.
      Call up an army against Babylon.
Wave your hand to encourage them
      as they march into the palaces of
      the high and mighty.
3 I, the LORD, have dedicated these
      soldiers for this task.
   Yes, I have called mighty warriors
      to express my anger,
   and they will rejoice when
      I am exalted."

4 Hear the noise on the mountains!
      Listen, as the vast armies march!
   It is the noise and shouting
      of many nations.

The LORD of Heaven's Armies has
called this army together.
5 They come from distant countries,
from beyond the farthest
horizons.
They are the LORD's weapons to
carry out his anger.
With them he will destroy the
whole land.

6 Scream in terror, for the day
of the LORD has arrived—
the time for the Almighty
to destroy.
7 Every arm is paralyzed with fear.
Every heart melts,
8 and people are terrified.
Pangs of anguish grip them,
like those of a woman in labor.
They look helplessly at one another,
their faces aflame with fear.

9 For see, the day of the LORD is
coming—
the terrible day of his fury and
fierce anger.
The land will be made desolate,
and all the sinners destroyed
with it.
10 The heavens will be black above
them;
the stars will give no light.
The sun will be dark when
it rises,
and the moon will provide
no light.

11 "I, the LORD, will punish the world
for its evil
and the wicked for their sin.
I will crush the arrogance of the
proud
and humble the pride of the
mighty.
12 I will make people scarcer than
gold—
more rare than the fine gold
of Ophir.
13 For I will shake the heavens.
The earth will move from its place
when the LORD of Heaven's Armies
displays his wrath
in the day of his fierce anger."

14 Everyone in Babylon will run about
like a hunted gazelle,
like sheep without a shepherd.
They will try to find their own
people
and flee to their own land.
15 Anyone who is captured will be
cut down—
run through with a sword.
16 Their little children will be dashed
to death before their eyes.
Their homes will be sacked, and
their wives will be raped.

17 "Look, I will stir up the Medes
against Babylon.
They cannot be tempted by silver
or bribed with gold.
18 The attacking armies will shoot
down the young men with
arrows.
They will have no mercy on
helpless babies
and will show no compassion for
children."

19 Babylon, the most glorious of
kingdoms,
the flower of Chaldean pride,
will be devastated like Sodom and
Gomorrah
when God destroyed them.
20 Babylon will never be inhabited
again.
It will remain empty for
generation after generation.
Nomads will refuse to camp there,
and shepherds will not bed down
their sheep.
21 Desert animals will move into the
ruined city,
and the houses will be haunted by
howling creatures.
Owls will live among the ruins,
and wild goats will go there to
dance.
22 Hyenas will howl in its fortresses,
and jackals will make dens in its
luxurious palaces.
Babylon's days are numbered;
its time of destruction will
soon arrive.

14:1But the LORD will have mercy on the descendants of Jacob. He will choose Israel as his special people once again. He will bring them back to settle once again in their own land. And people from many different nations will come and join them there and unite with the people of Israel.* 2The nations of the world will help the LORD's people to return, and those who come to live in their land will serve them. Those who captured Israel will themselves be captured, and Israel will rule over its enemies.

3In that wonderful day when the LORD gives his people rest from sorrow and fear, from slavery and chains, 4you will taunt the king of Babylon. You will say,

> "The mighty man has been
>   destroyed.
>   Yes, your insolence* is ended.
> 5 For the LORD has crushed your
>   wicked power
>   and broken your evil rule.
> 6 You struck the people with endless
>   blows of rage
>   and held the nations in your
>   angry grip
>   with unrelenting tyranny.
> 7 But finally the earth is at rest and
>   quiet.
>   Now it can sing again!
> 8 Even the trees of the forest—
>   the cypress trees and the cedars
>   of Lebanon—
>   sing out this joyous song:
> 'Since you have been cut down,
>   no one will come now to cut
>   us down!'
>
> 9 "In the place of the dead* there is
>   excitement
>   over your arrival.
> The spirits of world leaders and
>   mighty kings long dead
>   stand up to see you.
> 10 With one voice they all cry out,
>   'Now you are as weak as we are!
> 11 Your might and power were buried
>   with you.*
>   The sound of the harp in your
>   palace has ceased.

> Now maggots are your sheet,
>   and worms your blanket.'
>
> 12 "How you are fallen from heaven,
>   O shining star, son of the
>   morning!
> You have been thrown down
>   to the earth,
>   you who destroyed the nations
>   of the world.
> 13 For you said to yourself,
>   'I will ascend to heaven and set
>   my throne above God's stars.
> I will preside on the mountain
>   of the gods
>   far away in the north.*
> 14 I will climb to the highest heavens
>   and be like the Most High.'
> 15 Instead, you will be brought down to
>   the place of the dead,
>   down to its lowest depths.
> 16 Everyone there will stare at you
>   and ask,
>   'Can this be the one who shook
>   the earth
>   and made the kingdoms of the
>   world tremble?
> 17 Is this the one who destroyed the
>   world
>   and made it into a wasteland?
> Is this the king who demolished the
>   world's greatest cities
>   and had no mercy on his
>   prisoners?'
>
> 18 "The kings of the nations lie in
>   stately glory,
>   each in his own tomb,
> 19 but you will be thrown out of your
>   grave
>   like a worthless branch.
> Like a corpse trampled underfoot,
>   you will be dumped into a mass
>   grave
>   with those killed in battle.
> You will descend to the pit.
> 20   You will not be given a proper
>   burial,
>   for you have destroyed your nation
>   and slaughtered your people.
> The descendants of such an evil
>   person
>   will never again receive honor.

21 Kill this man's children!
    Let them die because of their
        father's sins!
    They must not rise and conquer the
        earth,
        filling the world with their cities."

22 This is what the LORD of Heaven's
        Armies says:
    "I, myself, have risen against
        Babylon!
    I will destroy its children and its
        children's children,"
        says the LORD.

23 "I will make Babylon a desolate place
        of owls,
        filled with swamps and marshes.
    I will sweep the land with the broom
        of destruction.
    I, the LORD of Heaven's Armies,
        have spoken!"

24 The LORD of Heaven's Armies has
sworn this oath:

    "It will all happen as I have planned.
    It will be as I have decided.

25 I will break the Assyrians when they
        are in Israel;
    I will trample them on my
        mountains.
    My people will no longer be their
        slaves
        nor bow down under their
        heavy loads.

26 I have a plan for the whole earth,
    a hand of judgment upon all the
        nations.

27 The LORD of Heaven's Armies has
        spoken—
    who can change his plans?
    When his hand is raised,
    who can stop him?"

28 This message came to me the year
King Ahaz died:*

29 Do not rejoice, you Philistines,
        that the rod that struck you is
        broken—
        that the king who attacked you
        is dead.
    For from that snake a more
        poisonous snake will be born,

a fiery serpent to destroy you!

30 I will feed the poor in my pasture;
    the needy will lie down in peace.
    But as for you, I will wipe you out
        with famine
    and destroy the few who remain.

31 Wail at the gates! Weep in the cities!
    Melt with fear, you Philistines!
    A powerful army comes like smoke
        from the north.
    Each soldier rushes forward eager
        to fight.

32 What should we tell the Philistine
messengers? Tell them,

    "The LORD has built Jerusalem*;
        its walls will give refuge to his
        oppressed people."

12:6 Hebrew *Zion.*   14:1 Hebrew *the house of Jacob.*
The names "Jacob" and "Israel" are often interchanged
throughout the Old Testament, referring sometimes
to the individual patriarch and sometimes to the nation.
14:4 As in Dead Sea Scrolls; the meaning of the Masoretic
Text is uncertain.   14:9 Hebrew *Sheol;* also
in 14:15.   14:11 Hebrew *were brought down to Sheol.*
14:13 Or *on the heights of Zaphon.*   14:28 King Ahaz died
in 715 B.C.   14:32 Hebrew *Zion.*

2 CORINTHIANS 13:1-13

This is the third time I am coming to
visit you (and as the Scriptures say, "The
facts of every case must be established
by the testimony of two or three witnesses"*). 2I have already warned those
who had been sinning when I was there
on my second visit. Now I again warn
them and all others, just as I did before,
that next time I will not spare them.

3I will give you all the proof you want
that Christ speaks through me. Christ is
not weak when he deals with you; he is
powerful among you. 4Although he was
crucified in weakness, he now lives by
the power of God. We, too, are weak, just
as Christ was, but when we deal with you
we will be alive with him and will have
God's power.

5Examine yourselves to see if your
faith is genuine. Test yourselves. Surely
you know that Jesus Christ is among
you*; if not, you have failed the test of
genuine faith. 6As you test yourselves, I
hope you will recognize that we have not
failed the test of apostolic authority.

7We pray to God that you will not do

what is wrong by refusing our correction. I hope we won't need to demonstrate our authority when we arrive. Do the right thing before we come—even if that makes it look like we have failed to demonstrate our authority. 8For we cannot oppose the truth, but must always stand for the truth. 9We are glad to seem weak if it helps show that you are actually strong. We pray that you will become mature.

10I am writing this to you before I come, hoping that I won't need to deal severely with you when I do come. For I want to use the authority the Lord has given me to strengthen you, not to tear you down.

11Dear brothers and sisters,* I close my letter with these last words: Be joyful. Grow to maturity. Encourage each other. Live in harmony and peace. Then the God of love and peace will be with you.

12Greet each other with Christian love.* 13All of God's people here send you their greetings.

14*May the grace of the Lord Jesus Christ, the love of God, and the fellowship of the Holy Spirit be with you all.

13:1 Deut 19:15.   13:5 Or *in you.*   13:11 Greek *Brothers.*
13:12 Greek *with a sacred kiss.*   13:14 Some English translations include verse 13 as part of verse 12, and then verse 14 becomes verse 13.

PSALM 57:1-11

For the choir director: A psalm of David, regarding the time he fled from Saul and went into the cave. To be sung to the tune "Do Not Destroy!"

1 **H**ave mercy on me, O God, have mercy!
    I look to you for protection.
I will hide beneath the shadow of
        your wings
    until the danger passes by.
2 I cry out to God Most High,*
    to God who will fulfill his purpose
        for me.
3 He will send help from heaven to
        rescue me,
    disgracing those who hound me.
                                Interlude
My God will send forth his unfailing
    love and faithfulness.

4 I am surrounded by fierce lions
    who greedily devour human
        prey—
whose teeth pierce like spears
        and arrows,
    and whose tongues cut like swords.

5 Be exalted, O God, above the highest
        heavens!
    May your glory shine over all the
        earth.

6 My enemies have set a trap for me.
    I am weary from distress.
They have dug a deep pit in my path,
    but they themselves have fallen
        into it.   *Interlude*

7 **My heart is confident in you,
        O God;
    my heart is confident.
    No wonder I can sing your
        praises!**
8 **Wake up, my heart!
    Wake up, O lyre and harp!
    I will wake the dawn with
        my song.**
9 I will thank you, Lord, among
        all the people.
    I will sing your praises among
        the nations.
10 For your unfailing love is as high
        as the heavens.
    Your faithfulness reaches
        to the clouds.

11 Be exalted, O God, above the
        highest heavens.
    May your glory shine over
        all the earth.

57:2 Hebrew *El-Elyon.*

PROVERBS 23:9-11

Don't waste your breath on fools, for they will despise the wisest advice. □Don't cheat your neighbor by moving the ancient boundary markers; don't take the land of defenseless orphans. For their Redeemer* is strong; he himself will bring their charges against you.

23:11 Or *redeemer.*

SEPTEMBER
14

ISAIAH 15:1–18:7

This message came to me concerning Moab:

In one night the town of Ar will be
leveled,
and the city of Kir will be
destroyed.
2 Your people will go to their temple
in Dibon to mourn.
They will go to their sacred
shrines to weep.
They will wail for the fate of Nebo
and Medeba,
shaving their heads in sorrow and
cutting off their beards.
3 They will wear burlap as they
wander the streets.
From every home and public
square will come the sound
of wailing.
4 The people of Heshbon and Elealeh
will cry out;
their voices will be heard as far
away as Jahaz!
The bravest warriors of Moab will
cry out in utter terror.
They will be helpless with fear.

5 My heart weeps for Moab.
Its people flee to Zoar and
Eglath-shelishiyah.
Weeping, they climb the road to
Luhith.
Their cries of distress can be
heard all along the road to
Horonaim.
6 Even the waters of Nimrim are
dried up!
The grassy banks are scorched.
The tender plants are gone;
nothing green remains.
7 The people grab their possessions
and carry them across the Ravine
of Willows.
8 A cry of distress echoes through the
land of Moab

from one end to the other—
from Eglaim to Beer-elim.
9 The stream near Dibon* runs red
with blood,
but I am still not finished
with Dibon!
Lions will hunt down the survivors—
both those who try to escape
and those who remain behind.

16:1SEND lambs from Sela as tribute
to the ruler of the land.
Send them through the desert
to the mountain of beautiful Zion.
2 The women of Moab are left like
homeless birds
at the shallow crossings of the
Arnon River.
3 "Help us," they cry.
"Defend us against our enemies.
Protect us from their relentless
attack.
Do not betray us now that we
have escaped.
4 Let our refugees stay among you.
Hide them from our enemies
until the terror is past."

When oppression and destruction
have ended
and enemy raiders have
disappeared,
5 then God will establish one of
David's descendants as king.
He will rule with mercy and truth.
He will always do what is just
and be eager to do what is right.

6 We have heard about proud Moab—
about its pride and arrogance and
rage.
But all that boasting has
disappeared.
7 The entire land of Moab weeps.
Yes, everyone in Moab mourns
for the cakes of raisins from
Kir-hareseth.
They are all gone now.
8 The farms of Heshbon are abandoned;
the vineyards at Sibmah are
deserted.
The rulers of the nations have
broken down Moab—

that beautiful grapevine.
Its tendrils spread north as far as the
town of Jazer
and trailed eastward into the
wilderness.
Its shoots reached so far west
that they crossed over the
Dead Sea.*

⁹ So now I weep for Jazer and the
vineyards of Sibmah;
my tears will flow for Heshbon
and Elealeh.
There are no more shouts of joy
over your summer fruits and
harvest.
¹⁰ Gone now is the gladness,
gone the joy of harvest.
There will be no singing in the
vineyards,
no more happy shouts,
no treading of grapes in the
winepresses.
I have ended all their harvest joys.
¹¹ My heart's cry for Moab is like a
lament on a harp.
I am filled with anguish for
Kir-hareseth.*
¹² The people of Moab will worship at
their pagan shrines,
but it will do them no good.
They will cry to the gods in their
temples,
but no one will be able to save
them.

¹³The LORD has already said these
things about Moab in the past. ¹⁴But now
the LORD says, "Within three years,
counting each day,* the glory of Moab
will be ended. From its great population,
only a few of its people will be left alive."

¹⁷:¹THIS message came to me concerning Damascus:

"Look, the city of Damascus will
disappear!
It will become a heap of ruins.
² The towns of Aroer will be deserted.
Flocks will graze in the streets and
lie down undisturbed,
with no one to chase them away.

³ The fortified towns of Israel* will
also be destroyed,
and the royal power of Damascus
will end.
All that remains of Syria*
will share the fate of Israel's
departed glory,"
declares the LORD of Heaven's
Armies.

⁴ "In that day Israel's* glory will
grow dim;
its robust body will waste away.
⁵ The whole land will look like a
grainfield
after the harvesters have gathered
the grain.
It will be desolate,
like the fields in the valley of
Rephaim after the harvest.
⁶ Only a few of its people will be left,
like stray olives left on a tree after
the harvest.
Only two or three remain in the
highest branches,
four or five scattered here and
there on the limbs,"
declares the LORD, the God of
Israel.

⁷ Then at last the people will look to
their Creator
and turn their eyes to the Holy
One of Israel.
⁸ They will no longer look to their
idols for help
or worship what their own hands
have made.
They will never again bow down to
their Asherah poles
or worship at the pagan shrines
they have built.
⁹ Their largest cities will be like a
deserted forest,
like the land the Hivites and
Amorites abandoned*
when the Israelites came here so
long ago.
It will be utterly desolate.
¹⁰ Why? Because you have turned from
the God who can save you.
You have forgotten the Rock who
can hide you.

So you may plant the finest
grapevines
and import the most expensive
seedlings.
[11] They may sprout on the day you set
them out;
yes, they may blossom on the very
morning you plant them,
but you will never pick any grapes
from them.
Your only harvest will be a load of
grief and unrelieved pain.

[12] Listen! The armies of many nations
roar like the roaring of the sea.
Hear the thunder of the mighty
forces
as they rush forward like
thundering waves.
[13] But though they thunder like
breakers on a beach,
God will silence them, and they
will run away.
They will flee like chaff scattered
by the wind,
like a tumbleweed whirling
before a storm.
[14] In the evening Israel waits in terror,
but by dawn its enemies are dead.
This is the just reward of those who
plunder us,
a fitting end for those who
destroy us.

18:1 LISTEN, Ethiopia*—land of
fluttering sails*
that lies at the headwaters of the
Nile,
[2] that sends ambassadors in swift
boats down the river.

Go, swift messengers!
Take a message to a tall, smooth-
skinned people,
who are feared far and wide
for their conquests and destruction,
and whose land is divided by
rivers.

[3] All you people of the world,
everyone who lives on the earth—
when I raise my battle flag on the
mountain, look!

When I blow the ram's horn,
listen!
[4] For the LORD has told me this:
"I will watch quietly from my
dwelling place—
as quietly as the heat rises on a
summer day,
or as the morning dew forms
during the harvest."
[5] Even before you begin your attack,
while your plans are ripening like
grapes,
the LORD will cut off your new
growth with pruning shears.
He will snip off and discard your
spreading branches.
[6] Your mighty army will be left dead
in the fields
for the mountain vultures and
wild animals.
The vultures will tear at the corpses
all summer.
The wild animals will gnaw at the
bones all winter.

[7] At that time the LORD of Heaven's
Armies will receive gifts
from this land divided by rivers,
from this tall, smooth-skinned
people,
who are feared far and wide for
their conquests and
destruction.
They will bring the gifts to Jerusalem,*
where the LORD of Heaven's
Armies dwells.

15:9 As in Dead Sea Scrolls, some Greek manuscripts, and
Latin Vulgate; Masoretic Text reads *Dimon;* also in 15:9b.
16:8 Hebrew *the sea.*   16:11 Hebrew *Kir-heres,* a variant
spelling of Kir-hareseth.   16:14 Hebrew *Within three
years, as a servant bound by contract would count them.*
17:3a Hebrew *of Ephraim,* referring to the northern
kingdom of Israel.   17:3b Hebrew *Aram.*   17:4 Hebrew
Jacob's. See note on 14:1.   17:9 As in Greek version;
Hebrew reads *like places of the wood and the highest bough.*
18:1a Hebrew *Cush.*   18:1b Or *land of many locusts;*
Hebrew reads *land of whirring wings.*   18:7 Hebrew *to
Mount Zion.*

GALATIANS 1:1-24

This letter is from Paul, an apostle. I was
not appointed by any group of people or
any human authority, but by Jesus
Christ himself and by God the Father,
who raised Jesus from the dead.
[2] All the brothers and sisters* here

join me in sending this letter to the churches of Galatia.

³**May God our Father and the Lord Jesus Christ* give you grace and peace. ⁴Jesus gave his life for our sins, just as God our Father planned, in order to rescue us from this evil world in which we live. ⁵All glory to God forever and ever! Amen.**

⁶I am shocked that you are turning away so soon from God, who called you to himself through the loving mercy of Christ.* You are following a different way that pretends to be the Good News ⁷but is not the Good News at all. You are being fooled by those who deliberately twist the truth concerning Christ.

⁸Let God's curse fall on anyone, including us or even an angel from heaven, who preaches a different kind of Good News than the one we preached to you. ⁹I say again what we have said before: If anyone preaches any other Good News than the one you welcomed, let that person be cursed.

¹⁰Obviously, I'm not trying to win the approval of people, but of God. If pleasing people were my goal, I would not be Christ's servant.

¹¹Dear brothers and sisters, I want you to understand that the gospel message I preach is not based on mere human reasoning. ¹²I received my message from no human source, and no one taught me. Instead, I received it by direct revelation from Jesus Christ.*

¹³You know what I was like when I followed the Jewish religion—how I violently persecuted God's church. I did my best to destroy it. ¹⁴I was far ahead of my fellow Jews in my zeal for the traditions of my ancestors.

¹⁵But even before I was born, God chose me and called me by his marvelous grace. Then it pleased him ¹⁶to reveal his Son to me* so that I would proclaim the Good News about Jesus to the Gentiles.

When this happened, I did not rush out to consult with any human being.* ¹⁷Nor did I go up to Jerusalem to consult with those who were apostles before I was. Instead, I went away into Arabia, and later I returned to the city of Damascus.

¹⁸Then three years later I went to Jerusalem to get to know Peter,* and I stayed with him for fifteen days. ¹⁹The only other apostle I met at that time was James, the Lord's brother. ²⁰I declare before God that what I am writing to you is not a lie.

²¹After that visit I went north into the provinces of Syria and Cilicia. ²²And still the Christians in the churches in Judea didn't know me personally. ²³All they knew was that people were saying, "The one who used to persecute us is now preaching the very faith he tried to destroy!" ²⁴And they praised God because of me.

1:2 Greek *brothers;* also in 1:11.   1:3 Some manuscripts read *God the Father and our Lord Jesus Christ.*   1:6 Some manuscripts read *through loving mercy.*   1:12 Or *by the revelation of Jesus Christ.*   1:16a Or *in me.*   1:16b Greek *with flesh and blood.*   1:18 Greek *Cephas.*

PSALM 58:1-11
For the choir director: A psalm of David, to be sung to the tune "Do Not Destroy!"

¹ **J**ustice—do you rulers* know the meaning of the word?
Do you judge the people fairly?
² No! You plot injustice in your hearts.
You spread violence throughout the land.
³ These wicked people are born sinners;
even from birth they have lied and gone their own way.
⁴ They spit venom like deadly snakes;
they are like cobras that refuse to listen,
⁵ ignoring the tunes of the snake charmers,
no matter how skillfully they play.

⁶ Break off their fangs, O God!
Smash the jaws of these lions, O LORD!
⁷ May they disappear like water into thirsty ground.
Make their weapons useless in their hands.*
⁸ May they be like snails that dissolve into slime,

like a stillborn child who will
never see the sun.
⁹ God will sweep them away, both
young and old,
faster than a pot heats over
burning thorns.

¹⁰ The godly will rejoice when they see
injustice avenged.
They will wash their feet in the
blood of the wicked.
¹¹ Then at last everyone will say,
"There truly is a reward for those
who live for God;
surely there is a God who judges
justly here on earth."

58:1 Or *you gods.*   58:7 Or *Let them be trodden down and wither like grass.* The meaning of the Hebrew is uncertain.

PROVERBS 23:12
Commit yourself to instruction; listen carefully to words of knowledge.

SEPTEMBER 15

ISAIAH 19:1–21:17
This message came to me [Isaiah] concerning Egypt:

Look! The LORD is advancing against
Egypt,
riding on a swift cloud.
The idols of Egypt tremble.
The hearts of the Egyptians melt
with fear.

² "I will make Egyptian fight against
Egyptian—
brother against brother,
neighbor against neighbor,
city against city,
province against province.
³ The Egyptians will lose heart,
and I will confuse their plans.
They will plead with their idols for
wisdom
and call on spirits, mediums, and
those who consult the spirits
of the dead.
⁴ I will hand Egypt over
to a hard, cruel master.
A fierce king will rule them,"
says the Lord, the LORD of
Heaven's Armies.

⁵ The waters of the Nile will fail to rise
and flood the fields.
The riverbed will be parched
and dry.
⁶ The canals of the Nile will dry up,
and the streams of Egypt will
stink
with rotting reeds and rushes.
⁷ All the greenery along the riverbank
and all the crops along the river
will dry up and blow away.
⁸ The fishermen will lament for lack
of work.
Those who cast hooks into the
Nile will groan,
and those who use nets will lose
heart.
⁹ There will be no flax for the
harvesters,
no thread for the weavers.
¹⁰ They will be in despair,
and all the workers will be
sick at heart.

¹¹ What fools are the officials of Zoan!
Their best counsel to the king
of Egypt is stupid and wrong.
Will they still boast to Pharaoh of
their wisdom?
Will they dare brag about all their
wise ancestors?
¹² Where are your wise counselors,
Pharaoh?
Let them tell you what God plans,
what the LORD of Heaven's
Armies is going to do to Egypt.
¹³ The officials of Zoan are fools,
and the officials of Memphis*
are deluded.
The leaders of the people
have led Egypt astray.
¹⁴ The LORD has sent a spirit of
foolishness on them,
so all their suggestions are wrong.
They cause Egypt to stagger

like a drunk in his vomit.
¹⁵ There is nothing Egypt can do.
All are helpless—
the head and the tail,
the noble palm branch and the
lowly reed.

¹⁶In that day the Egyptians will be as weak as women. They will cower in fear beneath the upraised fist of the LORD of Heaven's Armies. ¹⁷Just to speak the name of Israel will terrorize them, for the LORD of Heaven's Armies has laid out his plans against them.

¹⁸In that day five of Egypt's cities will follow the LORD of Heaven's Armies. They will even begin to speak Hebrew, the language of Canaan. One of these cities will be Heliopolis, the City of the Sun.*

¹⁹In that day there will be an altar to the LORD in the heart of Egypt, and there will be a monument to the LORD at its border. ²⁰It will be a sign and a witness that the LORD of Heaven's Armies is worshiped in the land of Egypt. When the people cry to the LORD for help against those who oppress them, he will send them a savior who will rescue them. ²¹The LORD will make himself known to the Egyptians. Yes, they will know the LORD and will give their sacrifices and offerings to him. They will make a vow to the LORD and will keep it. ²²The LORD will strike Egypt, and then he will bring healing. For the Egyptians will turn to the LORD, and he will listen to their pleas and heal them.

²³In that day Egypt and Assyria will be connected by a highway. The Egyptians and Assyrians will move freely between their lands, and they will both worship God. ²⁴And Israel will be their ally. The three will be together, and Israel will be a blessing to them. ²⁵For the LORD of Heaven's Armies will say, "Blessed be Egypt, my people. Blessed be Assyria, the land I have made. Blessed be Israel, my special possession!"

²⁰:¹IN the year when King Sargon of Assyria sent his commander in chief to capture the Philistine city of Ashdod,*

²the LORD told Isaiah son of Amoz, "Take off the burlap you have been wearing, and remove your sandals." Isaiah did as he was told and walked around naked and barefoot.

³Then the LORD said, "My servant Isaiah has been walking around naked and barefoot for the last three years. This is a sign—a symbol of the terrible troubles I will bring upon Egypt and Ethiopia.* ⁴For the king of Assyria will take away the Egyptians and Ethiopians* as prisoners. He will make them walk naked and barefoot, both young and old, their buttocks bared, to the shame of Egypt. ⁵Then the Philistines will be thrown into panic, for they counted on the power of Ethiopia and boasted of their allies in Egypt! ⁶They will say, 'If this can happen to Egypt, what chance do we have? We were counting on Egypt to protect us from the king of Assyria.'"

²¹:¹THIS message came to me concerning Babylon—the desert by the sea*:

Disaster is roaring down on you
from the desert,
like a whirlwind sweeping
in from the Negev.
² I see a terrifying vision:
I see the betrayer betraying,
the destroyer destroying.
Go ahead, you Elamites and Medes,
attack and lay siege.
I will make an end to all the
groaning Babylon caused.
³ My stomach aches and burns
with pain.
Sharp pangs of anguish are
upon me,
like those of a woman in labor.
I grow faint when I hear what God
is planning;
I am too afraid to look.
⁴ My mind reels and my heart races.
I longed for evening to come,
but now I am terrified of the dark.

⁵ Look! They are preparing a great feast.
They are spreading rugs for
people to sit on.
Everyone is eating and drinking.

But quick! Grab your shields and
   prepare for battle.
You are being attacked!

6 Meanwhile, the Lord said to me,
   "Put a watchman on the city wall.
   Let him shout out what he sees.
7 He should look for chariots
   drawn by pairs of horses,
and for riders on donkeys and
   camels.
   Let the watchman be fully alert."

8 Then the watchman* called out,
   "Day after day I have stood on the
   watchtower, my lord.
   Night after night I have remained
   at my post.
9 Now at last—look!
Here comes a man in a chariot
   with a pair of horses!"
Then the watchman said,
   "Babylon is fallen, fallen!
All the idols of Babylon
   lie broken on the ground!"
10 O my people, threshed and
   winnowed,
   I have told you everything the
   LORD of Heaven's Armies
   has said,
   everything the God of Israel has
   told me.

11 This message came to me concerning Edom*:

Someone from Edom* keeps calling
   to me,
   "Watchman, how much longer until
   morning?
   When will the night be over?"
12 The watchman replies,
   "Morning is coming, but night will
   soon return.
   If you wish to ask again, then
   come back and ask."

13 This message came to me concerning Arabia:

O caravans from Dedan,
   hide in the deserts of Arabia.
14 O people of Tema,
   bring water to these thirsty
   people,

food to these weary refugees.
15 They have fled from the sword,
   from the drawn sword,
from the bent bow
   and the terrors of battle.

16 The Lord said to me, "Within a year,
counting each day,* all the glory of Kedar will come to an end. 17 Only a few of
its courageous archers will survive. I, the
LORD, the God of Israel, have spoken!"

19:13 Hebrew *Noph.*   19:18 Or *will be the City of
Destruction.*   20:1 Ashdod was captured by Assyria in
711 B.C.   20:3 Hebrew *Cush;* also in 20:5.   20:4 Hebrew
Cushites.   21:1 Hebrew *concerning the desert by the sea.*
21:8 As in Dead Sea Scrolls and Syriac version; Masoretic
Text reads *a lion.*   21:11a Hebrew *Dumah,* which means
"silence" or "stillness." It is a wordplay on the word *Edom.*
21:11b Hebrew *Seir,* another name for Edom.
21:16 Hebrew *Within a year, as a servant bound by
contract would count it.* Some ancient manuscripts read
Within three years, as in 16:14.

GALATIANS 2:1-16

Then fourteen years later I [Paul] went
back to Jerusalem again, this time with
Barnabas; and Titus came along, too. 2 I
went there because God revealed to me
that I should go. While I was there I met
privately with those considered to be
leaders of the church and shared with
them the message I had been preaching
to the Gentiles. I wanted to make sure
that we were in agreement, for fear that
all my efforts had been wasted and I
was running the race for nothing. 3 And
they supported me and did not even demand that my companion Titus be circumcised, though he was a Gentile.*

4 Even that question came up only
because of some so-called Christians
there—false ones, really*—who were secretly brought in. They sneaked in to spy
on us and take away the freedom we have
in Christ Jesus. They wanted to enslave us
and force us to follow their Jewish regulations. 5 But we refused to give in to them
for a single moment. We wanted to preserve the truth of the gospel message for
you.

6 And the leaders of the church had
nothing to add to what I was preaching.
(By the way, their reputation as great
leaders made no difference to me, for
God has no favorites.) 7 Instead, they saw

that God had given me the responsibility of preaching the gospel to the Gentiles, just as he had given Peter the responsibility of preaching to the Jews. ⁸For the same God who worked through Peter as the apostle to the Jews also worked through me as the apostle to the Gentiles.

⁹In fact, James, Peter,* and John, who were known as pillars of the church, recognized the gift God had given me, and they accepted Barnabas and me as their co-workers. They encouraged us to keep preaching to the Gentiles, while they continued their work with the Jews. ¹⁰Their only suggestion was that we keep on helping the poor, which I have always been eager to do.

¹¹But when Peter came to Antioch, I had to oppose him to his face, for what he did was very wrong. ¹²When he first arrived, he ate with the Gentile Christians, who were not circumcised. But afterward, when some friends of James came, Peter wouldn't eat with the Gentiles anymore. He was afraid of criticism from these people who insisted on the necessity of circumcision. ¹³As a result, other Jewish Christians followed Peter's hypocrisy, and even Barnabas was led astray by their hypocrisy.

¹⁴When I saw that they were not following the truth of the gospel message, I said to Peter in front of all the others, "Since you, a Jew by birth, have discarded the Jewish laws and are living like a Gentile, why are you now trying to make these Gentiles follow the Jewish traditions?

¹⁵**"You and I are Jews by birth, not 'sinners' like the Gentiles. ¹⁶Yet we know that a person is made right with God by faith in Jesus Christ, not by obeying the law.** And we have believed in Christ Jesus, so that we might be made right with God because of our faith in Christ, not because we have obeyed the law. For no one will ever be made right with God by obeying the law."*

2:3 Greek *a Greek.*   2:4 Greek *some false brothers.*
2:9 Greek *Cephas;* also in 2:11, 14.   2:16 Some translators hold that the quotation extends through verse 14; others through verse 16; and still others through verse 21.

PSALM 59:1-17
For the choir director: A psalm of David, regarding the time Saul sent soldiers to watch David's house in order to kill him. To be sung to the tune "Do Not Destroy!"

¹ **R**escue me from my enemies,
    O God.
  Protect me from those who have
    come to destroy me.
² Rescue me from these criminals;
    save me from these murderers.
³ They have set an ambush for me.
  Fierce enemies are out there
    waiting, LORD,
  though I have not sinned or
    offended them.
⁴ I have done nothing wrong,
    yet they prepare to attack me.
  Wake up! See what is happening
    and help me!
⁵ O LORD God of Heaven's Armies, the
    God of Israel,
  wake up and punish those hostile
    nations.
  Show no mercy to wicked traitors.
                                Interlude

⁶ They come out at night,
    snarling like vicious dogs
    as they prowl the streets.
⁷ Listen to the filth that comes from
    their mouths;
  their words cut like swords.
  "After all, who can hear us?"
    they sneer.
⁸ But LORD, you laugh at them.
  You scoff at all the hostile nations.
⁹ You are my strength; I wait for you
    to rescue me,
  for you, O God, are my fortress.
¹⁰ In his unfailing love, my God will
    stand with me.
  He will let me look down in
    triumph on all my enemies.

¹¹ Don't kill them, for my people soon
    forget such lessons;
  stagger them with your power,
    and bring them to their knees,
  O Lord our shield.
¹² Because of the sinful things they say,

because of the evil that is on
   their lips,
let them be captured by their pride,
   their curses, and their lies.
¹³ Destroy them in your anger!
   Wipe them out completely!
Then the whole world will know
   that God reigns in Israel.*

Interlude

¹⁴ My enemies come out at night,
   snarling like vicious dogs
   as they prowl the streets.
¹⁵ They scavenge for food
   but go to sleep unsatisfied.*

¹⁶ But as for me, I will sing about your
   power.
   Each morning I will sing with joy
      about your unfailing love.
For you have been my refuge,
   a place of safety when I am in
      distress.
¹⁷ O my Strength, to you I sing praises,
   for you, O God, are my refuge,
   the God who shows me unfailing
      love.

59:13 Hebrew *in Jacob.* See note on 44:4.   59:15 Or *and
growl if they don't get enough.*

PROVERBS 23:13-14
Don't fail to discipline your children.
They won't die if you spank them. Physical discipline may well save them from
death.*

23:14 Hebrew *from Sheol.*

SEPTEMBER
16

ISAIAH 22:1–24:23
This message came to me [Isaiah]
concerning Jerusalem—the Valley of
Vision*:

What is happening?
   Why is everyone running to the
      rooftops?

² The whole city is in a terrible
   uproar.
   What do I see in this reveling city?
Bodies are lying everywhere,
   killed not in battle but by famine
      and disease.
³ All your leaders have fled.
   They surrendered without
      resistance.
The people tried to slip away,
   but they were captured, too.
⁴ That's why I said, "Leave me alone to
   weep;
   do not try to comfort me.
Let me cry for my people
   as I watch them being destroyed."

⁵ Oh, what a day of crushing defeat!
   What a day of confusion and
      terror
brought by the Lord, the LORD of
   Heaven's Armies,
   upon the Valley of Vision!
The walls of Jerusalem have been
   broken,
   and cries of death echo from the
      mountainsides.
⁶ Elamites are the archers,
   with their chariots and
      charioteers.
   The men of Kir hold up the
      shields.
⁷ Chariots fill your beautiful valleys,
   and charioteers storm your gates.
⁸ Judah's defenses have been
   stripped away.
   You run to the armory* for your
      weapons.
⁹ You inspect the breaks in the walls
   of Jerusalem.*
   You store up water in the lower
      pool.
¹⁰ You survey the houses and tear
   some down
   for stone to strengthen the walls.
¹¹ Between the city walls, you build a
   reservoir
   for water from the old pool.
But you never ask for help from the
   One who did all this.
   You never considered the One
      who planned this long ago.

¹² At that time the Lord, the LORD of
    Heaven's Armies,
    called you to weep and mourn.
    He told you to shave your heads in
        sorrow for your sins
    and to wear clothes of burlap to
        show your remorse.
¹³ But instead, you dance and play;
    you slaughter cattle and kill
        sheep.
    You feast on meat and drink wine.
    You say, "Let's feast and drink,
    for tomorrow we die!"

¹⁴The LORD of Heaven's Armies has revealed this to me: "Till the day you die,
you will never be forgiven for this sin."
That is the judgment of the Lord, the
LORD of Heaven's Armies.

¹⁵ This is what the Lord, the LORD of
Heaven's Armies, said to me: "Confront
Shebna, the palace administrator, and
give him this message:

¹⁶ "Who do you think you are,
    and what are you doing here,
    building a beautiful tomb for
        yourself—
    a monument high up in the rock?
¹⁷ For the LORD is about to hurl you
        away, mighty man.
    He is going to grab you,
¹⁸ crumple you into a ball,
    and toss you away into a distant,
        barren land.
    There you will die,
    and your glorious chariots will be
        broken and useless.
    You are a disgrace to your master!

¹⁹"Yes, I will drive you out of office,"
says the LORD. "I will pull you down
from your high position. ²⁰And then I
will call my servant Eliakim son of Hilkiah to replace you. ²¹I will dress him in
your royal robes and will give him your
title and your authority. And he will be a
father to the people of Jerusalem and
Judah. ²²I will give him the key to the
house of David—the highest position in
the royal court. When he opens doors,
no one will be able to close them; when
he closes doors, no one will be able to
open them. ²³He will bring honor to his
family name, for I will drive him firmly
in place like a nail in the wall. ²⁴They
will give him great responsibility, and
he will bring honor to even the lowliest
members of his family.*"

²⁵But the LORD of Heaven's Armies
also says: "The time will come when I
will pull out the nail that seemed so
firm. It will come out and fall to the
ground. Everything it supports will fall
with it. I, the LORD, have spoken!"

²³:¹THIS message came to me concerning Tyre:

    Weep, O ships of Tarshish,
        for the harbor and houses of Tyre
        are gone!
    The rumors you heard in Cyprus*
        are all true.
² Mourn in silence, you people
        of the coast
    and you merchants of Sidon.
    Your traders crossed the sea,
³   sailing over deep waters.
    They brought you grain from Egypt*
        and harvests from along the Nile.
    You were the marketplace of the
        world.

⁴ But now you are put to shame, city
        of Sidon,
    for Tyre, the fortress of the
        sea, says,
    "Now I am childless;
    I have no sons or daughters."
⁵ When Egypt hears the news
        about Tyre,
    there will be great sorrow.
⁶ Send word now to Tarshish!
    Wail, you people who live
        in distant lands!
⁷ Is this silent ruin all that is left of
        your once joyous city?
    What a long history was yours!
    Think of all the colonists you sent
        to distant places.

⁸ Who has brought this disaster
        on Tyre,
    that great creator of kingdoms?
    Her traders were all princes,
    her merchants were nobles.

⁹ The LORD of Heaven's Armies has
     done it
   to destroy your pride
   and bring low all earth's nobility.
¹⁰ Come, people of Tarshish,
     sweep over the land like the
       flooding Nile,
     for Tyre is defenseless.*
¹¹ The LORD held out his hand over
     the sea
   and shook the kingdoms of the
     earth.
   He has spoken out against Phoenicia,*
     ordering that her fortresses be
       destroyed.
¹² He says, "Never again will you rejoice,
     O daughter of Sidon, for you have
       been crushed.
   Even if you flee to Cyprus,
     you will find no rest."

¹³ Look at the land of Babylonia*—
     the people of that land are gone!
   The Assyrians have handed Babylon
     over
   to the wild animals of the desert.
   They have built siege ramps against
     its walls,
     torn down its palaces,
     and turned it to a heap of rubble.

¹⁴ Wail, O ships of Tarshish,
     for your harbor is destroyed!

¹⁵For seventy years, the length of a
king's life, Tyre will be forgotten. But
then the city will come back to life as in
the song about the prostitute:

¹⁶ Take a harp and walk the streets,
     you forgotten harlot.
   Make sweet melody and sing your
     songs
   so you will be remembered again.

¹⁷Yes, after seventy years the LORD
will revive Tyre. But she will be no different than she was before. She will
again be a prostitute to all kingdoms
around the world. ¹⁸But in the end her
profits will be given to the LORD. Her
wealth will not be hoarded but will provide good food and fine clothing for the
LORD's priests.

²⁴:¹LOOK! The LORD is about to destroy
     the earth
   and make it a vast wasteland.
   He devastates the surface
     of the earth
   and scatters the people.
² Priests and laypeople,
     servants and masters,
     maids and mistresses,
     buyers and sellers,
     lenders and borrowers,
     bankers and debtors—none will
       be spared.
³ The earth will be completely
     emptied and looted.
   The LORD has spoken!

⁴ The earth mourns and dries up,
     and the crops waste away and
       wither.
   Even the greatest people on earth
     waste away.
⁵ The earth suffers for the sins of
     its people,
   for they have twisted God's
     instructions,
   violated his laws,
     and broken his everlasting covenant.
⁶ Therefore, a curse consumes the
     earth.
   Its people must pay the price for
     their sin.
   They are destroyed by fire,
     and only a few are left alive.
⁷ The grapevines waste away,
     and there is no new wine.
   All the merrymakers sigh and
     mourn.
⁸ The cheerful sound of tambourines
     is stilled;
   the happy cries of celebration are
     heard no more.
   The melodious chords of the harp
     are silent.
⁹ Gone are the joys of wine and song;
     alcoholic drink turns bitter in the
       mouth.
¹⁰ The city writhes in chaos;
     every home is locked to keep out
       intruders.
¹¹ Mobs gather in the streets, crying
     out for wine.

Joy has turned to gloom.
Gladness has been banished from
the land.
¹² The city is left in ruins,
its gates battered down.
¹³ Throughout the earth the story is
the same—
only a remnant is left,
like the stray olives left on the tree
or the few grapes left on the vine
after harvest.

¹⁴ But all who are left shout and sing
for joy.
Those in the west praise the
LORD's majesty.
¹⁵ In eastern lands, give glory to the LORD.
In the lands beyond the sea, praise
the name of the LORD, the God
of Israel.
¹⁶ We hear songs of praise from the
ends of the earth,
songs that give glory to the
Righteous One!

But my heart is heavy with grief.
Weep for me, for I wither away.
Deceit still prevails,
and treachery is everywhere.
¹⁷ Terror and traps and snares will be
your lot,
you people of the earth.
¹⁸ Those who flee in terror will fall into
a trap,
and those who escape the trap
will be caught in a snare.

Destruction falls like rain from the
heavens;
the foundations of the earth shake.
¹⁹ The earth has broken up.
It has utterly collapsed;
it is violently shaken.
²⁰ The earth staggers like a drunk.
It trembles like a tent in a storm.
It falls and will not rise again,
for the guilt of its rebellion is
very heavy.

²¹ In that day the LORD will punish the
gods in the heavens
and the proud rulers of the
nations on earth.

²² They will be rounded up and put
in prison.
They will be shut up in prison
and will finally be punished.
²³ Then the glory of the moon will wane,
and the brightness of the sun
will fade,
for the LORD of Heaven's Armies will
rule on Mount Zion.
He will rule in great glory in
Jerusalem,
in the sight of all the leaders of
his people.

22:1 Hebrew *concerning the Valley of Vision.*
22:8 Hebrew *to the House of the Forest;* see 1 Kgs 7:2-5.
22:9 Hebrew *the city of David.*   **22:24** Hebrew *They will hang on him all the glory of his father's house: its offspring and offshoots, all its lesser vessels, from the bowls to all the jars.*   **23:1** Hebrew *Kittim;* also in 23:12.   **23:3** Hebrew *from Shihor,* a branch of the Nile River.   **23:10** The meaning of the Hebrew in this verse is uncertain.   **23:11** Hebrew *Canaan.*   **23:13** Or *Chaldea.*

GALATIANS 2:17–3:9

But suppose we [Paul and other believers] seek to be made right with God through faith in Christ and then we are found guilty because we have abandoned the law. Would that mean Christ has led us into sin? Absolutely not! ¹⁸Rather, I am a sinner if I rebuild the old system of law I already tore down. ¹⁹For when I tried to keep the law, it condemned me. So I died to the law—I stopped trying to meet all its requirements—so that I might live for God. ²⁰**My old self has been crucified with Christ.* It is no longer I who live, but Christ lives in me. So I live in this earthly body by trusting in the Son of God, who loved me and gave himself for me.** ²¹I do not treat the grace of God as meaningless. For if keeping the law could make us right with God, then there was no need for Christ to die.

³:¹OH, foolish Galatians! Who has cast an evil spell on you? For the meaning of Jesus Christ's death was made as clear to you as if you had seen a picture of his death on the cross. ²Let me ask you this one question: Did you receive the Holy Spirit by obeying the law of Moses? Of course not! You received the Spirit because you believed the message you

heard about Christ. ³How foolish can you be? After starting your Christian lives in the Spirit, why are you now trying to become perfect by your own human effort? ⁴Have you experienced* so much for nothing? Surely it was not in vain, was it?

⁵I ask you again, does God give you the Holy Spirit and work miracles among you because you obey the law? Of course not! It is because you believe the message you heard about Christ.

⁶In the same way, "Abraham believed God, and God counted him as righteous because of his faith."* ⁷The real children of Abraham, then, are those who put their faith in God.

⁸What's more, the Scriptures looked forward to this time when God would declare the Gentiles to be righteous because of their faith. God proclaimed this good news to Abraham long ago when he said, "All nations will be blessed through you."* ⁹So all who put their faith in Christ share the same blessing Abraham received because of his faith.

2:20 Some English translations put this sentence in verse 19.   3:4 Or *Have you suffered.*   3:6 Gen 15:6. 3:8 Gen 12:3; 18:18; 22:18.

PSALM 60:1-12

For the choir director: A psalm of David useful for teaching, regarding the time David fought Aram-naharaim and Aram-zobah, and Joab returned and killed 12,000 Edomites in the Valley of Salt. To be sung to the tune "Lily of the Testimony."

¹ **Y**ou have rejected us, O God, and
    broken our defenses.
  You have been angry with us; now
    restore us to your favor.
² You have shaken our land and split
    it open.
  Seal the cracks, for the land
    trembles.
³ You have been very hard on us,
    making us drink wine that
    sent us reeling.
⁴ But you have raised a banner for
    those who fear you—
  a rallying point in the face
    of attack.   *Interlude*

⁵ Now rescue your beloved people.
  Answer and save us by your power.
⁶ God has promised this by his holiness*:
  "I will divide up Shechem with joy.
  I will measure out the valley
    of Succoth.
⁷ Gilead is mine,
    and Manasseh, too.
  Ephraim, my helmet, will produce
    my warriors,
  and Judah, my scepter, will
    produce my kings.
⁸ But Moab, my washbasin, will
    become my servant,
  and I will wipe my feet on Edom
  and shout in triumph over
    Philistia."

⁹ Who will bring me into the fortified
    city?
  Who will bring me victory over
    Edom?
¹⁰ Have you rejected us, O God?
  Will you no longer march with
    our armies?
¹¹ Oh, please help us against our enemies,
    for all human help is useless.
¹² With God's help we will do mighty
    things,
  for he will trample down our foes.

60:6 Or *in his sanctuary.*

PROVERBS 23:15-16

My child,* if your heart is wise, my own heart will rejoice! Everything in me will celebrate when you speak what is right.
23:15 Hebrew *My son;* also in 23:19.

SEPTEMBER
17

ISAIAH 25:1–28:13
  O Lord, I [Isaiah] will honor and
    praise your name,
  for you are my God.
  You do such wonderful
    things!

You planned them long ago,
and now you have accomplished
them.
2 You turn mighty cities into heaps
of ruins.
Cities with strong walls are turned
to rubble.
Beautiful palaces in distant lands
disappear
and will never be rebuilt.
3 Therefore, strong nations will
declare your glory;
ruthless nations will fear you.

4 But you are a tower of refuge
to the poor, O Lord,
a tower of refuge to the needy
in distress.
You are a refuge from the storm
and a shelter from the heat.
For the oppressive acts of ruthless
people
are like a storm beating against
a wall,
5   or like the relentless heat of
the desert.
But you silence the roar of foreign
nations.
As the shade of a cloud cools
relentless heat,
so the boastful songs of ruthless
people are stilled.

6 In Jerusalem,* the Lord of Heaven's
Armies
will spread a wonderful feast
for all the people of the world.
It will be a delicious banquet
with clear, well-aged wine and
choice meat.
7 There he will remove the cloud
of gloom,
the shadow of death that hangs
over the earth.
8 He will swallow up death
forever!*
The Sovereign Lord will wipe
away all tears.
He will remove forever all insults
and mockery
against his land and people.
The Lord has spoken!

9 In that day the people will proclaim,
"This is our God!
We trusted in him, and he saved us!
This is the Lord, in whom we trusted.
Let us rejoice in the salvation he
brings!"
10 For the Lord's hand of blessing will
rest on Jerusalem.
But Moab will be crushed.
It will be like straw trampled
down and left to rot.
11 God will push down Moab's people
as a swimmer pushes down water
with his hands.
He will end their pride
and all their evil works.
12 The high walls of Moab will be
demolished.
They will be brought down to the
ground,
down into the dust.

26:1In that day, everyone in the land of
Judah will sing this song:

Our city is strong!
We are surrounded by the walls
of God's salvation.
2 Open the gates to all who are
righteous;
allow the faithful to enter.
3 You will keep in perfect peace
all who trust in you,
all whose thoughts are fixed on you!
4 Trust in the Lord always,
for the Lord God is the eternal
Rock.
5 He humbles the proud
and brings down the arrogant city.
He brings it down to the dust.
6 The poor and oppressed trample
it underfoot,
and the needy walk all over it.

7 But for those who are righteous,
the way is not steep and rough.
You are a God who does what is right,
and you smooth out the path
ahead of them.
8 Lord, we show our trust in you by
obeying your laws;
our heart's desire is to glorify
your name.

⁹ All night long I search for you;
  in the morning I earnestly seek
    for God.
For only when you come to judge
    the earth
  will people learn what is right.
¹⁰ Your kindness to the wicked
  does not make them do good.
  Although others do right, the wicked
    keep doing wrong
  and take no notice of the LORD's
    majesty.
¹¹ O LORD, they pay no attention to
    your upraised fist.
  Show them your eagerness to
    defend your people.
  Then they will be ashamed.
  Let your fire consume your enemies.

¹² LORD, you will grant us peace;
  all we have accomplished is really
    from you.
¹³ O LORD our God, others have ruled us,
  but you alone are the one we
    worship.
¹⁴ Those we served before are dead
    and gone.
  Their departed spirits will
    never return!
  You attacked them and destroyed
    them,
  and they are long forgotten.
¹⁵ O LORD, you have made our
    nation great;
  yes, you have made us great.
  You have extended our borders,
  and we give you the glory!

¹⁶ LORD, in distress we searched
    for you.
  We prayed beneath the burden
    of your discipline.
¹⁷ Just as a pregnant woman
  writhes and cries out in pain
    as she gives birth,
  so were we in your presence,
    LORD.
¹⁸ We, too, writhe in agony,
  but nothing comes of our
    suffering.
  We have not given salvation
    to the earth,
  nor brought life into the world.

¹⁹ But those who die in the LORD
    will live;
  their bodies will rise again!
Those who sleep in the earth
  will rise up and sing for joy!
For your life-giving light will fall
    like dew
  on your people in the place
    of the dead!

²⁰ Go home, my people,
  and lock your doors!
Hide yourselves for a little while
  until the LORD's anger has passed.
²¹ Look! The LORD is coming from
    heaven
  to punish the people of the earth
    for their sins.
The earth will no longer hide those
  who have been killed.
  They will be brought out for
    all to see.

²⁷:¹IN that day the LORD will take his terrible, swift sword and punish Leviathan,* the swiftly moving serpent, the
coiling, writhing serpent. He will kill the
dragon of the sea.

² "In that day,
  sing about the fruitful vineyard.
³ I, the LORD, will watch over it,
  watering it carefully.
  Day and night I will watch so no one
    can harm it.
⁴   My anger will be gone.
  If I find briers and thorns growing,
    I will attack them;
  I will burn them up—
⁵   unless they turn to me for help.
  Let them make peace with me;
    yes, let them make peace with me."
⁶ The time is coming when Jacob's
    descendants will take root.
  Israel will bud and blossom
  and fill the whole earth with fruit!

⁷ Has the LORD struck Israel
  as he struck her enemies?
Has he punished her
  as he punished them?
⁸ No, but he exiled Israel to call her
    to account.

She was exiled from her land
as though blown away in a storm
from the east.
9 The LORD did this to purge Israel's*
wickedness,
to take away all her sin.
As a result, all the pagan altars will
be crushed to dust.
No Asherah pole or pagan shrine
will be left standing.
10 The fortified towns will be silent
and empty,
the houses abandoned, the streets
overgrown with weeds.
Calves will graze there,
chewing on twigs and branches.
11 The people are like the dead
branches of a tree,
broken off and used for kindling
beneath the cooking pots.
Israel is a foolish and stupid nation,
for its people have turned away
from God.
Therefore, the one who made them
will show them no pity or mercy.

12 Yet the time will come when the
LORD will gather them together like hand-
picked grain. One by one he will gather
them—from the Euphrates River* in the
east to the Brook of Egypt in the west.
13 In that day the great trumpet will
sound. Many who were dying in exile in
Assyria and Egypt will return to Jerusalem to worship the LORD on his holy
mountain.

28:1 WHAT sorrow awaits the proud city
of Samaria—
the glorious crown of the drunks
of Israel.*
It sits at the head of a fertile valley,
but its glorious beauty will fade
like a flower.
It is the pride of a people
brought down by wine.
2 For the Lord will send a mighty
army against it.
Like a mighty hailstorm and
a torrential rain,
they will burst upon it like a surging
flood

and smash it to the ground.
3 The proud city of Samaria—
the glorious crown of the drunks
of Israel*—
will be trampled beneath its
enemies' feet.
4 It sits at the head of a fertile valley,
but its glorious beauty will fade
like a flower.
Whoever sees it will snatch it up,
as an early fig is quickly picked
and eaten.

5 Then at last the LORD of Heaven's
Armies
will himself be Israel's glorious
crown.
He will be the pride and joy
of the remnant of his people.
6 He will give a longing for justice
to their judges.
He will give great courage
to their warriors who stand
at the gates.

7 Now, however, Israel is led by drunks
who reel with wine and stagger
with alcohol.
The priests and prophets stagger
with alcohol
and lose themselves in wine.
They reel when they see visions
and stagger as they render
decisions.
8 Their tables are covered with vomit;
filth is everywhere.
9 "Who does the LORD think we are?"
they ask.
"Why does he speak to us
like this?
Are we little children,
just recently weaned?
10 He tells us everything over and over—
one line at a time,
one line at a time,
a little here,
and a little there!"

11 So now God will have to speak
to his people
through foreign oppressors who
speak a strange language!
12 God has told his people,

"Here is a place of rest;
  let the weary rest here.
This is a place of quiet rest."
  But they would not listen.
13 So the LORD will spell out his
      message for them again,
  one line at a time,
      one line at a time,
  a little here,
      and a little there,
  so that they will stumble and fall.
  They will be injured, trapped,
      and captured.

25:6 Hebrew *On this mountain;* also in 25:10.   **25:8** Greek version reads *Death is swallowed up in victory.* Compare 1 Cor 15:54.   **27:1** The identification of Leviathan is disputed, ranging from an earthly creature to a mythical sea monster in ancient literature.   **27:9** Hebrew *Jacob's.* See note on 14:1.   **27:12** Hebrew *the river.*   **28:1** Hebrew *What sorrow awaits the crowning glory of the drunks of Ephraim,* referring to Samaria, capital of the northern kingdom of Israel.   **28:3** Hebrew *The crowning glory of the drunks of Ephraim;* see note on 28:1.

GALATIANS 3:10-22

But those who depend on the law to make them right with God are under his curse, for the Scriptures say, "Cursed is everyone who does not observe and obey all the commands that are written in God's Book of the Law."* 11So it is clear that no one can be made right with God by trying to keep the law. For the Scriptures say, "It is through faith that a righteous person has life."* 12This way of faith is very different from the way of law, which says, "It is through obeying the law that a person has life."*

13But Christ has rescued us from the curse pronounced by the law. When he was hung on the cross, he took upon himself the curse for our wrongdoing. For it is written in the Scriptures, "Cursed is everyone who is hung on a tree."* 14Through Christ Jesus, God has blessed the Gentiles with the same blessing he promised to Abraham, so that we who are believers might receive the promised* Holy Spirit through faith.

15Dear brothers and sisters,* here's an example from everyday life. Just as no one can set aside or amend an irrevocable agreement, so it is in this case. 16God gave the promises to Abraham and his child.* And notice that the Scripture doesn't say "to his children,*" as if it meant many descendants. Rather, it says "to his child"—and that, of course, means Christ. 17This is what I am trying to say: The agreement God made with Abraham could not be canceled 430 years later when God gave the law to Moses. God would be breaking his promise. 18For if the inheritance could be received by keeping the law, then it would not be the result of accepting God's promise. But God graciously gave it to Abraham as a promise.

19Why, then, was the law given? It was given alongside the promise to show people their sins. But the law was designed to last only until the coming of the child who was promised. God gave his law through angels to Moses, who was the mediator between God and the people. 20Now a mediator is helpful if more than one party must reach an agreement. But God, who is one, did not use a mediator when he gave his promise to Abraham.

21Is there a conflict, then, between God's law and God's promises?* Absolutely not! If the law could give us new life, we could be made right with God by obeying it. 22**But the Scriptures declare that we are all prisoners of sin, so we receive God's promise of freedom only by believing in Jesus Christ.**

3:10 Deut 27:26.   **3:11** Hab 2:4.   **3:12** Lev 18:5.
3:13 Deut 21:23 (Greek version).   **3:14** Some manuscripts read *the blessing of the.*   **3:15** Greek *Brothers.*
3:16a Greek *seed;* also in 3:16c, 19. See Gen 12:7 and 13:15.   **3:16b** Greek *seeds.*   **3:21** Some manuscripts read *and the promises?*

PSALM 61:1-8

For the choir director: A psalm of David, to be accompanied by stringed instruments.

1 **O** God, listen to my cry!
    Hear my prayer!
2 From the ends of the earth,
    I cry to you for help
    when my heart is overwhelmed.
  Lead me to the towering rock of
      safety,
3   for you are my safe refuge,

a fortress where my enemies
cannot reach me.
4 Let me live forever in your
sanctuary,
safe beneath the shelter
of your wings!   *Interlude*

5 For you have heard my vows, O God.
You have given me an inheritance
reserved for those who fear
your name.
6 Add many years to the life of the
king!
May his years span the
generations!
7 May he reign under God's protection
forever.
May your unfailing love and
faithfulness watch over him.
8 Then I will sing praises to your
name forever
as I fulfill my vows each day.

PROVERBS 23:17-18
Don't envy sinners, but always continue
to fear the LORD. You will be rewarded
for this; your hope will not be dis-
appointed.

SEPTEMBER
18

ISAIAH 28:14–30:11
Therefore, listen to this message
from the LORD,
you scoffing rulers in Jerusalem.
15 You boast, "We have struck a
bargain to cheat death
and have made a deal to dodge
the grave.*
The coming destruction can never
touch us,
for we have built a strong refuge
made of lies and deception."

16 Therefore, this is what the Sovereign
LORD says:

"Look! I am placing a foundation
stone in Jerusalem,*
a firm and tested stone.
It is a precious cornerstone that is
safe to build on.
Whoever believes need never
be shaken.*
17 I will test you with the measuring
line of justice
and the plumb line of
righteousness.
Since your refuge is made of lies,
a hailstorm will knock it down.
Since it is made of deception,
a flood will sweep it away.
18 I will cancel the bargain you made
to cheat death,
and I will overturn your deal
to dodge the grave.
When the terrible enemy sweeps
through,
you will be trampled into the
ground.
19 Again and again that flood will come,
morning after morning,
day and night,
until you are carried away."

This message will bring terror
to your people.
20 The bed you have made is too short
to lie on.
The blankets are too narrow to
cover you.
21 The LORD will come as he did
against the Philistines at Mount
Perazim
and against the Amorites at
Gibeon.
He will come to do a strange thing;
he will come to do an unusual
deed:
22 For the Lord, the LORD of Heaven's
Armies,
has plainly said that he is
determined to crush the
whole land.
So scoff no more,
or your punishment will be even
greater.

23 Listen to me;
listen, and pay close attention.

²⁴ Does a farmer always plow and
         never sow?
    Is he forever cultivating the soil
         and never planting?
²⁵ Does he not finally plant his seeds—
         black cumin, cumin, wheat,
              barley, and emmer wheat—
    each in its proper way,
         and each in its proper place?
²⁶ The farmer knows just what to do,
         for God has given him
              understanding.
²⁷ A heavy sledge is never used to
         thresh black cumin;
    rather, it is beaten with a light
         stick.
    A threshing wheel is never rolled
         on cumin;
         instead, it is beaten lightly with
              a flail.
²⁸ Grain for bread is easily crushed,
         so he doesn't keep on pounding it.
    He threshes it under the wheels
         of a cart,
    but he doesn't pulverize it.
²⁹ The LORD of Heaven's Armies is a
         wonderful teacher,
    and he gives the farmer great
         wisdom.

²⁹:¹"WHAT sorrow awaits Ariel,* the
         City of David.
    Year after year you celebrate your
         feasts.
² Yet I will bring disaster upon you,
    and there will be much weeping
         and sorrow.
    For Jerusalem will become what her
         name Ariel means—
    an altar covered with blood.
³ I will be your enemy,
         surrounding Jerusalem and
              attacking its walls.
    I will build siege towers
         and destroy it.
⁴ Then deep from the earth you
         will speak;
         from low in the dust your words
              will come.
    Your voice will whisper from the
         ground

like a ghost conjured up from
     the grave.

⁵ "But suddenly, your ruthless
         enemies will be crushed
    like the finest of dust.
    Your many attackers will be driven
         away
    like chaff before the wind.
    Suddenly, in an instant,
⁶   I, the LORD of Heaven's Armies,
         will act for you
    with thunder and earthquake and
         great noise,
         with whirlwind and storm and
              consuming fire.
⁷ All the nations fighting against
         Jerusalem*
    will vanish like a dream!
    Those who are attacking her walls
         will vanish like a vision in the
              night.
⁸ A hungry person dreams of eating
         but wakes up still hungry.
    A thirsty person dreams of drinking
         but is still faint from thirst when
              morning comes.
    So it will be with your enemies,
         with those who attack Mount Zion."

⁹ Are you amazed and incredulous?
         Don't you believe it?
    Then go ahead and be blind.
         You are stupid, but not from wine!
         You stagger, but not from liquor!
¹⁰ For the LORD has poured out on you
         a spirit of deep sleep.
    He has closed the eyes of your
         prophets and visionaries.

¹¹All the future events in this vision
are like a sealed book to them. When
you give it to those who can read, they
will say, "We can't read it because it is
sealed." ¹²When you give it to those
who cannot read, they will say, "We
don't know how to read."

¹³ And so the Lord says,
    "These people say they are mine.
    They honor me with their lips,
         but their hearts are far from me.
    And their worship of me

is nothing but man-made rules
learned by rote.*

14 Because of this, I will once again
astound these hypocrites
with amazing wonders.
The wisdom of the wise will pass
away,
and the intelligence of the
intelligent will disappear."

15 What sorrow awaits those who
try to hide their plans from
the Lord,
who do their evil deeds in the
dark!
"The Lord can't see us," they say.
"He doesn't know what's
going on!"

16 How foolish can you be?
He is the Potter, and he is
certainly greater than you,
the clay!
Should the created thing say to the
one who made it,
"He didn't make me"?
Does a jar ever say,
"The potter who made me
is stupid"?

17 Soon—and it will not be very long—
the forests of Lebanon will
become a fertile field,
and the fertile field will yield
bountiful crops.

18 In that day the deaf will hear words
read from a book,
and the blind will see through the
gloom and darkness.

19 The humble will be filled with fresh
joy from the Lord.
The poor will rejoice in the Holy
One of Israel.

20 The scoffer will be gone,
the arrogant will disappear,
and those who plot evil will
be killed.

21 Those who convict the innocent
by their false testimony will
disappear.
A similar fate awaits those who use
trickery to pervert justice
and who tell lies to destroy
the innocent.

22 That is why the Lord, who redeemed
Abraham, says to the people of Israel,*

"My people will no longer be
ashamed
or turn pale with fear.

23 For when they see their many
children
and all the blessings I have
given them,
they will recognize the holiness of
the Holy One of Israel.
They will stand in awe of the
God of Jacob.

24 Then the wayward will gain
understanding,
and complainers will accept
instruction.

30:1 "What sorrow awaits my
rebellious children,"
says the Lord.
"You make plans that are contrary
to mine.
You make alliances not directed
by my Spirit,
thus piling up your sins.

2 For without consulting me,
you have gone down to Egypt
for help.
You have put your trust in Pharaoh's
protection.
You have tried to hide in his shade.

3 But by trusting Pharaoh, you will be
humiliated,
and by depending on him, you
will be disgraced.

4 For though his power extends
to Zoan
and his officials have arrived
in Hanes,

5 all who trust in him will be ashamed.
He will not help you.
Instead, he will disgrace you."

6 This message came to me concerning
the animals in the Negev:

The caravan moves slowly
across the terrible desert to
Egypt—
donkeys weighed down with riches
and camels loaded with
treasure—

all to pay for Egypt's protection.
They travel through the wilderness,
   a place of lionesses and lions,
   a place where vipers and
     poisonous snakes live.
All this, and Egypt will give you
   nothing in return.
7 Egypt's promises are worthless!
Therefore, I call her Rahab—
   the Harmless Dragon.*

8 Now go and write down these
   words.
Write them in a book.
They will stand until the end of time
   as a witness
9 that these people are stubborn
   rebels
who refuse to pay attention to the
   LORD's instructions.
10 They tell the seers,
   "Stop seeing visions!"
They tell the prophets,
   "Don't tell us what is right.
Tell us nice things.
Tell us lies.
11 Forget all this gloom.
Get off your narrow path.
Stop telling us about your
   'Holy One of Israel.'"

28:15 Hebrew *Sheol;* also in 28:18.   28:16a Hebrew *in Zion.*   28:16b Greek version reads *Look! I am placing a stone in the foundation of Jerusalem* (literally *Zion*), / *a precious cornerstone for its foundation, chosen for great honor. / Anyone who trusts in him will never be disgraced.* Compare Rom 9:33; 1 Pet 2:6.   29:1 *Ariel* sounds like a Hebrew term that means "hearth" or "altar."   29:7 Hebrew *Ariel.*   29:13 Greek version reads *Their worship is a farce, / for they teach man-made ideas as commands from God.* Compare Mark 7:7.   29:22 Hebrew *of Jacob.* See note on 14:1.   30:7 Hebrew *Rahab who sits still.* Rahab is the name of a mythical sea monster that represents chaos in ancient literature. The name is used here as a poetic name for Egypt.

GALATIANS 3:23–4:31

Before the way of faith in Christ was available to us, we were placed under guard by the law. We were kept in protective custody, so to speak, until the way of faith was revealed.

24Let me put it another way. The law was our guardian until Christ came; it protected us until we could be made right with God through faith. 25And now that the way of faith has come, we no longer need the law as our guardian.

26For you are all children* of God through faith in Christ Jesus. 27And all who have been united with Christ in baptism have put on the character of Christ, like putting on new clothes.* 28There is no longer Jew or Gentile,* slave or free, male and female. For you are all one in Christ Jesus. 29And now that you belong to Christ, you are the true children* of Abraham. You are his heirs, and God's promise to Abraham belongs to you.

4:1THINK of it this way. If a father dies and leaves an inheritance for his young children, those children are not much better off than slaves until they grow up, even though they actually own everything their father had. 2They have to obey their guardians until they reach whatever age their father set. 3And that's the way it was with us before Christ came. We were like children; we were slaves to the basic spiritual principles* of this world.

4But when the right time came, God sent his Son, born of a woman, subject to the law. 5God sent him to buy freedom for us who were slaves to the law, so that he could adopt us as his very own children.* 6And because we* are his children, God has sent the Spirit of his Son into our hearts, prompting us to call out, "Abba, Father."* 7Now you are no longer a slave but God's own child.* And since you are his child, God has made you his heir.

8Before you Gentiles knew God, you were slaves to so-called gods that do not even exist. 9So now that you know God (or should I say, now that God knows you), why do you want to go back again and become slaves once more to the weak and useless spiritual principles of this world? 10You are trying to earn favor with God by observing certain days or months or seasons or years. 11I fear for you. Perhaps all my hard work with you was for nothing. 12Dear brothers and sisters,* I plead with you to live as I do in freedom from these things, for I have become like you Gentiles—free from those laws.

You did not mistreat me when I first preached to you. [13]Surely you remember that I was sick when I first brought you the Good News. [14]But even though my condition tempted you to reject me, you did not despise me or turn me away. No, you took me in and cared for me as though I were an angel from God or even Christ Jesus himself. [15]Where is that joyful and grateful spirit you felt then? I am sure you would have taken out your own eyes and given them to me if it had been possible. [16]Have I now become your enemy because I am telling you the truth?

[17] Those false teachers are so eager to win your favor, but their intentions are not good. They are trying to shut you off from me so that you will pay attention only to them. [18]If someone is eager to do good things for you, that's all right; but let them do it all the time, not just when I'm with you.

[19]Oh, my dear children! I feel as if I'm going through labor pains for you again, and they will continue until Christ is fully developed in your lives. [20]I wish I were with you right now so I could change my tone. But at this distance I don't know how else to help you.

[21]Tell me, you who want to live under the law, do you know what the law actually says? [22]The Scriptures say that Abraham had two sons, one from his slave-wife and one from his freeborn wife.* [23]The son of the slave-wife was born in a human attempt to bring about the fulfillment of God's promise. But the son of the freeborn wife was born as God's own fulfillment of his promise.

[24]These two women serve as an illustration of God's two covenants. The first woman, Hagar, represents Mount Sinai where people received the law that enslaved them. [25]And now Jerusalem is just like Mount Sinai in Arabia,* because she and her children live in slavery to the law. [26]But the other woman, Sarah, represents the heavenly Jerusalem. She is the free woman, and she is our mother. [27]As Isaiah said,

"Rejoice, O childless woman,
  you who have never given birth!
Break into a joyful shout,
  you who have never been in labor!
For the desolate woman now has
    more children
  than the woman who lives with
    her husband!"*

[28]And you, dear brothers and sisters, are children of the promise, just like Isaac. [29]But you are now being persecuted by those who want you to keep the law, just as Ishmael, the child born by human effort, persecuted Isaac, the child born by the power of the Spirit. [30]But what do the Scriptures say about that? "Get rid of the slave and her son, for the son of the slave woman will not share the inheritance with the free woman's son."* [31]So, dear brothers and sisters, we are not children of the slave woman; we are children of the free woman.

3:26 Greek *sons.*   **3:27** Greek *have put on Christ.*
3:28 Greek *Jew or Greek.*   **3:29** Greek *seed.*   **4:3** Or *powers;* also in 4:9.   **4:5** Greek *sons;* also in 4:6.
4:6a Greek *you.*   **4:6b** *Abba* is an Aramaic term for "father."   **4:7** Greek *son;* also in 4:7b.   **4:12** Greek *brothers;* also in 4:28, 31.   **4:22** See Gen 16:15; 21:2-3.
4:25 Greek *And Hagar, which is Mount Sinai in Arabia, is now like Jerusalem;* other manuscripts read *And Mount Sinai in Arabia is now like Jerusalem.*   **4:27** Isa 54:1.
4:30 Gen 21:10.

PSALM 62:1-12
For Jeduthun, the choir director: A psalm of David.

[1] I wait quietly before God,
    for my victory comes from him.
[2] He alone is my rock and my
      salvation,
    my fortress where I will never
      be shaken.

[3] So many enemies against one man—
    all of them trying to kill me.
  To them I'm just a broken-down wall
    or a tottering fence.
[4] They plan to topple me from my
      high position.
    They delight in telling lies
      about me.
  They praise me to my face
    but curse me in their hearts.
                              Interlude

⁵ Let all that I am wait quietly
   before God,
      for my hope is in him.
⁶ He alone is my rock and my
   salvation,
      my fortress where I will not be
      shaken.
⁷ My victory and honor come from
   God alone.
      He is my refuge, a rock where no
      enemy can reach me.
⁸ O my people, trust in him at all
   times.
      Pour out your heart to him,
      for God is our refuge.   *Interlude*

⁹ Common people are as worthless as
   a puff of wind,
      and the powerful are not what
      they appear to be.
   If you weigh them on the scales,
      together they are lighter than a
      breath of air.

¹⁰ Don't make your living by extortion
   or put your hope in stealing.
   And if your wealth increases,
      don't make it the center
      of your life.

¹¹ God has spoken plainly,
      and I have heard it many times:
   Power, O God, belongs to you;
¹²   unfailing love, O Lord, is yours.
   Surely you repay all people
      according to what they have
      done.

PROVERBS 23:19-21
My child, listen and be wise: Keep your heart on the right course. Do not carouse with drunkards or feast with gluttons, for they are on their way to poverty, and too much sleep clothes them in rags.

SEPTEMBER
19

ISAIAH 30:12–33:9
This is the reply of the Holy One of Israel:

"Because you [Israel] despise what
   I tell you
      and trust instead in oppression
      and lies,
¹³ calamity will come upon you
   suddenly—
      like a bulging wall that bursts
      and falls.
   In an instant it will collapse
      and come crashing down.
¹⁴ You will be smashed like a piece
   of pottery—
      shattered so completely that
   there won't be a piece big enough
      to carry coals from a fireplace
      or a little water from the well."

¹⁵ This is what the Sovereign LORD,
   the Holy One of Israel, says:
   "Only in returning to me
      and resting in me will you be
      saved.
   In quietness and confidence is
      your strength.
   But you would have none of it.
¹⁶ You said, 'No, we will get our help
   from Egypt.
      They will give us swift horses for
      riding into battle.'
   But the only swiftness you are going
   to see
      is the swiftness of your enemies
      chasing you!
¹⁷ One of them will chase a thousand
   of you.
      Five of them will make all
      of you flee.
   You will be left like a lonely flagpole
   on a hill
      or a tattered banner on a distant
      mountaintop."

¹⁸ So the LORD must wait for you to
   come to him

so he can show you his love and
compassion.
For the LORD is a faithful God.
Blessed are those who wait
for his help.

¹⁹ O people of Zion, who live in
Jerusalem,
you will weep no more.
He will be gracious if you ask
for help.
He will surely respond to the
sound of your cries.
²⁰ Though the Lord gave you adversity
for food
and suffering for drink,
he will still be with you to teach you.
You will see your teacher with
your own eyes.
²¹ Your own ears will hear him.
Right behind you a voice
will say,
"This is the way you should go,"
whether to the right or to the left.
²² Then you will destroy all your silver
idols
and your precious gold images.
You will throw them out like filthy
rags,
saying to them, "Good riddance!"

²³Then the LORD will bless you with
rain at planting time. There will be wonderful harvests and plenty of pastureland for your livestock. ²⁴The oxen and
donkeys that till the ground will eat
good grain, its chaff blown away by the
wind. ²⁵In that day, when your enemies
are slaughtered and the towers fall,
there will be streams of water flowing
down every mountain and hill. ²⁶The
moon will be as bright as the sun, and
the sun will be seven times brighter—
like the light of seven days in one! So it
will be when the LORD begins to heal his
people and cure the wounds he gave
them.

²⁷ Look! The LORD is coming from
far away,
burning with anger,
surrounded by thick, rising
smoke.

His lips are filled with fury;
his words consume like fire.
²⁸ His hot breath pours out like a flood
up to the neck of his enemies.
He will sift out the proud nations for
destruction.
He will bridle them and lead them
away to ruin.

²⁹ But the people of God will sing
a song of joy,
like the songs at the holy festivals.
You will be filled with joy,
as when a flutist leads a group
of pilgrims
to Jerusalem, the mountain of
the LORD—
to the Rock of Israel.
³⁰ And the LORD will make his majestic
voice heard.
He will display the strength of his
mighty arm.
It will descend with devouring flames,
with cloudbursts, thunderstorms,
and huge hailstones.
³¹ At the LORD's command, the
Assyrians will be shattered.
He will strike them down with his
royal scepter.
³² And as the LORD strikes them with
his rod of punishment,
his people will celebrate with
tambourines and harps.
Lifting his mighty arm, he will
fight the Assyrians.
³³ Topheth—the place of burning—
has long been ready for the
Assyrian king;
the pyre is piled high with wood.
The breath of the LORD, like fire
from a volcano,
will set it ablaze.

^{31:1}WHAT sorrow awaits those who look
to Egypt for help,
trusting their horses, chariots, and
charioteers
and depending on the strength of
human armies
instead of looking to the LORD,
the Holy One of Israel.
² In his wisdom, the LORD will send
great disaster;

he will not change his mind.
He will rise against the wicked
and against their helpers.
3 For these Egyptians are mere
humans, not God!
Their horses are puny flesh, not
mighty spirits!
When the LORD raises his fist
against them,
those who help will stumble,
and those being helped will fall.
They will all fall down and die
together.

4But this is what the LORD has told me:

"When a strong young lion
stands growling over a sheep it
has killed,
it is not frightened by the shouts
and noise
of a whole crowd of shepherds.
In the same way, the LORD of
Heaven's Armies
will come down and fight on
Mount Zion.
5 The LORD of Heaven's Armies will
hover over Jerusalem
and protect it like a bird
protecting its nest.
He will defend and save the city;
he will pass over it and rescue it."

6Though you are such wicked rebels,
my people, come and return to the
LORD. 7I know the glorious day will
come when each of you will throw away
the gold idols and silver images your
sinful hands have made.

8 "The Assyrians will be destroyed,
but not by the swords of men.
The sword of God will strike them,
and they will panic and flee.
The strong young Assyrians
will be taken away as captives.
9 Even the strongest will quake
with terror,
and princes will flee when they
see your battle flags,"
says the LORD, whose fire burns
in Zion,
whose flame blazes from
Jerusalem.

32:1LOOK, a righteous king is coming!
And honest princes will rule
under him.
2 Each one will be like a shelter from
the wind
and a refuge from the storm,
like streams of water in the desert
and the shadow of a great rock in
a parched land.

3 Then everyone who has eyes will be
able to see the truth,
and everyone who has ears will be
able to hear it.
4 Even the hotheads will be full of
sense and understanding.
Those who stammer will speak
out plainly.
5 In that day ungodly fools will not be
heroes.
Scoundrels will not be respected.
6 For fools speak foolishness
and make evil plans.
They practice ungodliness
and spread false teachings about
the LORD.
They deprive the hungry of food
and give no water to the thirsty.
7 The smooth tricks of scoundrels
are evil.
They plot crooked schemes.
They lie to convict the poor,
even when the cause of the poor
is just.
8 But generous people plan to do what
is generous,
and they stand firm in their
generosity.

9 Listen, you women who lie around
in ease.
Listen to me, you who are so
smug.
10 In a short time—just a little more
than a year—
you careless ones will suddenly
begin to care.
For your fruit crops will fail,
and the harvest will never take
place.
11 Tremble, you women of ease;
throw off your complacency.
Strip off your pretty clothes,

and put on burlap to show your
grief.

12 Beat your breasts in sorrow for your
bountiful farms
and your fruitful grapevines.

13 For your land will be overgrown with
thorns and briers.
Your joyful homes and happy
towns will be gone.

14 The palace and the city will be
deserted,
and busy towns will be empty.
Wild donkeys will frolic and flocks
will graze
in the empty forts* and
watchtowers

15 until at last the Spirit is poured out
on us from heaven.
Then the wilderness will become
a fertile field,
and the fertile field will yield
bountiful crops.

16 Justice will rule in the wilderness
and righteousness in the fertile
field.

17 And this righteousness will bring
peace.
Yes, it will bring quietness and
confidence forever.

18 My people will live in safety, quietly
at home.
They will be at rest.

19 Even if the forest should be
destroyed
and the city torn down,

20 the LORD will greatly bless his
people.
Wherever they plant seed,
bountiful crops will spring up.
Their cattle and donkeys will
graze freely.

33:1 WHAT sorrow awaits you Assyrians,
who have destroyed others*
but have never been destroyed
yourselves.
You betray others,
but you have never been betrayed.
When you are done destroying,
you will be destroyed.
When you are done betraying,
you will be betrayed.

2 But LORD, be merciful to us,
for we have waited for you.
Be our strong arm each day
and our salvation in times
of trouble.

3 The enemy runs at the sound
of your voice.
When you stand up, the nations
flee!

4 Just as caterpillars and locusts strip
the fields and vines,
so the fallen army of Assyria will
be stripped!

5 Though the LORD is very great and
lives in heaven,
he will make Jerusalem* his home
of justice and righteousness.

6 In that day he will be your sure
foundation,
providing a rich store of salvation,
wisdom, and knowledge.
The fear of the LORD will be your
treasure.

7 But now your brave warriors weep
in public.
Your ambassadors of peace cry
in bitter disappointment.

8 Your roads are deserted;
no one travels them anymore.
The Assyrians have broken their
peace treaty
and care nothing for the promises
they made before witnesses.*
They have no respect for anyone.

9 The land of Israel wilts in mourning.
Lebanon withers with shame.
The plain of Sharon is now a
wilderness.
Bashan and Carmel have been
plundered.

32:14 Hebrew *the Ophel.*   33:1 Hebrew *What sorrow
awaits you, O destroyer.* The Hebrew text does not
specifically name Assyria as the object of the prophecy in
this chapter.   33:5 Hebrew *Zion;* also in 33:14.   33:8 As
in Dead Sea Scrolls; Masoretic Text reads *care nothing for
the cities.*

GALATIANS 5:1-12

So Christ has truly set us free. Now
make sure that you stay free, and don't
get tied up again in slavery to the law.

2Listen! I, Paul, tell you this: If you are
counting on circumcision to make you

right with God, then Christ will be of no benefit to you. ³I'll say it again. If you are trying to find favor with God by being circumcised, you must obey every regulation in the whole law of Moses. ⁴For if you are trying to make yourselves right with God by keeping the law, you have been cut off from Christ! You have fallen away from God's grace.

⁵**But we who live by the Spirit eagerly wait to receive by faith the righteousness God has promised to us. ⁶For when we place our faith in Christ Jesus, there is no benefit in being circumcised or being uncircumcised. What is important is faith expressing itself in love.**

⁷You were running the race so well. Who has held you back from following the truth? ⁸It certainly isn't God, for he is the one who called you to freedom. ⁹This false teaching is like a little yeast that spreads through the whole batch of dough! ¹⁰I am trusting the Lord to keep you from believing false teachings. God will judge that person, whoever he is, who has been confusing you.

¹¹Dear brothers and sisters,* if I were still preaching that you must be circumcised—as some say I do—why am I still being persecuted? If I were no longer preaching salvation through the cross of Christ, no one would be offended. ¹²I just wish that those troublemakers who want to mutilate you by circumcision would mutilate themselves.*

5:11 Greek *Brothers;* similarly in 5:13.   5:12 Or *castrate themselves, or cut themselves off from you;* Greek reads *cut themselves off.*

PSALM 63:1-11

A psalm of David, regarding a time when David was in the wilderness of Judah.

¹ **O** God, you are my God;
    I earnestly search for you.
My soul thirsts for you;
    my whole body longs for you
in this parched and weary land
    where there is no water.

² I have seen you in your sanctuary
and gazed upon your power
    and glory.
³ Your unfailing love is better than life
    itself;
    how I praise you!
⁴ I will praise you as long as I live,
    lifting up my hands to you in
    prayer.
⁵ You satisfy me more than the
    richest feast.
    I will praise you with songs of joy.

⁶ I lie awake thinking of you,
    meditating on you through
    the night.
⁷ Because you are my helper,
    I sing for joy in the shadow of
    your wings.
⁸ I cling to you;
    your strong right hand holds
    me securely.

⁹ But those plotting to destroy me will
    come to ruin.
    They will go down into the depths
    of the earth.
¹⁰ They will die by the sword
    and become the food of jackals.
¹¹ But the king will rejoice in God.
    All who trust in him will praise
    him,
    while liars will be silenced.

PROVERBS 23:22

Listen to your father, who gave you life, and don't despise your mother when she is old.

SEPTEMBER 20

ISAIAH 33:10–36:22

But the LORD says: "I will stand up and show my power and might. ¹¹You Assyrians produce nothing but dry grass and stubble.
    Your own breath will turn to fire
    and consume you.

¹² Your people will be burned up
        completely,
    like thornbushes cut down and
        tossed in a fire.
¹³ Listen to what I have done, you
        nations far away!
    And you that are near,
        acknowledge my might!"

¹⁴ The sinners in Jerusalem shake
        with fear.
    Terror seizes the godless.
    "Who can live with this devouring
        fire?" they cry.
    "Who can survive this all-
        consuming fire?"
¹⁵ Those who are honest and fair,
    who refuse to profit by fraud,
    who stay far away from bribes,
    who refuse to listen to those who
        plot murder,
    who shut their eyes to all
        enticement to do wrong—
¹⁶ these are the ones who will dwell
        on high.
    The rocks of the mountains will
        be their fortress.
    Food will be supplied to them,
        and they will have water in
        abundance.

¹⁷ Your eyes will see the king in all
        his splendor,
    and you will see a land that
        stretches into the distance.
¹⁸ You will think back to this time of
        terror, asking,
    "Where are the Assyrian officers
        who counted our towers?
    Where are the bookkeepers
        who recorded the plunder taken
        from our fallen city?"
¹⁹ You will no longer see these fierce,
        violent people
    with their strange, unknown
        language.

²⁰ Instead, you will see Zion as a place
        of holy festivals.
    You will see Jerusalem, a city quiet
        and secure.
    It will be like a tent whose ropes
        are taut

and whose stakes are firmly fixed.
²¹ The LORD will be our Mighty One.
    He will be like a wide river of
        protection
    that no enemy can cross,
        that no enemy ship can sail upon.
²² For the LORD is our judge,
        our lawgiver, and our king.
    He will care for us and save us.
²³ The enemies' sails hang loose
        on broken masts with useless
        tackle.
    Their treasure will be divided by
        the people of God.
    Even the lame will take their
        share!
²⁴ The people of Israel will no longer
        say,
    "We are sick and helpless,"
        for the LORD will forgive their
        sins.

³⁴:¹COME here and listen, O nations of
        the earth.
    Let the world and everything in it
        hear my words.
² For the LORD is enraged against the
        nations.
    His fury is against all their armies.
    He will completely destroy* them,
        dooming them to slaughter.
³ Their dead will be left unburied,
    and the stench of rotting bodies
        will fill the land.
    The mountains will flow with
        their blood.
⁴ The heavens above will melt away
    and disappear like a rolled-up
        scroll.
    The stars will fall from the sky
    like withered leaves from a
        grapevine,
    or shriveled figs from a fig tree.

⁵ And when my sword has finished its
        work in the heavens,
    it will fall upon Edom,
    the nation I have marked for
        destruction.
⁶ The sword of the LORD is drenched
        with blood
    and covered with fat—
    with the blood of lambs and goats,

with the fat of rams prepared for
sacrifice.
Yes, the LORD will offer a sacrifice
in the city of Bozrah.
He will make a mighty slaughter
in Edom.
⁷ Even men as strong as wild oxen
will die—
the young men alongside the
veterans.
The land will be soaked with blood
and the soil enriched with fat.

⁸ For it is the day of the LORD's revenge,
the year when Edom will be paid
back for all it did to Israel.*
⁹ The streams of Edom will be filled
with burning pitch,
and the ground will be covered
with fire.
¹⁰ This judgment on Edom will never
end;
the smoke of its burning will rise
forever.
The land will lie deserted from
generation to generation.
No one will live there anymore.
¹¹ It will be haunted by the desert owl
and the screech owl,
the great owl and the raven.*
For God will measure that land
carefully;
he will measure it for chaos and
destruction.
¹² It will be called the Land of Nothing,
and all its nobles will soon be
gone.*
¹³ Thorns will overrun its palaces;
nettles and thistles will grow
in its forts.
The ruins will become a haunt
for jackals
and a home for owls.
¹⁴ Desert animals will mingle there
with hyenas,
their howls filling the night.
Wild goats will bleat at one another
among the ruins,
and night creatures* will come
there to rest.
¹⁵ There the owl will make her nest
and lay her eggs.

She will hatch her young and
cover them with her wings.
And the buzzards will come,
each one with its mate.

¹⁶ Search the book of the LORD,
and see what he will do.
Not one of these birds and animals
will be missing,
and none will lack a mate,
for the LORD has promised this.
His Spirit will make it all come
true.
¹⁷ He has surveyed and divided the
land
and deeded it over to those
creatures.
They will possess it forever,
from generation to generation.

³⁵:¹EVEN the wilderness and desert will
be glad in those days.
The wasteland will rejoice and
blossom with spring crocuses.
² Yes, there will be an abundance of
flowers
and singing and joy!
The deserts will become as green as
the mountains of Lebanon,
as lovely as Mount Carmel or the
plain of Sharon.
There the LORD will display his glory,
the splendor of our God.
³ With this news, strengthen those
who have tired hands,
and encourage those who have
weak knees.
⁴ Say to those with fearful hearts,
"Be strong, and do not fear,
for your God is coming to destroy
your enemies.
He is coming to save you."

⁵ And when he comes, he will open
the eyes of the blind
and unplug the ears of the deaf.
⁶ The lame will leap like a deer,
and those who cannot speak will
sing for joy!
Springs will gush forth in the
wilderness,
and streams will water the
wasteland.

7 The parched ground will become
   a pool,
   and springs of water will satisfy
      the thirsty land.
   Marsh grass and reeds and rushes
      will flourish
   where desert jackals once lived.

8 And a great road will go through that
      once deserted land.
   It will be named the Highway of
      Holiness.
   Evil-minded people will never travel
      on it.
   It will only be for those who walk
      in God's ways;
   fools will never walk there.
9 Lions will not lurk along its course,
   nor any other ferocious beasts.
   There will be no other dangers.
   Only the redeemed will walk on it.
10 Those who have been ransomed by
      the LORD will return.
   They will enter Jerusalem*
      singing,
   crowned with everlasting joy.
   Sorrow and mourning will
      disappear,
   and they will be filled with joy and
      gladness.

36:1 IN the fourteenth year of King Hezekiah's reign,* King Sennacherib of Assyria came to attack the fortified towns of Judah and conquered them. 2 Then the king of Assyria sent his chief of staff* from Lachish with a huge army to confront King Hezekiah in Jerusalem. The Assyrians took up a position beside the aqueduct that feeds water into the upper pool, near the road leading to the field where cloth is washed.*

3 These are the officials who went out to meet with them: Eliakim son of Hilkiah, the palace administrator; Shebna the court secretary; and Joah son of Asaph, the royal historian.

4 Then the Assyrian king's chief of staff told them to give this message to Hezekiah:

"This is what the great king of Assyria says: What are you trusting in that makes you so confident? 5 Do you think that mere words can substitute for military skill and strength? Who are you counting on, that you have rebelled against me? 6 On Egypt? If you lean on Egypt, it will be like a reed that splinters beneath your weight and pierces your hand. Pharaoh, the king of Egypt, is completely unreliable!

7 "But perhaps you will say to me, 'We are trusting in the LORD our God!' But isn't he the one who was insulted by Hezekiah? Didn't Hezekiah tear down his shrines and altars and make everyone in Judah and Jerusalem worship only at the altar here in Jerusalem?

8 "I'll tell you what! Strike a bargain with my master, the king of Assyria. I will give you 2,000 horses if you can find that many men to ride on them! 9 With your tiny army, how can you think of challenging even the weakest contingent of my master's troops, even with the help of Egypt's chariots and charioteers? 10 What's more, do you think we have invaded your land without the LORD's direction? The LORD himself told us, 'Attack this land and destroy it!'"

11 Then Eliakim, Shebna, and Joah said to the Assyrian chief of staff, "Please speak to us in Aramaic, for we understand it well. Don't speak in Hebrew,* for the people on the wall will hear."

12 But Sennacherib's chief of staff replied, "Do you think my master sent this message only to you and your master? He wants all the people to hear it, for when we put this city under siege, they will suffer along with you. They will be so hungry and thirsty that they will eat their own dung and drink their own urine."

13 Then the chief of staff stood and shouted in Hebrew to the people on the wall, "Listen to this message from the great king of Assyria! 14 This is what the king says: Don't let Hezekiah deceive you. He will never be able to rescue you.

¹⁵Don't let him fool you into trusting in the LORD by saying, 'The LORD will surely rescue us. This city will never fall into the hands of the Assyrian king!'

¹⁶"Don't listen to Hezekiah! These are the terms the king of Assyria is offering: Make peace with me—open the gates and come out. Then each of you can continue eating from your own grapevine and fig tree and drinking from your own well. ¹⁷Then I will arrange to take you to another land like this one—a land of grain and new wine, bread and vineyards.

¹⁸"Don't let Hezekiah mislead you by saying, 'The LORD will rescue us!' Have the gods of any other nations ever saved their people from the king of Assyria? ¹⁹What happened to the gods of Hamath and Arpad? And what about the gods of Sepharvaim? Did any god rescue Samaria from my power? ²⁰What god of any nation has ever been able to save its people from my power? So what makes you think that the LORD can rescue Jerusalem from me?"

²¹But the people were silent and did not utter a word because Hezekiah had commanded them, "Do not answer him."

²²Then Eliakim son of Hilkiah, the palace administrator; Shebna the court secretary; and Joah son of Asaph, the royal historian, went back to Hezekiah. They tore their clothes in despair, and they went in to see the king and told him what the Assyrian chief of staff had said.

34:2 The Hebrew term used here refers to the complete consecration of things or people to the LORD, either by destroying them or by giving them as an offering; similarly in 34:5.   34:8 Hebrew *to Zion*.   34:11 The identification of some of these birds is uncertain.   34:12 The meaning of the Hebrew is uncertain.   34:14 Hebrew *Lilith*, possibly a reference to a mythical demon of the night.   35:10 Hebrew *Zion*.   36:1 The fourteenth year of Hezekiah's reign was 701 B.C.   36:2a Or *the rabshakeh;* also in 36:4, 11, 12, 22.   36:2b Or *bleached*.   36:11 Hebrew *in the dialect of Judah;* also in 36:13.

GALATIANS 5:13-26

For you have been called to live in freedom, my brothers and sisters. But don't use your freedom to satisfy your sinful nature. Instead, use your freedom to serve one another in love. ¹⁴For the whole law can be summed up in this one command: "Love your neighbor as yourself."* ¹⁵But if you are always biting and devouring one another, watch out! Beware of destroying one another.

¹⁶So I say, let the Holy Spirit guide your lives. Then you won't be doing what your sinful nature craves. ¹⁷The sinful nature wants to do evil, which is just the opposite of what the Spirit wants. And the Spirit gives us desires that are the opposite of what the sinful nature desires. These two forces are constantly fighting each other, so you are not free to carry out your good intentions. ¹⁸But when you are directed by the Spirit, you are not under obligation to the law of Moses.

¹⁹When you follow the desires of your sinful nature, the results are very clear: sexual immorality, impurity, lustful pleasures, ²⁰idolatry, sorcery, hostility, quarreling, jealousy, outbursts of anger, selfish ambition, dissension, division, ²¹envy, drunkenness, wild parties, and other sins like these. Let me tell you again, as I have before, that anyone living that sort of life will not inherit the Kingdom of God.

²²**But the Holy Spirit produces this kind of fruit in our lives: love, joy, peace, patience, kindness, goodness, faithfulness, ²³gentleness, and self-control. There is no law against these things!**

²⁴Those who belong to Christ Jesus have nailed the passions and desires of their sinful nature to his cross and crucified them there. ²⁵Since we are living by the Spirit, let us follow the Spirit's leading in every part of our lives. ²⁶Let us not become conceited, or provoke one another, or be jealous of one another.

5:14 Lev 19:18.

PSALM 64:1-10

For the choir director: A psalm of David.

¹ **O** God, listen to my complaint.
    Protect my life from my enemies' threats.
² Hide me from the plots of this
    evil mob,

from this gang of wrongdoers.
³ They sharpen their tongues like swords
and aim their bitter words like
arrows.
⁴ They shoot from ambush at the
innocent,
attacking suddenly and fearlessly.
⁵ They encourage each other to do evil
and plan how to set their traps in
secret.
"Who will ever notice?" they ask.
⁶ As they plot their crimes, they say,
"We have devised the perfect plan!"
Yes, the human heart and mind
are cunning.

⁷ But God himself will shoot them
with his arrows,
suddenly striking them down.
⁸ Their own tongues will ruin them,
and all who see them will shake
their heads in scorn.
⁹ Then everyone will be afraid;
they will proclaim the mighty acts
of God
and realize all the amazing things
he does.
¹⁰ The godly will rejoice in the LORD
and find shelter in him.
And those who do what is right
will praise him.

PROVERBS 23:23
Get the truth and never sell it; also get
wisdom, discipline, and good judgment.

SEPTEMBER
21

ISAIAH 37:1–38:22
When King Hezekiah heard their report, he tore his clothes and put on burlap and went into the Temple of the
LORD. ²And he sent Eliakim the palace
administrator, Shebna the court secretary, and the leading priests, all dressed
in burlap, to the prophet Isaiah son of

Amoz. ³They told him, "This is what
King Hezekiah says: Today is a day of
trouble, insults, and disgrace. It is like
when a child is ready to be born, but the
mother has no strength to deliver the
baby. ⁴But perhaps the LORD your God
has heard the Assyrian chief of staff,*
sent by the king to defy the living God,
and will punish him for his words. Oh,
pray for those of us who are left!"

⁵After King Hezekiah's officials delivered the king's message to Isaiah, ⁶the
prophet replied, "Say to your master,
'This is what the LORD says: Do not be disturbed by this blasphemous speech
against me from the Assyrian king's messengers. ⁷Listen! I myself will move
against him,* and the king will receive a
message that he is needed at home. So he
will return to his land, where I will have
him killed with a sword.'"

⁸Meanwhile, the Assyrian chief of
staff left Jerusalem and went to consult
the king of Assyria, who had left Lachish and was attacking Libnah.

⁹Soon afterward King Sennacherib
received word that King Tirhakah of
Ethiopia* was leading an army to fight
against him. Before leaving to meet the
attack, he sent messengers back to Hezekiah in Jerusalem with this message:

¹⁰"This message is for King
Hezekiah of Judah. Don't let your
God, in whom you trust, deceive you
with promises that Jerusalem will
not be captured by the king of
Assyria. ¹¹You know perfectly well
what the kings of Assyria have done
wherever they have gone. They have
completely destroyed everyone who
stood in their way! Why should you
be any different? ¹²Have the gods of
other nations rescued them—such
nations as Gozan, Haran, Rezeph,
and the people of Eden who were
in Tel-assar? My predecessors
destroyed them all! ¹³What
happened to the king of Hamath
and the king of Arpad? What
happened to the kings of
Sepharvaim, Hena, and Ivvah?"

¹⁴After Hezekiah received the letter from the messengers and read it, he went up to the Lord's Temple and spread it out before the Lord. ¹⁵And Hezekiah prayed this prayer before the Lord: ¹⁶"O Lord of Heaven's Armies, God of Israel, you are enthroned between the mighty cherubim! You alone are God of all the kingdoms of the earth. You alone created the heavens and the earth. ¹⁷Bend down, O Lord, and listen! Open your eyes, O Lord, and see! Listen to Sennacherib's words of defiance against the living God.

¹⁸"It is true, Lord, that the kings of Assyria have destroyed all these nations. ¹⁹And they have thrown the gods of these nations into the fire and burned them. But of course the Assyrians could destroy them! They were not gods at all—only idols of wood and stone shaped by human hands. ²⁰Now, O Lord our God, rescue us from his power; then all the kingdoms of the earth will know that you alone, O Lord, are God.*"

²¹Then Isaiah son of Amoz sent this message to Hezekiah: "This is what the Lord, the God of Israel, says: Because you prayed about King Sennacherib of Assyria, ²²the Lord has spoken this word against him:

"The virgin daughter of Zion
despises you and laughs
at you.
The daughter of Jerusalem
shakes her head in derision
as you flee.

²³ "Whom have you been defying and
ridiculing?
Against whom did you raise your
voice?
At whom did you look with such
haughty eyes?
It was the Holy One of Israel!
²⁴ By your messengers you have defied
the Lord.
You have said, 'With my many
chariots
I have conquered the highest
mountains—
yes, the remotest peaks of Lebanon.

I have cut down its tallest cedars
and its finest cypress trees.
I have reached its farthest heights
and explored its deepest forests.
²⁵ I have dug wells in many foreign
lands*
and refreshed myself with their
water.
With the sole of my foot,
I stopped up all the rivers of Egypt!'

²⁶ "But have you not heard?
I decided this long ago.
Long ago I planned it,
and now I am making it happen.
I planned for you to crush fortified
cities
into heaps of rubble.
²⁷ That is why their people have so
little power
and are so frightened and
confused.
They are as weak as grass,
as easily trampled as tender green
shoots.
They are like grass sprouting on
a housetop,
scorched* before it can grow
lush and tall.

²⁸ "But I know you well—
where you stay
and when you come and go.
I know the way you have raged
against me.
²⁹ And because of your raging
against me
and your arrogance, which I have
heard for myself,
I will put my hook in your nose
and my bit in your mouth.
I will make you return
by the same road on which you
came."

³⁰Then Isaiah said to Hezekiah, "Here is the proof that what I say is true:

"This year you will eat only what
grows up by itself,
and next year you will eat what
springs up from that.
But in the third year you will plant
crops and harvest them;

you will tend vineyards and eat
their fruit.
³¹ And you who are left in Judah,
who have escaped the ravages of
the siege,
will put roots down in your own soil
and grow up and flourish.
³² For a remnant of my people will
spread out from Jerusalem,
a group of survivors from Mount
Zion.
The passionate commitment of the
LORD of Heaven's Armies
will make this happen!

³³"And this is what the LORD says about
the king of Assyria:

"'His armies will not enter Jerusalem.
They will not even shoot an arrow
at it.
They will not march outside its gates
with their shields
nor build banks of earth against
its walls.
³⁴ The king will return to his own
country
by the same road on which he came.
He will not enter this city,'
says the LORD.
³⁵ 'For my own honor and for the sake
of my servant David,
I will defend this city and
protect it.'"

³⁶That night the angel of the LORD
went out to the Assyrian camp and killed
185,000 Assyrian soldiers. When the
surviving Assyrians* woke up the next
morning, they found corpses everywhere. ³⁷Then King Sennacherib of Assyria broke camp and returned to his
own land. He went home to his capital of
Nineveh and stayed there.

³⁸One day while he was worshiping in
the temple of his god Nisroch, his sons
Adrammelech and Sharezer killed him
with their swords. They then escaped to
the land of Ararat, and another son, Esarhaddon, became the next king of Assyria.

³⁸:¹ABOUT that time Hezekiah became
deathly ill, and the prophet Isaiah son of
Amoz went to visit him. He gave the
king this message: "This is what the
LORD says: 'Set your affairs in order, for
you are going to die. You will not recover from this illness.'"

²When Hezekiah heard this, he
turned his face to the wall and prayed to
the LORD, ³"Remember, O LORD, how I
have always been faithful to you and
have served you single-mindedly, always doing what pleases you." Then he
broke down and wept bitterly.

⁴Then this message came to Isaiah
from the LORD: ⁵"Go back to Hezekiah
and tell him, 'This is what the LORD, the
God of your ancestor David, says: I have
heard your prayer and seen your tears. I
will add fifteen years to your life, ⁶and
I will rescue you and this city from the
king of Assyria. Yes, I will defend this
city.'

⁷"And this is the sign from the LORD
to prove that he will do as he promised:
⁸I will cause the sun's shadow to move
ten steps backward on the sundial* of
Ahaz!' " So the shadow on the sundial
moved backward ten steps.

⁹When King Hezekiah was well
again, he wrote this poem:

¹⁰ I said, "In the prime of my life,
must I now enter the place of the
dead?*
Am I to be robbed of the rest of
my years?"
¹¹ I said, "Never again will I see the
LORD GOD
while still in the land of the living.
Never again will I see my friends
or be with those who live in this
world.
¹² My life has been blown away
like a shepherd's tent in a storm.
It has been cut short,
as when a weaver cuts cloth from
a loom.
Suddenly, my life was over.
¹³ I waited patiently all night,
but I was torn apart as though
by lions.
Suddenly, my life was over.
¹⁴ Delirious, I chattered like a swallow
or a crane,

and then I moaned like a
mourning dove.
My eyes grew tired of looking to
heaven for help.
I am in trouble, Lord.
Help me!"

15 But what could I say?
For he himself sent this sickness.
Now I will walk humbly throughout
my years
because of this anguish I have
felt.
16 Lord, your discipline is good,
for it leads to life and health.
You restore my health
and allow me to live!
17 Yes, this anguish was good for me,
for you have rescued me from
death
and forgiven all my sins.
18 For the dead* cannot praise you;
they cannot raise their voices in
praise.
Those who go down to the grave
can no longer hope in your
faithfulness.
19 Only the living can praise you
as I do today.
Each generation tells of your
faithfulness to the next.
20 Think of it—the LORD is ready to
heal me!
I will sing his praises with
instruments
every day of my life
in the Temple of the LORD.

21Isaiah had said to Hezekiah's servants, "Make an ointment from figs and spread it over the boil, and Hezekiah will recover."

22And Hezekiah had asked, "What sign will prove that I will go to the Temple of the LORD?"

37:4 Or *the rabshakeh;* also in 37:8.   37:7 Hebrew *I will put a spirit in him.*   37:9 Hebrew *of Cush.*   37:20 As in Dead Sea Scrolls (see also 2 Kgs 19:19); Masoretic Text reads *you alone are the LORD.*   37:25 As in Dead Sea Scrolls (see also 2 Kgs 19:24); Masoretic Text lacks *in many foreign lands.*   37:27 As in Dead Sea Scrolls and some Greek manuscripts (see also 2 Kgs 19:26); most Hebrew manuscripts read *like a terraced field.*   37:36 Hebrew *When they.*   38:8 Hebrew *the steps.*   38:10 Hebrew *enter the gates of Sheol?*   38:18 Hebrew *Sheol.*

GALATIANS 6:1-18

Dear brothers and sisters, if another believer* is overcome by some sin, you who are godly* should gently and humbly help that person back onto the right path. And be careful not to fall into the same temptation yourself. 2Share each other's burdens, and in this way obey the law of Christ. 3If you think you are too important to help someone, you are only fooling yourself. You are not that important.

4Pay careful attention to your own work, for then you will get the satisfaction of a job well done, and you won't need to compare yourself to anyone else. 5For we are each responsible for our own conduct.

6Those who are taught the word of God should provide for their teachers, sharing all good things with them.

7Don't be misled—you cannot mock the justice of God. You will always harvest what you plant. 8Those who live only to satisfy their own sinful nature will harvest decay and death from that sinful nature. But those who live to please the Spirit will harvest everlasting life from the Spirit. 9**So let's not get tired of doing what is good. At just the right time we will reap a harvest of blessing if we don't give up.** 10**Therefore, whenever we have the opportunity, we should do good to everyone—especially to those in the family of faith.**

11NOTICE WHAT LARGE LETTERS I USE AS I WRITE THESE CLOSING WORDS IN MY OWN HANDWRITING.

12Those who are trying to force you to be circumcised want to look good to others. They don't want to be persecuted for teaching that the cross of Christ alone can save. 13And even those who advocate circumcision don't keep the whole law themselves. They only want you to be circumcised so they can boast about it and claim you as their disciples.

14As for me, may I never boast about anything except the cross of our Lord Jesus Christ. Because of that cross,* my

interest in this world has been crucified, and the world's interest in me has
also died. [15]It doesn't matter whether
we have been circumcised or not. What
counts is whether we have been transformed into a new creation. [16]May
God's peace and mercy be upon all who
live by this principle; they are the new
people of God.*

[17]From now on, don't let anyone
trouble me with these things. For I bear
on my body the scars that show I belong
to Jesus.

[18]Dear brothers and sisters,* may the
grace of our Lord Jesus Christ be with
your spirit. Amen.

6:1a Greek *Brothers, if a man.*   6:1b Greek *spiritual.*
6:14 Or *Because of him.*   6:16 Greek *this principle, and
upon the Israel of God.*   6:18 Greek *Brothers.*

PSALM 65:1-13
*For the choir director: A song. A psalm of
David.*

[1] **W**hat mighty praise, O God,
        belongs to you in Zion.
     We will fulfill our vows to you,
[2] for you answer our prayers.
        All of us must come to you.
[3] Though we are overwhelmed
            by our sins,
        you forgive them all.
[4] What joy for those you choose to
            bring near,
        those who live in your holy courts.
     What festivities await us
        inside your holy Temple.

[5] You faithfully answer our prayers
            with awesome deeds,
        O God our savior.
     You are the hope of everyone
            on earth,
        even those who sail on distant
            seas.
[6] You formed the mountains by
            your power
        and armed yourself with mighty
            strength.
[7] You quieted the raging oceans
        with their pounding waves
        and silenced the shouting of the
            nations.

[8] Those who live at the ends of the
            earth
        stand in awe of your wonders.
     From where the sun rises to where
            it sets,
        you inspire shouts of joy.

[9] You take care of the earth and
            water it,
        making it rich and fertile.
     The river of God has plenty of water;
        it provides a bountiful harvest of
            grain,
        for you have ordered it so.
[10] You drench the plowed ground
            with rain,
        melting the clods and leveling
            the ridges.
     You soften the earth with showers
        and bless its abundant crops.
[11] You crown the year with a bountiful
            harvest;
        even the hard pathways overflow
            with abundance.
[12] The grasslands of the wilderness
            become a lush pasture,
        and the hillsides blossom with joy.
[13] The meadows are clothed with
            flocks of sheep,
        and the valleys are carpeted
            with grain.
        They all shout and sing for joy!

PROVERBS 23:24
The father of godly children has cause
for joy. What a pleasure to have children who are wise.*

23:24 Hebrew *to have a wise son.*

SEPTEMBER
22

ISAIAH 39:1-41:16
Soon after this, Merodach-baladan son
of Baladan, king of Babylon, sent Hezekiah his best wishes and a gift. He had
heard that Hezekiah had been very sick

and that he had recovered. [2]Hezekiah was delighted with the Babylonian envoys and showed them everything in his treasure-houses—the silver, the gold, the spices, and the aromatic oils. He also took them to see his armory and showed them everything in his royal treasuries! There was nothing in his palace or kingdom that Hezekiah did not show them.

[3]Then Isaiah the prophet went to King Hezekiah and asked him, "What did those men want? Where were they from?"

Hezekiah replied, "They came from the distant land of Babylon."

[4]"What did they see in your palace?" asked Isaiah.

"They saw everything," Hezekiah replied. "I showed them everything I own—all my royal treasuries."

[5]Then Isaiah said to Hezekiah, "Listen to this message from the LORD of Heaven's Armies: [6]'The time is coming when everything in your palace—all the treasures stored up by your ancestors until now—will be carried off to Babylon. Nothing will be left,' says the LORD. [7]'Some of your very own sons will be taken away into exile. They will become eunuchs who will serve in the palace of Babylon's king.'"

[8]Then Hezekiah said to Isaiah, "This message you have given me from the LORD is good." For the king was thinking, "At least there will be peace and security during my lifetime."

40:1"COMFORT, comfort my people,"
says your God.
[2] **"Speak tenderly to Jerusalem.**
Tell her that her sad days are gone
and her sins are pardoned.
Yes, the LORD has punished her
twice over
for all her sins."

[3] Listen! It's the voice of someone shouting,
"Clear the way through the wilderness
for the LORD!
Make a straight highway through the wasteland
for our God!

[4] Fill in the valleys,
and level the mountains and hills.
Straighten the curves,
and smooth out the rough places.
[5] Then the glory of the LORD will be revealed,
and all people will see it together.
The LORD has spoken!"*

[6] A voice said, "Shout!"
I asked, "What should I shout?"

"Shout that people are like the grass.
Their beauty fades as quickly
as the flowers in a field.
[7] The grass withers and the flowers fade
beneath the breath of the LORD.
And so it is with people.
[8] The grass withers and the flowers fade,
but the word of our God stands forever."

[9] O Zion, messenger of good news,
shout from the mountaintops!
Shout it louder, O Jerusalem.*
Shout, and do not be afraid.
Tell the towns of Judah,
"Your God is coming!"
[10] Yes, the Sovereign LORD is coming in power.
He will rule with a powerful arm.
See, he brings his reward with him as he comes.
[11] He will feed his flock like a shepherd.
He will carry the lambs in his arms,
holding them close to his heart.
He will gently lead the mother sheep with their young.

[12] Who else has held the oceans in his hand?
Who has measured off the heavens with his fingers?
Who else knows the weight of the earth
or has weighed the mountains and hills on a scale?
[13] Who is able to advise the Spirit of the LORD?*
Who knows enough to give him advice or teach him?

¹⁴ Has the Lord ever needed anyone's
  advice?
  Does he need instruction about
    what is good?
  Did someone teach him what is right
    or show him the path of justice?

¹⁵ No, for all the nations of the world
    are but a drop in the bucket.
  They are nothing more
    than dust on the scales.
  He picks up the whole earth
    as though it were a grain of sand.
¹⁶ All the wood in Lebanon's forests
    and all Lebanon's animals would
      not be enough
    to make a burnt offering worthy
      of our God.
¹⁷ The nations of the world are worth
    nothing to him.
  In his eyes they count for less
    than nothing—
  mere emptiness and froth.

¹⁸ To whom can you compare God?
  What image can you find to
    resemble him?
¹⁹ Can he be compared to an idol
    formed in a mold,
  overlaid with gold, and decorated
    with silver chains?
²⁰ Or if people are too poor for that,
    they might at least choose wood
      that won't decay
  and a skilled craftsman
    to carve an image that won't fall
      down!

²¹ Haven't you heard? Don't you
    understand?
  Are you deaf to the words of God—
  the words he gave before the world
    began?
  Are you so ignorant?
²² God sits above the circle of the
    earth.
  The people below seem like
    grasshoppers to him!
  He spreads out the heavens like
    a curtain
  and makes his tent from them.
²³ He judges the great people of
    the world

  and brings them all to nothing.
²⁴ They hardly get started, barely
    taking root,
  when he blows on them and they
    wither.
  The wind carries them off
    like chaff.

²⁵ "To whom will you compare me?
  Who is my equal?" asks the
    Holy One.

²⁶ Look up into the heavens.
  Who created all the stars?
  He brings them out like an army,
    one after another,
  calling each by its name.
  Because of his great power and
    incomparable strength,
  not a single one is missing.
²⁷ O Jacob, how can you say the Lord
    does not see your troubles?
  O Israel, how can you say God
    ignores your rights?
²⁸ Have you never heard?
  Have you never understood?
  The Lord is the everlasting God,
    the Creator of all the earth.
  He never grows weak or weary.
  No one can measure the depths
    of his understanding.
²⁹ He gives power to the weak
    and strength to the powerless.
³⁰ Even youths will become weak
    and tired,
  and young men will fall in
    exhaustion.
³¹ But those who trust in the Lord will
    find new strength.
  They will soar high on wings
    like eagles.
  They will run and not grow weary.
  They will walk and not faint.

^{41:1} "Listen in silence before me, you
    lands beyond the sea.
  Bring your strongest arguments.
  Come now and speak.
    The court is ready for your case.

² "Who has stirred up this king from
    the east,
  rightly calling him to God's service?

Who gives this man victory over
   many nations
   and permits him to trample their
      kings underfoot?
   With his sword, he reduces armies
      to dust.
   With his bow, he scatters them
      like chaff before the wind.
³ He chases them away and goes
      on safely,
   though he is walking over
      unfamiliar ground.
⁴ Who has done such mighty deeds,
   summoning each new generation
      from the beginning of time?
   It is I, the LORD, the First and
      the Last.
   I alone am he."

⁵ The lands beyond the sea watch
      in fear.
   Remote lands tremble and
      mobilize for war.
⁶ The idol makers encourage one
      another,
   saying to each other, "Be strong!"
⁷ The carver encourages the
      goldsmith,
   and the molder helps at the anvil.
   "Good," they say. "It's coming
      along fine."
   Carefully they join the parts together,
   then fasten the thing in place so it
      won't fall over.

⁸ "But as for you, Israel my servant,
   Jacob my chosen one,
   descended from Abraham my
      friend,
⁹ I have called you back from the ends
      of the earth,
   saying, 'You are my servant.'
   For I have chosen you
      and will not throw you away.
¹⁰ Don't be afraid, for I am with you.
   Don't be discouraged, for
      I am your God.
   I will strengthen you and help you.
   I will hold you up with my
      victorious right hand.

¹¹ "See, all your angry enemies lie there,
   confused and humiliated.

   Anyone who opposes you will die
      and come to nothing.
¹² You will look in vain
      for those who tried to conquer you.
   Those who attack you
      will come to nothing.
¹³ For I hold you by your right hand—
   I, the LORD your God.
   And I say to you,
   'Don't be afraid. I am here to
      help you.
¹⁴ Though you are a lowly worm,
      O Jacob,
   don't be afraid, people of Israel,
      for I will help you.
   I am the LORD, your Redeemer.
   I am the Holy One of Israel.'
¹⁵ You will be a new threshing
      instrument
   with many sharp teeth.
   You will tear your enemies apart,
      making chaff of mountains.
¹⁶ You will toss them into the air,
   and the wind will blow them
      all away;
   a whirlwind will scatter them.
   Then you will rejoice in the LORD.
   You will glory in the Holy One of
      Israel."

40:3-5 Greek version reads *He is a voice shouting in the wilderness, / "Prepare the way for the LORD's coming! / Clear a road for our God! / Fill in the valleys, / and level the mountains and hills. / And then the glory of the LORD will be revealed, / and all people will see the salvation sent from God. / The LORD has spoken!"* Compare Matt 3:3; Mark 1:3; Luke 3:4-6. **40:9** Or *O messenger of good news, shout to Zion from the mountaintops! Shout it louder to Jerusalem.* **40:13** Greek version reads *Who can know the LORD's thoughts?* Compare Rom 11:34; 1 Cor 2:16.

EPHESIANS 1:1-23

This letter is from Paul, chosen by the will of God to be an apostle of Christ Jesus.

I am writing to God's holy people in Ephesus,* who are faithful followers of Christ Jesus.

²May God our Father and the Lord Jesus Christ give you grace and peace.

³All praise to God, the Father of our Lord Jesus Christ, who has blessed us with every spiritual blessing in the heavenly realms because we are united with Christ. ⁴Even before he made the world, God loved us and chose us in

Christ to be holy and without fault in his eyes. [5]God decided in advance to adopt us into his own family by bringing us to himself through Jesus Christ. This is what he wanted to do, and it gave him great pleasure. [6]So we praise God for the glorious grace he has poured out on us who belong to his dear Son.* [7]He is so rich in kindness and grace that he purchased our freedom with the blood of his Son and forgave our sins. [8]He has showered his kindness on us, along with all wisdom and understanding.

[9]God has now revealed to us his mysterious plan regarding Christ, a plan to fulfill his own good pleasure. [10]And this is the plan: At the right time he will bring everything together under the authority of Christ—everything in heaven and on earth. [11]Furthermore, because we are united with Christ, we have received an inheritance from God,* for he chose us in advance, and he makes everything work out according to his plan.

[12]God's purpose was that we Jews who were the first to trust in Christ would bring praise and glory to God. [13]And now you Gentiles have also heard the truth, the Good News that God saves you. And when you believed in Christ, he identified you as his own* by giving you the Holy Spirit, whom he promised long ago. [14]The Spirit is God's guarantee that he will give us the inheritance he promised and that he has purchased us to be his own people. He did this so we would praise and glorify him.

[15]Ever since I first heard of your strong faith in the Lord Jesus and your love for God's people everywhere,* [16]I have not stopped thanking God for you. I pray for you constantly, [17]asking God, the glorious Father of our Lord Jesus Christ, to give you spiritual wisdom* and insight so that you might grow in your knowledge of God. [18]I pray that your hearts will be flooded with light so that you can understand the confident hope he has given to those he called—his holy people who are his rich and glorious inheritance.*

[19]I also pray that you will understand the incredible greatness of God's power for us who believe him. This is the same mighty power [20]that raised Christ from the dead and seated him in the place of honor at God's right hand in the heavenly realms. [21]Now he is far above any ruler or authority or power or leader or anything else—not only in this world but also in the world to come. [22]God has put all things under the authority of Christ and has made him head over all things for the benefit of the church. [23]And the church is his body; it is made full and complete by Christ, who fills all things everywhere with himself.

1:1 The most ancient manuscripts do not include *in Ephesus.*   1:6 Greek *to us in the beloved.*   1:11 Or *we have become God's inheritance.*   1:13 Or *he put his seal on you.*   1:15 Some manuscripts read *your faithfulness to the Lord Jesus and to God's people everywhere.*   1:17 Or *to give you the Spirit of wisdom.*   1:18 Or *called, and the rich and glorious inheritance he has given to his holy people.*

PSALM 66:1-20

For the choir director: A song. A psalm.

[1] **S**hout joyful praises to God, all the earth!
[2]   Sing about the glory of his name!
      Tell the world how glorious he is.
[3] Say to God, "How awesome are your deeds!
      Your enemies cringe before your mighty power.
[4] Everything on earth will worship you;
      they will sing your praises,
      shouting your name in glorious songs."   *Interlude*

[5] Come and see what our God has done,
      what awesome miracles he performs for people!
[6] He made a dry path through the Red Sea,*
      and his people went across on foot.
      There we rejoiced in him.
[7] For by his great power he rules forever.
      He watches every movement of the nations;
      let no rebel rise in defiance.
                                    Interlude

[8] Let the whole world bless our God
      and loudly sing his praises.

⁹ Our lives are in his hands,
　　and he keeps our feet from
　　　stumbling.
¹⁰ You have tested us, O God;
　　you have purified us like silver.
¹¹ You captured us in your net
　　and laid the burden of slavery on
　　　our backs.
¹² Then you put a leader over us.*
　　We went through fire and flood,
　　but you brought us to a place of
　　　great abundance.

¹³ Now I come to your Temple with
　　　burnt offerings
　　to fulfill the vows I made to you—
¹⁴ yes, the sacred vows that I made
　　when I was in deep trouble.
¹⁵ That is why I am sacrificing burnt
　　　offerings to you—
　　the best of my rams as a pleasing
　　　aroma,
　　and a sacrifice of bulls and male
　　　goats.　　　　　　　*Interlude*

¹⁶ Come and listen, all you who fear
　　　God,
　　and I will tell you what he did
　　　for me.
¹⁷ For I cried out to him for help,
　　praising him as I spoke.
¹⁸ If I had not confessed the sin
　　in my heart,
　　the Lord would not have listened.
¹⁹ But God did listen!
　　He paid attention to my prayer.
²⁰ Praise God, who did not ignore my
　　　prayer
　　or withdraw his unfailing love
　　　from me.

66:6 Hebrew *the sea.*　**66:12** Or *You made people ride over
our heads.*

PROVERBS 23:25-28

So give your father and mother joy! May
she who gave you birth be happy.
□O my son, give me your heart. May
your eyes take delight in following my
ways. A prostitute is a dangerous trap; a
promiscuous woman is as dangerous as
falling into a narrow well. She hides and
waits like a robber, eager to make more
men unfaithful.

SEPTEMBER
23

ISAIAH 41:17–43:13

"**W**hen the poor and needy search
　　for water and there is none,
　　and their tongues are parched
　　　from thirst,
　　then I, the Lord, will answer them.
　　I, the God of Israel, will never
　　　abandon them.
¹⁸ I will open up rivers for them on the
　　　high plateaus.
　　I will give them fountains of water
　　　in the valleys.
　　I will fill the desert with pools
　　　of water.
　　Rivers fed by springs will flow
　　　across the parched ground.
¹⁹ I will plant trees in the barren
　　　desert—
　　cedar, acacia, myrtle, olive,
　　　cypress, fir, and pine.
²⁰ I am doing this so all who see this
　　　miracle
　　will understand what it
　　　means—
　　that it is the Lord who has done this,
　　the Holy One of Israel who
　　　created it.

²¹ "Present the case for your idols,"
　　says the Lord.
　　"Let them show what they can do,"
　　says the King of Israel.*
²² "Let them try to tell us what
　　　happened long ago
　　so that we may consider the
　　　evidence.
　　Or let them tell us what the future
　　　holds,
　　so we can know what's going
　　　to happen.
²³ Yes, tell us what will occur in the
　　　days ahead.
　　Then we will know you are gods.
　　In fact, do anything—good or bad!
　　Do something that will amaze and
　　　frighten us.

²⁴ But no! You are less than nothing
    and can do nothing at all.
  Those who choose you pollute
    themselves.

²⁵ "But I have stirred up a leader who
    will come from the north.
  I have called him by name from
    the east.
  I will give him victory over kings
    and princes.
  He will trample them as a potter
    treads on clay.

²⁶ "Who told you from the beginning
    that this would happen?
  Who predicted this,
    making you admit that he was
    right?
  No one said a word!
²⁷ I was the first to tell Zion,
    'Look! Help is on the way!'*
  I will send Jerusalem a messenger
    with good news.
²⁸ Not one of your idols told you this.
  Not one gave any answer when
    I asked.
²⁹ See, they are all foolish, worthless
    things.
  All your idols are as empty as
    the wind.

⁴²:¹ "Look at my servant, whom
    I strengthen.
  He is my chosen one, who
    pleases me.
  I have put my Spirit upon him.
    He will bring justice to the
    nations.
² He will not shout
    or raise his voice in public.
³ He will not crush the weakest reed
    or put out a flickering candle.
  He will bring justice to all who
    have been wronged.
⁴ He will not falter or lose heart
    until justice prevails throughout
    the earth.
  Even distant lands beyond the sea
    will wait for his instruction.*"

⁵ God, the Lord, created the heavens
    and stretched them out.

  He created the earth and
    everything in it.
  He gives breath to everyone,
    life to everyone who walks the
    earth.
  And it is he who says,
⁶ "I, the Lord, have called you to
    demonstrate my righteousness.
  I will take you by the hand and
    guard you,
  and I will give you to my people,
    Israel,
  as a symbol of my covenant
    with them.
  And you will be a light to guide
    the nations.
⁷ You will open the eyes of the blind.
  You will free the captives from
    prison,
    releasing those who sit in dark
    dungeons.

⁸ "I am the Lord; that is my name!
  I will not give my glory to anyone
    else,
  nor share my praise with carved
    idols.
⁹ Everything I prophesied has come
    true,
  and now I will prophesy again.
  I will tell you the future before it
    happens."

¹⁰ Sing a new song to the Lord!
    Sing his praises from the ends
    of the earth!
  Sing, all you who sail the seas,
    all you who live in distant
    coastlands.
¹¹ Join in the chorus, you desert
    towns;
    let the villages of Kedar rejoice!
  Let the people of Sela sing for joy;
    shout praises from the
    mountaintops!
¹² Let the whole world glorify the Lord;
    let it sing his praise.
¹³ The Lord will march forth like a
    mighty hero;
  he will come out like a warrior,
    full of fury.
  He will shout his battle cry
    and crush all his enemies.

¹⁴ He will say, "I have long been silent;
  yes, I have restrained myself.
But now, like a woman in labor,
  I will cry and groan and pant.
¹⁵ I will level the mountains and hills
  and blight all their greenery.
I will turn the rivers into dry land
  and will dry up all the pools.
¹⁶ I will lead blind Israel down a new
    path,
  guiding them along an unfamiliar
    way.
I will brighten the darkness before
    them
  and smooth out the road ahead
    of them.
Yes, I will indeed do these things;
  I will not forsake them.
¹⁷ But those who trust in idols,
  who say, 'You are our gods,'
  will be turned away in shame.

¹⁸ "Listen, you who are deaf!
  Look and see, you blind!
¹⁹ Who is as blind as my own people,
    my servant?
  Who is as deaf as my messenger?
Who is as blind as my chosen
    people,
  the servant of the LORD?
²⁰ You see and recognize what is right
  but refuse to act on it.
You hear with your ears,
  but you don't really listen."

²¹ Because he is righteous,
  the LORD has exalted his
    glorious law.
²² But his own people have been
    robbed and plundered,
  enslaved, imprisoned, and
    trapped.
They are fair game for anyone
  and have no one to protect them,
  no one to take them back home.

²³ Who will hear these lessons from
    the past
  and see the ruin that awaits you in
    the future?
²⁴ Who allowed Israel to be robbed
  and hurt?

It was the LORD, against whom
    we sinned,
for the people would not walk in
    his path,
  nor would they obey his law.
²⁵ Therefore, he poured out his fury
    on them
  and destroyed them in battle.
They were enveloped in flames,
  but they still refused to
    understand.
They were consumed by fire,
  but they did not learn their
    lesson.

⁴³:¹BUT now, O Jacob, listen to the LORD
    who created you.
  O Israel, the one who formed
    you says,
"Do not be afraid, for I have
    ransomed you.
  I have called you by name; you
    are mine.
² When you go through deep waters,
  I will be with you.
When you go through rivers of
    difficulty,
  you will not drown.
When you walk through the fire
    of oppression,
  you will not be burned up;
  the flames will not consume you.
³ For I am the LORD, your God,
  the Holy One of Israel, your
    Savior.
I gave Egypt as a ransom for your
    freedom;
  I gave Ethiopia* and Seba
    in your place.
⁴ Others were given in exchange
    for you.
  I traded their lives for yours
because you are precious to me.
  You are honored, and I love you.

⁵ "Do not be afraid, for I am with you.
  I will gather you and your
    children from east and west.
⁶ I will say to the north and south,
  'Bring my sons and daughters
    back to Israel
  from the distant corners
    of the earth.

⁷ Bring all who claim me as their God,
  for I have made them for my
  glory.
It was I who created them.'"

⁸ Bring out the people who have eyes
  but are blind,
  who have ears but are deaf.
⁹ Gather the nations together!
  Assemble the peoples of the
  world!
Which of their idols has ever
  foretold such things?
Which can predict what will
  happen tomorrow?
Where are the witnesses of such
  predictions?
Who can verify that they spoke
  the truth?

¹⁰ "But you are my witnesses, O Israel!"
  says the LORD.
"You are my servant.
You have been chosen to know me,
  believe in me,
  and understand that I alone
  am God.
There is no other God—
  there never has been, and there
  never will be.
¹¹ I, yes I, am the LORD,
  and there is no other Savior.
¹² First I predicted your rescue,
  then I saved you and proclaimed
  it to the world.
No foreign god has ever done this.
  You are witnesses that I am the
  only God,"
  says the LORD.
¹³ "From eternity to eternity I am God.
No one can snatch anyone out
  of my hand.
No one can undo what I have
  done."

41:21 Hebrew *the King of Jacob.* See note on 14:1.
41:27 Or *'Look! They are coming home.'*   42:4 Greek
version reads *And his name will be the hope of all the
world.* Compare Matt 12:21.   43:3 Hebrew *Cush.*

EPHESIANS 2:1-22

●nce you [believers] were dead because of your disobedience and your
many sins. ²You used to live in sin, just
like the rest of the world, obeying the

devil—the commander of the powers in
the unseen world.* He is the spirit at
work in the hearts of those who refuse
to obey God. ³All of us used to live that
way, following the passionate desires
and inclinations of our sinful nature. By
our very nature we were subject to
God's anger, just like everyone else.

⁴But God is so rich in mercy, and he
loved us so much, ⁵that even though we
were dead because of our sins, he gave us
life when he raised Christ from the dead.
(It is only by God's grace that you have
been saved!) ⁶For he raised us from the
dead along with Christ and seated us
with him in the heavenly realms because
we are united with Christ Jesus. ⁷So God
can point to us in all future ages as examples of the incredible wealth of his grace
and kindness toward us, as shown in all
he has done for us who are united with
Christ Jesus.

⁸**God saved you by his grace when
you believed. And you can't take
credit for this; it is a gift from God.
⁹Salvation is not a reward for the
good things we have done, so none of
us can boast about it.** ¹⁰For we are
God's masterpiece. He has created us
anew in Christ Jesus, so we can do the
good things he planned for us long ago.

¹¹Don't forget that you Gentiles used
to be outsiders. You were called "uncircumcised heathens" by the Jews, who
were proud of their circumcision, even
though it affected only their bodies and
not their hearts. ¹²In those days you
were living apart from Christ. You were
excluded from citizenship among the
people of Israel, and you did not know
the covenant promises God had made
to them. You lived in this world without
God and without hope. ¹³But now you
have been united with Christ Jesus.
Once you were far away from God, but
now you have been brought near to him
through the blood of Christ.

¹⁴For Christ himself has brought
peace to us. He united Jews and Gentiles
into one people when, in his own body on
the cross, he broke down the wall of hostility that separated us. ¹⁵He did this by

ending the system of law with its commandments and regulations. He made
peace between Jews and Gentiles by cre-
ating in himself one new people from the
two groups. ¹⁶Together as one body,
Christ reconciled both groups to God by
means of his death on the cross, and our
hostility toward each other was put to
death.

¹⁷He brought this Good News of peace
to you Gentiles who were far away from
him, and peace to the Jews who were
near. ¹⁸Now all of us can come to the Father through the same Holy Spirit because of what Christ has done for us.

¹⁹So now you Gentiles are no longer
strangers and foreigners. You are citizens along with all of God's holy people.
You are members of God's family. ²⁰To-
gether, we are his house, built on the
foundation of the apostles and the
prophets. And the cornerstone is Christ
Jesus himself. ²¹We are carefully joined
together in him, becoming a holy temple for the Lord. ²²Through him you
Gentiles are also being made part of this
dwelling where God lives by his Spirit.

2:2 Greek *obeying the commander of the power of the air.*

PSALM 67:1-7

For the choir director: A song. A psalm, to be
accompanied by stringed instruments.

¹ May God be merciful and bless us.
   May his face smile with favor
      on us.   *Interlude*

² May your ways be known
      throughout the earth,
   your saving power among people
      everywhere.
³ May the nations praise you, O God.
   Yes, may all the nations praise
      you.
⁴ Let the whole world sing for joy,
   because you govern the nations
      with justice
   and guide the people of the
      whole world.   *Interlude*

⁵ May the nations praise you, O God.
   Yes, may all the nations praise
      you.

⁶ Then the earth will yield its harvests,
   and God, our God, will richly
      bless us.
⁷ Yes, God will bless us,
   and people all over the world will
      fear him.

PROVERBS 23:29-35

Who has anguish? Who has sorrow?
Who is always fighting? Who is always
complaining? Who has unnecessary
bruises? Who has bloodshot eyes? It is
the one who spends long hours in the
taverns, trying out new drinks. Don't
gaze at the wine, seeing how red it is, how
it sparkles in the cup, how smoothly it
goes down. For in the end it bites like a
poisonous snake; it stings like a viper.
You will see hallucinations, and you will
say crazy things. You will stagger like a
sailor tossed at sea, clinging to a sway-
ing mast. And you will say, "They hit me,
but I didn't feel it. I didn't even know it
when they beat me up. When will I wake
up so I can look for another drink?"

SEPTEMBER 24

ISAIAH 43:14–45:10

This is what the LORD says—your Redeemer, the Holy One of Israel:

"For your sakes I will send an army
      against Babylon,
   forcing the Babylonians* to
      flee in those ships they are so
      proud of.
¹⁵ I am the LORD, your Holy One,
   Israel's Creator and King.
¹⁶ I am the LORD, who opened a way
      through the waters,
   making a dry path through
      the sea.
¹⁷ I called forth the mighty army
      of Egypt
   with all its chariots and horses.

I drew them beneath the waves, and
they drowned,
their lives snuffed out like a
smoldering candlewick.
18 "But forget all that—
it is nothing compared to what I
am going to do.
19 For I am about to do something
new.
See, I have already begun! Do you
not see it?
I will make a pathway through the
wilderness.
I will create rivers in the dry
wasteland.
20 The wild animals in the fields will
thank me,
the jackals and owls, too,
for giving them water in the
desert.
Yes, I will make rivers in the dry
wasteland
so my chosen people can be
refreshed.
21 I have made Israel for myself,
and they will someday honor me
before the whole world.

22 "But, dear family of Jacob, you
refuse to ask for my help.
You have grown tired of me,
O Israel!
23 You have not brought me sheep or
goats for burnt offerings.
You have not honored me with
sacrifices,
though I have not burdened and
wearied you
with requests for grain offerings
and frankincense.
24 You have not brought me fragrant
calamus
or pleased me with the fat from
sacrifices.
Instead, you have burdened me with
your sins
and wearied me with your faults.

25 "I—yes, I alone—will blot out your
sins for my own sake
and will never think of them
again.

26 Let us review the situation together,
and you can present your case to
prove your innocence.
27 From the very beginning, your first
ancestor sinned against me;
all your leaders broke my laws.
28 That is why I have disgraced your
priests;
I have decreed complete
destruction* for Jacob
and shame for Israel.

44:1 "BUT now, listen to me, Jacob my
servant,
Israel my chosen one.
2 The LORD who made you and helps
you says:
Do not be afraid, O Jacob, my
servant,
O dear Israel,* my chosen one.
3 For I will pour out water to quench
your thirst
and to irrigate your parched
fields.
And I will pour out my Spirit on your
descendants,
and my blessing on your children.
4 They will thrive like watered grass,
like willows on a riverbank.
5 Some will proudly claim, 'I belong to
the LORD.'
Others will say, 'I am a descendant
of Jacob.'
Some will write the LORD's name on
their hands
and will take the name of Israel as
their own."

6This is what the LORD says—Israel's
King and Redeemer, the LORD of Heav-
en's Armies:

"I am the First and the Last;
there is no other God.
7 Who is like me?
Let him step forward and prove to
you his power.
Let him do as I have done since
ancient times
when I established a people and
explained its future.
8 Do not tremble; do not be afraid.

Did I not proclaim my purposes
     for you long ago?
You are my witnesses—is there any
     other God?
No! There is no other Rock—
     not one!"

⁹ How foolish are those who
     manufacture idols.
These prized objects are really
     worthless.
The people who worship idols don't
     know this,
so they are all put to shame.
¹⁰ Who but a fool would make his
     own god—
an idol that cannot help him
     one bit?
¹¹ All who worship idols will be
     disgraced
along with all these craftsmen—
     mere humans—
who claim they can make a god.
They may all stand together,
     but they will stand in terror
     and shame.

¹² The blacksmith stands at his forge
     to make a sharp tool,
     pounding and shaping it with all
          his might.
His work makes him hungry and
     weak.
     It makes him thirsty and faint.
¹³ Then the wood-carver measures
     a block of wood
     and draws a pattern on it.
He works with chisel and plane
     and carves it into a human figure.
He gives it human beauty
     and puts it in a little shrine.
¹⁴ He cuts down cedars;
     he selects the cypress and the oak;
he plants the pine in the forest
     to be nourished by the rain.
¹⁵ Then he uses part of the wood to
     make a fire.
     With it he warms himself and
          bakes his bread.
Then—yes, it's true—he takes the
     rest of it
     and makes himself a god to
          worship!

He makes an idol
     and bows down in front of it!
¹⁶ He burns part of the tree to roast
     his meat
     and to keep himself warm.
He says, "Ah, that fire feels good."
¹⁷ Then he takes what's left
     and makes his god: a carved idol!
He falls down in front of it,
     worshiping and praying to it.
"Rescue me!" he says.
     "You are my god!"

¹⁸ Such stupidity and ignorance!
     Their eyes are closed, and they
          cannot see.
     Their minds are shut, and they
          cannot think.
¹⁹ The person who made the idol never
     stops to reflect,
     "Why, it's just a block of wood!
I burned half of it for heat
     and used it to bake my bread and
          roast my meat.
How can the rest of it be a god?
     Should I bow down to worship
          a piece of wood?"
²⁰ The poor, deluded fool feeds on
     ashes.
     He trusts something that can't
          help him at all.
Yet he cannot bring himself to ask,
     "Is this idol that I'm holding in my
          hand a lie?"

²¹ "Pay attention, O Jacob,
     for you are my servant, O Israel.
I, the LORD, made you,
     and I will not forget you.
²² I have swept away your sins like
     a cloud.
     I have scattered your offenses like
          the morning mist.
Oh, return to me,
     for I have paid the price to set
          you free."

²³ Sing, O heavens, for the LORD has
     done this wondrous thing.
     Shout for joy, O depths of the
          earth!
Break into song,

O mountains and forests and
every tree!
For the Lord has redeemed Jacob
and is glorified in Israel.

24 This is what the Lord says—
your Redeemer and Creator:
"I am the Lord, who made all things.
I alone stretched out the heavens.
Who was with me
when I made the earth?
25 I expose the false prophets as liars
and make fools of fortune-tellers.
I cause the wise to give bad advice,
thus proving them to be fools.
26 But I carry out the predictions of my
prophets!
By them I say to Jerusalem,
'People will live here again,'
and to the towns of Judah, 'You will
be rebuilt;
I will restore all your ruins!'
27 When I speak to the rivers and say,
'Dry up!'
they will be dry.
28 When I say of Cyrus, 'He is my
shepherd,'
he will certainly do as I say.
He will command, 'Rebuild
Jerusalem';
he will say, 'Restore the Temple.'"

45:1This is what the Lord says to Cyrus,
his anointed one,
whose right hand he will
empower.
Before him, mighty kings will be
paralyzed with fear.
Their fortress gates will be
opened,
never to shut again.
2 This is what the Lord says:

"I will go before you, Cyrus,
and level the mountains.*
I will smash down gates of bronze
and cut through bars of iron.
3 And I will give you treasures hidden
in the darkness—
secret riches.
I will do this so you may know that I
am the Lord,

the God of Israel, the one who
calls you by name.

4 "And why have I called you for this
work?
Why did I call you by name when
you did not know me?
It is for the sake of Jacob my servant,
Israel my chosen one.
5 I am the Lord;
there is no other God.
I have equipped you for battle,
though you don't even know me,
6 so all the world from east to west
will know there is no other God.
I am the Lord, and there is no other.
7   I create the light and make the
darkness.
I send good times and bad times.
I, the Lord, am the one who does
these things.

8 "Open up, O heavens,
and pour out your righteousness.
Let the earth open wide
so salvation and righteousness
can sprout up together.
I, the Lord, created them.

9 "What sorrow awaits those who
argue with their Creator.
Does a clay pot argue with its
maker?
Does the clay dispute with the one
who shapes it, saying,
'Stop, you're doing it wrong!'
Does the pot exclaim,
'How clumsy can you be?'
10 How terrible it would be if a
newborn baby said to its father,
'Why was I born?'
or if it said to its mother,
'Why did you make me this way?'"

43:14 Or *Chaldeans*.   43:28 The Hebrew term used here
refers to the complete consecration of things or people to
the Lord, either by destroying them or by giving them as an
offering.   44:2 Hebrew *Jeshurun*, a term of endearment
for Israel.   45:2 As in Dead Sea Scrolls and Greek version;
Masoretic Text reads *the swellings*.

EPHESIANS 3:1-21

When I think of all this, I, Paul, a prisoner of Christ Jesus for the benefit of
you Gentiles* . . . 2assuming, by the way,
that you know God gave me the special

responsibility of extending his grace to you Gentiles. ³As I briefly wrote earlier, God himself revealed his mysterious plan to me. ⁴As you read what I have written, you will understand my insight into this plan regarding Christ. ⁵God did not reveal it to previous generations, but now by his Spirit he has revealed it to his holy apostles and prophets.

⁶And this is God's plan: Both Gentiles and Jews who believe the Good News share equally in the riches inherited by God's children. Both are part of the same body, and both enjoy the promise of blessings because they belong to Christ Jesus.* ⁷By God's grace and mighty power, I have been given the privilege of serving him by spreading this Good News.

⁸Though I am the least deserving of all God's people, he graciously gave me the privilege of telling the Gentiles about the endless treasures available to them in Christ. ⁹I was chosen to explain to everyone* this mysterious plan that God, the Creator of all things, had kept secret from the beginning.

¹⁰God's purpose in all this was to use the church to display his wisdom in its rich variety to all the unseen rulers and authorities in the heavenly places. ¹¹This was his eternal plan, which he carried out through Christ Jesus our Lord.

¹²Because of Christ and our faith in him,* we can now come boldly and confidently into God's presence. ¹³So please don't lose heart because of my trials here. I am suffering for you, so you should feel honored.

¹⁴When I think of all this, I fall to my knees and pray to the Father,* ¹⁵the Creator of everything in heaven and on earth.* ¹⁶I pray that from his glorious, unlimited resources he will empower you with inner strength through his Spirit. ¹⁷Then Christ will make his home in your hearts as you trust in him. Your roots will grow down into God's love and keep you strong. ¹⁸And may you have the power to understand, as all God's people should, how wide, how long, how high, and how deep his love is.

¹⁹May you experience the love of Christ, though it is too great to understand fully. Then you will be made complete with all the fullness of life and power that comes from God.

²⁰**Now all glory to God, who is able, through his mighty power at work within us, to accomplish infinitely more than we might ask or think. ²¹Glory to him in the church and in Christ Jesus through all generations forever and ever! Amen.**

3:1 Paul resumes this thought in verse 14: "When I think of all this, I fall to my knees and pray to the Father." 3:6 Or *because they are united with Christ Jesus.* 3:9 Some manuscripts omit *to everyone.* 3:12 Or *Because of Christ's faithfulness.* 3:14 Some manuscripts read *the Father of our Lord Jesus Christ.* 3:15 Or *from whom every family in heaven and on earth takes its name.*

PSALM 68:1-18

For the choir director: A song. A psalm of David.

¹ **R**ise up, O God, and scatter your
        enemies.
    Let those who hate God run for
        their lives.
² Blow them away like smoke.
    Melt them like wax in a fire.
    Let the wicked perish in the
        presence of God.
³ But let the godly rejoice.
    Let them be glad in God's
        presence.
    Let them be filled with joy.
⁴ Sing praises to God and to his name!
    Sing loud praises to him who
        rides the clouds.
His name is the LORD—
    rejoice in his presence!

⁵ Father to the fatherless, defender
        of widows—
    this is God, whose dwelling is holy.
⁶ God places the lonely in families;
    he sets the prisoners free and
        gives them joy.
But he makes the rebellious live in a
        sun-scorched land.

⁷ O God, when you led your people out
        from Egypt,
    when you marched through the
        dry wasteland,   *Interlude*

⁸ the earth trembled, and the heavens
    poured down rain
  before you, the God of Sinai,
  before God, the God of Israel.
⁹ You sent abundant rain, O God,
    to refresh the weary land.
¹⁰ There your people finally settled,
    and with a bountiful harvest,
    O God,
  you provided for your needy people.

¹¹ The Lord gives the word,
    and a great army* brings the
    good news.
¹² Enemy kings and their armies flee,
    while the women of Israel divide
    the plunder.
¹³ Even those who lived among the
    sheepfolds found treasures—
  doves with wings of silver
    and feathers of gold.
¹⁴ The Almighty scattered the enemy
    kings
  like a blowing snowstorm on
    Mount Zalmon.

¹⁵ The mountains of Bashan are
    majestic,
  with many peaks stretching high
    into the sky.
¹⁶ Why do you look with envy,
    O rugged mountains,
  at Mount Zion, where God has
    chosen to live,
  where the Lord himself will live
    forever?

¹⁷ Surrounded by unnumbered
    thousands of chariots,
  the Lord came from Mount Sinai
    into his sanctuary.
¹⁸ When you ascended to the heights,
    you led a crowd of captives.
  You received gifts from the people,
    even from those who rebelled
    against you.
  Now the Lord God will live
    among us there.

68:11 Or *a host of women.*

PROVERBS 24:1-2

Don't envy evil people or desire their
company. For their hearts plot violence,
and their words always stir up trouble.

SEPTEMBER 25

ISAIAH 45:11–48:11

This is what the Lord says—
  the Holy One of Israel and
  your Creator:
"Do you question what I do for
  my children?
  Do you give me orders about the
  work of my hands?
¹² I am the one who made the earth
  and created people to live on it.
With my hands I stretched out the
  heavens.
All the stars are at my command.
¹³ I will raise up Cyrus to fulfill my
  righteous purpose,
  and I will guide his actions.
He will restore my city and free my
  captive people—
  without seeking a reward!
  I, the Lord of Heaven's Armies,
  have spoken!"

¹⁴This is what the Lord says:

"You will rule the Egyptians,
  the Ethiopians,* and the Sabeans.
They will come to you with all their
  merchandise,
  and it will all be yours.
They will follow you as prisoners in
  chains.
  They will fall to their knees in
  front of you and say,
'God is with you, and he is the
  only God.
  There is no other.'"

¹⁵ Truly, O God of Israel, our Savior,
  you work in mysterious ways.
¹⁶ All craftsmen who make idols will
  be humiliated.
  They will all be disgraced together.
¹⁷ But the Lord will save the people
  of Israel
  with eternal salvation.
  Throughout everlasting ages,

they will never again be
  humiliated and disgraced.

18 For the LORD is God,
  and he created the heavens
    and earth
  and put everything in place.
He made the world to be lived in,
  not to be a place of empty chaos.
"I am the LORD," he says,
  "and there is no other.
19 I publicly proclaim bold promises.
  I do not whisper obscurities in
    some dark corner.
I would not have told the people of
    Israel* to seek me
  if I could not be found.
I, the LORD, speak only what is true
  and declare only what is right.

20 "Gather together and come,
  you fugitives from surrounding
    nations.
What fools they are who carry
    around their wooden idols
  and pray to gods that cannot save!
21 Consult together, argue your case.
  Get together and decide what
    to say.
Who made these things known
    so long ago?
  What idol ever told you they
    would happen?
Was it not I, the LORD?
  For there is no other God but me,
a righteous God and Savior.
  There is none but me.
22 Let all the world look to me for
    salvation!
  For I am God; there is no other.
23 I have sworn by my own name;
  I have spoken the truth,
  and I will never go back on
    my word:
Every knee will bend to me,
  and every tongue will confess
    allegiance to me.*"
24 The people will declare,
  "The LORD is the source of all my
    righteousness and strength."
And all who were angry with him
  will come to him and be ashamed.

25 In the LORD all the generations of
    Israel will be justified,
  and in him they will boast.

46:1BEL and Nebo, the gods of Babylon,
  bow as they are lowered to the
    ground.
They are being hauled away on
    ox carts.
  The poor beasts stagger under
    the weight.
2 Both the idols and their owners are
    bowed down.
  The gods cannot protect the
    people,
and the people cannot protect
    the gods.
  They go off into captivity together.

3 "Listen to me, descendants of Jacob,
  all you who remain in Israel.
I have cared for you since you
    were born.
  Yes, I carried you before you
    were born.
4 I will be your God throughout your
    lifetime—
  until your hair is white with age.
I made you, and I will care for you.
  I will carry you along and save you.

5 "To whom will you compare me?
  Who is my equal?
6 Some people pour out their silver
    and gold
  and hire a craftsman to make
    a god from it.
Then they bow down and
    worship it!
7 They carry it around on their
    shoulders,
  and when they set it down, it stays
    there.
  It can't even move!
And when someone prays to it,
    there is no answer.
  It can't rescue anyone from
    trouble.

8 "Do not forget this! Keep it in mind!
  Remember this, you guilty ones.
9 Remember the things I have done
    in the past.
  For I alone am God!

I am God, and there is none like me.
10 Only I can tell you the future
    before it even happens.
  Everything I plan will come to pass,
    for I do whatever I wish.
11 I will call a swift bird of prey from
    the east—
  a leader from a distant land to
    come and do my bidding.
  I have said what I would do,
    and I will do it.

12 "Listen to me, you stubborn people
    who are so far from doing right.
13 For I am ready to set things right,
    not in the distant future, but
    right now!
  I am ready to save Jerusalem*
    and show my glory to Israel.

47:1"COME down, virgin daughter of
    Babylon, and sit in the dust.
  For your days of sitting on a
    throne have ended.
  O daughter of Babylonia,* never
    again will you be
  the lovely princess, tender and
    delicate.
2 Take heavy millstones and grind
    flour.
  Remove your veil, and strip off
    your robe.
  Expose yourself to public view.
3 You will be naked and burdened
    with shame.
  I will take vengeance against you
    without pity."

4 Our Redeemer, whose name is the
    LORD of Heaven's Armies,
  is the Holy One of Israel.

5 "O beautiful Babylon, sit now in
    darkness and silence.
  Never again will you be known
    as the queen of kingdoms.
6 For I was angry with my chosen
    people
  and punished them by letting
    them fall into your hands.
  But you, Babylon, showed them
    no mercy.
  You oppressed even the elderly.

7 You said, 'I will reign forever as
    queen of the world!'
  You did not reflect on your actions
    or think about their consequences.

8 "Listen to this, you pleasure-loving
    kingdom,
  living at ease and feeling secure.
  You say, 'I am the only one, and
    there is no other.
  I will never be a widow or lose
    my children.'
9 Well, both these things will come
    upon you in a moment:
  widowhood and the loss of your
    children.
  Yes, these calamities will come
    upon you,
  despite all your witchcraft
    and magic.

10 "You felt secure in your wickedness.
    'No one sees me,' you said.
  But your 'wisdom' and 'knowledge'
    have led you astray,
  and you said, 'I am the only one,
    and there is no other.'
11 So disaster will overtake you,
    and you won't be able to charm
    it away.
  Calamity will fall upon you,
    and you won't be able to buy your
    way out.
  A catastrophe will strike you suddenly,
    one for which you are not prepared.

12 "Now use your magical charms!
    Use the spells you have worked
    at all these years!
  Maybe they will do you some good.
    Maybe they can make someone
    afraid of you.
13 All the advice you receive has made
    you tired.
  Where are all your astrologers,
  those stargazers who make
    predictions each month?
  Let them stand up and save you
    from what the future holds.
14 But they are like straw burning
    in a fire;
  they cannot save themselves from
    the flame.

You will get no help from them
at all;
their hearth is no place to sit
for warmth.
¹⁵ And all your friends,
those with whom you've done
business since childhood,
will go their own ways,
turning a deaf ear to your cries.

^{48:1} "Listen to me, O family of Jacob,
you who are called by the name
of Israel
and born into the family of Judah.
Listen, you who take oaths in the
name of the Lord
and call on the God of Israel.
You don't keep your promises,
²   even though you call yourself the
holy city
and talk about depending on the
God of Israel,
whose name is the Lord of
Heaven's Armies.
³ Long ago I told you what was going
to happen.
Then suddenly I took action,
and all my predictions came true.
⁴ For I know how stubborn and
obstinate you are.
Your necks are as unbending
as iron.
Your heads are as hard as bronze.
⁵ That is why I told you what would
happen;
I told you beforehand what I was
going to do.
Then you could never say, 'My idols
did it.
My wooden image and metal god
commanded it to happen!'
⁶ You have heard my predictions and
seen them fulfilled,
but you refuse to admit it.
Now I will tell you new things,
secrets you have not yet heard.
⁷ They are brand new, not things
from the past.
So you cannot say, 'We knew that
all the time!'

⁸ "Yes, I will tell you of things that are
entirely new,

things you never heard of before.
For I know so well what traitors you
are.
You have been rebels from birth.
⁹ Yet for my own sake and for the
honor of my name,
I will hold back my anger and not
wipe you out.
¹⁰ I have refined you, but not as silver
is refined.
Rather, I have refined you in the
furnace of suffering.
¹¹ I will rescue you for my sake—
yes, for my own sake!
I will not let my reputation be
tarnished,
and I will not share my glory
with idols!"

45:14 Hebrew *Cushites*.   **45:19** Hebrew *of Jacob*. See note
on 14:1.   **45:23** Hebrew *will confess;* Greek version reads
will confess and give praise to God. Compare Rom 14:11.
46:13 Hebrew *Zion*.   **47:1** Or *Chaldea;* also in 47:5.

EPHESIANS 4:1-16

Therefore I [Paul], a prisoner for serving
the Lord, beg you to lead a life worthy of
your calling, for you have been called by
God. ²Always be humble and gentle. Be
patient with each other, making allowance for each other's faults because of
your love. ³Make every effort to keep yourselves united in the Spirit, binding
yourselves together with peace. ⁴For
there is one body and one Spirit, just as
you have been called to one glorious
hope for the future. ⁵There is one Lord,
one faith, one baptism, ⁶and one God and
Father, who is over all and in all and living
through all.

⁷However, he has given each one of us
a special gift* through the generosity of
Christ. ⁸That is why the Scriptures say,

"When he ascended to the heights,
he led a crowd of captives
and gave gifts to his people."*

⁹Notice that it says "he ascended." This
clearly means that Christ also de-
scended to our lowly world.* ¹⁰And the
same one who descended is the one
who ascended higher than all the heavens, so that he might fill the entire uni-
verse with himself.

[11]Now these are the gifts Christ gave to the church: the apostles, the prophets, the evangelists, and the pastors and teachers. [12]Their responsibility is to equip God's people to do his work and build up the church, the body of Christ. [13]This will continue until we all come to such unity in our faith and knowledge of God's Son that we will be mature in the Lord, measuring up to the full and complete standard of Christ.

[14]Then we will no longer be immature like children. We won't be tossed and blown about by every wind of new teaching. We will not be influenced when people try to trick us with lies so clever they sound like the truth. **[15]Instead, we will speak the truth in love, growing in every way more and more like Christ, who is the head of his body, the church. [16]He makes the whole body fit together perfectly. As each part does its own special work, it helps the other parts grow, so that the whole body is healthy and growing and full of love.**

4:7 Greek *a grace.*   4:8 Ps 68:18.   4:9 Or *to the lowest parts of the earth.*

PSALM 68:19-35

Praise the Lord; praise God our savior!

For each day he carries us in his arms.   *Interlude*

[20] Our God is a God who saves!
The Sovereign LORD rescues us from death.

[21] But God will smash the heads of his enemies,
crushing the skulls of those who love their guilty ways.

[22] The Lord says, "I will bring my enemies down from Bashan;
I will bring them up from the depths of the sea.

[23] You, my people, will wash your feet in their blood,
and even your dogs will get their share!"

[24] Your procession has come into view, O God—

the procession of my God and King as he goes into the sanctuary.

[25] Singers are in front, musicians behind;
between them are young women playing tambourines.

[26] Praise God, all you people of Israel;
praise the LORD, the source of Israel's life.

[27] Look, the little tribe of Benjamin leads the way.
Then comes a great throng of rulers from Judah
and all the rulers of Zebulun and Naphtali.

[28] Summon your might, O God.
Display your power, O God, as you have in the past.

[29] The kings of the earth are bringing tribute
to your Temple in Jerusalem.

[30] Rebuke these enemy nations—
these wild animals lurking in the reeds,
this herd of bulls among the weaker calves.
Make them bring bars of silver in humble tribute.
Scatter the nations that delight in war.

[31] Let Egypt come with gifts of precious metals*;
let Ethiopia* bow in submission to God.

[32] Sing to God, you kingdoms of the earth.
Sing praises to the Lord.   *Interlude*

[33] Sing to the one who rides across the ancient heavens,
his mighty voice thundering from the sky.

[34] Tell everyone about God's power.
His majesty shines down on Israel;
his strength is mighty in the heavens.

[35] God is awesome in his sanctuary.
The God of Israel gives power and strength to his people.

Praise be to God!

68:31a Or *of rich cloth.*   68:31b Hebrew *Cush.*

PROVERBS 24:3-4

A house is built by wisdom and becomes strong through good sense. Through knowledge its rooms are filled with all sorts of precious riches and valuables.

SEPTEMBER
26

ISAIAH 48:12–50:11

"Listen to me, O family of Jacob,
Israel my chosen one!
I alone am God,
the First and the Last.
13 It was my hand that laid the
foundations of the earth,
my right hand that spread out the
heavens above.
When I call out the stars,
they all appear in order."

14 Have any of your idols ever told
you this?
Come, all of you, and listen:
The LORD has chosen Cyrus as his
ally.
He will use him to put an end to
the empire of Babylon
and to destroy the Babylonian*
armies.

15 "I have said it: I am calling Cyrus!
I will send him on this errand and
will help him succeed.
16 Come closer, and listen to this.
From the beginning I have told
you plainly what would
happen."

And now the Sovereign LORD and
his Spirit
have sent me with this message.
17 This is what the LORD says—
your Redeemer, the Holy One of
Israel:
"I am the LORD your God,
who teaches you what is good
for you

and leads you along the paths
you should follow.
18 Oh, that you had listened to my
commands!
Then you would have had peace
flowing like a gentle river
and righteousness rolling over
you like waves in the sea.
19 Your descendants would have been
like the sands along the
seashore—
too many to count!
There would have been no need
for your destruction,
or for cutting off your family
name."

20 Yet even now, be free from your
captivity!
Leave Babylon and the
Babylonians.*
Sing out this message!
Shout it to the ends of the earth!
The LORD has redeemed his
servants,
the people of Israel.*
21 They were not thirsty
when he led them through
the desert.
He divided the rock,
and water gushed out for them
to drink.
22 "But there is no peace for
the wicked,"
says the LORD.

49:1LISTEN to me, all you in distant
lands!
Pay attention, you who are far
away!
The LORD called me before my birth;
from within the womb he called
me by name.
2 He made my words of judgment as
sharp as a sword.
He has hidden me in the shadow
of his hand.
I am like a sharp arrow in his
quiver.

3 He said to me, "You are my servant,
Israel,
and you will bring me glory."

⁴ I replied, "But my work seems
        so useless!
   I have spent my strength for
        nothing and to no purpose.
   Yet I leave it all in the LORD's hand;
        I will trust God for my reward."

⁵ And now the LORD speaks—
        the one who formed me in my
           mother's womb to be his
           servant,
        who commissioned me to bring
           Israel back to him.
   The LORD has honored me,
        and my God has given me
           strength.
⁶ He says, "You will do more than
        restore the people of Israel
        to me.
   I will make you a light to the
        Gentiles,
        and you will bring my salvation
           to the ends of the earth."

⁷ The LORD, the Redeemer
        and Holy One of Israel,
   says to the one who is despised and
        rejected by the nations,
        to the one who is the servant
           of rulers:
   "Kings will stand at attention when
        you pass by.
        Princes will also bow low
   because of the LORD, the faithful
        one,
        the Holy One of Israel, who has
           chosen you."

⁸This is what the LORD says:

"At just the right time, I will respond
        to you.*
        On the day of salvation I will
           help you.
   I will protect you and give you to
        the people
        as my covenant with them.
   Through you I will reestablish the
        land of Israel
        and assign it to its own people
           again.
⁹ I will say to the prisoners, 'Come out
        in freedom,'

and to those in darkness, 'Come
        into the light.'
   They will be my sheep, grazing in
        green pastures
        and on hills that were previously
           bare.
¹⁰ They will neither hunger nor thirst.
        The searing sun will not reach
           them anymore.
   For the LORD in his mercy will lead
        them;
        he will lead them beside cool
           waters.
¹¹ And I will make my mountains into
        level paths for them.
        The highways will be raised above
           the valleys.
¹² See, my people will return from
        far away,
        from lands to the north and west,
        and from as far south as Egypt.*"

¹³ Sing for joy, O heavens!
        Rejoice, O earth!
        Burst into song, O mountains!
   For the LORD has comforted his
        people
        and will have compassion on
           them in their suffering.

¹⁴ Yet Jerusalem* says, "The LORD has
        deserted us;
        the Lord has forgotten us."

¹⁵ "Never! Can a mother forget her
        nursing child?
        Can she feel no love for the child
           she has borne?
   But even if that were possible,
        I would not forget you!
¹⁶ See, I have written your name on the
        palms of my hands.
        Always in my mind is a picture
           of Jerusalem's walls in ruins.
¹⁷ Soon your descendants will
        come back,
        and all who are trying to destroy
           you will go away.
¹⁸ Look around you and see,
        for all your children will come
           back to you.
   As surely as I live," says the LORD,

"they will be like jewels or bridal
ornaments for you to display.

19 "Even the most desolate parts of
your abandoned land
will soon be crowded with your
people.
Your enemies who enslaved you
will be far away.

20 The generations born in exile will
return and say,
'We need more room! It's
crowded here!'

21 Then you will think to yourself,
'Who has given me all these
descendants?
For most of my children were killed,
and the rest were carried away
into exile.
I was left here all alone.
Where did all these people
come from?
Who bore these children?
Who raised them for me?'"

22 This is what the Sovereign LORD
says:
"See, I will give a signal to the
godless nations.
They will carry your little sons back
to you in their arms;
they will bring your daughters
on their shoulders.

23 Kings and queens will serve you
and care for all your needs.
They will bow to the earth before
you
and lick the dust from your feet.
Then you will know that I am the
LORD.
Those who trust in me will never
be put to shame."

24 Who can snatch the plunder of war
from the hands of a warrior?
Who can demand that a tyrant*
let his captives go?

25 But the LORD says,
"The captives of warriors will be
released,
and the plunder of tyrants will be
retrieved.
For I will fight those who fight you,

and I will save your children.

26 I will feed your enemies with their
own flesh.
They will be drunk with rivers of
their own blood.
All the world will know that I, the
LORD,
am your Savior and your Redeemer,
the Mighty One of Israel.*"

50:1 THIS is what the LORD says:

"Was your mother sent away
because I divorced her?
Did I sell you as slaves to my
creditors?
No, you were sold because of your
sins.
And your mother, too, was taken
because of your sins.

2 Why was no one there when I came?
Why didn't anyone answer when
I called?
Is it because I have no power to rescue?
No, that is not the reason!
For I can speak to the sea and make
it dry up!
I can turn rivers into deserts
covered with dying fish.

3 I dress the skies in darkness,
covering them with clothes of
mourning."

4 The Sovereign LORD has given me
his words of wisdom,
so that I know how to comfort
the weary.
Morning by morning he wakens me
and opens my understanding to
his will.

5 The Sovereign LORD has spoken to me,
and I have listened.
I have not rebelled or turned
away.

6 I offered my back to those who
beat me
and my cheeks to those who
pulled out my beard.
I did not hide my face
from mockery and spitting.

7 Because the Sovereign LORD helps me,
I will not be disgraced.

Therefore, I have set my face like
a stone,
determined to do his will.
And I know that I will not be put
to shame.
[8] He who gives me justice is near.
Who will dare to bring charges
against me now?
Where are my accusers?
Let them appear!
[9] See, the Sovereign LORD is on
my side!
Who will declare me guilty?
All my enemies will be destroyed
like old clothes that have been
eaten by moths!

[10] Who among you fears the LORD
and obeys his servant?
If you are walking in darkness,
without a ray of light,
trust in the LORD
and rely on your God.
[11] But watch out, you who live in your
own light
and warm yourselves by your
own fires.
This is the reward you will receive
from me:
You will soon fall down in great
torment.

48:14 Or *Chaldean.* **48:20a** Or *the Chaldeans.*
48:20b Hebrew *his servant, Jacob.* See note on 14:1.
49:8 Greek version reads *I heard you.* Compare 2 Cor 6:2.
49:12 As in Dead Sea Scrolls, which read *from the region of
Aswan,* which is in southern Egypt. Masoretic Text reads
from the region of Sinim. **49:14** Hebrew *Zion.* **49:24** As
in Dead Sea Scrolls, Syriac version, and Latin Vulgate (also
see 49:25); Masoretic Text reads *a righteous person.*
49:26 Hebrew *of Jacob.* See note on 14:1.

EPHESIANS 4:17-32

With the Lord's authority I [Paul] say
this: Live no longer as the Gentiles do,
for they are hopelessly confused.
[18]Their minds are full of darkness; they
wander far from the life God gives because they have closed their minds and
hardened their hearts against him.
[19]They have no sense of shame. They
live for lustful pleasure and eagerly
practice every kind of impurity.

[20]But that isn't what you learned
about Christ. [21]Since you have heard
about Jesus and have learned the truth

that comes from him, [22]throw off your
old sinful nature and your former way
of life, which is corrupted by lust and
deception. [23]Instead, let the Spirit renew your thoughts and attitudes. [24]Put
on your new nature, created to be like
God—truly righteous and holy.

[25]So stop telling lies. Let us tell our
neighbors the truth, for we are all parts
of the same body. [26]And "don't sin by
letting anger control you."* Don't let the
sun go down while you are still angry,
[27]for anger gives a foothold to the devil.

[28]If you are a thief, quit stealing. Instead, use your hands for good hard
work, and then give generously to others in need. [29]**Don't use foul or abusive language. Let everything you say
be good and helpful, so that your
words will be an encouragement to
those who hear them.**

[30]And do not bring sorrow to God's
Holy Spirit by the way you live. Remember, he has identified you as his own,*
guaranteeing that you will be saved on
the day of redemption.

[31]Get rid of all bitterness, rage, anger,
harsh words, and slander, as well as all
types of evil behavior. [32]Instead, be kind
to each other, tenderhearted, forgiving
one another, just as God through Christ
has forgiven you.

4:26 Ps 4:4. **4:30** Or *has put his seal on you.*

PSALM 69:1-18

*For the choir director: A psalm of David,
to be sung to the tune "Lilies."*

[1] **S**ave me, O God,
for the floodwaters are up
to my neck.
[2] Deeper and deeper I sink
into the mire;
I can't find a foothold.
I am in deep water,
and the floods overwhelm me.
[3] I am exhausted from crying for help;
my throat is parched.
My eyes are swollen with weeping,
waiting for my God to help me.
[4] Those who hate me without cause
outnumber the hairs on my head.

Many enemies try to destroy me
with lies,
demanding that I give back what
I didn't steal.

5 O God, you know how foolish I am;
my sins cannot be hidden from
you.
6 Don't let those who trust in you be
ashamed because of me,
O Sovereign Lord of Heaven's
Armies.
Don't let me cause them to be
humiliated,
O God of Israel.
7 For I endure insults for your sake;
humiliation is written all over
my face.
8 Even my own brothers pretend they
don't know me;
they treat me like a stranger.

9 Passion for your house has
consumed me,
and the insults of those who
insult you have fallen on me.
10 When I weep and fast,
they scoff at me.
11 When I dress in burlap to show
sorrow,
they make fun of me.
12 I am the favorite topic of town
gossip,
and all the drunks sing about me.

13 But I keep praying to you, Lord,
hoping this time you will show
me favor.
In your unfailing love, O God,
answer my prayer with your
sure salvation.
14 Rescue me from the mud;
don't let me sink any deeper!
Save me from those who hate me,
and pull me from these deep
waters.
15 Don't let the floods overwhelm me,
or the deep waters swallow me,
or the pit of death devour me.

16 Answer my prayers, O Lord,
for your unfailing love is
wonderful.
Take care of me,

for your mercy is so plentiful.
17 Don't hide from your servant;
answer me quickly, for I am in
deep trouble!
18 Come and redeem me;
free me from my enemies.

PROVERBS 24:5-6
The wise are mightier than the strong,*
and those with knowledge grow stronger and stronger. So don't go to war
without wise guidance; victory depends
on having many advisers.

24:5 As in Greek version; Hebrew reads *A wise man is
strength.*

SEPTEMBER 27

ISAIAH 51:1–53:12
"Listen to me, all who hope for
deliverance—
all who seek the Lord!
Consider the rock from which you
were cut,
the quarry from which you
were mined.
2 Yes, think about Abraham, your
ancestor,
and Sarah, who gave birth to
your nation.
Abraham was only one man when
I called him.
But when I blessed him, he
became a great nation."

3 The Lord will comfort Israel* again
and have pity on her ruins.
Her desert will blossom like Eden,
her barren wilderness like the
garden of the Lord.
Joy and gladness will be found there.
Songs of thanksgiving will fill
the air.

4 "Listen to me, my people.
Hear me, Israel,
for my law will be proclaimed,

and my justice will become a light
to the nations.
⁵ My mercy and justice are coming
soon.
My salvation is on the way.
My strong arm will bring justice
to the nations.
All distant lands will look to me
and wait in hope for my powerful
arm.
⁶ Look up to the skies above,
and gaze down on the earth
below.
For the skies will disappear like
smoke,
and the earth will wear out like
a piece of clothing.
The people of the earth will die
like flies,
but my salvation lasts forever.
My righteous rule will never end!

⁷ "Listen to me, you who know right
from wrong
you who cherish my law in your
hearts.
Do not be afraid of people's scorn,
nor fear their insults.
⁸ For the moth will devour them
as it devours clothing.
The worm will eat at them as
it eats wool.
But my righteousness will last
forever.
My salvation will continue from
generation to generation."

⁹ Wake up, wake up, O LORD! Clothe
yourself with strength!
Flex your mighty right arm!
Rouse yourself as in the days of old
when you slew Egypt, the dragon
of the Nile.*
¹⁰ Are you not the same today,
the one who dried up the sea,
making a path of escape through
the depths
so that your people could cross
over?
¹¹ Those who have been ransomed by
the LORD will return.
They will enter Jerusalem*
singing,

crowned with everlasting joy.
Sorrow and mourning will
disappear,
and they will be filled with joy
and gladness.

¹² "I, yes I, am the one who comforts
you.
So why are you afraid of mere
humans,
who wither like the grass and
disappear?
¹³ Yet you have forgotten the LORD,
your Creator,
the one who stretched out the
sky like a canopy
and laid the foundations
of the earth.
Will you remain in constant dread
of human oppressors?
Will you continue to fear the
anger of your enemies?
Where is their fury and anger now?
It is gone!
¹⁴ Soon all you captives will be
released!
Imprisonment, starvation, and
death will not be your fate!
¹⁵ For I am the LORD your God,
who stirs up the sea, causing
its waves to roar.
My name is the LORD of Heaven's
Armies.
¹⁶ And I have put my words in your
mouth
and hidden you safely in
my hand.
I stretched out* the sky like
a canopy
and laid the foundations
of the earth.
I am the one who says to Israel,
'You are my people!'"

¹⁷ Wake up, wake up, O Jerusalem!
You have drunk the cup of the
LORD's fury.
You have drunk the cup of terror,
tipping out its last drops.
¹⁸ Not one of your children is
left alive
to take your hand and guide you.

¹⁹ These two calamities have fallen
  on you:
     desolation and destruction,
     famine and war.
  And who is left to sympathize
     with you?
  Who is left to comfort you?*
²⁰ For your children have fainted and
  lie in the streets,
     helpless as antelopes caught
     in a net.
  The LORD has poured out his fury;
     God has rebuked them.

²¹ But now listen to this, you afflicted
  ones
     who sit in a drunken stupor,
     though not from drinking wine.
²² This is what the Sovereign LORD,
     your God and Defender, says:
  "See, I have taken the terrible cup
     from your hands.
  You will drink no more
     of my fury.
²³ Instead, I will hand that cup to your
  tormentors,
     those who said, 'We will trample
     you into the dust
     and walk on your backs.'"

⁵²:¹WAKE up, wake up, O Zion!
  Clothe yourself with strength.
  Put on your beautiful clothes, O holy
  city of Jerusalem,
     for unclean and godless people
     will enter your gates no longer.
² Rise from the dust, O Jerusalem.
  Sit in a place of honor.
  Remove the chains of slavery from
  your neck,
     O captive daughter of Zion.
³ For this is what the LORD says:
  "When I sold you into exile,
     I received no payment.
  Now I can redeem you
     without having to pay for you."

⁴This is what the Sovereign LORD
says: "Long ago my people chose to live
in Egypt. Now they are oppressed by Assyria. ⁵What is this?" asks the LORD.
"Why are my people enslaved again?
Those who rule them shout in exulta-
tion. My name is blasphemed all day
long.* ⁶But I will reveal my name to my
people, and they will come to know its
power. Then at last they will recognize
that I am the one who speaks to them."

⁷ How beautiful on the mountains
  are the feet of the messenger
     who brings good news,
  the good news of peace and
     salvation,
     the news that the God of Israel*
     reigns!
⁸ The watchmen shout and sing
  with joy,
     for before their very eyes
     they see the LORD returning to
     Jerusalem.*
⁹ Let the ruins of Jerusalem break into
  joyful song,
     for the LORD has comforted his
     people.
  He has redeemed Jerusalem.
¹⁰ The LORD has demonstrated his holy
  power
     before the eyes of all the nations.
  All the ends of the earth will see
     the victory of our God.

¹¹ Get out! Get out and leave your
  captivity,
     where everything you touch
     is unclean.
  Get out of there and purify
  yourselves,
     you who carry home the sacred
     objects of the LORD.
¹² You will not leave in a hurry,
  running for your lives.
  For the LORD will go ahead of you;
     yes, the God of Israel will protect
     you from behind.

¹³ See, my servant will prosper;
  he will be highly exalted.
¹⁴ But many were amazed when they
  saw him.*
     His face was so disfigured he
     seemed hardly human,
     and from his appearance, one
     would scarcely know he was a
     man.
¹⁵ And he will startle* many nations.

Kings will stand speechless
in his presence.
For they will see what they had not
been told;
they will understand what they
had not heard about.*

53:1 WHO has believed our message?
To whom has the LORD revealed
his powerful arm?
2 My servant grew up in the LORD's
presence like a tender green
shoot,
like a root in dry ground.
There was nothing beautiful or
majestic about his appearance,
nothing to attract us to him.
3 He was despised and rejected—
a man of sorrows, acquainted
with deepest grief.
We turned our backs on him and
looked the other way.
He was despised, and we did
not care.

4 Yet it was our weaknesses he
carried;
it was our sorrows* that weighed
him down.
And we thought his troubles were a
punishment from God,
a punishment for his own sins!
5 **But he was pierced for our
rebellion,
crushed for our sins.
He was beaten so we could be
whole.
He was whipped so we could
be healed.**
6 All of us, like sheep, have strayed
away.
We have left God's paths to follow
our own.
Yet the LORD laid on him
the sins of us all.

7 He was oppressed and treated
harshly,
yet he never said a word.
He was led like a lamb to the
slaughter.
And as a sheep is silent before
the shearers,

he did not open his mouth.
8 Unjustly condemned,
he was led away.*
No one cared that he died without
descendants,
that his life was cut short in
midstream.*
But he was struck down
for the rebellion of my people.
9 He had done no wrong
and had never deceived anyone.
But he was buried like a criminal;
he was put in a rich man's grave.

10 But it was the LORD's good plan to
crush him
and cause him grief.
Yet when his life is made an
offering for sin,
he will have many descendants.
He will enjoy a long life,
and the LORD's good plan will
prosper in his hands.
11 When he sees all that is
accomplished by his anguish,
he will be satisfied.
And because of his experience,
my righteous servant will make
it possible
for many to be counted righteous,
for he will bear all their sins.
12 I will give him the honors of a
victorious soldier,
because he exposed himself
to death.
He was counted among the rebels.
He bore the sins of many and
interceded for rebels.

51:3 Hebrew *Zion;* also in 51:16.   **51:9** Hebrew *You slew
Rahab; you pierced the dragon.* Rahab is the name of a
mythical sea monster that represents chaos in ancient
literature. The name is used here as a poetic name for
Egypt.   **51:11** Hebrew *Zion.*   **51:16** As in Syriac version
(see also 51:13); Hebrew reads *planted.*   **51:19** As in Dead
Sea Scrolls and Greek, Latin, and Syriac versions; Masoretic
Text reads *How can I comfort you?*   **52:5** Greek version
reads *The Gentiles continually blaspheme my name because
of you.* Compare Rom 2:24.   **52:7** Hebrew *of Zion.*
52:8 Hebrew *to Zion.*   **52:14** As in Syriac version; Hebrew
reads *you.*   **52:15a** Or *cleanse.*   **52:15b** Greek version
reads *Those who have never been told about him will see, /
and those who have never heard of him will understand.*
Compare Rom 15:21.   **53:4** Or *Yet it was our sicknesses he
carried; / it was our diseases.*   **53:8a** Greek version reads
He was humiliated and received no justice. Compare Acts
8:33.   **53:8b** Or *As for his contemporaries, / who cared
that his life was cut short in midstream?* Greek version
reads *Who can speak of his descendants? / For his life was
taken from the earth.* Compare Acts 8:33.

EPHESIANS 5:1-33

Imitate God, therefore, in everything you do, because you are his dear children. ²Live a life filled with love, following the example of Christ. He loved us* and offered himself as a sacrifice for us, a pleasing aroma to God.

³Let there be no sexual immorality, impurity, or greed among you. Such sins have no place among God's people. ⁴Obscene stories, foolish talk, and coarse jokes—these are not for you. Instead, let there be thankfulness to God. ⁵You can be sure that no immoral, impure, or greedy person will inherit the Kingdom of Christ and of God. For a greedy person is an idolater, worshiping the things of this world.

⁶Don't be fooled by those who try to excuse these sins, for the anger of God will fall on all who disobey him. ⁷Don't participate in the things these people do. ⁸For once you were full of darkness, but now you have light from the Lord. So live as people of light! ⁹For this light within you produces only what is good and right and true.

¹⁰Carefully determine what pleases the Lord. ¹¹Take no part in the worthless deeds of evil and darkness; instead, expose them. ¹²It is shameful even to talk about the things that ungodly people do in secret. ¹³But their evil intentions will be exposed when the light shines on them, ¹⁴for the light makes everything visible. This is why it is said,

"Awake, O sleeper,
    rise up from the dead,
    and Christ will give you light."

¹⁵So be careful how you live. Don't live like fools, but like those who are wise. ¹⁶Make the most of every opportunity in these evil days. ¹⁷Don't act thoughtlessly, but understand what the Lord wants you to do. ¹⁸Don't be drunk with wine, because that will ruin your life. Instead, be filled with the Holy Spirit, ¹⁹singing psalms and hymns and spiritual songs among yourselves, and making music to the Lord in your hearts. ²⁰And give thanks for everything to God the Father in the name of our Lord Jesus Christ.

²¹And further, submit to one another out of reverence for Christ.

²²For wives, this means submit to your husbands as to the Lord. ²³For a husband is the head of his wife as Christ is the head of the church. He is the Savior of his body, the church. ²⁴As the church submits to Christ, so you wives should submit to your husbands in everything.

²⁵For husbands, this means love your wives, just as Christ loved the church. He gave up his life for her ²⁶to make her holy and clean, washed by the cleansing of God's word.* ²⁷He did this to present her to himself as a glorious church without a spot or wrinkle or any other blemish. Instead, she will be holy and without fault. ²⁸In the same way, husbands ought to love their wives as they love their own bodies. For a man who loves his wife actually shows love for himself. ²⁹No one hates his own body but feeds and cares for it, just as Christ cares for the church. ³⁰And we are members of his body.

³¹As the Scriptures say, "A man leaves his father and mother and is joined to his wife, and the two are united into one."* ³²This is a great mystery, but it is an illustration of the way Christ and the church are one. ³³So again I say, each man must love his wife as he loves himself, and the wife must respect her husband.

5:2 Some manuscripts read *loved you.*   5:26 Greek *washed by water with the word.*   5:31 Gen 2:24.

PSALM 69:19-36

You [LORD] know of my shame,
        scorn, and disgrace.
    You see all that my enemies
        are doing.
²⁰ Their insults have broken my heart,
        and I am in despair.
    If only one person would show
        some pity;
        if only one would turn and
        comfort me.
²¹ But instead, they give me poison*
        for food;

they offer me sour wine for
my thirst.

²² Let the bountiful table set before
them become a snare
and their prosperity become
a trap.*
²³ Let their eyes go blind so they
cannot see,
and make their bodies shake
continually.*
²⁴ Pour out your fury on them;
consume them with your burning
anger.
²⁵ Let their homes become desolate
and their tents be deserted.
²⁶ To the one you have punished, they
add insult to injury;
they add to the pain of those you
have hurt.
²⁷ Pile their sins up high,
and don't let them go free.
²⁸ Erase their names from the
Book of Life;
don't let them be counted among
the righteous.

²⁹ I am suffering and in pain.
Rescue me, O God, by your saving
power.
³⁰ Then I will praise God's name with
singing,
and I will honor him with
thanksgiving.
³¹ For this will please the LORD more
than sacrificing cattle,
more than presenting a bull with
its horns and hooves.
³² The humble will see their God at
work and be glad.
Let all who seek God's help
be encouraged.
³³ For the LORD hears the cries
of the needy;
he does not despise his
imprisoned people.

³⁴ Praise him, O heaven and earth,
the seas and all that move
in them.
³⁵ For God will save Jerusalem*
and rebuild the towns of Judah.
His people will live there

and settle in their own land.
³⁶ The descendants of those who obey
him will inherit the land,
and those who love him will live
there in safety.

69:21 Or *gall.*   **69:22** Greek version reads *Let their
bountiful table set before them become a snare, / a trap that
makes them think all is well. / Let their blessings cause them
to stumble, / and let them get what they deserve.* Compare
Rom 11:9.   **69:23** Greek version reads *and let their backs
be bent forever.* Compare Rom 11:10.   **69:35** Hebrew
Zion.

PROVERBS 24:7

Wisdom is too lofty for fools. Among
leaders at the city gate, they have nothing to say.

SEPTEMBER
28

ISAIAH 54:1–57:14

"**S**ing, O childless woman,
you who have never given birth!
Break into loud and joyful song,
O Jerusalem,
you who have never been in labor.
For the desolate woman now has
more children
than the woman who lives with
her husband,"
says the LORD.
² "Enlarge your house; build an
addition.
Spread out your home, and spare
no expense!
³ For you will soon be bursting
at the seams.
Your descendants will occupy
other nations
and resettle the ruined cities.

⁴ "Fear not; you will no longer live
in shame.
Don't be afraid; there is no more
disgrace for you.
You will no longer remember the
shame of your youth
and the sorrows of widowhood.

5 For your Creator will be your
    husband;
        the LORD of Heaven's Armies is
        his name!
    He is your Redeemer, the Holy One
    of Israel,
        the God of all the earth.
6 For the LORD has called you back
    from your grief—
        as though you were a young wife
        abandoned by her husband,"
        says your God.
7 "For a brief moment I abandoned
    you,
        but with great compassion I will
        take you back.
8 In a burst of anger I turned my face
    away for a little while.
        But with everlasting love I will
        have compassion on you,"
        says the LORD, your Redeemer.

9 "Just as I swore in the time of Noah
    that I would never again let a
    flood cover the earth,
    so now I swear
        that I will never again be angry
        and punish you.
10 For the mountains may move
    and the hills disappear,
    but even then my faithful love for
    you will remain.
        My covenant of blessing will
        never be broken,"
        says the LORD, who has mercy
        on you.

11 "O storm-battered city,
    troubled and desolate!
    I will rebuild you with precious
    jewels
        and make your foundations from
        lapis lazuli.
12 I will make your towers of sparkling
    rubies,
        your gates of shining gems,
        and your walls of precious stones.
13 I will teach all your children,
    and they will enjoy great peace.
14 You will be secure under a
    government that is just
    and fair.
        Your enemies will stay far away.

You will live in peace,
    and terror will not come near.
15 If any nation comes to fight you,
    it is not because I sent them.
        Whoever attacks you will go down
        in defeat.

16 "I have created the blacksmith
    who fans the coals beneath
    the forge
    and makes the weapons of
    destruction.
        And I have created the armies
        that destroy.
17 But in that coming day
    no weapon turned against you
    will succeed.
    You will silence every voice
    raised up to accuse you.
    These benefits are enjoyed by the
    servants of the LORD;
        their vindication will come
        from me.
        I, the LORD, have spoken!

55:1 "Is anyone thirsty?
    Come and drink—
        even if you have no money!
    Come, take your choice of wine
    or milk—
        it's all free!
2 Why spend your money on food that
    does not give you strength?
        Why pay for food that does you
        no good?
    Listen to me, and you will eat
    what is good.
        You will enjoy the finest food.

3 "Come to me with your ears wide
    open.
    Listen, and you will find life.
    I will make an everlasting covenant
    with you.
        I will give you all the unfailing
        love I promised to David.
4 See how I used him to display my
    power among the peoples.
    I made him a leader among the
    nations.
5 You also will command nations you
    do not know,

and peoples unknown to you will
    come running to obey,
because I, the LORD your God,
    the Holy One of Israel, have made
    you glorious."

6 Seek the LORD while you can find
    him.
    Call on him now while he is near.
7 Let the wicked change their ways
    and banish the very thought of
    doing wrong.
    Let them turn to the LORD that he
    may have mercy on them.
    Yes, turn to our God, for he will
    forgive generously.

8 "My thoughts are nothing like your
    thoughts," says the LORD.
    "And my ways are far beyond
    anything you could imagine.
9 For just as the heavens are higher
    than the earth,
    so my ways are higher than
    your ways
    and my thoughts higher than
    your thoughts.

10 "The rain and snow come down
    from the heavens
    and stay on the ground to water
    the earth.
    They cause the grain to grow,
    producing seed for the farmer
    and bread for the hungry.
11 It is the same with my word.
    I send it out, and it always
    produces fruit.
    It will accomplish all I want it to,
    and it will prosper everywhere
    I send it.
12 You will live in joy and peace.
    The mountains and hills will burst
    into song,
    and the trees of the field will clap
    their hands!
13 Where once there were thorns,
    cypress trees will grow.
    Where nettles grew, myrtles will
    sprout up.
    These events will bring great honor
    to the LORD's name;

they will be an everlasting sign of
    his power and love."

56:1 THIS is what the LORD says:

"Be just and fair to all.
    Do what is right and good,
    for I am coming soon to rescue you
    and to display my righteousness
    among you.
2 Blessed are all those
    who are careful to do this.
    Blessed are those who honor my
    Sabbath days of rest
    and keep themselves from doing
    wrong.

3 "Don't let foreigners who commit
    themselves to the LORD say,
    'The LORD will never let me be
    part of his people.'
    And don't let the eunuchs say,
    'I'm a dried-up tree with no
    children and no future.'
4 For this is what the LORD says:
    I will bless those eunuchs
    who keep my Sabbath days holy
    and who choose to do what
    pleases me
    and commit their lives to me.
5 I will give them—within the walls
    of my house—
    a memorial and a name
    far greater than sons and
    daughters could give.
    For the name I give them is an
    everlasting one.
    It will never disappear!

6 "I will also bless the foreigners who
    commit themselves to the
    LORD,
    who serve him and love his name,
    who worship him and do not
    desecrate the Sabbath day
    of rest,
    and who hold fast to my covenant.
7 I will bring them to my holy
    mountain of Jerusalem
    and will fill them with joy in my
    house of prayer.
    I will accept their burnt offerings
    and sacrifices,
    because my Temple will be called

a house of prayer for all
nations.

8 For the Sovereign LORD,
who brings back the outcasts
of Israel, says:
I will bring others, too,
besides my people Israel."

9 Come, wild animals of the field!
Come, wild animals of the forest!
Come and devour my people!

10 For the leaders of my people—
the LORD's watchmen, his
shepherds—
are blind and ignorant.
They are like silent watchdogs
that give no warning when danger
comes.
They love to lie around, sleeping and
dreaming.

11   Like greedy dogs, they are never
satisfied.
They are ignorant shepherds,
all following their own path
and intent on personal gain.

12 "Come," they say, "let's get some
wine and have a party.
Let's all get drunk.
Then tomorrow we'll do it again
and have an even bigger party!"

57:1Good people pass away;
the godly often die before their
time.
But no one seems to care or
wonder why.
No one seems to understand
that God is protecting them from
the evil to come.

2 For those who follow godly paths
will rest in peace when they die.

3 "But you—come here, you witches'
children,
you offspring of adulterers and
prostitutes!

4 Whom do you mock,
making faces and sticking out
your tongues?
You children of sinners and liars!

5 You worship your idols with great
passion

beneath the oaks and under every
green tree.
You sacrifice your children down
in the valleys,
among the jagged rocks in the
cliffs.

6 Your gods are the smooth stones
in the valleys.
You worship them with liquid
offerings and grain offerings.
They, not I, are your inheritance.
Do you think all this makes
me happy?

7 You have committed adultery on
every high mountain.
There you have worshiped idols
and have been unfaithful to me.

8 You have put pagan symbols
on your doorposts and behind
your doors.
You have left me
and climbed into bed with these
detestable gods.
You have committed yourselves
to them.
You love to look at their naked
bodies.

9 You have given olive oil to Molech*
with many gifts of perfume.
You have traveled far,
even into the world of the dead,*
to find new gods to love.

10 You grew weary in your search,
but you never gave up.
Desire gave you renewed strength,
and you did not grow weary.

11 "Are you afraid of these idols?
Do they terrify you?
Is that why you have lied to me
and forgotten me and my words?
Is it because of my long silence
that you no longer fear me?

12 Now I will expose your so-called
good deeds.
None of them will help you.

13 Let's see if your idols can save you
when you cry to them for help.
Why, a puff of wind can knock
them down!
If you just breathe on them, they
fall over!

But whoever trusts in me will inherit
    the land
and possess my holy mountain."

[14] God says, "Rebuild the road!
    Clear away the rocks and stones
so my people can return from
    captivity."

57:9a Or *to the king.*   57:9b Hebrew *into Sheol.*

EPHESIANS 6:1-24

Children, obey your parents because
you belong to the Lord,* for this is the
right thing to do. [2]"Honor your father
and mother." This is the first commandment with a promise: [3]If you
honor your father and mother, "things
will go well for you, and you will have
a long life on the earth."*

[4]Fathers, do not provoke your children to anger by the way you treat them.
Rather, bring them up with the discipline and instruction that comes from
the Lord.

[5]Slaves, obey your earthly masters
with deep respect and fear. Serve them
sincerely as you would serve Christ. [6]Try
to please them all the time, not just when
they are watching you. As slaves of Christ,
do the will of God with all your heart.
[7]Work with enthusiasm, as though you
were working for the Lord rather than
for people. [8]Remember that the Lord will
reward each one of us for the good we do,
whether we are slaves or free.

[9]Masters, treat your slaves in the
same way. Don't threaten them; remember, you both have the same Master in heaven, and he has no favorites.

[10]A final word: Be strong in the Lord
and in his mighty power. [11]Put on all of
God's armor so that you will be able to
stand firm against all strategies of the
devil. [12]**For we* are not fighting
against flesh-and-blood enemies,
but against evil rulers and authorities of the unseen world, against
mighty powers in this dark world,
and against evil spirits in the heavenly places.**

[13]Therefore, put on every piece of
God's armor so you will be able to resist

the enemy in the time of evil. Then after
the battle you will still be standing firm.
[14]Stand your ground, putting on the belt
of truth and the body armor of God's
righteousness. [15]For shoes, put on the
peace that comes from the Good News
so that you will be fully prepared.* [16]In
addition to all of these, hold up the
shield of faith to stop the fiery arrows of
the devil.* [17]Put on salvation as your
helmet, and take the sword of the Spirit,
which is the word of God.

[18]Pray in the Spirit at all times and on
every occasion. Stay alert and be persis-
tent in your prayers for all believers
everywhere.

[19]And pray for me, too. Ask God to
give me the right words so I can boldly
explain God's mysterious plan that the
Good News is for Jews and Gentiles
alike.* [20]I am in chains now, still preaching this message as God's ambassador.
So pray that I will keep on speaking
boldly for him, as I should.

[21]To bring you up to date, Tychicus
will give you a full report about what I am
doing and how I am getting along. He is a
beloved brother and faithful helper in
the Lord's work. [22]I have sent him to you
for this very purpose—to let you know
how we are doing and to encourage you.

[23]Peace be with you, dear brothers
and sisters,* and may God the Father
and the Lord Jesus Christ give you love
with faithfulness. [24]May God's grace be
eternally upon all who love our Lord
Jesus Christ.

6:1 Or *Children, obey your parents who belong to the Lord;*
some manuscripts read simply *Children, obey your parents.*
6:2-3 Exod 20:12; Deut 5:16.   6:12 Some manuscripts
read *you.*   6:15 Or *For shoes, put on the readiness to
preach the Good News of peace with God.*   6:16 Greek *the
evil one.*   6:19 Greek *explain the mystery of the Good
News;* some manuscripts read simply *explain the mystery.*
6:23 Greek *brothers.*

PSALM 70:1-5

*For the choir director: A psalm of David,
asking God to remember him.*

[1] Please, God, rescue me!
    Come quickly, LORD, and help me.
[2] May those who try to kill me
    be humiliated and put to shame.

May those who take delight in my
trouble
be turned back in disgrace.
³ Let them be horrified by their
shame,
for they said, "Aha! We've got
him now!"
⁴ But may all who search for you
be filled with joy and gladness
in you.
May those who love your salvation
repeatedly shout, "God is great!"
⁵ But as for me, I am poor and needy;
please hurry to my aid, O God.
You are my helper and my savior;
O LORD, do not delay.

PROVERBS 24:8
A person who plans evil will get a reputation as a troublemaker.

SEPTEMBER
29

ISAIAH 57:15–59:21
The high and lofty one who lives
in eternity,
the Holy One, says this:
"I live in the high and holy place
with those whose spirits are
contrite and humble.
I restore the crushed spirit of the
humble
and revive the courage of those
with repentant hearts.
¹⁶ For I will not fight against you
forever;
I will not always be angry.
If I were, all people would pass
away—
all the souls I have made.
¹⁷ I was angry,
so I punished these greedy
people.
I withdrew from them,
but they kept going on their
own stubborn way.

¹⁸ I have seen what they do,
but I will heal them anyway!
I will lead them.
I will comfort those who mourn,
¹⁹   bringing words of praise to
their lips.
May they have abundant peace, both
near and far,"
says the LORD, who heals them.
²⁰ "But those who still reject me are
like the restless sea,
which is never still
but continually churns up mud
and dirt.
²¹ There is no peace for the wicked,"
says my God.

58:1 "SHOUT with the voice of a trumpet
blast.
Shout aloud! Don't be timid.
Tell my people Israel* of their sins!
²   Yet they act so pious!
They come to the Temple every day
and seem delighted to learn all
about me.
They act like a righteous nation
that would never abandon the
laws of its God.
They ask me to take action on their
behalf,
pretending they want to be
near me.
³ 'We have fasted before you!'
they say.
'Why aren't you impressed?
We have been very hard on
ourselves,
and you don't even notice it!'

"I will tell you why!" I respond.
"It's because you are fasting to
please yourselves.
Even while you fast,
you keep oppressing your
workers.
⁴ What good is fasting
when you keep on fighting and
quarreling?
This kind of fasting
will never get you anywhere
with me.
⁵ You humble yourselves

by going through the motions
of penance,
bowing your heads
like reeds bending in the wind.
You dress in burlap
and cover yourselves with ashes.
Is this what you call fasting?
Do you really think this will please
the LORD?

6 "No, this is the kind of fasting I want:
Free those who are wrongly
imprisoned;
lighten the burden of those who
work for you.
Let the oppressed go free,
and remove the chains that bind
people.
7 Share your food with the hungry,
and give shelter to the homeless.
Give clothes to those who need
them,
and do not hide from relatives
who need your help.

8 "Then your salvation will come like
the dawn,
and your wounds will quickly
heal.
Your godliness will lead you
forward,
and the glory of the LORD will
protect you from behind.
9 Then when you call, the LORD will
answer.
'Yes, I am here,' he will quickly
reply.

"Remove the heavy yoke of
oppression.
Stop pointing your finger and
spreading vicious rumors!
10 Feed the hungry,
and help those in trouble.
Then your light will shine out from
the darkness,
and the darkness around you will
be as bright as noon.
11 The LORD will guide you continually,
giving you water when you are dry
and restoring your strength.
You will be like a well-watered
garden,

like an ever-flowing spring.
12 Some of you will rebuild the
deserted ruins of your cities.
Then you will be known as a
rebuilder of walls
and a restorer of homes.

13 "Keep the Sabbath day holy.
Don't pursue your own interests
on that day,
but enjoy the Sabbath
and speak of it with delight as the
LORD's holy day.
Honor the Sabbath in everything
you do on that day,
and don't follow your own
desires or talk idly.
14 Then the LORD will be your delight.
I will give you great honor
and satisfy you with the inheritance
I promised to your ancestor
Jacob.
I, the LORD, have spoken!"

59:1 LISTEN! The LORD's arm is not too
weak to save you,
nor is his ear too deaf to hear
you call.
2 It's your sins that have cut you
off from God.
Because of your sins, he has
turned away
and will not listen anymore.
3 Your hands are the hands of
murderers,
and your fingers are filthy
with sin.
Your lips are full of lies,
and your mouth spews
corruption.

4 No one cares about being fair and
honest.
The people's lawsuits are based
on lies.
They conceive evil deeds
and then give birth to sin.
5 They hatch deadly snakes
and weave spiders' webs.
Whoever falls into their webs
will die,
and there's danger even in getting
near them.

⁶ Their webs can't be made into clothing,
    and nothing they do is productive.
All their activity is filled with sin,
    and violence is their trademark.
⁷ Their feet run to do evil,
    and they rush to commit murder.
They think only about sinning.
    Misery and destruction always
    follow them.
⁸ They don't know where to find
    peace
    or what it means to be just and
    good.
They have mapped out crooked roads,
    and no one who follows them
    knows a moment's peace.

⁹ So there is no justice among us,
    and we know nothing about
    right living.
We look for light but find only
    darkness.
    We look for bright skies but walk
    in gloom.
¹⁰ We grope like the blind along a wall,
    feeling our way like people
    without eyes.
Even at brightest noontime,
    we stumble as though it were
    dark.
Among the living,
    we are like the dead.
¹¹ We growl like hungry bears;
    we moan like mournful doves.
We look for justice, but it never
    comes.
    We look for rescue, but it is far
    away from us.
¹² For our sins are piled up before God
    and testify against us.
Yes, we know what sinners we are.
¹³ We know we have rebelled and have
    denied the LORD.
    We have turned our backs on
    our God.
We know how unfair and oppressive
    we have been,
    carefully planning our deceitful
    lies.
¹⁴ Our courts oppose the righteous,
    and justice is nowhere to be
    found.

Truth stumbles in the streets,
    and honesty has been outlawed.
¹⁵ Yes, truth is gone,
    and anyone who renounces evil
    is attacked.

The LORD looked and was displeased
    to find there was no justice.
¹⁶ He was amazed to see that no one
    intervened
    to help the oppressed.
So he himself stepped in to save
    them with his strong arm,
    and his justice sustained him.
¹⁷ He put on righteousness as his body
    armor
    and placed the helmet of
    salvation on his head.
He clothed himself with a robe of
    vengeance
    and wrapped himself in a cloak
    of divine passion.
¹⁸ He will repay his enemies for their
    evil deeds.
    His fury will fall on his foes.
    He will pay them back even to the
    ends of the earth.
¹⁹ In the west, people will respect the
    name of the LORD;
    in the east, they will glorify him.
For he will come like a raging
    flood tide
    driven by the breath of the LORD.*

²⁰ "The Redeemer will come to
    Jerusalem
    to buy back those in Israel
who have turned from their sins,"*
    says the LORD.

²¹"And this is my covenant with
them," says the LORD. "My Spirit will not
leave them, and neither will these words
I have given you. They will be on your
lips and on the lips of your children and
your children's children forever. I, the
LORD, have spoken!"

58:1 Hebrew *Jacob.* See note on 14:1.   **59:19** Or *When the
enemy comes like a raging flood tide, / the Spirit of the LORD
will drive him back.*   **59:20** Hebrew *The Redeemer will
come to Zion / to buy back those in Jacob / who have turned
from their sins.* Greek version reads *The one who rescues
will come on behalf of Zion, / and he will turn Jacob away
from ungodliness.* Compare Rom 11:26.

PHILIPPIANS 1:1-26

This letter is from Paul and Timothy, slaves of Christ Jesus.

I am writing to all of God's holy people in Philippi who belong to Christ Jesus, including the elders* and deacons.

²May God our Father and the Lord Jesus Christ give you grace and peace.

³Every time I think of you, I give thanks to my God. ⁴Whenever I pray, I make my requests for all of you with joy, ⁵for you have been my partners in spreading the Good News about Christ from the time you first heard it until now. ⁶And I am certain that God, who began the good work within you, will continue his work until it is finally finished on the day when Christ Jesus returns.

⁷So it is right that I should feel as I do about all of you, for you have a special place in my heart. You share with me the special favor of God, both in my imprisonment and in defending and confirming the truth of the Good News. ⁸God knows how much I love you and long for you with the tender compassion of Christ Jesus.

⁹I pray that your love will overflow more and more, and that you will keep on growing in knowledge and understanding. ¹⁰For I want you to understand what really matters, so that you may live pure and blameless lives until the day of Christ's return. ¹¹May you always be filled with the fruit of your salvation—the righteous character produced in your life by Jesus Christ*—for this will bring much glory and praise to God.

¹²And I want you to know, my dear brothers and sisters,* that everything that has happened to me here has helped to spread the Good News. ¹³For everyone here, including the whole palace guard,* knows that I am in chains because of Christ. ¹⁴And because of my imprisonment, most of the believers* here have gained confidence and boldly speak God's message* without fear.

¹⁵It's true that some are preaching out of jealousy and rivalry. But others preach about Christ with pure motives. ¹⁶They preach because they love me, for they know I have been appointed to defend the Good News. ¹⁷Those others do not have pure motives as they preach about Christ. They preach with selfish ambition, not sincerely, intending to make my chains more painful to me. ¹⁸But that doesn't matter. Whether their motives are false or genuine, the message about Christ is being preached either way, so I rejoice. And I will continue to rejoice. ¹⁹For I know that as you pray for me and the Spirit of Jesus Christ helps me, this will lead to my deliverance.

²⁰**For I fully expect and hope that I will never be ashamed, but that I will continue to be bold for Christ, as I have been in the past. And I trust that my life will bring honor to Christ, whether I live or die. ²¹For to me, living means living for Christ, and dying is even better.** ²²But if I live, I can do more fruitful work for Christ. So I really don't know which is better. ²³I'm torn between two desires: I long to go and be with Christ, which would be far better for me. ²⁴But for your sakes, it is better that I continue to live.

²⁵Knowing this, I am convinced that I will remain alive so I can continue to help all of you grow and experience the joy of your faith. ²⁶And when I come to you again, you will have even more reason to take pride in Christ Jesus because of what he is doing through me.

1:1 Or *overseers;* or *bishops.*   1:11 Greek *with the fruit of righteousness through Jesus Christ.*   1:12 Greek *brothers.* 1:13 Greek *including all the Praetorium.*   1:14a Greek *brothers in the Lord.*   1:14b Some manuscripts read *speak the message.*

PSALM 71:1-24

⊙ LORD, I have come to you for
    protection;
    don't let me be disgraced.
² Save me and rescue me,
    for you do what is right.
  Turn your ear to listen to me,
    and set me free.
³ Be my rock of safety
    where I can always hide.
  Give the order to save me,

for you are my rock and my
fortress.
⁴ My God, rescue me from the power
of the wicked,
from the clutches of cruel
oppressors.
⁵ O Lord, you alone are my hope.
I've trusted you, O Lord, from
childhood.
⁶ Yes, you have been with me from
birth;
from my mother's womb you
have cared for me.
No wonder I am always
praising you!

⁷ My life is an example to many,
because you have been my
strength and protection.
⁸ That is why I can never stop
praising you;
I declare your glory all day long.
⁹ And now, in my old age, don't set
me aside.
Don't abandon me when my
strength is failing.
¹⁰ For my enemies are whispering
against me.
They are plotting together to
kill me.
¹¹ They say, "God has abandoned him.
Let's go and get him,
for no one will help him now."

¹² O God, don't stay away.
My God, please hurry to help me.
¹³ Bring disgrace and destruction on
my accusers.
Humiliate and shame those who
want to harm me.
¹⁴ But I will keep on hoping for your
help;
I will praise you more and more.
¹⁵ I will tell everyone about your
righteousness.
All day long I will proclaim your
saving power,
though I am not skilled with
words.*
¹⁶ I will praise your mighty deeds,
O Sovereign Lord.
I will tell everyone that you
alone are just.

¹⁷ O God, you have taught me from my
earliest childhood,
and I constantly tell others about
the wonderful things you do.
¹⁸ Now that I am old and gray,
do not abandon me, O God.
Let me proclaim your power to this
new generation,
your mighty miracles to all who
come after me.

¹⁹ Your righteousness, O God, reaches
to the highest heavens.
You have done such wonderful
things.
Who can compare with you,
O God?
²⁰ You have allowed me to suffer much
hardship,
but you will restore me to life
again
and lift me up from the depths
of the earth.
²¹ You will restore me to even greater
honor
and comfort me once again.

²² Then I will praise you with music
on the harp,
because you are faithful to your
promises, O my God.
I will sing praises to you with a lyre,
O Holy One of Israel.
²³ I will shout for joy and sing your
praises,
for you have ransomed me.
²⁴ I will tell about your righteous deeds
all day long,
for everyone who tried to hurt me
has been shamed and humiliated.

71:15 Or *though I cannot count it.*

PROVERBS 24:9-10
The schemes of a fool are sinful; everyone detests a mocker. □ If you fail
under pressure, your strength is too
small.

SEPTEMBER
30

ISAIAH 60:1–62:5

"**A**rise, Jerusalem! Let your light
    shine for all to see.
  For the glory of the LORD rises to
    shine on you.
2 Darkness as black as night covers all
    the nations of the earth,
  but the glory of the LORD rises
    and appears over you.
3 All nations will come to your light;
    mighty kings will come to see
    your radiance.

4 "Look and see, for everyone is
    coming home!
  Your sons are coming from
    distant lands;
  your little daughters will be
    carried home.
5 Your eyes will shine,
    and your heart will thrill with joy,
  for merchants from around the
    world will come to you.
  They will bring you the wealth of
    many lands.
6 Vast caravans of camels will
    converge on you,
    the camels of Midian and Ephah.
  The people of Sheba will bring gold
    and frankincense
  and will come worshiping the
    LORD.
7 The flocks of Kedar will be given
    to you,
  and the rams of Nebaioth will be
    brought for my altars.
  I will accept their offerings,
    and I will make my Temple
    glorious.

8 "And what do I see flying like clouds
    to Israel,
  like doves to their nests?
9 They are ships from the ends
    of the earth,
    from lands that trust in me,
    led by the great ships of Tarshish.

They are bringing the people of
    Israel home from far away,
    carrying their silver and gold.
  They will honor the LORD your God,
    the Holy One of Israel,
    for he has filled you with splendor.

10 "Foreigners will come to rebuild
    your towns.
    and their kings will serve you.
  For though I have destroyed you
    in my anger,
  I will now have mercy on you
    through my grace.
11 Your gates will stay open around
    the clock
    to receive the wealth of many
    lands.
  The kings of the world will be led
    as captives
    in a victory procession.
12 For the nations that refuse to serve
    you
    will be destroyed.

13 "The glory of Lebanon will be yours—
    the forests of cypress, fir, and
    pine—
  to beautify my sanctuary.
    My Temple will be glorious!
14 The descendants of your tormentors
    will come and bow before you.
  Those who despised you
    will kiss your feet.
  They will call you the City of the LORD,
    and Zion of the Holy One of Israel.

15 "Though you were once despised
    and hated,
    with no one traveling through
    you,
  I will make you beautiful forever,
    a joy to all generations.
16 Powerful kings and mighty nations
    will satisfy your every need,
  as though you were a child
    nursing at the breast of a queen.
  You will know at last that I, the LORD,
    am your Savior and your Redeemer,
    the Mighty One of Israel.*
17 I will exchange your bronze for gold,
    your iron for silver,
    your wood for bronze,

and your stones for iron.
I will make peace your leader
and righteousness your ruler.
18 Violence will disappear from your
land;
the desolation and destruction
of war will end.
Salvation will surround you like
city walls,
and praise will be on the lips of all
who enter there.

19 "No longer will you need the sun to
shine by day,
nor the moon to give its light by
night,
for the LORD your God will be your
everlasting light,
and your God will be your glory.
20 Your sun will never set;
your moon will not go down.
For the LORD will be your everlasting
light.
Your days of mourning will come
to an end.
21 All your people will be righteous.
They will possess their land
forever,
for I will plant them there with my
own hands
in order to bring myself glory.
22 The smallest family will become a
thousand people,
and the tiniest group will become
a mighty nation.
At the right time, I, the LORD, will
make it happen."

61:1 THE Spirit of the Sovereign LORD is
upon me,
for the LORD has anointed me
to bring good news to the poor.
He has sent me to comfort the
brokenhearted
and to proclaim that captives will
be released
and prisoners will be freed.*
2 He has sent me to tell those who
mourn
that the time of the LORD's favor
has come,*
and with it, the day of God's anger
against their enemies.

3 To all who mourn in Israel,*
he will give a crown of beauty
for ashes,
a joyous blessing instead of
mourning,
festive praise instead of despair.
In their righteousness, they will be
like great oaks
that the LORD has planted for his
own glory.

4 They will rebuild the ancient ruins,
repairing cities destroyed long
ago.
They will revive them,
though they have been deserted
for many generations.
5 Foreigners will be your servants.
They will feed your flocks
and plow your fields
and tend your vineyards.
6 You will be called priests of the LORD,
ministers of our God.
You will feed on the treasures
of the nations
and boast in their riches.
7 Instead of shame and dishonor,
you will enjoy a double share
of honor.
You will possess a double portion of
prosperity in your land,
and everlasting joy will
be yours.

8 "For I, the LORD, love justice.
I hate robbery and wrongdoing.
I will faithfully reward my people
for their suffering
and make an everlasting covenant
with them.
9 Their descendants will be
recognized
and honored among the nations.
Everyone will realize that they are
a people
the LORD has blessed."

10 I am overwhelmed with joy in the
LORD my God!
For he has dressed me with the
clothing of salvation
and draped me in a robe of
righteousness.

I am like a bridegroom in his
  wedding suit
  or a bride with her jewels.
11 The Sovereign LORD will show his
  justice to the nations of the
  world.
Everyone will praise him!
His righteousness will be like a
  garden in early spring,
  with plants springing up
  everywhere.

62:1BECAUSE I love Zion,
  I will not keep still.
Because my heart yearns for
  Jerusalem,
  I cannot remain silent.
I will not stop praying for her
  until her righteousness shines
  like the dawn,
  and her salvation blazes like a
  burning torch.
2 The nations will see your
  righteousness.
  World leaders will be blinded by
  your glory.
And you will be given a new name
  by the LORD's own mouth.
3 The LORD will hold you in his hand
  for all to see—
  a splendid crown in the hand
  of God.
4 Never again will you be called "The
  Forsaken City"*
  or "The Desolate Land."*
Your new name will be "The City
  of God's Delight"*
  and "The Bride of God,"*
for the LORD delights in you
  and will claim you as his bride.
5 Your children will commit
  themselves to you, O Jerusalem,
  just as a young man commits
  himself to his bride.
Then God will rejoice over you
  as a bridegroom rejoices over
  his bride.

60:16 Hebrew *of Jacob.* See note on 14:1.   61:1 Greek
version reads *and the blind will see.* Compare Luke 4:18.
61:2 Or *to proclaim the acceptable year of the LORD.*
61:3 Hebrew *in Zion.*   62:4a Hebrew *Azubah,* which
means "forsaken."   62:4b Hebrew *Shemamah,* which
means "desolate."   62:4c Hebrew *Hephzibah,* which
means "my delight is in her."   62:4d Hebrew *Beulah,*
which means "married."

PHILIPPIANS 1:27–2:18

Above all, you must live as citizens of
heaven, conducting yourselves in a man-
ner worthy of the Good News about
Christ. Then, whether I come and see you
again or only hear about you, I will know
that you are standing side by side, fighting together for the faith, which is the
Good News. 28Don't be intimidated in
any way by your enemies. This will be a
sign to them that they are going to be destroyed, but that you are going to be
saved, even by God himself. 29For you
have been given not only the privilege of
trusting in Christ but also the privilege of
suffering for him. 30We are in this struggle together. You have seen my struggle
in the past, and you know that I am still in
the midst of it.

2:1Is there any encouragement from belonging to Christ? Any comfort from his
love? Any fellowship together in the
Spirit? Are your hearts tender and com-
passionate? 2Then make me truly happy
by agreeing wholeheartedly with each
other, loving one another, and working
together with one mind and purpose.

3**Don't be selfish; don't try to im-
press others. Be humble, thinking of
others as better than yourselves.
4Don't look out only for your own interests, but take an interest in others,
too.**

5You must have the same attitude
that Christ Jesus had.

6 Though he was God,*
  he did not think of equality with
  God
  as something to cling to.
7 Instead, he gave up his divine
  privileges*;
  he took the humble position
  of a slave*
  and was born as a human being.
  When he appeared in human form,*
8   he humbled himself in obedience
  to God
  and died a criminal's death
  on a cross.

⁹ Therefore, God elevated him to the
place of highest honor
and gave him the name above all
other names,
¹⁰ that at the name of Jesus every knee
should bow,
in heaven and on earth and under
the earth,
¹¹ and every tongue confess that Jesus
Christ is Lord,
to the glory of God the Father.

¹²Dear friends, you always followed
my instructions when I was with you.
And now that I am away, it is even more
important. Work hard to show the results of your salvation, obeying God
with deep reverence and fear. ¹³For God
is working in you, giving you the desire
and the power to do what pleases him.

¹⁴Do everything without complaining and arguing, ¹⁵so that no one can
criticize you. Live clean, innocent lives
as children of God, shining like bright
lights in a world full of crooked and per-
verse people. ¹⁶Hold firmly to the word
of life; then, on the day of Christ's return, I will be proud that I did not run
the race in vain and that my work was
not useless. ¹⁷But I will rejoice even if I
lose my life, pouring it out like a liquid
offering to God,* just like your faithful
service is an offering to God. And I want
all of you to share that joy. ¹⁸Yes, you
should rejoice, and I will share your joy.

2:6 Or *Being in the form of God.*   2:7a Greek *he emptied
himself.*   2:7b Or *the form of a slave.*   2:7c Some English
translations put this phrase in verse 8.   2:17 Greek *I will
rejoice even if I am to be poured out as a liquid offering.*

PSALM 72:1-20
A psalm of Solomon.

¹ **G**ive your love of justice to the king,
O God,
and righteousness to the king's
son.
² Help him judge your people in the
right way;
let the poor always be treated
fairly.
³ May the mountains yield prosperity
for all,
and may the hills be fruitful.

⁴ Help him to defend the poor,
to rescue the children of the
needy,
and to crush their oppressors.
⁵ May they fear you as long as the
sun shines,
as long as the moon remains
in the sky.
Yes, forever!

⁶ May the king's rule be refreshing
like spring rain on freshly cut
grass,
like the showers that water the
earth.
⁷ May all the godly flourish during
his reign.
May there be abundant prosperity
until the moon is no more.
⁸ May he reign from sea to sea,
and from the Euphrates River* to
the ends of the earth.
⁹ Desert nomads will bow before him;
his enemies will fall before him
in the dust.
¹⁰ The western kings of Tarshish and
other distant lands
will bring him tribute.
The eastern kings of Sheba and Seba
will bring him gifts.
¹¹ All kings will bow before him,
and all nations will serve him.

¹² He will rescue the poor when they
cry to him;
he will help the oppressed, who
have no one to defend them.
¹³ He feels pity for the weak and the
needy,
and he will rescue them.
¹⁴ He will redeem them from
oppression and violence,
for their lives are precious
to him.

¹⁵ Long live the king!
May the gold of Sheba be given
to him.
May the people always pray for him
and bless him all day long.
¹⁶ May there be abundant grain
throughout the land,
flourishing even on the hilltops.

May the fruit trees flourish like the
 trees of Lebanon,
and may the people thrive like
 grass in a field.
17 May the king's name endure
 forever;
may it continue as long as the
 sun shines.
May all nations be blessed through
 him
and bring him praise.

18 Praise the LORD God, the God of Israel,
 who alone does such wonderful
 things.
19 Praise his glorious name forever!

Let the whole earth be filled with
 his glory.
Amen and amen!

20 (This ends the prayers of David son
 of Jesse.)

72:8 Hebrew *the river.*

PROVERBS 24:11-12

Rescue those who are unjustly sentenced to die; save them as they stagger to their death. Don't excuse yourself by saying, "Look, we didn't know." For God understands all hearts, and he sees you. He who guards your soul knows you knew. He will repay all people as their actions deserve.